A WEALTH OF INSIGHTS

A WEALTH OF INSIGHTS

HUMANIST THOUGHT SINCE THE ENLIGHTENMENT

BILL COOKE

Prometheus Books
59 John Glenn Drive
Amherst, New York 14228-2119

Published 2011 by Prometheus Books

A Wealth of Insights: Humanist Thought Since the Enlightenment. Copyright © 2011 by Bill Cooke. All rights reserved. No part of this publication may be reproduced, stored in a retrieval system, or transmitted in any form or by any means, digital, electronic, mechanical, photocopying, recording, or otherwise, or conveyed via the Internet or a website without prior written permission of the publisher, except in the case of brief quotations embodied in critical articles and reviews.

Cover design by Grace M. Conti-Zilsberger

Inquiries should be addressed to
Prometheus Books
59 John Glenn Drive
Amherst, New York 14228–2119
VOICE: 716–691–0133
FAX: 716–691–0137
WWW.PROMETHEUSBOOKS.COM

15 14 13 12 11   5 4 3 2 1

Library of Congress Cataloging-in-Publication Data

Cooke, Bill, 1956–
 A wealth of insights : humanist thought since the Enlightenment / Bill Cooke.
  p. cm.
 Includes bibliographical references and index.
 ISBN 978–1–59102–727–0 (hardcover : alk. paper)
 1. Humanism—History. I. Title.

B821.C67 2011
144.09—dc22

2009017861

Printed in the United States on acid-free paper

CONTENTS

Introduction   11

Acknowledgments   17

PART ONE: OUT OF THE SHADOW OF HEGEL

Chapter 1: Out of the Shadow of Hegel:
Humanism's First Century   21
   Friedrich Immanuel Niethammer and the Birth of Humanism   23
   Arnold Ruge, Ludwig Feuerbach, and the Stream of History   30
   George Jacob Holyoake and the Arrival of Humanism in England   35
   The Humanism of "What Might We Become?"   41
   Burckhardt, Symonds, and the Move from *Umanista* to *Humanist*   43
   English Usages of *Humanism* in the Later Nineteenth Century   46

Chapter 2: Protagoras's Cheerleader: F. C. S. Schiller and
Humanism's New Beginning   53
   F. C. S. Schiller and the Humanistic View of Life   54
   F. C. S. Schiller and the New Understanding of *Humanism*   56
   Why Did F. C. S. Schiller's Humanism Not Take Root?   62

Chapter 3: Making the Manifesto:
Humanism between F. C. S. Schiller
and John Dewey   67
   Humanism in Britain after F. C. S. Schiller   67
   Bertrand Russell and "The Free Man's Worship"   74
   George Santayana and the Life of Reason   76
   Irving Babbitt and the Humanism of Character   80
   Richard Haldane and the Lonely Path   83
   The Birth of American Religious Humanism   85
   Roy Wood Sellars and the Next Step in Religion   87
   The High Tide of American Religious Humanism   90

Chapter 4: The Rise and Fall of Scientific Humanism — 97
- Lothrop Stoddard and the Inauspicious Start — 97
- Julian Huxley and the Developed Religion — 99
- The Marxists and Dialectical Materialism — 104
- Cyril Joad and the Rationalist's Charter — 109
- John Dewey and the Common Faith — 114
- Bertrand Russell and the Unflinching Perception — 119
- H. G. Wells and the Open Conspiracy — 120
- Scientific Humanism Finds Its Feet—Too Late — 129

Chapter 5: British Humanism Since World War II — 133
- Harold Blackham and the Plain View — 133
- Bertrand Russell and the Faith of a Rationalist — 136
- Herbert Read and the Sensuous Apprehension of Being — 139
- Amber Blanco White and the New Woman — 141
- Margaret Knight and Morals without Religion — 143
- Hector Hawton and Reason in Action — 147
- Julian Huxley and Evolutionary Humanism — 149
- A. J. Ayer's Ambivalent Legacy — 154
- Alan Bullock and the Humanist Tradition — 158
- Isaiah Berlin and the Crooked Timber of Humanity — 161
- Recent Expressions of Humanism in Britain — 163
- Linda Smith and the Gift of Humor — 169

Chapter 6: American Humanism Since World War II — 173
- Corliss Lamont and the Philosophy of Humanism — 173
- Sidney Hook, the Humanist Cold Warrior — 181
- Paul Kurtz and the *Humanist Manifesto II* — 183
- Paul Kurtz and the *Secular Humanist Declaration* — 187
- Why *Secular* Humanism? — 193
- The Debate over *Eupraxsophy* — 198
- Humanism among the Children of Nimrod — 200
- Pragmatist, Naturalist, and Secular Humanism after a Century of Debate — 205
- Does Humanism Have a Future in America? — 208

PART TWO: TOWARD PLANETARY HUMANISM

Chapter 7: **Bildung** *to* **Laïcité***: European Humanism*   213
   Thomas Mann, the Reluctant Humanist   215
   Albert Camus and the Absurd Rebel   220
   Is Existentialism a Humanism?   225
   Martin Heidegger and Primordial Being   227
   Karl Jaspers and Limitless Communication   230
   The Rise and Fall of Socialist Humanism   235
   Socialist Humanism's Last Gasp   241
   Postmodern Humanism and Humanistics   244
   Tzvetan Todorov and the Imperfect Garden   250

Chapter 8: Christian Humanism: Athens versus Jerusalem   253
   The Failed Promise of Catholic Humanism   256
   Charles Hartshorne and the Move Beyond   263
   The New Humanism and the Death of God   266
   American Evangelicals and the "Religion of Secular Humanism"   275
   Lloyd Geering and the Spiritual Schizophrenia   279
   Albert Schweitzer and the Reverence for Life   284

Chapter 9: Indian Humanism: One Long, Rich Argument   289
   Two Ancient Humanist Traditions of India   290
   Swami Vivekananda and the Realization of Religion   294
   Rabindranath Tagore and the Religion of Man   296
   Dr. Ambedkar and the Plight of the Dalits   301
   Rationalism in India   304
   M. N. Roy and Radical Humanism   306
   Gora and the Atheist Centre   310
   Periyar and Dravidar Kazagham   314
   Jawaharlal Nehru and Indian Secularism   318

Chapter 10: The Spirit of Chinese Humanism   323
   Confucius and the Way of Shu   324
   Confucianism from Qin to Qing   327

Confucianism's Century from Hell ... 333
The Rise of the New Confucians ... 341
The Venerable Master Xingyun and Humanistic Buddhism ... 347

Chapter 11: Humanism in the Muslim World: Rethinking **Ijtihad** ... 355
Nurturing a Strategy of Refusal ... 356
Muʻtazilism, Ibn Rushd, and the Heyday of Muslim Free Thought ... 359
Islamic Modernism and the Reinvention of Ijtihad ... 362
The Difficult Intersection between Islam and Secularism ... 371
The Rise of the Refuseniks ... 378
Are There Grounds for Hope? ... 384

Chapter 12: Humanism in Africa: From **Uhuru** *to* **Ubuntu** ... 387
What Is Meant by *African Humanism*? ... 388
A Short History of Organized Humanism in Africa ... 393
Humanism in South Africa ... 396
Kenneth Kaunda and Christian Humanism ... 399
Humanism in Nigeria from Tai Solarin to Wole Soyinka ... 402
Ugandan Humanism and the Promise of Education ... 408

Chapter 13: A World without Walls: Planetary Humanism ... 413
Ecohumanism and the Awareness of Interdependence ... 414
H. G. Wells and the Federation of Humanity ... 424
Julian Huxley, Boyd Orr, and United Nations Programs ... 426
The International Humanist and Ethical Union ... 429
Bertrand Russell and the Peril of Man ... 432
John Rawls and the Law of Peoples ... 434
Planetary Humanism and the Twenty-First Century ... 437
Grounded Cosmopolitanism and the Identity of the Future ... 444

Epilogue: The Main Features of Twenty-First-Century Humanism ... 449
Life Is Intrinsically Worth Living ... 449
A Sufficient Grounding in Humility ... 450

Not Against or Beyond Nature, but Within It	451
Learning from and Valuing the Past	452
Grounded in Our Culture, Yet beyond Nations	453
Placing a High Value on Learning	453

Notes 455

Bibliography 497

Index 521

INTRODUCTION

"If the humanism that makes civilization civilized is to be preserved into this new century, it will need advocates. Those advocates will need a memory, and part of that memory will need to be of an age in which they were not alive."[1] Nothing could sum up more effectively what this book is about. It comes from Clive James at the start of his contribution to the retention of that memory. This book is my contribution.

When James speaks of humanism, he has in mind the European tradition of cultural refinement and sensitivity. This book is trying something broader. It will talk of that strand of humanism, but it will also speak of its other strands, which go by various names: *secular*, *religious*, *reflective*, *empirical*, *scientific*, and many others. In this way, *A Wealth of Insights* is a work of synthesis. I have tried to bring together a broad range of thinkers who could be called humanist, or who called themselves humanist, to see what they were saying and what motivated them, and to learn something about humanism as a result. As with any work of synthesis, I will inevitably skate lightly over areas others have specialist knowledge of and I apologize in advance for any offense that might cause. It's getting a bit formulaic to subtitle books "Toward a new understanding of . . . ," but this book should be seen very much in that light.

People have lived and behaved along humanistic lines for as long as people have lived together. The core humanist insight of according to others the consideration one would have accorded to oneself, called *reciprocal altruism* by evolutionary psychologists, and *the golden rule* by moralists, is the foundation of civil society. As well as this long history, we know of the humanistic quality of much inter- and intracultural discourse. Humanist thinking forms the bedrock of Chinese civilization and has contributed significantly to the *nastika* tradition of unorthodox thought in India. It may well represent minority opinion there, but there is no stigma attached to being "unorthodox" in India as there is in any monotheist tradition. And in Greece, the pre-Socratic thinkers inquired into the world as it is, rather than as it should be or as the gods would wish it.

Humanism, in other words, is the most transcultural mode of thought ever conceived. One of the many exciting points about this is that these three cultural traditions, China, India, and Greece, operated quite happily without the word we now associate with them. So far as we know, the word *humanism* was coined in 1808, so this book can conveniently be seen as a bicentenary history of the word and the excellent adventures it has had over that time. It seems high time that this word be subjected to some historical assessment and that stock be taken of what it might mean at the beginning of its third century. This book will illustrate the wisdom of another of Clive James's observations, when he said that the "collective mentality" of humanism is made up of the connections between phrases and written thoughts of otherwise disparate people around the world.[2] We will be doing a lot of that.

On the one hand this book is going to relish the breadth of the humanist discourse, but on the other hand it will try to gather the strands into some order, but not too much. The confusion that surrounds the word at present is testimony to its shadowy origins. In much of the academic literature at present we are likely to come across scientific realists speaking of humanists as postmodernist relativists inhabiting humanities departments. But we are just as likely to read those very people criticizing the "residual humanism" among scientific realists. We have grown used to theists and atheists calling themselves humanists, but we have also seen theists and atheists competing in their denunciation of humanism.

The problem gets no easier to understand when we look at what opponents of humanism accuse it of being responsible for. Postmodernists accuse humanism of being out of step with modernity by virtue of its modernism. Protestant evangelicals, by contrast, accuse it of being all too representative of modernity. Scientific realists fear humanism is too romantic, while mystics accuse it of not being romantic enough. Conventional Christian believers accuse humanism of being too secular while hardline atheists are quite sure it is not secular enough. Some environmentalist thinkers and defenders of mystery accuse humanism of hubris. Depending on the prejudices of the accuser, humanism is too vague or too literal, too shallow or too cerebral. Not infrequently at the same time.

To illustrate the problem, two of the most influential of the recent critiques of humanism have used the word in quite different ways. In his major work *A Secular Age*, Charles Taylor has spoken of "exclusive humanism," by which he means an arid, flat naturalism. The major weakness of Taylor's thesis is his extraordinary unfamiliarity with what humanists themselves have written. He makes no mention, even in passing, of the vast majority of humanist thinkers discussed in this book. Another study, by David Cooper, though based on sounder knowledge of what humanists have actually said, has defined humanism in a way few humanists would recognize. He has spoken of humanism as a form of subjectivism that holds that no describable world exists independently of human beings. What Taylor calls *exclusive humanism* Cooper calls *scientific realism* or *absolutism*. Cooper also says that humanism suits his purposes because it "doesn't have much of a pedigree in the philosophical lexicon, so there is less danger of confusing the intended sense with others."[3]

While I doubt this book will improve the tainted pedigree of humanism in the philosophical lexicon, it will have served its purpose if people don't mind that too much. If this book must have a disciplinary category, it is a work of intellectual history; what used to be called the history of ideas. So, in that vein, two—at times unrelated—things will be attempted. It will trace the evolution of the word *humanism*, while at the same time outlining the development of humanist thinking. There is a bigger gap between these two projects than one might at first suppose. Indeed, it is one of the central paradoxes of this book that on more than one occasion the people specifically employing the word *humanist* require more explanation and apology now than those who do not use the word but exemplify its ideals in some way or other.

Inevitably a project such as this requires a great deal of selection on my part. It is straightforward enough to gather together all those who have spoken specifically of humanism and to subject their thoughts to scrutiny. But it takes more selection to isolate certain figures who are then held up as exemplars of humanism in practice. It is relatively unproblematic that some people should be included. John Dewey, for example, rarely spoke directly of humanism and found himself in a whole lot of trouble when he did. But it is clearly not running counter to Dewey's thought to speak of him as an exemplar of humanism. Then there are people like Bertrand Russell who was, at best, indifferent to the idea of humanism, being distrustful of the anthropocentrism he saw as inherent in it. But a history of contemporary humanism would obviously be incomplete without mentioning Russell, whose work was humanistic even if he was skeptical about humanism. Then there are those who were enthusiastic about humanism and used the word, but whose thinking or behavior was an embarrassment to most other humanists—people ranging from Lothrop Stoddard through Irving Babbitt to Kenneth Kaunda. Also included are some who would, in all probability, shudder in horror at being included among contemporary humanists and yet are spoken of here as humanists. I have in mind people like Jamal-al-din al-Afghani or Syed Ahmad Khan. A book can only be so long, and generous inclusion of all thinkers over the past two centuries who have exemplified significant elements of humanist thinking would blow this book out to a length beyond all reason. The reader can judge whether the selection process has been a success.

Since the manuscript for this book was completed, important changes have taken place within American humanism. Paul Kurtz, long recognized as that country's leading advocate of secular humanism, has been eased out of all positions of control of the Center for Inquiry, the latest incarnation of the organization he formed in 1980. As well as the perennial issues of intergenerational succession, the split runs along deeper fissures, especially as regards humanism's proper attitude toward religion. Is the relation between humanism and religion necessarily one of conflict? Can humanism have a religious quality—variously understood—and remain coherent? These questions will need to be tackled in the twenty-first century, but differently to the way they were tackled in the nineteenth and the twentieth centuries. It is hoped that this book will provide some insights as to how issues such as these were approached in the past, in the hope, at least, of not repeating some of the more egregious errors.

So it's not a straight-forward set of choices. Different chapters operate along different criteria. The people included as humanists in the chapter dealing with the Middle East would in all likelihood not warrant inclusion in the chapter on British humanism. I have not wanted to exclude people who have spoken specifically about humanism because I find their use of the word unsatisfactory in some way or other. To do so strikes me as a sectarian way of operating, and thus it would be contrary to my understanding of humanism. The main justification for exclusion is that the thinker in question has said things about humanism that has not already been said by somebody else. I have also included slightly more biographical material than is usual in books of this type. It seemed important to establish some sort of context.

Neither have I devoted much space to the many criticisms of humanism from without. It is not that this would not be useful. It would. But it is not what this book is about. It is a history of the word *humanism* and the ideas that have been associated with it over the past two centuries. Criticisms of humanism from within the discourse will, however, be canvased fully. So many criticisms of humanism, glaringly so in the case of Charles Taylor, have been made with little or no knowledge of this history that their value as criticisms seems highly questionable. Let's actually find out what humanists have said before laying into them.

Of all the themes of humanism one could choose to concentrate on, this book pursues three: humanism and anthropocentrism, humanism and freedom, and humanism and transcultural values. Why these ones? Because in trying to articulate an understanding of humanism that is relevant for the twenty-first century, it seems to me that these are the most important. A humanism freed from anthropocentrism will be best able to grapple with the environmental challenges the twenty-first century is going to face. These challenges, in turn, will affect notions of freedom and transcultural values. Get these right and humanism has something relevant and important to say. While I would count myself a humanist, I am not intending this book to act as a standard piece of apologetics. As will become apparent, I am critical of much that has passed as humanist thinking over the past two centuries. So this book could well be seen as a critical history.

And while this book is a work of synthesis, I have refrained from tidying up messy edges or ensuring a clean, but misleading, continuity. Many people have observed that humanism is a moveable feast, and this book shall certainly provide evidence of that. For many, the vagueness of humanism, the fact it does appeal across so many cultures, counts against it. But it is just possible that, in the twenty-first century, this could be its greatest asset.

ACKNOWLEDGMENTS

As is ever the case, a lot of people and some institutions assisted in very significant ways the completion of this book. Chapter 1 was added to considerably by Sascha Nolden, who translated some the passages from Niethammer's *Philanthropinismus—Humanismus* into English, the first time, to my knowledge, this has been done. He also helped me with some background on Philanthropinism. Fred Donnelly also provided some worthwhile criticism. Chapter 2 was looked over and commented on by John Shook, himself an authority on F. C. S. Schiller. I'm grateful for his comments and suggestions. And this chapter is due to appear in a memorial issue of *Intellectual News*, the predecessor to the excellent refereed journal, *Intellectual History Review*, run by the International Society of Intellectual History (ISIH) of which I am a member. I thank the ISIH for permission to use the chapter in my book. Chapter 3 was assisted in no small way by Wayne Facer, who provided me with a large amount of difficult-to-find material on early American religious humanism and Unitarianism. Mr. Facer also supplied me with copies of some rare material from the library of the Auckland Unitarian Church. Chapter 12 received some absolutely crucial assistance. While attending a conference of the New Zealand Association for the Study of Religion, South African scholar Paul Prinsloo alerted me to the concept of *ubuntu*. And while attending the twenty-second World Congress of Philosophy in Seoul, Mogobe Ramose gave me a copy of his important work *African Philosophy through Ubuntu*, for which I am especially grateful. Ebenezer Obadare then helped a lot by offering some valuable observations of an early draft of the chapter. Dr. Obadare also made some very helpful suggestions for further reading. And Norm Allen Jr. sent me some very useful back issues of the *African American Examiner*, which filled in some important gaps in my knowledge.

I would also like to acknowledge the ongoing support and criticism of Emeritus Professor of Philosophy Ray Bradley. Ray does me the honor of saying in no uncertain terms when I have cut intellectual corners or, more simply, erred. I am very grateful for this sort of intellectual friendship. He is unlikely to agree with everything written here, so the debate will continue.

Thanks also for the support, criticism, and encouragement from lots of people: David Ross, Floris van den Berg, Greg Dawes, Bert Gasenbeek, Bruce Cathey, Max Wallace, Ben Radford, and Imran Aijaz. And in Australia, Hannah Taylor introduced me to the Internet world of Facebook, and sites of that nature, and in so doing helped acquaint me with the twenty-first century.

Of the institutions to mention, two libraries were of special assistance: the Center for Inquiry library at Amherst, New York, the best library of its kind in the world; and the library of the New Zealand Association of Rationalists & Humanists, not far behind in range and quality. This book could not have been written without material from those two excellent libraries. Manukau Institute of Technology, where I worked until 2008, funded several of the research trips to India, China, the United States, and to the twenty-second World Congress of Philosophy in Seoul, each of which was invaluable for the development of this book.

Most important, though, is the ongoing support of my loving wife, partner, and friend, Bobbie Douglas Cooke, who dealt with the world at large while I buried myself in the intellectual history of humanism. She also read the finished manuscript, corrected grammatical infelicities and cleared away awkward or bulky passages. As ever, responsibility for whatever errors remain is mine.

PART ONE

OUT OF THE SHADOW OF HEGEL

CHAPTER 1

OUT OF THE SHADOW OF HEGEL: HUMANISM'S FIRST CENTURY

1808 is not usually a date to conjure with. It's not one of those evocative years, like 1066, 1776, 1945, or 2001. And yet the close of the eighteenth century and the first two decades of the nineteenth were among the most pivotal in Western history. In his classic study of the early nineteenth century, Eric Hobsbawm listed some words that came into circulation at about this time. Words like *capitalist*, *socialism*, *scientist*, *ideology*, *liberal*, *conservative*, *middle class*, and *working class*.[1] And, as Raymond Williams noted, it was also a time when old words started being used in disturbingly new ways—words like *industry*, *democracy*, *class*, *art*, and *culture*.[2] Elsewhere I have read that the word *international* was first used by Jeremy Bentham at about this time. Imagine a world without these words!

It is not surprising that these words were born or came to their current meanings at this time. Since Newton and Galileo, awareness was slowly dawning of a universe vastly larger and more complex than they had hitherto been allowed to imagine. As a result, much eighteenth-century conversation consisted in dismantling the old ideas of a God who intervened in human history and who demanded worship, got into moods, and bestowed rewards and punishments. God, according to the Deists, may well have created things and may even retain an afterlife, but all the rest of the time we are encouraged to behave according to our own lights and to study nature in the knowledge that such activity is really a form of worship, and a more practical one at that.

Emerging as a consequence of this radically new understanding of the cosmos, the eighteenth century had initiated a conversation about democracy and the sort of human being who could flourish in conditions of democracy.

The American War of Independence and the French Revolution brought with them new conception of the rights man. The two outstanding documents of the age were the American Constitution along with the Bill of Rights and the French *Declaration of the Rights of Man and of the Citizen*. Ideas were having political consequences more rapidly than ever before. And some of the most significant ideas were coming from Immanuel Kant (1724–1804), whose philosophy placed the focus on the human subject, in particular the faculties of a self-conscious subject—faculties like reason, judgment, imagination, and instinct. Immaturity, Kant wrote, is the lack of "resolution and courage to use one's own understanding without the guidance of another." Against this, his clarion call was to dare us to use our own understanding.[3] The most valuable possession any person can have, Kant argued, is an unfettered will. Whatever the source of the fetters, be they nature, God, tradition, government, or custom, Kant set himself against them insofar as they impinged on the central fact of human freedom. And he passed on to his readers a sense of the gravity of the change that had transpired since Copernicus. Between Kant and Hume—who had awoken him from his dogmatic slumbers—the Enlightenment *philosophes*, and the great changes their thought had helped unleash, it is not surprising that those who followed them would need a radically new and revised vocabulary.[4]

The old language, that which the Enlightenment had displaced, was theological, passive, sin-besotted, and supernaturalist. But at the start of the nineteenth century, some thinkers were beginning to appreciate that the language preferred by Enlightenment thinkers also had its limitations. With all the talk of man as a machine, of physical systems, and of laws, human value was being lost somewhere. And then there were the horrors of the Terror to account for. The optimism and exhilaration of the first years of the French Revolution had given way to altogether darker thoughts and actions. So for many thinkers living in the wake of both the Enlightenment and the Terror, a need was felt for a language that understood humanity's place in nature while still according a value on being human. The old, supernaturalist standards and assumptions were no longer workable, but some of the new ideas generated problems of their own no less troubling, so a new set of standards, and a new set of words to convey those standards, was needed. And as all the developments were moving in the direction of human needs, sufferings, and wants, it was only a matter of time before the word *humanist* should find itself reworked in service of this new vision of the potentialities of being human. And on top of these very significant changes, the eighteenth century had created something else quite new: a reading public that understood this problem. The existence of this educated readership, keen to express itself in public, and the new political systems that encouraged this, were the ideal breeding ground for the range of new words that entered service at this time.

The word *humanist* is thought to have been first used in 1589, although it can be traced back in various Latin renderings to Roman times. When we now speak of a *Renaissance humanist*, we have a positive and a negative meaning. Negatively, a humanist referred to the itinerant scholars who, like the sophists of old, traveled in search of sponsors. They had a reputation as hard-living, hard-drinking men who one wouldn't want to invite to the family table. Positively, a humanist was a genteel man of letters, a scholar of independent means who had the leisure and inclination to pursue knowledge in the arts and sciences for no other reason than that knowledge was there to pursue. These distinctions weren't articulated until the middle of the nineteenth century. But at the start of the nineteenth century, people had not seen the need to speak of human*ism*. Humanists were not in the business of inventing new modes of looking at the world. They were more interested in understanding once more the old ways, the way of Greece and Rome, with a view to improving the thought, religion, and manners of the day.

These first years of the nineteenth century were when ism words were being coined. At the same time the need was felt to speak of humanism, Friedrich Heinrich Jacobi (1743–1819) invented the word *nihilism*, a word which, in so many ways, is humanism's polar opposite. Robert Owen first spoke of socialism in 1817. Of all the new ism words, it could be argued that *humanism* best encapsulates the core of each of the words cited by Hobsbawm and Williams and is one of the most foundational words relating to our current understanding of the world. This book will trace the fluctuating fortunes of the word *humanism* in the two centuries of its existence.

FRIEDRICH IMMANUEL NIETHAMMER AND THE BIRTH OF HUMANISM

Credit usually goes to the German thinker and politician Friedrich Immanuel Niethammer (1766–1848) as the coiner of the word *humanism*.[5] Strictly speaking, however, the claim is not true, as there had already been occasional references in French periodicals to *humanisme* from around the 1760s.[6] It's possible Niethammer knew of the word from these sources, although he seemed under the impression that the word was indeed his creation. This caveat duly noted, it's still fair to credit Niethammer with being the first person not just to speak of humanism but to articulate what he meant by it. It is astonishing how little attention Niethammer has attracted from humanists. Only since the Dutch humanist Jaap van Praag (1911–1981) drew attention to Niethammer's work have humanists even known his name, with most accounts making fleeting mention of the word's birth at this time, before quickly moving on. Nobody has taken the trouble to understand Niethammer and what he meant by *humanism*. It is the purpose of this chapter to fill that gap.

So who, then, was Friedrich Immanuel Niethammer and, of all the people who could have coined the word *humanism*, why this one? Niethammer's importance lies not so much in what he knew, but in who he knew. He was ideally placed to be at the center of the intellectual ferment in Germany at the time. Like many other influential Germans of his generation, he had began his study at Tübingen, then in a state of decline. The contrast of Tübingen's stuffy orthodoxy with the inspiring changes then taking place in revolutionary France could hardly have been more stark. He was at Jena when this small, provincial university enjoyed its short career as the center of German intellectual life. Among his friends included his old Tübingen colleague Friedrich Hölderlin (1770–1843), often said to be Germany's finest poet, and the philosophers Friedrich Schelling (1775–1854), Johann Christoph Friedrich Schiller (1759–1805) and Johann Gottlieb Fichte (1762–1814). There has long been a legend, in all likelihood apocryphal, of a meeting at Niethammer's house in Jena of the poet Novalis (1772–1801), Hölderlin, and Fichte in the summer of 1795. Even if not true, as is likely, this story indicates the importance of Niethammer at the time. But more important than any of these people, from our point of view, was Niethammer's close friendship with Georg Wilhelm Friedrich Hegel (1770–1831), who devoted his career to providing Germany with a new outlook for what they all believed was a new age. Along with Hegel and some others, Niethammer devoted his career to encouraging Germany to learn from the French experiment and grow strong as a result. It was his good fortune to constantly be well placed to realize this ambition.

Why 1808? The German intellectual ferment generated by the Enlightenment and the French Revolution were still new. Kant had been dead only four years and Schiller only three. Schiller's stress on the need to reassert our humanity and understand our own role as creators of value was still fresh in people's thought. And Fichte, in *The Destiny of Man* (1800), reworked Kant's rather imposing moral imperatives by giving them content as rational principles in the hearts of men, under the authority of God. Fichte was the first philosopher to argue that an outlook on life is ethical only insofar as it enables us to recognize that a necessarily abstract devotion to the universe is "grounded in the nature of the world and of life."[7]

But a ferment of ideas is one thing; what made 1808 special was that it offered the ideal opportunity for these ideas to be put into practice. This is because 1808 was pretty much the high point of the Napoleonic domination of Europe and therefore also the high point of the influence of the ideas from the Enlightenment, as mediated through Bonapartism. And Bavaria under Crown Prince Maximilian Joseph (1756–1825) and was one of Napoleon's strongest allies, a loyalty that was rewarded with a royal marriage between Maximilian's daughter Augusta (1788–1851) and Eugene de Beauharnais (1781–1824), the only son of Napoleon's wife Josephine by her first marriage. Unlike Prussia, Bavaria had not sustained serious and humiliating defeats on the battlefield that in turn nurtured festering resentment against all things French. In 1807 Napoleon "suggested" to King Maximilian I, as the crown prince had now become, that Bavaria adopt the Code Napoleon. With that in mind Bavaria inaugurated, in 1808, its first constitution. The inspiration behind this was King Maximilian's capable first minister Maximilian Josef Garnerin, Count von Montgelas (1759–1838), a man imbued with secular, anticlerical, liberal views we now see as archetypal Enlightenment principles.

As part of this comprehensive program of reform and emancipation, Friedrich Immanuel Niethammer was appointed, in 1808, to a prominent position in the Bavarian education system, the Central Commissioner of Education and Consistory, no less. Education in Bavaria had traditionally been left to the Catholic Church, but the new leadership realized full well that, if their reforms were to last, the education system must be brought into their control. In this vein a university had been established at Würzburg that was free from clerical influence. To advance his thought he wrote the book, published in 1808, that was the birthplace of humanism: *The Dispute between*

Philanthropinism and Humanism in the Theory of Educational Instruction of Our Time.
Niethammer's best chance of seeing his reform program through was to initiate it in the newly acquired northern districts of Bavaria, where the Catholic interest was not as deeply entrenched and where there was a tradition, if now a bit dilapidated, of Protestant schools going back to the Reformation. In particular was the Nuremberg Gymnasium, which could trace its history back to 1526 and which had once embodied many of the values Niethammer wanted to reintroduce. This is an important point to note. Niethammer's educational reforms looked back as well as forward. He was no more a Utopian futurist than he was a knee-jerk reactionary. And he coined the word *humanism* precisely to avoid either extreme. This characteristic of humanism as a middle course between extremes has stayed with it ever since.

Into this sensitive project Niethammer appointed Hegel, his friend from Jena, as headmaster of a model school in Nuremburg. Between 1809 and 1815, Hegel did his best to ensure the success of the new vision of humanist education project under way. The aim was to produce autonomous, cultivated individuals, a condition known in German as *bildung*, a term we will discuss again in chapter 7 and elsewhere. *Bildung* refers both to the business of educating a person and to the attainment of these qualities as the end result of that education.[8] The bildung advanced by Hegel and Niethammer was not original to them. Goethe, Wilhelm von Humboldt, and others said similar things, as had Fichte in his *Address to the German Nation* (1807–1808), which spoke passionately of the moral rearmament Germany needed to undergo, not just so as to recover from the military defeats at the hands of Napoleon's armies, but also to contribute in the manner Germany deserved to the moral progress of the world. The bildung preferred by Niethammer and Hegel had less of the romantic sermonizing and overt nationalism of many of their contemporaries. Though just as concerned as Fichte was to see Germany develop, Niethammer and Hegel retained a more cosmopolitan approach. This has been another very significant legacy to humanism's subsequent development.[9]

The next question to answer is, why did Niethammer need a new word to encapsulate what he meant? And why did he settle on *humanism* as that word? Niethammer's generation was the first one to be caught up in the fundamental changes unleashed by the French Revolution. It is difficult in the twenty-first century, with its disillusionment with ideologies, to recapture the zeal and excitement that young men had for the new ideals and the age they were living in, even though many of them would all too quickly go through their own stage of disillusionment. Once the first wave of enthusiasm for the revolution died away following the excesses of the Terror, Niethammer's generation—those who did not fall back into blank reaction—still saw a unique opportunity to rid the world of despotisms, dungeons, and the old religious ways. Indeed, it was the very failure of the first rush of enthusiasm that helped generate their various responses.[10] The men of Niethammer's generation, like his friend Hegel, dedicated their lives to the reconciliation of the secular and divine in light of the new world conditions. How, then, to take the best of the revolutionary ideals and integrate them into what was worth preserving from the *ancien regime*? *Humanism*, like no other word, was custom-built for the task.

The humanism Niethammer spoke of had progressive and conservative elements. It was progressive in the sense that it valued individual autonomy with its associated right—even duty—to think for oneself, and promotion by merit rather than by birth. It was with this in mind that Niethammer's humanism championed Greek language over Latin as the true language of European culture. Latin had become the language of the church and of the aristocrats. Greek, however, was the language of the world's earliest democracies. With Greek one could think as an individual and could cultivate a true bildung. Niethammer's generation was deeply imbued with Greek ideals of "wholeness." Like the people we now call *Renaissance humanists*, the German reformers of the late eighteenth century and early nineteenth century were steeped in reverence for antiquity. But they tempered this with an essentially forward-looking outlook. As Georg Henrik von Wright observed, the humanist "holds a peculiar middle position between the old and the new, the past and the future. He belongs to both and at the same time he belongs to neither."[11]

When Niethammer spoke of humanism, he had in mind a broad-ranging program of moral education designed to create a new generation of leaders, people imbued with the contemporary zeitgeist. He also probably had in mind the schooling of his native Württemberg, which was unique in Germany for the provision of a general education to a non-noble elite. The education system in Württemberg went back to the middle of the sixteenth century and derived ultimately from the Renaissance. And in the spirit of the Greek and

Renaissance antecedents, the humanism espoused by Niethammer and supported by his friend Hegel was pan-European in flavor. Unlike most German intellectuals of the day, Hegel and Niethammer were not enthusiastic supporters of the Romantic notions of "organic" communities. Such talk, they recognized, could easily descend into a backward-looking xenophobia.[12] And neither were Niethammer nor Hegel opposed in principle to the education of women. They believed women were capable of bildung, if only for the purposes of complementing their menfolk, who alone had a proper role in the working world. During his time in Nuremberg Hegel was an active supporter of education for girls in the city. These were seen as progressive ideas at the time—scandalously so by the upholders of faith and privilege.

There were two main rival theories to Niethammer's reformism. On the one hand there was the knee-jerk reactionary opposition of the Catholic Church, which saw any change to the status quo as a dangerous innovation to the timeless principles of hierarchy and obedience. And at the other extreme there was Philanthropinism, a movement deeply influenced by Jean-Jacques Rousseau (1712–1778). The movement was the creation of Johann Bernhard Basedow (1723–1790), an academic and dreamer who, with the support of Prince Leopold Friedrich Franz von Anhalt-Dessau, established a progressive school, the Philanthropin, in 1774 and which ran until 1793, although not before inspiring the foundation of several other schools run along similar lines around Germany. *Philanthropinism* came to be understood as a term for this range of theories and schemes devoted to educational reform. It was little interested in rote learning the classics, valuing instead practical and physical education and emphasizing self-directed learning at the expense of rigidity, rules, and coercion. Most alarming of all, it was freethinking in tone, which to its critics meant it was antireligious and eccentric.

If Niethammer saw little compromise possible with the aggrieved Catholic Church, with the Philanthropinists things were different. Against them he spoke of humanism as defending humanity's spiritual nature and stressing our independence from the physical world. Philanthropinism could be given, he mused, the more insulting epithet of *animalism*, but he demurred to do so. Humanism was more than simply the pedantic inculcation of the humanities. It was the general nurturing of bildung, the condition of being generously educated in the broadest sense of the term. He then went on to make another important qualification. His use of the words *humanism* and *Philanthropinism* served only to highlight the distinction between educating toward the humanity of the student, rather than toward the animality. He went on to insist that the words are, in most other respects, unnecessary, "given how quickly they may be criticized as descriptors of sects, [and they] may be disadvantageous and undesirable."[13] This recognition of the dangers of fetishizing over words is another important feature of humanism that we owe to Niethammer.

Early in his book, Niethammer outlined the core differences between humanism as he viewed it, and Philanthropinism. Far from being simple either-or polarities, the differences were those of degree. Humanism viewed educational instruction as being not so much about the accumulation of specific knowledge but more about the general bildung of the student, or about "the exercising of the *Geist*."[14] Why train the body, he asked, when only sacred things matter in the end? In the end, though, Niethammer saw room for both approaches. He agreed with the Philanthropinists that a degree of autonomy in learning was valuable, though he was not prepared to go as far as they preferred. If Germany was to prosper, the earlier models of education had to be radically overhauled, but without jumping to the opposite extreme of the wholesale sloughing off the values of the past, which he associated with Philanthropinism. What was needed was a creative fusion of the best of Philanthropinism with the best of humanism.

With the advantage of two centuries' worth of hindsight we can see how Niethammer's humanism was as conservative as it was radical. It applied, in the main, to middle class men and was an education intent on preparing these people to rule. It was disdainful of technical training, which it saw as of lesser use in the acquisition of taste than a sound training in philosophy, in the classics, and in Greek. But equally, Niethammer's conception of humanism had a clear understanding of the value of dialogue, particularly in its concern not to dismiss Philanthropinism or the values of the past out of hand. It was also commendably concerned not to atrophy into simply one more sect clamoring for attention, to the extent of not paying undue attention to the word *humanism*. It was, in short, self-critical, dialogical, and open. And finally, we should savor for a moment the irony of humanism developing originally as an attempt to preserve and rehabilitate tried and trusted values against supposedly animalistic social innovations. Reading the more hysterical critics of humanism today is to be told of such values being under unique level of threat from humanism. This is only the first of many such ironies this book will encounter.

It is easier to say what Niethammer's conception of humanism was not. It was not Enlightenment rationalism. Neither was it sentimental Romanticism. It was neither reactionary nor futurist. It was a complex mix of all these influences, seeing value in all of them, and wanting, in the name of bildung, to press them all into service. There is much in Niethammer's mix of motivations and predispositions that has remained with humanism to this day.

ARNOLD RUGE, LUDWIG FEUERBACH, AND THE STREAM OF HISTORY

Clearly, humanism could well have died in the 1840s. It had not carried on in the sense Niethammer had used it. After the fall of Napoleon, the modernizing forces in Bavaria were slowly rolled back by a reaction inspired by ultramontane Catholicism and enforced by the Metternich system. Count Montgelas was eased out of office in 1817, leaving Niethammer's educational reforms exposed. In the years that followed, they were slowly ground down, frustrated, and betrayed. Discouraged, Niethammer reverted to a relatively orthodox Lutheranism and spoke less of reformist humanism. The next significant figure to take up humanism also took it in interesting new directions. In his short and terse account of the development of humanism, Nicholas Walter argued that the key transition of the word from German *humanismus* to *humanism* came via Arnold Ruge (1802–1880), a radical scholar and man of letters whose views landed him in trouble over and over again.[15] We need to examine this important claim.

Like so many bright young men of his generation, Ruge was profoundly influenced by Hegel. But he was more instrumental than most other second-wave Hegelians (i.e., those born after 1800) in reimagining a new use of Hegelianism. Many other Hegelians of his generation were retreating from concentration on politics in favor of art, religion, and academic philosophy. This was part of their accommodation with the political and social realities of a resurgent Prussia. In stark contrast to this, Ruge went to prison in 1825 for five years for his activities in the cause of a united Germany. During his incarceration he translated Thucydides and a play of Aeschylus into German and wrote a tragedy of his own. After his release, he went to Halle University, where he became a professor of pedagogy and aesthetics. But in 1838 he once again jeopardized his future when he cofounded the *Hallische Jahrbücher*. Though originally open to centrist and leftist Hegelian views, Ruge's journals tracked his escalating trajectory toward the radical end of the Left Hegelian outlook. And as other, moderate, Hegelian journals had already fallen foul of censorship authorities, it was only a matter of time before Ruge's more radical version would attract the same sort of attention. The *Hallische Jahrbücher* was suppressed in 1840 and its still more radical successor journal, the *Deutsche Jahrbücher* operated until its final suppression in January 1843. Despite its brief career, the *Jahrbücher* was one of the most influential of its kind in nineteenth-century Germany. For a short while Ruge cooperated with Karl Marx, but didn't follow him into socialism. It was during this brief collaboration that Marx wrote the article that contained his famous "opium of the people" phrase.[16] In 1847 Ruge opened a bookshop in Leipzig, but continued harassment forced it to close in 1851. He was briefly elected to the parliament at Frankfurt, but unrest following the 1848 revolutions forced him to flee. He moved first to France, then to Switzerland, and then to Britain, where he lived the rest of his life, earning his money as a schoolmaster.

It is true that Ruge was not an original thinker and is therefore less important in the story of Left Hegelianism than the likes of David Friedrich Strauss (1808–1874), Bruno Bauer (1809–1882) or Ludwig Feuerbach (1804–1872). But for the purposes of our story, Ruge is, after Feuerbach, the most important Left Hegelian. This is because of Ruge's use of the word *humanism*. When he took up humanism, he did so with the background to the young word we have essayed. But in an article called "The Religion of Our Time," published in *Die Akademie* (1848), Ruge spoke of humanism as a transcendence of religion, an apotheosis of all that had come before. He developed these ideas in *Our System* (1850) and *The Lodge of Humanism* (1852). He argued for the liberation of social ethics and values from their supernaturalist associations. He devoted a great deal of time and effort to justify the role of opposition in democracy. The authoritarian Prussian state he worked so conscientiously against was unused to the notion of opposition being a good thing for democracy. Left Hegelians had placed a great deal of hope in the new Prussian king, Frederick William IV (reigned 1840–1861) and once they realized their hopes were unfounded, they moved to other, more radical solutions. To Ruge's credit, he stuck with notions of democracy. As part of this campaign for a healthy democracy that could tolerate, even value, a loyal opposition, Ruge called for free education, freedom of religious association, free speech, and a lively intellectual life encouraged by academies for the propagation of the arts and sciences. And he advocated a free market although, he was quick to add, within a context of what we now call *social justice*. This was his vision of humanism. In 1869 Ruge wrote *Addresses on Religion*, which developed a more extensive materialist critique of religion.

As a by-product of this practical, empirical reformism, Ruge was a consistent opponent of Romanticism. In a manner reminiscent of Niethammer, Ruge saw the nationalist, mythologizing irrationalism in Romanticism as a source of strength to authoritarianism and, therefore, a movement opposed to humanism. He was probably less conscious than Niethammer of the elements of Romanticism that he retained. The *Hallische Jahrbücher* devoted considerable space to criticizing Romanticism before its suppression in 1840.

So Ruge matters. He was, in part, responsible for carrying *humanismus* over to *humanism*. But it was not so much that he was pioneering a new path as popularizing the thoughts of others, in particular Hegel and Feuerbach. In fact, Ruge was among the first people to notice that Hegel's method could be dissociated from his conclusions.[17] This was a momentous insight and should be enough to cement Ruge's place in the humanist pantheon, even if his reworking of Hegelianism did not last. He was instrumental in transforming Hegel's philosophy from a retrospective look at the uses to which philosophy was made in the past to a prophetic tool that looked toward the future. Hegel had no particular interest in the future because his entire philosophy was a study of its final consummation in Christianity, Germanic freedom, the modern state—all exhaustively and idiosyncratically defined—and his own thought. Hegel's extraordinary influence lay in his releasing philosophy into the stream of history, and it was the achievement of Hegelian thinkers to re-envisage the course the stream of history might take.

While Hegel saw the stream of history winding its way inexorably to the semidemocratic, bourgeois constitutional monarchies then emerging in Europe, the Left Hegelians like Ruge could see the stream of history moving in new directions. Ruge saw the stream of history moving in the direction of humanism, by which he meant a "realized Christianity," in the sense of the humanistic goals expressed by Christianity (as by other systems of belief) finally being able to do some good by virtue of being shorn of the reactionary dogmas that for so long shackled the gospel of Jesus. Hegel, too, had been content to dismiss virtually all items of Christian dogma as metaphors for the essential truth of Christianity as the final vehicle by which *Geist* can be apprehended. *Geist*, or Spirit, was the only meaningful understanding of God, and only Christianity moved people toward *Geist*. Ruge made the next step when he spoke of humanism transcending both Christianity and philosophy. He wrote: "Only the free man is a real human being—the realization of the theoretical freedom is free humanity. Such humanizing of the world we call *humanism*."[18]

Ruge is important to our story because of the uses he put humanism to. But he was only really reworking the more profound insights of people like Feuerbach, who, more than anyone else, recalibrated the debate after Hegel's star began to wane. What is interesting about Feuerbach is that he grew up in Bavaria during the years Niethammer was building an education program modeled on humanism. Ludwig's father, Paul Johann Anselm von Feuerbach (1775–1833), had a similar role: being in charge of reforming Bavaria's penal code. And like Niethammer and Ruge, Ludwig Feuerbach wanted to chart a course between unpalatable extremes, in his case his father's Enlightenment rationalism on the one side and emotive Romanticism on the other.

Feuerbach recognized that, claims to a presuppositionless philosophy notwithstanding, Hegel's philosophy was a product of his time and circumstances and could not therefore presume to contain absolute truth, valid for all time.[19] And, crucially, Feuerbach took a much more naturalistic view of historical change than Hegel could ever have done. "Time," he wrote, "and not the Hegelian dialectic, is the medium of uniting opposites, contradictories, in one and the same subject."[20] And neither was Feuerbach interested in arguing for this or that doctrine. Instead he sidestepped all the sectarian noise by seeing religion in psychological terms, as a human need. Religion, Feuerbach argued, was a projection of our anthropocentric conceit. "Man distinguishes himself from Nature. This distinction of his is his God: the distinguishing of God from Nature is nothing else than the distinguishing of man from Nature."[21] This profound insight is an important foundation for a humanist ecology that began to be articulated a century later by Frederick Woodbridge, the American naturalist philosopher, whose work we will follow in chapter 13. As Feuerbach's thought developed, he came to emphasize more what he called the *I-Thou* relationship with nature and with our situation in nature. He rejected the Romantic image of the isolated individual able to operate in glorious separation from the world. Indeed, without this *I-Thou* dynamic being embedded in human nature, there would be no morality.

God, in Feuerbach's view, was the projection of our own conceit. The more we projected our greatest values onto a construct called *God*, the more we demonstrated our alienation from the world and from each other. What Feuerbach wanted to do was to alert people to the nature of this illusion, not in order to reject religion, but in order to be religious in the proper way. This, at least, was what he originally wanted. But as he read further, he came to a more comprehensively naturalist rejection of religion and sought a transformation of philosophy where humans would accept their limitations in the real world and come to terms with themselves more fully as a result.

The reputations of Ruge and Feuerbach suffered greatly at the hands of the Marxists, who never forgave either of them for their refusal to abandon liberal humanism. Ruge's public split with Marx meant he was written off as a bourgeois fellow traveler. And it is true that, late in his career, Ruge became an enthusiastic supporter of Bismarck and, for the last two years of his life, received a pension from the Prussian state. But Marx, who lived for many years on the credit of the capitalist Engels was not really in a position to criticize on this score. At the other end of the scale, the rationalist historian J. M. Robertson described Ruge as a man who "gave his life to a disinterested propaganda of democracy and light."[22] It is neither a profound nor an original insight on my part to suggest that the truth lies in between these two assessments. Ruge's true successors are Europe's non-Marxist socialists and social democrats—people like Jean Jaurès (1859–1914) in France, Edouard Bernstein (1850–1932) in Germany, and the English Fabians. And Feuerbach's true successors are most of the humanist thinkers this book will examine.

Before leaving Continental Europe, mention must be made of a curious irruption of humanism in Denmark. Gabriel Sibbern (1824–1903) was the son of Frederik Christian Sibbern (1785–1872), a prominent philosopher at the university in Copenhagen. While Frederik Sibbern was broadly critical of Hegelianism, preferring Schelling's brand of idealism, his son was more broadly skeptical. Gabriel was a strong influence on Georg Brandes (1842–1927), who went on to become one of Denmark's—and Europe's—most influential literary critics. In his memoirs, Brandes remembered Sibbern as old before his time, bald and suffering from gout, despite having lived an abstemious life. Sibbern was to Brandes an "emancipating phenomenon," having divested himself of all Danish prejudices, including supernatural religion. In 1866 Sibbern helped the young Brandes write a pamphlet called *Dualism in Our Modern Philosophy* (1866). Brandes helped introduce positivism and empiricism into Denmark, and from 1906 he was an honorary associate of the Rationalist Press Association (RPA) in Britain.

Sibbern brought his thoughts together in *Om Humanisme* (1858), which spoke of humanism as a way of life guided by reason and opposed to teleology and the claims of revelation. Not specifically atheistic, Sibbern took a broadly Confucian view of the gods, allowing their existence but seeing little value in devoting time to their consideration. Things were driven by "general forces" and the proper role of humanity was the open-ended and non-mediated study of these forces.[23] It would be good to see more work in English done on Sibbern.

GEORGE JACOB HOLYOAKE AND THE ARRIVAL OF HUMANISM IN ENGLAND

Whatever Gabriel Sibbern's influence on the Continent was, he had little direct influence on the spread of humanism in Britain. Here is where Ruge reenters the story. Once in England, it was natural that he should become acquainted with George Jacob Holyoake (1817–1906), an indomitable campaigner for secularism and cooperation. As early as 1854 the two men cooperated in the publication as a pamphlet one of Ruge's articles on German politics. And in 1859 Holyoake published a short work *The Principles of Secularism Briefly Explained*, in which humanism is mentioned. Secularist principles, Holyoake explained, included "humanism, moralism, utilitarian unity: humanism the physical perfection of this life—moralism founded on the laws of nature as the guidance of this life—materialism as the means of nature for the secular improvement of this life—unity upon this three-fold ground of positivism."[24]

Later in his life, Holyoake availed himself of the help of some of his better-educated acquaintances, people like John Stuart Mill and Francis William Newman (1805–1897), and rewrote his handbook on secularism. Holyoake's ideas on secularism in the 1890s were no less humanistic than they had been forty years earlier, although he no longer used the word *humanism* to describe them. What makes Holyoake interesting is that he anticipated many of the priorities and concerns of twentieth-century humanism, which took the rejection of supernaturalism as a given, asking what we put in its place. Secularism was Holyoake's answer to that question. In *The Origin and Nature of Secularism* (1896) Holyoake suggested that the scholarship of the day had revealed several negative insights: "That God is unknown; that a future life is unprovable; that the Bible is not a practical guide; that Providence sleeps; that prayer is futile; that original sin is untrue; and that eternal perdition is unreal."[25] This was no more than all the other radicals of the day were saying. Holyoake's contribution was the next step. "When we call out to men that they are going down the wrong road," he wrote, "we are more likely to arrest their attention if we can point out the right road to take."[26] Holyoake's right road was then itemized in this way:

(1) Study the laws and nature of the universe rather than its origin;
(2) Make wise use of this life rather than pining for a future life;
(3) Employ observation, investigation, and experience rather than revelation;
(4) Respect the providence of science over the Providence of scripture;
(5) Favor self-help over prayer;
(6) Strive for moral excellence rather than succumb to the defeatism of original sin, which denies it; and
(7) Worry more about breaking the laws of nature rather than eternal perdition for apparently breaking the laws of God.[27]

What is significant in Holyoake's prescription is its open-endedness. Rather than replacing one set of imperious truth-claims with another, Holyoake understood the need for a process humanism; a meliorist humanism of free inquiry and openness to new experiences. "The aim of secularism is to educate the conscience in the service of man. It puts duty into freethought."[28] We will return frequently through the course of this book to the notion of meliorism, so it's worth stopping and defining it carefully. *Meliorism* is the idea that the world can be made better, but that this is only going to happen by human effort. This is not the same as the sanguine confidence in progress; that things will automatically get better because that's how history works. Meliorism understands, in ways progressionism or dialectics do not, human fallibility and the ever-present reality of stagnation, decay, and disillusionment in history. Nothing happens easily and many things that do transpire have effects unforeseen by those who campaigned for them, leading to a new set of problems. For things to get better, people need to put aside their own little comforts and preferences and devote time to some aspect of making the world a better place. There is no shortage of causes for people to contribute time, effort, and money in the service of. But nothing will happen if we all stay at home and watch DVDs, or if we throw our hands up in horror, in the manner of some contemporary pessimists, and say that problems are too big. Meliorism is a core concept of humanism.

Holyoake has had a bad press from within the humanist movement and is now undeservedly forgotten. He was not as brave and forthright a person as his rival Charles Bradlaugh (1833–1891), was sometimes petty in disputation, and was too fawning of his social superiors. But, more than Bradlaugh, Holyoake saw the need for the nonreligious to take the next step after recognizing the error of religion to work out a coherent set of humanist ethics. And neither did he commit the error of the positivists who created little more than a quasi "me-too" religion or of the Marxists who replaced one set of absolutist commandments with another. Holyoake's secularism was unambiguously nontheistic without being exclusionary, something twentieth-century humanism strove long and hard to become. So while Holyoake, in all probability, took the word *humanism* from Ruge, I suspect that he also dropped the word because it came from Ruge. It is a tantalizing possibility that the very English and practical Holyoake dropped *humanism* in favor of *secularism* partly because of the dense, quasi-teleological gloss Ruge had given it.

So we can say with reasonable confidence that Arnold Ruge brought the word *humanism* to Britain and that George Jacob Holyoake popularized it, at least for a while, in his writings on secularism. But for the word to take hold there had to be a wider need for it. It had to fill a gap. And so there was, although it was a long time before humanism found its natural constituency. Two large potential constituencies were available. On the one hand was the radical tradition epitomized by Thomas Paine (1737–1809), who wrote *Rights of Man* (1971). It was through Holyoake that humanism entered this tradition, although it took another century for anything productive to arise from the union. The other constituency was the Whig tradition of constitutional reform, informed by the group known as the Philosophical Radicals, and which later turned into Liberalism.[29] It is not my intention to retell these stories here, even in the briefest detail, save to offer a mere sketch of two of the greatest figures of English reformism: Jeremy Bentham (1748–1832) and John Stuart Mill (1806–1873). Bentham's whole life was essentially humanistic, although he became a democrat and radical relatively late in his life. He was a convinced atheist, referring to Christianity as "Jug[gernaut]." Along with the historian George Grote (1794–1871), Bentham wrote *Analysis of the Influence of Natural Religion on the Temporal Happiness of Mankind* (1822). This remarkable document anticipated evolutionary psychology a century and a half later when it outlined the irrational nature of religion and argued that it can be explained entirely in naturalistic terms. It went even further by arguing that religion is damaging to society. But the criticism of religion was a relatively unimportant part of Bentham's lifework. He was, at heart, a practical reformer. In *Introduction to the Principles of Morals and Legislation* (1789), he said that the standard by which legislation should be judged is the degree to which happiness is maximized for the greatest number of sentient creatures, which he defined a lot more generously than was common.

> The French have already discovered that the blackness of the skin is no reason why a human being should be abandoned without redress to the caprice of a tormentor. It may come one day to be recognized, that the number of legs, the villosity of the skin, or the termination of the *os sacrum*, are reasons equally insufficient for abandoning a sensitive being to the same fate.[30]

To this end, he devised the principle of utility to give measure to happiness in each instance. He was not appealing to a supposed inherent rationality, but to the simpler measure; the ability to suffer. That he should apply this principle to animals, in defiance of millennia of theological tradition, was truly groundbreaking.

By any application of the principle of utility, much of England at the time was going to score very poorly indeed. Bentham was appalled by the state of hospitals and prisons in England, and the unalloyed misery they— and the beliefs that sustained them—engendered. He outlined various new layouts for schools and prisons, objecting, for example, to the mixing of hardened criminals with first offenders and teenagers. In order to attract public attention to these sorts of issues, he helped establish the *Westminster Review* in 1823, which went on to become very influential, not least when, many years later, it was edited by George Eliot (1819–1880). Bentham helped found Birkbeck College and University College, London, and he was a supporter of Robert Owen's visionary social experiment at New Lanark. Bentham understood, as many of his detractors have not, that problems need to be studied on-site and with as few metaphysical presuppositions as possible. When the Whigs returned to power in 1830, they brought with them some important ideas from Bentham. More than a century after his death, the humanist scholar and author E. Royston Pike (1896–1980) penned an appreciation of Bentham's achievements in a short work called "The Humanist Library," written for a series published by the Rationalist Press Association and called *Pioneers of Social Change*. "When today we turn," Pike wrote, "as we do as a matter of course, to parliament as the instrument of reform and the remover of abuses, we should sometimes remember that it was Jeremy Bentham who first suggested this particular way for us."[31]

One of the most telling criticisms of Bentham was that his measure of happiness was unhelpfully crude. How was one to measure happiness and would such a project make sense? Bentham was fortunate that John Stuart Mill was able to offer a credible solution to this problem. In *Utilitarianism* (1863) Mill developed and improved Bentham's crude utilitarianism by arguing that we should seek to maximize the happiness not of ourselves, but of others. He also spoke more of the *quality* of happiness than its *quantity*. This is why we should value liberty, Mill wrote. Who knows what sort of happiness is right for us? The good society, therefore, is the one that allows us maximum scope to find our happiness.

Mill was brought up in what even by nineteenth-century standards was an unloving and exceptionally demanding home environment. Throughout his life he suffered from depression, for which the poetry of Wordsworth and contemplation of the beauties of ancient Greece were important cures. He wrote of his upbringing very movingly in his revealing and honest *Autobiography* (1873). It is almost as easy to mock Mill as it is Bentham, and many have taken the opportunity to do so. But his wisdom, humanity, and wish to overcome his deficits are all admirable traits. Indeed, his successful resolution of the rationalist utilitarianism he was brought up with and the passion of the Romantics provided the framework for his humanism. Like Niethammer and Feuerbach, Mill was seeking out a viable middle ground between narcissistic Romanticism on the one hand and arid rationalism on the other.

Mill's essay *On Liberty* (1859) remains one of the foundational documents of the humanist tradition, even if his standard of liberty would be too laissez-faire for many. So many subsequent works have either taken it as their point of inspiration or have sought to continue its work in some way or another.[32] He declared liberty was essential to the health of the individual and the wider society. It followed from this that danger lies in intolerance and the tyranny of the majority, a message just as valid in the twenty-first century as in his own. Mill deserves recognition for being the first thinker in the Anglo American tradition to treat diversity as something beneficial rather than as a problem to overcome.[33] This is not to say he succumbed to a bland cultural relativism. He retained the duty to condemn practices that run against the grain of the ideal of liberty as he saw it. He defended Richard Carlile's right to publish books the majority disapproved of, and he was a staunch supporter of the North during the American Civil War. Other causes Mill supported included proportional representation, votes for women, national education, and the abolition of discrimination based on religion. He also gave public support to the embattled atheist campaigner Charles Bradlaugh, which probably cost him his seat in parliament in 1868. Not since Robert Owen had a respectable person of social standing been brave enough to publicly declare his own nonreligious views.[34]

Not even defending atheists got Mill in more trouble than his advocacy of the rights of women. Mill was an instinctive feminist, outlining his thoughts in *The Subjection of Women* (1869), although he had supported feminist views since he was eighteen. Not since Plato had it crossed anyone's mind to make a case for the equality of women. This book, and several others (notably *On Liberty*), was written with the help of Harriet Taylor (1807–1858), Mill's longtime companion and eventual wife. In some ways, Mill's open acknowledgement of Harriet's central importance as intellectual co-worker is what marks him out. In the way that Spinoza is seen as the "God-intoxicated" philosopher, Mill was the "Harriet-intoxicated" philosopher, and who's to say who had the better deal? More than most, before or after him, Mill acknowledged his love for someone else as a central motivation and correction for his life's work. Maybe that's where his true importance lies.

The point of all this is that, in the climate of opinion that Bentham and Mill had done so much to foster, there was a market for a concept like humanism. It is a commonplace for intellectual historians to speak of this climate of opinion as "liberal humanism."[35] These men were charting a middle course between reactionary conservatism on the one hand and destructive revolution on the other. They valued education and cosmopolitanism and eschewed supernaturalism without making the mistake of replacing one abstraction for another, whether based on nationality or class. And to their left was the radicalism in the tradition of Thomas Paine, secularism, and what came to be known as rationalism. But it took more than a century for either of these tendencies to either habitually be described as humanist or to specifically adopt the word as that which best expressed these virtues.[36] But the immediate future belonged more to words that divided people along class lines (socialism) or along lines of race (nationalism, imperialism). The time was not ready.

THE HUMANISM OF "WHAT MIGHT WE BECOME?"

Richard Rorty observed that the nineteenth century was the first time philosophers developed serious doubts about the traditional philosophical quest of discovering timeless truths to which humanity should conform. Under the influence of Hegel and Darwin, Rorty argues, the prime philosophical question moved from being, what are we? to, what might we become?[37] This builds on an observation made by Karl Löwith about Hegel. For all the deficiencies of detail, Löwith writes, Hegel remains the first philosopher to see history as infinite progress.[38] In *The Philosophy of History* Hegel says, "By nature man is not what he ought to be; only through a transforming process does he arrive at truth."[39] Where Kant saw the moral law as something stitched into the fabric of the cosmos, Hegel understood that both God and the moral law needed to be temporal and historical in order to be believable.[40] But Hegel left very little space for an ethically aware individual to consciously look toward self-improvement or to participate more ethically with the world. This was the task the Left—Hegelians set themselves. The history of the Left Hegelians–people like Feuerbach and Ruge—is the history of dissent about the nature of that progress and of its ultimate consummation. They were, in Löwith's words, preparatory philosophers.[41] An important implication of this is that there exists, at least in principle, the possibility that we might have developed differently. And the moment this possibility is seen to exist, humanity is charged with the task of working out what indeed we are to become.

What we can now see with the advantage of hindsight is that the Left Hegelians misunderstood what it was we were preparing for. If it was not the infinite stasis of the reactionaries, neither was it infinite progress, in the sense of things continually improving for humanity in accordance with some law of the universe. This is why the growth of socialism in the second half of the nineteenth century meant the corresponding sidelining of humanism as a distinct body of thought, which sees no cosmic law or principle at work in the dynamic of directionless change. So, as far as the story of humanism is concerned, the trail runs cold as the humanism of the Left Hegelians is turned by the Marxists into something quite different. And in Britain, the humanistic socialism of Robert Owen was slowly replaced by the more class-oriented socialism derived from Marx and Engels. Put crudely, Marx's question was not, what *might* we become? but, what I declare we *will* become! He replaced the meliorism implicit in the *might* with the teleological certainty of *will*. Marx divided the world into those on the right side of history and those on the wrong side. And, even more problematically, he then projected his understanding of history into a prophecy as to how the future will unfold. There is little direct communication between Marxism and humanism until the twentieth century, the story of which will be told in chapters 4 and 7.

Neither will time be spent here on the massive impact of Darwinism on humanism. This is because, as with Marxism, that teleological dynamic needed time to play itself out, which did not happen until the twentieth century. But it is clear that Darwinism radically altered the dimensions of any question about what we might become. But humanism, certainly in the nineteenth century, has little role in this story because it could contribute little to the understandings of evolution preferred at the time. In the second half of the nineteenth century it seemed blindingly obvious that evolution operated in teleological terms, maybe in the way set out by Herbert Spencer, maybe not, but teleological nonetheless. No less than Marx, Spencer was telling us what cosmic evolution, as revealed in his Synthetic Philosophy, had in store for human beings. Humanism had yet to emerge from the shadow of teleology, whether metaphysical or biological. This, over the past two centuries, is what humanism has been doing.

Another person who had a lot to say about what we might become was Friedrich Nietzsche. But once again, the cross-fertilization of Nietzsche's thought and humanism did not take place until the twentieth century. For many decades, Nietzsche's atheism was a barrier to his being seen as a humanist, rather than the essential starting point it was later to become for many. Nietzsche was an atheist, one of the world's greatest atheists, but the highly charged and problematic nature of his humanism took a lot longer to emerge. This did not become clear until Nietzsche's work found its finest twentieth-century interpreter, Walter Kaufmann.[42]

In other words, most of the later nineteenth-century accounts of what we might become had their moment in the sun with little reference to humanism. Feuerbach, Ruge, Mill, and Holyoake all offered their insights but were buried by the grander teleological systems of their rivals. Feuerbach and Ruge, in particular, were sufficiently deep within the shadow of Hegel to ask Hegelian sorts of questions but close enough to the edge of the shadow to see light beyond. And others like Bentham, Mill, and Holyoake were asking, what might we become? with even fewer teleological assumptions and without speaking directly of humanism. The story of contemporary humanism is the story of the evolution of the question, what might we become? in the light of new information. But it took another half century before this question could be asked in humanist terms. The rest of this chapter will trace the career of humanism in the second half of the nineteenth century.

BURCKHARDT, SYMONDS, AND THE MOVE FROM *UMANISTA* TO *HUMANIST*

While Ruge and Sibbern are both interesting and attractive figures, I don't, in the end, think that naming rights can go unequivocally to either of them. Sibbern was unknown in English-speaking circles, and while Ruge did indeed bring *humanism* into English usage, we know the word was already there. Neither is there much evidence of influential scholars taking the word up from Ruge. Too many of his works remain untranslated into English for his work to have had a broad influence. And Feuerbach had written by far the best humanist account of things to date, but had not spoken of this as humanism at all frequently enough for the connection to be made in the public mind.

At about the same time *humanism* came into usage in English, it was also being used to very different ends by James Gardner in a bulky, two-volume reference work called *The Faiths of the World* (1858–1861). This work included an entry on "humanists" but insisted on linking them to the Philanthropinists, the very people the word *humanism* was coined in opposition to. Gardner attacked the Philanthropinists as "thoroughly infidel, their chief aim being to sink the *Christian* in the *man*. Hence the name given to their system, which was usually called *humanism*."[43] Gardner's hostile application of *humanism* may have derived from earlier usages of the word in English in which its being at odds with Christian orthodoxy was more apparent than on the Continent. In England *humanism* had developed in the theological sense as the belief that Jesus Christ was merely and only human. Samuel Taylor Coleridge (1772–1834) used the word in this context in a marginal note that was later published in *Omniana* (1812), a collection of ephemera and left-over items gathered together by his friend Robert Southey (1774–1843), who then added a larger number of his own. In one of these items, titled "Religion," though actually a criticism of the Socinian heresy, Coleridge attacked those who had "passed from orthodoxy to Arianism to the barest humanism."[44] So, among English-speakers, *humanism* began its career as denoting very unpopular beliefs that would guarantee social ostracism. This goes a long way to explaining the longer time it took the word to gain acceptance in England than was the case on the Continent. Neither Ruge nor even Holyoake was in a position to reassure people of *humanism*'s respectability.

There is more evidence that *humanism*, when understood in its positive sense, entered into English usage through the growing body of Renaissance scholarship. Georg Voigt (1827–1891) was a German historian who, along with Jacob Burckhardt (1818–1897), was a significant figure in the creation of the idea of the Renaissance. Voigt's book *Wiederbelebung des classischen Altertums oder das erste Jahrhunderte des Humanismus* (*Revival of Classical Antiquity or the First Century of Humanism*), published in 1859, spoke of the Renaissance as the cradle of contemporary humanism. Indeed, it was Voigt who first spoke systematically of "Renaissance humanism." An earlier historian, Karl Hagen, had spoken of humanism in his three-volume *Deutschlands literarische und religiöse Verhältnisse im Reformationszeitalter. Mit besonderer Rücksicht auf Wilibald Pirkheimer* (1841–1844). These are the people who may well have read Niethammer and taken the word from him. Some

German-language scholars may well have already detected this line of descent. Until further work is done here, I can only speculate.

The most influential historian of the Renaissance was Jacob Burckhardt, whose *The Civilization of the Renaissance in Italy* (1860) was translated into many other languages and had a long life as the standard historical account of the period. Burckhardt had originally intended to join the church, but he lost his faith while studying theology. As Voigt had done, Burckhardt distinguished between *humanism*, which he defined broadly, and *humanists*, the itinerant scholars who lived a precarious life traveling between appointments, educating their clients in the ways of antiquity. These "Renaissance humanists" were spoken of disparagingly, on account of their reputation for being dissolute and irreligious. Humanism, by contrast, was characterized as "the discovery of the world and of man," the title he gave to the section of his book that dealt with the intellectual achievements of the Renaissance.

Burckhardt's history was translated into English in 1878, but by that time the first three volumes of what ended up as a seven-volume account by the Englishman John Addington Symonds (1840–1893) had appeared. *Renaissance in Italy* (1875-1886) introduced readers to a more effusive account of Renaissance humanism than Burckhardt had attempted. Following Burckhardt, Symonds gave a largely negative account of the wandering humanist scholars. But he was closer to Voigt when he brought humanism into the story, and in the very positive account he gave of it as the general outlook the Renaissance gave to the world. Niethammer had been completely forgotten at this stage, and Symonds did little more than note that *humanism* was a new word and had a German sound to it. The meaning Symonds gave to *humanism* is important and worth quoting at length.

> The essence of humanism consisted in a new and vital perception of the dignity of man as a rational being apart from theological determinations, and in the further perception that classic literature alone displayed human nature in the plenitude of intellectual and moral freedom. It was partly a reaction against ecclesiastical despotism, partly an attempt to find the point of unity for all that had been thought and done by man, within the mind restored to consciousness of its own sovereign faculty. Hence the single-hearted devotion to the literature of Greece and Rome that marks the whole Renaissance era. Hence the watchword of that age, the *Litterae Humaniores*. Hence the passion for antiquity, possessing thoughtful men, and substituting a new authority for the traditions of the Church. Hence the so-

called Paganism of centuries bent on absorbing and assimilating a spirit no less life-giving from their point of view than Christianity itself. Hence the persistent effort of philosophers to find the meeting point of two divergent inspirations. Hence, too, the ultimate antagonism between the humanists, or professors of the new wisdom, and those uncompromising Christians who, like St. Paul, preferred to remain fools for Christ's sake.[45]

Symonds was influential. He hoped to do for the Renaissance what Gibbon did for Rome. Gibbon was widely regarded as an essential element in any educated person's intellectual and social portfolio, and Symonds wished his work to be held in the same esteem and used in the same way. While not achieving that level of prestige, *Renaissance in Italy* is quoted liberally through humanist works of the first half of the twentieth century and helped shape the understanding of *humanism* at that time. And it was often the same people who read Gibbon who were reading Symonds. The people who learned that Rome was brought down by the combination of barbarians and Christianity also learned from Symonds that the humanism of the Renaissance was the progenitor of the rationalism then effecting major changes in theology, philosophy, and other disciplines. We can see, then, that *humanism* had been overshadowed on the left by more teleological gospels of progress, but it found a new home as the name given to virtues of the past that bourgeois historians favored.

ENGLISH USAGES OF *HUMANISM* IN THE LATER NINETEENTH CENTURY

Symonds was the first to graft *humanism* onto *progress* in a systematic way that was not teleological. After the Renaissance historians, the question, what might we become? took on a historical flavor. The question was asked by people wanting to show, in the light of the new naturalistic outlook revealed by Darwin, what we might become by looking at where we have come from. Humanism could now be seen as part of our development from a more primitive or tribal supernaturalism. The teleology of the first half of the century had altered its coloring slightly by taking on the form of what we would now call *progressionism*.

Evidence that this understanding of humanism as a naturalistic alternative to supernaturalism had reached English-speaking thinkers can be found in a late work by William Kingdon Clifford (1845–1879). In 1877, during an ongoing controversy in the influential journal *The Nineteenth Century*, Clifford argued that the decline of religion does not necessarily lead to a decline in morality. He made the perfectly reasonable observation that virtue may well be expressed in the language of the established beliefs of the day, but that does not mean that virtue is intimately beholden to them. "I neither admit the moral influence of theism in the past," he wrote, "nor look forward to the moral influence of humanism in the future. Virtue is a habit, not a sentiment or an ism."[46] It is interesting that while Clifford was distancing himself from the moral influence of humanism in the future, he was not denying in advance that possible outcome. He was simply saying that one can no more use the future as a mine from which evidence can be extracted as we can the past. In this way, Rorty's observation that the nineteenth century was speaking of what we may become in the future remains true with Clifford, even if the path is more difficult than others might suggest. And as an aside, it is worth noting that William James's classic essay "The Will to Believe" was written in response to Clifford's best-known essay, "The Ethics of Belief." And James was more specifically concerned to place truth as a future goal we strive for.[47] Here we have two strands of contemporary Western humanism in a nutshell: the *scientific rationalism* of Clifford and the more *individualistic pragmatism* (as it would later be called) of James. Both are postponing the final acquisition of truth to the indefinite future; where they differ is in the value to be placed on having a final goal at all, and what we can reliably use as evidence for our journey.

After Symonds's introduction of *humanism* and Clifford's use of the word in a setting unrelated to the Renaissance, it was a small step to encounter *humanism* spoken of in historical accounts of the nineteenth century. The earliest example I am aware of is from the British scholar J. M. Robertson (1856–1933). Dubbed "Britain's forgotten genius," Robertson remains an underappreciated scholar of daunting breadth. Most remembered for his views on the myth theory of Jesus, in fact his best works were intellectual histories of free thought, which avoided the mistakes his myth theory works were based on. In 1891 he brought together a series of lectures under the title "Modern Criticisms of Life" in a book called *Modern Humanists*. The book was subtitled *Sociological Studies of Carlyle, Mill, Emerson, Arnold, Ruskin and Spencer, With an Epilogue on Social Reconstruction*. As a friend of

Charles Bradlaugh, Robertson was familiar with words like *atheist*, *rationalist*, and *freethinker*, and yet he was happy here to speak of *humanist*. None of those other words would apply to all the people he was considering, while *humanist* was new enough, and general enough to apply to them all. He saw no need to justify his use of the word *humanist* in this context, and he understood it in the sense Matthew Arnold understood poetry as the criticism of life. As poetry was the criticism of life, it was a small step for the humanist to become the critic of life.[48] Two further collections with similar themes came out; *Pioneer Humanists* (1907) grew out of a series of articles that appeared originally in a variety of journals, principally the *Reformer*, a short-lived radical publication run by Hypatia Bradlaugh Bonner (1858–1935), Charles Bradlaugh's daughter. The people considered were, in this order: Machiavelli, Francis Bacon, Hobbes, Spinoza, Shaftesbury, Bernard Mandeville, Gibbon, and Mary Wollstonecraft. And in 1927, *Modern Humanists Reconsidered* returned to the thinkers he had considered in 1891.

More specific was the British philosopher and historian Alfred William Benn (1843–1915), who wrote a brief history of modern philosophy for the Rationalist Press Association, which also published Robertson's works. Benn was best known as the author of a substantial history of nineteenth century thought in Britain. This shorter and slightly broader account was published in 1912 in what was called the *History of Science* series. Benn's fifth and final chapter was titled "The Humanists of the Nineteenth Century." Unlike Robertson, Benn felt moved to offer some explanation for his use of the term.

> As applied to the culture of the Renaissance, *humanism* meant a tendency to concentrate interest on this world rather than on [the] next, using classic literature as the best means of understanding what man had been and again might be. At the period on which we are entering human interests again become ascendant; but they assume the widest possible range. Claiming for their dominion the whole of experience—all that has ever been done or known or imagined or dreamed or felt.[49]

Benn then outlined the story, taking care to include a few more European thinkers than was common among British philosophers at the time. Interestingly, he did not mention Ruge. The use of *humanism* made by Robertson and Benn suggest the line of influence runs from Burckhardt and Symonds rather than from Ruge, let alone Sibbern.

While *humanism* was making its first appearances in Britain as a catchall term for the study of the world without undue reference to supernaturalism, in the United States, *humanism* returned very deliberately to the cultural usage Niethammer had given it. This was largely the work of Irving Babbitt (1865–1933), a conservative literary critic. In 1895 Babbitt gave a lecture called "What Is Humanism?" in which he criticized Jean-Jacques Rousseau, who epitomized everything he disliked about Romanticism. Whereas earlier in the century Niethammer spoke of humanism as a corrective to the radical implications of Philanthropinism, at the end of the century Babbitt used humanism as a corrective to the radical implications of Romanticism. And Niethammer and Babbitt both found in the notion of humanism an important corrective to the dangers they espied in the doctrines of Rousseau. We will return to Babbitt in chapter 3.

Neither was Babbitt alone in taking humanism in this direction. Just as well known in his day was Edward Howard Griggs (1868–1951), an ethicist and literary critic from Stanford who made a career as a moralist and public intellectual espousing humanism in the sense of a cultured synthesis of classical and Christian virtues, particularly as revealed in the Renaissance. Griggs's professional work involved poetry and literary criticism, with studies of Dante, Goethe, Tennyson, and Robert Browning. But he also produced an extensive body of work for nonspecialists. One of the earliest of them was *The New Humanism: Studies in Personal and Social Development*. Published in 1899, this book had a long life, going through at least eight editions. Griggs did not specifically expound on *humanism*, being content to imply the word as the one best suited to his cultured synthesis of virtues. This is a remarkably modern-sounding book. With a few stylistic alterations, it could be published today with little need of explanation or apology. He was skeptical of ecclesiastical authority and formal creeds. "Not in great churchly establishments, not in the formal worship detached from daily life, not in inherited creeds and formulae lies the ethical inspiration for tomorrow."[50] He also warned against undue optimism that a golden new age is dawning. The answers lie not in escapism, asceticism, or acceptance of static formulae of thought. Griggs's ideal, and what he implied amounted to humanism, was a world of individuals committed to social living. As he put it, "The truest teaching is living; and the primary philanthropy is to live a good life."[51]

Griggs fits into a long American tradition of cultivated moralists who are suspicious of orthodoxy and who can employ current phrases and turns of thought to restate what are fairly conventional concerns and preferences. His slant was to popularize the idea of the Renaissance humanist as an ideal we can aspire to. He was, in effect, reworking for the benefit of American readers the notion of bildung, one which, given his field of study, he would almost certainly have been familiar with. He also deserves to be remembered as one of the first people who can usefully be thought of as a religious humanist. The way Griggs put it, if the Christian ideal was the higher one, then the Greek ideal was the broader and the saner one.

Coming from a different perspective, but in his way epitomizing just as central an aspect of humanism was Winwood Reade (1838–1875). An unusual man, a writer and a prophet, Reade was born into a comfortable middle-class family and was nephew of Charles Reade (1814–1884), the successful dramatist and novelist best remembered for his historical novel *The Cloister and the Hearth* (1861). Perhaps in imitation of his uncle, Winwood Reade hoped to make his name as a novelist but in this he was unsuccessful. His best-known novel was *The Outcast* (1875), a strange, tortured work that explored a sensitive man's loss of faith, social ostracism, and eventual suicide. Ironically, Reade is remembered not for his novels but for his visionary work *The Martyrdom of Man* (1872), which looked to an age when science, having freed humanity from its material needs, would permit us to attend to our psychological and emotional needs and build a perfect society on Earth. Reade was only thirty-three when he wrote *The Martyrdom of Man*, which went through twenty-two editions and sold more than two hundred thousand copies over the next fifty years. It had a profound influence on many people, perhaps the most notable being Winston Churchill (1874–1965), H. G. Wells (1866–1946) and George Orwell (1903–1950). Reade died of tuberculosis at the age of thirty-seven. A maniacal salvationist woman broke into the house where he lay dying and prayed noisily for his soul before being removed.

It has become almost mandatory to dismiss Reade's work. He has been accused of progressionism, scientism, utopianism, and superficial optimism, among other things. Biographers of Churchill and Wells are often bemused by Reade's influence and seek to explain it away, with apologies. But Reade's view of the future was not as crass as his critics imply. It is true that Reade indulges in a periodizing of history that is no longer the done thing. The crucial point, however, is that there is nothing inevitable, nothing teleological, about Reade's sense of history. Neither is there any melodrama about great men, the destiny of nations, or anything of that sort. In this respect he compares favorably with many of his theistic-minded contemporaries like William Swinton (1833–1892), whose popular histories combined progressionism with Christian triumphalism and racism.[52]

Reade's vision of progress was wistful and melancholic. It was one of the first of the biological visions; history was a stream of humanity. The progress of human life, he wrote, "is caused first by the mental efforts which are made at first from necessity to preserve life, and secondly from the desire to obtain distinction." Human development could not take place when one section of people advanced at the expense of others. "The progress of a nation is the sum total of the progress of the individuals composing it. If certain parts of the body politic are stifled in their growth by means of artificial laws, it is evident that the growth of the whole will be arrested; for the growth of each part is dependent on the growth of all."[53]

Reade was a humanist in the way Ruge was: a radical democrat not willing to embrace socialism but deeply moved by the long history of human suffering that oligarchy and orthodoxy have perpetrated. And if he took longer views than Bentham or Mill, he was motivated in a similar way. Science and technology *have* accomplished many of the things Reade spoke about. If later generations have been unable to manage science and technology effectively, the fault lies with us, not with Reade, who gave future generations the benefit of the doubt. Neither was Reade's progressionism as uncritical as later commentators have claimed. He understood the commitment, even sacrifices, that must be made in building a humane society of the future. The last sentences of *The Martyrdom of Man* spoke almost as a lament. In a style reminiscent of Matthew Arnold, Reade wrote: "The soul must be sacrificed; the hope in immortality must die. A sweet and charming illusion must be taken from the human race, as youth and beauty vanish, never to return."[54]

By the end of the nineteenth century, three important strands of humanist thinking had begun their career. *Humanism* as a term for cultural refinement, erudition, and a love of learning, often associated with the Renaissance, was now an established idea. But there was also the very different notion of humanism as a radical alternative to theism and the reactionary establishment that propped it up. For the first part of the century it had been known as *humanism*, among other things, but as the century progressed and the lines of opposition hardened, this usage fell away. As the intellectual trajectory of humanism moved away from metaphysically justified teleology, it became estranged from Marxism. And standing in the wings, as yet unaware of its common purpose with humanism, stood non-Marxist materialism, as championed by people such as Ludwig Büchner (1824–1899). And finally, there was the third arm of humanism, the one least aware of itself in this sense. This was the tradition of moderate, constitutional reform, which, in England at any rate, was championed by people like Bentham and Mill and later articulated by sociologists and liberals like Graham Wallas (1858–1932) and L. T. Hobhouse (1864–1929). This is the tradition many historians now call *liberal humanism*. Over the next century the first of these strands, the moralists taking their cue from the Renaissance, drifted away into more conservative positions or reconciled themselves with traditional religion. But the second and the third strands were destined to see a lot more of each other through the course of the twentieth century.[55] Radical visionaries like Reade and his successors found they had more in common with constitutional reformers like Mill and his successors than either of them did with advocates of violent revolution like Marx.

What is apparent in this account of nineteenth-century humanism was how little it intersected with major trajectories of atheist and other non-Christian thought. Arthur Schopenhauer and Friedrich Nietzsche, to name the two most important of these thinkers, were atheists and non-Christians, and it has really been only since World War II that Nietzsche, in particular, has become a significant intellectual force in world humanism. But as we will see in chapter 7 and elsewhere, this relationship has never been an easy one.

CHAPTER 2

PROTAGORAS'S CHEERLEADER: F. C. S. SCHILLER AND HUMANISM'S NEW BEGINNING

As *humanism* approached its first centenary, we have seen that it had been put to several different usages, each of which was justified in some manner or other as a legitimate continuation of the word from its Renaissance origins. But *humanism* could easily have sunk once more without trace. Outside a small coterie of Renaissance scholars and aficionados of post-Hegelian thought, the word had little traction. Indeed, nineteenth-century philosophical thought had moved along trajectories which were antithetical to humanism: metaphysical theories of history, nationalism, and the will. And during the 1890s there had been a return to various forms of irrationalism, known by its detractors as the "flight from reason."

There had also developed, stimulated in no small part by William James's essay "The Will to Believe," a climate of opinion that legitimated one's beliefs because of what they did for the believer, rather than whether or not they were true according to some apparently absolute external standard. Belief was no longer simply a matter of dutifully accepting what one believed to be true. It was believed because the sense of commitment the belief involved was worth more, in the end, than whether the proposition believed was true. The person who developed this insight most fully was not James, but his ally F. C. S. Schiller. And what makes this most interesting from our point of view was his decision to repackage this as *humanism*. By this roundabout route, Schiller was the person who flung the word into the twentieth century.

F. C. S. SCHILLER AND THE HUMANISTIC VIEW OF LIFE

Ferdinand Canning Scott Schiller (1864–1937) was an exuberant, even garrulous man with an interesting background. He was born to a German family in the Danish part of Schleswig, in the year the majority of that province was placed under Prussian administration after the first of the series of brief wars that created the German Empire. The family had made its fortune in India and settled in England. He was educated at Rugby and Balliol College, Oxford. In 1897, after a short but significant spell at Cornell University in the United States, he returned to Corpus Christi College, Oxford, where he taught until 1926. While in the United States, Schiller was exposed to what became known as *pragmatism*, especially as articulated by William James. Schiller spent his career championing his variety of pragmatism. But his work fell on increasingly deaf ears in England, so from 1926 onward, Schiller spent part of each year lecturing at the University of Southern California. In 1935, he moved there permanently and, aged seventy-one, married. He died on August 9, 1937.

In his day, Schiller was routinely listed as one of the most significant exponents of pragmatism. Now his name is all but forgotten. But for the purpose of this history, Schiller is once again important. It is not my intention to outline a history of pragmatism, but it is important to look thoroughly at Schiller's version of pragmatism. While acknowledging William James's importance, Schiller took pragmatism in more of a relativist direction than his mentor advocated. Schiller resolutely opposed any form of foundationalism, or what today is called *essentialism*, although, as we will see, he was not altogether consistent about this.

But the real importance of Schiller for our purposes is his use of the word *humanism* to describe his variation of pragmatism. He wrote a great deal, though the most relevant titles for our purposes are *Humanism: Philosophical Essays* (1903), *Studies in Humanism* (1907) and *Our Human Truths* (1939). His prose was dense but was made readable by the clarity of his thinking and the vigor of his opinions. The main point, as I say, is that what James called *pragmatism*, Schiller chose to call *humanism*. This was not a casual change. In speaking of humanism, Schiller wanted to anthropomorphize pragmatism. Indeed, in his first book, *The Riddle of the Sphinx*, published in 1891, he spoke of anthropomorphism to express his views. In his influential essay of 1902, "Axioms as Postulates," he acknowledged the existence of pragmatism, and the following year he introduced humanism. Why humanism? He doesn't say. There is no evidence either way, but it is tempting to speculate that Schiller knew of and might even have read *Om Humanisme*, written by the Danish thinker Gabriel Sibbern. Far more likely would have been his knowledge of the word through the classical scholars like Cicero and from the historians of the Renaissance. It is also more than likely he had read Clifford, if only because William James, his mentor, had reacted so strongly to him.

As is so often the case with humanists, of whichever stripe, Schiller took inspiration from the ancient world. Which particular ancient one takes prime inspiration from tells a lot about the sort of humanism one will espouse. For Schiller it was Protagoras (ca. 485–411 BCE), the pre-Socratic philosopher best known for his maxim that "man is the measure of all things." Schiller extolled Protagoras as providing the most sound and convenient starting point for humanism. Fairly interpreted, Schiller writes, "this is the truest and most important thing that any thinker has ever propounded."[1] Near the end of his life, Schiller praised Protagoras as the first ancestor "of the humanistic attitude toward life in general."[2] His fullest discussions of Protagoras came in the form of two dialogues that expanded on the "man is the measure" maxim. So central was Protagoras to Schiller's entire philosophy that in an address titled "The Humanistic View of Life," Schiller felt he was doing the topic justice by telling once again the story of his mentor's life and drawing conclusions from that.

Schiller was especially anxious to protect Protagoras from the suspicion of atheism. Protagoras had written: "concerning the gods I have never been able to discover whether they exist or not: life is too short and the subject too obscure." Far from suggesting atheism, Schiller countered, Protagoras simply wanted to know about the gods, and his persecutors took one sentence out of context and charged him with impiety.[3] It's not that such a scenario is unlikely, but there is little evidence that can be offered either way. It is significant that Schiller never saw fit to apply this argument to his own use of Protagoras's "man is the measure of all things." Neither did Schiller discuss Protagoras's statement on the gods as a prototype of agnosticism, as opposed to atheism.

F. C. S. SCHILLER AND THE
NEW UNDERSTANDING OF *HUMANISM*

But we are getting ahead of ourselves. We need first to understand the distinction Schiller drew between pragmatism and humanism. He outlined the differences in a 1905 essay, "The Definition of Pragmatism and Humanism." His account of pragmatism was straightforward enough. Whereas all previous philosophical or theological systems sought to determine what the truth was, pragmatism "essays to trace out the actual 'making of truth,' the actual ways in which discriminations between the true and false are effected, and derives from these its generalizations about the method of determining the nature of truth. It is from such empirical observations that it derives its doctrine that when an assertion claims truth, *its consequences are always used to test its claim.*"[4] From this, Schiller arrived at the first step in his seven-point definition of pragmatism.

The first point about pragmatism as Schiller understood it was that it is a doctrine that states "*truths are logical values*, and as the method which systematically tests claims to truth in accordance with this principle."[5] This accords with James's understanding of pragmatism as "first, a method; and second, a genetic theory of what is meant by truth."[6] From this core principle, Schiller extrapolated the following six points: (1) the truth of any claim depends on its application, with the result that "abstract" truths are not "fully truths at all." From this it followed that (2) the meaning of a rule must also lie in its application, which in turn implied (3) that all meaning depends on purpose. This led to what he called the "most essential feature of pragmatism," which was the claim that (4) "all mental life is purposive." This, he argued, was a major feature of pragmatism's revolt against naturalism which, in his mind, was a purposeless void of atoms. His central theme came in the next dictum, which spoke of pragmatism as (5) "a systematic protest against all ignoring of the purposiveness of actual knowing, alike whether it is abstracted from for the sake of the imaginary 'pure' or 'absolute' reason of the rationalists, or eliminated for the sake of an equally imaginary 'pure mechanism' of the materialists." While pragmatism may point to "a metaphysic" (rather than being one), Schiller insisted pragmatism's real gift was as (6) an "epistemological method which really describes the facts of actual knowing."[7] He now offered his summative definition of pragmatism as (7) "*a conscious application to epistemology (or logic) of a teleological psychology, which implies, ultimately a voluntaristic metaphysic.*"[8]

This is very unsatisfactory definition, not the least reason being that it in turn needs to be explained and clarified. And this will not be the last time we will come across this sort of problem. More important for our story, however, is the transition from pragmatism to humanism that Schiller now makes. Humanism was pragmatism writ large. "What is really important, however, is not this or that formulation, but the spirit in which it approaches, and the method by which it examines, its problems. The method we have observed; it is empirical, teleological, and concrete. Its spirit is a bigger thing, which may fitly be denominated humanism."[9] So humanism, in Schiller's mind, was the animating heart of pragmatism. It is, he wrote, the more universal application of pragmatism, not just to the theory of knowledge, but to all fields of human endeavor. It is one of the paradoxes of this story that Schiller is not better known, given the significance of this step. William James is often acknowledged as broadening the scope of pragmatism from the more focused applications in logic that motivated Charles Peirce. Why, then, is Schiller not credited for expanding the scope of humanism? There are three main reasons: Schiller's personality, the narrowness of his conception of humanism, and the rise of people who ended up broadening the range of humanism so much better.

The first point to note, of course, was that Schiller was unsuccessful in persuading James to adopt his usage of *humanism* over *pragmatism*, notwithstanding Louis Menand's claim to the contrary.[10] This seems unlikely, not least because the chronology is wrong. James spoke of pragmatism in 1898, five years before Schiller began to speak of humanism. Once Schiller began speaking of humanism, it seems James made some effort to accommodate his ally, but in the end he chose not to take humanism up as Schiller wished. In his 1904 article "Humanism and Truth," James recommended *humanism* be adopted as the name for Schiller's more expansive view, partly, one can't help suppose, to ensure a gap between the two ideas.[11] In a letter to Schiller in April 1907, James apologized that it was too late for replacing *pragmatism* with *humanism* in his forthcoming book because it was already in type. It must have been apparent to Schiller how lame this excuse was. James was familiar with Schiller's use of the word and had had plenty of time to make the changes to his 1907 lectures had he wished to do so. The 1907 lectures duly came out under the title "Pragmatism." And once again, James spoke about humanism, linked the word with Schiller's usage of it, and left it at that.[12] James's unwillingness to take humanism on, particularly when he had the opportunity with his 1907 lectures, spelled the end of Schiller's attempt to replace *pragmatism* with *humanism*.

So Schiller was on his own. But he probably was not unduly fazed by this, as he was a confident man. For most of his career he saw humanism as the middle ground between Hegelian absolutism and Christian theology on the one hand and science and materialism on the other. James used different terminology when he spoke of pragmatism but agreed that this was the correct placement. Humanism was the middle ground in that it avoided the worst excesses of determinism and dogmatism without lapsing into solipsism and skepticism. What is more, the ability of humanism to affect this amounted to a transcendence of the earlier outlooks. Later on, Schiller changed tack slightly when he said humanism dealt only with logic and the theory of knowledge and "is not concerned with theology at all."[13]

So how did Schiller go about his quest of building humanism as an extension of pragmatism? He argued that pragmatism frees us "from what constitutes perhaps the worst and most paralyzing horror of the naturalistic view of life, the nightmare of an *indifferent* universe."[14] He always expressed this particular fear with greater emphasis than James, and it had a large role in his idea of humanism as the next step up from pragmatism. For James, pragmatism was not there to save us from anything, and still less to provide consolations. But it was for Schiller. So while Schiller settled on *humanism* as his preferred vehicle in preference to *anthropomorphism*, the change of word was purely tactical, because his humanism was essentially anthropomorphic. "Thus in the last resort the anthropomorphic 'humanism' of our whole treatment of experience is unavoidable and obvious; and must finally confess that to escape anthropomorphism he would have to escape from self."[15]

There is a very reasonable and uncontroversial point here as well as a contentious one. The reasonable point was echoed by Bernard Williams, who reiterated Schiller's point made eight decades previously, that seeing the world from a human point of view is not an unreasonable or absurd thing for us to do. After all, from what other point of view can we use? Humanism, in that sense, is not a prejudice. But Williams made sure to go on, in a way Schiller did not, to aver any idea that this legitimized anthropocentric thinking. "It is not, as the strongest forms of ethical theory would have it, that reason drives us to get beyond humanity. The most urgent requirements of humanity are, as they have always been, that we should assemble as many resources as we can to help us to respect it."[16]

Schiller did not make that crucial next step that Williams made, which led to the contentious part: his anthropocentrism. Whereas Williams would urge us to assemble resources from a clear-eyed look at the world as it actually is, Schiller was content we would create a world of our own to stave off the void. He was concerned about the sort of world in which the "ultimate significance of our ideals was denied." A world like that would enthrone despair in a ways that "hopelessness would disarm even the suicide's hand.... The foundations of the cosmos would be shattered, and we should have to realize that nothing is worth doing because nothing has any worth, because human valuations have no significance in establishing the nature of things."[17] So as to prevent, or at least fend off, this nightmare, we must create the belief of a moral universe. We can't prove that the universe is moral, but that matters little. We need this belief, and that is justification enough. We "cannot organize our moral experience without this assumption, and in the course of moral development our confidence in it grows."[18] And into this moral universe we can happily insert anthropocentric conceits like immortality, a belief that, because it is needed, will be impervious to the findings of science.

In the face of this shrine to our anthropocentrism, it is not surprising Schiller had little or no interest in criticizing religion. He was critical of Christian theology in the sense that it was dogmatic. Dogmas "are not really intellectual products at all, and therefore cannot be attacked (or defended) as such. No religion really rests on the impersonal support of pure reason; nor can it be kept from moving with the times by chains of rusty syllogisms. For the truth is that dogmas are essentially secondary expressions of the vital value of a religion, the by-products of a spiritual life that was never nourished on pure intellect."[19] One of Schiller's most memorable maxims came to light in this context when he said, "In making dogmas it is hard to avoid making heretics."[20] This is reminiscent of Spinoza's equally valid observation that there is no heretic without a text.[21]

Dogma and the real core of religion were, for Schiller, quite different things. This comes to one of the core areas humanists have been unable to agree upon. Hardline critics of religion tend to take dogmatic claims seriously and see value in confronting them head-on. The English sociologist Colin Campbell has called this *strand abolitionism*. Then there are those who are happier to simply ignore dogma and try to refashion religion in their own image. Campbell calls this tendency *substitutionism*.[22] By this measure,

Schiller was a radical substitutionist. He was entirely unconcerned about the truth or falsity of dogmatic claims. Religions are "deserving of respectful and sympathetic consideration from a humanist philosophy. They are pragmatically very potent influences on human life, and the religious instinct is one of the deepest in human nature."[23] This was a consistent thread through his philosophical career. In one of his later essays, he wrote of religions as being vehicles where "appeals for supernatural and superhuman aid when human powers fail."[24] He was uninterested in any claim as to whether or not the supernatural agency being appealed to existed. All that mattered was whether it worked for the appellant. "I do not see why a humanist should not turn naturalist or supernaturalist upon occasion, when his human resources have left him in the lurch. For the supreme and overriding principle to guide our attitude toward life must always be the pragmatic principle, and we should not allow any metaphysical prejudices to stand in the way of our salvation."[25]

One of the many objections to this approach is that, while it's all very well to simply step aside from the phantoms of theology and dogma, can one take the same attitude toward the physical world, and toward science, the most effective means by which we learn how the physical world operates? This has been an ongoing problem for pragmatism and against which they reacted defensively. Schiller illustrates these problems more graphically than any other pragmatist philosopher. The simplest illustration of the problems he got into is his confusion of relativity with relativism, a mistake he shares with many postmodernist and sociology-of-science critics eight or nine decades later. Humanism and relativity "are, of course, forms of relativism in the wider sense, and humanism naturally sympathizes with relativity insofar as it breaks away from the naïve absolutism of Newtonian physics, which ascribed absoluteness to space and time and barely conceded the relativity of motion."[26] Reassured that science could no longer claim any privileged status as a method by which reliable knowledge can be gleaned, Schiller was able to take from science what he wanted.

For Schiller, scientific law implied determinism, with all the horrors of a purposeless void he so feared. He also saw that what was called a law of nature one day was a discredited shibboleth the next, and he concluded from this that science can produce no reliable knowledge. "In all the sciences 'laws of nature' are being rejected, reenacted, revised and remodeled daily. They are 'true' only insofar as they work and are able to anticipate results which experience confirms. There is no more mystical nor higher test of their truth."[27] With scientific method suitably dethroned, Schiller could proceed to impose upon science his preferred nostrums.

With respect to evolution, Schiller was reluctant to make any concessions to Darwinism. He gave this full treatment in "Darwinism and Design," published originally in 1897 and reproduced in *Humanism: Philosophical Essays*. It was Schiller's strongly held desire to retain room for teleology in evolution. With that in mind, he used a phrase which has since become notorious: *intelligent design*.[28] It is no surprise, then, that some of Schiller's weakest, most question-begging arguments can be found in this context. In a piece of sleight of hand many of his descendants would be proud of, Schiller concluded his lengthy essay insisting that evolution "is not necessarily bound to be mechanical; it is perfectly possible to regard it as the gradual working out of a divine purpose."[29] Two things are going on here. First, it is perfectly *possible* to do a lot of things, but that doesn't make them valid. And second, he seems to assume that these are the only available options. He almost recognizes this when he concludes that neither side can appeal uncontestably to the facts, it boils down to choice: "the exercise of our 'will to believe'; it rests, like all the ultimate assumptions of our knowledge, upon an act of faith."[30]

One of the strongest motivating forces for Schiller to keep some wiggle room for teleology was his Lamarckist preconceptions. For instance, he consistently reiterated the uniqueness of *Homo sapiens*. Once all the other points have been conceded, he insisted, the very least that can said is that humans are not automata. "In us at least, therefore, intelligent effort is a source of adaptation."[31] He went on to give an account of the problems with variation he saw Darwinism suffering from, specifically identifying his conclusions with Lamarckism in the process. What gave design the edge as an explanatory tool was the fact of progress. The only "method of discriminating between the results of 'design' and 'chance' is to observe a *deviation* from the fortuitous distribution (which betrays no preference for any particular result) in the direction of what may be conceived as a *more valuable result*."[32] The fact of these more valuable results was what built up human progress. For Schiller it was a telling blow when he declared that all "mechanical laws of evolution, from Spencer's law of differentiation downward, fail just where Darwinism pure and simple failed—viz., in accounting for the historical fact of progress."[33]

Schiller's Lamarckism, progressionism, and teleology were all in the service of his other, and most deeply held "scientific" notion, that of eugenics. A founding member of the Eugenics Society, he served on its board on several occasions. One of his most important points against Darwinism was that it gave no support for eugenics. At one point he spoke of the "idiot, or lunatic, or weakling, or wastrel [who] clearly possess only negative value for social purposes. . . . Clearly, therefore, society would be better without them, and if science could prevent their birth, it would unquestionably do so; if it could detect them after birth, it would extinguish them as speedily as possible. No sentiment of pity or prejudice about justice and right would impede its mercilessly reasonable calculations."[34]

WHY DID F. C. S. SCHILLER'S HUMANISM NOT TAKE ROOT?

Schiller's understanding of humanism did not survive him. There are several reasons for this. Not the least significant was Schiller's personality. More than once has it been observed that defenders of openness, toleration, and flexibility are themselves so often closed, intolerant, and inflexible. It's one of those human foibles. By the standards of late Victorian and Edwardian philosophy, Schiller was combative, even truculent. He was right and everyone else was wrong, very wrong indeed. There was little room for compromise; all the prominent philosophers of the day—Bradley in particular, but also Lotze and McTaggart—were, at best, hopelessly lost and misguided. Oxford never came to terms with Schiller's combative style, and pragmatism remained entirely beyond the pale as a result. Bertrand Russell thought that Schiller rather liked being hated by his Oxford colleagues.[35] An early biographer of Bertrand Russell noted, "Schiller's philosophy was supposed to be humanistic, but in argument he was dogmatic and dry. Russell had a philosophy which was cold and logical; but in argument he was warm and human."[36] Even Schiller's widow acknowledged this weakness. In a foreword to a posthumous collection of his essays, Louise Schiller described her late husband's work as "occasionally flashing into thunder and lightning, and sharp riposte, impatient with stupidity, in many places at the same time, fluid as mercury, rushing in upon his truth from many directions."[37]

Against this unattractive picture, it should be added that Schiller also had a sense of humor. A lot can be forgiven a person who has a sense of humor. This was given most famous expression in 1901 when he wrote a spoof issue of the prestigious philosophical journal, *Mind*. The full title was *Mind! A Unique Review of Ancient and Modern Philosophy, Edited by A. Troglodyte, with the Cooperation of the Absolute and Others*. Contributors to Schiller's parody included I. Cant on "The Critique of Pure Rot." There was also a history of philosophy written entirely in limericks. Many of the targets of this parody never forgave him. Later in his life Schiller penned an essay called "Must Philosophy Be Dull?" But even much of his humor was at the expense of his philosophical foes.

Also relevant is the fact that Schiller had no thoughts of humanism becoming a mass movement. Humanists are not amateurs, he wrote, but "hard-working professionals, themselves leading the academic life, and exposed to all the rigors of the academic atmosphere."[38] One can only imagine Schiller's reaction to Richard Rorty's demand that Philosophy, with a capital *P*, be dismantled in favor of philosophy, to be conducted in the manner of cultural criticism by name-dropping generalists of the chattering classes.[39] And yet it must still have come as something of a surprise to the framers of the *Humanist Manifesto* when Schiller replied so negatively to their invitation to comment on the draft as it then stood. We will explore this further in the next chapter.

But neither of these can be the whole answer. One has only to consider the posthumous career of Martin Heidegger to appreciate that neither an unattractive personality nor the distinct lack of popular appeal need stand in the way of achieving a broad influence. A larger part of the answer lies in the limitations of what Schiller was trying to do. His goal was in fact relatively narrow: the discrediting of his philosophical opponents of the 1900s. Schiller saw his understanding of humanism as the middle ground between the Scylla of Hegelian absolutists and the Charybdis of scientific materialism. But Scylla soon collapsed and Charybdis changed its character considerably, leaving Schiller's humanism becalmed in the doldrums rather than charting a bold new course. Hegelian absolutism was in mortal decline by 1910 and was largely irrelevant to the philosophical climate after World War I.

In fact, Hegel's influence on the pragmatism he championed was no less significant. One historian of religious humanism has credited Hegel with two core insights of pragmatism and, from there, religious humanism. The first of these insights is the idea that truth can be seen as developmental and the second is the related idea that reality and our experience of reality are part of an ongoing dynamic.[40] And many philosophers have noted the strong influence of these Hegelian notions on Dewey's thought. So, if Hegelianism was more flexible intellectually than Schiller allowed for, so was his other bete noire, scientific materialism, which had also changed considerably rather than petered out. The atomism of Ludwig Büchner and the talk of substance led by Ernst Haeckel had gone, but Darwinian evolution had not. And in the hands of people like Roy Wood Sellars, Frederick Woodbridge, and others, evolutionary naturalism was to take on a new lease of life and stimulate new conceptions of humanism. This is another line we will follow in a later chapter. And the narrowness of Schiller's goals also limited the need critics felt to give full attention to his work. If they intended to criticize pragmatism, they not unreasonably went to James rather than to Schiller. And as Dewey built up a reputation, people increasingly turned to him as well. And only later on did Charles Peirce receive his due as the true founder of the school.

And finally, in a very important respect Schiller has simply been proved wrong. He saw scientific materialism as a flawed dogmatism of the past that his radically subjectivist version of humanism had transcended. He vented his spleen in this rather confusing polemical flourish: "The rattling of dry bones can no longer fascinate respect nor plunge a self-suggested horde of fakirs in hypnotic stupor. The agnostic maunderings of impotent despair are flung aside by the young, the strong, the virile."[41] This has not happened. What has been flung aside are most attempts at offering transcendental fig leafs. In fact, each pillar of Schiller's understanding of science has collapsed: Lamarckism, progressionism, teleology, psychical research, and eugenics.

But despite it all, Schiller deserves an important place in the history of humanist thinking. Wrong-headed and truculent as he was, it was Schiller, more than anyone else, who gave humanism a new lease of life. Alongside the better-known Bertrand Russell and G. E. Moore, Schiller deserves praise for his slash-and-burn assault on Hegelian absolutism. Crude and misdirected as his assault was, he severed the links between humanism and grandiose system building and teleology. The severing was achieved partly by the strength of Schiller's arguments against it, and the links with teleology were severed partly because of the weakness of his arguments in favor of it. This left the ground clear for others to follow in his footsteps and cut the last links, in particular between teleology and humanism, which hung on for a while. The people who developed humanism after Schiller followed paths he did not approve of, but he is not alone in suffering that fate, and neither is such a fate inimical to his philosophy.

Schiller also deserves credit for his strong engagement with real issues. No bloodless toying with language for Schiller. He was interested in the big questions and not afraid to pose big solutions. And finally, Schiller's pluralism was deep and abiding. Once allowance is made for his personal foibles, he was an important example of how different philosophical persuasions can muddle along together. And he never shirked the responsibility for ongoing study and reflection. He may not have practiced it as completely as he could—hardly a crime unique to him—but he realized the importance of rejecting the easy absolutes and taking responsibility for one's intellectual destiny. "The notion of an absolute truth suggested itself as an expedient for escaping the continuous revaluation and transvaluation of truths, which forms the history of knowledge."[42] Reuben Abel says Schiller's "unique contribution to philosophy may be stated as his emphasis on the effective creativity of the mind of man."[43] That probably overstates the case, but it remains true that this wise warning cannot be repeated too frequently.

CHAPTER 3

MAKING THE MANIFESTO: HUMANISM BETWEEN F. C. S. SCHILLER AND JOHN DEWEY

This chapter tells the odd, disjointed story of developments in humanism after F. C. S. Schiller. We have already noted that his influence in Britain ranged between negative and negligible and that only in the United States did he attract a hearing. But the humanism that grew up in the United States quickly revealed a much broader range of influences than Schiller could possibly have approved of.

HUMANISM IN BRITAIN AFTER F. C. S. SCHILLER

Ferdinand Schiller failed to pass on his conception of humanism, but this does not mean that humanism's career came to an end. But it had to cross the Atlantic to find a congenial home. In Britain humanism went into cold storage for the best part of forty years. Several people referred to humanism, but nobody adopted the word wholeheartedly. Two of the more important of these incidental usages were *Lectures on Humanism* (1907) by the Scottish ethicist John Stuart Mackenzie (1860–1935) and R. B. Haldane's *The Philosophy of Humanism* (1922), which we will consider presently. Mackenzie was at this time a professor of logic and philosophy at the University College of South Wales and on the editorial board of the *International Journal of Ethics*. His most important work was a *Manual of Ethics*. First published in 1883, this book was still being reprinted in 1946, having gone through six editions. If a little unexciting by contemporary standards, the *Manual of Ethics* is an impressive textbook of sound ethical thinking.

Mackenzie was briefly an honorary associate of the Rationalist Press Association, accepting the title along with twelve others when the RPA first created them in 1899. Clearly uncomfortable with the title, he resigned a year later, the first RPA honorary associate to do so. He was more at home in the ethical movement, where he remained active for most of the rest of his life. Among other things, he contributed an essay to an anthology issued to commemorate the twenty-first anniversary of the Union of Ethical Societies. The anthology, *A Generation of Religious Progress* (1916), can be seen as the British version of *Humanist Sermons*, an influential collection of essays edited by Curtis Reese, which we will discuss later in this chapter. *A Generation of Religious Progress* is weaker than the American collection; the writing is more pedestrian and the bland assumption of time being on their side is all the more incongruous, given that it was published as the battle of the Somme raged.

The most concerted attempt to employ humanism came in 1917 when the ethical movement began a magazine called *The Humanist* (subtitled *A New Religion*) under the editorship of Charles T. Gorham (1856–1933), who also served at that time as secretary of the Rationalist Press Association. Gorham was a respected and frequent contributor in the RPA's journal, the *Literary Guide*, and he had written several short works of rationalist criticism. Each issue of *The Humanist* ran what it called "The Enlarging Vision." Placed in italics, this statement served as the rallying cry for the ethical movement. In today's parlance, it would be described as *religious humanism*:

> There can be no Nirvana in our ethical religion. In the moral life every attained objective is but the starting-point for fresh effort. The moral end achieved becomes the normal, and further ends that we had not seen before open out to our spiritual vision.[1]

Despite its strengths, *The Humanist* did not survive. Gorham resigned in 1920 and was succeeded by Mrs. M. I. Joad, wife of C. E. M. Joad (1891–1953), who went on to have a noisy career as journalist and philosophical popularizer. It folded soon after. The problem with *The Humanist* was that it had not managed to establish a niche for itself that was not already being covered by the *Literary Guide*, or by other organs of liberal religious opinion. Its format was too close to the *Guide*, and many of its contributors also wrote in both journals. Humanism, in the sense later to be understood as religious humanism, could not find a place to stand on its own that was sufficiently distinct from the secularist wing, represented by the RPA on the one side and liberal religious bodies like the Unitarians or the Quakers on the other.

A prominent contributor to *The Humanist* (as he was to the *Literary Guide*) was Frederick James Gould (1855–1938), a Victorian moral education campaigner and passionate advocate for the substutitionist wing of organized free thought. Quite influential in his day, Gould is important not so much for charting a new humanist outlook as for his contacts and energy. When he came to write his autobiography, he called it *The Life Story of a Humanist*. Published in 1923, this book was already something of an anachronism because it told a very Victorian story of Gould's earnest and painful transition from Christianity. Each new item of Christian dogma presented further opportunity for an agonized search for truth. In place of Christian theology, Gould variously embraced rationalism, Ethical Culture, positivism, and the vitalist philosophy of Henri Bergson, each of which was supported with a great deal of writing. Gould sought to apply his various enthusiasms in a program of moral education, barely distinguishable from what civics teachers would favor nowadays but radical in its day because it was not tied to a package of supernaturalist dogma. He produced a series of textbooks for use in moral education that achieved a relatively wide circulation in the first two decades of the century, even reaching India. He was the leading figure in the Moral Education League, another creation of the Union of Ethical Societies. The League's president was John Stuart Mackenzie, who we encountered earlier. It is gratifying to see that some of Gould's works of moral instruction have been revived online in what is called the Baldwin Project.

"I will merely claim," Gould declared in his autobiography, "that I have trudged by the sixty-seventh milestone of life, and retain a joyful freedom from the dictatorship of any creed, or program, or polity, or imposing *ism*."[2] He went on to demonstrate this by finding some fault with most of the major creeds he had examined over his life. Positivists had underestimated the labor and suffrage questions, Ethical Societies were too prone to exaggerate the power of exhortation, while moralists exaggerate the power of censure. Socialists and Marxists were also shown to exhibit what Gould called *spiritual rheumatism*.

Nowhere in his autobiography does Gould outline what he meant by *humanism*, but we can surmise he meant it in the general sense of being an educated man of letters, a humanitarian not bound by creed. He occasionally spoke of humanism, taking his cue, I suspect, from J. M. Robertson. In 1907, for instance, Gould wrote an article for the *Literary Guide* that surveyed the year just finished and speculated on the year to come. There he urged closer collaboration of what he called "the humanist force" and later "the humanist army." What is interesting is Gould's use of *humanist* as a catch-all category for all forms of free thought. In this context Gould mentioned the Rationalist Press Association, the secularists, the Ethical Societies, the positivists, and the pantheists as natural allies who could engage in concerted efforts on issues of mutual concern.[3] So far as I have found, Gould was the first person to speak of a humanist movement in this way.

It was Gould's use of *humanism* in this sense that caught the imagination of John Dietrich (1878–1957), who took the idea up with such commitment that he is now spoken of as the father of American religious humanism.[4] Gould was the single most significant conduit between the rapidly developing humanism in the United States and organized rationalism and ethicism in the United Kingdom. His understanding of humanism was probably best articulated in an article he wrote in 1882 and was liked enough to reproduce in his autobiography, forty years later:

> Here are the four pillars of the new religion—the love of man to woman, the love of parent to child, the love of man to man, the love of man to nature. Is not this a better gospel than that of miracles, of deities, of angels, of heavens, of hells, of elect peoples, and [of] ruined souls?[5]

Gould's embrace of love of man to man was, of course, entirely figurative. I doubt it would have crossed his mind that it could be read any other way. This rhetorical appeal to a simple humanity was what he meant by *humanism*.

Gould's links with and appreciation of American religious humanism was given an airing in an article in the *Literary Guide* of September 1931 under the title "The New Humanism." He spoke of his having met the young Edwin H. Wilson in London and of having corresponded with most of the significant religious humanists of the day: John Dietrich, H. J. Adlard, and Charles H. Lyttle. Gould began the article by defining *humanism* for his British readers:

> Humanism is a joyous and progressive comradeship in social service, which passes beyond theology and draws its inspiration from the story of humanity's

struggles, achievements in science, creations of beauty, increasing cooperations, and valiant facing of the universe.[6]

Humanism, Gould insisted, is future oriented, and that future consists primarily of three aspects: economics, education, and internationalism. Gould finished the article with one of his beloved rhetorical flourishes.

These three impulses will be stages in the "Everlasting March"—stages only; many an "untried way" will lie in front. I think Europe is already stepping. I salute the American Humanists. The rumble of an awakening world is heard, while Atropos, with her scissors, glides near to the thread of God.[7]

Gould's reference to Atropos was quite characteristic of his thought. Atropos was one of the three fates in Greek mythology. While Lachesis spreads luck randomly for people to chance upon, Clotho spins the thread of life, assuring some sort of balance to portions of luck. And the third fate is Atropos, who has the sterner duty of discharging the fate that cannot be avoided. It is evidence of the strength of Comte's influence on Gould that he should have chosen Atropos as the fate to invoke for the future.

If F. J. Gould invoked Atropos as the appropriate fate of humanism, Joseph McCabe (1867–1955) was more under the spell of Lachesis. This is because McCabe toyed with humanism as an idea briefly before giving it away. He first speaks of humanism in *The Religion of Woman*, a work from 1905 designed as his contribution to the suffrage campaign. McCabe denounced the commonly repeated assertion that women were necessarily more religious than men, due in large part to a greater need to be sheltered from the hard truths of the world, which the males shouldered nobly on their behalf. Christian writing of the time abounds with this sort of thinking. After outlining the significant problems facing contemporary Christianity as it comes to terms with the findings of modern scholarship while still wanting to preserve a place for faith, McCabe said, "I see no sound moral reason why these things should be hidden from women."[8] The final chapter was called "The Humanism of Tomorrow," in which he attempted a Wellsian flourish of a new world peopled by autonomous and self-actualized people, free from the shackles of theology and creed. He wrote: "In the solid facts of life and history, in the plain teaching of experience as to what is needed to bring gladness into our lives, we have a broad and massive foundation to build upon. This is humanism."[9]

Two years later McCabe wrote a short article titled "Fore-gleams of Humanism in Dante," published in the *Agnostic Annual* for 1907. Here he made some perfectly reasonable but unexceptionable observations of Dante's anticipation of significant elements of Renaissance humanism. He illustrated his claim in three ways: the relative ease with which Dante ignored orthodox theology in the interests of a broader understanding of Christianity; the greater influence of Aristotle and Cicero than that of St. Thomas Aquinas or St. Bonaventure; and the lavish praise given to pagans like Virgil and the scorn of many popes, who find themselves in the furthest reaches of hell.[10]

For our purposes, the interest lies in McCabe's use of *humanism* both in the scholarly sense of Renaissance humanism, and in the contemporary sense of a comprehensive lifestance that downplays supernaturalism. But after this, he stopped speaking of humanism, being unhappy with both the Comtean and the pragmatist influences permeating humanism at the time. Neither resonated with his sturdy rationalism. He said little more about humanism until late in his career, when his opinion on the word had turned distinctly hostile.

A contemporary of McCabe in the British free thought movement was Adam Gowans Whyte (1875–1950), a Scottish journalist, novelist and activist. The seventh of nine children, Whyte's father was a dentist of gentle, epicurean habits, who hoped his son would become an artist. Adam's skills lay elsewhere, however, and his father died when he was only twelve years old. In 1898 Whyte moved south to London, where he remained for the rest of his life and earned his living as a journalist. He joined the board of the Rationalist Press Association at its foundation in 1899 and remained a board member for fifty-one years, a record nobody has come near to matching. Whyte's formal job after 1901 was editor of the journal *Electrical Industries*, but his real love was rationalist writing. His best book was *The Religion of the Open Mind*, published originally in 1913; it went through four editions, remaining in print until the late 1940s. This book is still worth reading. It encapsulates some of the finer humanist ideas and emphases without once speaking of humanism. Whyte spoke of rationalism, which "does not simply substitute a positive creed for a supernatural creed. It does not simply take away the Bible and replace it by another volume which contains the new Ten Commandments and the new Sermon on the Mount. It has no dogma save this: that salvation is by knowledge alone."[11] He acknowledged that, to some, the "religion of the open mind may seem nothing more than the apotheosis of uncertainty."[12] So, where we spoke of McCabe's "sturdy rationalism" as an alternative to humanism, in Whyte's rationalism we can see a line of thinking indistinguishable from what in another decade have been labeled *humanism*.

Whyte's religion of the open mind (lovely phrase) was a humble acceptance of life as it is and an alive openness to its possibilities and joys. The religion of the open mind atones for the loss of a delusional "other world" by leading us to realize fully the possibilities of this world. "Moreover, by an apparent paradox, this yea-saying of life is the best preparation for the acceptance of death."[13] One can trace a direct line from Whyte's religion of the open mind to books like Richard Holloway's essay on spirituality, *Looking in the Distance*, published almost a century later.[14]

As we have seen with this survey, British nonreligious and liberal religious thought skirted around the edges of what we would now call *humanism*. But the existing nonreligious organizations, the National Secular Society (founded in 1866) and the Rationalist Press Association (founded in 1899) had each adopted their flagship term and saw no particular need to take on this newer one. This reluctance was only confirmed when those who did speak of humanism were either actively hostile to free thought (as Schiller was) or blandly confident they were "the next big thing." And the organization that was most enamored of humanism, the Union of Ethical Societies, was the least equipped to take the word on and make something of it.

And, just as an example of how ideas can travel on the merest zephyr, humanism turned up in New Zealand, at the other end of the Earth, in 1906. But *humanism* was not on the lips of intellectuals or technocrats, but on those of Richard John Seddon (1845–1906), the bluff, Lancastrian-born publican-turned-politician who rose to become premier of the thriving colony. Seddon served as premier from 1893 until his death in 1906, one of the longest terms in office. So dominating did Seddon become that he was universally known as King Dick. The Liberal administration Seddon presided over has gone down in the country's history as a high-water mark of progressive legislation. In fact, most of it was passed, or had begun, during the term in office of Seddon's Liberal predecessor, the freethinker John Ballance (1839–1893). Votes for women, old age pensions, and advanced industrial legislation helped create an image of New Zealand as a social workshop for progressive legislation, an image it has retained for itself ever since.

Seddon had not supported all the progressive legislation but was enough of an opportunist to take credit for it once its popularity was beyond doubt. In one of his relatively few reflective moods, shortly before his death in June 1906, Seddon described himself as a humanist. "All legislation which I have brought to bear upon the human side of life is the legislation which counts most with me. . . . I am a Humanist. I desire to improve the conditions of the people, to inspire them with hope, to provide for their comfort and to improve them socially, morally, and politically."[15] Seddon was the first national leader to speak of himself in this way.

It remains a mystery from where Seddon picked up this term. It was presumably one of the buzzwords sweeping around Wellington at the time, as people caught up with news from England. For Seddon, humanism was a straightforward humanitarianism, although expressed as his desire for social, moral, and political improvement, it has a reformist, progressive edge and without the implications of earlier phrases like *free thought*, or *rationalism*. Seddon always had a sharp ear for what the public would handle. It has the sound of Edward Howard Griggs.

BERTRAND RUSSELL AND "THE FREE MAN'S WORSHIP"

While all this was happening, a major milestone in the modern history of humanism was quietly being put together. In the same year Schiller's *Humanism* appeared, a journal called the *Independent Review* published an essay by Bertrand Russell called "The Free Man's Worship." Russell's biographer, Ronald W. Clark, calls this his most famous essay. Russell was still very much an unknown in 1903, with a reputation extending to only the tiny academic community centered round Cambridge University. His formal philosophical work had been dauntingly technical and was quite inaccessible even to the educated general reader. The same year "The Free Man's Worship" appeared, Russell was preparing for the publication of *The Principles of Mathematics*, widely thought to be his most outstanding contribution to philosophy. "The Free Man's Worship" was written in Italy at a time when Russell was painfully aware of the deadening spaces between people, the gnawing loneliness of a great deal of modern life. It is not a new observation to him of course, and it has been restated poignantly many times since, as when Henry David Thoreau said, "The mass of men lead lives of quiet desperaration."

Russell set out in clear and ringing tones the transience of human life and achievement. Nothing we do will last, nor is it meant to. We ourselves are but the "accidental collocations of atoms" and no achievement, no matter how magnificent, will survive beyond our brief years. And neither is humanity itself nor even the Earth that sustains it any more exempt from the iron law that hangs over individual human beings. But this is not something we must flee from or pretend is not there. "Only within the scaffolding of these truths, only on the firm foundation of unyielding despair, can the soul's habitation henceforth be safely built."[16] With this core insight firmly in place, we can proceed. Once radically shorn of our tendency to anthropocentric conceit, we can, with due recognition of our limitations, seek to transcend them. "In spite of death, the mark and seal of the parental control, man is yet free, during his brief years, to examine, to criticize, to know, and in imagination to create."[17]

What Russell was taking seriously was the consequences for human pretensions of a universe in which human life is a peripheral accident in an uncharted byway. This is the core metaphysical insight of naturalistic philosophies. Humanity does not matter to the universe. It is not important in the larger scheme of things, and supernaturalist constructions of a God looking over us and taking an interest in our trivial pursuits are fanciful delusions. Once we have taken that truth fully to heart, we can then proceed and look to creating a more modest, more real worldview, which places ultimate value on the extraordinary joy of living in the face of such forces that conspire against us. Feuerbach recognized before Russell the anthropocentric nature of belief in God, but Russell took further the Spinozist conclusions that should be reached from this insight. Spinoza spoke in terms of *sub specie aeternitatis*, or "from the viewpoint of eternity." It is difficult to succumb to the temptations of anthropocentrism from this perspective, and Russell was consistent in recommending its advantages to his readers.[18]

Russell was ambivalent about this essay in later years, not because he came to doubt what he had said, but because the Romanticism of his writing and the suggestions of Platonism in some of his assumptions were no longer valid for him. But the core insight of "The Free Man's Worship" remained unchanged. "I still believe," Russell wrote, "that, in times of moral difficulty and emotional stress, the attitude expressed in this essay is, at any rate for temperaments like my own, the one which gives most help in avoiding moral shipwreck."[19] Russell may have been ambivalent about "The Free Man's Worship," but it went on to inspire people for much of the twentieth century, people as varied as Joseph Conrad (1857–1924), one of the century's greatest novelists, and the English journalist and editor Kingsley Martin (1897–1969). Many others cite this essay as either the first of his they read or the one that remained the most vivid in their imaginations. It stands, in my view, as a major milestone in the coming together of humanism and naturalism that took place in the twentieth century.

GEORGE SANTAYANA AND THE LIFE OF REASON

A contemporary of Schiller and Russell was George Santayana, the reading of whose work has been the most enjoyable part of the research for this book. One of the finest writers of philosophical prose since Plato, Santayana justifies inclusion because of the richness of his thought and because of its humanistic quality, rather than for any active employment of the word in his own writings. In fact, part of the problem here is to justify calling Santayana a *humanist* when he—like Bertrand Russell—preferred not to use the word.

George Augustín Nicolás Ruiz de Santayana (1863–1952) was born in Madrid to Spanish parents, was brought to Boston at the age of nine, and was educated at the Boston Latin School. He studied at Harvard under William James and the idealist philosopher Josiah Royce (1855–1916) and spent his academic career there. But his impatience with American life slowly built up, and in 1912 he resigned from Harvard and emigrated to Europe. In 1924 he settled in Italy and remained there for the rest of his life.

Most brief surveys of Santayana acknowledge that he wrote a great deal but is best remembered for *The Life of Reason* (five volumes, 1905–1906) and his novel, *The Last Puritan* (1936). While these two works are important, there is so much of Santayana's work that one can still read with pleasure and profit. He is also standing refutation of the oft-repeated accusation that humanism must somehow be dull or that is unable to appreciate the finer things in life. Santayana's humanism was deeply imbued with the ideals of the naturalism and humanism of ancient Greece as filtered through the cosmic perspective of Spinoza. He scorned dualism and Romanticism and advocated what he called the *Aristotelian principle*: all ideals have a natural basis, but all natural processes are capable of ideal fulfillment. This developed into his theory of essences, which I don't propose to discuss here, beyond agreeing with those supporters of Santayana who remain unconvinced that his essence theory sits comfortably or necessarily with his naturalism. And if we are to object—as we should—to the presumption of directional change in notions of dialectic or teleology, surely we are no less bound to object to a theory of essences that serves to restrict any prospect of change.

The point is, then, that Santayana was no off-the-shelf materialist or rationalist. He contributed to an important collective work called *Essays in Critical Realism* (1920), but his realist colleagues became increasingly uncomfortable with his talk of essences, psyche, and spirit, notwithstanding the naturalist context he gave to them. And Santayana differed from the more extreme rationalists by thinking of reason as a higher-order impulse. An interesting parallel can be seen in *The Rational Good* (1921) by the English scholar L. T. Hobhouse, who spoke of impulse feeling as the touchstone of reason. Neither was Santayana an easy fit among atheists, because he saw good in religion, when understood properly, and was unconcerned by people retaining religious belief. Religion is part of one's social identity, which itself is a social need, and social needs have a basis in nature. At one point he wrote that, had he been a family man, he would have been happy for it to be a Catholic family. He said this in the context of firmly rejecting all items of Catholic dogma, but accepting the inescapable fact of having been born into a Catholic milieu. There is no God, Russell joked of Santayana, and Mary is his mother. Santayana's attitude is paralleled by Karl Jaspers's insight that he was Christian in the same sense he was German; it's just something he was born with. Santayana's attitude should not be seen as halfway-house religious humanism. In a letter to William James, Santayana states clearly that religion has been "found out" and that it is intolerable that one should participate in the "conspiracy of mock respect by which intellectual ignominy and moral stagnation are kept up in our society."[20] That remains as true today as it was in 1905.

In another context, Santayana spoke of Christianity as partly poetry and partly delusion. While Catholicism kept both in full measure, Protestantism had killed the poetry while keeping the delusion. It was typical of Santayana that this profound insight was casually thrown off in his novel. Several points arise from this observation. First, it is not limited to Christianity alone but applies to all religions. But it also has implications for humanism. Many people have complained, not entirely without justification, that the drier forms of humanism have killed both the delusion *and* the poetry.[21] Santayana's contribution was to have scotched firmly the delusions but to have kept—indeed to have contributed mightily—to the poetry of living.

Santayana's point also has implications for religious humanism and what now gets called *post-Christianity*, which claim people are naturally religious and that religion has an exclusive preserve on poetry and delusion. This is not true, but our need for poetry and delusion does seem to be well nigh universal. By virtue of its rejection of anthropocentric conceit, humanism is irrevocably set against delusion. The humanist commitment to science sets the tone here. But there is no reason why it should be set against poetry, when taken in the broader sense Santayana meant of an inspiring account of our place in the world. There is, in fact, a long tradition of art, poetry, music, and literature with a humanistic perspective and that has served to enrich people's lives. But it is time for this treasury to become a central part of the humanist experience, rather than an optional extra.

Santayana's dealings with Schiller were of a type, as Schiller's bombast and dogmatism put him off to no small degree. With William James, however, the situation was more complicated. Santayana was one of the few thinkers of the time to be neither warmed by James's personality nor impressed by his philosophy. The temperamental differences between the two men, and the very different axes of their respective views of the world worked against any closeness between them. Against this, some of Santayana's correspondence with James suggests strong intellectual collegiality, even when they did not agree, which was often enough.[22] As against the puritanism at the heart of James's pragmatism, Santayana was a freethinker. And both can legitimately be seen as expressions of humanism, whether or not they employed the word directly.

Santayana's thoughts on humanism are best illustrated in a passing remark he made in the first volume of his autobiography. In the context of some reminiscences on his Harvard teachers, he credits one of them, the classicist Louis Dyer (1851–1908), with making the distinction between the Dionysian/Apollonian drives before Nietzsche. Santayana went on to acknowledge his own Apollonian tradition and manner while "unhesitatingly accept[ing] the Dionysiac inspiration as also divine."

> It comes from the elemental god, from the chaotic but fertile bosom of nature; Apollo is the god of measure, the perfection of humanism. He is more civilized, but more superficial, more highly conditioned. His worship seems classic and established forever, and it does last longer and is more often revived than any one form of Dionysiac frenzy: yet the frenzy represents the primitive world soul, not at home in the world, not settled in itself, and merging again with the elements, half in helplessness and half in self-transcendence and mystic triumph.[23]

The Dionysian and Apollonian instincts need each other. The Dionysian devours itself too quickly in its short burst of self-absorbed enthusiasm. But there is always the Apollonian drive there to pick up the pieces and carry on. We could anticipate here the language of Irving Babbitt and liken the Apollonian with the will to refrain, the inner check. Once in a while the will to refrain needs to be let off its leash and given free rein, but it will soon exhaust itself and implode. Once this inevitable little trajectory has taken its course, normal Apollonian service will resume. Santayana saw the Apollonian as superficial in the sense of it not being sufficiently primordial. But it is also absolutely essential to human survival.

Bertrand Russell said much the same thing with respect to Romanticism in a little parable about tigers:

> Tigers are more beautiful than sheep, but we prefer them behind bars. The typical romantic removes the bars and enjoys the magnificent leaps with which the tiger annihilates the sheep. He exhorts men to imagine themselves tigers, and when he succeeds the results are not wholly pleasant.[24]

Santayana's thoughts on spirituality mirrored important elements of Russell's as expressed in "The Free Man's Worship." Santayana had a rarified idea of spirituality as the exclusive preserve of those who could cope with the truth that a genuine cosmic perspective would give to our pretensions as a species. Spiritual life is not the worship of values, much less supernatural dogmas. It is in fact the "disintoxication" from the influence of such forces. "Spirituality comes precisely of surrendering this animal arrogance and this moral fanaticism and substituting for them pure intelligence: not a discoursing cleverness or skepticism, but perfect candor and impartial vision."[25]

All this being the case, what are we to make of Santayana's refusal to speak of himself as a humanist? The key is to appreciate what it was he was rejecting. At one stage of his career he equated humanism with what he called the *genteel tradition*, which he lampooned in *The Genteel Tradition at Bay* (1931). Santayana disliked the thin-lipped moralism of the American genteel tradition and suspected that, as its decline became evident, it would return to its theocratic roots. But his core objection was the hubris that humanism as he understood it would lead to:

> In the Old Testament and even in the New, there were humanistic maxims, such as that the Sabbath was made for man, and not man for the Sabbath. Epicurus had crept into Ecclesiastes, and Plato into the Gospel of Saint John; and by a bolder stroke of humanism than anyone had yet thought of, God himself had been made man. Man consequently might be superlatively important in his own eyes, without offense to the higher powers.[26]

Late in his life, Santayana looked again at humanism, but from a slightly different perspective this time. In the course of thanking the American philosopher Corliss Lamont for a copy of *Humanism as a Philosophy*, Santayana had this to say: "In my mind *humanism* is a taste rather than a system, and those who make a system of it are obliged to explain away what is not human in the universe as a normal fiction; as Croce when one day he asked himself, 'But where can the idea of nature come in?'"[27] Like Russell, Santayana worried about the anthropocentric hubris he thought implicit in humanism. Humanity is clearly part of nature, but it is by no means the reason for nature nor the center of nature, let alone the center of the universe.

Santayana matters because he was deeply influential on the next generation of humanist thinkers: people as varied as Frederick Woodbridge, Corliss Lamont, and Horace Kallen in the United States and H. J. Blackham in Britain. Santayana's naturalism avoided the narrower scientism of the logical positivists by seeing value in scientific and literary endeavors. It epitomized the humanism that reaches across disciplines and sees value in an insight without regard to its source.

IRVING BABBITT AND THE HUMANISM OF CHARACTER

Santayana and Irving Babbitt (1865–1933) shared a deep distrust of the narcissism inherent in Romanticism, though unlike Santayana, Babbitt called his outlook *humanism*. Babbitt was a cultural historian and literary critic and, as we mentioned in chapter 1, was one of the first American scholars to speak of humanism. He and Paul Elmer More (1864–1937) were influential as the spokesmen for this tendency, which came to be known as the *new humanism*. The new humanism of Babbitt and More was in the context of morals education that valued elements of classical over modern education. In a way reminiscent of Niethammer a century before, Babbitt sought to find a middle way between radicalism and reaction. But the Scylla and Charybdis for Babbitt were sentimental humanitarianism on the one hand and scientism on the other.

Though a professor of French at Harvard, the principal thread of Babbitt's career was the stern criticism of what he called *sentimental humanitarianism*, which was built largely on a sunny view of people's natural goodness but which sapped our moral integrity and habits of self-control. The man chiefly responsible for this state of affairs was Babbitt's bete noir, Jean-Jacques Rousseau. But where conventional conservatives (then and now) did little more than demand a return to doctrinally orthodox religion, Babbitt spoke of humanism, which he knew to be an older tradition. While temperamentally sympathetic to religious experience, Babbitt's reading was too broad to be satisfied with acquiescence to one dogma. He was well read in, and highly sympathetic to, Theravada Buddhism.

So far as I have been able to discern, Babbitt first spoke of humanism in a lecture at Harvard in 1895, soon after taking up his position. But, being something of an outsider at Harvard, he had little impact on a wider audience until the 1920s, particularly after the publication of *Rousseau and Romanticism* in 1919, his best-known work. By this time his attention had focused on what he saw as the threat to civilization posed by Romanticism's imaginative extravagance and emotional irresponsibility. Christianity's great gift to civilization, he argued, was humility born of a strong sense of otherworldliness.

Classical humanism's great gift to civilization was decorum, tempered by a worldliness set within the limits of reason. Babbitt complained that Rousseau had assumed a natural goodness of humanity that was in no need of decorum of any type, preferring to give vent to the natural outflow of emotion. He looked to humanism to provide that moral integrity he knew command moralities were no longer capable of in any sense except the outward imposition of uniformity. Humanism was the cultural vehicle best equipped to foster the cultivation of what he called variously the *inner check* or the *will to refrain*, which is the ability to view life with a sense of proportion. At its darkest, the inner check is our built-in sense of right and wrong that helps us keep within the law. More positively, the inner check is the sense of commitment to a happy, purposeful, and harmonious life. Because we are not naturally good, the inner check is kept in place initially by an effort of will, but he allowed that it became easier to apply as one's sense of proportion and expectations slowly come to correspond with what is reasonable for us. He wrote: "The goal of the humanist is poised and creative living. This he hopes to accomplish by observing the law of measure."[28] His notion of decorum and measure resonate with many conceptions of bildung.

Among Babbitt's many critics was T. S. Eliot, who asked whether humanism could really stand alone from its supposedly Christian roots. To Eliot's mind, humanism was essentially parasitic on the Christian tradition from which he claimed it fed. More telling was the worry that Babbitt was too anxious to link religion and humanism against naturalism. A humanism seeking to stand alone from religion *and* naturalism is probably too tenuous a plant to thrive. This then becomes one of the ever-present strains within humanism. Does it lean more to religion, perhaps in the form of religious humanism, or to naturalism, perhaps in the form of secular humanism? Eliot had the extreme view that humanism was necessarily ancillary to religion. Extremist atheists, by contrast, see humanism as authentic only insofar as it rejects all things religious. This conundrum remains unsolved.

Babbitt's legacy has been ambivalent, and he's ended up falling through the cracks. Within the academy he has become the punching bag for postmodernist literary critics and has done more than most to shape what they understand by humanism, and why they reject it. Conventional religious supporters have seen little value in his humanism, and secular humanists have seen little value in his moral conservatism. This seems unfair, and it has been a mistake to ignore him. There is something relevant to the wiser, less gung-ho humanism of the twenty-first century in Babbitt's moral concerns. Western societies are no less superficial and addicted to consumerism as was the case in his day, and some return to ideas of a will to refrain is timely. Society at large is done no favors if sole authority to contribute on moral discussions is ceded to religious conservatives.

RICHARD HALDANE AND THE LONELY PATH

A book that defies any attempt to be slotted neatly in some understandable historical context is *The Philosophy of Humanism*. Richard Burdon Haldane (1856–1928) was a remarkable man who pursued successful careers in politics, philosophy, and law. He was born into a very prominent family—his parents were strict Baptists—but Haldane lost his religious beliefs during adolescence, after reading David Friedrich Strauss, Ernest Renan, and Lucretius. After undergoing adult baptism to please his parents, Haldane made a public declaration of his abandonment of Christianity. Anticipating the mantra of many religious humanists in later decades, Haldane declared that "God is not outside us, but within our breasts." Religious creeds were of symbolic significance only.

Haldane went to pursue distinguished careers in law and politics, serving several Liberal governments and the first Labor government, led by Ramsey MacDonald in 1924. His more important contributions include his role in establishing tertiary institutions alongside Oxford and Cambridge, which until then had existed solely to educate the ruling classes. Haldane also oversaw many of the changes in British military organization that had become necessary after the indifferent performance of British arms against the Boers between 1899 and 1902. And, against a background such as this, he showed great courage during the persecution of Oscar Wilde. Despite opinion having swung aggressively against Wilde, Haldane visited him in prison and arranged for a loosening of the austere regime imposed upon him of restricted visiting rights and his reading limited to *The Pilgrim's Progress*.

Through all this Haldane never dropped his interest in philosophy. In 1883 he participated in a collected work called *Essays in Philosophical Criticism*, which was an important milestone in establishing Hegel's influence in Britain. He was offered the chair in moral philosophy at St. Andrews after presenting the Gifford Lectures of 1903–1904, which were later published as *The Pathway to Reality* (1903). He turned down the invitation and continued with his career in law and politics. After the war he had a little more time to return to his philosophical work, and in 1921 he published *The Reign of Relativity*, which outlined the philosophical consequences of the general theory of relativity, having been vindicated in 1919 by scientists led by the Englishman Sir Arthur Eddington. Haldane's scientific knowledge was sufficiently sound for him to offer an intelligible, if dense, account of Einstein's theory. Unlike Schiller, Haldane was not fooled into thinking that relativity implied relativism. But he did appreciate that the days of dogmatic declarations of final, perfect truth were over.

The book that is of interest here is his next one, *The Philosophy of Humanism*, which appeared in 1922. On the few occasions this book is noticed in historical accounts of humanism, it is usually dismissed as having very little to say on the subject. This is unfair. Anticipating C. P. Snow three decades later, Haldane lamented the growing gap between the sciences and the humanities. Humanism was, he said, "the mode by which we render the abstractions of reality into concrete particulars."[29] And different people render these abstractions into particulars in different ways, whether it be through literature, art, music, religion, or science. Haldane was one of the few people who brought together in their thought strands what we now call *scientific*, *religious*, and *literary humanism*. No wonder he is ignored.

Haldane's scientific understanding was more profound than many of his contemporaries. In the light of the theory of relativity, he argued, it is not for humanism to concern itself with general rules or abstract concepts for which universal validity is claimed. Rather, its concern is the method by which our closest parallels to rules and concepts are given concrete application. Anticipating the systemism of Mario Bunge and much contemporary humanism, Haldane insisted that the humanist's task to was to appreciate the interdependence of things. "The doctrine that every department of knowledge belongs to a single entirety, and can be adequately interpreted only in its organic relation to the other departments, is of the very essence of humanism."[30] He recommended the Upanishads as exemplifying this insight most keenly.

As happened to Gabriel Sibbern, Haldane's conception of humanism has been pretty much universally ignored. *The Philosophy of Humanism* was too densely written to appeal to nonspecialist readers, and his earlier Neo-Hegelianism was too much in the minds of philosophers of 1922 to bother about. But if few people were interested in what former Neo-Hegelians had to say, neither were they motivated to pick up a book about humanism, after the example Schiller had set. Haldane himself seemed ambivalent about the book, not even mentioning it in his autobiography, written only six years later. This is a pity, because while by no means a popular manifesto or exercise in rhetoric, *The Philosophy of Humanism* has valuable things to say about what humanism is. It was essentially a protracted warning against hubris.

THE BIRTH OF AMERICAN RELIGIOUS HUMANISM

The demise of Schiller and the lack of impact of Haldane's work meant the fire went out for humanism in Britain for a few decades. We will examine the sporadic attempts to revive it in the 1930s under the guise of scientific humanism in the next chapter. We need once again to the cross the Atlantic and look at how what we now call *religious humanism* came to being. I don't intend in this section to repeat the story of American religious humanism, which has already been written. What I would like to do is discuss the career of humanism as an idea among American religious liberals. The trend toward a noncreedal Unitarianism was well under way by the beginning of the twentieth century. Since its foundation in Boston in 1825, American Unitarians had been markedly liberal and progressive in their theology, but they did not adopt humanism as their flagship concept until 1908. We have already encountered Irving Babbitt and Edward Howard Griggs speaking of humanism in the literary or cultural sense, but it was Frank Carleton Doan (1877–1927) who first spoke specifically of humanism in the philosophical or religious sense. Doan was a liberal theist and, at the time a professor of philosophy of religion and systematic theology at Meadville College, then based in Meadville, Pennsylvania. The college proved so successful it relocated to Chicago, where it became a center of progressive theology in the first half of the twentieth century.

With the advantage of a century's worth of hindsight, it is hard to warm to Doan's thought. He is too confident about human progress and too sanguine about the nobility of humanity for twenty-first-century readers. One example will suffice:

> The modern man is a religionist of humanity, the most exquisite example, so far, of all nature's finer products. In him the "struggle for the life of others" has come to full fruition. He yields his energies completely to the life of the whole he calls "humanity." All *his* wants, all *his* needs, center in a future Man. . . . This is his religion; the service of Man its only, holy office; his God is, shall be this Man-to-be.[31]

Two rival influences fought for Doan's soul. He was strongly influenced by the radical German theologian Albrecht Ritschl (1822–1889), who preferred to speak of religious statements as value judgments rather than statements of objective fact. And there are also strong strains of the *naturphilosophie* as articulated by Friedrich Schelling (1775–1854) and others. But sitting uncomfortably alongside the Germans was the other great influence: American pragmatism. And while probably not a direct influence, there are interesting parallels between the cosmic humanism of Frank Doan and what was called the *New Theology*, then subsiding in Britain after a couple of years of heady controversy. New Theology, championed by the Congregationalist clergyman R. J. Campbell (1867–1956), was a similar mix of what would now be called *religious humanism* or *post-Christianity*. The main difference is that the English strain was markedly less anthropocentric.

Doan put his thoughts together under the title *cosmic humanism*. At an address to the American Philosophical Association in December 1908, he positioned his cosmic humanism between "brute pragmatism" on the one hand and "unromantic realism" on the other. As with Schiller, Doan saw his brand of humanism as an extension and enlargement of pragmatism. But the trajectory of cosmic humanism was toward a quasi-mystical rendering of the world-soul idea. Like most religious humanists since, Doan was ready to concede that no God exists as a substantial entity. But he was not ready to abandon God-talk altogether. He summed up cosmic humanism in these terms:

> Cosmic humanism is thus anthropomorphic in its religious intention. In its essential terms it gratifies men's ingrained passion for human form in the divine life; i.e., by establishing in the place of the overturned God of hands and feet a real community of cerebral experience between man and the universal life. The physique of the cosmic life touches the physique of man in his most sensitive organ, the brain.[32]

William F. Schulz, a historian of American religious humanism, credits Doan with being the first person to speak of humanism in these terms in the United States. This is true as far as it goes, but we should take care to remember Edward Howard Griggs, who we discussed in chapter 1, and whose views resembled Doan's. It is true, however, to say that Doan was more influential in the development of religious humanism, if only because of the students he inspired, among them J. A. C. Fagginner Auer (1882–1964), who ended up at the Harvard Divinity School; and the prominent Unitarian Charles H.

Lyttle (1885–1980), who taught at Meadville. Both articulated variations of religious humanism through their lives.

Either way, having introduced cosmic humanism into the fertile soil of American progressive religion, Doan's eclectic interpretation was soon left behind. And, being a pacifist, he also ran up against the limits of what even progressive Christians would tolerate. He left Meadville in 1913 complaining of infringements on his academic freedom by the college. He held several Unitarian pastorates between 1914 and 1925, when he retired, due to ill health. At the end of his life a disillusioned Doan specifically distanced himself from British and American humanism, and linked himself instead with what he called "the *Continental spirit*—the spirit of a Lessing, a Herder, a Kant (he of the *Critique of the Practical Reason*), a Fichte, a Feuerbach."[33] One can't help noticing that a spirit incorporating such very different names would be a thoroughly fractious one.

ROY WOOD SELLARS AND THE NEXT STEP IN RELIGION

If Frank Doan was the first to employ the word *humanism* in North America in the sense now understood, Roy Wood Sellars (1880–1973) was far more successful in refining and developing what it actually meant. And Sellars approached the question from a radically different position than Doan or Schiller. Sellars spent his entire philosophical career at the University of Michigan, and he was a lifelong Unitarian while also being a confirmed naturalist, atheist, and socialist. Sellars was the intellectual backbone behind *critical realism*, a philosophical development that remains underappreciated in humanist circles to this day. His book by that title in 1916 criticized some of the more naïve assumptions of the earlier breed of naturalists, known as the *new realists*. The core of critical realism, as Sellars understood it, was a theory of perception whereby through what he called a "from-and-to" operation, we acquire a "direct, though mediated, knowledge about our surroundings."[34]

Critical Realism created enough interest that a collection of essays by a series of philosophers was published in 1920 that further explored elements of critical realism. As well as from Sellars, *Essays in Critical Realism* included essays from George Santayana, Arthur O. Lovejoy (1873–1962), and Durant Drake (1878–1933). It is also important that pragmatism came under criticism, not so much for any perceived basic errors as for having gone astray.

There are two main strengths of Sellars's outlook. The first was his successful integration of the changes to thinking about materialism to his evolutionary naturalism. Like Schiller, Sellars recognized nineteenth-century materialism had been overthrown, but unlike Schiller, Sellars understood the new naturalism that had replaced it. Matter is no longer an inanimate substance but is now a "patterned system capable of union with other systems in an evolutionary series."[35] Sellars saw some justification for philosophical idealism when science tended to reduce reality and human creativity to abstract matter, but with the new naturalism he spoke of, this was not the case now.

The second strength of Sellars's work was his appreciation of the underlying reality of transitoriness, even tragedy, in the world. Humanists are often accused of superficiality by virtue of a sanguine optimism in human perfectibility. Sellars did not have this weakness. He was perhaps a bit too confident that liberal religion would triumph over the forces of fundamentalism, but he is hardly alone in making that mistake. Neither was it an unreasonable expectation in the 1920s, considering the changes in that direction someone born in 1880 would have seen. But the quietness and gentleness of his writing, and his candid recognition of the brevity of life and achievement serve as a continuing check to anthropocentric conceit.

Like Arnold Ruge, Sellars believed that humanism was the zeitgeist of the age. But where Ruge thought in dialectical terms, Sellars had a more empirical understanding of history. The tragic defect of the modern age, Sellars wrote, was the spiritual vacuum of contemporary culture. Times were changing, but the religions were not changing with the times, leaving people washed up and confused. What was so desperately needed was a humanist religion, something to engage the mind and heart of living people, inspiring them to create the good life on earth. This is not an observation unique to Sellars, of course. Ruge and Feuerbach had thought similarly, however differently they expressed themselves. And, since Sellars, humanists as diverse as H. G. Wells, Julian Huxley, Peter Singer, Paul Kurtz, Gora, Xu Fuguan, Carl Sagan, and many others have spoken in these terms. Some have been content to speak of a humanist religion, but increasingly humanists have looked to express their thinking without recourse to religious language. In the United States the use or rejection of religious language is a central bone of contention.

On a secure basis of nonreductive philosophical naturalism, Sellars went on to posit a humanist approach to religion and ethics. And this was done in his more accessible works; he had an attractive, homely style of writing. *The Next Step in Religion* (1918) and *Religion Coming of Age* (1928) were very influential among American Unitarians, religious humanists, and liberal theists in presenting the outlines of a humanist outlook. Late in his life Sellars claimed *The Next Step in Religion* deserved priority over either Dewey or Julian Huxley in introducing humanism to the English-speaking world.[36] While it may be true that Sellars *deserves* that priority, it remains a fact that Schiller predated Sellars. What Sellars meant, but did not say, was that he was the first to introduce a systematic exposition of naturalistic humanism to the world. He was also able to provide one of the simplest definitions of *humanism*, the core of which he took to be "an emphasis on human activities and values and a rational concern for their clarification."[37]

The interesting paradox with Sellars—as it now appears—is that this pioneer of naturalistic humanism is usually bracketed with religious humanism, with the result that he is undeservedly forgotten. This is sad and doesn't do justice to Sellars, who made plain his disbelief in a personal God, immortality, and all the trappings of supernaturalism. And neither did he try, as Doan did, to reconfigure God into a cosmic principle. Agnosticism was dismissed as a "weasel word."[38] And he specifically repudiated the link often made between humanism and anthropocentrism. Humanism was anthropocentric, he argued, only in the existentialist sense of recognizing the human situation.[39] Recognition of the human situation in no way implies limiting one's perspective to that which profits *Homo sapiens* only.

The only area of his work that would raise eyebrows now is his willingness to speak of the humanism that is destined to replace religion, itself having religious elements to it. But this is a problem that would not make itself apparent until after Sellars's death. The fate of Sellars serves as a warning not to bracket people too firmly into the naturalistic or religious camp.

THE HIGH TIDE OF AMERICAN RELIGIOUS HUMANISM

Sellars was able to achieve the level of influence he did because there was a significant cohort of progressive religious thinkers and activists in the field in need of that sort of guidance. One of them was John H. Dietrich, who had already come across humanism from reading articles by the Englishman F. J. Gould. Dietrich was a minister in the Reformed Church when, in 1911, he was charged with heresy for denying the inerrancy of the Bible and most items of Christian dogma. He walked away from the Reformed Church and joined the Unitarians. After a spell in Spokane, Washington, he moved to Minneapolis in 1916, where he became one of the most progressive and influential Unitarian ministers in the country. That was the year Dietrich came across Gould's work, which had appeared in an English ethical journal the year previously. From this came Dietrich's essay "The Religion of Experience," which appeared on the cover of the Unitarian magazine the *Christian Register* in March 1919. This article is credited with launching religious humanist ideas to a wider Unitarian readership.

The other person Schulz credits with founding American religious humanism was Curtis W. Reese (1887–1961). Reese traveled even further than Dietrich to arrive at humanism. He was born in the remote Blue Ridge Mountains in North Carolina to a family staunchly fundamentalist even by the standards of that region. Reese trained to become a minister in the Southern Baptist Church but early on in his theological training found he was unable to accept uncritically the biblical literalism he was taught. He moved on to the Unitarians, much to the dismay of his entire family, who shunned him, declaring they would rather see him burn in hell. Reese went on to articulate his new beliefs in *Humanism* (1926); his edited collection, *Humanist Sermons* (1927); and *Humanist Religion* (1931). Later in his life, he wrote *The Meaning of Humanism* (1945), but times had moved on by then, and this book was less important.

Another person who deserves more mention than he has received is Charles Francis Potter (1885–1962). Like Reese, Potter was raised a fervent evangelical, coming from a family of Baptists in Marlboro, Massachusetts. So fervent was the young Potter that he was licensed to preach at the age of seventeen. But exposure to higher criticism while at theological college and then at Brown University ended his evangelical career. In 1914 he began a career as a Unitarian minister, where he was drawn into the influence of leading religious humanists like Dietrich and Reese. At this point, Potter began to see himself as a humanist. But despite an upbringing similar to other prominent religious humanists, Potter was something of an outsider. He came to national prominence following a series of debates with the prominent fundamentalist Baptist John Roach Straton (1875–1929) and then during the Scopes trial in 1925 when he assisted Clarence Darrow with his knowledge of the Bible. Potter called himself the "Bible expert for the defense."

The significant point about Potter's career, and the main reason for his lesser influence, was that he chose to go alone. Rather than work within the Unitarians, Potter founded in 1929 the First Humanist Society of New York. This was in effect a humanist church. Two of his books *Humanism: A New Religion* (1930) and *Humanizing Religion* (1933) were bestsellers and helped bring religious humanism to a wider audience. Potter signed the *Humanist Manifesto I*, although he was critical of elements of it. In turn, Potter was held in low regard by some of the more important people behind the manifesto, who undervalued his role as a popularizer and feared his superior ability to generate publicity. Potter was an active campaigner for abolition of the death penalty, for voluntary euthanasia, for birth control, and for women's rights. Later on he wrote *The Faiths Men Live By* (1955), a popular account of the world's major systems of belief and an autobiography.

The simplest, cleanest definition of *humanism* from these men came from Potter, who defined *humanism* as "faith in the supreme value and self-perfectibility of human personality." He expanded on that in this way: "Humanism is the conviction that personality is the explanation of the universe, that man himself is the highest manifestation of this personality, and that the powers resident in the individual and society are sufficient to ensure progress toward an ideal society of ideal persons."[40] Curtis Reese said much the same thing:

> Man is capable of achieving things heretofore thought utterly impossible. He is capable of so ordering human relations that life shall be preserved, not destroyed; that justice shall be established, not denied; that love shall be the rule, not the exception. It but remains for religion to place human responsibility at the heart of its gospel. When this is done, science and democracy and religion will have formed an alliance of wisdom, vision, and power. In this high concert of values, religion must be the servant and through service the master of all.[41]

A less-commented-on feature of American religious humanism is its peculiarly American flavor. American religious humanism of the 1920s and 1930s can be understood as a restatement of the brash optimism of what the nineteenth-century historians had discerned in fifteenth-century Italy. It also gave expression to a form of American exceptionalism. Religious humanism was seen as the cutting-edge development in human spirituality that required the mix of democracy, prosperity, and goodwill available in sufficient quantity in America. Toward the end of his chapter outlining the core elements of humanism as he understood it, Potter quoted John Symonds, who wrote of the history of the Renaissance in Italy. The passage from Symonds spoke of the essence of Renaissance humanism being a new and vital perception of the dignity of man as a rational being apart from the theological determinations. Potter warmly approved this idea. He added:

> Humanism in religion is built upon a recognition of man's essential and native dignity and his infinite possibilities of development. This renaissance in religion will come when man really recognizes his tremendous opportunities and parallel responsibilities.[42]

As the twentieth century wore on and the United States had occasion to question its role as the leader of the world to a new renaissance, so too did the message of religious humanism seem brittler.

The weaknesses of religious humanism are apparent from these passages. First, their appeal is mainly rhetorical and they retain a strong sense of sermonizing. Second, and a greater weakness, is its facile optimism, its straining after a sense of contrived uplift. One of the more common criticisms of humanism is that its optimism reveals its superficiality, its inability to recognize or empathize with suffering, loss, waste, and decay. The favorite criticism of religious conservatives is that humanism replaces God with man, with disastrous consequences for our sense of humility. This charge is less fair on Potter than on Reese or Dietrich, but is not entirely misplaced with any of them.

What is noticed less often is that this tendency to sanguine optimism is more commonly a feature of religiously motivated strands of humanism. It is true of humanist thinkers in the Renaissance and is quite frequently true of contemporary religious humanists. But the charge is very rarely true of the people it is most commonly made against: the atheist, the rationalist, and the secular humanist. This is because the rejection of the transcendental temptation is an act that, when made in full knowledge of the consequences, precludes anthropocentric presumption of any kind.

Reese had more difficulty than Potter in giving a brief synopsis of humanism and was more concerned to say what it is not. He began by telling us that humanism is not materialism, is not atheism, is not positivism, and is not rationalism. Even when he went on to state what humanism was, he did so in a negative way. What Reese called the "basal article of the faith of humanism" was that it is "the conviction that human life is of supreme worth and consequently must be treated as an end, not as a means." But he then went on to temper that with a series of negative qualifications:

> Man is not to be treated as a means to the glory of God. Man is not to be treated as a means to cosmic ends. Man is not to be treated as a means to a moral order. Man is not to be treated as a means to a world order. A man is not to be treated as a means to any other man.[43]

At some point along the way, these assertions have to involve atheism, materialism, and rationalism. It is just a point of where one draws the line. And this has long been a problem for religious humanism because the point at which one religious humanist has drawn the line has differed from another's, with no particular reason to prefer one cutoff point from another. Duncan Howlett called this the fatal flaw in religious liberalism. We will return to this theme in chapter 8.

It is not that the religious humanists were unaware of what they were doing. But they felt a strong need to offer another consolation, little more worthwhile than the one being rejected. One prominent religious humanist, A. Wakefield Slaten wrote: "Humanism may take away some of the old consolations, but it offers others more convincing. After we have borne the first chill blast, a warm glow suffuses us; we are heartened by vision of the World-Hope."[44] To many people in the Great Depression, it would have been the chill blast that would have been uppermost in their minds.

It was natural, then, that these men should look toward bringing together a coherent public declaration of their position. This was not the first time a humanist manifesto had been put together. An earlier one, four pages long, had been compiled in 1919 by the Swedish socialist and humanist Ivan Oljelund (1892–1978), and it attracted 138 signatories.[45] There is no direct evidence that the Americans knew of the Swedish predecessor, although the large Scandinavian community in Minnesota, Dietrich's state, make a link not unlikely. Roy Wood Sellars was approached to write the draft; a wise choice. The main middleman was the young Unitarian minister and officeholder Raymond Bragg (1902–1979), another product of Meadville. After his graduation in 1928 and a couple of years serving as a minister in Evanston, Illinois, Bragg succeeded Curtis Reese as secretary of the Western Unitarian Conference, the body established to promote Unitarianism in parts west of New York State. From this important position he helped organize *The Humanist Manifesto*. Sellars's original draft underwent considerable modification at the hands of Bragg, Reese, Edwin Wilson, and A. Eustace Haydon, the latter being particularly influential.[46]

The final draft consisted in fifteen points, working down from the cosmological sphere and through the biological, anthropological, sociological, and economic spheres. The first point revealed the fine line being drawn by religious humanism when it said, "Religious humanists regard the universe as self-existing and not created."[47] The next five points, which placed humanity in a naturalistic context, raised few difficulties for rationalists, atheists, and those who now call themselves secular humanists. But the seventh point returned to the mood of the first point, when it said that religion "consists of those actions, purposes, and experiences which are humanly significant. Nothing human is alien to the religious."[48] The next six points continued in that vein. The drafters of the manifesto understood that a problem existed, taking care in the preamble to lament that the word "religion" should be linked irrevocably with "doctrines and methods which have lost their significance."[49] As if their use of the word *religion* wasn't problematic enough, the fourteenth point provoked difficulties in a new direction, when it recommended a "socialized and cooperative economic order" to replace the "acquisitive and profit-motivated society."[50]

The Humanist Manifesto attracted relatively little press attention, and what attention it did attract was as likely to be hostile. Part of the problem was that interest in religious humanism was already on the wane, and the growing disaster of the Depression was concentrating people's minds in other directions.[51] Also, it has to be said that the manifesto was a mish-mash of contradictory ideas and contrasting attitudes. Its use of religious language put off those already nonreligious, and its acceptance of important elements of naturalist thought alienated the conventionally religious. It appealed to a small coterie of people stuck in between religion and irreligion.

It was understandable that the framers of the manifesto would ask Ferdinand Schiller to sign it. But they should not have been surprised at his indignant refusal to do so. He expressed his "great annoyance" at the adoption of the word for *The Humanist Manifesto*. "The Unitarian sort [of humanism] is antitheistic, mine is antiabsolutist and antinaturalist, but not antitheistic. Indeed, it will be seen that its personalistic implications render it inherently favorable to theism."[52] Schiller went on to object to the blandness of the God-idea being put forward, complaining that the God Unitarians spoke of "had been so much attenuated and had grown so impalpable and colorless that he might just as well be dropped altogether."[53]

Reactions to religious humanism from the atheist and rationalist communities was largely unchanged from before the manifesto. At the more extreme end, in the more rationalist-inclined *Truth Seeker*, Theodore Schroeder did little more than resort to abuse. His final words illustrate his tone:

> The humanist's pious emotions may prove to the psychoneurotic his own Godhood, give him some sublime self-righteous thrills, and ensure the applause of many morons. It can never lead up to that better mental hygiene which is a prerequisite for the use of more mature intellectual methods in finding solutions for our social problems.[54]

It is also interesting that American religious humanism, which was striking roots in the United States, failed to do so among English Unitarians. Even before the manifesto was published, the English attitude was pretty much set. An editorial from 1932 in *The Inquirer* had this to say:

> It seems to us that the weakness of modern, religious humanism is strikingly evident in its failure to provide a satisfactory cosmic setting for the human soul; it stops short: avowedly homocentric, it leaves man defiant and homeless in an unfriendly universe. . . . Modern religious humanism as such is Faustian, Promethean; defiant! And for this reason it fails to meet the requirements of a religion.[55]

Since the death of Robert Green Ingersoll in 1899, the Americans had been without a clearly secular alternative to orthodox religion. But they had seen plenty of fundamentalism, culminating in the Scopes trial of 1925. Add to this mix the clear directions set by John Dewey and Roy Wood Sellars, and we can see why American humanism moved to humanize religion. But in Britain, there were several viable nonreligious alternatives to orthodoxy in the form of the National Secular Society, the Rationalist Press Association, and the Ethical Union. And the generally negative impression Schiller had given of humanism meant there was less need felt among Unitarians and others on the religious left to take the path of religious humanism.

It is commonplace, particularly among American writers, to see the *Humanist Manifesto* as a landmark event in the history of humanism. I do not see it that way. The manifesto was too short, too much of its time, and too vague. Its superficial optimism, its loose usage of religious terminology, and its general philosophical incoherence has rendered the manifesto a liability rather than an asset to the development of a sustainable humanism. This is not, of course, to decry the earnestness of the authors or signatories, or the goodwill that lay behind it. But it remains true that, at the cerebral level, it mired the movement in an unhelpful seesaw debate about the boundaries between religion and irreligion. And at the practical level, *The Humanist Manifesto* was rushed into print without adequate preparation and attracted only thirty-three signatories along the way, thus drastically limiting its value as a publicity document.

The Humanist Manifesto also popularized the least helpful picture of humanism: man replacing God at the center of the universe; but by placing faith in Man (always a capitalized abstraction) the dialectic of progress would be sure to lumber on in its own beneficent way. Humanism in the twenty-first-century needs, with some urgency, to reject shallow optimism of this sort. Far from being a landmark in the history of humanism, *The Humanist Manifesto* was, at best, a relatively uninteresting sideshow, and at worst, a damaging wrong turn.

Little more will be said about American religious humanism in this book. But this should not be taken as a dismissal of the movement's worth or integrity. American religious humanism has become closely bound up with the Unitarian Universalist movement, the story of which has been told effectively elsewhere. But with respect to the history of the idea of humanism, which is the subject of this book, little new has been said. We need now to turn to the brand of humanism that claimed to be its final manifestation: *scientific humanism*.

CHAPTER 4

THE RISE AND FALL OF SCIENTIFIC HUMANISM

At the close of the first chapter we observed that the objectives of the constitutional reformers and the radical visionaries who rejected violent revolution had begun to coincide. They were both, in effect, working toward what we could call *scientific humanism*. But the sad irony of this term is that it spent much of its career in the hands of the very people who rejected this approach and who preferred violent revolution as justified by an imposing dialectic. By the time scientific humanism had rid itself of these associations, it was too late.

LOTHROP STODDARD AND THE INAUSPICIOUS START

Musing on this legacy would be a nice way to begin a discussion on scientific humanism. But none of these people spoke of themselves as scientific humanists. Sadly, however, we have an unattractive detour to make first. It is usually claimed that Walter Lippmann (1889–1974) was the first person to speak of scientific humanism, in his book *A Preface to Morals*, published in 1929. I wish this were true, but it's not. So far as I have found, the first book to appear using the title *Scientific Humanism* came from an altogether less attractive figure. Lothrop Stoddard (1883–1950) was the only child of a privileged Massachusetts Unitarian family, and took a doctorate at Harvard in 1914, having already studied law there. His dissertation, titled "The French Revolution in Santo Domingo," told of the horrific slaughter of whites by black slaves in the Caribbean. His fifteen other books all pursued this theme;

they followed his grand theory of a clash of civilizations. The best-known of them was *The Rising Tide of Color against White-World Supremacy* (1920) in which he warned of the dire consequences of the white races relinquishing their hold on the inferior colored peoples of the earth. *The New World of Islam* (1921) and *The Revolt against Civilization: The Menace of the Underman* (1922)—a study of Bolshevism—and *Racial Realities in Europe* (1924) all continued the theme. Not surprisingly, Stoddard was also an enthusiastic eugenicist and anti-Semite, and his works were cited in Nazi textbooks. In 1940, he traveled to Germany, where he met Adolf Hitler and Joseph Goebbels. The outcome of the war and the erosion of any scientific credibility for eugenics spelled the end of whatever influence he enjoyed during his lifetime, although excerpts of his more lurid works can still be found on white-supremacist websites.

When he came to write *Scientific Humanism* (1926), Stoddard put his more elegant face to the world. Much of it is an unremarkable account of the problems of the age as he saw them, and his remedy, which was the humanism of the Renaissance, suitably added to with the findings of science, the "defining feature of the age." *Scientific Humanism* is a plea for open-mindedness, respect for opposing points of view, and a reconciliation between science and religion. All's well and good, until we remember what he thought to be the findings of science. Stoddard was by no means alone in using science in this way. Eugenicist and racial xenophobia had been quite pronounced in the United States during the first two decades of the twentieth century, and it came from across the religious and political spectrum. But this was the first—and only—study of this kind done within the framework of scientific humanism. All that can be said in mitigation of this sorry episode is that Stoddard's conception of scientific humanism found no favor whatsoever in any other discussion of the topic that I have come across.[1] It was, at best, in inauspicious start to the career of scientific humanism.

If Lothrop Stoddard was not disadvantage enough for the career of scientific humanism, an early book from the Far Left was little, if any, improvement. In his disarmingly uncritical apologia for the Soviet Union, Leon Samson was even more enthusiastic for what he called *scientific humanism*. His book, *The New Humanism* (1930), spoke of the altogether newer and finer breed of person arising in the civilization being built by Stalin. All the noblest qualities among people could be found in the working class and only now was this obvious truth being brought to light in the Soviet Union. No book qualifies for the term "vulgar Marxism" more than *The New Humanism*. The book was panned by all but the most sectarian Marxist journals. It was reviewed very unfavorably in the British philosophical periodical *Mind* in 1931. The reviewer, of course, was Ferdinand Schiller.

JULIAN HUXLEY AND THE DEVELOPED RELIGION

If scientific humanism was going to have any worthwhile career at all, it would need to be relaunched. And this is what happened. A year after Stoddard's work was published, a book by a rising young English popularizer of science appeared, and it completely transformed the career of scientific humanism. The person was Julian Huxley (1887–1975) and the book was *Religion without Revelation*. Julian Huxley had an ace up his sleeve even before he began his career: his surname. As the grandson of Thomas Henry Huxley (1825–1895), Julian was assured of an audience. It is hard to overestimate T. H. Huxley's influence on the generations born in the second half of the nineteenth century, an influence significant enough to rub off on several generations of descendants. After education at Eton, Julian studied zoology at Balliol College, Oxford, and graduated in 1909. He then roamed for many years, in and out of various academic institutions in Britain and abroad, but he was not suited to teaching. He was a research associate at the Rice Institute in Houston, Texas, for six years until 1916, and in 1921 he organized an expedition to Spitzbergen. But Huxley's true contribution was as a public intellectual and popularizer of science. His *Essays in Popular Science* and *The Stream of Life* (both 1926) established him as a first-class communicator of science and the consequences of science to a wider readership, as his grandfather had done before him.

Huxley was an obvious candidate, then, for the publishing house Ernest Benn to have contribute to a series of books it was publishing under the title "What I Believe." After two conventional expositions, of theism and Catholicism, Ernest Benn must have been looking for something more controversial and edgy, without wandering off into the ghettos of fanaticism. Huxley accomplished this in *Religion without Revelation*, which combined a naturally religious disposition with a scientific training. Where his head said *scientific method* and *impersonal evolution*, his heart said *poetry, mysticism,* and *religious experience*. These strands came together while waiting for an operation in Colorado Springs, when he came across a comment from an essay by the English statesman and thinker John Morley (1838–1923) that the next great task of science will be to create a religion for humanity. This helped galvanize Huxley's own scientific training and personal crises into a plan of action for his life.

Huxley began *Religion without Revelation* by lamenting the growing gap between what the churches professed to be true and what thinking people knew was the case. This was a popular refrain; we have already seen Sellars begin *Religion Coming of Age* in the same manner. What Huxley did was to give the new zeitgeist a name.

> The moment does indeed seem to be approaching when man can and should begin constructing a new common outlook, a new habitation for his spirit, new from the foundations up, on the basis of a scientific humanism.[2]

And, again, like the American religious humanists, Huxley saw religious experience as something that could be dissociated entirely from all aspects of theology, creed, or ecclesiastical organization. He then made a lengthy survey of the history of religions from a comparative perspective, noting the weakening of ecclesiastical authority and of appeals to scriptural authority as well as the decline in belief in magic, miracles, and supernaturalism. From that survey, he arrived at this conclusion: "If the process continues—and in spite of conflict there is every appearance of its so doing—religious thought is due to enter on a new phase of relative stability, based upon the naturalistic and humanistic outlook brought in by the scientific spirit."[3]

Here we come to yet another of the many paradoxes that pop up through this history. Humanists like Huxley thought themselves much more insightful of the realities of religious experience than the hard and crusty rationalists who could only, as he saw it, criticize religion. And yet behind all this supposedly empathetic appreciation of religious experience was a bedrock of teleological condescension. Supernaturalist religion was going to wither away, and it was going to do so according to the lines Huxley decreed it would, toward naturalism and humanism. For all his understanding, Huxley was in fact more dismissive of religious experience than the rationalists he so despised because, in the manner of all teleological thinking, religion was *destined* to change as Huxley foretold. Rationalists, by contrast, were under no illusions that supernaturalism would wither and die at the first blast of criticism. Rationalists showed supernatural religion a great deal more respect than they have been given credit for, because they take supernaturalist truth-claims seriously. Humanists of Huxley's stamp, by contrast, are content to believe that supernaturalism is inevitably doomed and it's therefore a waste of time to engage with them, either in controversy or dialogue.

Another questionable hypothesis Huxley worked on was the ubiquity of a religious instinct, what some have called *Homo religiosus*. Man, "inheriting as he does certain instincts and mental capacities, and born into the physical environment of this planet and the human environment of a social life and tradition, is bound to have some religious life; though it is by no means necessary that this religious life shall be religious in any narrow or conventional sense."[4] Here is an important instance where Huxley fudged one of Darwinism's most significant implications: its serious undermining of many central items of Christian dogma. We mentioned some in the previous chapter.[5] Huxley's humanism is undermined by his commitment to these forms of essentialism and teleology. The issue has resurfaced more recently in the so-called "God gene" debate, which talks about an evolutionary-driven survival advantage for certain forms of anthropomorphism. This argument may or may not be sound, but even if it is, it is a big step to then insist that we are all naturally religious.

For this naturally religious species, Huxley conceived what he called *developed religion*, complete with its own secular trinity of power, idea, and spirit. As power, idea, and spirit were all elements of the same unity, this could even be called *God*, although Huxley acknowledged doing this would lead to problems. So, for the time being, he was content to call that unity the *sacred reality*. The developed religion would be an exercise in harmonizing the facts of the external world with one's inner set of values.

Conceptions of the sacred and the objects of religious feeling would come together by including man's destiny. The theology of the developed religion would amount to the application of the "pure force of intellect" to the problems of the world and the sacred beliefs would engage dynamically with ethics, always with human destiny at the forefront. The realization of the developed religion would be the outcome of humanity reaching its maturity. And with this maturity would come peace, because, as Huxley put it, "today humanity is facing the possibility of maturity. We cannot really think it tolerable that it should be faced with perpetual conflict at the central heart of its being."[6] Such a prospect may not be tolerable, but that doesn't make it untrue.

It is difficult not to see Huxley's developed religion as a replay of the positivism of Auguste Comte. The inevitability, the teleology, the harmonizing, and the eclectic borrowing from other religious traditions; all are reminiscent of positivism. But the incongruity of this observation is heightened when we recall that Thomas Henry Huxley, Julian's grandfather and mentor, had little time for this sort of system building, dismissing positivism as "Catholicism minus theology." Huxley's developed religion idea repeated another mistake popular among learned religious reformers: being too cerebral. And in being too cerebral, it misunderstands a very significant feature of religion. Religion is not in the end a cerebral activity. The growing strength of fundamentalist religion, flying in the face of two centuries of evidence against such a stance, is one of the more stark pieces of evidence for that claim. And writing less than two years after the Scopes trial, this should not have been a point about which Huxley needed reminding.

A few years later Huxley returned to the theme of scientific humanism in his collection of essays called *What Dare I Think?* He had wanted to call the book "Essays in Scientific Humanism," but he explained in the preface that he had come across an American work that had already taken the title *Scientific Humanism*, and it used the term in a way he was unhappy with. He doesn't name the author, but I suspect it was Lothrop Stoddard's work, which we examined at the beginning of the chapter. Huxley was more enthusiastic about the other trend in the United States where humanism was serving as the name for "an interesting brand of antisupernatural religion."

Among some straightforward exercises in popular biology, *What Dare I Think?* also expanded on what he meant by *scientific humanism*. Humanism, Huxley said, is the belief that the sole sources of values we can really know anything about are those created in the "commerce between mind and matter that we call life." What makes *scientific* humanism is the recognition that humanity is "endowed with infinite powers of control should he care to exercise them."[7]

The trouble with any label that attaches itself to the prefix "scientific" is that the label can rise or fall insofar as the bundle of values associated with it is properly scientific or not. Lothrop Stoddard saw scientific humanism as endorsing a Manichean racism. And reminiscent of Schiller, Julian Huxley saw it endorsing a comprehensive program of eugenics. He criticized pre-scientific codes of values that accord absolute value to human life.

> The value of human life becomes so absolute that it is murder to put away a deformed monster at birth, and criminal to suggest euthanasia; and we push on with our reduction of infant mortality until we save an excess of cripples and defectives to breed from.[8]

It is worth noting that Huxley thought sufficiently highly of this article that a minimally revised version of it appeared in a later collection of his essays, *The Uniqueness of Man*, published ten years after *What Dare I Think?* And in another essay from *The Uniqueness of Man*, Huxley went so far as to hope that eugenics "will inevitably become part of the religion of the future, or of whatever complex of sentiments may in the future take the place of organized religion."[9] Underlying this zeal for eugenics and his fondness for a teleological reading of evolution was his belief in the uniqueness of man. It is a truism of evolutionary thinking that *Homo sapiens* is an animal species, subject to the same biological needs and constraints of all other species on the planet. Part of the radical change that evolution has required of us is to see ourselves in this more modest way, shorn of the transcendental presumption that dominated our self-conception before evolution.[10] But Huxley retained a view more reminiscent of the great chain of being. "Man," he said "represents the culmination of that process of organic evolution which has been proceeding on this planet for over a thousand million years. That process, however wasteful and cruel it may be, and into however many blind alleys it may have been diverted, is also in one aspect progressive."[11] True, he went on to remind us that this uniqueness confers upon us a special responsibility, but this point could be made without declaring us to be the culmination of evolution and evidence of progress.

So clearly there are problems with Julian Huxley's notion of scientific humanism. Indeed, he suffers from the same weakness as Lothrop Stoddard, and with less excuse, as his scientific training was much greater. And while this condemnation of Huxley is easier with the advantage of hindsight—all condemnations are easier from such a position—it remains true that plenty of people knew the folly of eugenics at the time. Lancelot Hogben (1895–1975), who also spoke positively about scientific humanism was, like Huxley, a skilled scientist and a capable popularizer. But he was also an outspoken opponent of eugenics. Joseph McCabe was less consistent than Hogben, but at the time we are speaking of, he condemned eugenics as the new Calvinism. And Bertrand Russell disliked eugenics, not only for scientific reasons, but also because he distrusted the disinterestedness of any government to implement the program sufficiently carefully.[12] And McCabe and Russell criticized eugenics for its presumption of progress in evolution. It is interesting that Hogben, McCabe, and Russell were all from the rationalist wing of the free thought movement, unlike the supposedly more compassionate Huxley.

Few people spoke of scientific humanism in the way Huxley conceived it, and his version remained dormant for thirty years. When he came to discuss *Religion without Revelation* four decades later in his autobiography, Huxley no longer spoke of the humanism he was then espousing as scientific. He then spoke of it as religious humanism and linked his thoughts not with biology or evolution but with the nineteenth-century loss-of-faith angst as detailed in the popular novel *Robert Elsmere* (1888) written by his aunt, Mary Augusta Ward (1851–1920), who was known at the time as Mrs. Humphry Ward.[13] One can't help feel this is a more accurate placement. We will return to Huxley's evolving conception of humanism in the next chapter.

THE MARXISTS AND DIALECTICAL MATERIALISM

The career of scientific humanism was launched by the wrong person with the wrong ideas in the United States. Lothrop Stoddard's scientific humanism was at best a fig leaf to cover naked and primitive racism. And Leon Samson simply adopted a currently fashionable term for his apology for Soviet Marxism. In Britain, scientific humanism found a more worthy champion in Julian Huxley. Although clearly a more humane man than Stoddard and a wiser one than Samson, Huxley's eclectic a mix of ideas was little better qualified to support a convincing version of scientific humanism, although it took longer for that to become apparent. We now need to consider another group of people who have been associated with scientific humanism: the Marxists.

Leon Samson, as we saw, was keen to associate scientific humanism with Soviet civilization. But the relationship between Marx, Marxism, and humanism is a great deal more troubled than that. One question always worth bearing in mind is, which Marx was being put on display at this time? It is often claimed that the "early Marx" was broadly humanist, but that this changed in his later work. At a superficial level, this distinction is plausible. After all, the word *humanism* appeared regularly in Marx's writings only between 1843 and 1845, after which it practically disappears. This coincides with the years when Marx collaborated with Arnold Ruge and wrote his influential *Contribution to the Critique of Hegel's Philosophy of Right* (or sometimes *Law*) (1844), which included the famous phrase "opium of the people." But Marx and Ruge soon fell out. Ruge would not follow Marx into socialism, which he saw as a coercive means to reduce everyone to a lowest common denominator. For Marx, the state is, and will be until the triumph of socialism, a class state. And the single most important historical dynamic is class conflict. Ruge could not accept that. Later that year, Marx went public in his criticism of his former ally, finding fault in particular with Ruge's skepticism about the chances of a socialist revolution happening in Germany. The basis of Marx and Ruge's differences lay in their respective views on revolution. By the time Marx and Engels had written *The Communist Manifesto* in 1848, the divergence was irrevocable. In the spirit of the most fiery Old Testament prophet, the manifesto painted a Manichean picture of bourgeois evil and proletarian virtue. It offered readers "certainty, hope, and revenge."[14] So, while it is true that there was a time when Marx spoke of humanism, followed by a time when he did not, this does not mean there was a fundamental shift in outlook to accompany this transition. What happened was that the disappointments hardened and made more rancorous Marx's already significant dislike of the bourgeois and impatience with history's unwillingness to cooperate. As Isaiah Berlin noted, the shift was merely from the young Marx who believed in "swift blows and putsches" to the older Marx who was resigned to the long revolutionary preparation.[15]

Just as important is the fact that the "early Marx" is a relatively late invention. Some of his early writing—the texts cited when pointing to the humanistic Marx—were locked away in short-lived journals that time and censorship had ensured would be known to only very few people. And much of this work did not see the light of day until after his death, in several cases not until the twentieth century. For example, *Theses on Feuerbach* was written in 1845 but was not published until 1888. Another important document for the "humanist Marx," which became known as *The Economic and Philosophical Manuscripts*, was originally planned as a series of significant monographs on the problems of the day. But the project got no further than these drafts on economic and philosophical issues. Though written in 1844, it was not published until the Marx-Engels Institute in Moscow got around to it in 1932. *Contribution to the Critique of Hegel's Philosophy of Right* was written, as we saw, in 1844, and *The German Ideology* in 1845 and 1846.[16] But neither did these see the light of day until 1932. It is also highly relevant that these works were published in the Soviet Union only once it was known that they were being published by anti-Stalinist Marxists in the West with a political goal in mind. So, prior to their republication in the 1930s, it is difficult to see how the "early Marx" had much influence on any but a tiny group of initiates. And even then, there was little or no reason to stress the humanist qualities of Karl Marx, given the favorable direction the dialectic of history seemed to be moving in. And Stalin's strong dislike of the word *humanist* would not have been an irrelevant factor.[17] It was not until the 1960s that Marx's early works became readily available in English. But by then it was too late.

There is another significant problem for "early Marx" theorists. Even his early work is permeated with a teleological certainty that runs counter to the melioristic spirit of humanism. That teleological certainty was later christened *dialectical materialism*. This is how Marx characterized humanism in *The Economic and Philosophical Manuscripts*. Atheism is, Marx wrote, "humanism mediated with itself through the supersession of religion, and communism is humanism mediated with itself through the supersession of private property. Only through the supersession of this mediation, which is, however, a necessary precondition, does positive humanism that begins with itself come into being."[18] Elsewhere in the same document, Marx spoke of communism as the apotheosis of a naturalism and humanism.[19] Historical supersessionism is a dangerous doctrine. It puts great power into the hands of the learned few who are privy to the details and provides them with the justification to persecute those who would dissent. Christian scholars are beginning to acknowledge the dangers of supersessionism in their religion with respect to the Jews. The sorry tale of Christian anti-Semitism is the story of Christian claims to have superseded the religion of the Jews. Marxist supersessionism is no more immune to the objections Christians are beginning to grapple with. So the "humanist Marx" is something of a misnomer and had little or no role in the development of humanism. Mark that down as another paradox of this story.[20]

The Marx who mattered before the 1950s was the Marx of dialectical materialism, of violent revolution led by a militant and self-conscious proletariat against which a foredoomed bourgeois would approach its Ragnarok. This was the Marxism that Friedrich Engels (1820–1895) had a great deal of influence in developing, although the actual term *dialectical materialism* was coined by Georgii Plekhanov (1856–1918). Marxism, especially in its more dialectical forms, runs against humanism in several ways. Its conception of history is teleological, or, in the worst sense of the more recent word, a metanarrative. Any sophisticated worldview has a philosophy of history, and humanism is no exception, but teleological views of history bestow special knowledge and destiny upon one group, be that the chosen people, the elect, the proletariat, or the born-again. This divides people into firmly segregated groups of people, those who can safely be demonized as unheedful of history and those who are deemed the bearers of historical truth, that is, themselves. In many ways the core insight of humanism is that there are no divisions between human beings worthy of enshrining in law or custom. Monotheistic religions are fundamentally anti-humanistic when they divide humans into the righteous—those who share my beliefs—and the heretics, those who do not. The Marxist division by class serves the same antihumanistic ends and works in the same tradition. One of the clearest of the humanist refutations of dialectical materialism came from Bertrand Russell, who objected to the feeling of certainty about the future that a dialectical mind-set encouraged.[21]

So long as they felt history was on their side, orthodox Marxists were unconcerned about what they saw as bourgeois carping. Dialectical materialism instilled in those who believed it to be true a tremendous confidence that history was on their side. Humanists and others were condescended to as only partially enlightened fellow travelers. The first of the major tremors in the course of dialectical progress came in 1939. When Communists read their newspapers on August 23, 1939, they learned that Stalin had signed a treaty of alliance with Nazi Germany. Only the day before they had been urging full mobilizing against Hitler as the paramount concern, alongside which all other considerations counted for nothing. But overnight, the war against Hitler had turned into an irrelevant squabble between varying brands of discredited imperialism. But once the news broke of Operation Barbarossa on June 22,

1941, the war was transformed once again into a crusade against the greatest evil the world had known. It took a dedicated type of person to effect, at short notice, such basic reorientations of the dialectical path.

Much of the appeal of the title *scientific humanism* lay in its claim to scientific levels of objectivity. So it is not surprising, then, that some scientists should favor the term, particularly if, like J. B. S. Haldane (1892–1964), they also happened to be Marxists. Haldane's work on this subject, *The Marxist Philosophy and the Sciences* (1939), brings together some of the more unhelpful elements of scientific humanism, particularly when shot through with doctrinaire Marxism. In particular, his insistence upon the identity of communism with the scientific attitude.[22]

Haldane is a prime example of what one contemporary philosopher of science, Susan Haack, has called the *Old Deferentialism*. Old Deferentialists, like Haldane, believed science to be entirely a rational undertaking and concluded that it could be articulated solely by means of formal logic. What this process left out was the world, with all its problems, contingency, and mess.[23] One scientist largely free of Old Deferentialism was C. H. Waddington (1905–1975). As well as being a highly respected developmental biologist, Conrad Hal Waddington was unusually well-read in the arts and in philosophy, which he had also studied. He married Justin, the daughter of Amber Blanco White, whose work we will examine in the next chapter. Waddington did not speak of scientific humanism, but his influential paperback *The Scientific Attitude* (1941) was emblematic of it. What makes his approach interesting is his sensitive treatment of science and his avoidance of all the pitfalls that later critics were apt to pounce on and that have come to be called *scientism*. He was not, he insisted, writing some "pontifical utterance" in the name of science, and neither is there some "critical point at which we must 'introduce science' or all is lost."[24]

By *science*, Waddington meant "the organized attempt of mankind to discover how things work as causal systems." And the scientific attitude of mind is interested in such questions, an outlook that anticipated contemporary philosophers of science, such as Susan Haack. If Waddington was free of Old Deferentialism, he also avoided the triumphalism of the Marxist theorists of science like J. B. S. Haldane, J. D. Bernal (1901–1971), or Benjamin Farrington (1891–1974). And Haldane made many of the same caveats about Marxism that Waddington made about science: not a final dogma but a method, and so on. But while Waddington was far more enamored of communism than would now seem intellectually acceptable, he maintained enough critical distance to differ from Haldane on its supposed identity with science. He noted, for example, that the dogma of dialectical materialism and the placing of the working class as its final test of value meant that, in the end, communism could not claim to be the extension of the scientific attitude into the world.[25]

But if Waddington could articulate a scientific humanism that was free of most of the Old Deferentialism, scientism, and other errors, we should also recall, even if only in passing, the long list of humanist scholars who were deeply critical of Marxism, particularly in its more teleological guises. The first of them was Bertrand Russell's *The Practice and Theory of Bolshevism* (1920), which Alan Ryan hailed as being thirty years ahead of its time. Others, like George Orwell's *Animal Farm* (1945), would count among some of the classics of twentieth-century literature.[26] Despite their differences of approach and emphasis, all these writers objected in one way or another to the unthinking progressionism implied in dialectical materialism. None of these critics was under any illusion about the scale of effort and sacrifice that would be needed over time for development to take place.

Marxist thinkers did not discover the latent humanism in Marx until it was apparent that the dialectic Marx had been discredited. Three things had conspired to destroy the dialectical Marx (1) the historical evidence that had revealed his forecasts to be false; (2) the corruption of Marxism into Stalinism (and then Maoism); and (3) the ongoing humanistic criticism, some of which is listed above. But by the time Marxists saw a pressing need to reinvent the "humanist Marx," it was too late. We will return to this story in chapter 7.

CYRIL JOAD AND THE RATIONALIST'S CHARTER

Part of the reason scientific humanism stuttered in Britain was the taint it quickly acquired of being bound up with Marxism. Among non-Marxists Julian Huxley was clearly the best-known apologist. But neither the Marxists nor Huxley had much success in convincing the free thought community. For instance, scientific humanism came to the Rationalist Press Association in 1931 in unfortunate circumstances because it was the catchphrase for a younger generation of RPA members who wanted change. Challenges to the leadership of organizations from young turks is a fascinating process. Throughout history such challenges have been made, and while the issues are never the same, the underlying dynamics are rarely that different. The RPA had been drifting somewhat since the end of the Great War. Its publications and emphases reflected the priorities of the country before the war. The RPA was not alone in this condition of course. Most people in responsible positions who had reached maturity before the war, found themselves in this state, almost willing themselves back to the world of 1913. But the younger ones knew that this was no longer possible or desirable. Among freethinkers, the prewar emphases of great men without religion, Christian evidences, and the controversy over evolution held little interest for the younger ones. For them biology was old hat, physics was now the happening science. For them it was taken for granted that Christian truth-claims were not valid, for them the question was, what now? And for many of them the worthwhile answers to pressing questions came from Sigmund Freud rather than Charles Darwin, or Aldous rather than T. H. Huxley.

Scientific humanism reared its head in the RPA in 1931 when J. B. Coates, one of the younger members, wrote a letter to the *Literary Guide* urging a new outlook. While the RPA had done a splendid job, Coates acknowledged, in combating superstition, religious obscurantism, and intolerance, was it not time for a new approach? Had not the time come, Coates wrote, "when the RPA and kindred societies, without abandoning their fundamental skepticism, should throw in their lot more definitely with the cause of scientific humanism?" There was a clear distinction between the work of the nineteenth-century rationalists (the people he was criticizing) and contemporary scientific humanism. Coates saw the work of the RPA as "out of harmony with the modern spirit."

> It must abandon its perhaps excessive preoccupation with Christian evidences and Christian theology; it must abandon also a certain tendency which I think it shows to a type of individualism which it has inherited from nineteenth-century liberalism, and accept the proposition, which is axiomatic to the modern humanist, that the higher moral possibilities of mankind cannot be realized without the scientific control of the political and economic mechanism of the world.[27]

The exemplars of scientific humanism for Coates were H. G. Wells, Julian Huxley, Walter Lippmann and, later on, Bertrand Russell. Coates may well have had a clear idea of what he meant, but thanks to F. J. Gould, the call for scientific humanism was quickly made messy and incoherent. This is because, the month after Coates's letter was published, Gould wrote in support of change, but in the service of a quite different notion of humanism. As we saw in the previous chapter, Gould was not speaking of scientific humanism at all but of the religious humanism then developing strongly in the United States. Instead of Julian Huxley, Bertrand Russell, or H. G. Wells, Gould spoke of John Dietrich, Edwin H. Wilson, Meadville Theological College, and the various humanist publications from the States.[28]

Two letters that came in over the next couple of months were probably more influential than most in scuppering Coates's rebellion. J. B. S. Haldane made a telling point when he noted that Wells, Russell, and Huxley disagreed on significant issues like behaviorism, Marxism, and eugenics.[29] A month later, a very grumpy J. M. Robertson weighed in with further observations about the lack of any coherent scientific humanist attitude toward political and social issues, such as free trade, proportional representation, the League of Nations, and birth control.[30] And both men insisted that even should unanimity on these issues be reached, they would count for little until such time as the fog of religious obscurantism had been lifted from people. This goes back to the classic struggle between the two wings of organized free thought. Which is the proper priority? Should freethinkers criticize religion first and foremost in the knowledge that while people still hold to supernaturalist nostrums, they will have no inclination to explore other ideas and ways of living? Or should they discuss the other ideas and ways of living in the hope of attracting all people of goodwill and, in the process, subverting old dogmatisms along the way? It is the central faultline of contemporary free thought, and it remains unsolved to this day.

Neither was Robertson above the more basic challenge of asking why, if rationalism was so unfashionable, did the aggrieved scientific humanists not go off and form their own organization and magazine? In all probability, Robertson knew the answer. In April 1929 a journal had been launched amid much fanfare called *The Realist, A Journal of Scientific Humanism*. The editorial board included Wells, Julian and Aldous Huxley, Rebecca West, Arnold Bennett, and Harold Laski. Originally it was thought that the lavish magazine was to be funded by Lord Melchett (Alfred Moritz Mond), then chairman of ICI (Imperial Chemical Industries). It soon became apparent that this was not the case, and after ten issues *The Realist* ceased publication at the beginning of 1930.

The failure of the initiative begun by J. B. Coates has been told elsewhere and need not be told once again.[31] Suffice it so say that scientific humanism did not storm the barricades of rationalism and was not to be heard from again until conditions had changed very significantly. The RPA did eventually reprint *Religion without Revelation* as Number 83 of its influential Thinker's Library, but only in 1941, after it was rejected as unsuitable in 1935. And the abridged version the RPA reprinted did not include most of the references to scientific humanism.

Having failed to secure in the Rationalist Press Association the name of scientific humanism, some of the dissidents went off and founded a new grouping to promote the cause. The Federation of Progressive Societies and Individuals (FPSI) was intended to act as an umbrella grouping, a popular front for all left-leaning tendencies. It pulled together an impressive though eclectic gathering of progressive thinkers and writers, including Vera Brittain, Leonard Woolf, Bertrand Russell, Aldous Huxley, H. G. Wells, Barbara Wootton, J. B. Coates and Norman Haire. Several of its leading figures did what they could to promote the FPSI's aims. In 1932, Cyril Joad produced *The Book of Joad*, which included what he called "A Charter for Rationalists." It was no such thing, of course, because the Rationalist Press Association had only just rejected him, his allies, and their priorities. But Joad's charter can be taken as representing fairly closely what he and his allies had in mind when they spoke of scientific humanism. The twelve points of the charter included, in this order:

- repeal of the divorce laws
- repeal of discriminatory laws against homosexuality
- diffusion of knowledge on birth control
- legalization of abortion
- sterilization of the feeble-minded
- abolition of censorship on plays, films, and books
- abolition of all Sabbath restrictions
- disendowment and disestablishment of the Church of England
- conservation of the countryside, curbing urban development, creation of national parks
- prohibition of exhibitions of performing animals
- abolition of licensing restrictions
- unilateral and complete disarmament[32]

But the FPSI's principal publication was a collection of articles, edited by Joad, published in 1934, and called *Manifesto*. Subtitled *Being the Book of the Federation of Progressive Societies and Individuals*, *Manifesto* hoped to set a new social and political agenda according to its lights. There was a brief introduction by H. G. Wells and then a series of eleven articles covering the FPSI program. Joad outlined the goals and ideals of the FPSI, then came articles on economics; disarmament; pacifism; education; and law reform in several areas, notably sexuality, the need for planning, secularization, and "a psychology for progressives." Care was taken to include a short summary of its program, which was almost identical to Joad's earlier charter. The summary divided the FPSI's program into three main areas. In "Economic and Social," it spoke of regional and world planning, and reorganization of world finance and world government. In "Educational," it had one goal: the establishment of a planetary education system. And under "Social," the *Manifesto* called for divorce law reform, birth control, legal abortion, penal law reform, town and country planning, and the abolition of censorship and of the blasphemy laws.[33] With the prominent exception of the support for eugenics, which was opposed by a wide range of humanist thinkers, it is interesting to note how many of these goals have become an accepted part of our lives now.

The choice of the title *Manifesto* for this work, only a year after the *Humanist Manifesto* had been published in the United States is unlikely to be coincidental. In some ways, the FPSI may have learned from the mistakes made by the Americans, in that its program was more down-to-earth and less couched in abstractions. It also followed its program with a nine-point plan of how these aims would be realized. The book included an application for membership form at the end, complete with areas the applicant could register an interest or competence in. Nothing is unusual about any of this now, but it represented a serious new commitment to social agitation at the time.

All this attention to detail and the support of big names came to nothing. By the time *Manifesto* was published in 1934, it was apparent that the FPSI had not succeeded in becoming the all-purpose umbrella organization for progressive societies it had hoped. Virtually no societies that might have been expected to show an interest opted to join. Societies that shared one goal may have had no policy on, or been specifically opposed to, another of the FPSI program, so FPSI ended up satisfying nobody. The FPSI was composed almost exclusively of individuals, almost invariably people already committed to its program. It later renamed itself the Progressive League. It is not that the aims outlined in the *Manifesto* were unpopular, being a fair representation of the views of Britain's left-leaning activists at the time. But most people thought that existing organizations, particularly the Labor Party, were better positioned to realize them. If American humanists are sometimes despondent about the relative failure of the *Humanist Manifesto* to create the waves they hoped it would, they should look to the fate of the FPSI for consolation.

JOHN DEWEY AND THE COMMON FAITH

We have already observed, more than once, that the people who articulated the finest, most nuanced, and most humane vision of scientific humanism were those who never spoke of themselves as scientific humanists. Bertrand Russell and George Santayana have already been offered as examples. The others would be John Dewey and H. G. Wells. Turning to Dewey first, we need to justify examining him in a chapter on scientific humanism (a phrase he didn't adopt) and not in the chapter on pragmatism, of which he is routinely listed as a champion. It is largely because, in a history of contemporary humanism, the discontinuities between Schiller and Dewey are more significant than the continuities. We have seen that Schiller set his task as opening pragmatism up to his broader conception of humanism. And we have seen that, by and large, he failed. Paradoxically, John Dewey succeeded in doing this, despite never declaring specifically that this was his task. Indeed, he rarely spoke of humanism, preferring to speak of naturalism. Dewey saw Peirce primarily as a logician, where William James was "an educator and humanist" (one of the few times Dewey uses the word) who worked to convince the wider public that the philosophical problems pragmatism concerned itself with "have a real importance for mankind, because the beliefs which they bring into play lead to very different modes of conduct."[34] It is difficult not to see the unsaid subtext following this, to the effect that Dewey was continuing this process of educating and broadening.

Dewey claimed to have "great regard" for Schiller's writings, but he did not support the "unduly subjectivist turn" he gave humanism. In a letter to Corliss Lamont, Dewey observed shrewdly that Schiller was so interested "in bringing out the elements of human desire and purpose neglected in traditional philosophy that he tends . . . to a virtual isolation of man from the rest of nature."[35] He was right about this. He was so much more successful than Schiller in propagating his version of pragmatism because he always linked humanity to nature. He gave his readers a grounding, which Schiller was never able to do. And this was the ground of his scientific humanism. Another reason for Dewey's success was his willingness to paint on a broader canvas. Where Schiller was aiming at the Hegelian absolutists and more rigid Christian theologians, Dewey was concerned about the entire corpus of knowledge in the wake of the Copernican and Darwinian revolutions. Where Schiller's solution was a narrowly conceived set of epistemological fine-tuning, Dewey sought nothing less than a comprehensive new worldview that takes seriously the changed intellectual climate of the modern age. But while he was convinced of the need for a new worldview, he was equally determined not to simply offer up another list of absolutist nostrums. Nowhere is this better illustrated than in *The Quest for Certainty*, the book that emerged from his Gifford Lectures of 1929. The quest for certainty, he wrote, "is a quest for a peace which is assured, an object which is unqualified by risk and the shadow of fear which action casts."[36] In contrast to this, Dewey spoke of the scientific attitude, which "may almost be defined as that which is capable of enjoying the doubtful; scientific method is, in one aspect, a technique for making a productive use of doubt by converting it into operations of definite inquiry."[37] At the beginning of the twenty-first century we often hear of the pressing need for such an attitude. And not infrequently this is said in the context of a postmodernist critique of the supposed dogmatism of naturalism and certainty of science. But when we take the trouble to read the said naturalists, we find in fact that they were no less eloquent in their warnings before the current generation of commentators was born.

Dewey's solutions were much more flexible and open to reinterpretation than Schiller's. He spoke of *experimentalism, intelligent action,* and the *social intelligence*—terms that can be explained without recourse to jargon and for which the meaning can be made clear to any intelligent reader. Schiller, by contrast, was anxious to limit his humanism to a narrow elite of academicians. And Dewey understood that progress, in the sense of fixed goods being finally and fully attained until paradise has arrived, was untenable. Indeed, he reserved some of his harshest condemnation for this attitude, calling it "pitifully juvenile."[38] Dewey was, like most humanists, a meliorist. Things would improve only if we understood the issues sufficiently clearly and worked sufficiently diligently.

Dewey understood the fundamentalists' fear of the modern world because he understood that their theology could not survive in it. One of the many paradoxes of this study is that it is those further along the secular end of the humanist spectrum who appreciate more fully what it is that fundamentalists stand to lose. This has often been put down to a psychological and epistemological similarity between atheistic and theistic hardliners. This is true for the very extremes of either end, but the vast majority of secular humanists arrive at their understanding by taking what fundamentalists say more seriously than their supposedly more reasonable allies from the religious humanist community. We will address this issue again in chapter 6.

The book that gave Dewey more aggravation than any other of his large corpus was *A Common Faith* (1934), his brief foray into the relation between religion and humanism. This short work is still a source of division among American humanists and an iconic focus of hatred from American fundamentalists. Dewey began with the state of intellectual crisis of the modern world brought about by the dysfunction between what the traditional monotheist religions thought the universe was like, and what science since Copernicus has shown it was actually like. Between the two conceptions lies an abyss, which he then named *supernaturalism*. The depth and breadth of this abyss had stranded many thinking people in the modern world with no respectable way to call themselves religious. Unable to still believe the claims about the way the world works shouted at them from the other side of the chasm, people assume they must therefore be nonreligious. For Dewey, this was a mistake, a category mistake, as Gilbert Ryle would later describe it.

Dewey wanted to rescue notions of God, of religion, of faith, for use in a secular world by people who understood the changes in outlook brought on by science in the last four centuries. Rather than being the irascible patriarch of traditional understanding, Dewey spoke of God as the "active relation between the idea and the actual."[39] And the common faith he spoke of was our collective duty as citizens to do our bit to make things better for those who follow us. This idea has a lot in common with the later writings of H. G. Wells, as we will see later in this chapter.

The issue that has divided humanists was whether Dewey was correct to reemploy religious language in this way. He recognized the problems with it and was content to leave it up to individual decision. In a letter to Corliss Lamont in 1935, once it was clear just how confused the issue had become, Dewey admitted:

> I made a bad slip which accounts for the fact that you thought I was making a recommendation. The meaning in my mind was essentially: If the word *God* is used, this is what is *should* stand for; I didn't have a recommendation in mind beyond the proper use of a word. . . . I got my auxiliary verbs mixed.[40]

Lamont, and later Alan Ryan, were correct when they questioned the possibility of appropriating religious language for social uses without wanting to pay the epistemological price for it.[41] In other words, religious language is too tightly bound up with common understandings of the words and with intellectual baggage too reminiscent of the other side of the intellectual abyss for successful transplantation on this side.

Dewey himself offered a prize example of the dangers involved in attempts such as this to reconfigure religious language. As part of his attempt to make ground between aggressive atheism and humanistic religion, he spoke of retaining words like *God* and *divine* as helping "protect man from a sense of isolation and from consequent despair or defiance."[42] Here is the crux of the problem. It seems to confuse things unnecessarily to seek to offer consolations of this sort while at the same time recognizing the bankruptcy of supernaturalism. There either is a supernatural realm, with all that is said to entail for human beings, or there is not. And if there is not, then it is ill-advised to get in the business of offering consolations that have meaning only in a context of what is being denied. The people Dewey denounced as "aggressive atheists" have always understood that important point better than he did.

Dewey was trying to pave a way between what he saw as aggressive atheism and humanistic religion. He was not the first to see aggressive atheism as a mirror image of the supernaturalism he wanted to bypass. But he was no more prepared to seek refuge in agnosticism, which he described as "a shadow cast by the eclipse of the supernatural."[43] By this he meant that agnosticism ceases to be able to offer anything once our focus is directed to the way the world actually works. But against agnosticism, Dewey saw faults in humanistic religion, which, "if it excludes our relation to nature, is pale and thin, as it is presumptuous when it takes humanity as an object of worship."[44] He doesn't expand on this comment, but it's hard not to suppose he has the religious humanists in mind. Only the year before writing *A Common Faith*, Dewey had signed the *Humanist Manifesto*. He took no active role in helping draft or publicize the manifesto beyond lending his signature to it.

So, with these caveats in mind, it's fair to think of Dewey as a scientific humanist. Alan Ryan concurred with this, conceding that "scientific humanist" is as good a description of Dewey's position as any, so long as we do not mean by that the vulgar Marxist notion of inevitable progress.[45] Like many others who were uncomfortable with aspects of humanism, he was a meliorist. Progress was not written into the fabric of the cosmos, whether the stitching is theological, teleological, or dialectical. And yet, he was able to offer a vision of the future in purely naturalistic terms:

> We who live are parts of a humanity that extends into the remote past, a humanity that has interacted with nature. The things of civilization we most prize are not of ourselves. They exist by grace of the doings and sufferings of the continuous human community in which we are a link. Ours is the responsibility of conserving, transmitting, rectifying, and expanding the heritage of values we have received that those who come after us may receive it more solid and secure, more widely accessible, and more generously shared than we have received it.[46]

This was Dewey's common faith: grounded, melioristic, yet inspiring.

Before crossing the Atlantic once again, note should be taken of another experiment in scientific humanism. This came from the American philosopher Oliver Reiser (1885–1974), another signatory of the *Humanist Manifesto*. Not only did Reiser speak specifically of scientific humanism, at one stage he unveiled an ambitious plan to institutionalize it. Nothing came of this plan. Over the course of his long life he experimented with various forms of humanism, ending up with a mystical form of cosmic humanism not unrelated to the ideas of his friend Rabindranath Tagore, whose thought we will discuss in chapter 9. But during the 1940s, Reiser advocated scientific humanism which, by and large, was free of many of the problems of overweening historical determinism we have complained of in this chapter. He took care to locate humanity in a fragile and interdependent world and stressed our inability to gain certain knowledge of anything or to even arrive at enduring solutions. Two of his five tenets of scientific humanism involved recognition of human imperfection and fallibility [47] While there is much of value in Reiser's work, it strikes me that we can explore many of his insights better by examining Tagore, as will happen in chapter 9.

BERTRAND RUSSELL AND THE UNFLINCHING PERCEPTION

Bertrand Russell's star waned somewhat between the wars. He married Dora Black in 1921 and worked with her at their alternative school project at Beacon Hill in rural Sussex for several years until the very messy collapse of their marriage between 1932 and 1935. No longer employed at a university, Russell needed to make money by writing popular philosophy and through journalism. The general consensus is that Russell's attitude toward religion hardened during these years, largely due to the influence of the more militantly rationalist Dora. And Russell's outspoken criticism of Bolshevism set him at odds with many people who called themselves scientific humanists. So neither the scientific humanists nor the religious humanists were attractive options to him at the time.

Russell's discomfort with humanism as being articulated in the United States rested on a reasonable suspicion of the degree of anthropocentrism still lurking within it, with too much extravagant talk of limitless possibilities, man as the apogee of nature, and man's ability to control and transform nature to its own ends—what Tzvetan Todorov has later to call "proud humanism." Russell wrote to his American acquaintance Corliss Lamont that he still preferred the word *rationalism*.[48] The framers of the *Humanist Manifesto* understood this and made no formal approach to solicit Russell's signature.

Despite all this, Russell can legitimately be seen as a scientific humanist because of the role he accorded science as the means by which we can learn reliable information about the world, and because of the benefit this knowledge will bring to human beings. As he said in his best-known address of the period, "Science can teach us, and I think our own hearts can teach us, no longer to look round for imaginary supports, no longer to invent allies in the sky, but rather to look to our own efforts here below to make this world a fit place to live in, instead of the sort of place the churches in all these centuries have made it."[49]

The overwhelming conclusion of all science since Copernicus, Russell said on many occasions, was the unimaginable littleness of humanity in the scheme of things. Through all the changes in his outlook, this position remained much the same through his long life. His essays in the 1920s reworked the core insight of "The Free Man's Worship," but without the Romanticism, the poetry, and the lingering Platonism. In their place was the same sense of cosmic modesty, but told in new language. Modern science will not have done its job until our view of the world fully recognizes the inescapable fact of our cosmic irrelevance. Then, and only then, can humanity move on. There is, he wrote, "stark joy in the unflinching perception of our true place in the world, and a more vivid drama than any that is possible to those who hide behind the enclosing walls of myth."[50]

One of the few occasions Russell made specific mention of *humanism* was in his essay "My Mental Development," written in 1943, and which appeared in the Library of Living Philosophers volume devoted to his work. Once again, he distanced himself from making a religion of humanism, but this time he acknowledged human beings are, necessarily, the sole bearers of anything he could value. So, while his head went with the humanists, he admitted his "emotions violently rebel" at the prospect.[51] This remained his view for the rest of his life.

H. G. WELLS AND THE OPEN CONSPIRACY

In many ways the most representative thinker who could be described as a scientific humanist was H. G. Wells, although, like Dewey and Russell, he did not use this term himself. Wells (1866–1946), a novelist, prophet, and thinker, was one of the twentieth century's most multitalented publicists. Born in modest circumstances in Kent, he narrowly avoided a life a penury and obscurity in the drapery trade his mother planned for him. He studied at the Normal School of Science at South Kensington (now the Royal College of Science and part of the University of London) under T. H. Huxley, and taught for a while, before he was able to earn a living as a writer. His first published work was a series of scientific romances. This genre, now known as *science fiction*, was then in its infancy. The best of these works, *The Time Machine* (1895), *The Island of Dr. Moreau* (1896), *The Invisible Man* (1897), and *The War of the Worlds* (1898) remain classics in their field to this day.

Common wisdom says that these works represent Wells at his best, but his writing career lasted another forty-five years, and included some very significant books, fiction and nonfiction. World War I brought on a series of personal conflicts for Wells, as it did for many people, and his writing changed as a result. His wartime books reflected the tension he felt between his deep love of England and his suspicion of jingoism. The best of them were *Mr. Britling Sees It Through* (1916) and *The Undying Fire* (1919). His output after the war was prodigious, but the best of the novels were *Christina Alberta's Daughter* (1925), *Mr. Blettsworthy on Rampole Island* (1928), and *The Bulpington of Blup* (1932). *Mr. Blettsworthy*, in particular, deserves much more recognition than it has had, being a study of the breakdown of the easy Edwardian consensus about progress. Wells is unfairly said to have been an apostle of progress, only to have been disillusioned in his last days. This is untrue because it overlooks the stream of pessimism about humanity's anthropocentric conceit from the very early days of his writing career. This underlies the lasting appeal of his science fiction and reappears periodically, as in *Mr. Blettsworthy*.

The crisis Wells experienced during World War I took the form of a religious crisis. Finding that the beliefs he had gone into the war with seemed misplaced and unsatisfactory, he looked around for something else. His books between about 1916 and 1919 reflect this restlessness. The main nonfiction work of this time where these thoughts found expression was *God the Invisible King* (1917). Even Wells's biographers tend to skirt around this book, usually picking up on the same embarrassment Wells felt about it in later years. Wells spoke of the God he was brought up with. For many of us, he wrote, God "first came into our lives to denote a wanton, irrational restraint, as Bogey, as the All-Seeing and quite ungenerous Eye."[52] Wells never reconciled himself to this conception of God, and his reading of the National Secular Society's magazine, the *Freethinker*, would have helped arm him against this version of the God-idea very effectively. But the war rendered opposition to this notion of God no less unhelpful than the original notion itself. He had spoken with William James on these matters and now, under the pressure of the war, put them together. Wells began *God the Invisible King* maintaining complete agnosticism in the matter of God the Creator, and "entire faith in the matter of God the Redeemer."[53] Then, as so often happens, he went on to outline what he did *not* mean with respect to *God*. What was left was a deified humanism, not unlike the cosmic humanism of

Frank Doan or the religion of man Rabindranath Tagore spoke of, which we will examine in chapter 9. None of the ideas were original to him, Wells said, he was being but the "scribe to the spirit of [his] generation." What he claimed to have done that was new was to restate in religious language what had already been said in scientific language. He ended the book, "Modern religion has no revelation and no founder; it is the privilege and possession of no coterie of disciples or exponents. . . . It is a process of truth, guided by the divinity of men."[54]

God the Invisible King provoked a great deal of debate, from all manner of positions. This was Wells's genius. He *was* the scribe of his generation. Over the next two years he carried on playing with these ideas in his next three novels: *The Soul of a Bishop, Joan and Peter* and *The Undying Fire*. *The Soul of a Bishop* features the crisis of faith of Edward Scrope, bishop of Princhester. Scrope's crisis is brought on by the war, by biblical and historical criticism, and by his own health. Toward the end of his drug-induced vision of God, Scrope came to his final realization:

> He had not seen the Invisible but only its sign and visible likeness. He knew now that all such presentations were true and that all such presentations were false. Just as much and just as little was God the darkness and the brightness of the ripples under the bows of the distant boat, the black beauty of the leaves and twigs of those trees now acid-clear against the flushed and deepening sky. These riddles were beyond the compass of common living.[55]

In *Joan and Peter*, Wells returns to the theme, but this time using the fresh and idealistic youth Peter Stubland as his principal mouthpiece. Where Edward Scrope has to deconstruct a lifetime's worth of attitudes and reassess the privileges the acceptance of those attitudes has secured for him, Peter Stubland is just starting out in life. His war experiences sharpen his understanding of life. As befitting a novel about youth, *Joan and Peter* is more about education than about religion, although therein lies the rub. In a delirious state brought on by a war wound, Peter has a long conversation with God, who, in the end, tells him that if he wants change in the world, he will have to bring it about by his own efforts.

Without question the best of Wells's discussion novels from this stage in his life was *The Undying Fire*. In a conscious retelling of the story of Job, the main character, Job Huss, headmaster of Woldingstanton School, is afflicted with a seemingly overwhelming series of calamities to his school, to his family, and to his health. But the wager between God and Satan in this case is not whether Job Huss should curse God, but whether he should even remember him. While recovering from a series of calamities and preparing for a major operation, three prominent members of the Woldingstanton school board of governors visit Huss and tell him of their plans to remove him as head and change the school's direction. Whereas Huss wanted his pupils to understand the world they were entering so as to participate in it knowingly and meaningfully, the governors wanted to make the students compliant tools in a society they did not understand. Like Eliphaz the Temanite, Bildad the Shuhite, and Zophar the Naamanite in the biblical story, Job Huss's three interlocutors are unimaginative in their notions of God, society, duty, reward, and friendship. Sir Eliphaz Burrows, William Dad, and Joseph Farr each had a Pecksniffian quality of smugness about them.

The book revolves around the conversation Huss has with Burrows, Dad, and Farr about the future direction of the school and the worldviews which sustain them in those thoughts. Huss has a Spinozistic quality about him, in that his God is all-pervasive and the best means to understand him is though knowledge and work. Some of the best renderings of how I imagine Spinoza's *sub specie aeternitatis*, or "under the aspect of eternity," are to be found in *The Undying Fire*.

> I feel that life is a weak and inconsequent stirring amidst the dust of space and time, incapable of overcoming even its internal dissensions, doomed to phases of delusion, to irrational and undeserved punishments, to vain complainings and at last to extinction.[56]

But on that backdrop of cosmic modesty, Wells builds a worldview of poetic beauty, warm melancholy, and sublime joy. Against this Sir Eliphaz Burrows gives a Panglossian apology for things as they are (for he is wealthy) and declares man the planned-for apogee of evolution.

What makes *The Undying Fire* so interesting as a transitional work is that Wells introduces another character who not only criticizes the three interlocutors but also sees the weaknesses in Huss's arguments, and by implication, in Wells's own excursion into attenuated supernaturalism. Elihu

Barrack is the doctor in attendance of Huss. A man who lost a leg in the Great War, Barrack is a no-nonsense agnostic. He is invited to share his thoughts late in the book, after Huss had condemned the egotism of personal immortality, saying it is not men who go on living but Man the Universal. In *God the Invisible King* this would have been a major event in the book, given as much rhetorical flourish as Wells could muster. But only two years later, Wells has Dr. Barrack see through Huss's fancies no less than the conventional conceits of the three interlocutors. Where Huss spoke of Man the Universal, the undying fire that is the only true immortality, Elihu Barrack spoke only of evolution, or as he put it, the Process.

> Put everything of yourself into the Process. If the Process wants you it will accept you; if it doesn't you will go under. You can't help it—either way. You may be the bit of marble that is left in the statue, or you may be the bit of marble that is thrown away. You can't help it. *Be yourself!*[57]

Huss replies to this, making some criticisms of the fatalism inherent in Barrack's agnosticism, but one can't help feeling that Barrack wins the day. In the end Huss admits to Barrack that his notion of the God-concept of Man the Universal is "metaphorical and inexact." And, interestingly, Wells doesn't return to the God and Satan wager in any depth at the end of the novel, so we must assume that God was content with Huss's minimal endorsement.

Barrack's victory is apparent in Wells's later novels. In the three-volume *World of William Clissold* (1926), Wells examines the world and his beliefs at some length. And Clissold has no truck with God-talk. "We realize the complete indifference of the universe to us and our behavior. We know we are exposed and unprotected." And Clissold finds he is relieved to be free of the idea that some supernatural busybody is looking over his shoulder and tut-tutting his every thought and motivation. Later still, in *The Fate of Homo Sapiens* (1939) Wells specifically distances himself from the many attempts to evade the unreality of God. He mentions not his Invisible King but many of the alternatives; the Absolute, the "force not ourselves making for righteousness," the "whisper of conscience," the "brainless Thinker responsible for the mathematical order of the world," are all recognized as evasions and subterfuges. It is a natural, though regrettable, human disposition to want to believe we are being taken care of, he sighed.[58] But behind his fiction Wells had a far simpler explanation why he had abandoned all his God-talk. In a letter from 1920 to his lover Rebecca West (1892–1983), Wells said "God has no thighs and no life."[59] Scandalous, even blasphemous to those so inclined, but no less true for that. You can't turn over in bed and speak about your joys and sorrows to some bloodless abstraction. But you can to a living human being.

Before moving on, it should be noted that *The Undying Fire* is a standing reprimand to unthinking critics who repeat the old canard that Wells lost faith in a superficial progressionist optimism in the last year of his life. He never was superficially optimistic. He had stages in his career of relative optimism, and stages where that optimism, as in 1919, was tinged with the warm sadness of the cosmic perspective. As a true meliorist, Wells was all too aware of the human effort that positive change would require, and as he got older his faith that humanity possessed that will diminished.

After *The Undying Fire*, Wells had played out his theistic phase and returned to what he called "the sturdy atheism of my youthful days."[60] He then went on to write what became known as his three textbooks for the world: *The Outline of History* (1920), *The Science of Life* (1931), and *The Work, Wealth and Happiness of Mankind* (1932). Each of these was very influential, despite receiving sniffy reviews from academics. They can be seen as core documents of scientific humanism at its best.

It has become so much the norm to deprecate Wells's nonfiction that this claim might seem outlandish. I will defend it with only one example, for fear this chapter blow out of all proportion. *The Outline of History* is, we are told, derivative, a pastiche of ideas lifted from the *Encyclopedia Britannica*, even that it was plagiarized from a Canadian woman. More recent criticism prefers to accuse it of being a metanarrative for some hegemonic modernism. The truth is simpler. On any fair reading of *The Outline of History*, it should be apparent that Wells was no positivist. At no time in his career did he embrace a monolithic scientific method that could be applied in all circumstances. As Krishnan Kumar has correctly observed, "Science *in* society was one thing, and a supremely urgent and important one; a science *of* society was quite another and, in Wells's view, impossible and undesirable."[61] Wells was passionate about history as a discipline and critical of the way it was usually taught, being funneled down lines of nationality, class, or religion. Inspired by Winwood Reade, he was skeptical of golden ages, great men, and turning points in history—common historical devices then and now. He also treated periodizing of history with little of the standard reverence. In fact, his appreciation of social movements in history as expressed in changing conceptions of money, gender, and slavery mark him off as distinctly contemporary in his understanding of history. He was also more aware of the history of the world outside Europe than was common at the time. Wells saw history as an organic process of muddling from one blundering innovation to another. Far from presenting people with a grandiose metanarrative, Wells outlined a melioristic account of human history nowhere more clearly stated than when he said that history had become a race between education and catastrophe. Like any historian, he hoped that *The Outline of History* would help people understand how and why they were as they were. Wells wrote in the introduction, "A sense of history, as the common adventure of mankind is as necessary for peace within as it is for peace between nations."[62] Is that so unreasonable?

The Outline of History was written with the advice and editorial help of some of the most distinguished scholars of the day: Sir E. Ray Lankester, Gilbert Murray, Ernest Barker, and Sir H. H. Johnston. None of these men were of the type to sit by and let their names and reputations be tainted by amateurish generalizations. And at frequent intervals through the revised version I have (published 1921), they appear in footnotes and present a dissenting view to the one offered in Wells's main text. It is very instructive to follow these dissenting footnotes through the course of the work. As one epoch is succeeded by another, a new historian takes issue with Wells over this or that claim. To take two examples from very many, Ernest Barker obviously disagreed with Wells about his description of some legal occupations in classical Athens as "hereditary barristers." Barker takes twelve lines to essay his opposition, charging it with being unjust to Athens. As another example, late in the second volume, Gilbert Murray suggests that Britain's policy in the years leading to the First World War was clearer than the "heavy ambiguity" Wells speaks of. So, on the same page that readers came across Wells's comment, they also had the dissenting view from his panel of specialists. It is difficult to support the charge that a singular metanarrative is being force-fed to readers when dissent of this sort punctuates the text at frequent intervals.[63]

Neither was Wells unaware of ecological thinking, as Julian Huxley claimed in his memoirs. In fact, Wells was more ecologically aware than Huxley. Wells was under no illusions about the periodic extinctions that have swept away whole categories of species. The general history of life, he wrote in 1939, is marked more by failure and defeat than by adaptation. And he understood that each new extinction "is a swift, distressful impoverishment of life that is now going on."[64] In fact, it was their contrasting attitudes toward *Homo sapiens* that most distinguished Julian Huxley from H. G. Wells. A constant feature of Wells's writing, both his fiction and his nonfiction, was his awareness of the need to overcome the anthropocentric conceit. Huxley retained an exaggerated notion of the exceptionalism of *Homo sapiens*, even to the point of not fully throwing off old great chain of being ideas. The contrast with Wells could hardly be more stark. In *The War of the Worlds*, Wells challenges "our" sense of outrage that the Martians should be so bold as to seek to exterminate us. "We" had destroyed the Tasmanians, Wells reminded his readers, so what grounds for complaint have we if the Martians make war in the same spirit?[65] Four decades later, he began his gloomy *The Fate of* Homo Sapiens (1939) by itemizing the lessons we have failed to learn. We are not at the center of the universe, as the old religious systems so presumptuously declared, but are the denizens of "a very second rate planet."[66] And following on from that, Charles Darwin forced upon our reluctant attention the recognition that our species is not magically set apart from the laws that determine the destinies of any other species. *Homo sapiens* "prospers or suffers under the same laws."[67] He returned to this theme in his last novel; *You Can't Be Too Careful*, published in 1941. This unjustly neglected work is, in essence, a retelling of *The Fate of* Homo Sapiens in novel form. Very near the end of the book, he makes his major point: "Mankind has to be debunked. When Man realizes his littleness, his greatness can appear. But not before."[68] The Nietzschean flavor of this statement reflects Wells's reading at the time. His next book, *The Conquest of Time* (1942) also featured some Nietzschean ideas and turns of phrase.

Most well-read people today are aware of the dangers of anthropocentrism, of the need for an ecological awareness, and of the urgent need for concerted effort in order to save the day. But in 1939 few people were. It was not a theme popular writers on evolution dwelled upon, preferring instead the themes of onward and upward progress. And this was a failing not by any means confined to nonreligious writers. If anything it was more pronounced among theistic evolutionists. What makes Wells an attractive figure is not simply that he saw the problems ahead of many others, he also had the courage to offer some solutions. One of his more imaginative ideas was the open conspiracy, which he conceived of as a groundswell of popular opinion in favor of world government and planetary cooperation and planning. He introduced the idea in his three-volume novel *The World of William Clissold*, which was published in 1926. He liked it enough to return to it in two subsequent works, *The Open Conspiracy: Blueprints for a World Revolution* (1928) and *What Are We to Do to With Our Lives?* (1931). Interestingly, the term had already been used by Arnold Ruge, who we discussed in chapter 1. Ruge meant an open conspiracy in the sense of being desirous of change to the established order, but without resorting to the violence preferred by Marx and other revolutionaries. Along with the open conspiracy, Ruge spoke of an "invisible church of humanity," and "voluntary freemasonry" to illustrate his intentions.

But for Wells the problem was not so much active persecution as blank incomprehension. He struggled against the undirected drift of purposeless and motiveless societies, and his campaign was directed against inertia. The open conspiracy foretold not a domineering world directorate so beloved by writers of dystopias. He saw no need for a capital city or a flag or grand congresses at which mountains of words are built and scaled. Rather, he spoke of a revolution in ideas, led by newspapermen, businessmen, and teachers, toward bypassing old loyalties based on class, nationality, race, or religion. The open conspiracy was to be a popular front led by motivated, socially concerned young men and young women to sweep aside the self-serving obscurantism of the vested interests and reactionaries, and work together to build a new world of rational, compassionate, humanistic planning and building. It was to be an intellect rebirth. The open conspiracy was followed by the World Brain. A major reason for the muddle, waste, lethargy, and short-sightedness that Wells campaigned so passionately against was the fractured and disorganized state of the world's knowledge. In speaking of the World Brain, Wells looked forward to the time when the world's knowledge would be organized and accessible to anyone who cared to use it. He devoted a book to the subject in 1938, but it peppered his writing for several years before World War II.

There are, doubtless, many things Wells can justifiably be criticized for. But through all the criticisms, he remains an engaging figure. He is fun to read and he cared passionately about the world he lived in. Though he never described himself in these terms, Wells is an exemplar of the best kind of scientific humanism. We will return to Wells in his role as prophet of planetary humanism in the last chapter.

SCIENTIFIC HUMANISM FINDS ITS FEET—TOO LATE

It is yet another irony of this story that the clearest, most level-headed expositions of scientific humanism were not produced until well after the term's use-by date had expired. As if to add to the irony, one of them came not from a firebrand Marxist or peddler in teleological certainties. Instead, it came from Antony Flew (1923–2010), one of Britain's most prolific and successful postwar philosophers and a lifelong political conservative. After editing or coediting some very influential essays in the 1950s with people like Alasdair MacIntyre, Flew wrote some important works in the 1960s, such as *Hume's Philosophy of Belief* (1961) and the atheist classic *God and Philosophy* (1966). This was only one of a series of works on philosophical atheism that helped cement his reputation as a formidable thinker. His early paper, "Theology and Falsification," and later concepts such as the *presumption of atheism* and the related *Stratonician presumption* have become standard features on the atheist philosophical landscape.

So, both from a philosophical and a political perspective, Flew's thoughts on scientific humanism would be interesting. As one of the century's most consistent expositors of David Hume, Flew's version of scientific humanism took pains to distinguish questions of fact from those of value. The scientific part of the equation deals with matters of fact while the humanist part deals with matters of value. He attempted no grand definition or synthesis. He understood scientific humanism as a means by which to refuse to place any abstraction, be it God, progress, or the dialectic, ahead of humanity. Instead, it accepted "as ultimate in all matters of fact and real existence the appeal to the evidence of experience alone; a court subordinate to no higher authority, to be overridden by no prejudice however comfortable."[69] This straightforward understanding was what most of Flew's predecessors had in mind with the term as well, but, unlike Flew, they assumed their other beliefs were equally uncontroversial and in harmony with science.

Another person who gave admirable expression of what could be called *scientific humanism* was Jacob Bronowski (1908–1974). Born in Lodz, then part of Russian Poland, Bronowski was the son of an observant Jewish father and an atheist, communist mother. The family fled their hometown at the beginning of the First World War and lived in Germany until 1920, when they migrated to Britain. He studied mathematics at Cambridge and spent part of

World War II engaged in military research. He spent part of 1945 in Nagasaki, monitoring the effects of the plutonium bomb that had been dropped on that city on August 9. In 1964 he moved to the United States, where he worked at the Salk Institute for Biological Studies in California.

Bronowski was one of the best popularizers of science in the twentieth century. His early work *Science and Human Values* (1958) brought together a series of articles written for the *New York Times* about nuclear science and the morality of nuclear weapons. *The Identity of Man* (1965) sought to find a viable humanist account of what it is to be human in an era of mechanization. And he cowrote with the American historian Bruce Mazlish *The Western Intellectual Tradition* (1960), a magisterial intellectual history of thought from the Renaissance to the nineteenth century. But he's best remembered for the thirteen-part BBC television documentary *The Ascent of Man*, which was issued as a book in 1973. This series epitomized his characteristically Continental mix of high culture and scientific awareness. We could discuss Bronowski just as happily in chapter 7 where we examine the bildung tradition of European humanism.

When he's remembered at all, Bronowski has had a bad press since his death, being accused, among other things, of scientism. It's difficult to see how this charge can be sustained. A quick survey of his article titled "The Values of Science," which appeared in the *Rationalist Annual* in 1960 should illustrate the point. We are not taught values by the facts of science, Bronowski said. People valued truth before we had science. But the *activity* of science, which is committed to truth, has ramifications for us all, such as a commitment to ongoing inquiry, originality, and dissent, and the ability to distinguish seeing an opponent as mistaken from seeing them as wicked.[70] A more memorable counterexample would be from his *Ascent of Man* television series, when Bronowski knelt in a puddle outside Auschwitz, lamenting the fate of his loved ones and of humanity in general. It was not dehumanizing science that permitted the slaughter of so many people, disgorging their ashes into the puddle where he then stood. It was arrogance. It was dogma and it was ignorance. "We have to cure ourselves," he said, "of the itch for absolute knowledge and power. We have to close the distance between the push-button order and the human act. We have to touch people."[71]

Antony Flew gave scientific humanism its simplest and cleanest definition, and Jacob Bronowski best epitomized its values. But, despite their efforts, the career of scientific humanism as a stand-alone category was coming to an end. An interesting feature of the demise of scientific humanism is that its principal accusers were fellow nonreligious thinkers. For example, the English philosopher Stephen Toulmin criticized scientific humanism in a radio program in 1957, calling it a "religion substitute." He accused scientific humanism of retaining the same proselytizing urge that rationalism had before it. Agnostics, he claimed, lacked this urge. What is notable about this otherwise unremarkable claim is that Toulmin made this point while speaking on a program titled "On Remaining an Agnostic." Toulmin's broadcast was important, not because of what he said but because he was allowed to say it on BBC and he was not accompanied by a clergyman to act as spiritual chaperone. But his criticism of scientific humanism revealed a point of deeper importance. Britain was becoming more secular, and with that secularity came a larger range of viewpoints, including nonreligious ones.

Another incident, again, not important on its own, illustrates the problem. Early in 1963 the Irish historian Benjamin Farrington (1891–1974) resigned his membership of the RPA because of his opposition to the label *scientific humanism*, which he thought had become unhealthily dominant. In a letter explaining his position, Farrington wrote:

> A *humanist*, as I understand the word, is interested not only in science but in art, literature, scholarship, philosophy, religion, and many other things. His claim to the title *humanist* depends not on the side he takes in the infinite perplexities that arise in all spheres, but on refusing to push any quarrel over opinions to such an extreme as to forget that his opponent is a man.[72]

Farrington was precisely the sort of man scientific humanism should have appealed to. He was a capable historian of ideas whose history of Greek science, for example, is still an informative and useful book. What mars its value, though, is his insistence every now and then to nudge Greek intellectual history into the straitjacket of Marxist historiography. But even a Marxist like Farrington was becoming sufficiently impatient of the contradictions he perceived in scientific humanism by the 1960s. The association with doctrinaire Marxism, coupled with growing suspicion of science and fears of scientism, combined to fatally undermine *scientific humanism* as a uniting term. By the 1960s being "scientific" was no longer an uncontroversially good thing and so the coupling of *scientific* with *humanism* was serving to divide humanists more than it was to unite them.

It would be a mistake, however, to conclude from this that scientific humanism was shown to be fatally flawed. It's worth reiterating the important point that many critics of scientific humanism were nonetheless deeply sympathetic to the general principles it was thought to represent. From Benjamin Farrington in the 1960s to Susan Haack four decades later, the most perceptive critics of scientific humanism have been those who are, in the broadest sense, scientific humanists. Their criticisms were not against the principle of what was being put across but against the suppositions "scientific" humanism was thought to carry. Haack, for example, has observed that what used to be called a *scientific attitude* is not the preserve of scientists alone. And neither is there a single scientific attitude, any more than there is a single religious attitude. What is really being recommended is a critical attitude to the evidence and a degree of caution in accepting whatever answer is being urged. Bertrand Russell and John Dewey, despite their strong differences on other matters, both said as much. Even a figure as unlikely as Karl Jaspers, whose thought is examined in chapter 7, was quite clear that "there can be no integrity, reason, or human dignity without a true scientific attitude."[73] Phrases like *scientific humanism* or *scientific attitude* presume such things are the exclusive preserve of scientists or humanists. This, of course, is not the case; these qualities are present in all people with an inquiring mind. Haack understood this when she spoke of her version of the scientific attitude as *critical common-sensism*.[74] If scientific humanism had started out with a more homely label like this, it might have enjoyed a longer career, or at least a less fraught one.

CHAPTER 5

BRITISH HUMANISM SINCE WORLD WAR II

As we saw in chapter 3, it was F. J. Gould who, in 1907, first spoke of a humanist movement in the collective sense it has come to mean pretty much a century after the term was first used. And yet it took another half century for a humanist movement in the form Gould envisaged to actually come about in Britain. This chapter will explore why that was and look at what British humanism has become.

HAROLD BLACKHAM AND THE PLAIN VIEW

At the end of World War II humanism had little traction in Britain. Ferdinand Schiller's noisy championing of his relatively narrow version of humanism had died with him. And the few who followed him had little more success, in some cases for similar reasons. For example, Stanton Coit (1857–1944) spoke in terms very similar to the American religious humanists, with whom he shared many ideas, although he was less certain about *humanism* as the word to best express what he meant. A highly intelligent man, Coit was born and educated in the United States, and he was deeply impressed by the transcendentalism of Ralph Waldo Emerson before moving on to Felix Adler's Ethical Culture movement. The rest of his life was devoted to Ethical Culture, in the United States and, after 1894, in England. He was instrumental in creating the Union of Ethical Societies (1896), which later became the Ethical Union (1920). He wrote widely; his most important books were *The Message of Man* (1902), *National Idealism* (1908), and *The Soul of America* (1914). He was also fluent in German and translated several important works into English, including, between 1931 and 1932, Nicolai Hartmann's *Ethics*. Hartmann (1882–1950) was an important nontheistic philosopher, although underappreciated in English-speaking countries.

Even Coit's friends admitted he was a difficult man, not easy to get along with. In the time-honored manner in such situations, his friends often resorted to describing him as "complex." He was an odd, though not unusual, combination of an intolerant tyrant who devoted his life to the message of tolerance and democracy. He toyed with the idea of taking up the new word *humanist* for the movement, but he decided not to in the end because of the several ways the word was being used at the time. At heart, he was a Platonist who believed in the ideal of Truth.[1] He tended to equate humanism with Modernism within the church.[2]

As Coit and the older generation moved on, the decaying shell of the Ethical Culture movement in Britain fell into the lap of a virtual unknown. Harold Blackham (1903–2009) found himself pretty well in charge of the movement in the middle of the 1930s and from there went on to become one of the leading figures in twentieth-century English humanism. Born near Birmingham, the son of a lay preacher, Blackham left school at sixteen and worked on a farm, so as to work with horses. His entry into adult life came during the general strike in 1926, when he volunteered to join a militia to help suppress the coal miners. After this, he decided he needed more of an education, so he enrolled in university to train as a teacher. He studied divinity with a view to teaching, but he realized he had lost his faith, so felt the need to move on again. After drifting for a while, he answered an advertisement from Stanton Coit to work in the Ethical Church in London, now in serious decline. After war service in the London Fire Brigade, Blackham set about the task of redirecting the ethical movement in a humanist direction. For the rest of his active career, he did what he could to promote the concept of humanism as a positive ethical alternative to traditional religion. His preferred vehicle for this was the Ethical Union's journal, *Plain View*, which he began in 1944 and edited until 1965. He was less interested in the criticism of religion that had been the staple of the Rationalist Press Association, and more in the promotion of ethical alternatives to religion. The *Plain View* had a strictly limited readership, but its earnest tone earned it some measure of respect.

Blackham went on to write some important books. The most influential of them was *Six Existentialist Thinkers* (1952), which went through several editions and is still in print. It is a sympathetic account, and it contrasts well with the more critical *The Feast of Unreason* (1952), written by Blackham's contemporary—and rival—Hector Hawton, from the Rationalist Press Association. Blackham's other important book is *Humanism* (1968), a book designed to popularize humanism to a wide reading audience. Unfortunately, his rather flat writing style worked against that and disguised the book's real value. His other main works include *Political Discipline in a Free Society* (1961), *Religion in a Modern Society* (1966), and *The Future of Our Past* (1994).

Blackham was also a consistent critic of *rationalism*, at the time still the most common description British non-Christians would use to describe themselves. This inevitably made his relationship with some leading members of the Rationalist Press Association a trifle strained at times. For Blackham, rationalism fell between the cracks. On the one hand rationalism's message of reason was insipid enough to be entirely uncontroversial. But on the other hand there was a dogmatism to what he saw as its militant atheism and teleological positivism that turned off a lot of people otherwise sympathetic. And above all, rationalism could not hope to illuminate the lives of people by only criticizing. In one his rare resorts to italics, he declared in an essay from 1956: "*To destroy you must replace.*"[3]

There was nothing particularly new in these criticisms. George Jacob Holyoake had said this almost a century earlier. And in 1933 J. A. Hobson (1858–1940) had said much the same thing in a lecture to the South Place Ethical Society. But beyond articulating the need for this change, Hobson made no attempt to specify what he meant by *humanism*.[4] Blackham made it his task to fill this need. What makes Blackham important is that he was no more enamored of the label *scientific humanist*, which he thought too narrow and that overlooked the very real limitations of rational thinking.[5] In fact, he opposed any prefixing to the core notion of *humanism*, something he dismissed as mutilation with an epithet.[6] This has remained a strongly held feeling in British humanism ever since. Blackham's preference was for a more restrained, modest humanism: "Humanists cannot possibly discharge the responsibility they take on; like others, they can only do their best and strive to do better, steering between complacency and demoralization and despair."[7] As befitting a man who was strongly impressed by the existentialists, he was of the view that we are not born human, it is something we have to grow into. The virtues he most wished we could cultivate were candor and generosity, fortitude and fairness.[8] Blackham understood and sympathized with the bildung tradition.

BERTRAND RUSSELL AND THE FAITH OF A RATIONALIST

Harold Blackham was looking to establish *humanism* as the default word to describe commitment to democracy, open-mindedness, and rationality without rationalism. At one level, he was joined by Bertrand Russell, who was just as motivated to defend these virtues, though no less ambivalent about thinking of them as *humanism* than he had been earlier in his life. Soon after his return from the United States, where he had been for most of the war, Russell quickly found his way back into the spotlight of public life. He was reappointed to Trinity College, Cambridge, from which he had been dismissed in the previous war for his opposition to the fighting. The joy this gave him soon palled, however, once he learned that some of his colleagues and most of the students thought him old hat, particularly when compared with Wittgenstein, whose star was then in its ascendant. But among the reading public, Russell's name was never more prominent. His *History of Western Philosophy* was published in Britain in 1946 and quickly became a bestseller.

Two main issues exercised Russell through the ten years after the war. The most important was his concern to show how science was the surest means by which reliable answers can be found while at the same time not wanting to concoct some technological absolutism or scientism. His most significant work devoted to this was *Human Knowledge: Its Scope and Nature* (1948), which Russell regarded as a major restatement of his thinking and a significant contribution to naturalistic philosophy. Its aim was to show the strict limits to what we can really know about the world around us, the impossibility of foundationalism (though he didn't use that term), and then offer a series of postulates, the use of which could help us determine what was very probably true. He noted that knowledge is a significantly less precise concept than is generally assumed and that the roots of knowledge are, as evolutionary psychologists now say, in our "embedded and unverbalized animal behavior."[9] At the end of the book Russell proposed five postulates, the job of which was to justify external realism and in so doing, provide a means by which we can acquire reliable knowledge about the world.

Human Knowledge received an almost universally negative reception. It was the wrong book at the wrong time. But that doesn't make the book wrong, just unfashionable. In 1948, linguistic philosophy was king, and

Wittgenstein was very much the philosopher of choice. Since then, however, linguistic philosophy has fallen into disfavor, having been charged with not having any real philosophical problems to ask. *Human Knowledge*, by contrast, had some pressing questions to ask, took the subject seriously, and made a valiant attempt to provide an answer.

The dismal response to *Human Knowledge* had little effect on Russell's growing prestige among general readers, which was derived mainly from his shorter, more popular books, essays, and lectures. For instance, in 1946 Russell gave a lecture to the National Book League in which he outlined his notion of Liberalism (his capitals) as the need of the hour. What Russell was calling Liberalism was indistinguishable from what others would call humanism. "The Liberal creed, in practice, is one of live-and-let-live, of toleration and freedom as far as public order permit, of moderation and absence of fanaticism in political programs."[10] Russell was restating the creed of his godfather, John Stuart Mill, whose outlook is now called *liberal humanism*. At much the same time in the United States, Morris Cohen (1880–1947) was expressing a similar mix of liberal humanism in his selected essays, *The Faith of a Liberal*.[11]

The following year, in another popular address, called *The Faith of a Rationalist*, Russell returned to themes he had thought about since "The Free Man's Worship" more than forty years previously. Once again, he was concerned to disabuse any anthropocentric conceit humans may wish to arrogate to themselves.

> Apart from the minuteness and brevity of the human species, I cannot feel that it is a worthy climax to such an enormous prelude. There is a rather repulsive smugness and self-complacency in the argument that man is so splendid as to be evidence of infinite wisdom and infinite power in his Creator.[12]

Arising directly from this rejection of anthropocentrism, Russell found two motivating sources for his life's work: kindly feeling and veracity. These humanistic virtues arose not *in spite* of his rationalist understanding of the universe but *because* of them. And the order in which these developed was important; hence his ambivalence toward humanism as he perceived it.

Russell's views on rationalism were reflected at about the same time by Karl Popper, when he spoke of *critical rationalism*, toward the end of the two-volume work, *The Open Society and Its Enemies* (1945). Popper distinguished *critical* from *pseudo, uncritical,* and *excessive* forms of rationalism, each of which he criticized at length. What he meant by *critical rationalism* was identical to what others have called *humanism.* "In short, the rationalist attitude, or, as I may perhaps label it, the 'attitude of reasonableness,' is very similar to the scientific attitude, to the belief that in the search for truth we need cooperation, and that, with the help of argument, we can in time attain something like objectivity."[13] He said as much toward the end of another article, written originally in 1951, and which appeared in *Conjectures and Refutations.* In one of the few times he spoke directly of humanism Popper asked the rhetorical question, if humanism is concerned with the growth of the human mind, what then is the tradition of humanism if not a tradition of criticism and reasonableness?[14]

In this respect, Russell was not saying anything greatly different either from Popper or Blackham. But what Blackham did was to shift the usage from *rationalism* to *humanism.* Being a generation older, Russell still preferred the older words, *liberalism* and *rationalism.* But he wasn't going to die in a ditch for them. When the Rationalist Press Association made the change to *humanism* in the mid-1950s, not only did Russell not object, he accepted the honorary position of president and retained it for the rest of his life.[15] And when asked by the American Humanist Association in 1951 whether he was a humanist, Bertrand Russell replied that that he preferred the older term *rationalist.* "I should not have any inclination to call myself a humanist, as I think, on the whole, that the nonhuman part of the cosmos is much more interesting and satisfactory than the human part. But if anybody feels inclined to call me a humanist, I shall not bring an action for libel."[16] Russell's sardonic reply says a lot about his attitude toward *humanism.* His enduring contribution to scientific humanism was to take the implications of science with respect to humanity to its logical conclusion. He had an abiding dislike of the anthropocentric conceit in all its forms, something that humanists, particularly those of a more "religious humanist" disposition, are not immune.

The other issue that exercised Russell during the 1940s and 1950s was the felt need to help people resist the temptation, in troubled times, to lapse into the easy comforts of absolutism. Whether emanating from Rome or Moscow, "great systems of dogma lie in wait for the modern man when his spirit is weary."[17] Russell hoped to provide the moral courage for people to resist these easy consolations and look life fully in the face. His anticommunism, which had forced him to the periphery of advanced opinion between the wars, now placed him center stage. We will discuss this last phase of Russell's long life in chapter 13.

The ten years from the end of the war until his move to radical peace activism are probably the least favored by professional philosophers today, to the point almost of competing with each other for ever more comprehensive dismissals of Russell's work from this period. It remains a fact, however, that a whole generation of intelligent general readers grew up on these works and were guided by them. More than anyone else, it was Russell who established the link with *humanism* and *classical liberalism*, creating in the process a market for a notion like *liberal humanism*.

HERBERT READ AND THE SENSUOUS APPREHENSION OF BEING

At this point it seems important to break from the story as it is normally understood and to mention two significant, though now largely forgotten, humanists. One person never mentioned in histories of humanism is the art critic and theorist Herbert Read (1893–1968). During his long and successful career, Read was at various times a professor of fine art, editor of the *Burlington Magazine*, and director of Britain's first major design consultancy. He was also a prolific poet, critic, and writer; he even wrote a successful novel, *The Green Child* (1935). Read lost his faith during World War I. He wrote many years later of his cynical response to seeing roadside shrines or churches destroyed by the process of war. As so often happens, Read's standing has suffered since his death, in his case because his two most passionately held causes, psychoanalysis and Jungianism, have not proved to be the bold new insights he believed them to be. Freud was a brilliant man who made a lasting contribution to twentieth-century thought, but his chief creation, psychoanalysis, has not survived critical scrutiny in academic psychology. And the extravagant edifice of Jungian psychology never achieved the level of acceptance of Freudianism and has ceased to have influence outside of New Age circles. In fact, Herbert Read is one of the few serious thinkers strongly influenced by Jung whose work is not irrevocably tarnished as a result.

Part of the reason for this is that Read was more than a fellow traveler. He compared Freudian and Jungian psychology to medieval scholasticism, being "an extensive corpus of expert knowledge for the most part written in a repulsive jargon."[18] He wanted the insights of these psychologies to be mediated by a humane literature. And, on the reverse side, he saw humanism as in dire need of these insights if it was not to remain a shallow fabianism. One can't build a meaningful and vibrant humanism by tinkering with the edges of the welfare state, he insisted.

In an essay titled "The Creative Nature of Humanism," Read made the case for a humanism in the sense of a "sensuous apprehension of being." In deference to a youthful exposure to the work of the German nihilist Max Stirner (1806–1856), he was anxious to avoid the abstracting of *Man,* which, suitably capitalized, becomes as tyrannical and jealous as Yahweh, Der Führer, or the proletariat. So he wrote not for or about "Man," or even men, but for and about you and me. Read's humanism was essentially a revivified Renaissance humanism: a humanism of letters and the cultivation of character, of appreciation of the tragic dimension of life, and of bildung. The sensuous apprehension of being was Read's understanding of the goal of the Renaissance humanists. A culture that encourages our appreciation of these and other insights is a humanist culture. It was Read's view that the best of the contemporary artists and poets had captured some element of the sensuous apprehension of being and that abstract art was the twentieth century's specific response to the confusions of its time. A phrase Read used was the inspiration for the title of this book. He spoke of a *wealth of concrete insights*—that is the point: humanism is the creation of a wealth of such concrete insights."[19] Once again, we can almost feel the quivering of Friedrich Niethammer's shadow at this point.

Why is Read ignored in the history of humanism? Part of the answer lies in the taxonomies that have emerged and hardened. Making distinctions between secular, religious, and cultural humanism is an interesting exercise so long as we use these distinctions to deepen our understanding of what humanism is about. But, like all categories, it quickly becomes a means by which some people can be forgotten. This is a great pity, and humanism seems diminished as a result.

AMBER BLANCO WHITE AND THE NEW WOMAN

Another humanist thinker who is easily forgotten and who deserves better is Amber Blanco White (1887–1981), daughter of the prominent politician and historian William Pember Reeves and his wife Maud, a suffrage campaigner. After a political career in New Zealand, the Reeves family moved to England when Amber was nine years old. She went to Newnham College, Cambridge, in 1905 and blossomed in student life, joining, predictably, the Cambridge University Fabian Society, which boasted H. G. Wells as one of its speakers. Their mutual admiration became a physical affair, the news of which caused a huge scandal that threatened to wreck Wells's career and Amber's life. There is the marvelous story of Wells and Reeves making love in the countryside, cavorting atop a newspaper that featured an article by Mrs. Humphry Ward lamenting the decline in morals of the young.[20] Quite unchastened, Wells provoked the scandal by writing about it, thinly disguised in his novel, *Ann Veronica*, which appeared at its height in 1909. While the circumstances of the fictional Ann Veronica Stanley are somewhat different to those of Amber Reeves, one gets the feeling that the feisty, passionate, and intelligent young woman portrayed in the novel was closely based. Pretty soon Amber was pregnant with Wells's baby. A marriage with George Rivers Blanco White was hastily cobbled together in May, and Anna Jane was born, safely legitimate, in December. Wells dedicated *Ann Veronica* to "A. J."

Had Amber Blanco White kept to script, she would have retreated into provincial obscurity to live out her days in shame. But she never regretted her affair with Wells. She went on to work actively for women's suffrage and, after that, for a range of progressive causes. In the early 1930s she provided important assistance to Wells, who was working on *The Work, Wealth and Happiness of Mankind*, which appeared in 1932. This ambitious work was designed to serve as a guide to the general reader to how the world actually works. It was the third of Wells's great "textbooks for the world" projects which had already produced *The Outline of History* and *The Science of Life*. Blanco White supplied a wealth of research for the book and influenced it throughout. And although the chapter on the role of women in the world was her suggestion, it did not reflect her views. Working with Wells helped propel her name into the wider public. She stood as Labor candidate for Hendon in 1933 and 1935, but it was really as an educator that she found her niche. Over her thirty-seven-year career lecturing at Morley College in

London, Amber Blanco White became an inspiration for successive generations of younger women. Her novels included *The Reward of Virtue* (1911), *A Lady and Her Husband* (1914), and *Helen in Love* (1916). Nonfiction titles included *The New Propaganda* (1938) and *Worry in Women* (1941). But it was *Ethics for Unbelievers* (1949) that she felt most closely expressed her own views.[21]

Ethics for Unbelievers is still worth reading. At no time did Blanco White justify the need for a book of this sort: she simply presupposed a large constituency of non-Christians for whom a coherent ethical outlook free from supernatural appeals can be constructed. Neither did she presume to be saying anything particularly new. She was, in her words, restating the humanitarian tradition, what in chapter 1 we called the tradition of liberal humanism that Bentham and Mill articulated so thoroughly. What was unusual was her broad reading of Confucian thought and her warm, though critical, sympathy with it. The simple fact that Amber Blanco White was a woman was the most remarkable feature of the book. Books like this had appeared before, and some had included chapters on "the woman problem," or something of that sort, but this was the first time a woman had given voice to expressing a humanist outlook. Unlike some of her male contemporaries, Blanco White's discussion on sexual ethics was relatively sober and devoid of shock value. True to her own experience, she counseled caution with respect to premarital sex but did not rule it out as a legitimate form of experience.[22]

Looked at several decades later, the single biggest flaw in *Ethics for Unbelievers* was Blanco White's identification of Freudianism as the scientific attitude that could provide a coherent, nonsupernaturalist outlook. Even here though, her attitude was critical; she was critical of the blank pessimism of *Civilization and Its Discontents*, for example.[23] And Blanco White valued Freud's thought without the zealous espousal of psycho-analysis that afflicts so many people of this persuasion. As with Read and Jungianism, Blanco White was sufficiently critical of her sources so as not to be dragged down once her star ceased to shine.

MARGARET KNIGHT AND MORALS WITHOUT RELIGION

If Blackham laid the groundwork for humanism in Britain, it was not his work that propelled it into people's living rooms. Neither was it the important book by Corliss Lamont, which we will examine in depth in the next chapter, or the works of people like Herbert Read or Amber Blanco White. Lamont's important book *Humanism as a Philosophy* received a lukewarm response in the United Kingdom. The *Literary Guide* didn't even give it a full review, relegating it instead to the "Short Notices" section. The unsigned notice (my bet is that Hector Hawton wrote it) was complimentary, praising its readability and erudition, but expressing unease that dialectical materialism is an ally of humanism.[24]

Ethics for Unbelievers was not reviewed at all by the *Literary Guide*. This is not to say, of course, that these books were not influential in moving the British rationalist movement to take *humanism*. But clearly not everybody in the movement was taking up the word, as we saw with Bertrand Russell, who preferred the older words to express broadly similar thoughts.

If there was a single series of events that helped establish humanism as an idea across Britain, a very good case can be made for it being the controversy Margaret Knight ignited when she gave a radio broadcast about morals without religion. I have written at some length about Knight elsewhere but make no apology for covering similar ground here.[25] Her story is sufficiently important and interesting to warrant a bit of repetition. Margaret Knight (1903–1983) had a career that was successful and worthwhile—not always the same thing—at a time when such things were not usually open to women.

Like so many people, Margaret Knight began university conventionally religious and left it an atheist. One could almost ask how anyone could *not* leave Cambridge in the 1930s as an atheist, particularly when she cited her main influences as Bertrand Russell and the Hegelian atheist J. M. E. McTaggart (1866–1925). In the nineteenth century it was often the case that the shedding of religious beliefs was a long and painful exercise, but for people in the twentieth century, it was just as often spoken about as a joyful release. Knight later recalled letting her religious beliefs go "with a profound sense of relief, and ever since I have lived happily without them."[26]

After leaving Cambridge she worked for ten years at the National Institute of Industrial Psychology before following Rex, her husband, to take up a lectureship in psychology at Aberdeen. The war provided Knight an opportunity to serve as acting head of department, while her husband was on war service. Upon his return, she stepped down and took on a part-time role and developed her career within the confines of what was allowable at the time. In particular she cowrote with her husband the highly successful textbook *A Modern Introduction to Psychology*, which went through several editions and remained in print for more than twenty years. In 1950 she was asked to edit the works of William James and provide an introductory essay for a Pelican series on psychology. This book went through six editions. Rex Knight died suddenly and unexpectedly in 1959, leaving Margaret a widow for the rest of her life.

In 1953, by now a respected academic psychologist, Margaret Knight turned her attention to the issue of radio broadcasting on moral education. Her initial approaches to the BBC were scornfully rejected, but she persisted until, in July 1954, her third proposal for a series of talks was accepted. The main theme Knight wanted to pursue was the inculcation of sound moral education of children outside a formal religious setting. Once having taken on the concept of the talks, the BBC was surprisingly open to the sorts of comments and criticisms it was prepared to allow her to make. Not only did the BBC agree to the idea that children could be raised successfully without religious instruction, it was also happy for her to offer advice specifically tailored to nonreligious parents.

The key to the success of the talks was Knight's knowledge of her audience. She began the first talk by speaking frankly of the position most parents found themselves in. They may have married in church and baptized their children, and they may even attend church every now and then. But they don't believe a word of it. "Their general feeling is that it does not much matter what views a man holds on the higher management of the universe, so long as he has the right views on how to behave to his neighbor. And they are not at all troubled about religion, except for one thing: what shall they teach the children?"[27] She went on to outline a straightforward and eminently reasonable account of raising morally aware children free from dogma. She denied that Christianity and communism were the great alternatives of the day, suggesting instead that both are dogmatic systems and, as such, stood together against scientific humanism. There is much to be learned from the Bible, just as there is much to be learned from any mythology. The essence of humanism was held to be disinterestedness, or not letting our own claims blind us to those of other people.

Reading Knight's talks today, it is hard to fathom the level of invective they provoked, so straightforward they now appear. Indeed, one often hears the same ideas being espoused by religious educators, as if these insights are original to them. But at the time Margaret Knight's "Morals without Religion" talks were highly controversial, not least because they were advanced by a woman. The *Daily Telegraph* was incensed the BBC permitted what it called "atheistical propaganda" on the air and called on God and the BBC to prohibit the second broadcast. The *Sunday Graphic* focused more on its sense of outrage that a woman should say such things. Under a two-inch heading "The Unholy Mrs. Knight," readers were warned, "Don't let this woman fool you.... She looks—doesn't she—just like the typical housewife; cool, comfortable, harmless. But Mrs. Margaret Knight is a menace. A dangerous woman. Make no mistake about that." A range of prominent churchmen, ranging from the Catholic bishop of Liverpool to the Dean of Windsor lamented the talks had been permitted. The bishop of Coventry dismissed her as a "brusque, so-competent, bossy female."[28]

But hard on the heels of the first wave of indignation came the second wave of reaction, either from those in favor of the broadcasts, or from those who favored people's right to hear them. No less a figure than the Dean of St. Paul's, the Very Reverend W. R. Matthews acknowledged that Knight's broadcasts had in fact been moderate and courteous. Even more important, he admitted that her views better reflected the actual state of thought in Britain at the time than those of her detractors. The *Church of England Newspaper* was admirably candid when it said, "If the Christian faith can only reply to such a person as Mrs. Knight with personal abuse and can find no compelling answer, it deserves to fail and will, in fact, disappear.... Big Brother is no less sinister for wearing a dog collar."[29]

Without a doubt, the virulence of the reaction is partly explained by the fact that a woman was saying these things. Gone was the comforting old prejudice that the bosom of the mother was the same as the bosom of the church. The other reason was probably that saying these things on national radio exposed these thoughts to an altogether larger audience than had they been locked away in some book or obscure journal. But the main reason why this furore was so splenetic was that it had finally exposed what everyone knew to be true but nobody had actually dared say. Knight paraphrased the theme: "'Someone's said it at last!' For years there had been an elaborate pretence that we were, with negligible exceptions, a nation of Christian believers. Now I had 'blown the gaff.'"[30]

Margaret Knight's broadcast series on morals without religion was a significant milestone in the making of a post-Christian Britain. It demonstrated to Britain that it was in fact a nation of diverse beliefs. It had long been true, but now it was known to be true. It had just needed someone to stand up and say that the emperor had no clothes. While the church continued to enjoy a privileged level of access to radio and, shortly, television, never again would it be so presumptuous as to assume it deserved the privilege. The Margaret Knight controversy linked humanism in the public mind with down-to-earth concerns about raising one's children well. Friedrich Immanuel Niethammer would have approved.

The furore over the "Morals Without Religion" broadcasts made Margaret Knight a highly sought-after speaker. It was during the course of her speaking on humanism at British universities that she saw the need for a single-volume anthology of humanist thought. This was her next important contribution. *Humanist Anthology: From Confucius to Bertrand Russell* was a great success. Beginning with Laozi and Confucius, then going through the Greeks and Romans down to Albert Einstein and E. M. Forster, Knight brought together a variety of thinkers who disagreed on many very significant issues but shared a commitment to humanity and to reason. *Humanism*, Knight wrote in her introduction, had moved on from the beginning of the twentieth century when it meant someone educated in the humanities.

> Rather, it implies that he sees no reason for believing in a supernatural God, or in a life after death; that he holds that man must face his problems with his own intellectual and moral resources, without invoking supernatural aid; and that authority, supernatural or otherwise, should not be allowed to obstruct inquiry in any field of thought.[31]

From this, Knight saw humanism supposing two corollaries: that virtue is a matter of promoting human well-being rather than displaying obedience to a supernatural lawgiver, and that the mainsprings to social action have biological roots and that are just as conducive to altruism and cooperation as to competition and aggression. Both of these corollaries have been amply fulfilled by the resurgence of thinking in virtue ethics and evolutionary psychology.

It is easy to quibble about who is and who is not included in a book such as this. Despite Knight's inclusion of Laozi and Confucius, the list is overwhelmingly European. It's also overwhelmingly male. And Americans might justifiably feel underrepresented. Corliss Lamont, in particular, could justifiably have felt miffed at not being included. Schiller's absence, by contrast, was a sign of how humanism had changed since his day—and the degree to which it had not moved as he would have wished. Having said all this, though, Margaret Knight's *Humanist Anthology* is an admirable collection and did a great deal of positive work to expand the horizons, both of the non-specialist inquirer who delved into the book, and of humanists who were exposed to new names from the tradition. The first twelve were ancient thinkers and there was a generous sprinkling of novelists, journalists, and politicians. And the inclusion of Spinoza, Thomas Paine, and Arthur Schopenhauer expanded the horizons of people normally listed as humanists. Others were rescued from obscurity, such as Georg von Gizycki (1851–1896), in his time a prominent German ethicist and critic of supernaturalism. Gizycki's works, incidentally, were translated into English by Stanton Coit.

An interesting little transition made in Knight's anthology was that Bertrand Russell's famous essay "The Faith of a Rationalist" was reprinted under the headline "The Faith of a Humanist." As we have already essayed, Russell was uncomfortable with the idea of *humanism*, as it suggested a level of anthropocentrism he thought unwarrantable. But Knight was wise to make this transition for Russell's beautiful essay and Russell, presumably, gave her permission for the change. For all its condemnation of anthropocentrism, the essay begins by extolling the simple, human virtues of kindly feeling and veracity. The change of name gave Russell's essay a new lease of life, and the new title has stuck: in 1983 the National Secular Society reprinted it under the new heading. But probably the most important contribution of Knight's *Humanist Anthology* was to reveal the diversity of what can legitimately be called humanist thinking. The range of thoughts, the various styles of expression, the different emphases and approaches—in other words the absence of any orthodoxy: these were, and remain, humanism's greatest asset. Here, truly, we could see a wealth of insights.

HECTOR HAWTON AND REASON IN ACTION

Coming from the same generation as Blackham and Margaret Knight, yet with a different path to humanism, was Hector Hawton (1901–1975). Like so many humanists, especially self-educated ones, Hawton has been neglected since his death, and his broad-minded and extensive contribution has not received the attention it deserves. Hector Hawton was born into an ardently Protestant family and raised on *Foxe's Book of Martyrs* and *The Pilgrim's Progress*. Partly in rebellion against his upbringing, he converted to Catholicism at the age of fifteen, remaining a Catholic until his early thirties when study of science and philosophy led him briefly to Marxism before becoming a humanist.

Hawton built a career around his ability to write. He worked as a journalist before setting up as a freelance writer in the early 1930s, where he turned his hand to detective stories, children's adventures, even romances. During World War II he worked for Bomber Command's Group 4 at Heslington Hall in York, during which time he wrote two books on aspects of the Royal Air Force's war effort. After the war, he became active in the humanist movement, working first for the South Place Ethical Society until he took over the editorship of the *Literary Guide*, the magazine of the Rationalist Press Association in 1953. He also oversaw a radical downsizing of the RPA, which saved the organization from financial ruin.[32]

Hawton's unusually wide reading and clarity of style made his humanist books among the best then available. His humanism, like his writing, was straightforward and unpretentious. As late as 1950 he still preferred to speak of *rationalism* rather than *humanism*. His book of that year, *The Thinker's Handbook*, was a nonspecialist's guide to a morally engaged, skeptical, and atheistic outlook that had been the core of organized British rationalism since at least the 1880s. Many years later Blackham recalled Hawton teasing him that humanism was no more than a gleam in his eye. And until the mid-1950s it was. But, to Hawton's credit, once he took the word up he did more to promote it intelligently than most other people in Britain. This was his single most important contribution. His first move was to oversee the transition of the *Literary Guide*, as the RPA's journal had been called since its inception in 1885, to *The Humanist*. Under his editorship, which lasted from 1953 until 1971 and again from 1974 until his death in 1975, *The Humanist* enjoyed one of its finest periods, with the years between 1954 and 1968 standing out as especially strong. During those years, many of the leading thinkers of Britain were published in the *The Humanist* at some time or other. And under a series of pseudonyms, Hawton contributed mightily himself, mostly notably as "R. J. Mostyn."

Hawton never made the mistake of replacing one creed for another. In an editorial in 1959, he set out his views:

> We [humanists] are obviously a coalition of different schools of philosophy with common ground in our rejection of supernaturalism. Any attempt to devise a set of dogmas would be the negation of humanism. There is no humanist answer book and those who wish to be told what to believe must look elsewhere.[33]

Like Amber Blanco White, Hawton was keen to bring a more transcultural approach to British humanism, and so opened the pages of *The Humanist* to explorations of Confucianism, Taoism, Buddhism, and Indian thought. But Hawton's common sense kept him and *The Humanist* from wandering off on a puff of incense. He was enough of a rationalist not to want to load up *humanism* with a whole lot of unhelpful baggage. As he was an early critic of the extravagances of existentialism, he was also one of the more perceptive critics of *The Humanist Frame* and of Julian Huxley's infatuation with Teilhard de Chardin. He saw more clearly than Huxley the dangers tied up with a teleological account of the universe. Finding inspiration in Teilhard's work comes at a cost that Huxley took insufficient account of. Is it possible, Hawton asked, for a godless universe to have a direction?[34] If it has a direction, it needs some sort of force that sets the course of that direction. In other words, one cannot claim to have shed a religious outlook and still believe the universe has a direction. It followed from that that Hawton was also skeptical of Huxley's confidence that traditional religious concepts could be reformulated and made the basis for a new humanistic religion.[35] By all means, let us embrace humanism as an affirmation of life and diversity, but why do so using religious language?

JULIAN HUXLEY AND EVOLUTIONARY HUMANISM

The tremendous exposure humanism received in the "Morals without Religion" affair stimulated a succession of new books on the subject. The highest-profile of them came from Julian Huxley who, having retired from UNESCO, had time on his hands, and having championed humanism in one guise or another for thirty years, it is not at all surprising that he should reenter the fray. Aspects of Huxley's humanist thinking at the end of the 1950s and early 1960s were much the same as during his younger years, but other facets had changed a lot. His first move was to issue a revised edition of *Religion without Revelation,* which had sold well thirty years previously and had been included in the popular Thinker's Library series of the Rationalist Press Association in 1941. What is not widely known is that Huxley did not do any of the revisions himself. He entrusted the job to his friend in the humanist movement, H. J. Blackham.[36]

The revised *Religion without Revelation* enjoyed a wide success, as the first edition had. But Huxley's new direction of thought was aired much more fully in a work that he edited and that appeared in 1961 called *The Humanist Frame.* Huxley drew on his extensive contacts around the world and ensured an impressive line-up of twenty-six prestigious contributors. This ambitious book was an attempt to present a general account of humanist perspectives across all the pressing issues of the day. The core idea of the book was summed up in the opening paragraph of Huxley's introduction:

> Man is embarked on the psychosocial stage of evolution. Major advance in that stage of the evolutionary process involves radical change in the dominant idea-systems. It is marked by the passage from an old to a new general organization of thought and belief; and the new pattern of thinking and attitude is necessitated by the increase of knowledge, demanding to be organized in new and more comprehensive ways, and by the failure of older ideas which attempted to organize beliefs round a core of ignorance.[37]

The key word in that paragraph is organize. *The Humanist Frame* was about persuading people that the old ideas were no longer adequate to the new problems appearing around the world, and that no coherent response to them was possible without organization along broadly humanist lines. *Evolutionary humanism* was the preferred paradigm within which this organization should take place. And in this respect it was an extension of scientific humanism. Huxley saw evolutionary humanism as the effective marriage of science as the most effective means by which we acquire reliable knowledge about the world, and religion, the longest-standing way by which we interpret it. "For the first time in history," Huxley wrote, "science can become the ally of religion instead of its rival or its enemy, for it can provide a 'scientific' theology, a scientifically ordered framework of belief, to whatever new religion emerges from the present ideological disorder."[38] This was the main addition of evolutionary humanism: a gospel of progress.

> The central belief of evolutionary humanism is that existence can be improved, that vast untapped possibilities can be increasingly realized, that greater fulfillment can replace frustration. This belief is now firmly grounded in knowledge: it could become in turn the firm ground for action.[39]

It was Huxley's intention that *The Humanist Frame* should serve as a textbook for the technocrats of this new progress, an intention learned from H. G. Wells. The new element was the more sanguine attitude toward religion. There may have been a need at one stage for *militant rationalism* that focused on negative criticism, but that time was now passed. "What the world now needs is not merely a rationalist denial of the old but a religious affirmation of something new."[40] Such a short sentence, and yet two very significant errors lie within it. To begin with, militant rationalism at the turn of the twentieth century was nowhere near the exclusively negative criticism of orthodoxy Huxley—and so many others—have claimed. Second, and even more important, though the affirmation of something new is clearly a valuable thing to do, why did it need to be a *religious* affirmation?

This is the sort of question that so exasperates people outside the humanist fold. It seems a mere quibble over semantics. But it really isn't. If the distinctions between species matter, or the boundary between a planet and an asteroid, then delineating the boundaries of religion also matters. Huxley was as firm as any other humanist in what he rejected. Humanism has no truck with any absolutes, "including absolute truth, absolute morality, absolute perfection, and absolute authority, but insists it can find standards to which our actions and our aims can properly be related."[41] What Huxley hoped evolutionary humanism could do was to reformulate traditional religious concepts in light of the new knowledge. Religious concepts are, after all, human constructs, so why can we not reconstruct them?

There are many serious objections to this approach. To begin with, attempts to give religious language new life and meaning assume the success of the earlier rationalist criticism that Huxley so disparaged. Another serious weakness with Huxley's revisionism was his assumption that religion had been defanged and did not pose a serious threat to the humanist frame he was urging on his readers. He also assumed that religion had sportingly recognized this fact and was happy to be subsumed into a broader humanist consensus. But as subsequent events have shown, this was not the case at all. Each of the monotheistic faiths has, in their different way, become more conservative, even reactionary, and the sort of criticism and thinking then going on within the churches would now provoke loud and organized dissent from evangelicals, resulting in, at best, a stifling compromise to appease their wrath. Huxley's confidence that criticizing religion was no longer a constructive activity assumed that religion was evolving slowly toward humanism, but that is not what happened. Oddly enough, it is the so-called militant rationalists who have understood religion better and have accorded it greater respect by taking doctrinal claims seriously and subjecting them to criticism.

In the end, evolutionary humanism as articulated in *The Humanist Frame* was not so different from the scientific humanism he had spoken of thirty years before. And, like its predecessor, it was better seen as a form of religious humanism. What was needed, he said, was the divinization of existence, with a notion of the divine that is free from any connotation of the supernatural. At the end of the lengthy discussion of Huxley's thought between the wars, he finished with the observation that, once we get to the core of his work, the chief inspiration was not science or scientists, but his aunt, Mrs. Humphry Ward, whose novels—*Robert Elsmere* in particular—expressed a late-Victorian ethical social gospel without reference to revelation or doctrine. We can imagine *The Humanist Frame* suiting Robert Elsmere's grandson, now a successful technocrat.

The Humanist Frame never achieved the status Huxley hoped it would. Despite the quality of the contributions and the eminence of the contributors, the book never found a true home. One gets the feeling Huxley himself rather gave up on it. He gave humanism some attention in his two-volume autobiography but made no specific mention of *The Humanist Frame*. By underestimating the power of supernaturalist doctrine, Huxley managed to be equally uncomprehending of the humanist and religious positions. And to make matters worse, his infatuation with the Catholic mystic Pierre Teilhard de Chardin excited the suspicion of evolutionists and humanists alike. Teilhard's works achieved a celebrity among nonspecialist readers for several years but never achieved the recognition from the scientific community he wanted. Huxley had written a foreword for Teilhard's main work *The Phenomenon of Man* (1959), claiming the work was an important reconciliation between science and religion. He never understood the criticism he received from humanists and fellow evolutionists over this.

Huxley's championing of Teilhard had a bearing on who appeared in *The Humanist Frame* and who did not. Corliss Lamont, with whom Huxley had stayed in New York on several occasions, was not among them. Neither was Bertrand Russell, A. J. Ayer, or Margaret Knight, none of whom shared Huxley's confidence in religion as an agent of positive change. It is also interesting to compare the contributors to *The Humanist Frame* with those who contributed to *The Humanist Outlook*, another anthology of humanist thought, this one edited by A. J. Ayer and which we will discuss in the next section. The only person included in both works was the sociologist Morris Ginsberg. This is probably not a coincidence because in both works Ginsberg addressed aspects of the humanist notion of progress.

Another problem with *The Humanist Frame* was the gatekeeper Julian Huxley appointed to provide the final chapter. This was his brother, Aldous, who had already become a very controversial figure within the humanist movement and elsewhere, thanks to his accounts of the use of mind-expanding drugs. Aldous Huxley's chapter was called "Human Potentialities," which spoke of the need for educating people "on the nonverbal level of first-order psychophysical experience," for which Tantric training was particularly recommended.[42] It is useless, Huxley wrote, "to preach the life of reason to people who find that life is flat, stale and unprofitable."[43] Very probably true, but it is dubious that drug-induced escapism is an improvement. Julian Huxley consistently defended his younger brother, even calling him one of the twentieth century's most outstanding humanists.[44] This overstates the case. Aldous Huxley was one of the century's finest novelists, but his role as an apologist for drug use and its supposed benefits of mind expansion calls into question his credentials as a humanist. He bears a lot of the responsibility for the commonly held view that humanism has been morally permissive and a symptom of social decay. Like the equally well-meaning Corliss Lamont, who unwittingly contributed toward saddling humanism with the charge of being "soft on communism," Aldous Huxley provided ammunition for those who have wanted to accuse humanism of being "soft on drugs."

One would think there is little more that can be said about evolutionary humanism, but only a year after *The Humanist Frame* was published, Huxley returned to this theme in a lecture called "Education and Humanism." Here he left behind the quasi-religious language and spoke of evolutionary humanism more in ecological terms; a subtle new slant that quite altered its drift. "Man is not merely the latest dominant type produced by evolution, but its sole active agent on earth. His destiny is to be responsible for the whole future of the evolutionary process on this planet."[45] This, he said, was the gist of evolutionary humanism. The change here, though slight, is profound. With the replacement of a few words, the emphasis has moved from anthropocentric progressionism to an awareness of ecological interdependence and stewardship. And with this shift in emphasis came a shift in implications, which were now seen as achieving greater fulfillment for more human beings while also living in "responsible partnership" with the environment rather than "irresponsible exploitation." He also defended his use of "evolutionary" humanism. Evolution is, quite simply, the "most powerful and comprehensive idea that has ever arisen on earth."[46] This is because it places us squarely on and of the earth, with all the naturalistic and ecological consequences that entails. We can see here the germs of *evolutionary psychology* and *planetary humanism*; two terms with a surprising amount in common. Here, at the end of his productive life, Julian Huxley gave expression to the clearest workable formula for humanism for the twenty-first century. After all the false starts and confusions with language of the previous forty years, Huxley's essential goodness and scientific education resolved themselves into a powerful new conception of humanism understanding its relationship with nature in terms both naturalistic and humble.

A. J. AYER'S AMBIVALENT LEGACY

Alfred Jules Ayer (1910–1989) makes an interesting contrast to Julian Huxley. Ayer was such a prominent twentieth-century philosopher as well as a committed humanist that one would think considerable space would need to be devoted to his career. But that's not so. It is true that Ayer was a lifelong atheist, rationalist, and humanist, but his contributions in these areas have not been memorable. The reason for this lies in his philosophical interests. His reputation was made with his first book, *Language, Truth and Logic* (1936), which argued boldly for the elimination of many philosophical problems simply by seeing them as meaningless. In a long career in academic philosophy, Ayer held prestigious chairs, such as the Grote professorship in philosophy at University College (1946–1959), London, and the Wykeham professorship in philosophy at New College, Oxford (1959–1977).

Ayer believed that philosophy could not solve problems by asking large, metaphysical questions. He also said that it is silly and presumptuous for a philosopher to pose as a champion of virtue. On the face of it, this is true enough, but the fear of being seen in this way has ended up dissuading many philosophers from even addressing issues of vital concern let alone offering some sort of solution. The sort of philosophy Ayer made his career out of had nothing to say to the general reader. It was only late in his career and after he had retired, that he produced some of his most worthwhile and accessible works. *Russell* (1971) and *Hume* (1980) remain among the best short introductions to these philosophers and *Voltaire* (1986) and *Thomas Paine* (1988) are worthwhile studies of these men and their legacy to the modern world. *The Central Questions of Philosophy* (1973) is more difficult but worth the effort because it provides a valuable introduction to some of philosophy's main problems. But his deep suspicion about asking the big questions automatically disqualified him from offering any large account of humanism.

Ayer also wrote two volumes of autobiography and almost completely ignored his long record of service to the humanist movement. An honorary associate of the Rationalist Press Association from 1947, he also served as vice president and president of the British Humanist Association. His strongest direct contribution to humanist thinking was as editor of *The Humanist Outlook* (1968), one of the major publishing projects of the humanist movement in Britain in the 1960s. Like *The Humanist Frame* seven years previously, *The Humanist Outlook* assembled an impressive line-up of contributors. If it avoided the extravagances of Huxley's collection, it lost something of its unity of purpose. *The Humanist Outlook* talked relevantly about humanism and the arts, humanism and this, and humanism and that; but it said relatively little about humanism. The collection had a complacent, "we're all humanists now" flavor to it. After Ayer's competent, if uninspiring, introduction, the collection opened unfortunately with the British educator Cyril Bibby (1914–1987) urging readers on the need for a scientific humanist culture in all the least helpful ways. The real reason science "must move right into the center of culture is so as ensure that each citizen is part of the spirit of the age."[47] Well, that really depends on who is interpreting the spirit of the age. One suspects the zeitgeist of 1968 would have been better expressed with hallucinogenic drugs, long hair, and little red books.

Ayer's most important contribution to humanism was his warning against complacency. Humanism is worth little, he wrote, if it can only be applied fully by the comfortably well-off, well-fed, well-housed, and gainfully employed.

> For those who are ignorant, helpless and in material want, it is small consolation only that their miseries will end with death, and throughout history the majority of human beings have been in this condition. It would therefore be insensitive, if not hypocritical, for humanists to preach their doctrines unless they believed that the values which they set on human experience and achievement were capable of being realized not merely by a privileged minority but by mankind in general. Even if they cannot be assured that this will ever be so, they at least have the moral obligation to do what they can to make it possible.[48]

Quite the most extraordinary feature of *The Humanist Outlook* is what it omits. Earlier in the same year the English sociologist Ronald Fletcher (1921–1992) had penned a marvelous synopsis of humanism. Fletcher was sufficiently highly thought of to be given the job of contributing the first essay to the Rationalist Press Association's annual journal in 1968, recently relaunched under the name *Question*. The RPA's annual, under various titles, had been an important vehicle for articulating nontheistic positions. Its contributors are a veritable who's who of twentieth-century thought. But it was symptomatic of the times that the old title was becoming more of a liability. When the RPA established itself in 1899, the word *rationalist* was an uncontroversial word meaning "reasonable." But seven decades later, *rationalist* was more likely to conjure up visions of hard-bitten, narrow thinking that repeated the old dualist mistakes of distinguishing and exalting reason over unreason. This had never been the case, but by the 1960s it seemed easier just to acknowledge that this misperception was not going to go away. In introducing the new journal, with its new name, Hector Hawton explained why they hadn't simply replaced *rationalist* with *humanist*. To do that, Hawton wrote, would imply "that there is an important ideological difference." It was thought, he wrote, "that in the conditions of today a title that suggested the search rather than the answer would be most appropriate."⁴⁹ But it was clearly still felt necessary to begin *Question*'s career with a definition. In asking Fletcher to take this on, Hawton and his advisory board chose well.

A few years previous, Fletcher had attracted widespread attention with a tongue-in-cheek offering published in the *New Society* that was called *The Humanist's Decalogue*. Before long it was taken up by Pioneer Press, which was aligned with the National Secular Society, and turned into a pamphlet. *The Humanist's Decalogue* was as follows:

(1) Never accept authority, unless, in your own seriously considered view, there are good grounds to do so.
(2) Base your conduct upon simple human principles.
(3) Strive to eliminate war.
(4) Strive to eliminate poverty and work for greater prosperity for everyone.
(5) Don't be a snob, don't worry about labels, and work for a broader fellowship in society.
(6) In sexual behavior, use your brains as well as your genitals, and always in that order.
(7) Take the necessary steps to enjoy family life and marriage.
(8) Keep the law.
(9) Commit yourself to active citizenship.
(10) Have confidence in the modern world and in your powers to improve it.⁵⁰

Fletcher's intelligence, sense of humor, and general decency are apparent in all this. He brought this easy humanity to his more sustained attempt to kick-start *Question* with a sound, new understanding of *humanism*. Humanism is, he pointed out, not a creed but an approach. To speak of humanism in this way is to recognize that the human mind is a profoundly limited thing and that what we know can "never be final or dogmatic, but always be limited, uncertain, open to question."⁵¹ Fletcher was also careful to add that humanism is human centered, but that does not mean it is human confined. "A sensitive vulnerability to all the dimensions of our entanglement in the world, and the desire to probe and to articulate the experience of some deeply sensed meaning in it all, are not exclusive to religions."[52] In this spirit of intellectual humility, he then reiterated the importance of toleration, self-responsibility, opposition to the arbitrary imposition of authority, and the development of character. And perhaps most important of all, Fletcher addressed the old worry that humanism must necessarily be at once naively optimistic and devoid of hope.

> Humanism, it seems to me, has to recognize an inescapable undertone of tragedy in the world. Ultimately, the situation of mankind in the world is a tragic one. Human life is transient. . . . All that we are, all that we love, all those things, people, and values to which and to whom we are attached by love, perish. Nothing of an individual nature seems permanent. Nothing is certain. Humanism can offer no consolation.[53]

What humanism can offer in the light of this reality is the awareness that we can value people, ideas, and things no less, despite knowing they are transient. The recognition of the tragic undertone to human existence is what gives our love of it while we are alive a special poignancy and color. Fletcher's vision of humanism remains one of the finest in the British humanist tradition. Ayer, who was a member of *Question*'s advisory board, would have known of Fletcher's article. There must be a good reason why it didn't take pride of place in *The Humanist Outlook*, but I don't know what that reason is.

ALAN BULLOCK AND THE HUMANIST TRADITION

The contribution to humanist thinking made by the historian Alan Bullock could just as easily appear in the chapters dealing with European and American humanism. Bullock himself was quintessentially English, but the venue for his thoughts was the United States, and the principal drift of his humanism was European. Alan Bullock (1914–2004), the son of a Unitarian minister, is best remembered for his groundbreaking study *Hitler: A Study in Tyranny* (1952), and a three-volume study of the Labor Party politician Ernest Bevin (1881–1951), whose politics and background paralleled his own. He was knighted in 1972. Bullock was a senior and respected member of the intellectual establishment of Britain. He was an insider.

Bullock had no connections at all with the humanist movement and didn't call himself a humanist, thinking it "a confusing word, an impossible word."[54] But in 1984 he delivered a series of lectures on the humanist tradition in the West, in New York. His venue was uniquely American: a well-heeled think tank emerging out of that country's genteel tradition. The Aspen Institute was founded in 1950 by the American businessman Walter Paepcke (1896–1960), a man very much in the mold of Edward Howard Griggs, whose work we surveyed in chapter 1. Paepcke had been inspired by the Great Books Program, which was run by Mortimer Adler, and he founded the Aspen Institute for Humanistic Studies to carry that work on. The year before founding the Aspen Institute, Paepcke had hosted a bicentenary celebration of Goethe, bringing in guests like Albert Schweitzer for the occasion. One of Paepcke's other European contacts, Ortega y Gasset, had suggested the "Humanistic Studies" subtitle for the institute, but by the early 1980s, the institute was sufficiently worried about the term to downplay it. It now prefers the silkier slogan "Timeless values, enlightened leadership."

In the way these things go, Bullock's lectures were soon published. *The Humanist Tradition in the West* was attractively illustrated and accessible to nonspecialist readers. The humanism Bullock espoused here was the humanism of bildung, which he described as "the capacity of individuals to develop themselves to a point where their inner conflicts would be overcome and they would live in harmony with their fellow men and with nature."[55] He reiterated the idea that humanism is not a doctrine but rather

> a broad tendency, a dimension of thought and belief, a continuing debate within which at any one time there will be found very different—at times opposed—views, held together not by a unified structure but by certain shared assumptions and a preoccupation with certain characteristic problems and topics, which change from one period to the next.[56]

As we have seen frequently in this book, Bullock's emphasis was on humanism as an ongoing inquiry—limitless communication, in Jaspers's language. What makes Bullock interesting is that he also took the next step, one that is made much less often, when he outlined the features of humanist debate. They were for him focusing on humanity as a part of the natural order, acknowledging the intrinsic value possessed by humans, and putting a high value on ideas and their ongoing movement and evolution.[57] He was insistent that, while humanist discourse did not focus on theological views, it did not exclude them. At this point he aimed a barb at the humanist movement when he said, "Humanist attitudes toward religion in fact cover a much wider spectrum than rationalist hostility to anything which smacks of the supernatural or the mystical."[58] Though Bullock did his best to distance his humanism from secularism and rationalism, the British humanist movement saw no need to reciprocate the hostility. Jim Herrick, editor of the *New Humanist*, interviewed Bullock in 1986 and drew out the common threads in their understanding of humanism very well.

The Humanist Tradition in the West began with ancient Greece and sketched briefly the ever-changing discourse of humanism in Europe. Perhaps the most useful single feature of the book was the discussion on the possibility of humanism in the wake of the horrors of the twentieth century. How can one speak of humanism, with its notions of the perfectibility of man, so the complaint goes, in the face of such wickedness? Nobody could accuse Bullock of hiding from these calamities. His historical career was built on articulating and understanding their horror. But to write off humanism in the wake of this horror is to betray a lack of understanding as to what humanism is about. If we take seriously the idea of humanism as an ongoing discourse, it is quite wrong to pick one relatively brief chapter in that discourse and single it out as representing the essence of the whole tradition. This complaint assumes that all humanism is nothing more than eighteenth- and nineteenth-century positivist progressionism. For this accusation to work, it must ignore the humanism of the Stoics, or of Montaigne, which emerged out of the horrors of the Wars of Religion. It must also ignore the humanist thinkers who emerged after the period of positivist progressionism—Bullock mentioned Thomas Mann, Ibsen, Freud, and Max Weber—who understood the divisions and irrationality at the core of human existence.[59] Bullock didn't make this parallel, but it's true that few people would think Christianity irrevocably discredited by making reference solely to the Crusades or to the Inquisition.

There are also some important parallels between Bullock's humanism and that of Irving Babbitt. Like Babbitt, Bullock distinguished three distinct modes of Western thought. There was the supernatural or transcendental discourse, which focused on God; and there was the natural or scientific, which focused on nature and treated humanity as part of nature. Then there was the humanist mode, which focused on humankind and experience as a starting point for knowledge of oneself and of God.[60] Bullock didn't speak directly of a will to refrain as Babbitt did, but his notion of bildung as something that helps one *overcome* inner turmoil and live comfortably thereafter is strongly reminiscent of it.

If Bullock's humanism resembled Babbitt's, it also shared some of the same weaknesses. Barbara Smoker noted that Bullock had skewed his historical account of the humanist tradition in the West by simply ignoring the naturalist and atheist strand. From the Atomists to Charles Bradlaugh, from Lucretius to Bertrand Russell, Bullock simply passed them by, offering no justification for this beyond simply asserting that atheism is dogmatic. Indeed, he seemed incapable of saying the word *atheist* without prefixing *dogmatic* to it. Smoker was quite right, and her insight helps provide part of the motivation for this book, which has sought to gather all major expressions of humanism together in one book, without regard to whether or not I agree with them, and to see what transpires.

ISAIAH BERLIN AND THE CROOKED TIMBER OF HUMANITY

In the process of drawing *The Humanist Tradition in the West* to a close, Bullock asked what conclusion he could draw from his lifetime of scholarship. "I would put it into five words: the future is not predictable."[61] Few people would have agreed more heartily than another prominent academic humanist from his generation: Isaiah Berlin (1909–1992). The person who became England's foremost historian of ideas in the twentieth century was born in Riga, then part of the Russian Empire, now capital of Latvia. His family's escape to England in 1921 gave Berlin a lifelong love of his adopted country and a strong inoculation against Marxism. He taught at Oxford in the 1930s, where he befriended most of England's leading philosophers. For a short while he was enamored of logical positivism but soon came to see that the principle of verification did not work as comprehensively as its defenders claimed. The decisive moment in his life was an intense series of meetings with the Russian poet Anna Akhmatova (1889–1966) in 1945 and 1946. These meetings galvanized Berlin's appreciation of the Enlightenment principles he valued and confirmed his already sharp detestation of Marxism. He then spent a career investigating the lives and motivations of the leading opponents of the open society that he so cherished. Only late in his life, thanks largely to the work of Henry Hardy, his editor, did much of Berlin's work become widely available to the reading public.

Berlin was once asked if he thought of himself as a *critical humanist*. He replied by saying he did not know what that meant, but he went on to restate his commitment to an open society that permits criticism.[62] Elsewhere he was happy to call himself a *liberal rationalist*.

> The values of the Enlightenment, what people like Voltaire, Helvetius, Holbach, [and] Condorcet preached, are deeply sympathetic to me. Maybe they were too narrow, and often wrong about the facts of human experience, but these people were great liberators. They liberated people from horrors, obscurantism, fanaticism, monstrous views.[63]

Where Berlin moved on from the Enlightenment thinkers was his recognition of the difficulty inherent in any exercise of choice. Each choice we make involves a loss of some equally worthwhile quality. If we as a society opt for greater equality, we shall sacrifice elements of our liberty. But if we opt for greater liberty, we shall just as surely need to abandon the ideal of equality. In this way, we can never reach a perfect state, let alone a state of perfection. It follows from this that the first requirement of a decent society is not the construction of some unachievable Camelot but the maintenance of "a precarious equilibrium that will prevent the occurrence of desperate situations."[64] And for this, a certain humility is necessary.

Berlin's career was an extended commentary on Kant's wise observation (which he translated rather more elegantly than the original phrase allows for): "Out of the crooked timber of humanity no straight thing was ever made."[65] The process of making straight things out of the crooked timber of humanity goes under various names: absolutism, fundamentalism, totalitarianism. All of them Berlin abhorred. Isaiah Berlin was a humanist. One of the best the twentieth century produced.

If this is all true, why did Berlin have so little to do with the humanist movement? The obvious reasons first: Berlin was not an organization man and was temperamentally averse to "movements," no matter how congenial. And from the humanist movement's point of view, Berlin was largely unknown outside the top echelons of the academic world. Many of his essays did not become widely available until late in his life. So leaders of the humanist movement, people like Blackham and Hawton, could be forgiven for overlooking him. All this said, there was more to their nonattachment than simply missing each other in the mist. Although explicitly atheist, Berlin saw little value in emphasizing it. "Stone-dry atheists," as he called them, "don't understand what men live by."[66]

RECENT EXPRESSIONS OF HUMANISM IN BRITAIN

It would take a book to do justice to the humanist strands within contemporary British intellectual life, so one symbolic illustration will have to do. It comes from the bishop of Oxford, Richard Harries, who, in an essay on Richard Dawkins (in all likelihood, the world's best-known atheist), praises him as a "fellow humanist," by which he means "one who believes in the importance, dignity, and utter worthwhileness of being a human being and of trying to live humanely."[67] Just imagine what the bishop of Oxford would have said about the world's best-known atheist in 1808! In the past two centuries, people from across the metaphysical spectrum have come to speak of themselves and others as *humanists* in a spirit of finding common ground. For all its faults and weaknesses, a tremendous amount can be forgiven a word if it can do that.

Christianity's troubled relations with humanism are the subject of chapter 8, but here we must briefly trace a late-flowering attempt to develop an English variety of religious humanism. This came in the form of the Sea of Faith, a movement created by Don Cupitt (1934–), a radical English theologian. Cupitt had already become a controversial figure in the Anglican Church with his book *Taking Leave of God* (1980), which earned him a personal reprimand from the archbishop of Canterbury. The Sea of Faith movement began in 1984 after a six-part television series and a book (both of that name) written by Cupitt created a great deal of interest. The phrase *sea of faith* was taken from Matthew Arnold's poem "Dover Beach," which lamented the decline of orthodox Christianity. Cupitt is frankly humanistic, and in effect atheistic, but the Sea of Faith movement has charted a slightly more eclectic course, incorporating post-Christian, Jungian, and avowedly secular strands of thought. Most Sea of Faith groups agree that, while the actual truth-claims of religions are invalid, there nonetheless remains a valuable experiential core to religion, which is useful. Cupitt's goal is to help create a "postdogmatic and nonsupernatural religion of the future."

The Sea of Faith resembles elements of the religious humanism popular in the United States between the wars, although its development owes nothing to the American movement. The Sea of Faith arose out of ongoing dissatisfaction with the English churches, particularly as they moved toward more conservative, even reactionary positions, in the decades since John Robinson's *Honest to God*, which appeared in 1963. Emerging as it did in the 1980s, the Sea of Faith was keen to tone down the progressionism and anthropocentrism of American religious humanism and to tone up the valuation of mythology, stories, and (in some cases) postmodernist relativism. In some instances, this has ended up simply replacing one brand of progressionism with another. One lesser Sea of Faith theorist, in an attempt to articulate a contemporary account of religious humanism, urged humanists to appreciate the reality of the postmodern condition and even felt sure that most people are now comfortable with taking Christian scripture as myth and metaphor.[68] Three major objections present themselves: (1) the briefest acquaintance with some fundamentalists should be enough to dispel such sanguine confidence, (2) the confidence that *postmodernism* has replaced *modernism* as the default social and intellectual condition seems premature, and (3) relegating Christian scripture to the mythical and metaphorical does violence to nineteen centuries of church history. Apart from that, I'm sure it's a valuable insight.[69]

Cupitt's understanding, though not free of problems, is more sophisticated than this. His vision of what religion will look like in the twenty-first century is not reassuring for conventional believers. It may have a role as a repository of values or as a means by which people express themselves in a private realm or simply as a counterculture. Religion, he says, is not about supernatural doctrine but "an experiment in selfhood."[70] But, he adds, it is the "last supernaturalist illusion," that "we can find salvation by retreating into some fenced-off and privileged area: a personal spirituality, a local vocabulary, an ethnic group, a traditional certainty."[71] In the place of traditional certainties, Cupitt has posited what he calls *solar ethics*, which draws inspiration from Matthew 5:14, which says: "You are a light to the world." As the sun shines seemingly forever from its own energy, so can our purpose and happiness be created and sustained by understanding ourselves and living a full life in accordance with that understanding. While taking his cue from the New Testament, he has jettisoned all elements of conventional Christian doctrine and happily concedes that one need not have even heard of Christianity to be able to embrace solar ethics.

Religious humanism has a small niche in Britain, and may well grow in the years to come as the Church of England rigidifies still further. But it remains true that British humanism is, in the main, secular, rationalist, and frankly atheist. Most British humanists see more value in pursuing a humanist outlook consciously distanced from, and critical of, any form of religious expression. Here the legacy of rationalism is still evident. Chief among them is A. C. Grayling, who can be seen as the most prominent defender of the strand of liberal humanism articulated a century and a half ago by John Stuart Mill. Like Isaiah Berlin, Grayling is a stone-dry atheist, although unlike Berlin, Grayling works with and through his atheism and has a clear understanding of the role atheism plays in his view of things. This is one reason why Grayling has associated himself with the humanist movement in a way Berlin (let alone Bullock) did not. After a long career in formal philosophy, since the 1990s Grayling has been more interested in writing for the general reader, in the manner of Bertrand Russell. Grayling's antipathy to Christianity is as pronounced as Russell's and, if anything, more so than Richard Dawkins's. With this in mind, his popular writing is devoted to articulating a humanist account of living and of history, one that stands in sharp distinction from the Christian account.

In *What Is Good?* (2003), Grayling concludes a historical survey by identifying the six key humanist values: individual liberty, the pursuit of knowledge, the cultivation of pleasures that do not harm others, the satisfaction of art, personal relationships, and a sense of belonging to the human community.[72] He takes care to leave these values broad, so as to permit freedom of expression and action within them. In the wrong hands, lists of values can quickly degenerate into prescriptions. His concluding definition of what constitutes the good life sound very much like a definition of *humanism*: "The considered life—free, creative, informed, and chosen, a life of achievement and fulfillment, of pleasure and understanding, of love and friendship; in short, the best human life in a human world, humanely lived."[73] Despite otherwise major differences of approach, belief, and cultural priority, I doubt a single humanist in this book would find undue fault with this understanding. *Inclusive* has become such a fashionable word that

I hesitate to use it here, and yet it illustrates what humanism, at its best, is about. Four years later, Grayling retains the historical theme in *Towards the Light* (2007), this time to give an account of the struggle for the rights we now take for granted and are now seeing eroded in the face of the so-called war on terror. It's an account that will annoy postmodernists, who like to claim they are "beyond" such grand narratives, despite being the beneficiaries of the very rights and freedoms the struggles for liberty produced. *Towards the Light* is, in Grayling's own words, a paean to "pluralism, secularism, and humanism. These, one feels pressed to argue, are the fields in which the harvest of liberty grows."[74]

The existence of a well-established humanist movement in Britain means there is no shortage of works looking to introduce humanism as a comprehensive worldview. One such work is *Humanism: An Introduction* (2003) by Jim Herrick (1944–), a longtime activist and editor, at various times, of most of the major humanist publications in Britain. In the interests of unity and clarity of purpose, Herrick reiterates the long-held British preference for a humanism without adjectives.[75] But on the same page, he states that humanists are atheists and agnostics. The problem with this is that, if unity is valued, surely it is problematic to insist humanists must be either atheists or agnostics. And if clarity of purpose is the aim, maybe an adjective would help. This is one of those distinctions that matter to those inside the movement but which seems abstruse, even bizarre, to people looking from without.

One of the strong points of Herrick's book, and a fair indication of the strength of humanism in Britain, is the care he takes to outline the practical applications of humanism to living a morally engaged life without reference to supernaturalism. This is also a feature of a similar introductory account by Barbara Smoker (1923–), another veteran humanist campaigner in Britain. Over a long life, she has served the cause in a variety of capacities: president of the National Secular Society from 1971 until 1996; chair of the Voluntary Euthanasia Society from 1981 until 1985; speaker, broadcaster, writer, commentator and activist. Smoker's work is interesting because it was designed for secondary school students; imagine *that* happening in the United States! *Humanism* was first published in 1973 by the respected publisher Ward Lock Educational. In 2004 it went into its fourth edition, this one published by the South Place Ethical Society. Much like Herrick's book, Smoker's is simple and honest. Short chapters outline the history of humanism since the Greeks before they deal with questions of God, belief, and faith. The basics of humanist morality are then covered, ending with practical elements of living as a humanist. The whole book runs to less than eighty pages. Smoker's humanism is a confident, happy, engaged humanism.

Coming at humanism from a different angle was Nicholas Walter (1934–2000), author of a nuggety monograph called *Humanism: What's in the Word* (1997). After working as a journalist and gaining some notoriety as an anarchist activist, Walter had a long career in the Rationalist Press Association, serving in editorial and administrative roles.[76] His short history of the various uses of the word *humanism* has been influential for this book, which is attempting a similar task, though on a larger scale. An exasperating scholar, Walter managed to be exhaustive and insightful while also being unhelpfully terse and clipped. Running to only ninety-one pages, his work has an almost Wittgensteinian level of compactness. But, as Wittgenstein scholars can attest, the pressure of that sort of compactness does not necessarily lead to clarity. Like his writing, Walter's humanism was brisk, lean, and impatient of what he thought of as unnecessary add-ons. He didn't even like the word *humanism* that much, noting sardonically that "we are stuck with it and should make the best of it."[77] He was especially suspicious of the attempts to rework humanism into a coherent movement with agreed positions on the issues of the day. He loathed the various neologisms employed to galvanize the movement: *lifestance, eupraxsophy, worthship*, and so on. He was content with a minimal understanding of humanism, which for him was "a combination of the negative rejection of the idea of anything superhuman as a guide to thought and the positive recognition of common humanity as a guide to action."[78] Our job, he wrote, "is not to convert people to humanism but to encourage them to be human."[79] What at first glance looks like modesty lies a far greater level of presumption.

The best of the recent examinations of humanism come from Jeaneane Fowler and Richard Norman. Fowler's *Humanism: Beliefs and Practices* (1999) is a scholarly yet accessible general introduction to the various meanings of *humanism*, and its areas of interest. She disagrees with Walter by seeing value in the notion of humanism as a lifestance. How can humanism *not* be a lifestance? Any outlook that has a view on how to live cannot but be a lifestance, and Fowler is correct to see that it would be a mistake to opt out of this position in fear of being seen as religious.[80] Her awareness of the ways anthropocentric thinking undermines humanism is another valuable feature of her book. And her familiarity with humanist trends in the United States and ability to resist the almost automatic rejection of American thinking common in British and European thinkers is a refreshing change. She is also comfortable with humanism as a movable feast, or, in the language of this book, a wealth of insights. "Lack of definition can be a distinct advantage!"[81] That said, Fowler gives a clear account of naturalistic humanism as she understands it, making along the way a worthwhile distinction when she says humanism "has no creed but many convictions."[82]

The other good single-volume study is from Richard Norman, a philosopher from the University of Kent. *On Humanism* (2004) was part of a series of books called *Thinking in Action*, which looked to presenting accessible accounts of topical issues to a general reading public. Norman makes a valuable point, one for which I hope this book has provided evidence: it is a mistake to see a clear and fast distinction between the various strands of humanism. While cultural humanism, religious humanism, and secular humanism all have different emphases and trajectories, it is, he writes, not a coincidence that they have come to be known by the same name. In adopting the word *humanism*, freethinkers, rationalists, atheists, agnostics, and secularists are all paying tribute to the older tradition that looked to the "celebration of what is finest in human thought and creativity."[83] Shades of Herbert Read. This is important because it deals with the long-standing objection that humanism somehow misses an important dimension of what it means to be human. Indeed, most of the important dimensions of what it means to be human are make-believe constructs, of which an immortal soul fashioned in the image of God is simply the most obvious. Norman takes all the right steps in the direction of a humanism not imbued with shallow confidence in progress, the dignity of man, let alone Man. It has the ring of being an authentic twenty-first-century humanism. Like Ronald Fletcher, Norman recognizes the element of tragedy in life without losing a sense of humor and lightness of touch. The main weakness with Norman's book, as with Fowler's, is the inattention to the humanist traditions outside the West. Part 2 of this book will be looking to fill that gap.

LINDA SMITH AND THE GIFT OF HUMOR

As with the range of books outlining humanism, so does Britain enjoy a range of humanist associations, all with different histories and emphases. As this is an account of the history of humanism, mention shall be made only of the British Humanist Association (BHA). In many ways the most significant single act of British humanists since the war was the formation of the BHA. It is not the intention here to give an account of the history of this organization, beyond simply noting it was formed on May 17, 1963, when two hundred people gathered at the House of Commons as the guests of Laurie Pavitt, MP. Sir Julian Huxley became president and A. J. Ayer became vice president. It had been intended that the BHA would supersede and encompass the all the existing free thought and rationalist organizations, in particular the Ethical Union, the Rationalist Association (formerly the Rationalist Press Association) and the National Secular Society. This was never that likely to happen, as each organization had different emphases and was run by people who did not always find cooperation as easy as would have been ideal. This said, the *New Humanist*, technically the organ of the Rationalist Association, is also the organ of the BHA.

While the BHA has not become the single humanist organization in Britain, it has gone on to become a major voice for defending the secular state, articulating humanist ethics, and providing services to members—most notably the secular celebrants service. The popularity of humanist weddings, baby namings, and funerals has grown consistently as Britain has become post-Christian. The BHA also hosts conferences that consider various questions of religion and the state and of ethical issues. And it provides support for the dozens of local humanist groups and fellowships around Britain. It has also arrived at one of the more straightforward conceptions of humanism yet proposed. The BHA understands humanism as "the belief that we can live good lives without religious or superstitious beliefs. Humanists make sense of the world using reason, experience, and shared human values. We seek to make the best of the one life we have by creating meaning and purpose for ourselves. We take responsibility for our actions and work with others for the common good."[84]

The BHA's other focus is on education. The association has long campaigned for a broadening of scope in religious education to include humanism in British schools. Though not a religion, it is a comprehensive worldview that deserves to be considered alongside religions. Accordingly, it does not oppose religious education as such, it simply wants religious education's focus to expand to reflect the real contours of belief in British society. The BHA has produced some highly regarded resources for teachers who want to deal with social or ethical issues. The BHA sponsors the Humanist Philosophers' Group, which publishes occasional pamphlets on topical issues. One of this group's pamphlets devised one of the cleverest understandings of humanism to date. At the end of the work, after all manner of warnings that definitions are problematic, provisional, and even antithetical to humanism, they conclude:

> If someone were to insist that we summarize our account in the form of a definition, perhaps the best that we could offer would be something like this: Humanism is an evolving tradition of thought which starts from the rejection of religious beliefs and attempts, through rational argument and debate, to work out the positive implications of that starting point.[85]

There is a lot to like about this. It captures the spirit of so much of what has been said and what is still to come in this book. I am entirely in sympathy with it, but it has the problem of ignoring large sectors of humanist thought that have not rejected religious beliefs or that have claimed that not believing religious beliefs to be true does not constitute a rejection of the poetry thought to underlie them. But maybe this is just something else that the ongoing tradition of humanist debate and argument can reconcile in the years to come.

To end this chapter, probably the most worthwhile point to be made about the BHA, and about humanism in Britain at the start of the twenty-first century, can be made by profiling the association's president from 2004 until her untimely death two years later. Linda Smith (1958–2006) was not a philosopher nor a scientist nor any sort of public intellectual in the sense we usually understand that term. She was a comedian. The daughter of a railway worker, Smith was born in the London suburb of Erith and attended the local school (where she lost her religious beliefs), before going on to Sheffield University (where she studied English and drama).

After a spell in Sheffield theater, Smith found her strength in stand-up comedy. Her ability to tease out the absurdities of ordinary situations and in oddly juxtaposed language earned her a large and devoted audience. In 1993

Smith and her partner Warren Lakin, moved to London, where she complemented her work in stand-up comedy with new ventures in radio and television. She appeared in a range of BBC programs, like *News Quiz*, *Just a Minute*, *Call My Bluff*, and the satirical news show *The Treatment*. Her success in these shows earned her the chance with her own sitcom series called *A Brief History of Time Wasting*. An appearance Smith made on the radio show *Devout Skeptics* attracted the attention of the British Humanist Association, who invited her to assume the presidency of that organization. She took on the role in July 2004. Her easy manner and natural sense of humor made her an ideal face for humanism in Britain. Tragically, this happy state did not last long. Smith was diagnosed with ovarian cancer in 2002 and died on March 2, 2006, aged forty-eight.

The career of Linda Smith may well tell us more about British humanism than many lengthy disquisitions on the peregrinations of learned men. E. M. Forster (1879–1970), one of Britain's finest twentieth-century novelists, and a humanist, commented frequently that the absence of humor in the New Testament was such as made his blood chilled.[86] In many ways, British humanism has found its best expression in humor: think of Douglas Adams, *Monty Python's Flying Circus*, and their subsequent film *The Life of Brian*; television programs like *Father Ted*; and comedians like Peter Cook, Billy Connolly, Dave Allen, and Ben Elton. A very good case could be made for describing Eric Idle, author of several of *Monty Python*'s most iconic songs, as one of the most influential humanists of the second half of the twentieth century. This tradition of irreverent humor, continued by Linda Smith, may well constitute one of British humanism's more important gifts to the world.

CHAPTER 6

AMERICAN HUMANISM SINCE WORLD WAR II

The interest generated by the *Humanist Manifesto* came and went as economic depression and war took over public attention. Rival varieties of *humanism*, especially that of Irving Babbitt, confused people as to what the word really meant, and attention to things nonreligious had been distracted by the brief career of the more popular and strident American Association for the Advancement of Atheism. But the "Four A's," as it was known, succumbed to the Depression in the same way the humanist movement did.

Organized humanism languished in the 1930s, and it was to deal with this situation, as well as to provide a clear humanist voice, that the American Humanist Association (AHA) was founded in 1941. Its first president was Raymond B. Bragg (1902–1979), another graduate of Meadville Theological School, later a minister in the Unitarian Church and a signatory of the *Humanist Manifesto I*. Another signatory, Edwin Wilson (1899–1993), ran the AHA and edited its journal for many years. The AHA was the successor to the Humanist Press Association, which had been named in imitation of the Rationalist Press Association in Britain. The AHA's new journal, *The Humanist*, intended taking over where its predecessor, the *New Humanist*, which ran from 1928 until 1936, had left off. *The Humanist* is still published today.

CORLISS LAMONT AND THE PHILOSOPHY OF HUMANISM

What the AHA and American humanism needed was a new face and a new direction. This came in the form of Corliss Lamont, the most significant and coherent new humanist voice after World War II. Lamont brought to humanism the social concern that Dewey had manifested; the appreciation of science as a means to generate reliable knowledge about the world; and a genuine appreciation of art, beauty, and stillness. He combined, in other words, the pragmatist, the naturalist, and the literary strands of humanism. Unlike the religious humanists, he did not seek to redeploy religious language, nor was he unduly anthropocentric.

Like Bertrand Russell, Corliss Lamont (1902–1995) was born into the very upper reaches of society. He could trace the arrival of his father's family in the United States to the 1750s and his Scottish ancestry back to the thirteenth century. His mother's family was no less illustrious, going back to William Bradford (1589–1657), who arrived on the *Mayflower* and later served as Governor of Plymouth Colony. Another ancestor on his mother's side, Elihu Corliss, fought at Bunker Hill. His father, Thomas Lamont (1870–1948), was a business partner of the industrialist J. P. Morgan (1867–1943), and his mother had taken a master of arts degree in philosophy at Cornell in 1898. Lamont was born on Good Friday, which his mother took as a good omen for his future piety.

She was to be disappointed. While still a student, Lamont became familiar with atheist and socialist thinking, something Sidney Hook claimed the credit for.[1] Lamont's doctorate, taken at Columbia in 1932 under the naturalist philosopher Frederick J. E. Woodbridge (1867–1940), was later published as *The Illusion of Immortality* (1935). He began his study while holding conventional religious views, including belief in life after death, and he ended it an atheist. *The Illusion of Immortality* was the first systematic study of death from a humanist viewpoint since Feuerbach's *Thoughts on Death and Immortality*, published in 1830. Having begun his study into this question as a believer, Lamont understood and sympathized with the wish for immortality. But facts are facts, and it was clear that it was incompatible with a naturalistic account of things. This said, he did more than simply debunk traditional conceptions of immortality; he also broadened the range of ways we could think about it, which involved many more perspectives than a naively dualistic personal immortality. He identified *ideal immortality*, or the eternal moment that Spinoza and Santayana spoke of; *material immortality*, where the material that makes us up is subsumed after death back into nature; *historical immortality*, or the simple fact of our existence in time; *biological immortality*, or our continued existence through our children; and *social immortality*, or the survival through the memory of our achievements.[2] Like most first books, *The Illusion of Immortality* is a bit labored, but it remains a classic study of the subject, going through several new editions and revisions.

Lamont's other discovery at this time was socialism. This wasn't as new for him as atheism, as he had heard discussion on socialism at the dinner table with guests like H. G. Wells.[3] Lamont visited the Soviet Union twice in the 1930s and wrote laudatory accounts of his experiences there. And he was less inclined than Wells or Russell to distinguish sharply between socialism as an ideal and support for the Soviet Union as its most appropriate exemplar. That it took Lamont much longer than most people of his generation to review his attitude toward the Soviet Union remains the millstone around his neck with respect to his legacy as a humanist thinker and leader.

Lamont was a major target of Senator Joseph McCarthy (1909–1957) during the years of anticommunist hysteria. He showed great courage in standing up to McCarthy's bullying, and the legal contest that ensued helped turn the tide against McCarthy. Lamont's claim that McCarthy's Senate Permanent Subcommittee on Investigations had no legal or constitutional authority to conduct its inquisitions was upheld and was a significant blow to McCarthy's already-waning prestige. Neither was this the only significant legal battle Lamont had to take on; he went all the way to the Supreme Court to regain his First Amendment rights to receive his mail untampered with. He also fought suits against the CIA and FBI with respect to the surveillance these agencies had put him under.

Lamont's major work was *Humanism as a Philosophy* (1949), which developed out of a course he taught at Columbia called "Philosophy of Naturalist Humanism," which ran from 1947 until 1959. It was the first systematic attempt to offer, in a single book, an outline of what *naturalistic humanism* means and how it works. As such, *Humanism as a Philosophy* was a different sort of book than anything Schiller, the Unitarian religious humanists, or Irving Babbitt could have produced. This is because of the prominence then enjoyed by the philosophical naturalism pioneered by his mentor Woodbridge and given expression in an influential group of essays, *Naturalism and the Human Spirit*, which was published in 1944. Lamont was deeply sympathetic with this brand of philosophical naturalism, and it was his unique contribution to reorient humanism in that direction, without overshooting into dry positivism. Woodbridge had a low view of humanism, dismissing it as suggesting "a polite superiority of character of a pleasant medicine for that spiritual nostalgia which sickens the soul when faith has apparently lost its foundations."[4] Lamont was more indulgent toward religious humanism than that, but he was just as concerned to position humanism as a natural ally of naturalism.

Humanism as a Philosophy went through many editions, several translations, and a change of name—*The Philosophy of Humanism*—and it became one of the most influential twentieth-century statements on humanism. And with good reason. His willingness to offer humanism as a philosophy of living attracted praise from reviewers, whether or not they agreed with him. It is all very well, he wrote, for philosophy to analyze and criticize, "but I believe that it achieves its highest role in successful synthesis."[5] He also appreciated the genuinely transnational nature of humanism. It was not, he recognized, the "Eurocentric discourse" postmodernists would later try to characterize it as.

More important still, Lamont was the first systematic thinker to appreciate fully the cosmic perspective as a precondition for humanism. Many others had spoken of the lessons of Copernicus and Darwin in dethroning *Homo sapiens* from the pedestal it had rather presumptuously built for itself. And many criticisms of religion had been made with this in mind. But Lamont was the first to put it all together in a single, accessible package. The other contribution Lamont made so effectively was in his simple affirmations of what humanism is for, as opposed to his denunciations of what it is against:

> Humanism is an *affirmative* philosophy.... We mortals delight in the sweetness of living rather than lamenting over its brevity. And we rejoice in being able to hand on the torch of life to future generations. Yes, this life is enough; this earth is enough; this great and eternal Nature is enough.[6]

As part of his packaging of humanism for nonspecialist readers, Lamont outlined eight central propositions of the humanist philosophy:

(1) The universe is best understood naturalistically as a constantly changing system of events that exists independently of human consciousness and that gives no support to supernatural ideas.

(2) Humanity is an evolutionary product entirely within nature, with the consequence, among other things, of there being no afterlife.

(3) Human thinking is as natural as walking or breathing, and thoughts do not exist in any capacity outside the human brain.

(4) It has ultimate faith in humanity to solve its own problems and realize its own potential through reason and science applied with courage and vision.

(5) Creative freedom of human beings is best realized "within reasonable limits," by those who are masters of their own destiny.

(6) All human values are grounded in this-earthly experiences and relationships, and our highest loyalty is to humanity in general.

(7) Aesthetic experience becomes a pervasive reality in people's lives when the widest possible development of art and awareness of beauty are permitted to flourish.

(8) Worldwide "democracy and peace [are realized and based] on the foundations of a flourishing and cooperative economic order, both national and international."[7]

These points, he concluded, embodied humanism in its most acceptable modern form. That is probably true, but they also illustrated well the historical roots and the transcultural core of humanism. Although he doesn't make the parallel himself, I can't help feeling he would have known of the Eight Steps as outlined by Confucianists and would have appreciated the likenesses. In order to realize the Three Ways of achieving clear character, loving the people and abiding in the highest good, the Confucianist work *The Great Learning* posited the Eight Steps. They are, in order:(1) investigation of things; (2) extension of knowledge; (3) sincerity of the will; (4) rectification of the mind; (5) cultivation of the personal life; (6) regulation of the family; (7) national order; and (8) world peace. Like the Confucianist Eight Steps, Lamont's eight central propositions of humanist philosophy proceed in a specific order. Superficially, the Confucian order differs from the contemporary humanist order, but in fact they build from similar insights. Where the Confucianists began from within the individual (investigation of things, extension of knowledge, sincerity of the will, rectification of the mind and cultivation of personal life), Lamont proposed a series of propositions about the universe that reinforce a cosmic perspective and have in mind ends similar to the Confucian steps. Both are seeking to shed the individual of anthropocentric conceit and hubris. And both work on the supposition that if everyone could manage this, then world peace and harmony (the last point in both systems) could be achieved.

This neat parallel with the Confucian Eight Steps was lost in later editions when Lamont adjusted and added to his eight propositions so that, by the fifth edition, published in the 1960s, there were now ten central propositions in humanist philosophy. Altogether a less happy parallel to work with. The third proposition was dropped, Lamont having recognized it was essentially a repetition of the second. He then added three new propositions. Slotted into the sixth proposition (the original fourth, fifth, and sixth propositions all moving up a number) was a statement about the good life:

> Humanism believes that the individual attains the good life by harmoniously combining personal satisfactions and continuous self-development with significant work and other activities that contribute to the welfare of the community.[8]

He then added at the end two further propositions. The ninth seems confused and not entirely to the point—it dealt with the "complete social implementation of reason and scientific method; and thereby in the use of democratic procedures, including full freedom of expression and civil liberties, throughout all areas of economic, political, and cultural life." The third addition, slotting in as proposition number ten, made more sense: "Humanism, in accordance with [the] scientific method, believes in the unending questioning of basic assumptions, including its own."[9] Very important observation, that. It is a significant point of difference for humanism that it alone enshrines the ongoing criticism of itself as part of its central propositions.

Lamont also took care to thread his conception of humanism back through history and was as much at home among literature, poetry, and music as he was with philosophy. He outlined a magnificent, transcultural appreciation of the humanistic impulse, citing people as varied as Confucius and Swinburne, Beethoven and Euripides, George Eliot and Erasmus. It's a shame he didn't develop this theme because, with the space constraints of the chapter devoted to it, he was able to do little more than rattle off a list of great names.

Humanism as a Philosophy was, and remains, a good book. It is always easy to pick holes in a book that's a half a century old, but two flaws do seem worth mentioning, even if they both require healthy doses of hindsight to bring to light. The first of these weaknesses, when viewed from the twenty-first century, is a certain complacency, a confidence that history was moving inexorably in the direction of humanism; that progress and secularization were the same thing; and that superstition was self-evidently a thing of the past. So confident was Lamont about this that he even felt able to question the law of entropy. "Genuine humanists," Lamont wrote, "cannot for a moment admit that man must necessarily be defeated in his career in the universe."[10] And yet fifty years later it seems that genuine humanists must acknowledge that very point, and even make it central to their humanism. And as an offshoot of this complacency was an inconsistency in fully ridding our thoughts of anthropocentric conceit. "Whenever a thinker in any field treats the this-worldly welfare of man as central, he treads on humanist ground."[11] Comments like these were in the context of a general awareness of the dangers and delusions of anthropocentrism. He was critical, for instance, of supernatural religion and idealist philosophies for having "made man central in a perverse and exaggerated way," and for teaching "a cosmology of deceit and a superstitious anthropomorphism that militates against men's true good in their one and only life."[12] And a key element in his criticism of personal immortality was the anthropocentric conceit it requires to presume oneself worthy of such a destiny. Lamont was also one of the first naturalistic humanists to observe the weakness in much previous humanist writing with respect to nature as an aesthetic object and the "philosophical relevance of nature appreciation."[13] I say "one of the first," because a good case can be made that H. G. Wells preceded Lamont on this point.

Much more damaging, both for Lamont's reputation and for the credibility of humanism, was his inability to cast as critical an eye over his support for the Soviet Union as he did over most other matters. This needs less hindsight to observe, as he was criticized at the time for his pro-Soviet views. But even here, he wasn't always the unthinking propagandist he has been made out to be. He was wrong to whitewash the Stalinist show trials as he did, but after the war he became somewhat more critical, for instance, of the tendency exhibited by many Marxists to see the victory of socialism as inevitable. His attempts to defend Marxist theory from this charge, however, were less convincing and awkwardly placed. Toward the end of *Humanism as a Philosophy*, Lamont felt the need for a passionate claim to democracy as a core humanist commitment. He could easily have just wound the book up with a flurry of platitudes, but instead he developed the claim by isolating twelve intersecting elements of democracy. Beginning with political democracy, he argued convincingly for civil liberties and democracy before the law as sufficiently important to deserve special attention. He then listed eight subsets of democracy that must all be active and healthy for a political democracy to be considered thriving. They still read well half a century later: organizational democracy; economic democracy; social democracy; cultural and intellectual democracy; religious and philosophic democracy; democracy between sexes, ages, and races. He wrapped the list up with international democracy.[14]

All is well and good, until, on just the next page, he indulged in a lengthy apology for the Soviet Union, declaring it "patently unrealistic to expect the Russians and the Chinese would be able to advance immediately to a fully natured democratic way of life."[15] Lamont's apology for communist failures had the effect of drastically undermining his wise articulation of democracy on preceding pages. And opponents of humanism were not so slow to notice his circumlocutions for Stalinism came on the heels of ringing denunciations of the many shortfalls in the realization of American democracy. It was passages such as these that so enraged his critics inside and outside the humanist movement and weakened his argument. Lamont recognized this by dropping these pages of apology for the Soviet record on democracy from later editions. But by then it was too late: in the feverish atmosphere of the 1950s, humanism had been linked irrevocably with being "soft on communism." Opponents of humanism, from Senator Joseph McCarthy to Tim LaHaye, have fed on this link ever since. And within the movement, Sidney Hook led an ongoing and frequently bad-tempered debate on this over five decades. Right up until his autobiography, written in the 1980s, Hook was still sniping at Lamont for views he had expressed in the 1930s. The dispute came to an end only with Hook's death in 1989.

If Hook's persistence was unattractive, it has to be said that he had a point. Lamont's well-meant but misguided support for the Soviet Union was enough to undo much of the good he did in an otherwise wise and civilized rendition of humanism. He had helped consummate the marriage between humanism and naturalism. He also showed far greater appreciation of nature than had been the case before him. He had a more genuine appreciation for the arts as an intrinsic part of the humanist experience. And he was a bold champion for civil liberties and for unpopular causes. But his fatal flaw ended up doing humanism as much harm as good.

SIDNEY HOOK, THE HUMANIST COLD WARRIOR

The perception of strong, even necessary, links between humanism and Marxism has left deep scars. It has allowed the opponents of humanism to caricature it as "antifreedom," "anti-American," anti-this and anti-that. More recently, some antihumanist critics have wanted to lay the responsibility for the suffering, the purges, and the gulags on the "atheistic humanism" of communism. But criticisms such as these ignore three inconvenient truths: (1) communism was far from being a variety of humanism (a point we have already explored at some length); (2) Stalin and Mao both specifically spoke against humanism; and (3) not all Christians were staunch opponents of communism. Influential Christian Marxists like Hewlett Johnson (the "Red Dean") and Conrad Noel, whose credulous works found ready acceptance in the Left Book Club were just as avidly read as the longer and more ponderous tomes of Sidney Hook and Beatrice Webb. And finally, lumping communism in with humanism ignores the long record of opposition to communism from most leading humanist thinkers of the twentieth century: people like Bertrand Russell, Karl Popper, Tzvetan Todorov, Sidney Hook, and others.

Hook's opposition to communism was the overriding fact of his life. His autobiography, *Out of Step* (1987), is little more than a retelling of every battle against Soviet fellow travelers. Sidney Hook (1902–1989) was born and raised in New York, and the vast majority of his entire career was also spent there. He worked as professor of philosophy at New York University from 1932 to 1972, during which time he was intensely active politically, being involved with a succession of organizations, conferences, manifestos, publications, and appeals. As a young man he had been a fervent Marxist, but he soon changed his mind, and the rest of his life was dominated by his ever-stronger opposition to the Soviet Union and all it stood for. This was manifested in some trenchant anticommunism during the McCarthy period, and in his support for the Vietnam War, neither position endearing him to many leftist thinkers who would otherwise have been his natural allies. Hook was not an easy man to pigeon hole. Though a staunch and vigorous opponent of the Soviet Union and of communism, he remained a convinced social democrat and secular humanist, sometimes to the embarrassment of his neoconservative backers and followers. But it was the turn of his leftist allies to feel embarrassed in 1986 when Hook accepted the Presidential Medal of Freedom, America's highest civilian award, from the Reagan administration.

Hook spoke of himself as a secular humanist but acknowledged an important place for religion in people's personal lives.[16] And as if to demonstrate that he meant this, he devoted relatively little time to the criticism of religion. Neither did he write at great length on humanism, preferring to define it negatively as being a series of freedoms from various intellectual and social constraints. Part of the reason for this reticence was that, for him, *humanism* meant American religious humanism such as we discussed in chapter 3. Unlike Dewey, Hook did not endorse the use of religious language in moral discourse.[17] Ever the Cold Warrior, his humanist ideal was pressed into service in the service of the principled (to his friends) or noisy (to his detractors) rejection of any support for totalitarianism. His brand of engaged philosophy in the real world was a great influence on his students, including Paul Kurtz, whose priorities, methods, and values derived in large part from his teacher.

The most lasting of Hook's contributions that concern us was his 1959 essay "Pragmatism and the Tragic Sense of Life," which addressed the frequently heard accusation that pragmatism was little more than shallow American entrepreneurial optimism made to sound philosophical. Not so, Hook argued. In contrast to some ponderous dialectic that dismisses one's suffering as an inescapable by-product of history or the consolations of supernaturalism, pragmatism takes tragedy seriously. He also took a new look at what tragedy is. Tragedy is more than the brute facts of illness, old age, and death. These are built in to the fabric of life and as such may be pitiful but are not tragic. Tragedy is when alternate goods require of us a choice that cannot but involve diminishment somewhere.[18] There are also conflicts between some sense of the good against an equally significant conception of the right.

Hook is also interesting on his proposed solution. He thought Russell's defiance in "The Free Man's Worship" a bit too romantic. But he was more critical of the semi-Catholic mystic Miguel de Unamuno (1864–1936), who castigated reason as the enemy of his form of mystical sentimentalism. We cannot escape from the limitations of life, Hook wrote, but we need to be able to resist the temptation to lapse into lamentation, defiance, or make-believe. We do this in the context of a sustainable meliorism. "To the meliorist the recognition of the gamut of tragic possibilities is what feeds his desire to find some method of negotiating conflicts of value by intelligence rather than war, or brute force."[19] This awareness of the fragility of the good things in life is an important insight for twenty-first-century humanism to take on board. It represents the right blend of reason and Romanticism that has been a hallmark of successful humanism since Friedrich Immanuel Niethammer in 1808.

PAUL KURTZ AND *THE HUMANIST MANIFESTO II*

Like Hook, Paul Kurtz has always been keen to distance humanism from dogmatic allies of whatever stripe. And like John Dewey, Kurtz has wanted to emphasize the positive elements of humanism; its program for living rather than its record of accusations against religion. But it was Kurtz's fate to be prominent at a time of resurgent fundamentalism, which required a whole new approach to problems his mentors thought long dealt with. New Jersey–born, Kurtz's university study was interrupted by volunteering for military service. When he was not quite nineteen, his unit was rushed to the front during the height of the Battle of the Bulge. A few months later he was among the forces that liberated Dachau concentration camp. He stayed with the American forces in Germany for eighteen months after the war before being demobilized.

Upon his return to civilian life, Kurtz resumed his studies at New York University before moving on to Columbia University, where he took his doctorate in 1952. Kurtz had studied under Hook and retained a lifelong relationship with the older philosopher. And through Hook, Kurtz stands in direct line from John Dewey. Kurtz's doctoral dissertation was called *The Problem of Value Theory*, and his academic career was devoted mainly to justifying the methods of objective inquiry. And like Dewey and Hook, Kurtz was never happy restricting his activities to the academy; when he was offered the editorship of *The Humanist*, the magazine of the American Humanist Association in 1967 (and not to be confused with the magazine of the same name Hector Hawton ran in Britain for the Rationalist Press Association), he took it. At the time he took over editorship of the *Humanist* in 1967, Kurtz was very much the young man in a hurry. Shortly after taking the editorship, he wrote:

> A person who leaves the traditional church in revolt does not want a warmed-over dish of platitudes as a weak substitute, as he has been often

served by organized humanism in the United States. If one reads what many professional humanists write about, one often finds the same old clichés and slogans. Humanism should be concerned with moral choice and social change, and not just theorize about them.[20]

It was in this spirit of engaged philosophy that Kurtz led the campaign in 1973 for a revised humanist manifesto. The *Humanist Manifesto* was now four decades old and was in many respects unsatisfactory and obsolete. Over several issues Kurtz featured opinions from leading humanists as to what the *Humanist Manifesto* had achieved forty years previous and to which aspects of it were now in need of renewal. Most people whose views found their way into print agreed that the manifesto needed updating. Several of the signatories of the original manifesto took part in the debate. Corliss Lamont thought it was no longer appropriate to advocate socialism and favored instead points outlining a humanist position on democracy, ecology, and gender relations.[21] Roy Wood Sellars, in one of the last letters written before his death at the age of ninety-three, restated what he had being arguing all through his life:

> Humanism must concentrate on institutions and objectives of promise. This is already beginning: birth control, lessening of pollution, stress on the quality of education and equal opportunities, and lasting peace. Love and compassion must be harnessed to intelligent endeavor. In this atmosphere, religion will come of age.[22]

Another, more problematic, legacy from the original manifesto was the relationship between humanism and religion. The 1933 document had spoken of religious humanism, which the 1973 manifesto dropped. The *Humanist Manifesto II* was much more specific in its rejection of traditional monotheistic religion. It also distanced itself from religious humanism:

> Some humanists believe we should reinterpret traditional religions and reinvest them with meanings appropriate to the current situation. Such redefinitions, however, often perpetuate old dependencies and escapisms; they easily become obscurantist, impeding the free use of the intellect. We need, instead, radically new human purposes and goals.[23]

This unambiguous rejection of the religious elements of humanism went on to have important and unhelpful consequences for the unity of the humanist movement in the United States. But it hasn't stopped American fundamentalists continuing to accuse humanism of being "just another religion." This accusation is almost always made at the expense of the facts. For instance, we find quotations from both manifestoes, and from other sources all thrown together, with no allowance made for the different usages of *religion* and *religious*. Neither is any space given to the no-less frequent criticisms of religious usage and language in organized humanism.[24]

Alongside the rejection of the religious humanism of the first manifesto, the *Humanist Manifesto II* was also anxious not to strike a note of facile optimism that been a feature of its predecessor.

> Nazism has shown the depths of brutality of which humanity is capable. Other totalitarian regimes have suppressed human rights without ending poverty, Science has sometimes brought evil as well as good. Recent decades have shown that inhuman wars can be made in the name of peace.[25]

Other contemporary evils listed included abuse of power by military and industrial elites, racism, and sexism. So the second manifesto set an altogether darker scene than its predecessor.

Humanist Manifesto II made eighteen main points, grouped into the fields of religion, ethics, the individual, democratic society, and humanity as a whole. The main points were:

(1) Moral values derive from human experience.
(2) Reason and intelligence are humanity's most effective instruments.
(3) Economic systems should be judged by how they help humanity, rather than along ideological lines.
(4) Affirming the moral equality of all.
(5) A call to transcend the limits of national sovereignty.
(6) Adopting planetary solutions to planetary problems.

Without using the phrase, this manifesto made a call for *planetary humanism*. "What more daring a goal for humankind," it concluded, "than for each person to become, in ideal as well as in practice, a citizen of a world community. It is a classical vision; we can now give it new vitality."[26]

The manifesto attracted a full media response, in America and around the world. It was front-page news on the August 26 issue of the *New York Times* and received good coverage in a large number of other prominent American papers. Within weeks of publication it was being translated into Korean. Some of the signatories signed at some risk to their personal safety. Andrei Sakharov was hauled before the Soviet deputy prosecutor general and warned about his "collaboration" with anti-Soviet media. And in Yugoslavia, Svetozar Stojanovic was subjected to media criticism for being a "pseudo-humanist" and "anarcho-liberal." Some of the domestic reaction was no less hysterical. The Knights of Columbus inveighed against the "devastating cancer" threatening to undermine Western civilization, while Garry Wills bemoaned, at the same time, its supposed dogmatism and moral laxity. More interesting was the criticism from within the movement. The reaction of British humanists was phlegmatic. Harold Blackham wrote a short, rather terse notice of the manifesto for the *New Humanist*, noting that it is "a bugle call not a battle plan; but rationalists are not a light brigade; they are called to serious strategic thinking by the ringing phrases of this document."[27]

To its credit, *The Humanist* ran a series of letters from people who were not willing to sign the manifesto. There is no particular theme to these criticisms. They all expressed general support for what was being said but stopped short at one particular feature that was important to them. John Hospers felt unable to lend his name to a document that saw virtue in world government. Sidney Hook was also unhappy with this aspect of the manifesto, but not sufficiently so to withhold his signature. Brigid Brophy criticized the lack of attention given to animal rights. Several others lamented the low value placed on mysticism. What is interesting is how little opposition from religious humanists there was. Many prominent religious humanists signed *Humanist Manifesto II*, despite whatever reservations they must have felt.

Ever the skilled publicist, Kurtz also edited a collection of essays that was designed to complement the manifesto. *The Humanist Alternative* is a good book, better than either Huxley's *Humanist Frame* or Ayer's *Humanist Outlook*, the two other attempts of the period to offer a comprehensive account of humanism from a variety of perspectives. The essays in *The Humanist Alternative* are shorter, snappier, and come from a wider range of viewpoints than Huxley's or Ayer's works. They also seem more to the point, actually discussing *humanism* and what it means to them. While less transnational than would now be seen as adequate, *The Humanist Alternative* made some effort to include humanists from outside the Anglo American world. Gora, an Indian social crusader whose career we will follow in chapter 9, got his first major international exposure in this book.

The overriding impression of this collection is of the variety of viewpoints from people who called themselves humanists. Kurtz addressed this issue in his essay, which he used as a conclusion to *The Humanist Alternative*. Under the title "Is Everyone a Humanist?" he welcomed the apparent trends toward openness in both the Catholic Church and the Marxist countries, both of which used the word *humanism*, though suitably prefixed by *Christian* and *Socialist* respectively. But, he added, "we should surely insist that a theistic or totalitarian ideology cannot be considered humanistic in its essential nature if one of the most basic of human rights—the right of individuals to the free use of knowledge—is ignored."[28] Needless to say, this clear affirmation of the secular principles of humanism is ignored by fundamentalist critics.

The *Humanist Manifesto II* was a great improvement on the original, being better thought out, better prepared, and better marketed than its predecessor. Kurtz had gathered 114 signatories by the time of publication and altogether 261 prominent thinkers from around the world put their name to it. It was more specific about what humanism actually is and what it is not. It also canvassed a wider range of issues than the simpler original. And while the *Humanist Manifesto II* was a more consistently secular document, it was not antireligious in an unhelpful way. It acknowledged that religion can inspire dedication to commendable ethical ideals. And finally, the *Humanist Manifesto II* was very careful not to set itself up as a rival creed. Sections of the humanist movement, particularly in Britain, have been uncomfortable with manifestos of any sort, fearing their prescriptive implications. But Kurtz's manifesto did not do this. "These affirmations are not a final credo or dogma but an expression of a living and growing faith. We invite others in all lands to join us in further developing and working for these goals."[29]

PAUL KURTZ AND THE *SECULAR HUMANIST DECLARATION*

The *Humanist Manifesto II* appeared in 1973, the same year of the *Roe v. Wade* Supreme Court decision that legalized abortion in the United States.

This was an unhappy coincidence for secular humanism. It is also true that 1973 is often seen as a fulcrum year when the conditions that had prevailed since World War II fractured and the messier, less stable conflicts of the twenty-first-century were conceived. "The history of the twenty years after 1973," wrote Eric Hobsbawm, "is that of a world which lost its bearings and slid into instability and crisis."[30]

International politics took an alarming turn after the Yom Kippur War in October of that year, with Western economies for the first time being called to account by the predominantly Muslim oil-producing countries for their support of Israel. The "Oil Shock," as it was known, came to realign fundamentally the faultlines of international politics, leading to what in the 1990s some called the "clash of civilizations." To all appearances, the Cold War between the capitalism of the West and the state socialism of the Soviet Union and its satellites was still the main attraction. As late as 1983 important commentators like Jean-Francois Revel could still predict the imminent triumph of socialism. But in one respect the Cold War was well and truly over. After 1968, the year the Soviet Union invaded Czechoslovakia, the Soviet model was no longer a serious contender for the hearts and minds of reform-minded people. Communist China had a brief honeymoon among disillusioned Westerners, but the excesses of the Cultural Revolution soon put an end to that.

But the Western world was mired in its own difficulties and could inspire little sense of involvement or commitment from young people. The decade began with the American decision to extend its war in Vietnam across the border to Cambodia. This provoked widespread unrest in the United States, culminating in the deaths of students at Kent State University in Ohio. And then came Watergate. Americans were used to a certain level of corruption in their political arrangement, most commonly with officeholders arranging for their pecuniary advantage at the expense of the public good. But Watergate was an altogether nastier type of corruption and at significantly higher levels than had previously been thought to exist.

This general mood of pessimism and decline had unforeseen consequences. The United States had been on a rightward trajectory since 1968 when Richard Nixon turned the solid Democratic south into the solid Republican south. But for the large evangelical minority in the United States, things were going from bad to worse. A succession of issues, from gay rights, women's rights, abortion, bussing, and affirmative action became prominent and posed a significant challenge to the evangelical view of what America was about. In the wake of its defeat in Vietnam in 1975, the United States was restless and ill at ease with itself. The country seemed uncertain of the proper use of its global policeman role. And the 1976 election of Jimmy Carter, a born-again Christian, further disappointed evangelicals around the country. Rather than see a moral renaissance, things from their perspective continued to decline. Evangelicals felt betrayed by Carter. Many Americans voted for Reagan because they wanted an end to what they perceived as an America demoralized within and weakened abroad. Reagan symbolized an America they thought they remembered from their childhood. But for observers outside the United States, the election of Reagan produced a bemused shock. Reagan's election was the beginning of the feeling, which has since grown around the world, that the United States is on a different planet.

It was against this background of growing irrationalism and paranoia in public discourse that the *Secular Humanist Declaration* was published and *Free Inquiry* magazine was launched at the end of 1980. Only seven years previously, the *Humanist Manifesto II* had been widely praised. Even the *New York Times* called it a philosophy for survival. But in seven short years the climate had changed considerably. In 1973 Kurtz could plausibly ask if everyone was a humanist, but in 1980 humanism looked more like a quaint relic of the past, to its friends, or a vicious plot to undermine all that was best in America, to a lot of other people. Many sections of society were anxious about the growing fundamentalist threat, but few seemed able or willing to organize any coherent response. The politicians were scared of the voting strength of the fundamentalists, the business community was happy that this distraction should deflect attention from itself, and the academic community was too busy arguing within itself to notice. Many in the academic community were pleased to dismiss humanists as no more than the opposite side of the same coin as fundamentalists.[31]

Under Kurtz's editorship, *The Humanist* had become more topical and political. The magazine's influence was probably at its height during the campaign to promote the *Humanist Manifesto II* in 1973. But through these years his relations with the American Humanist Association began to unravel. While still involved with the AHA, Kurtz was a central figure in establishing the Committee for the Scientific Investigation of Claims of the Paranormal in 1976. But the following year he resigned his editorship of *The Humanist*, and a long estrangement between him and the AHA set in. Determined now to operate according to his own thoughts, Kurtz set up the Council for Democratic and Secular Humanism (CODESH) in 1980. The *Secular Humanist Declaration* and *Free Inquiry* became Kurtz's principal means by which to propagate his version of humanism.

The core of Kurtz's philosophy of life can be found in *The Transcendental Temptation* (1986); *Forbidden Fruit: The Ethics of Humanism* (1988); *Eupraxophy: Living without Religion* (1989); and *Skepticism: Inquiry and Reliable Knowledge* (1992). Like Hook, Kurtz has always been keen to distance humanism from dogmatic interpretations and unsavoury allies. And like Dewey, Kurtz has wanted to emphasize the positive elements of nonreligious living. Perhaps the most significant difference between Dewey and Kurtz is in their respective attitudes toward religion and religious language. Kurtz warned against the transcendental temptation and rather than insisting humanism is a "me too" religion, coined the word *eupraxsophy* to explain the humanist love of life, profound respect for nature, and willingness to live an active life.

Kurtz's academic books have had a mixed career, having been largely ignored by the academic community. In part this can be put down to being out of step when academic fashions have moved to other questions. But neither have they enjoyed the influence they might have among the general humanist readership, particularly outside the United States, where Kurtz's writing style has found less favor. They have fallen into the trap of being not academic enough for the specialists but too academic for the nonspecialists. The most successful of them was *Forbidden Fruit: The Ethics of Humanism*, which has been translated into many languages.

In some ways, his shorter books have been the most successful. They have flown below the radarscope of the academics and have gone straight to the nonspecialist reader. With the exception of Hector Hawton, and, more recently, Richard Norman in the United Kingdom and Corliss Lamont in the United States, there had been a shortage of good outlines of humanism for the nonspecialist. Books like *Exuberance* (1978), *The Courage to Become* (1996), *Affirmations* (2004), and *What Is Secular Humanism?* (2007) were written to fill that need. These books offer a clear understanding of humanism as a secular and this-worldly philosophy.

> Human life has no meaning independent of itself. There is no cosmic force or deity to give it meaning or significance. There is no ultimate destiny for

man. Such a belief is an illusion of humankind's infancy. The meaning of life is what we choose to give it. Meaning grows out of human purposes alone.[32]

And once more, this passage, and the many others like it, was ignored by the fundamentalists who were determined to prove against all odds that humanism was a religion. Passages such as these were also ignored by those in the academic community who contrived to see secular humanists as the opposite side of the coin as fundamentalists.

So, with a backdrop of the defeat of Jimmy Carter at the hands of a Republican Party on a sharp rightward trajectory, Paul Kurtz felt the need for a new voice. In announcing *Free Inquiry*, Kurtz wrote:

> The task of this new magazine will be to define and defend the positions of freedom and secularism in the contemporary world. In recent years the world has witnessed a massive resurgence of fanatical dogmas and doctrines. The fundamental premises of the modern world and the Enlightenment are either being forgotten or [being] completely ignored. The commitment to scientific evidence and reason as a method of knowing, belief in the value of the individual freedom and dignity, and the view that superstition can be eradicated by increased education and affluence—all of these have been replaced by positions which are often blatantly irrational.[33]

Among the dangers named specifically were Christian fundamentalism, Islamic sects, cults, and the paranormal. But Kurtz was no less critical of authoritarian ideologies, such as Marxism-Leninism and Nazism. Kurtz criticized the traditional leftist orientation of the humanist movement, arguing that conventional distinctions between Right and Left were rapidly becoming anachronistic. He called for a broad coalition of Left and Right, neoliberals and social democrats, to defend the free society. His rallying cry in the inaugural issue of *Free Inquiry* came from a long line of liberal thinking, a tradition that can be traced back to ancient Greece. It was the "liberal humanism" we spoke of in chapter 1 now being articulated under its own name. He was also anxious to make clear that secular humanism is not simply antireligious. Antifundamentalist, antisectarian, yes; antireligious, no. In stark contrast to the line adopted by the fundamentalists, the *Secular Humanist Declaration* was specifically inclusive:

> We are apprehensive that modern civilization is threatened by forces antithetical to reason, democracy, and freedom. Many religious believers will no doubt share with us a belief in many secular humanist and democratic values, and we welcome their joining with us in the defense of these ideals.[34]

The declaration went on to itemize these ideals. They were four main types of ideals mentioned: free inquiry, reason; ethics based on critical intelligence and education, including moral education; commitment to science and technology and the findings of science, such as evolution; and the separation of church and state, the ideal of freedom, religious skepticism. Kurtz ended the declaration with this call:

> We believe that it is possible to bring about a more humane world, one based upon the methods of reason and the principles of tolerance, compromise, and the negotiations of difference. We recognize the need for intellectual modesty and the willingness to revise beliefs in the light of criticism. Thus consensus is sometimes attainable. While emotions are important, we need not resort to the panaceas of salvation, to escape through illusion, or to some desperate leap toward passion and violence. We deplore the growth of intolerant sectarian creeds that foster hatred. In a world engulfed by obscurantism and irrationalism it is vital that the ideals of the secular city not be lost.[35]

The first point to note about this passage is how little support it lends the critics of humanism, whether from academics such as Ehrenfeld or from the fundamentalists. This passage, which concluded the *Secular Humanist Declaration*, is not arrogant nor speciesist nor dogmatic nor hegemonic nor optimistic nor any of the other accusations so frequently made against humanism. It is, rather, a radical call to renew our commitment to a transnational tradition that has provided a level of knowledge, safety, community awareness, longevity, and chance of fulfillment that is unparalleled in world history.

The pages of *Free Inquiry* were open to all manner of criticisms in the months to follow. Apparently unaware of the irony of the situation, John P. Roche, Phyllis Schafly, Roscoe Drummond, and Pat Buchanan, all accused the declaration of (to varying degrees) dogmatism, elitism, anti-Americanism, and being an enemy of freedom.[36] The reaction from the British humanists was more measured but generally unenthusiastic. For example, the prominent

English ethicist James Hemming thought the declaration "intellectually faultless but desperately weak on the subjective side of human development and functioning."[37] I suspect Hemming's qualms reflected the majority opinion outside the United States.

WHY *SECULAR* HUMANISM?

The point not considered so far is why Kurtz now started to speak of *secular humanism*. We need to answer this in the roundabout way of asking first where *secular humanism* came from. The most commonly repeated claim is that secular humanism began its career in 1961 when Justice Hugo Black used the term in the *Torcaso v. Watkins* Supreme Court case, which decided that the state cannot require a religious test for public office. Roy Torcaso (1910–2007), an atheist, had been removed from his position as notary public for the state of Maryland after his views became known. The state constitution required all government employees to believe in the existence of God. In a footnote to the decision, Justice Black noted that "secular humanism" should, for legal purposes, be seen as a religion. Black could not anticipate that fundamentalists would use his peripheral comment as justification for censorship in public schools and the promotion of religious instruction. Comments made in footnotes have no legal validity, and many subsequent decisions affirmed that secular humanism is not a religion.

This is not where *secular humanism* originated. In all probability Justice Black took the term from the distinguished jurist Leo Pfeffer (1910–1993), who used it in his book *Creeds in Competition* (1958). The point of Pfeffer's book was that the separation of church and state, so finely balanced in the United States, was the surest guarantee of the ongoing health of organized religion. He spoke of creeds in competition in a positive sense of healthy competition. The US Constitution, Pfeffer reminded his readers, was drafted at a time when the Christian religion was at a low ebb and when none of the first seven American presidents was formally affiliated with any church. He outlined this history in a section of his book called "Secular Humanism," which he thought simply a more modern term than *deistic rationalism*, which he observed was the guiding principle of the US Constitution. By *secular humanism*, he did not mean "a consciously nontheistic movement, but merely the influence of those unaffiliated with organized religion and concerned with human values."[38] The critical point is that Pfeffer was on the team of attorneys defending Roy Torcaso, making it highly likely that this is where Justice Black picked up the term. Pfeffer was also insistent that secular humanism was not a religion.

In the years that followed, the fundamentalists seized on *secular humanism* as the catchall term to denote all they opposed. In particular, they turned Justice Black's marginal comment that secular humanism should be seen as a religion for legal purposes into the very different claim that the Supreme Court had identified secular humanism as a religion, with all the implications this had for the separation of church and state. From that day to this, American fundamentalists have repeated this claim and have demanded that "the religion of secular humanism" be removed from the nation's schools, particularly in its guise as the teaching of evolution, sex education, and what they call *moral relativism*. In Kurtz's view, this growing campaign from the fundamentalist Right made the claim of the American Humanist Association that humanism is indeed a religion very risky indeed. Over and above all the older, more academic arguments about the meaning of words and their proper use, the AHA's view was playing into the hands of the religious Right. So when Kurtz went out on his own, he was happy to take up the term *secular humanism* as a means both to counter fundamentalist campaigning and to highlight the differences between his position and that of the AHA.

It was inevitable that the *Secular Humanist Declaration* should attract some intemperate condemnation from its opponents. But even some allies worried about aspects of the declaration. Many people, allies and opponents of humanism, objected to religion being exposed to criticism. To this Kurtz replied:

> We share with many religionists their commitment to the values of a free society. But some dogmatic religionists are intolerant and wish to impose their views on others. Part of their growing influence may be attributed to the fact that the views they express often go unchallenged. Some skeptics ask, "Why take them seriously?" Others behave ostrichlike, hoping that they will go away. But doctrinaire religions must be taken seriously, for they have a powerful influence on the lives of countless people. That is why we believe that religions should not be immune to free inquiry or critical scrutiny.[39]

This has remained a central element of the secular humanist worldview, one that Daniel Dennett reiterated at the start of his critique of religion, *Breaking the Spell* (2006). Humanists are often attacked for criticizing religion, the suggestion being that such behavior implies lack of respect. The very opposite is true. As Kurtz said, secular humanists show religions the courtesy of taking their truth-claims seriously and seeing it as a worthwhile exercise to expose those truth-claims to scrutiny. This is one of the main features which distinguish humanists from the vast mass of nonreligious people. Millions of people around the world have given up on religion, but relatively few can give coherent reasons why they have done so. It is not that they have actively rejected religion, it is that they can't be bothered with it. Humanists share with religious people the appreciation that asking questions about the purpose of life and wanting to abide by the consequences of the answer arrived at is a worthwhile way to live a life. This shared emphasis is very rarely commented upon, let alone appreciated by religious apologists for whom the most important thing is whether the answers arrived at are the same as their own.

It remains a fact, however, that significant sections of the humanist community have remained unconvinced by the value of a specifically *secular* humanism. *Free Inquiry* devoted extensive space to this question in the 1980s. The most indicative of these debates took place toward the end of 1985, and featured some very prominent thinkers across the range of the divide. The core of the argument revolved around the appropriate use of religious language. But there were important political considerations as well, something observers from outside the United States have not appreciated as fully as they might. The first salvo in this exchange came from Paul Beattie (1937–1989), a prominent American religious humanist who thought of religion in broader, looser ways than many of his secular humanist allies. Religion, Beattie wrote, consists of two parts:

> First, a religion is an individual's response to life. It is the core of attitudes and values out of which a person lives. Second, a religion possesses an institutional and community aspect.[40]

Beattie was entirely at one with secular humanists on the first of his points. It was the second where he saw secular humanism having something positive to learn from conventional religious institutions. Beattie's position was comprehensively challenged by Joseph Fletcher (1905–1991), a prominent American philosopher best known for his influential work, *Situation Ethics*. Fletcher began adult life as an Episcopalian minister before devoting his life to philosophy, where he pioneered the new field of medical ethics, taking an especial interest in the question of voluntary euthanasia. Over the course of his life he moved from conventional believer through various positions that would now be called *post-Christian*, to a full-fledged secular humanism. Beattie, Fletcher charged, was guilty of the "fallacy of indefinition," that is, of lumping quite contrary notions together in an effort of contrived syncretism. Beattie also failed to say what a secular humanist is not. If secular humanism is a religion, then there is no meaningful difference between the truth-claims of an ardent evangelical or that of a Darwinian naturalist.

> To be a *secular* humanist, to thus qualify the noun, means to be a certain kind of humanist; to think, that is, about men and their problems and prospects without God or heaven *or any other religious ideas and aspirations* entering in.[41]

Fletcher ended his article; "No more worship of either God or man." But he understood that this was more than just a scrap over words and terms. Unlike Beattie, Fletcher was not going to add fuel to the fundamentalist lobby, then very actively trying to engineer a ban of "the religion of secular humanism" from American public schools. Whether the strategists of American fundamentalism actually believed this to be true is open to question, but it was a very shrewd move politically, playing on the American instinct for fair play. Beattie dismissed the fundamentalist threat as "so *intellectually deficient* that it will fall of its own weight."[42] Intellectually deficient it may be, but that has not stopped arguments from achieving dangerous levels of popular acceptance and political influence. Beattie's flaw here is another example of what has been commented upon already: the worst flaws associated with the humanist outlook—a sanguine confidence in progress, reason, and the perfectibility of man—are more a feature of religious humanist thought than of secular or naturalistic humanist thought.

A few years after this controversy, another series of criticisms were made of secular humanism, but this time in the interests of redefining the argument. After a long career in the ethical culture movement and with an interest in moral education, Howard Radest (1928–), lamented that since

American humanism had taken the descriptor *secular*, the movement had lost the initiative. Although a signatory of the *Humanist Manifesto II* and the *Secular Humanist Declaration*, he worried that secular humanism had retreated into a fundamentalism indistinguishable from its religious mirror image, and with the same zeal for criticism. Oddly, he exempted the criticism of secular humanism from the same charge. As noted in previous chapters, this question of determining the correct priority which criticism of religion should be given as opposed to the articulation of a positive humanist alternative is perhaps the single most intractable issue dividing religious and secular humanists. Few people have understood this dilemma more than Paul Kurtz, and nobody has done more to try to find a happy balance. Radest sought to redefine the argument by adding that secular humanism remained unhelpfully tied to Enlightenment values.[43] What he did not do was articulate any humanist values that are "beyond" those of the Enlightenment while not also being those of secular humanism.

The debate between religious and secular expressions of humanism in the United States has continued, with no signs of being any closer to resolution. One of the more concerted attempts to define *secular humanism* was made in 2002 by Tom Flynn, editor of *Free Inquiry* and editor of the *New Encyclopedia of Unbelief* (2007). Flynn discussed the issues in an exclusively American context and defined secular humanism in ways conducive to the American situation. The "American situation" being the ongoing squabble between secular and religious humanism. Flynn ended up defining secular humanism as "a comprehensive nonreligious life stance that incorporates a naturalistic philosophy, a cosmic outlook rooted in science, and a consequentialist ethical system."[44] This is all very well, but a definition that uses terms which themselves require explanation is always going to run into trouble. Flynn assumes people know what the term *lifestance* refers to and that they understand *consequentialist ethics*. Even more problematic, in the long run, is that this definition was offered in the context of delineating a clear boundary between religious and secular humanism. What was left unexplored was whether such an exercise was useful.[45]

In many ways the debate about the religious or secular nature of humanism is a peculiarly American affair, bound as it is with political considerations about humanism's status as a religion. However, it is also about more simple things, like the rivalry between organizations. As such, it's had little traction in British or European humanist circles. When mentioned at all outside the United States, it is often in a spirit of impatience at so much time-consuming disputation.[46] However, much of this criticism overlooks the reasons for the development of a consciously secular humanism in the United States. This spirit of impatience rests on a far too sanguine confidence of the irrelevance of fundamentalism and a lack of appreciation for the urgent political reasons American humanists have had to insist that humanism is not a religion. At its worst, the Anglo European objection to secular humanism is little more than a knee-jerk anti-Americanism.

THE DEBATE OVER *EUPRAXSOPHY*

It was partly in response to this divisive and round about debate over the boundaries between humanism's relationship with religion that Kurtz felt the need for a new direction. In the context of reviewing the first decade of *Free Inquiry* magazine, he argued that the criticism of religion should continue, but, he announced "secular humanism must go beyond criticism and affirm a positive outlook."[47] It is important to recall that America's best-known atheist at the time was Madalyn Murray-O'Hair (1919–1995), whose abusive antics served to confirm people's worst fears about nonbelievers. While acknowledging that secular humanism *is* atheistic, Kurtz didn't want to limit it in that way. But he was just as anxious not to make the AHA's mistake, as he saw it, of employing religious vocabulary while speaking of humanism. With these aims in mind, Kurtz developed a word he hoped would transcend these differences. The word was *eupraxsophy*.

Eupraxsophy was Kurtz's attempt to condense into one word the spirit of what the religious and the secular humanists were all about. With the religious humanists, he recognized the insufficiency of atheism as an all-encompassing description of the nonreligious experience. But, like Joseph Fletcher, he was not prepared to take on the religious vocabulary to express an essentially secular orientation. Kurtz has gone to great lengths to demonstrate that humanist ethics are independent of theistic ethics. One can be awed by the beauty of the universe, love life to distraction, find fulfillment in other people, and live openly and actively without being religious, and it was the intention of *eupraxsophy* to encapsulate that.

Kurtz's neologism owes an intellectual debt to Aristotle's concept of *eudaimonia*, and yet it goes further in one crucial sense. Aristotle saw the final goal as the contemplative life, whereas eupraxsophy seeks a dynamic fusion of contemplation and action. The nub of the question, Kurtz wrote, is to love not just wisdom but the *practice* of it. Here is where the debt to Dewey is a positive one, because eupraxsophy owes a lot to Dewey's slogan of intelligent action. Eupraxsophy is an amalgam of *eu* (good, well), *praxis* (conduct, practice), and *sophia* (scientific and philosophic wisdom). Brought together, *eupraxsophy* stands for "good wisdom and practice in conduct." The word was initially spelled as "eupraxophy," but after some confusion about how the word should be pronounced, an *s* was added after the *x*. It is unlikely that this helped.

Eupraxsophy was a commendable idea based on a perceptive reading of the needs of the humanist movement. The genius of religions is their provision of different types of religiosity to appeal to different personalities while being able to wrap them up in an apparently coherent package. Kurtz saw a similar need in humanism, so that simple goodness, social activism, and intellectual breadth—all features one admires in a humanist—can come together in one recognizable fusion and gain strength and coherence from doing so. Like the saint, the sage, or the *arhat*, the eupraxsopher would bring under one roof the humanist ideals of goodness, activism, and wisdom and would not need to be defined solely by what he or she rejected.

But it would be naïve not to see its faults. Two objections have dogged eupraxsophy since its inception. One line of criticism asked, why bother with a new term at all? Tim Madigan, at the time editor of *Free Inquiry*, offered in response the historical parallel of T. H. Huxley who, in 1869, felt the need for a new term. Being unable to identify with any of the theological or philosophical titles then on offer, he coined the word *agnostic*, which has remained in use to this day.[48] What this attempted parallel did not address, however, was whether *eupraxsophy* did actually fill a need in the way that *agnostic* did. A second line of criticism asked, why *that* term? One critic said that, whatever the faults of humanism as a label, it is at least accessible. "Better stay on the ground (and, if necessary, in the mud) struggling to retain clarity with other people than to retreat to the stratosphere with a dictionary."[49] Outside the United States, which didn't properly appreciate Kurtz's motivations, the reaction was one of blinking incomprehension. In Britain, in the context of a generally supportive review of the word, the reviewer was skeptical about what he saw as an "ungainly neologism."[50]

But Kurtz had more in mind than coining a neologism, ungainly or otherwise. He also had in mind the creation of what he called Eupraxsophy Centers, which would become places for people to meet to discuss the issues raised by living naturalistically. Eupraxsophy Centers would be meeting rooms, community centers, lecture halls, places where people may marry, where counseling could take place, and so on. In a letter to *Free Inquiry*, a perceptive English writer commented: "Forget the new buildings, Paul, Eupraxsophy Centers already exist! In England we call them pubs."[51] This irreverent response captures the flavor of much of the response outside the United States to the whole eupraxsophy idea.

Another, more theoretical, problem with eupraxsophy was Kurtz's anxiety to put as much distance between his new concept and religion. He did this by way of a robust critique of functionalist approaches to religion, stressing instead the differences in what humanists and religionists believe. But at the same time, he wanted eupraxsophy to get beyond the squabbling over details he felt atheists and evangelicals were engaged in. But by insisting the "positive outlook" of eupraxsophy could arise only from a naturalistic perspective, Kurtz shut down the possibility of forging common ground with like-minded religious progressives while also rendering the term unnecessary to those already within the humanist movement. Eupraxsophy was a good idea, but, despite Kurtz's efforts, it has not been taken up by the humanist community. In chapter 13, we will take up Kurtz's more recent attempts to redefine and invigorate humanism.

HUMANISM AMONG THE CHILDREN OF NIMROD

It would seem, judging from the story so far, that American humanism has a strongly academic flavor about it, and an overwhelmingly WASP flavor. But that would be untrue. American secular Jews, for example, have taken the lead in building new organizations for themselves. This interesting story has been told elsewhere. The story of African American humanism, however, still needs to be told fully. What follows here is a brief overview of a story still emerging from the shadows.

The stereotype of black religiosity is almost as pervasive as that of female religiosity. People of African descent, so the story goes, are more naturally attuned to the cadences of religion. And neither has this account come from only white writers. John Mbiti, whose *African Religions and Philosophy* (1969) was for a long time one of the most influential books on African religious studies, argued in this way. We will discuss Mbiti more in chapter 12. Among African Americans, the perception of a natural black religiosity was very much the case until the publication of William R. Jones's work *Is God a White Racist?* (1973). It took another quarter century for Jones's work to be taken seriously among African American scholars.

One of the more important thinkers to take Jones seriously, and indeed to move on from his work, is Anthony B. Pinn. Like so many people who grow up as committed humanists, Pinn grew up in an atmosphere of total immersion in religion. Growing up in Buffalo, New York, Pinn was earmarked early as a church leader, and he expressed his desire to become a preacher. By the time he graduated, Pinn had abandoned his uncritical supernaturalism and his plans to become a preacher. The question that began his process of unraveling was an old one: Given that black people are so devoted to God, why do they continue to suffer disproportionately in American society? Pinn went on to have a distinguished career in the field of religious studies, focusing on the history of the African American religious experience.

Pinn relates the myth of Nimrod as most befitting people of African descent. The tenth chapter of Genesis tells of Nimrod, the son of Cush and grandson of Ham. Nimrod was a "mighty hunter before the Lord" and ruled as king in Mesopotamia. His association with the construction of the Tower of Babel is the key to his subsequent reputation. From the earliest church fathers, Nimrod was the archetype for despotism, hubris, and revolt against God. For many centuries he was characterized as black, and the sufferings of the black races, so the story went, was legitimate punishment for the sins of Nimrod. But the Nimrod story can also be read as a Promethean attempt to forge a means by which humans could be united without recourse to God. Pinn urges African Americans to take up this account and call themselves the "children of Nimrod—those who seek to celebrate and safeguard human creativity, potential, and responsibility."[52]

Pinn outlined five principles of African American humanism. Most are unremarkable: being accountable for the human condition and responsible for its improvement; rejection of supernaturalism; a "controlled optimism" with respect to human potential; and a commitment to "individual and societal transformation." The only principle that marked this list off from others was the third; "an appreciation for African American cultural production and a perception of traditional forms of black religiosity as having cultural importance as opposed to any type of 'cosmic' authority."[53] This is an aspect of a black humanist studies discipline he would like to see developed. Pinn follows in Dewey's footsteps when he sees black humanism as a variety of religious expression. Like Dewey, and many religious humanists, he is careful to dissociate any form of supernaturalism from his understanding of religion, seeing it in broad terms as "the creation of identity or complex subjectivity (realization of full humanity), understood in terms of the individual and community."[54]

Pinn's willingness to see black humanism as a form of religion, as well as his third principle, highlights the obvious fact, which he is certainly not denying or underplaying, that churches have played a major part in the life of African Americans. But he is also right to point out that this does not mean an untroubled acceptance of all things Christian can be assumed. For example James Baldwin (1924–1987) one of black America's greatest writers, denounced the principles of the churches he grew up in as "blindness, loneliness and terror, the first principle necessarily cultivated in order to deny the two others."[55] Inevitably, the issue that exercised African Americans most was the gulf between what was said by white Christians and what they did or what they condoned. This in turn provoked a sharp version of the problem of evil: how could a loving God permit such suffering? For many African Americans, there was no convincing answer to this outside of assuming that no God existed in the first place.

One of the least-known facts about the civil rights movement was that one of the four people usually credited as the movement's leaders was a humanist. James Farmer (1920–1999) was the son of a preacher in Marshall, Texas. Rising quickly through the education given him, Farmer went to Wiley College in Marshall before going off to Howard University's School of Religion, from which he graduated in 1941. After graduation, Farmer refused to become a Methodist minister because he opposed that denomination's practice of segregating congregants. Instead he joined the Quaker Fellowship for Reconciliation. And in 1942, he helped found the Congress of Racial Equality (CORE), a civil rights organization intent on nonviolent protest against segregation and inequality. Farmer's mentor was Gandhi, whose insistence on nonviolence was paying huge dividends in India. Under Farmer's leadership, CORE organized the "Freedom Rides" throughout the

South as a protest against segregation in buses. He narrowly escaped being lynched in Plaquemine, Louisiana, for his efforts. Predictably, it was Farmer who ended up in jail after that incident, apparently for "disturbing the peace." He listened to Martin Luther King Jr.'s "I have a dream" speech in prison. In Farmer's absence, an aide read his speech on that day.

These and other activities meant Farmer is seen as one of the four most prominent black civil rights leaders of the 1960s, known as the "Big Four." The other three were Martin Luther King Jr. (1929–1968), Whitney Young (1921–1971), and Roy Wilkins (1901–1981). Farmer was also instrumental in recruiting Michael Schwerner and his two friends, who were murdered by white supremacists in 1964. Farmer left CORE in the later 1960s, when it began to move away from its nonviolent roots. From 1968 until 1971 he had a political career as a Republican, serving in the Nixon administration as assistant secretary of health, education, and welfare. In 1998, President Clinton awarded Farmer the Presidential Medal of Freedom. As happens so often, Farmer's humanism is ignored in the obituaries and accounts of his life. The fact is that James Farmer was a signatory to the *Humanist Manifesto 2000* and was on the advisory board of African Americans for Humanism.

As with the civil rights movement, so with the Harlem Renaissance, a period of great intellectual and cultural vitality in African American thought, which lasted from about 1917 until 1935. One of the more significant figures of this period was Langston Hughes, regarded by many as the African American poet laureate. Langston Hughes (1902–1967) was born in Joplin, Missouri, to a white father and a black mother. His parents divorced when he was very young, and he was brought up by his grandmother until he was thirteen. In the 1920s, he emerged as a major poetic talent. Two of the strongest influences on Hughes were Walt Whitman and Claude McKay (1889–1948), a Jamaican-born African American poet with humanist leanings.

As a youth, Hughes lost his faith, and some of his most powerful poems relate his views on religion. His early poem, "Goodbye Christ," written after a trip to the Soviet Union, attacked the church and praised communism, all of which landed him in a lot of trouble, particularly during the McCarthy years. He later apologized for writing "Goodbye Christ," not to appease his accusers, but because it no longer reflected his views. There were other poems which made his views on religion quite clear, including "Christ in Alabama." Another work, *I, Too, Sing America*, was a strong influence on Martin Luther King Jr. His first published work of poetry was *The Weary*

Blues (1926). He went on to publish twelve more volumes of poetry, and the *Collected Works of Langston Hughes* appeared in 1994. Hughes also wrote novels and drama. His first novel, *Not without Laughter* (1930) won the Harmon gold medal for literature. Despite these successes, his life was not easy. Though he earned a living from his writing, he was never far from the poverty line. He also struggled with being homosexual. Hughes did not use the word *humanist* to describe himself, but was explicitly atheist.

But beyond these few individuals, there was little or no infrastructure catering to African American humanists until late in the 1980s. A couple of courageous pioneers worked, without much reward, to build and sustain liberal religious or secular humanist organizations. Egbert Ethelred Brown (1875–1956) kept alive a patchy Unitarian presence in Harlem for thirty years, preaching a liberal Christianity. More directly humanist was Lewis A. McGee (1893–1979), who arrived at religious humanism in the late 1920s, but who hid his beliefs from his Methodist congregation for more than twenty years. Eventually he was able to leave, and in 1946 he enrolled at (where else?) Meadville Theological School, by this time known as Meadville Lombard. The following year he established the Free Religious Fellowship in Chicago, which was home to an eclectic mix of liberal theists, humanists, and atheists. It also crossed the racial divide. But Brown and McGee struggled at the periphery of their churches. Even the Unitarians had difficulties finding placements for black ministers.[56]

African American humanism needed to wait until the late 1980s before it could be adequately represented. The catalyst for the change was Paul Kurtz, who in 1989 employed Norm Allen to head up a branch of the Council for Secular Humanism devoted to African Americans. Allen had been raised in a God-fearing Pittsburgh family. His earliest memories of a religious nature were his prayers for deliverance from the interminable and boring church services that dominated his Sunday. The fact that the prayers went unanswered did not go unnoticed.[57] After periods of fervent evangelical Christianity, Black Power radicalism, Marxism, and Afrocentrism, Allen settled on humanism as his preferred lifestance. Now with the opportunity, care of Paul Kurtz, Allen set about establishing African Americans for Humanism (AAH), which began life in August 1989. His first move was to articulate a coherent program, and this came in the form of the *African American Humanist Declaration*. The goals of the AAH were listed as: fighting all forms of racism; incorporating an Afrocentric outlook into the broader world perspective; redressing the imbalance in historical studies that overlooks the contribution of Africans to world history; developing eupraxsophy among African American communities; improving the lot of African Americans through education and self-reliance; and building up self-help groups in the African American community.[58] The AAH has worked doggedly toward this end since then. But, as we will see in chapter 12, a good case could be made that AAH's finest hour was not in the United States at all, but in Africa.

PRAGMATIST, NATURALIST, AND SECULAR HUMANISM AFTER A CENTURY OF DEBATE

Paul Kurtz's career has been about trying to build a creative fusion between abolitionist humanism (which derives its strength from the criticism of supernaturalism) and substitutionist humanism (which focuses more on building a viable alternative to religious commitment and involvement). He has been trying to find a middle ground between rationalism and Romanticism, in the way we have seen thinkers since Niethammer trying to do. The other, related, bridge Kurtz has been working on is between pragmatism and scientific realism. Pragmatism had gone into a slump after World War II and remained alive on the edges of philosophical naturalism as articulated by Lamont, Hook, and Kurtz. This type of reconciliation remains a peculiarly American project because pragmatist-inclined humanism has always found its largest audience in America. Richard Rorty (1931–2007), the most prominent contemporary American pragmatist, became less patient with analytical philosophy and with the secular humanism he saw as dependent upon it. Rorty never ceased being a humanist, but he had a different way of expressing it than many of his colleagues. Rorty established his reputation with *Philosophy and the Mirror of Nature* (1979), which broke out against much of the Western intellectual tradition. His rebellion against traditional metaphysics and epistemology lies in what he sees as the long-standing mistake of philosophers to assume that their task is to reflect accurately a reality that is capable of accurate reflection. But to many of his colleagues' dismay he went on to agree with the proposition earlier generations of pragmatists had been anxious to avoid: that theories are true when people say they are true.

At no point in his career was Rorty opposed to all forms of Enlightenment rationalism. Its influence had, by and large, been beneficent. But, he added, does not philosophy lose too much when it dismisses from its ranks philosophers who aren't necessarily interested in addressing scientific issues, writing in a scientific way, or addressing a "canonical" list of approved philosophical problems? Indeed, not to do this was a mark of humanistic culture.[59] This is an entirely reasonable question, one we see humanists have answered in various ways since 1808. In the minds of many of his critics, however, the problem arose when Rorty was not content to leave it there. In *Contingency, Irony, and Solidarity* (1989), he developed his thoughts on the idea of a final vocabulary. This is the collection of words we carry around with us—and the ideas they are connected to—that we use when we describe ourselves to ourselves or to others. We will use our final vocabulary when we express admiration or condemnation and generally when we make sense of the world. But he goes on to say that there are two main personality types, which are understood in terms of how they relate to their own final vocabulary. There are the metaphysicians, who are those who search for the one true final vocabulary, and the ironists, who have deep doubts about their own final vocabulary (and are impressed by the strength with which others express theirs) but rather than adopt someone else's final vocabulary, remain ambivalent about the whole process.

Rorty had a distinct preference for the ironist, for a number of reasons. Metaphysicians delude themselves when they seek out the final vocabulary, assuming as they do the existence of one final truth above all others. For Rorty, the ironist is wise to abandon this futile quest and to enjoy the spirit of free inquiry as a sufficient end in itself. But rather than wallow in a nihilist morass, as his critics have accused him of leaving us with, Rorty insists on human solidarity, as we human beings, aware of our respective positions, work out a common purpose in the face of that pluralism. He specifically contrasts solidarity, as understood here, with objectivity, the more final-vocabulary-besotted goal of the positivist.

Critics accuse Rorty of throwing the baby out with the bathwater. It is one thing, they say, to see difficulties in getting an accurate picture of the world—an insight hardly original to Rorty. It is quite another to then declare that attempts at a comprehensive understanding of the world should be abandoned. Many antihumanists have said this, demanding along the way that science be declared simply one narrative among others. Rorty himself never went quite that far, although he has been criticized for seeing notions like "human rights" as being merely grammatical constructs, which has the effect of turning the protest at human rights violations into little more than an attempt at a discredited foundationalism. Edward Said was particularly critical in this respect.[60] For his part, Rorty thought his notion of solidarity took him beyond the hollow notion of deconstruction as an end in itself.

For a while Rorty spoke of himself as a postmodernist, although later he came to regret that usage. Certainly he is not to blame for the rapid descent of many postmodernists into precisely the sort of clannish insistence on prescribed sets of questions and a specific vocabulary with which to address them that he so deprecated. The problem remains, however, that postmodernism *has* become altogether a more pernicious regulator and censor of discourse and free inquiry than the so-called positivists ever were. In the end, Rorty remained a humanist, although he was happier along the porous boundary with literary humanism. Despite his reservations about naturalistic humanism, he accepted membership in 1988 of the International Academy of Humanism, an international symposium of humanist thinkers established by Paul Kurtz in 1983. And Rorty took particular care to identify with the humanist tradition anytime conspiracy theorists posited a fiendish plot by humanists and liberals to overthrow America. In the last interview before his death, he reiterated a point he made several times throughout his career. The development of a secularist moral tradition, one which "regards the free consensus of the citizens of a democratic society, rather than the Divine Will, as the source of moral imperatives," was the most important advance Western culture has made.[61] He sympathized with the European humanist tradition of civilized discourse that paid little attention to the divisions between disciplines, divisions which in the last half century have become armed walls in some cases. At this point Said agreed strongly with him, although he added that non-European traditions could also point to long traditions of humanist discourse, a point this book has, hopefully, underlined.[62]

If Rorty felt motivated to reject the narrower consequences of positivism, with its apparent willingness to prescribe and curtail, Daniel Dennett, by contrast, is motivated no less strongly against precisely the same tendencies within postmodernism. And both men call themselves humanists. In *Darwin's Dangerous Idea* (1995), Dennett identified himself as a secular humanist and, unlike Rorty, had less complaint with science's claim to a special position by virtue of its unique record of success in solving problems.[63] Somewhat confusingly, in more recent works, where he has criticized postmodernism and cultural relativists, who are happy to relativize everything in a barrage of verbiage, Dennett has labeled these people humanists.[64] This is the sort of confusion I lamented in the introduction.

Dennett is right to call his philosophy secular humanism. Along with evolutionary psychologists like Pascal Boyer and Scott Atran, Dennett refuses to talk of a fundamental divide between the natural and the supernatural. *All* thoughts and events take place within the context of the natural world in which we live, including supernatural constructs. Religion is a natural phenomenon in the sense that it "is a human phenomenon composed of events, organisms, objects, structure, patterns, and the like that all obey the laws of physics or biology, and hence do not involve miracles."[65] This important point has a long history in American philosophical naturalism and goes back to Frederick Woodbridge.[66] As such, religion needs to be studied as one would study any other natural phenomenon, with no special deference to the subject matter. Rorty would agree with this. The important insight here is the focus on the anthropomorphic elements in religion, where we project ourselves writ large across the universe. But where Feuerbach tolerated this and thought it understandable, even natural, the growing severity of the environmental crisis in the twenty-first century means we don't have this luxury. Thinking anthropocentrically may well be hardwired in us, but it is no less an encumbrance for that.

DOES HUMANISM HAVE A FUTURE IN AMERICA?

So, a century after religious humanists, pragmatists, and realists first crossed swords in America, the debate continues. The three principal strands of American humanism are there today, still contending with one another and still offering their respective visions to the world. Religious humanism is perhaps finding the current situation the most difficult, caught as it is with the legacy of a bland progressionism that is difficult to shake off. But the pragmatist and the naturalist variations of humanism are in good health and still have a great deal to contribute. Though differently balanced and with different emphases, all three are legitimate expressions of humanism. And neither is the divide between pragmatism and realism as deep as was once thought to be the case. The variation of pragmatism that has best weathered the philosophical storm over the last century is the naturalistic variant. The current naturalism is pragmatist by virtue of conducting its inquiries in a consistently empirical manner and in response to genuine human problems.[67] Corliss Lamont made the boldest attempt to fuse the naturalist, the pragmatist, and the cultural strands of humanism in one coherent package, but most of his successors have preferred to remain in one genre or another. Far from claiming to have achieved any great synthesis here, I am content to simply illustrate that humanists are capable of generating a wealth of insights.

At the start of the twenty-first century, the United States is well placed for a humanist future. This may seem an odd, even extraordinary statement, given its recent past. After all, several of the older generation of American philosophers have lamented the slide from what they remembered as pretty much a humanist consensus of the 1960s to the fractured state of things at the start of the twenty-first century.[68] But as against that, the Catholic philosopher Charles Taylor has lamented no less strongly the overwhelming secularist and humanist consensus in the academy today, although he does go on to add, correctly, that it has had less influence in disseminating its ideas beyond the gilded spires than European elites have.[69]

Taylor is correct to point to the strong hold that humanist outlooks, variously conceived, have in American academic life. Throughout the period we have examined, the line of tension has been between the variations of pragmatism and of naturalism or scientific realism. And, of course, there are now the so-called New Atheists, of whom three are based in the United States: Daniel Dennett, Sam Harris, and Christopher Hitchens. Dennett and Hitchens are scientific realists, but Harris holds a candle out for a variation of humanistically conceived Eastern thinking, particularly with respect to meditation. The vogue of the New Atheists is due largely to a new awareness among the post-9/11 public that fundamentalism is no longer a marginal nuisance one can afford to ignore.

Looking more broadly, there is evidence that the United States is becoming more diverse with respect to religion. The percentage of nonbelievers is growing, as is the percentage of adherents to non-Christian religions and systems of belief. And as Americans come to understand and appreciate the extent of this diversity, one can only hope they will also understand, in sufficient numbers, the pressing need for a secular state to give aid to all and special privileges to none. After all, as Susan Jacoby and others have shown, this is as authentically American an understanding as are those more inspired by religious exclusivism.[70] The reason to be hopeful is that this is understood as much by progressive religious thinkers as it is by secularists. The various humanist organizations remain relatively weak, particularly when compared to their vastly better-funded religious counterparts. But the calamitous Bush administration may well have been the high-water mark of the current wave of authoritarian Christian fundamentalism. Grave inroads into the separation of church and state have been made, but it is possible to hope that the secular core of American society will remain largely untouched long enough for the wounds to heal. The world needs this to happen.

PART TWO

TOWARD PLANETARY HUMANISM

CHAPTER 7

BILDUNG TO *LAÏCITÉ*: EUROPEAN HUMANISM

The humanism of Continental Europeans is of a different kind than that of the English-speaking world. Generally, the Europeans have remained closer to Niethammer's original use of the word in the sense of creating a cultural refinement, whereas the English-speaking world, in the twentieth century at least, devoted more attention to arguments around the existence of God and the ethical consequences arising from that. For many European humanists, the atheism of being contra-God was seen as coming from an earlier stage that had been passed through. Ludwig Feuerbach expressed this attitude very clearly in 1846:

> He who says no more of me than that I am an atheist, says and knows *nothing* of me. The question as to the existence or nonexistence of God, the opposition between theism and atheism belongs to the sixteenth and seventeenth centuries but not to the nineteenth. I deny God. But that means for me that I deny the negation of man. In place of the illusory, fantastic, heavenly position of man which in actual life necessarily leads to the degradation of man, I substitute the tangible, actual, and consequently also the political and social position of mankind.[1]

Such was the nature of his humanism that, though he had no doubt God was a human creation, Feuerbach thought no less of the notion of God for that. What mattered to Feuerbach was whether humans were aware of what they had created and of what that meant. As Sidney Hook put it in his insightful account of Feuerbach, whereas Descartes spoke of *cogito ergo sum*, Feuerbach proclaimed *sentio ergo sum*.[2] For most nonbelievers in the English-speaking world, the rejection of the God idea meant rejecting the value of that idea as well. This has been one of the more important faultlines running through world humanism in the past two centuries.

A great deal of European humanism can be explained as variations on the theme of understanding *sentio ergo sum*. One such strand of exploration and explanation is epitomized in the notion of *bildung*, a German word we introduced in chapter 1. *Bildung* is best understood in the broad sense as the full development of the individual. The person of bildung is the person of education and culture, with refined and developed tastes, and who is articulate, well read, and good company. What is more, bildung requires active effort, rather than the passive reception of received wisdom from figures of authority. This was the ideal of some of the most significant German humanists of the late eighteenth and early nineteenth centuries; men like Johann Wolfgang Goethe and Karl Wilhelm Humboldt (1767–1835) (whose profession of Christianity was nominal at best) and Johann Cristoph Friedrich von Schiller (who was an avowed pagan). And no relation to Ferdinand Schiller (whom we discussed in chapter 2. Hegel and Niethammer both assigned bildung an important place in their respective systems. For Hegel, history is the slow coming of humanity to consciousness of itself and of the central role freedom has with respect to oneself. And bildung has this role of gradually coming to consciousness of freedom in a more secular context than in its earlier, Christian auspices.

A very few words on Goethe's conception of bildung is necessary. Goethe spoke of Christianity as the ultimate religion, but his understanding of Christianity would not be recognized by most Christians. He also spoke of this "Jewish nonsense," and lamented that Homer had not remained the primary scripture of European peoples. This should not be taken as evidence of anti-Semitism. It has more to do with the division, which we will discuss in the next chapter, between the rational, Apollonian tradition and its more frenzied, faith-centered strand, that is, what have been called the "Athens" and "Jerusalem" strands of European Christianity. When Goethe spoke of Christianity he meant a radically attenuated religion of humanity. So radical was this attenuation, he did not even mean it in the sense of the perennial philosophy of the mystics or as an amalgam of the common beliefs of all religions. It was a highly abstracted conception of the elevated human condition. In this way, he thought of the crucifixion and resurrection of Christ as a confirmatory example of this elevated human condition. In his poem "Die Geheimnisse," Goethe wrote of the monk Humanus who leads a monastery with twelve knightly monks. Humanus is a personification of pure and universal humanity. Christianity is absorbed into humanity. Like Hegel, with whom he corresponded on these matters, Goethe had no concern at all for the details of Christian theology. "We shall all grow gradually," Goethe wrote, "from a Christianity of word and faith to a Christianity of disposition and deed."[3] The story of nineteenth-century bildung was the story of that unfolding.

Bildung can also be associated with what English speakers call a "Renaissance man," which means a cultured person well versed in the arts and sciences, who is active in civic affairs and who has a full family life. This was what Friedrich Immanuel Niethammer had in mind when he coined the word *humanism* and what Paul Kurtz had in mind when he coined the word *eupraxsophy*. Bildung has a great deal in common with the Confucian ideal of the *junzi*, or superior man. And despite the sexist origins of Renaissance man, superior man, and so on, there is no reason whatsoever that these notions need be limited in the future in the way they were in the past.

A less helpful element in bildung was the inference that the cultivation of the individual was best pursued by withdrawing oneself from active participation in the public affairs of the community. The civic-mindedness so prominent in the Greek conception of *paideia*, from which Western humanism developed, did not flower in the notion of bildung. The younger Thomas Mann was an exponent of the narrower form of bildung but came around to a more expansive understanding of the term, a change forced on him by the Nazi takeover. And Friedrich Nietzsche coined the word *bildungsphilister* to denote the mediocrity of one who cultivates cultural depth without ever really wanting it for its own sake or appreciating what it actually means. This said as much about Nietzsche's hatred of the middle classes as it did about the malady he claimed to have identified. Many European humanists now speak of *laïcité*, which can be loosely translated as "secularism," but which also invokes the committed moral secularism championed by George Jacob Holyoake and others.

THOMAS MANN, THE RELUCTANT HUMANIST

There are so many places one could begin a discussion of modern European humanism, but the discussion so far on the tradition of bildung goes a long way to justifying the choice made here. Thomas Mann (1875–1955) was the twentieth century's most important German novelist. But he was more than a novelist in the sense of simply being a storyteller. He was also a subtle and wide-ranging thinker whose own personal development is as interesting as his written work. Mann was born and raised in Lübeck, but much of his life in Germany was spent in Munich. Though his parents were German, his mother's family had origins in Brazil. While still only twenty-five years old, Mann wrote *Buddenbrooks* (1901), which told the tale of a German family, not unlike his own, which had declined over a few generations as robust business talent gave way to artistic leanings. This book is cited as the principal reason he was awarded the Nobel Prize for Literature in 1929. Mann became one of the greatest practitioners of what Germans call the *bildungsroman*, or the novel designed to show the intellectual, spiritual, and cultural development of the main character. An early short story with strong autobiographical overtones, *Tonio Kröger* (1903) has Kröger commit his life to writing without the customary and vehement rejection of all things bourgeois.[4] Neither did he have time for the romantic notion of art for art's sake—yet another example of humanism standing in opposition to Romanticism. Unlike so many of his contemporaries, Mann understood how central his bourgeois background was to his literary calling. You can't produce the bildungsroman without a bourgeois appreciation of bildung. And neither can one have bildung without educators to show us the way. Mann admired most artists who appreciated their role as educator, something that brought two of his main heroes together—Goethe and Tolstoy—despite their otherwise huge dissimilarities.

It took a long time for this to come together as humanism. For much of his early life, Mann was socially conservative, antidemocratic, and apolitical, something that led, especially after the Great War had set in, to serious strains with Heinrich, his older and more progressive brother. Thomas Mann's views found expression in *Confessions of an Unpolitical Man* (1918), in which he distinguished the debilitating notion of civilization, with its implications of internationalism, from *Kultur*, with its more nationalistic focus. Here he advanced the older, more conservative reading of bildung, which feared that association with politics only coarsened the individual. In the very same year Heinrich Mann published his novel *Man of Straw*, which exposed brilliantly the sham values of much of what Thomas had held up for admiration.

As German politics went from bad to worse, Thomas slowly revised his views, seeing his earlier stance as an evasion of responsibility. He came to see that Heinrich had been right and he had been wrong. From 1922, particularly after the assassination of Walther Rathenau by an anti-Semitic fanatic, Mann was supporting the Weimar government with a passion difficult to infer from his 1918 *Confessions*. Being apolitical, he now realized, was a luxury he could not afford. By the time the Nazis took power in Germany, he was, however reluctantly, a leading advocate of an active and humanistic notion of bildung, which encouraged involvement in political life. All this came too late for Germany.

Humanism features significantly in Thomas Mann's seminal novel *The Magic Mountain* (1924), in which the main character, Hans Castorp, is both spectator and target of two rival systems. Ludovico Settembrini stands in for the humanist tradition and Father Naphta is the reactionary Catholic who despises pretty much every aspect of modernity, as the Church of his day required of him. Humanists, Settembrini notes, have a pedagogical bent, there being a historical link between schoolmasters and humanism. In a passionate declaration of his humanist credo, Settembrini declares his aversion to the life-and-body-denying code of the ascetic.

> I affirm, honour and love the body, as I protest I affirm, honour, and love form, beauty, and freedom, gaiety, and enjoyment of life. I represent the world, the interest of this life, against a sentimental withdrawal and negation, classicism against Romanticism. . . . By all means I am a humanist, because I am a friend of mankind, like Prometheus, a lover of humanity and human nobility.[5]

But Settembrini is never given all the best parts and allowed to shine in a superficial way. On several occasions he illustrates the weaknesses of European humanism, being at times Eurocentric, even racist, as when he warns of accepting notions of time that come from the vast Asian wastelands. But for all his faults, Settembrini is a much more attractive character than the misanthropic Naphta.

It is often said that *The Magic Mountain* is about the poverty of the humanist and Christian systems as commonly conceived in the years before World War I. But whatever truth that claim may have is tempered by Mann's own enthusiasm for humanism while he was writing the book. In a letter to a correspondent in 1922, he spoke of his "infatuation with the idea of humanism, which I have noted in myself for some time . . ." and which he linked to his work on *The Magic Mountain*.[6] His humanism owed a great deal to Goethe, who had little time for Christian dogma but admired deeply what he saw as Christianity's civilizing, antibarbarian tendencies. This refinement and humanity was the essence of bildung, although Mann's other mentor, Nietzsche, ensured his rendering of bildung would never make any concessions to dogmatic religion.

Mann's enthusiasm for humanism was in the context of a defeated and increasingly chaotic Germany trying to find new roots for development. One such attempt was to recapture the educational sense of humanism, as scholars and intellectuals tried to devise a new system of education for a citizenry trained in the ways of democracy. There was, for instance a conference of educators and scholars in 1921 at Hanstein, near Göttingen. The proceedings of the conference were published in a pamphlet called *Humanismus, Hochshule, und Student*. It was the aim of this movement to introduce an interdisciplinary, organic style of education in the hope of producing well-rounded, autonomous citizens. The rigid disciplinary divisions and social inequalities of Wilhelmine education were to be replaced by confident, cosmopolitan new Germans able to manage uncertainty and change in life. It is one of Germany's—and the world's—tragedies that this movement was not successful. While the details of this educational humanism differ, it is in the same tradition as Friedrich Niethammer's work more than a century previous.

From the middle of the 1920s, Mann became increasingly alarmed by the rise of tribalism and irrationalism in general and of Nazism in particular. And it was in the context of this darkening of the European aspect that he came to appreciate the limitations of a passive, uninvolved bildung. The common bourgeois willingness to turn a blind eye to the destruction of democratic society revealed the impotence of an ascetic, cloistered bildung. It was no longer enough to assert blandly that "we" will be able to control the Nazis once they've done the service of destroying the Communists. In October 1930, after the Nazis achieved an electoral breakthrough, Mann wrote an open letter to the German people, warning of the dangers of allowing the Nazis to grow stronger and urging a common front against them. The open letter was called an "Appeal to Reason." He followed this up with a speech in Berlin that Nazis tried to disrupt. He must have been gratified when the hecklers were silenced by the crowd. All the same, he and his wife had to be led out of the building through some corridors to an unmarked exit after the meeting.

Mann continued his anti-Nazi work up to and beyond the moment when Hitler became chancellor on January 30, 1933. He left Germany shortly afterward, not to return for sixteen years, during which time he became the voice of the other Germany, the Germany of Goethe, Beethoven, and Schiller, the Germany of an engaged, civilized bildung. The vehicle for much of this work was a journal he helped establish, called *Mass und Wert* (*Measure and Worth*), which attracted a large number of exiled German thinkers and writers. During a speaking tour of East European capitals in 1936, he spoke of the need to articulate a "militant humanism" in the face of the dangers of fascism.[7] And his tours of, and eventual settling in, the United States also helped keep alive the memory of a civilized Germany in that country.

In the later part of his life, Mann contributed in no small way, however reluctantly at times, to overcoming the limitations of Settembrini's humanism he had articulated so well in *The Magic Mountain*. *Dr. Faustus* involves a dialogue between humanist and other outlooks. But in this later work, though the vulnerability of humanism is acknowledged, so also was its essential role as an agent of civilization. The narrator, Serenus Zeitblom, identifies himself repeatedly through the book as a humanist, and, for all of his failings—a want of humor and imagination—he is not encumbered with Settembrini's more obvious faults. Indeed, Mann has Zeitblom repeat some of his own denunciations of Nazism from his various speeches and addresses. The story is set through the first four decades of the twentieth century, but Mann has Zeitblom writing the story down in the last months of World War II, as the Germany of his youth and manhood crashes and burns. Adrian Leverkühn, the musical genius whose life Zeitblom is retelling, had consorted with the devil in return for his musical gifts. Leverkühn's moral disease is represented in a physical form as syphilis, working once again the leitmotif of disease serving as a metaphor for a broader, more psychosocial malady. And Leverkühn's death was given as August 25, 1940, pretty much the high point of Nazi power in Europe. So, whatever reconstruction of postwar Germany there was to be would take place not in the image of Leverkühn but of Zeitblom.

At the end of 1948, Mann was understandably more pessimistic about humanism and humanity in general. When asked by the journal of the American Humanist Association for his current views, he distanced himself from what he called *classical humanism*, saying that this stance was no longer possible. But the humanism he did articulate was of the same nuanced, civilized variety he had aired in *Dr. Faustus*. He went on to say:

[M]y hopes are aimed at the development of a new humanism which is no longer purely optimistic, but religiously tinged and deeply experienced in all the dark aspects of life, a humanism which derives its pride from the unique and mysterious position of man between nature and mind.[8]

Mann was far from advocating a religious humanism as understood in the United States. His use of *religious* was in no way supernatural or even transcendental. It is better understood as *existential* or simply *deep*. In another essay, Mann looked forward to the coming of a third humanism, one that "will not flatter mankind, looking at it through rose-colored glasses." This new humanism would, without romantic extravagance, recognize that humanity's beauty lies precisely in its fusion of the natural and the spiritual.[9] Once again, we feel the presence of Niethammer.

ALBERT CAMUS AND THE ABSURD REBEL

Another exemplar of the humanism of character is Albert Camus (1913–1960). Because he is so often pigeonholed as "one of the existentialists," it is difficult to speak of him in other contexts. But in fact, Camus consistently refused the label, replying that existentialism, like Marxism, presumes to have all the answers, and if there was anything central to Camus' thought, it is that there are no easy answers.

An important fact about Camus was that he was born not in mainland France but in French Algeria. His rubbing shoulders with the Muslim majority of Algeria should help give Camus a renewed relevance in the first half of the twenty-first century, as Westerners seek to do the same. The death of his father as a result of wounds from a shell blast at the Battle of the Marne in 1914 meant the family was brought up in poverty. Luckily for young Albert, his teachers recognized his intelligence and provision was made for him to have an education his family could not have afforded from its own means. An early literary influence was Thomas Mann's *The Magic Mountain*. Camus worked in Algeria as a journalist and playwright before moving to France only weeks before the German invasion. While in Algeria, he consistently opposed the reactionary French establishment, which maintained the system of disenfranchisement and inequality of the Muslim population. In the last months of the German occupation, he worked with the

French Resistance. Camus won the Nobel Prize for Literature in 1957. He died as a passenger in a car accident in 1960.

Camus met and befriended Jean-Paul Sartre in 1943, a friendship that ended in 1952 in a violent disagreement that became a *cause celèbre*. The split was more than a clash of personalities, or even of their sharply contrasting views on existentialism. For example, they had radically different views on the Soviet Union. Sartre became more dogmatically supportive of the Soviet Union and of Marxism while Camus was strongly anti-Communist. He had been a member of the Communist Party briefly in Algeria, mainly because it was the best organized vehicle for progressive agitation. He was always skeptical about Marxist thought and it wasn't long before Marxist practice looked just as suspect. Camus was expelled in 1937 for his opposition to Moscow's latest twist in foreign policy priorities, this time requiring a downscaling of anticolonialist activities. Camus was, we can see now, more consistent in his defense of freedom than Sartre, who juggled his views on freedom with belligerent apologetics for Marxism. And Camus' writing has stood the test of time in the way most of Sartre's has not.

Camus found his audience in the months after the liberation of Paris in August 1944. As a senior editorial journalist on the resistance journal *Combat*, he articulated a new morality, a new sense of urgency, and a new determination that the postwar France must not look like the prewar France. Camus' humanism found itself running up against the dogmatism of the reactionary Catholics on the one hand and of the communists on the other. The Catholic thinker François Mauriac (1885–1970) became particularly venomous about Camus, rarely turning down an opportunity for an attack. For example, in October 1944, Mauriac sneered that Camus could not desist from using Christian imagery in his writing about the new France. Camus responded that the Christian thinks injustice in the world is always compensated by justice in the afterlife. But we have chosen, he responded, "to accept human justice with its terrible imperfections, careful only to correct it through a desperately maintained honesty."[10] This would be one of the most eloquent expressions of meliorism encountered in this book.

Camus' genius was to articulate the ethical consequences of the fact that there is no God. In the manner of the passage from Feuerbach quoted at the beginning of this chapter, Camus took it as that the truth-claims of Christianity were untrue. He was not interested in the arguments for and against religion as they were carried out in English-speaking countries. He took his atheism seriously and wrote about the tragic freedom that wells up once one realizes that there is no God to hold one's hand. In this vein, Camus called his first major writing projects the "Three Absurds." These works began from the premise, itself unexplored, of atheism, and then went on to explore what he thought that meant for us. They were his novel *The Outsider*, his play *Caligula*, and, what many people consider his masterpiece, his essay "The Myth of Sisyphus." Here Camus placed his absurd between the Scylla of phenomenology as articulated by Husserl on the one hand and the Charybdis of the self-absorbed existentialism of Kierkegaard on the other. He saw little real difference between Husserl's abstract god and Kierkegaard's irrational commitment. And he made explicit his point of difference with existentialists. "The theme of the irrational, as it is conceived by the existentialists, is reason becoming confused and escaping by negating itself. The absurd is lucid reason noting its limits."[11] Camus' humanism revolved around the exploration of these limits.

> I don't know whether this world has a meaning that transcends it. But I know that I do not know that meaning and that it is impossible for me just now to know it. What can a meaning outside my condition mean to me? I can understand only in human terms. What I touch, what resists me—that is what I understand.[12]

The different modes of expression notwithstanding, this is much what Schiller was saying. Here is Schiller's Protagoras restating that "man is the measure," but in terms more modest and poetic than was in Schiller's blood to do. Certainly, Camus was unsympathetic to the man-is-the-measure notion when taken as an example of human hubris. He refers to this in *The Plague* (1947), his parable of the spread of evil, which he tells in the form of the plague overwhelming his hometown. Our townsfolk, he wrote,

> were like everybody else, wrapped up in themselves; in other words they were humanists; they disbelieved in pestilences. A pestilence isn't a thing made to man's measure; therefore we tell ourselves that pestilence is a mere bogey of the mind, a bad dream that will pass away. But it doesn't always pass away and, from one bad dream to another, it is men who pass away, and the humanists first of all, because they haven't taken their precautions.[13]

If humanists are taken to task for their lack of cosmic modesty, *The Plague* is a quintessentially humanist novel. Camus has Bernard Rieux, the main character, reject Father Paneloux's claim that he too is working for people's salvation. "Salvation's much too big a word for me. I don't aim so high. I'm concerned with man's health; and for me his health comes first."[14] Interestingly, Paneloux, who we meet first delivering a fire-and-brimstone sermon warning the people that the plague is God's punishment for their sins, wills his own death after seeing the death of a small boy, too young to have amassed the volume of sin to justify such a painful demise. And, of course, we should note the interesting coincidence of two great humanist novelists, Thomas Mann with *Dr. Faustus* and Albert Camus with *The Plague*, publishing in the same year works that used disease as a metaphor for moral and societal illness.

The year after *The Plague* was published, Camus returned to this ambiguous humanism when he addressed a Dominican monastery. There he said that though he is "pessimistic as to human destiny, I am optimistic as to man. And not in the name of a humanism that always seemed to me to fall short, but in the name of an ignorance that tries to negate nothing." Camus went on to conclude that it is wisest to pay attention not to what divides us but to what unites us.[15] So the *New York Times* editorial wasn't so wrong when, commenting on him receiving the Nobel Prize for Literature, it stated: "His is one of the few literary voices that has emerged from the chaos of the postwar world with the balanced, sober outlook of humanism."[16]

The first phase of Camus' writing career focused on the absurd and was individualist in orientation. But in the transition from *The Outsider* to *The Plague*, which was published five years later in 1947, the transition is to seeing things more socially. How things impact on others is the next step that a great deal of existentialist thinking never made. Camus consummated this transition with the other idea he is famous for exploring: the rebel. This is not to say there is anything new in writing about the rebel, of course. In many ways the rebel is the default archetype for freethinkers. Following the lead of Prometheus, freethinkers rebel against tyranny, even when the tyrant is Zeus himself. It takes a rebellious spirit to see through the conformism and anthropocentric conceit implicit in the god idea. The twentieth-century rationalist Joseph McCabe asked that his tombstone should read: "He was a rebel to his last breath." It did not, but he was. And Bertrand Russell said: "Without rebellion, mankind would stagnate, and injustice would be irremediable."[17] It would, and it would. And, as we saw in the previous chapter, Anthony B. Pinn has suggested that Nimrod could act as the rebel prototype for African Americans. But it was Camus who created the most memorable vision of the rebel, in a book by that name, published in 1951. The rebel is the person who says no, but who, in saying no, is not simply mouthing a renunciation. That primary act of rebellion is the essential preliminary to thinking for oneself.

Camus' rebellion is different from Christian forms of rebellion, which are quickly rendered futile by its promises of eternal life. It is of first importance to Camus that the rebellion takes place in the face of the certainty and utter finality of our death. The rebel is an atheist and the rebellion is against anthropocentric conceit. Camus' insight has provided the hitherto underappreciated tragic dimension to atheist thought. More recently, the idea has been carried on by the American philosopher Erik J. Wielenberg. In a study of humanist ethics, Wielenberg proposes the hero as the appropriate self-image the naturalist should adopt. Who but a hero—and by implication, a rebel—could reject the command moralities on offer and create instead a coherent and stable moral system; fashion an understanding of meaning, purpose, and the good life; and retain the unforced ability to love life and live for the moment?[18] Only a rebel would wish to do so and only a hero would succeed, or even fail with integrity. And yet it happens all the time. People outside conventional religious systems live happy, successful lives and raise united and stable families, all while being told they are somehow missing an essential element or that their lives are somehow empty.

Before we leave the notion of the absurd, it is worth noting that Camus was not alone in developing the notion of absurdity. Alongside the warm, nonanalytical, Mediterranean-inspired thinker was the Swedish secularist philosopher Ingemar Hedenius (1908–1982), who developed a philosophy of absurdism that owed more to Northern pessimism. For Hedenius, absurdism had two factors. The first is the recognition that in the world of humans, anything can happen, without regard to its awfulness, meanness of spirit, or downright stupidity. And it follows from this that absurd things happen all the time and always have. Everything from the rise of National Socialism to petty academic intrigues tended to confirm Hedenius's conviction in the ubiquity of the absurd. It also underscored his essentially melancholic view of life.

IS EXISTENTIALISM A HUMANISM?

Camus can be understood as a humanist just as well as he can as an existentialist. The pairing of Jean-Paul Sartre (1905–1980) with humanism has been a lot more controversial, with humanist thinkers from Hector Hawton to Clive James adamant in denying the link. James has gone so far as to suggest that Sartre's bad faith with respect to his resistance record during the war and his apologies for Soviet repression after it automatically disqualify his credentials as a humanist.[19] This is going too far, if only because it fails to take account of the stages in Sartre's career. For a few years after World War II, we can legitimately speak of a humanist Sartre. This phase began with his famous lecture, given in Paris at the end of the war, which is often cited as the day existentialism came to public attention.[20] The lecture was originally called "Existentialism Is a Humanism" and was translated into English into the blander "Existentialism and Humanism." Sartre's task of identification was made easier by recognizing only two types of humanism. As so many had done before him, he was careful to distance existentialism from the positivism of Comte, which he saw as holding humanity up as the supreme value. How can this be done when humanity is, as he put it "still to be determined"?

The only other humanism Sartre recognized was the type Schiller had spoken of four decades earlier: the humanism of Protagoras. There is, Sartre said, no other universe except the universe we perceive, the universe of human subjectivity. And again, while the language in which Sartre's appeal is couched, he is not saying anything that Schiller had not said all those years before. "This is humanism," Sartre wrote, "because we remind man that there is no legislator but himself; that he himself, thus abandoned, must decide for himself; also because we show that it is not by turning back upon himself, but always by seeking beyond himself, an aim which is one of liberation or of some particular realization, that man can realize himself as truly human."[21]

Where Sartre was advancing from Schiller was his recognition that existentialist humanism is taking the consequences of atheism seriously. There is no God, so how does one live? While many people, with some justice, have decried the subjectivism and narcissism at the heart of the existentialist project, they at least took this question seriously. But taking the question seriously did not mean it would be examined thoroughly. In this sense, existentialism was thoroughly European because, once identified as a core issue, it was then pretty much left alone. Sartre finished his lecture by saying that, in the end, it doesn't matter whether or not God exists. The real question is that each individual needs to find him- or herself, and this imperative remains true without regard to the status of God's existence. The core of existentialist humanism is the understanding that our freedom only has any meaning insofar as we understand the interdependence of our freedom with that of other people. This is an argument others fleshed out more thoroughly than Sartre did.

Despite the many criticisms that have been directed against it, existentialism was nonetheless a bold step forward. In 1945, many people found it difficult to imagine the basis upon which a coherent ground for living was possible. As in 1918, the aftermath of World War II revealed the shallowness and perniciousness of so many elements of European thought and morals. And even more than it did in 1918, it seemed more than likely that renewed hostilities, this time between the Americans and the Russians, were just around the corner. And this would be a nuclear conflict. So the problem of building a coherent morality in 1945, in the wake of Auschwitz and Hiroshima and in the shadow of the A-bomb, was a real one. Existentialism suggested a way. The fashionable pessimism and narcissism was still to come. At this time Sartre was still emphasizing the optimism of his brand of atheistic existentialism. Yes, personal decisions could be made, and, yes, those decisions mattered. We are not bound by tradition and convention unless we choose to be so bound. His ideas of authenticity and bad faith remain permanent contributions to ethics. People could understand them and could be empowered by them.

So Sartre was right in 1945. The existentialism of which he spoke then was indeed a humanism. A new type of humanism, to be sure; a humanism drifting away from many of the known landmarks humanists had come to rely on over the past century. But if Sartre was right in 1945, he was not right for long. Existentialism was a humanism, but only briefly. Sartre's growing willingness to hitch existentialism up with Marxism derailed what was already unstable freight. A plausible date to end Sartre's humanist phase could be 1950, when he broke off relations with David Rousset (1912–1997), a survivor of Buchenwald who wanted to extend the widespread revulsion to Nazi concentration camps to all existing camps, including those in the Soviet Union. Sartre and his friend Maurice Merleau-Ponty (1908–

1961) were fiercely critical of Rousset for making a blanket condemnation of all terror, regardless of where it is perpetrated. Sartre's split with Camus in 1952 sharpened the trajectory of his brand of existentialism away from humanism. Sartre was now fatally compromised as an apologist of the Soviet Union, leaving people like Rousset and Camus to articulate the tradition of radical freedom and decision that was best in existentialism. And, as we have seen, Camus consistently denied he was an existentialist.

MARTIN HEIDEGGER AND PRIMORDIAL BEING

One person who wanted nothing to do with the warm, vibrant existentialism of 1945 was the person often given much of the credit for generating the ideas that led to it. A year after Sartre's address, Martin Heidegger wrote the first draft of his "Letter on Humanism." Heidegger at this time was brooding resentfully under the restrictions placed upon him by the denazification process, restrictions he could see no earthly justification for. He was isolated, resentful, and ill. In this state, between December 1946 and the middle of 1947 he worked on the "Letter on Humanism." Heidegger scholars generally see the letter as one of his important later works because it signposted new directions from his magnum opus, *Being and Time*. The letter is important to us, obviously, because it deals with humanism, but also because of its influence on later antihumanist thought. Ostensibly, it was written in response to a question from a French correspondent as to whether meaning could be restored to the word *humanism*. In light of Sartre's considerable publicity, the query was timely and gave Heidegger the opportunity to put things straight, as he saw it. But the request also gave him an opportunity to frame his philosophy in the light of the postwar conditions. And anyone who hoped for some form of reassessment of his thought with a view to offering something like an apology for his past support for Nazism was to be disappointed. His response was characteristic. He returned to *das Man*, his dismissive term used in *Being and Time* to mean the average, uninitiated herd. Any ism is no more than the *das Man*'s clamour to deflect itself away from the primordial reality of Being. Constructing a worldview, speaking of ethics, physics, or humanism; all these are superficial noises made to drown out the quiet essence of Being.

Humanism, Heidegger argued, by virtue of its essentially metaphysical nature, is unable to ask the only serious question: the relation of Being to the essence of man. Humanism can do no more than think in terms of rational animals, as "one living creature among others in contrast to plants, beasts, and God."[22] But in this *animalitas*, Heidegger argues, the *humanitas* is forgotten. At this point, Heidegger introduces one of his notorious linguistic creations, often translated as *ek-sistence*, which "not only [is] the ground of the possibility of reason, *ratio*, but also is that in which the essence of man preserves the source that determines him."[23] Ek-sistence is a faculty available only to humans. He then went on to dissociate ek-sistence from traditional notions of the soul and mind. But his most emphatic rejection was reserved for science. He was left with nothing more than a blank assertion. "The fact that physiology and physiological chemistry can scientifically investigate man as an organism is no proof that in this 'organic' thing, that is, in the body scientifically explained, the essence of man consists."[24] By preserving this talk of essence, Heidegger retained, however eccentrically, an exalted sense of the uniqueness of humanity. His objection to humanism was not that it wrongly exalts humanity too much, but that it does not do so enough. Whether speaking of *animalitas*, or of man as special by virtue of having a soul, none come near to the primordial core Heidegger has revealed for us in the concept of ek-sistence. Man, he says, is the shepherd of Being, and humanism, locked as it is in futile metaphysics, can never come close to appreciating this.

Heidegger's attempt at an answer offers little consolation to his critics. Being, Heidegger writes, "is the nearest. Yet the near remains farthest from man."[25] And, significantly, Being, as the "dimension of the *ecstasis* of ek-sistence," is more essential than humanity.[26] One does not ascend to Being, one descends, "by climbing back down into the nearness of the nearest."[27] The core property is not humanity but Being.[28] Human values have no value because humans value them, that is mere "subjectivizing." Valuing does not let beings be, it requires them to be valid according to some arbitrary standard. This is "the greatest blasphemy imaginable against Being."[29] In effect, any human—and, by implication, any humanist—estimation of values is going at some point to offend the primordial claim of Being. Primordiality, another of Heidegger's favorite notions of the postwar years, is the nearest to man, and yet, because of our superficial adherence to metaphysics and values, the furthest away as well. It is hard not to see that the only way toward the required level of primordiality is to think with the blood, as Hermann Goering recommended, or simply not to think at all. Thinking, Heidegger said, never creates the house of Being.[30] Only primordiality, unmediated by metaphysics, can do that.

The important point for our purposes is that this is not humanism. Heidegger himself said as much insofar as humanism thinks metaphysically (according to his understanding of the word), or insofar as it is existentialism.[31] The essential factor is not humanity, Heidegger, said, but Being. Here he quoted Parmenides approvingly: "for there is Being." In the way that Protagoras's "man is the measure" summed it all up for Schiller, so did this passage from Parmenides for Heidegger. "The primal mystery for all thinking is concealed in this phrase."[32] And for Heidegger that may well be true, but no humanism can be built upon that phrase. In the event we decide to retain the word at all, *humanism* means "that the essence of man is essential for the truth of Being, specifically in such a way that the word does not pertain to man simply as such."[33]

More than one critic of Heidegger has observed his inability to give any clear guide on what Being is. In several places, including the "Letter on Humanism," he is careful to tell us what it is not. For instance, it is not God, or any other creation of metaphysics. Elsewhere he resorts to paradoxical statements about Being as "the ungraspable," or "self-disclosing," except to Heidegger of course. In the letter he is reduced to this: "Yet Being—what is Being? It is It itself. The thinking that is to come must learn to experience that and to say it."[34] On other occasions Heidegger stresses the all-embracingness of Being. Being is not simply something within us, which humans need to become aware of. It is out there, which we become aware of only by grace or the revelation of Being. But, Heidegger then wavers on the vital question of whether or not Being required beings. This inconsistency, noted by Paul Edwards, is central to Heidegger's project and was never resolved.[35] This inconsistency gets to the heart of the Heideggerian project, and it will not do, as Richard Rorty has done, to claim that the idea of Being is not essential to Heidegger's work, being nothing more than a "rhetorical blemish."[36] To do this is to talk of apple pie without the apples.

No more justifiable is the attempt by several Heideggerians to contextualize Heidegger's lament about humanity's forgetfulness of Being in terms of being estranged from nature or one's inner feelings. As Edwards has remarked, this misses the important point that, for Heidegger, such things as nature, our surroundings, even our feelings, are beings, not Being.[37] Thinkers have for centuries called us to take heed of our nature and our surroundings. We do not need Heidegger's barbarous prose to remind us of that. His gloomy prophecy that we can do nothing but wait for the time when Being "will become thought-provoking to man."[38] This reflects his growing realization that National Socialism had not proved to be the vehicle for this apotheosis he had so triumphantly announced in his *Rektoradsrede* in 1933.

It is perhaps best to see Heidegger as a Teutonic Taoist. His gnomic encapsulations of Being resemble attempts to speak of the Tao, if without the poetry. Neither Being nor the Tao can be spoken of outside the language of paradox. For those favorable to this strain of thought, it is an attempt to gather in the mystery of living. To those unmoved to it, such writing is, to use Susan Haack's term, *glossogonous word-salad*. But either way, it is not humanism. For all Heidegger's objections, his assertion—for that is all it is—that humans (and only humans) are potential bearers of a unique primordial grounding stands in the same tradition as claims about eternal souls, vital sparks, blood and soil, the Unconscious, and all other manifestations of anthropocentric conceit. But it is precisely this form of conceit that poses the single biggest obstacle to any genuine humanist exploration of the fragile, interdependent reality of being human. We should also note the paradox that Heidegger spoke approvingly of essences, claiming that humanism lacks or misses the only essence that matters, while his postmodernist heirs have derided humanism not so much for missing the true essence but for claiming an essence in the first place. Forgotten in all this is the neglected truth that humanists, certainly the more secular-oriented ones, have virtually never spoken of essences in the first place.

KARL JASPERS AND LIMITLESS COMMUNICATION

It has been Karl Jaspers's fate not only to be habitually lumped in as an existentialist but also, far more debilitating, to be forever in Heidegger's shadow. This is unfair because, unlike Heidegger, Jaspers (1883–1969) has much to say that is of value to humanism. Paul Tillich got the heart of the difference between the two when he said that Heidegger's core concern was what it means to *be*, while Jaspers wanted to understand what it means to *be a person.*[39] This is a skill that is going to be relevant in the twenty-first century. Karl Jaspers was born in Oldenburg, northwestern Germany, the son of a prosperous bank manager on his father's side and from a line of well-off farmers on his mother's. He graduated with a medical degree in 1909 after finding the Neo-Kantian philosophy he had originally studied dry and irrelevant. In 1910 he married Gertrude Mayer, a scholar of great ability, and a practicing Jew. Their marriage was happy and Gertrude was an invaluable supporter, critic, and colleague throughout his career. After World War I, Jaspers returned to philosophy, despite strong opposition from entrenched interests, who viewed him as an interloper. And when the Nazis took power, he was progressively shut out of the academic world, and he narrowly escaped being sent to an extermination camp at the end of the war.

Jaspers came into his own after the war as a major philosophical figure who had opposed the Nazis and who could help Germans deal with their burden of guilt. He stood in stark contrast to Heidegger in this respect, who never admitted any sense of guilt or responsibility for what the Nazis had done. For Heidegger the Nazis were a promise betrayed, while for Jaspers they were a threat realized. This could only affect their respective attitudes toward humanism. Jaspers identified much more closely with the bildung tradition and spoke of humanism as embodying the culture of European civilization. Its importance is not as a great system of philosophy but as "an attitude toward tradition and learning, an attitude of openness and human freedom, without which our Western life would be impossible."[40] Having just emerged from the Nazi years, Jaspers knew that was not an overstatement.

Though his influence in Germany after the war was great, he has not crossed over into English to the extent that Heidegger has. And though nowhere near as abstruse as Heidegger, Jaspers did tend toward the prolix. One of his core notions, *existenz*, was as elusive as many other existentialist terms, and indeed, not unlike some ruminations on the Tao. As he who seeks the Tao shall never find it, and as he who claims to understand the Tao never will, so is the case with existenz. But if at times Jaspers's thought meant a jumble of ideas, at others it meant a conceptual wealth of insights. He was, unlike Heidegger, a pluralist, both in the method and in the content of his thinking. And, in the tradition of the greatest humanist thinkers, Jaspers was concerned less with grandiose philosophical systems as with helping real people live their lives. Philosophy is too valuable to be left to the academic ghetto, and this, on its own, is sufficient reason why Jaspers earns his place in this book. Like so many other thinkers we have examined, philosophy was for Jaspers a living, breathing necessity. It was not simply a means to earn a living or to achieve personal acclaim.

Thanks perhaps to his early training in psychology, he had a keener appreciation of science than many of his contemporaries. Scientific facts are objectively true for all of us, without regard to our condition in life, cultural background, sexual orientation, or anything else. Jaspers was clear about that. Neither could we be indifferent to those objective facts of science, but it was part of our philosophical duty to incorporate them into our thinking. What's more, nonscientific beliefs are of a different order; they are fallible and in constant need of revision. But as against this, Jaspers was equally insistent that scientific language and thinking has no place outside science and that nonscientific language can "go deeper" than dispassionate scientific language. And, rather confusingly for the empirically minded English-speaking humanist, Jaspers called himself a Christian, despite recognizing no item of Christian dogma as being true. He was Christian in the same sense he was German, something he was born with.

In a way characteristic of the European tradition we are following in this chapter, Jaspers rejected theism and atheism alike, relegating them both to the status of symbols that should not be taken literally. When he spoke of God, he was usually tolerably clear that God was an expression of human authenticity and groundedness. We won't rehearse again the debate about the value of this sort of talk. What we can do is express some gratitude to Jaspers for at least employing this language back against the religious literalists. At one point he directed his attention to the popular accusation that secular modernity has dethroned God in favor of man, still today one of the most popular accusations made by religious conservatives. Those who make this accusation, he said, "fail to recognize that God does not speak through the commands and revelations of other men but in man's selfhood and through his freedom, not from without but from within. Any restriction on man's freedom, created by God and oriented through God, is a restriction upon the very thing through which God manifests himself."[41] Here, as the Death of God theologians tried to do after him, Jaspers put his interior, authentic-person God idea to sound use.

One of Jaspers's more important ideas was that of limitless communication (*Grenzenlose Kommunikation*), which became a central element of his thought. It referred to the ongoing dialogue between people as the reliable way to arrive at truth, which, Jaspers argued, is communicative in that it cannot be arrived at without people talking about what truth is. And, of course, it was a means by which the danger of overweening certainty could be avoided. "In the certainty of the moment the humility of the enduring question is indispensable."[42] So with limitless communication, and its necessary corollary of limitless listening, we can at least be pointed in the direction of some sort of truth. And the process of limitless communication takes place in this world, in sharp distinction with Heidegger, who saw Being as something apprehended only when we abandon the humanist project of limitless communication. Stephen Eriksen understood this divide when he thought Jaspers more Aristotelian, as against the Platonic, even Orphic, cast of Heidegger's thought.[43] Jaspers saw Being as something altogether more circumstantial, provisional, and transitory, and as something toward which limitless communication was a necessity, not an impediment. Limitless communication belongs to the same family as John Dewey's ideas of active intelligence and social intelligence. It also has similarities to Jürgen Habermas's recommendation of participating in an ongoing flow of communicative rationality.[44] And it is even related to Richard Rorty's idea that philosophy's principal purpose is as an ongoing discourse, although Jaspers would say this in a more positive sense; that is not *all* philosophy is good for. Forms of expression aside, like Dewey and Habermas, Jaspers took seriously the question, what could we become? If only for this distinction, we can call Jaspers a humanist and Heidegger an antihumanist.

Two other thinkers should be mentioned here, in the context of being praxis-and-communication-oriented humanists. The first of them was Gerhard Szczesny (1918–2002), an author, broadcaster, and controversialist. Szczesny was born in East Prussia and studied philosophy, literature, and journalism at Königsberg, Berlin, and Munich. After World War II, he acquired a reputation as an intellectual leader, largely through a series of essays under the title *Europe and the Anarchy of the Soul*. He went on to have a prominent career in radio broadcasting. In 1961, he was embroiled in a major controversy when, in a highly controversial broadcast, he compared West German Chancellor Willi Brandt (1913–1992), East German leader Walter Ulbricht (1893–1973), and Nazi propaganda chief Joseph Goebbels (1897–1945). As part of the fallout over this broadcast and in protest to ongoing interference by the Catholic Church in the cultural life of the country, Szczesny founded the Humanist Union. The Church had recently engineered the banning of Mozart's *Figaro* on the grounds of immorality. Unlike many other German free thought organizations, the Humanist Union has done well, attracting prominent people to its ranks.

Szczesny's best-known work relevant to our inquiry was *The Future of Unbelief: Contemporary Observations of a Non-Christian*, published originally in 1958. This book won the Heinrich Droste Literature Foundation award for the most outstanding treatment of a historico-cultural theme. His concerns were characteristic of European humanism. He began with the assumption that Europe is now post-Christian—a term he used—and was more concerned with how the disconnect between the outdated metaphysics and the new knowledge would work itself out.[45] He was quite uninterested in pursuing a critique of religion in the tradition of Anglo American humanism. Interestingly, however, this book, like many of its Anglo American counterparts, spent relatively little time on the nature of "unbelief," let alone its future. More recent material on the Humanist Union's website corrects this omission. The union's statement illustrates talks of "the liberation of people from the shackles of an authoritarian state and from clerical ties; the promulgation of human rights and civil duty; the expansion of educational, training, and care facilities—and the free expression of science, press, literature, and art."[46] One can't help feeling an earlier Munich-based humanist, Friedrich Immanuel Niethammer, would have approved.

The other important praxis-and-communication humanist who deserves mention is Jaap van Praag, a man who made three powerful contributions to twentieth-century humanism, one practical and two intellectual. His practical contribution was his work as the central linchpin of the International Humanist & Ethical Union for the first two decades of its career. We will outline this in chapter 13. The first of his two major contributions to the theory of humanism was his historical insight. He discerned more clearly than anyone else had done to date the various strands of humanist discourse, which he called the reflective, the social, and the scientific (or sometimes empirical) strands. The reflective strand of humanism goes back to Antiquity and is found in the Epicureans, Epictetus, philosophical Taoism, and German humanist thought down to Karl Jaspers. Social humanism, by contrast, goes back to Confucius and on through people as varied as Jeremy Bentham and M. N. Roy. Then there is empirical humanism, which can be traced back to the atomists and Wang Chong down to logical positivism, Bertrand Russell, and humanistic psychology.[47] The single most important point about these strands, Van Praag was at pains to point out, is the absence of clear lines of distinction between them. They have intertwined and cross-fertilized through history in one long, rich, and deeply rewarding conversation. This book is built on that insight. It was Van Praag's historical awareness that allowed him to see the importance of Niethammer and his humanism.

The second of Van Praag's theoretical insights was to represent humanism not by a number of creedal positions but by a series of postulates. A postulate, he wrote, "is not a hypothesis, which has to be proved by thought or experience, but rather a starting point that enables one to think and experience in a certain way."[48] His humanist postulates were: equality, secularity, liberty, fraternity, reason, experience, existence, completeness, contingency, and evolution. These postulates do not sum up humanist answers or define humanist thought. But they do, he argued, encapsulate the starting point, the common basis of humanist thought. Some strands might spend more time developing these postulates, while another strand will develop those postulates. It could be argued that the European concept of laïcité is the encapsulation in a single word of Van Praag's ten postulates of humanism.

THE RISE AND FALL OF SOCIALIST HUMANISM

We need now to resume the story begun in previous chapters on the tortured relations between Marxism and humanism. In the 1890s and again in the 1930s, many people were impatient with humanism for its ambivalent attitude toward socialism. After World War II the tide of disapproval began to turn. For these critics the new trend of socialist humanism looked like the way forward. But socialist humanism came and went so quickly that it never had enough time to make any long-term impact on humanism. In chapter 4 we sketched the career of dialectical materialism from the death of Marx and Engels until World War II. As the world emerged from that war, it was apparent that Marxism was not the harbinger of a new civilization, as some of its fellow travelers had insisted. Indeed, it was becoming a fair question whether Soviet Russia was a Marxist country in any serious sense at all. Up until the 1930s most Marxists saw no important fissure between the Soviet Union and the body of theory known as Marxism. But after the war, as the realities of Stalinism cast an ever-longer shadow, this became a more pressing dilemma for leftist intellectuals. At the Tenth International Congress of Philosophy, held in Amsterdam in 1948, the Soviet delegates did little more than insist loudly that the only true humanism was that embodied in the teachings of Lenin and Stalin, and all others were merely decadent bourgeois relics. This was one component of the doctrine recently drawn up by the Soviet theorist Andrei Zhdanov (1896–1948).

This clearly wasn't going to satisfy anyone except the diehards. While Jean-Paul Sartre is open to a great deal of criticism with respect to his Marxism, even he felt some need to articulate a "genuine" Marxist humanism. Sartre decided that the humanist existentialism he had until then been championing was no longer adequate for the times. He was also responding to Heidegger's criticism that he had underplayed the historical role in determining Being. So, in his monumental *Critique of Dialectical Reason* (1960), Sartre attempted a synthesis between Marxism and existentialism. It didn't work, and by the time it had been translated into English in 1976, the question was thoroughly dead.

Alongside Sartre, though operating along different lines of thought, was the movement that came to be known as *socialist humanism*. The most comprehensive anthology of this thinking can be found in *Socialist Humanism* (1965), a collection edited by Erich Fromm (1900–1980). Fromm was also a prominent publicist for the humanistic "early Marx" theory, which we have previously discussed at some length. He clearly liked this line of argument because he also claimed Jesus was essentially humanistic, as against the authoritarian Christianity that arose in his name.[49] This has even less to recommend it than the "early Marx" argument. Whatever value Fromm's anthology had was washed away in 1968, when Soviet tanks snuffed out the Prague Spring, the doomed attempt to put socialist humanism into practice. But between 1956 and 1968 socialist humanism was a live option. In the wake the invasion of Hungary and Krushchev's destalinization speech at the Twentieth Congress of the Communist Part of the Soviet Union, socialist humanism developed its core insight: alienation remained a problem in socialist societies no less than in capitalist ones. The socialist humanistics wanted to rescue Marxism—especially the so-called early Marx—from the link Engels had made with dialectical materialism and Lenin had with Soviet autocracy. The socialist humanists hoped to reinvigorate Marxism along humanist lines. With this in mind, there was a series of dialogues with Western humanists for a short while in the later 1960s, but the increasingly nervous Marxist governments became less keen on them, forcing the cancellation of planned meetings in 1972 and 1974. Part of the reason for Soviet reticence was that an important center of socialist humanist thought was Yugoslavia, which had been expelled in 1948 by Stalin from the international Communist community. Since its expulsion, socialist intellectuals had been trying to articulate a new vision of popular Marxism. Socialist humanist thought slowly converged on a small but influential group of philosophers who became known as the Praxis Group. These thinkers emphasized the so-called early Marx, who they took to be more open and free in his thinking and less inclined to the dialectical historicism and class-war theory of his major works. As one theorist (not one of the Praxis Group) put it, Marx's ultimate aim is not socialism at all:

> His ultimate aim is *human* society; society in which dehumanisation ceases, human labor is truly emancipated, and man has all the conditions necessary to his development and self-affirmation.[50]

The Praxis Group, as with the socialist humanist movement generally, was trying to use Marx not as a repository of scripture but as a body of work to assist the ongoing critique of society. The goal was not the final realization of Marxist dogma but an ongoing, open-minded process of learning as the means by which alienation will be eliminated. This was all a bit too much for Yugoslavia's dictator, Marshall Tito (1892–1980), who had spoken in similar terms himself but was anxious that such talk did not extend too far and challenge the power of the party. The relative freedom of the group was assured for as long as Tito remained anxious not to lose his reputation in the West as a maverick leader of a freer brand of Marxism. After several years of skirmishing and harassment, Tito's patience snapped in January 1975, and the Praxis Group was shut down. As Oskar Gruenwald, an informed commentator, observed, the party "bartered away the soul of Marxism in the hope of preserving the body. . . ."[51] Most of the philosophers lost their academic positions, but Tito shrank from imprisoning them. This was in part due to international pressure from Western intellectuals on their colleagues' behalf. Humanist intellectuals played a prominent role in this campaign. Not long after their suppression a leading member of the Praxis Group, Mihailo Markovic (1923–) released a series of essays titled *The Contemporary Marx*, which combined an enthusiastic endorsement of the humanistic "early

Marx" with biting criticisms of state socialism as it actually existed. During Tito's crackdown on the Praxis Group, the International Humanist & Ethical Union (IHEU) did what it could to support Markovic by nominating him as one of its three coleaders.[52] Most of the Praxis Group of philosophers went on to have important roles in building Serbia's post-Communist future in the 1990s. One of them, Svetozar Stojanovic, was a leading opponent to the dictatorial regime of Slobodan Milosevic, which was ousted in a popular revolution in 2002. Stojanovic is a member of the International Academy of Humanism, the brainchild of Paul Kurtz, a leading ally of the Praxis Group in the United States.

It is one of the many ironies of this book that two of the more articulate enthusiasts for the later, more authoritarian, Marx of the dialectic lived in democracies. One of them was George Novack (1905–1992), who led a lonely but spirited struggle on behalf of Trotskyite socialism in the United States. Under the Alien Registration Act of 1940, usually known as the Smith Act, after Congressman Howard Smith of Virginia, who sponsored the bill, Novack had been imprisoned for his beliefs during World War II. Undeterred, he remained a staunch Marxist for the rest of his life, writing a great deal along the way. In *Humanism and Socialism* (1973), he argued for what he called *revolutionary socialist humanism* and made some telling criticisms of the "early Marx idea." After all, Novack said, Marx did in fact move on, he was not content to remain a Feuerbachian. The "humanist Marx" was merely a precursor to the mature Marx of dialectical materialism. Novack also criticized the motivation behind the hunt for the "early Marx" which he likened to the Protestant reformers' search for primitive Christianity in the hope of "rediscovering" the simple faith of Jesus unsullied by Romish corruptions.[53] He accused the socialist humanists of making the same mistake non-Marxist humanists made: shrinking from the stark reality of the materialist conception of history, with its black-and-white choice of whether to accept or reject monopoly capitalism. Aspects of Novack's criticisms of socialist humanism were valid. The transition between the "early" and "late" Marx isn't as clear as socialist humanists made it out to be, and he was right to question the essentialist motivation behind their return to a few early texts, most of which were unfinished and which Marx was content to leave unpublished in his lifetime. But neither has history been kind to Novack's argument. Between 1989 and 1991, historical materialism did not ride the wave of history to consummate its inevitable success; it collapsed completely and utterly. And in the rubble of this collapse, the Marx of dialectical materialism died, never to reappear.

For many, the most telling critique of socialist humanism came as part of a general condemnation of any type of humanism. Its author was Louis Althusser (1918–1990), another Frenchman born in Algeria. Althusser came to Marxism in 1948 and retained a quality of total immersion in doctrine that he had earlier imbibed as a dedicated Catholic activist. His main contribution that interests us was to radically downplay the so-called early Marx, the humanistic Marx, in favor of the later Marx, the Marx of dialectical materialism. For Althusser, Marxism was not simply another philosophical system from which we could learn. It was "the *theoretical domain of a fundamental investigation*, indispensable not only to the development of the science of society and of the various 'human sciences,' but also to that of the natural sciences and philosophy."[54] His essay "Marxism and Humanism," published originally in 1964, and which appeared later in *For Marx*, was widely thought of as the intellectual foundation of theoretical antihumanism. Here he argued that Marx's move away from his supposedly humanistic earlier self was not just an incidental shift but was the key to his greatness and what made Marxism the scientific discovery he believed it to be.[55] His reworked dialectical materialism was a grimly determined process, one without a subject like "humanity." Indeed, Althusser insisted that the Marx he was defending, the post-1845 Marx of dialectical materialism, should be understood as theoretically antihumanist. Humanism was necessary in a reduced capacity as an ideology, but only one among others to be buffeted by the dialectic of history.[56] Human beings were consigned to the humble role of fetchers-and-carriers of the structures of history. Any objection to this radical demotion of human agency was dismissed as humanism. Althusser could see no point to socialist humanism. The Soviet Union was already living the dream that socialist humanists were only promising. The socialist humanists, for all their faults, were at least not suffering from that illusion.

A good case could be made that socialist humanism's most important contribution was a destructive one, made well after it had ceased to be a live option. This was E. P. Thompson's devastating reply to Althusser in *The Poverty of Theory* (1978). Thompson (1924–1993) was author of the classic work *The Making of the English Working Class* (1963) and was coeditor of the *New Reasoner*, a journal with the subtitle "A Quarterly Journal of Socialist Humanism." Like many leading British Marxists, he quit the Communist Party after the invasion of Hungary in 1956, and he went on to become a leading spokesman for a variation of social democratic humanism. And it was in this vein that he led, in *The Poverty of Theory*, the counterattack against Althusser's strident antihumanism. The details of Thompson's rebuttal don't matter particularly anymore. But his core objection illustrates clearly what socialist humanism, at its best, had to offer. Marxist theory, Thompson argued, is nothing if it is not the theory of "the real human project, in all its manifestations. . . ."[57] The history in *Das Kapital* is hypothesis, which in turn always needs to be tested and verified, which will inevitably entail revision and, when necessary, replacement. Literal-minded reverence helps neither the subject nor object of the reverence. "Following Marx" had to be done critically and with "an understanding of the provisional and exploratory nature of all theory, and the openness with which one must approach all knowledge."[58] And if this meant arguing against Marx, then so be it. This was socialist humanism's finest hour. But the price was high, because socialist humanism was at its best when defending liberal humanist ideas someone like John Stuart Mill would have championed a century earlier.

People continued to speak about and write about socialist humanism after 1968, but the heart had gone out of it. After 1968, the disillusioned leftist thinkers drifted into various expressions of postmodernism or toward any number of cults or into indifferentism. A few intellectuals sympathetic to Marxism started up a line of inquiry very much in the vein of Thompson's critique, in particular Ernesto Laclau and Chantal Mouffe in *Hegemony and Socialist Strategy* (1985). In what came to be known as post-Marxism, Laclau and Mouffe were candid about the theoretical failures of Marxist prophecy and the practical failures of state socialism, and they called for a realignment of priorities around emerging issues, like feminism, postcolonialism, and antimonopoly capitalism—what in a few years would become the antiglobalization movement. Jacques Derrida took elements of this argument on board in *Specters of Marx* (1994), but the specific antihumanism of Derrida's thinking takes him beyond the range of this book. The important point, though, is that few people outside the academic left were paying any attention to post-Marxism.

In the end, socialist humanism failed to sort out its own contradictions. It failed to reconcile orthodox Marxism with liberal humanism and failed to provide a stable ground for pluralism and freedom of thought within a Marxist dialectic of history that discounts such things as bourgeois irrelevances. Ironically, socialist humanism had the same sort of contradictions and difficulties liberal Christianity has between reconciling the authority of scripture and the shifting moral imperatives of a diverse and ever-changing world.

SOCIALIST HUMANISM'S LAST GASP

Before we leave the subject of socialist humanism, we have one more digression to make, and to a most unlikely place. It could be said that the last gasp of socialist humanism came from the least expected place: the Soviet Union itself. As the structural and economic failures of state socialism were becoming ever more apparent in the 1980s, the Soviet leadership began to look for ways to change the system. Once Mikhail Gorbachev took over as general secretary of the Communist Party in 1985, these changes gathered pace. Under the banner of *glasnost* and *perestroika*, Gorbachev hoped—so far as we can tell this close to events—to shake the foundations of state socialism.

One aspect of this realignment was a new attitude toward humanism. If the more rigorous aspects of state socialism and dialectical materialism were going to be quietly retired, the Soviet leadership was looking around for some sort of alternative ideology that could accommodate a naturalistic perspective with a respect for liberty. As most other patterns of thought were either too foreign or too implacably opposed to socialism, it was inevitable that the Russians should take another look at humanism. After all, the idea had been around ever since Marx himself. Typical of earlier Soviet statements on humanism is this one from 1963, when P. N. Fedoseyev wrote:

> Communists are undoubtedly the most consistent humanists. Communism is real humanism. The philosophy of Communism does not tolerate any forms of antihumanism, it shall never conclude any ideological truce with them.[59]

Maria Petrosyan (1911–1971), another senior Soviet academic, said much the same in a book-length study of humanism, published in English in 1972. Repeating a softer form of the Zhdanov Doctrine, Petrosyan argued true humanism could only be given full expression under the aegis of

Marxism-Leninism.[60] The line taken by Fedoseyev and Petrosyan remained the formal Soviet approach until the mid-1980s.

Nikita Krushchev was the last Soviet leader who really believed in Marxism. Under his successor Leonid Brezhnev (1906–1982), the Soviet Union became more ramshackle and corrupt. Halfhearted moves began even in his time to look for some idea with which to shore up the tottering Marxist edifice. But it was not until the 1980s, when things had deteriorated still further, that efforts in this direction took a new urgency. Late in the 1980s, Soviet emissaries began involving themselves in various international humanist events. No longer were they satisfied simply to castigate humanists as evading the reality of dialectical materialism in the interests of the bourgeois. They were genuinely interested in dialogue. A senior deputation of Soviet intellectuals and functionaries attended the Tenth World Humanist Congress, held in Buffalo, New York, in 1988, and the following year some senior American and European humanists visited the Soviet Union. The visitors were there for a conference titled "A Dialogue between Humanists and Atheists: Differences and Similarities." It was held in the generously appointed building used by the Institute of Scientific Atheism, which had been founded in 1963, but which had been conspicuously unsuccessful to date. The Institute was loathed by Russians for its intrusiveness as much as for its propagation of atheism. The Russian delegates knew that the institute was a liability but were nonplussed by the strong opposition of the Western humanists to the official propagation of atheism. What worried some of the Russians was the relationship between humanism and religion. Several of them had read a lot of Julian Huxley's works and were confused by his speaking of humanism in religious terms.

No less a person than Ivan Frolov (1929–) had signaled the new direction toward humanism. Frolov had a long career as a senior academician behind him and was an important Politburo ally of Gorbachev. From his position as editor of the Soviet philosophical journal *Viprosy Filosofia (Problems of Philosophy)*, Frolov was appointed as one of Gorbachev's three secretaries and had recently been named as editor of *Pravda*. One of Frolov's first acts as *Pravda* editor was to drop the tagline "Communist Party of the Soviet Union," suggesting it was now to be open to a range of viewpoints. So when he produced a book called *Man-Science-Humanism: A New Synthesis*, it could be reasonably inferred that this change reflected the mood at the very top of the Soviet hierarchy. The inevitable dialectic of history was de-emphasized and Marxism was seen as a science of emancipation and development. Kremlinologists undoubtedly picked through it, discerning the glacial tectonic shifts away from Zdhanov and through people like Fedoseyev and Petrosyan. But the true indicator of change was not what was being said but who was saying it. The attempt to effect a fusion of Marxism and humanism to create a "real humanism" was no longer simply an academic exercise. It was a last-ditch clutching of straws of a dying system.

Writing later, Paul Kurtz speculated on the reasons for this revived interest in humanism:

> The Soviets are groping for new answers and new formulae. The government killed off the Soviet free market and repressed the literary, artistic, and philosophical intelligentsia for so long that today's Soviet populace seems to lack the sparks of creativity. Refusing to allow the development of an open society, the government stifled new ideas, and the nation has stagnated. It has withdrawn from the world community and desperately wants to rejoin it.[61]

As we now know, the Soviet Union collapsed before it had time to develop humanism as a viable new formula for a more open society. When Paul Kurtz and other senior Western humanists visited the Soviet Union again early in 1991, it was clear things were beginning to unravel. The Institute for Scientific Atheism had been renamed the Institute for the Study of Religion and Atheism, and new legislation permitting a degree of freedom of conscience had been passed. A new Society for Secular Culture had been established to act as a conduit for state-sponsored humanism, especially through its main organ *Dispute*, which was set to have a print run of one hundred thousand.

But all this was too little, too late. As these initiatives were being pulled together, troops were being sent into the Baltic States in a last-ditch attempt to prevent their secession, and hard-liners were finding their way back into important Communist Party positions. It was becoming increasingly clear that the main focus for change lay outside the Communist Party. In some ways this represents the most extraordinary paradox of this book. After snubbing, belittling, and slandering liberal humanism since the 1840s, the orthodox Marxists and their heirs in the Soviet Union finally turned to them when they finally realized their own system was in its death throws. But by then it was far too late. We will pick up this thread once again in chapter 10 when we look at China's equally brief flirtation with humanism at roughly the same time. All the talk of a religious revival notwithstanding, humanism has done better in post-Soviet Russia than it ever did before. The Russian Humanist Society is thriving, well connected, and influential.

POSTMODERN HUMANISM AND HUMANISTICS

It will already be apparent to the reader that humanism has been interpreted in several, sometimes conflicting, ways. Sidney Hook commented on this with respect of the Tenth International Congress of Philosophy, which was held at Amsterdam in 1948. This was the first meeting of the Congress since the war, and the expectations were high. The conference theme reflected those expectations with the big-picture theme of "Man, Mankind, and Humanity." But instead of looking boldly at the big picture and offering some considered visions of the future, the Congress quickly got mired in technicalities and politics. Even more frustrating was that, despite the scale of the disagreements, virtually everybody at the Congress thought of themselves as humanists. At one end were the naturalists but at the other end were those who saw true humanism only being possible once recognition was made of whichever version of supernatural reality was being favored. These divisions then fractured still further, with the naturalist humanists being split between those who supported the Soviet Union or emanated from a Soviet Bloc country, and the non- or anti-Communist liberals from the West; people like Bertrand Russell and Sidney Hook.

For a short while in postwar Europe it looked as if everybody was becoming a humanist of some description of other. There was Catholic humanism and its Protestant rival, usually known simply as *Christian* humanism (to be discussed in the next chapter). Then among the nonreligious were the liberal, naturalistic, and socialist humanists, who were, in turn, bound up with the Frankfurt School, whose preoccupation with critical theory was moving along a similar trajectory. But by the later 1960s, the problems of prosperity and the growing inability of Marxism to offer a credible, nondogmatic alternative to capitalism, provoked the brief flurry of rhetorical antihumanism in the 1970s and 1980s. Building on a rereading of people as different as Marx, Nietzsche, Georges Sorel (1847–1922), and others, the antihumanists railed against what later became known as the essentializing of Man the abstraction. "Man," wrote Michel Foucault (1926–1984), one of the more vehement of the antihumanists, is an invention of Europe in the sixteenth century, and "one perhaps nearing its end."[62] Foucault is not referring to "Man" in the sense of *Homo sapiens*, but the cultural construct of "Man," that was first theorized about as part of the Renaissance revolt against medievalist Christianity.

Hopefully, readers will appreciate how irrelevant this particular criticism is, as relatively few humanists have actually written in this way. A century before Foucault, John Stuart Mill criticized Comte's Positive Philosophy in these terms. Awareness of artificiality of a capitalized abstraction "Man" permeates the writing of people as diverse as Santayana, Russell, Dewey, and Hook, among others. Tzvetan Todorov, whose work we will explore later in this chapter, observed: "In the eyes of the humanists, man is a potentiality rather than an essence: he can become this or that, act one way or another, he does not do it *out of necessity*."[63] Todorov is the latest in the long line of Continental humanists who have stressed the potential, what-we-may-become element in human beings over some static essence of what we supposedly are. The postmodernist antihumanists agreed that humanity has no essence, but they then went on to conclude that people are therefore entirely at the beck and call of passing trends, social construction, fads, and fancies. And the more extreme of them professed not to see any problem with this.

What renders the antihumanist critique of Man, suitably capitalized, even more problematic than its simple irrelevance is the underappreciated influence of the contempt for the general citizen as expressed most forcefully by Nietzsche and Heidegger. Nietzsche dismissed the general citizen as "the superfluous," "the many-too-many," or the "Last Man." Less poetic but even more disparaging, Martin Heidegger wrote of the general citizen as *das Man*, or "the they," whose main offense is their "undifferentiated primitive everydayness." Nietzsche yearned for a new nobility, lest time be handed over to the mob, in which case "drown all time in shallow waters."[64] It followed from this that people who wrote for "the they" were not merely wasting their time but were wilfully blind to the social reality. As Nietzsche made clear: "Books for everybody are always malodorous books: the smell of petty people cling to them."[65] It is with this in mind that the postmodernist theorist Gregory Bruce Smith admitted that "there is an unmistakable and unavoidable aristocratic element lurking within the essence of the genuinely postmodern."[66] How postmodernist antihumanism, which claims to have exposed the essentializing project of humanism, can itself have an essence is left unexplained.

So, while antihumanists have denounced humanism as a brutalizing, hegemonic metanarrative, their own criticisms, characterized by ambivalence toward democracy and a bleak view of human nature, seem little of an improvement. Equally problematic for the antihumanists is that their criticisms are not original to them. John Dewey expressed many of these concerns half a century before most antihumanists were born. More recently, psychology, particularly evolutionary psychology and neuropsychology, has gone much further toward breaking up our pretensions to possessing some central command post which we can flatter with names like *mind* or *soul*. But this debunking is the easy bit; the difficult bit comes after this: what does being human mean in the twenty-first century? How do we rebuild a credible sense of being human in the light of having no Cartesian theater, as Daniel Dennett calls it, to orchestrate our lives? This is one of the tasks of twenty-first-century humanism. Postmodern antihumanism, by definition, has nothing at all constructive to contribute to this discussion. Its deep suspicion of science condemns its work to an unhelpful one-sidedness. Norman Levitt was correct when he noted that the postmodernists have "considerable corrosive power but little capacity to build."[67] Indeed, it has been observed that antihumanism cannot ever rid itself of its humanist concerns because its very purpose is to unsettle and problematize the human subject so as to make him more human.[68] In this way, postmodernist antihumanism can only offer any constructive contribution when it is being humanist.

Nowhere is this better illustrated than in a short work, called *Humanism*, by the postmodernist critic Tony Davies. As a historian of English literature, Davies spends most of his time among the humanists of the sixteenth and seventeenth centuries, who are berated for their lack of postmodern sensitivities. Most of the strands of humanist thought outlined in this book are ignored. Toward the end of his book, having scolded humanists for their elitism, racism, sexism, Eurocentrism, and so on, Davies makes the following remarkable admission.

> At the same time, though it is clear that the master narrative of transcendental Man has outlasted its usefulness, it would be unwise simply to abandon the ground occupied by the historical humanisms. For one thing, some variety of humanism remains, on many occasions, the only available

alternative to bigotry and persecution. The freedom to speak and write, to organize and campaign in defense of individual or collective interests, to protest and disobey: all these, and the prospect of a world in which they will be secured, can only be articulated in humanist terms.[69]

Here, in starkly clear terms, lies revealed the hollowness of postmodernist antihumanism. For all its eloquent fatwas, it cannot do without that which it condemns. To the degree it articulates anything constructive, it needs to be done in the language of humanism.

In the wake of the demise of the antihumanists, there have been a few attempts to graft humanism with postmodernism, although one must keep in mind that it is literary humanism that many of these critics have in mind. One of the more useful came in 1992 from the American literary scholar and critic Stephen Yarbrough, who wrote that postmodernism can best be understood as "an intense awareness of the present-day incapacity to discover." The difference lay in what conclusion one drew from this. Unlike most antihumanists, postmodernist humanists saw this more as a problem to overcome rather than a condition to celebrate.[70] He also differed on the standard analysis of the conditions of the modern malaise, understanding in the way most fellow postmodernists did not, that the death of god, rather than ending all foundation for meaningful discourse, was "all we need to stand under our discourse."[71] He then set down his understanding of humanism as "an attitude toward theory rather than a theory in itself; it necessarily alters its style, method and stance as the situation in which it practices alters. It must change, if it is to remain the same."[72] The solution, he said, was too close to our eyes for us to see. So the task of contemporary humanism was to articulate a new account of common experience within the discourse of postmodernism. He emphasized this last point by recourse to italics. What he did not foresee was that postmodernism was not the immovable new paradigm he supposed it to be. The intellectual counterattack on postmodernism began in 1994 and culminated in 1996 with the Sokal hoax. Outside of a few disciplines, postmodernism has been in constant retreat since then. In the end, the postmodern humanists have very little to add. Their criticisms—those that do not attack a straw man—were anticipated by many people from within the humanist stream of thinking decades before the postmodernists stumbled upon them. And most of the criticisms that were new were the least convincing, being either unhelpfully nihilist, indecipherable, or tautologous.

This is not to say, of course, that postmodernism has disappeared. But it is remarkable how banal its claims have become, in comparison to its earlier, headier days. So much so, it is difficult to avoid the impression that postmodern humanists are trying to reinvent the wheel. One such postmodernist revision of humanism, called *Critical Humanisms*, is anxious to distance itself from naturalistic humanism, claiming it "will show humanism to be both a pluralistic and a self-critical tradition that folds in and over itself, provoking a series of questions and problems rather than necessarily providing consolation or education for individuals when faced with intractable economic, political, and social pressures."[73] Without psychoanalyzing "folding in and over itself" too deeply, hopefully readers will appreciate how irrelevant this criticism is. The postmodern presumption that it is bringing humanism back to these virtues is misplaced. Any serious reading of the major humanist thinkers will show that these virtues were not abandoned in the first place. Pluralism, self-criticism, and the rejection of pat consolations have permeated humanist thinking since the beginning of the tradition. And we have seen these virtues given eloquent expression by Thomas Mann, Albert Camus, Karl Jaspers, and others mentioned earlier in this chapter. More recently, Edward Said (1935–2003) took up this line in *Humanism and Democratic Criticism*, the last work published during his lifetime. Said had no doubts about the central role of humanism in open-ended criticism:

> [It] is the mark of humanistic scholarship, reading, and interpretation to be able to disentangle the usual from the unusual and the ordinary from the extraordinary in aesthetic works as well as in statements made by philosophers, intellectuals, and public figures. Humanism is, to some extent, a resistance to *idées reçues*, and it offers opposition to every kind of cliché and unthinking language.[74]

Said agreed that the "great books" approach to instilling a uniquely authoritative Western canon was no longer a workable idea, although he was not then prepared to simply dismiss them as yet more dead white men. What happened was that a new generation of humanist scholars arose that was more aware of the contributions across cultures. But this did not involve, as the antihumanists argued, the demise of humanism; it simply involved it in a new level of awareness and growth.

Contemporary European humanism is so rich and diverse that little more than a suggestion of one or two aspects of it can be given here, by way of finishing this chapter. One attempt to break new ground in humanist thinking comes in the form of *humanistics*, a word used mainly by the Dutch humanists. It was defined in 1992, at a time when postmodernism was still in the ascendant, as "humanities that are oriented toward everyday practices with specific attention to processes of giving meaning to life and 'humanizing.'"[75] It claims to be a unique fusion of existential and political examination of questions of personal identity and social inclusion. The home of humanistics is the University for Humanist Studies, founded in Utrecht, in the Netherlands in 1989. The principal purpose of the university is the training of counselors wishing to work in schools, hospitals, the armed forces, or prisons. It has since expanded to provide education for prospective teachers and those wishing to work as policymakers for government departments, for NGOs, and for academics. The university, also known as the University of Humanistics, offers a three-year bachelors program, a series of vocationally specific masters programs, and a doctoral degree.

While it may hesitate to speak of bildung, Dutch humanistics is in the same tradition of looking to nurture the full individual. In the tradition of European humanism, it is unconcerned, even impatient with the priorities of naturalistic or secular humanism as espoused in the English-speaking world. And in the Netherlands, with (until recently) little or no experience of fundamentalism, such an attitude is understandable. But it suggests a certain complacency, such as we saw with American religious humanism, to take for granted that the future lies with the open society and that those who work against it are doomed to fail. The growing incidence of fundamentalism among Muslim migrants to the Netherlands and the murder of the filmmaker Theo van Gogh in 2004 present challenges that this rather pacifist brand of humanism will not manage well. But in the sense of producing caring and capable counselors and caregivers, humanistics has much it can teach humanism around the world. Its value of learning, its concern for social inclusion, its provision for sex education to its teens (resulting in some of the lowest abortion and STD rates in the world), and its internationalism are all admirable features of humanistics in particular and of Dutch society in general.

TZVETAN TODOROV AND THE IMPERFECT GARDEN

To end this chapter, we should look to one of the most interesting of the recent exponents of the European strand of humanism. Tzvetan Todorov was born in Bulgaria in March 1939 but moved to France in 1963, where he has made a successful career as a literary and cultural critic, theorist, and intellectual historian. Todorov's upbringing in a totalitarian society has set the parameters for his life's work, articulating a twenty-first-century humanist and democratic ethos. Initially, one could be forgiven for fearing that his book *Imperfect Garden: The Legacy of Humanism* would get us nowhere, it consisting largely of examinations of Montaigne, Jean-Jacques Rousseau, and Benjamin Constant. Montaigne would take the least explanation; his humanism is warm, nonideological, down-to-earth and entirely devoid of anthropocentric conceit. Rousseau, however, is a particularly controversial figure, and we have seen several humanists—Irving Babbitt in particular—develop wide-ranging criticisms of him and all he stood for. But the central point of this seemingly obscure discussion is Todorov's articulation of humanism. There are two especially valuable contributions Todorov made to humanist thought. They have endearingly romantic titles: the three pillars of humanist morality and the humanist wager.

The core proposition of humanism, according to Todorov, is what he called *the humanist wager*. The humanist wager is built on the supposition that, because human beings are free, they are capable of the best behavior—and of the worst. In full knowledge of this, the humanist wager is that human beings will act willingly, fraternally, even lovingly, rather than grudgingly, selfishly, and spitefully. As well as the obvious reference to Pascal's Wager, there is something reminiscent here of Mencius's notion of human-heartedness. Todorov insists that the humanist wager is neither naïve in the sense of taking for granted that people will do the right thing, nor is it proud in the sense of believing humans will always rise to the occasion. "Modern humanism, far from ignoring Auschwitz and Kolyma, take them as a starting point."[76] The humanist wager stands in stark contrast to the Christian assumption that, because of original sin, humans will automatically behave in a depraved way. It also repudiates the postmodernist assertion that, in the wake of Auschwitz, humanism is impossible. Another of Todorov's works, *Hope and Memory*, explores the lives of people who exemplified a post-Holocaust humanism; people like Primo Levi (1919–1987) and David Rousset (who we mentioned briefly in our discussion of Sartre), both of whom devoted their lives to understanding fully the consequences of state-sponsored terror.

Grounded in this knowledge of what being human is about, Todorov outlines the three pillars of humanist morality in these terms: the autonomy of the *I*, the finality of the *you*, and the universality of the *they*. When we speak of the autonomy of the *I*, we mean that humanism prefers freely chosen acts over acts performed grudgingly or under some form of coercion. When we speak of the finality of the *you*, we mean that our neighbor is an end and not a means. It means we look to helping this or that individual, not the abstraction "humankind." Love, properly understood, is the finality of the *you*.[77] The Christian idea that we love because loving is what God wants us to do or because the recipient of our love is in God's image, reduces love to a means to an end, namely securing God's love. Humanist love, in that sense, is of a higher nature because it is not done for ulterior purposes. The goal is the *finality of the you*, not loving you so that God will love me. And finally, when we speak of the universality of the *they*, we mean recognizing the complete equality of all *Homo sapiens*. It also implies a rejection of any abstraction, ism, or "ology" that stands between the individual and his neighbor. In this way, totalitarianism, with its tendency to a Manichean division into "us" and "them," is fundamentally antihumanistic.[78] And democracy is the closest approximation we have so far managed to give practical expression to these ideals. Democracy, Todorov insists, is "founded on humanist thought."[79]

Humanist morality does not seek to prioritize any one of these pillars over the other. What it seeks is the interaction of these three rather than the priority of any one over the other. To the Anglo-Saxon reader, Todorov's next point seems to run counter to his general trajectory when he says humanism cannot tell us whether or not to be religious, neither can it teach us about our need to understand the world and live in harmony with it. These tasks he assigns to science and the "disinterested contemplation of nature."[80] Like Camus, Todorov identifies most with Sisyphus because humanism rejects the illusion of paradise on earth and must remain content in the knowledge that our garden, however well tended, "remains forever imperfect."[81]

CHAPTER 8

CHRISTIAN HUMANISM: ATHENS VERSUS JERUSALEM

Christianity is, according to Leszek Kolakowski, a painful compromise between Athens and Jerusalem. "The compromise has never been entirely happy and the intellectual history of the Church has been plagued by incessant attempts to challenge it from one side or another."[1] By "Athens," Kolakowski means the tradition of philosophy and rational thought that began in Greece. And by "Jerusalem," he means the Abrahamic tradition of faith and revelation as the principal agency by which we know and love a God who cannot be understood rationally. Until the last few centuries, the contest has been an unequal one in that Jerusalem held the high ground from which to conduct the debate. Faith, Jerusalem's weapon of choice, was continually called into service when the reasoning of Athens seemed in danger of undermining Christian belief. And when faith needed help, in came the faggots and the stake. For a while, in the seventeenth and eighteenth centuries, it looked as if a marriage between Athens and Jerusalem could be arranged. That soon proved impossible. Since then, relations have worsened, and Jerusalem has been on the back foot. Søren Kierkegaard (1813–1855), one of the thinkers most influential in modern theology, understood the problem when he distinguished modern secular philosophy as the consequence of *cogito ergo sum*, whereas the Christian outlook revolves around "As thou believest, so art thou; to believe is to be." *Cogito* and *credo*: they are antithetical.[2]

The central dynamic of modernity for Christianity has been the growing distance between its Athens and Jerusalem wings, between *cogito* and *credo*. Jerusalem, represented in our day by theological conservatives, evangelicals, and fundamentalists, needs to retain the central role for an external, supernatural agent that overlooks and is responsible for all human reality. And yet

Athens, represented by a spectrum of people ranging from relatively centrist Christian believers to people now called post-Christians, is moving steadily away from this notion, partly in response to the new scientific understanding of our universe, our planet, and ourselves; and partly from a moral need to rescue notions of human autonomy from supernaturalist proscriptions. This trendline of modernity in the direction of Athens is a corollary of secularization, one feature of which has been biblical criticism, which, since the eighteenth century, has revealed progressively the human authorships and motivations of the Bible. Other stimuli have been the impact of Darwinism, new attitudes about gender equality, growing frustration at religion's role in fomenting divisiveness and a preference to help people in this world rather than preparing them for the next.

A number of important theologians in the twentieth century tried to resolve this tension between Athens and Jerusalem, between *cogito* and *credo*, by articulating varying themes of Christian humanism. Thinking theologically, the basic task of Christian humanism has been to reformulate the doctrine of the Incarnation, which, more than any other, telescopes the tension between the Athens and the Jerusalem strands of Christianity. The doctrine of the Incarnation declares that Christ was "truly God and truly man." Christ has two natures, the divine and the human, but no division or confusion between these two natures is admitted. Through the Incarnation, God intervenes in history, making us partakers of the communion with him. As the Gospel according to John says: "I am come that they might have life, and that they might have *it* more abundantly" (10:10). Roger Shinn, a progressive theologian from Union Theological Seminary, called this passage "the charter of Christian humanism."[3] A lot is going to ride on the emphasis here. Is the promise of abundant life the key phrase, or is it rather that Jesus has come so we can have these things? If the former, then one could be seen as expressing Christian faith legitimately by working in the world to bring relief to distress. If the latter, then the priority shifts away from action in the world to right belief and full obedience to the Jesus who brings these things.

This passage from John's Gospel contains the key line of tension that bedevils contemporary Christianity in general and Christian humanism in particular. Many millions of people, in the West at least, have simply washed their hands of the whole business by walking away from religion. A much smaller number have left organized religion for some specific alternative. Among those left within the church, fundamentalists have planted their stake firmly in a narrowly conceived version of the Jerusalem tradition and have insisted that Athens conform. And a few religious thinkers have tried to rework Athens so that it can plausibly pass muster as a simulacrum of Jerusalem. The insight of the Death of God theologians was to see in the Incarnation the ground through which modern believers could, in all faith, will the death of God.[4]

More recently came Charles Taylor, whose massive work *A Secular Age* won the 2007 Templeton Prize for its attempt to bridge the divide between Athens and Jerusalem. Taylor reworked the divide by speaking instead of the basic split between what he calls the *immanent frame* and some sort of *higher time*. The immanent frame, the dominant zeitgeist of our age, is that "sensed context in which we develop our beliefs" in which humanist options are as easy to hold as traditional religious beliefs.[5] It is clear that Taylor's immanent frame would be the home for the range of ideas preferred by the Athens mode of Christian belief, while his more elusive higher time would be more suitable for Jerusalem-type thinking.

Whichever way this basic divide is portrayed, the main goal of Christian humanism has been to contrive some form of reconciliation between the two diverging axes. Faith without sacrificing the rational faculty, reason without abandoning faith and a sense of mystery. Most people cite Erasmus (1466–1536), whose elegant fusion of Scholasticism and Ciceronian humanism created what has remained the ideal of Christian humanism: engaged, learned, and seeing the goodness in the world as evidence of God's love. A more recent version of the tradition could well be Friedrich Schleiermacher (1768–1834), who was sufficiently disturbed by the biblical criticism of his day to seek a new way to understand the Bible. Schleiermacher's method was a humanist one: locate and emphasize what is universal in the religious message in the Gospels, and de-emphasize the rest, recognizing it to be peripheral. And more recently still, we have Charles Taylor, who urges us to live in awareness of the mystery of higher time while planted firmly in the immanent frame. In this chapter, an attempt will be made, by the judicious selection of a few prominent representatives of Christian humanism, to illustrate their various reconciliations of Athens and Jerusalem.

THE FAILED PROMISE OF CATHOLIC HUMANISM

It is one of the paradoxes—another of the paradoxes—of this story, that the career of Christian humanism, with its talk of the universal qualities of being human, took very different courses and died for different reasons in the Catholic and Protestant worlds. Taking up our story in 1808, in fact, highlights the extent of the chasm between the papacy and Napoleon, modernity's most powerful enforcer at the time. Relations between Napoleon and Pope Pius VII had deteriorated to such an extent since their concordat seven years previously that French troops were sent into the Papal States, which in 1809 were incorporated into France. Napoleon was promptly excommunicated, and the pope found himself under arrest. Once Pius VII was back in Rome following Napoleon's defeat, he took his revenge. In short order, all papal officials who had cooperated with the French were dismissed and the Jews were dispatched back to the ghettoes from which Napoleon had freed them. Things went so far that the recently installed street lighting was turned off and vaccinations were banned. Suitably traumatized by the threat modernity posed to its premodern outlook and privileges, the papacy in the nineteenth century issued a stream of reactionary encyclicals that excoriated everything humanism stood for: unfettered learning, social justice, and freedom of thought and expression. The popes of the early twentieth century sat in sullen silence in the Vatican, hoping that it was all a bad dream. The mildest dissent to this attitude invited, and not infrequently attracted, excommunication. Only after their concordats with the rising fascist powers did the Vatican once more begin to play a role in the secular world.

But, as against the papacy, a few Catholic thinkers made some effort to understand what was happening, rather than merely reacting against it. One of them was the English historian Lord Acton (1834–1902), who has been called a Catholic humanist in this respect. His profound respect for John Locke, for the American Constitution, and for the separation of church and state all attest to this. It was Acton who uttered the famous warning that power corrupts and absolute power corrupts absolutely. And he had good reason to think this, being one of the few prominent Catholics to resist the move at the First Vatican Council from 1869 to 1870 to declare the pope infallible on matters of faith and morals.

The first of the major Catholic theorists to speak specifically of humanism was Jacques Maritain (1882–1973). A devout apologist of Thomist Catholicism, Maritain had no intention to articulate a position in opposition to the Vatican or to question Catholic dogma. His task was to rearticulate Catholic thought in the cadences of humanism. This he did in a series of lectures in Spain in 1934, which was later published as *Humanisme Intégral* (1936) and appeared in an English translation two years after that. Maritain distinguished sharply between theocentric and anthropocentric humanism. Theocentric humanism looked remarkably like Thomist Catholicism: the center for man is God, who has bestowed grace and freedom on a humanity that is both sinner and redeemed.[6] But against this ideal stood a line of anthropocentric humanism emerging out of the Renaissance, punctuated along the way by Rousseau and Hegel and ending up in atheism, leaving in the end the contest between two "pure positions": atheism and Christianity.[7] For Maritain, the only true humanism was Christian and the only true Christian was Catholic. Humanism becomes integral only when the central role of God in determining humanity is acknowledged. It combined all the best features, he claimed, of socialist humanism, but without all the attendant errors.[8] W. M. Urban argued in much the same way in *Humanity and Deity*.[9]

Another Catholic intellectual who wrote at some length on humanism was the German theologian and classicist Werner Jaeger (1888–1961). He was born in Kempen in the Rhineland, very near the Dutch border and the hometown of Thomas a Kempis, author of the classic piece of Christian mysticism, the *Imitation of Christ*. Jaeger was a product of the German education system while it was at its greatest level of influence. He held a variety of academic positions in Germany and Switzerland before immigrating to the United States. Despite working with Nazi authorities fairly amicably at first, it was not long before his Jewish wife became a serious issue. Soon after he was banned from teaching in 1936, he left the country for good. In 1939, he became director of the newly formed Institute for Classical Studies at Harvard. Jaeger remained in the United States for the remainder of his life. He is best known for his three-volume study *Paideia, the Ideals of Greek Culture* (1933–1943), a celebration of Greek civilization for a European culture he believed was rapidly degenerating into barbarism.

Jaeger articulated his understanding of humanism in 1943 in the Aquinas Lectures, sponsored each year by the Aristotelian Society of Marquette University of Wisconsin. It was Jaeger's wish to construct a "third humanism," following on from the first two; that of antiquity and the Renaissance. Interestingly, even a historian of Jaeger's stature was unaware of the true origin of the word *humanism*. Along with many others, he attributed it to the German Renaissance historians and was quite unaware of Niethammer's earlier role.[10]

Jaeger was aware of the trend toward nonreligious usage of humanism, which he traced—again, not entirely fairly—back to Ferdinand Schiller. The key to any humanism, Jaeger insisted, is its classical underpinnings, a claim many nonreligious humanists would agree with. But Jaeger had a different set of classical underpinnings in mind. He had little time for the pre-Socratic philosophers and, in reaction to Schiller, spoke specifically against Protagoras. Jaeger's classical underpinnings were Socrates, Plato, and Aristotle, who, he insisted, "reestablished the certainty of God as the supreme principle of the natural and social world."[11] True *Paideia*, in Plato's mind, rests on the supreme reality of God. It is hard to see how a classicist of Jaeger's repute would be unaware of the fact that Socrates, Plato, and Aristotle each had vastly different notions of what *God* (not to mention *the gods*) meant from what Christians later supposed to be the case. But these theological distinctions mattered less to Jaeger than the general cultural drift. Jaeger's attitude toward humanism goes to the heart of the Catholic approach. Where Protestants often work on some theological rearrangement of Christ's mission, the Catholic thinkers are more concerned with a broader conjunction of *civilization* with *Catholicism*. As Jaeger said: "Theology was intended from its very beginning to transcend humanism but at the same time it was the true fulfillment of the task [that] humanism had formulated."[12]

It was only after World War II that these attempts to accommodate the demands of dogma with the language of humanism were seen as problematic. The Church's ambivalent role in the war and the moral pressures of a post-Holocaust world suggested to many that the earlier approach was simply not enough. For many people in the 1960s, the outstanding example of a successful Christian humanism came from the work of Pierre Teilhard de Chardin (1881–1955). Teilhard was a curious mix of Jesuit priest and active evolutionist. He was a leading figure in the discovery of the remains at Piltdown, in Sussex, which were claimed to have been the newly discovered pieces of a skull that supplied the famous missing link between ape and human. The Piltdown discoveries were never free from suspicion and were eventually proved to be frauds. Teilhard was the only participant in the whole affair not to have been implicated in some way or other. The Catholic

Church of the day remained deeply suspicious of evolution and even more so of Catholic evolutionists, so Teilhard was sent off to China and forbidden to write on the subject. Paradoxically, it was in China that he participated in the discovery of *Homo erectus*, the so-called Peking Man, which really was a momentous discovery in human evolution.

It was only after his death that friends and admirers defied the church ban by gathering up and publishing Teilhard's writings. His books enjoyed a brief vogue, especially *The Phenomenon of Man*, which was hailed as a spectacular reconciliation of science and religion and as the century's finest articulation of Christian humanism. Teilhard spoke of the need for a rebirth of humanism and of Christianity.[13] But the means he sought to affect this rebirth were unique to him. He set himself the task of writing evolutionary theory across the cosmos, taking care to embed elements of Catholic dogma along the way. The result was an extravagant monument of anthropocentrism. "What I depict," he wrote, "is not the past in itself, but as it must appear to an observer standing on the advanced peak where evolution has placed us."[14] Evolution was placed on a universal scale of progression from simple to more complex organisms, but the complexity was spiritual rather than merely physical, as earlier attempts at this sort of progressionism had been content with.

Once again, we see that the more anthropocentric expressions of humanism come not from naturalists but from apologists from some variation of supernaturalism. And not only was Teilhard's work fundamentally anthropocentric, it was also strikingly Eurocentric. It's not often one can use this already-overstrained pejorative accurately, but with Teilhard one can. We would be "allowing sentiment to falsify the facts if we failed to recognize that during historic time the principal axis of anthropogenesis has passed through the West."[15] And by "the West," he meant "Christianity." And by "Christianity" he meant "Catholicism." China apparently "lacked both the inclination and the impetus for deep renovation,"[16] and India "allowed itself to be drawn into metaphysics, only to become lost there."[17] In the wake of Christian thought, humanity was moving inexorably toward a perfect Oneness. "Alone, unconditionally alone, in the world today, Christianity shows itself able to reconcile, in a single living act, the All and the Person."[18]

Teilhard was criticized from a number of perspectives. He wanted his work to be seen as a work of science, but the scientific community would have none of it. As science, Teilhard's work had no standing whatever. His evolutionary thinking was too heavily influenced by Henri Bergson to achieve that sort of status; his teleological projections into the future broke some of the most basic principles of science. Neither did Teilhard's work win much support among fellow Catholic thinkers. Jacques Maritain was incensed at the implied abandonment of important items of Catholic dogma, like original sin. He also deprecated the anthropocentrism of Teilhard's work. Other, more sympathetic critics, like Martin D'Arcy, saw Teilhard's work as "an inspirational program rather than the beginning of a successful reconciliation of science, humanism, and religion."[19]

From the point of view of this book, the question of Teilhard's Christian humanism is what matters. A core claim being made here is that if humanism is to be a positive force for the good in the twenty-first century, it must be able to articulate a meaningful way of living that is as free of anthropocentric conceit as possible. One of the more commonly encountered forms of anthropocentric conceit is a teleological projection of humanity's glory into an even more glorious future. Such a presumption can do no good for establishing humanist credentials: it flies in the face of science while also being philosophically untenable in any other guise than metaphysical speculation. It is difficult to see Teilhard's vision as any style of humanism, let alone a successful one.

For many, the high point of the Roman Catholic strand of Christian humanism came during the Second Vatican Council, or Vatican II, as it's known, which sat between 1962 and 1965. Since its bloodcurdling condemnations of liberalism and modernity in the nineteenth century, the church had found itself ever more estranged from the world, and the newly elected John XXIII knew that things had to change. Most of these contortions are beyond the range of this book, but the Declaration on Religious Liberty (*Humanae Dignitatis*), which was passed shortly before the council closed, is directly relevant. The extent of the shift in thinking in the declaration was made most clear when it conceded the essentially Protestant (and humanist) point that religious belief is, more than anything, a matter of individual conscience. As such, it eschewed any form of coercion to manufacture consent. As one Catholic writer put it, the declaration "was nothing less than an effort to reconcile the teaching of the Church with the philosophical inheritance of the Enlightenment."[20]

For most of the 1960s, the Vatican was keen to see itself as the only genuine source of humanism, much in the manner Jacques Maritain had spoken of. The most authoritative statement of Catholic humanism came from Pope Paul VI in his encyclical *Populorum Progressio* (*On the Development of Peoples*) on March 26, 1967. In a wide-ranging attempt to position the Church at the center of the fast-moving global situation, Paul VI spoke several times of the need for a "transcendent humanism," a "complete humanism," or a "universal humanism."

> The ultimate goal is a full-bodied humanism. [Here he has a footnote reference to Maritain.] And does this not mean the fulfillment of the whole man and of every man? A narrow humanism, closed in on itself, and not open to the values of the spirit and to God who is their source, could achieve apparent success for man and can set about organizing terrestrial realities without God. But closed off from God they will end up being directed against man.... True humanism points the way toward God and acknowledges the task to which we are called, the task which offers us the real meaning of human life. Man is not the ultimate measure of man. Man becomes truly man only by passing beyond himself.[21]

Paul VI even addressed "men of goodwill" who were not Christians in this encyclical, although he still did so on the authority of being "the father of all men." In this spirit he had established in 1965 the Secretariat for Non-Believers as a permanent office in the Vatican bureaucracy. A few formal meetings and dialogues took place, but little came from them. Paul VI reiterated his core position in his Christmas message in 1969 when he said that the Roman Catholic Church was the only home for true humanism.

Many Catholics were deeply moved by these changes. Albert Dondeyne (1901–1985), a prominent theologian from Louvain, said at one of the dialogues that an urgent task for the Secretariat for Non-Believers was to dispel negative old prejudices with respect to non-Christian humanism. He acknowledged that humanists could justifiably feel aggrieved by Paul VI's 1969 Christmas message and other more recent comments.[22] The most sustained expression of the new optimism was *Humanism and Christianity*, by the English Jesuit Martin D'Arcy (1888–1976). D'Arcy enthused that the long Lent of the church was over, by which he meant the centuries the Church sat on the sidelines grumbling resentfully about the cultural and intellectual developments had come to close. Instead the church "has entered the lists not to fight the good secularist but to work side by side with him in the regeneration of society."[23] No less than Jaeger and Maritain before them, Dondeyne and

D'Arcy insisted that "true humanism" was impossible without God. But unlike the earlier advocates, the men of the Vatican II decade saw value in making an effort to understand the bases of nonreligious humanism and acknowledging that one can be morally authentic without being Catholic.[24]

It was all a bit too good to be true. The hopes of men like Dondeyne and D'Arcy that Paul VI was a true successor to the hopeful John XXIII were soon to be betrayed. Paul VI's "full-bodied humanism" became apparent a year after this encyclical when he issued *Humanae vitae*, which prohibited any use of contraceptives among Catholics. He also reaffirmed clerical celibacy in *Sacerdotalis coelibatus* (1967) and disapproval of marrying outside the Church in *Matrimonia mixta* (1970). The short effusion of Catholic humanism was over. The pontificates of John Paul II (1978–2005) and his successor accelerated the retreat from the heady days of Vatican II Catholic humanism to a more doctrinaire triumphalism. The retreat began with the shutting down of popular Catholic intellectuals who had been prominent in Vatican II, like Hans Küng. More drastic was the proscription of liberation theology. John Paul II had been happy to fight injustice when the agents of oppression were atheistic Marxists, but when the oppressors were Catholic juntas and the rebels espoused Marxism, it was a different story. The retreat from the heady days of Vatican II reached its nadir in 2000, in the form of the encyclical *Dominus Iesus: On the Unicity and Salvific Universality of Jesus Christ and the Church*, which reasserted Catholic superiority and exclusivity. *Dominus Iesus* was written by Cardinal Ratzinger, who succeeded John Paul II as Benedict XVI.

No more graphic illustration of the distance traveled between the 1960s and the 1990s can be offered than to make mention of John Carroll's 1993 work *Humanism: The Wreck of Western Culture*. The expansive, open-ended Catholicism of Vatican II had collapsed back into blank reaction. Calling works one disagrees with polemical and a caricature are all too easy and all too frequent and run the same risks as crying wolf; we become less likely to react when it is true, as it is here. The substance of Carroll's charges was not new, although the level of polemic was. His arguments retrace Jacques Maritain's jeremiads in his later years. Humanism, Carroll argued, was doomed to fail from the start, unable as it is to successfully dethrone God in favor of Man. In a flourish any backwoods fundamentalist would be proud of, Carroll decries Darwin and Marx as the "key wreckers" of Western culture.[25] He goes on, "the humanist will has atrophied to nothing, now it has lost its higher conscience, the 'I am' has degenerated into that of a chronic invalid watching life from the window of the hospital."[26] And so on.

This is not to say that no stirrings of Catholic humanism remain. But since *Humanae vitae* and the pontificate of John Paul II, they are necessarily the voices of dissent. The theologian John Haught has made some startlingly frank admissions about how much dogma needs to be jettisoned in order to reconcile evolutionary thought with a religious impulse. In the manner of Teilhard, Haught has attempted a "metaphysics of the future," with a drastically reduced notion of God exercising overall, though remote, governance over a universe operating along evolutionary lines.[27] And, more practically, reformist Catholic organizations like Catholics Speak Out give voice to a humanistic variant of religious commitment.[28] One must imagine them praying for another John XXIII.

CHARLES HARTSHORNE AND THE MOVE BEYOND

At the beginning of the twentieth century, among Protestant theologians at least, the move toward a humanistic expression of faith seemed assured. One of Germany's leading Protestant theologians, Adolf von Harnack (1851–1930) outlined a liberal creed in *The Essence of Christianity* (1900), which amounted to loving God, loving one's neighbor, and being a good citizen. And Charles Eliot (1834–1926), longtime president of Harvard University, spoke of a similar brand of applied Christianity as the religion of the future. But World War I put strain on this bland progressionism. The shallowness of Harnack's liberal Protestantism was revealed quickly once his country was embroiled in war and he signed up as an enthusiastic and influential advocate of the holiness of Germany's cause, as did many of his erstwhile followers in their respective countries.

World War I changed everything, including the attitude of Protestant thinkers toward humanism. The bankruptcy of the prewar liberal, progressionist Protestantism encouraged in the decades between the wars a new mood of hostility toward expressions of Protestant humanism. One of the first specific attempts by a leading Protestant thinker to grapple with humanism came from Arthur Balfour (1848–1930), theologian, former prime minister, and one of the most prominent men in Britain at the time. A Conservative in politics, he had long been a defender of theism, having made his theological reputation with books *A Defence of Philosophic Doubt* (1879) and *The Foundations of Belief* (1894). Balfour relied mainly on rather strained rhetorical appeals to design, usually in the interests of the God of the Church of England. So, when it was announced that his title for the 1914 Gifford Lectures was "Theism and Humanism," many must have thought they were going to get a systematic consideration of Schiller's controversial works.

This did not happen. Balfour did little more than rework the main themes from his previous books, in particular, his design argument.[29] The biggest disappointment, though, was his almost complete inattention to the humanist side of his title. Balfour's targets hadn't changed; he was still gunning for nineteenth-century materialists and agnostics, but it was humanism that was labeled as the enemy. There was no recognition of the fact that humanists like Schiller were probably closer to Balfour than to the materialists and agnostics on many points. In fact, there was no discussion of any sort of people who we may justly see as humanists. William James and the liberal Protestants were hinted at, though not mentioned specifically. The word *humanism* appeared only twice in the entire work. Balfour laid out his views at the end of the lectures: "My desire has been to show that all we think best in human culture, whether associated with beauty, goodness, or knowledge, requires God for its support, that humanism without theism loses more than half its value."[30] In the end, his approach was much the same as that of the Catholic scholars.

The growth of the humanist movement in the 1920s and 1930s prompted a series of more promising criticisms of humanism. Reinhold Niebuhr (1892–1971) was a prominent critic, but for our purposes the American Protestant theologian Charles Hartshorne (1897–2000) is worth some attention. In *Beyond Humanism* (1937), Hartshorne displayed a considerable knowledge of contemporary humanist writings and offered relevant arguments against them. And in a partial return to aspects of earlier liberal Protestantism, he was also prepared to jettison a great deal of the traditional orthodoxy that Balfour held dear. Traditional supernaturalism was no longer credible, and popular fundamentalism amounted to little more than a "boast or a bludgeon."[31] This is a significant concession from this strand of Protestant thinking. They are, to return to our language at the start of the chapter, willing to abandon most of Jerusalem in order to graft more effectively what they see as its core elements onto a newly spiritualized Athens.

What worried Hartshorne (along with Jaeger, Maritain, and many others) was what he saw as the excessive anthropocentrism of considering humanity the be-all and end-all of the universe. "If the man of today leaves humanism, it should be to go beyond and forward, not back to those things which the humanist has so acutely criticized and found wanting."[32] But unlike the more conservative theologians, Hartshorne understood that turning the clock back was hardly a constructive solution. Going forward involved embracing a neo-Spinozist panentheism sprinkled with A. N. Whitehead's philosophy of religion and Einstein's notions of cosmic religious feeling. God, according to Hartshorne's reading of the new theism is "simply nature as literally and profoundly lovable, and not merely as pleasant to our senses or interesting for us to think about."[33] As the title suggests, *Beyond Humanism* was devoted not so much to defending his brand of theism as to demonstrating the inadequacy of humanism.

The rest of the book was devoted to surveys of a range of prominent thinkers and to explanations of where they went wrong. Hartshorne's first target, unsurprisingly, was John Dewey, whose influential work *A Common Faith*, which we discussed in chapter 3, was then only three years old. His approach here was representative of the book. In point after point Hartshorne agreed with Dewey, insofar as his criticisms applied to traditional Catholic theology. The dangers of the split between supernatural and natural, the personal God, the problem of evil—Hartshorne conceded them all. But after each concession he would retort that the "new theism" had dealt with the problem. It is not the purpose of this book to enter into lengthy discussion of Hartshorne's new theism except to say that few people today would see much value in it. But he did at least engage with his humanist adversaries intelligently and honestly.

Having left the narrow path of criticizing his contemporaries, Hartshorne's work fell off dramatically. Quite in any way the weakest chapter is his eleven-page dash through the entire history of humanism, from the Buddha and Confucius to H. G. Wells and Clarence Day, where fault was found with everyone and everything in the most casual and sweeping terms. Here he looks more like the conventional apologists of the day. Buddhism is condemned as having contributed "next to nothing to the development of natural science." And "the Chinese" are said to lack an intense sense of the divine, a defect which explains "their somewhat cynical, disillusioned attitude toward social evils and their tendency toward sensuality."[34] A few words of dismissal see off ancient Greece, the Stoics, Epicureans, Nietzsche, Schopenhauer, and all the rest. Having outlined the "petulant arrogance" of Schopenhauer, the "humorless pedantry" of Comte, and so on, Hartshorne magnanimously concedes that "it is only fair to remark that the defects of character and sanity found in atheists of earlier generations may have been due in no small measure to the intolerance and unkindness with which they were treated by religious bigots."[35] He concludes the chapter thus: "Only by surveying the long-run and average effects of doctrines can one with any confidence pronounce upon their practical bearings."[36] How often have Christian apologists reacted with Olympian scorn when rationalists have drawn unfavorable conclusions about Christianity after making historical studies—often very thorough studies—of the Inquisition, the Crusades, burning witches, and so on? And yet when a Christian scholar does the same thing, and with a fraction of the evidence, he is lionized as a major intellect.

THE NEW HUMANISM AND THE DEATH OF GOD

Theologians between the wars were too conscious of human weaknesses and depravity to take kindly to notions of humanism, particularly as the word was being taken over, it seemed, by the American religious humanists. But after World War II a new attitude arose among churchmen, one that was more willing to engage with the challenges posed by humanism. But it was a specific understanding of humanism, laden with terminology borrowed from the existentialist philosophers, in particular Heidegger.

In their different ways, four theologians articulated aspects of this trend: Karl Barth, Dietrich Bonhoeffer, Rudolf Bultmann, and Paul Tillich. Karl Barth (1886–1968) is best remembered for his ferocious polemics written between the wars on behalf of God as "wholly other" and humanity's utter dependence on God's grace. But after World War II, he spoke for a while of the New Humanism. In his 1949 address "The Christian Message and the New Humanism," he declared that the Christian message is nothing less than "the message of the humanism of God." As he had done in his younger days, Barth still stressed humanity's utter dependence on God but placed more emphasis on an Incarnational theology of God and man being one in Jesus Christ.

Appealing as this may have been for a small coterie of theologically minded Christians, Barth's language and priorities were never going to travel beyond this small audience. More appealing to a broader readership was Dietrich Bonhoeffer (1906–1945), whose death at the hands of the Nazis only days before the end of the war added poignancy to his message, despite strong points of similarity with that of Barth. It was the fate of Bonhoeffer's legacy that he became the poster boy for a radical post-Christianity he would not have supported had he been alive. The Bonhoeffer favored by new humanist and Death of God thinkers was the radical Bonhoeffer who spoke of *religionless Christianity*, by which he meant a Christianity that has become a removable garment hindering free and spontaneous movement of the man of God. With Jesus' lament that God has forsaken him on his mind (Mark 15:34), Bonhoeffer wrote: "God is teaching us that we must live as men who can get along very well without him. . . . The God who makes us live in this world without using him as a working hypothesis is the God before whom we are ever standing."[37]

Another prominent theologian who came to speak of humanism in the years after the war was Rudolf Bultmann (1884–1976). Bultmann understood the growing divide between Athens and Jerusalem and made it his task to reinterpret the New Testament for the new world we live in. By acknowledging openly the mythological elements in the New Testament, Bultmann devoted his career to the radical transformation of an outmoded dogmatic theology into a set of existential challenges. So his foray into humanism was something of a digression for him, but it's worthwhile nonetheless for us to consider. Christianity and humanism, he wrote, will sink or swim together in the contest against arbitrariness, relativism, and nihilism.

> Humanistic faith in man is not at all faith in man as an empirically definable phenomenon, with his reason and his right and his ability to make the law for himself and for the world. Rather humanistic faith is faith in the idea of man which stands as a norm above his empirical life, prescribing his duty and thereby bestowing upon him dignity and nobility. Humanism is faith in the spirit of which man partakes, the spirit of whose power man creates the world of the true, the good, the beautiful, in science and philosophy, in law and in art.[38]

Bultmann argued that humanism and Christianity are one in seeing that a person is "a being that carries its meaning and value in itself."[39] But he was by no means arguing for a complete identity between humanism and Christianity. He was too far in Heidegger's debt for that. To the extent there is an "either-or," it lies in the perception of God. For the humanist, "God's Beyond is spirit of which man with his spirit partakes."[40] For the Christian, however, God is always "the hidden one and the coming one." Both forces acknowledge the authority of the spirit of man, but only Christianity attributes this to the agency of God. The challenge for the future, Bultmann argued, was not the victor of one or the other party but the progressive establishment of a creative balance between the diverging perspectives.

Bultmann has been a hugely influential theologian, and his position on the creative tension between humanism and Christianity has, with varying degrees of intensity, been taken up by nondogmatic Christian thinkers.[41] Another equally influential theologian who tackled these issues, though in a different way, was Bultmann's contemporary, Paul Tillich (1886–1965). From their different perspectives, Hartshorne and Bultmann agreed with the humanists that most items of Christian dogma were unsustainable, but they saw little improvement in the humanist position beyond their recognizing that simple fact. Tillich too saw little value in Christian dogma, to the point of being more openly supportive of the atheist rejection of the conventional personal God. "The first step to atheism," he wrote, "is always a theology [that] drags God down to the level of doubtful things."[42] But where Hartshorne went up into the ether to deposit the remnants of his God, Tillich went down into the human psyche. Recalling the then fashionable depth psychology, Tillich spoke of God as both "the ground of all being" and the "source of your being."[43]

At one point he turns directly to the unbeliever and invites him in.

> And believe me, you who are estranged from religion and far away from Christianity, it is not our purpose to make you religious and Christian when we interpret the call of Jesus for our time. We call Jesus the Christ not because He brought a new religion, but because He is the end of religion, above religion and irreligion, above Christianity and non-Christianity.[44]

It should come as no surprise that those who are estranged from religion have not heeded this call. Most humanists not closely connected with specifically Christian humanism have not seen a great deal of point in Jesus Christ, once every item of Christian dogma is abandoned, bearing in mind that "Jesus Christ" is an invention of Christian dogma. As the so-called Third Quest for the Historical Jesus has shown, the simple message of Rabbi Yeshua, a message entirely of its time, was directed entirely to his fellow Jews. But, over the next three centuries, Rabbi Yeshua's eschatological warnings were transformed into the theology of the universalizing Jesus Christ.

Tillich also seems to miss the point with respect to humanism.

> Glory without purity is the character of all pagan gods. And purity without glory is the character of all the humanistic ideas of God. Humanism has transformed the inaccessibility of God into the sublimity of His moral commands. Humanism has forgotten that God's majesty, as experienced by the prophet, implies the shaking of the foundations wherever He appears, and the veil of smoke whenever He shows Himself. When God is identified with an element of human nature, as in humanism, the terrifying and annihilating encounter with majesty becomes an impossibility.[45]

It is hard to imagine who Tillich had in mind with this construction of humanism, unless he is thinking only of Renaissance humanism. But it seems to miss the point in a major way. Humanism has not *forgotten* God's majesty, and neither does it recognize his moral commands as necessarily being sublime. And, insofar as it rejects firmly the more supernatural elements of the God idea, humanism is committed far more deeply to a shaking of the foundations than Tillich's studied ambiguity. Several critics, Walter Kaufmann in particular, have made the point that Tillich is simply trying to eradicate the gulf between religious belief and other forms of commitment by means of a thoroughly ambiguous exercise in redefinition. In one pithy summary, Kaufmann wrote: "Tillich wants to have his Nietzsche and eat his bread at communion, too."[46]

These weaknesses notwithstanding, Tillich's influence among progressive Protestants has been profound. Nowhere can this be seen more clearly than in the flurry of attempts in the 1960s to expound a variety of Christian humanism. In Britain the most public face of this trend was the bishop of Woolwich, J. A. T. Robinson (1919–1983), whose short tract, *Honest to God* (1963) had a brief vogue. *Honest to God* owed a massive debt to Bonhoeffer and Tillich in particular. Robinson wanted us to abandon a notion of god "out there" and embrace the god within. Whereas Julian Huxley was calling for a religion without revelation, Robinson—following Bonhoeffer—called for a Christianity without religion. It was not that Robinson's book was all that original, or even coherent. What made his work influential is that a bishop had written it. Neither was Robinson an out-and-out radical seeking a drastic demythologization. He reiterated constantly his reluctance to explore religion in the way that he was doing, but he felt the situation demanded it. He began *Honest to God* admitting that, when listening to radio discussions between Christians and humanists, his sympathies often lay with the humanists.[47]

Despite its wide circulation, the majority of the religious public rejected Robinson's deified humanism. And, following the archbishop of Canterbury's lead, most of his colleagues distanced themselves from him as well. And indeed the Church of England has retreated more and more into reaction since then. Robinson wrote more worthwhile books after *Honest to God*, but his fifteen minutes of fame had passed, and they were ignored. Those embracing Robinson's views continue to hold important positions and are influential, but the balance of power has passed back to religious conservatives. Religious critics, whether liberal or—like Robinson—quite conservative, have always been in the difficult position of recognizing the force of the rationalist critique of religion while wanting to preserve some increasingly hollow religious essence. In the end, however, *cogito* and *credo* don't mix.

In the United States the new humanism in theology was led by Harvey Cox and by the Death of God theologians. In *The Secular City*, Cox challenged the prevailing view that the secularization of society inevitably meant the retreat of Christianity. If by *Christianity* we meant the traditional hierarchy bound by dogmatic theology and obsolete supernaturalism, then this would be as true as it was welcome. But, Cox promised, if Christianity could embrace the conditions of the new secular humanity, with all its hope and energy, then a glorious future was in store. This was, in effect, a new vision of the Incarnation, cut to suit contemporary tastes. It was also blandly confident that things were on an infinite progression to better things. Once again, we can see that the more crass expressions of progressionism come from theistic-inclined humanists.

The trajectory of the new humanism was at this stage spiraling toward the most radical renunciation of pretty much every aspect of Christian dogma. No more so than the career of the so-called Death of God movement. The Death of God idea was never really popular enough to warrant being called a *movement*. But for a few years, particularly between 1961 and 1969 or so, it was influential. The high point in terms of popular recognition came in October 1965 when *Time* magazine ran a cover that asked the question, is God dead? As with Robinson and Cox, the core insight of the Death of God thinkers was not new to them. The first major thinker to speak specifically about the death of God was Hegel, but it was Friedrich Nietzsche, who, in *The Gay Science* (1882), wrote one of the more memorable passages of Western philosophy when a madman declared that "God is dead, and we have killed him." By "we," Nietzsche meant Western civilization.[48] But it wasn't the death of God being lamented so much as our lack of awareness of the magnitude of what was happening. And anyway, while Nietzsche was obviously important for the Death of God theologians, it was Kierkegaard by whom they were most influenced. Altizer described him as "the real creator of modern theology."[49]

When they spoke of the death of God, most of these theologians meant the end of any serious meaning to a transcendental God in contemporary society. What had died, they argued, was the cultural significance and relevance of God in people's lives. And, as some critics observed, what they were really saying had died was one particular *understanding* of God. Once again, this climactic event was understood in terms of the doctrine of Incarnation.

> Only the Christian can celebrate the Incarnation in which God has actually become flesh, and radical theology must finally understand the Incarnation itself as effecting the death of God.[50]

Paul van Buren expressed a similar point, though without recourse to Death of God language.

> The Christian is nothing if not one who is concerned for man, and his "humanism" is defined by the history of that man [Jesus] and his strange but human freedom, which has become contagious.[51]

What the Death of God theologians grasped was that Bultmann and Tillich, though happy to demythologize large areas of Christianity, were reluctant to extend the practice to Jesus Christ, who remained "the answer" in some way or another. Christ, in this way, remains transcendent and immanent. The Death of God theologians were not satisfied by this. Altizer was clearer as to the implications of biblical scholarship:

> When the biblical scholar arrived at a historical understanding of the eschatological foundation of Jesus' proclamation of the Kingdom of God, he brought to an end the contemporary relevance of the biblical forms of Jesus' message.[52]

And Ronald Gregor Smith, though not identified with Death of God theology, was saying much the same thing with his oft-quoted passage: "we may freely say that the bones of Jesus lie somewhere in Palestine."[53] The more conservative Death of God theologians like Vahanian still believed that God was alive and real, while the more radical thinkers like Altizer, William Hamilton, and Paul van Buren (1924–1998) spoke in terms of a "real loss of real transcendence." They were following on from Bonhoeffer's observation, made while he was incarcerated in 1944, that "men as they are now simply cannot be religious anymore."[54]

It has become customary to speak slightingly of the Death of God movement in the wake of the fundamentalist resurgence that has taken place since then. It was always foolish, the argument goes, to speak of the Death of God when God still has such power to inspire millions of people. This may be the case, but the fact remains that the Western world lives in a secular age. Even the Templeton Foundation–funded Charles Taylor has acknowledged as much. This can plausibly be called a post-Christian age, and the Death of God theologians were trying to find a place for faith in such an environment. A more telling criticism of this movement was its inability to draw the line at a reduced and yet still credible and emotionally satisfying religious belief. But this weakness is not unique to the Death of God theologians; it is ubiquitous among all contemporary theologians trying to reconcile Athens and Jerusalem.

The trajectory on both sides of the Atlantic since the end of the 1960s has been to return to a more conservative, doctrinal variant of Christianity. Nowhere is this shift more graphically illustrated than in the few attempts to fashion a Christian humanism in the light of this new conservatism. One of them emerged from the lesser colleges in the Midwest after the 1960s, where William Franklin and Joseph Shaw had an awkward time positioning themselves between antihumanist fundamentalism on the one hand and religious humanism and radical theology on the other. Their work, *The Case for Christian Humanism* (1991), insisted on the Christian nature of their humanism and heatedly denied they were peddling any radical theology. The

Risen Christ was at the center of their theology, not "the watered-down, good example" Christ of old-style liberalism."[55] On the basis of a very modest reading, secular humanism was simply abused, being dismissed at various times as extreme, strident, and antireligious. Religious humanism was denounced almost as strongly, but at least here some care was taken to offer an argument.

> One cause even claims the name "religious humanism," but it is in fact a naturalistic, secularistic humanism with a vengeance. It is unacceptable to Christians because it rejects the existence of any power superior to humans, transcending human life. What is also disturbing about "religious humanism" is that while it purports to honor humans by lauding their dignity, worth, and unlimited capabilities, it actually does them a disservice by treating them as natural objects. They are simply a part of nature, nothing more.[56]

Against the religious humanists, the Christian humanism of Franklin and Shaw took traditional Christian theology seriously and expressed it once again, in broadly humanistic terms. "Christian humanism rests on God taking human form, the doctrine of the Incarnation, and God's Son being rejected and killed, the doctrine of the Atonement. This is good news for *all* humanity."[57]

The Christian humanism of Franklin and Shaw was a great deal more conventional than either their New Humanist predecessors, or the similar expressions of Christian humanism appearing in Britain at the time. At about the same time their book appeared, an English liberal churchman, Anthony Freeman, penned a short work *God in Us: A Case for Christian Humanism* (1993), which carried on the course set by Bishop Robinson and acknowledged that religion is a human construct and that our relation to this construct is one based on faith rather than facts.[58] This was in sharp contrast to the Americans, who were pitted against any rejection of supernaturalism, any idea that human beings are part of the natural order, or any notion of Christ being merely human. For this they needed a conventional theology of Incarnation, a doctrine that was already under serious challenge, most notably by John Hick.[59] Franklin and Shaw stood for a humanitarian ethic by and through Christian living. But as Maritain had tried to conflate "true" humanism with Catholicism, so did Franklin and Shaw try to do with Protestantism. And Freeman was trying the same thing in the name of a postdoctrinal Christianity.

Yet despite their differences, both suffered a similar fate, being too conventionally Christian to appeal to any other type of humanist, and by even using the word *humanism*, ensuring they would have little traction within conventional Christendom. Its fate was shared by socialist humanism which, as we have seen, also had the problem of being caught between a rock and a hard place.

The central dilemma the New Humanists, and religious liberals generally, have been unable to resolve satisfactorily is the point at which one concession too many has been made and one can no longer meaningfully describe oneself as a Christian. The most insightful critic here was Walter Kaufmann (1921–1980), whose work has been supported in the decades since by a wide range of thinkers. Kaufmann noted correctly that it would not have crossed anyone's mind before the nineteenth century to determine charity as the key mark of the Christian. What made someone a Christian was conformity to dogma, what one believed. In conformity to the prevailing humanist ethos of the age, liberal Protestants have turned all this upside down, shedding items of dogma as time has passed until, in their nakedness, they claim to have returned to the ethical purity of Jesus. But this requires a very peculiar view of Jesus and a cavalier view of Christian history. It requires Jesus to look very much like a liberal Protestant in fact: dogma lite, but a really good guy. As Kaufmann notes, for liberal Protestantism to be right, Jesus would have to have been betrayed the moment his flesh was cold, by all arms of Christendom until such time as the world was made safe for liberal Protestants to recapture his essential message.[60]

A later critic, one who had spent his career as a liberal Protestant in the United States, was Duncan Howlett (1906–2003). After a lifetime of service to the Unitarian church, Howlett came to recognize the validity of Kaufmann's argument. There always comes a point, he wrote in 1995, when religious liberals have to stop asking questions. Too many questions and the religious believer will end up nonreligious. But where to draw the line? This will depend on each individual's disposition, confidence, and learning, but at the cost of giving an arbitrary feel to religious liberalism. This demilitarized zone inside each religious liberal between what is open to question and what is not results in a weak worldview and constitutes the fatal flaw in the heart of religious liberalism.[61] One can extend Howlett's critique by seeing it is not peculiar to liberal Christians. We will see this fatal flaw at work again in chapter 11. The fatal flaw is one of the principal faultlines that demarcates

Athens from Jerusalem. Christianity, in the end, is not a humanist enterprise. It is about the conquest of the human, not its fulfillment.[62] It is about finding oneself not through oneself and through others, but through submission to a body of propositions about something called *God*.

AMERICAN EVANGELICALS AND THE "RELIGION OF SECULAR HUMANISM"

The Christian critics of humanism in the first half of the twentieth century varied in the range of humanist material they were familiar with, which meant, of course, that their criticism varied in quality as well. But the criticisms were, for the most part, based on an adequate reading of humanist material. In the half century that followed, this changed. The overriding feature of Christian criticism of humanism in the later part of the twentieth century was its ever-greater fanaticism. The engine room of this acceleration came from the United States, and it was driven as much by its total rejection of the Christian humanism we have been summarizing as by any reaction to what secular-minded humanists were saying. And while the angst experienced by the United States in the seventies was by no means peculiar to that country, the solution many Americans sought to deal with the problem was. There was a general feeling through the West that intellectual and moral foundations of society were becoming ever more brittle and insupportable. But only in the United States did this angst focus, in the minds of many people, around a single concept. Only in the United States was the need felt for an all-purpose scapegoat. During a similar period of doubt and transition in Germany, that scapegoat was "the Jews." In the United States, it was secular humanism.

Among the academic community, the mood was captured by books like *The Arrogance of Humanism*, by David Ehrenfeld, at the time a professor of biology at Rutgers University. Ehrenfeld was not indulging in a general attack on humanism. "The better parts of humanism are not in question here," he wrote, "when the inappropriate religious elements have been removed, humanism will become what it ought to be, a gentle and decent philosophy and a trustworthy guide to nondestructive behavior."[63] But having said that, Ehrenfeld went on to make a systematic critique of much that he saw wrong in Western society, lumping it all under the general appellation of *humanism*. Anticipating many later postmodernists, Ehrenfeld was worried about the universalizing tendencies of reason, and while not using the term, he feared humanism was a brand of *speciesism*.

Ehrenfeld's critique was to be the last civil discussion of humanism for some time. Far more widely read were the heated attacks coming from outside the academy. The attack with the greatest pretensions to academic credibility came from Francis A. Schaeffer (1912–1984), a self-appointed evangelical jeremiah. In a long series of books, most notably *How Should We Then Live?* (1976), Schaeffer attacked what he saw as gradual loss of purpose in modernity toward an ever-growing fragmentation and despair. He had a particular interest in, although a crude understanding of, contemporary visual arts. Characteristic of Schaeffer's critique is the following passage:

> The historical flow is like this: The philosophers from Rousseau, Kant, Hegel and Kierkegaard onward, having lost their hope of a unity of knowledge and a unity of life, presented a fragmented concept of reality; then the artists painted that way.[64]

Providing a fragmented concept of reality has not been one of the more common accusations made against any of these thinkers, particularly Kant and Hegel. But with airy generalizations of this sort, Schaeffer achieved a following among evangelicals and fundamentalists.

Low-quality though this sort of critique was, Schaeffer's work was ivory tower in comparison with much of what was to follow. Among the many hysterical works assailing secular humanism at the time included a short monograph published out of Lubbock, Texas. Homer Duncan's work, titled *Secular Humanism: The Most Dangerous Religion in America*, built up a Manichean picture of a life-or-death struggle between the forces of good versus the forces of evil. A passage from Dr. L. Nelson Bell, Billy Graham's father-in-law, which was put in bold print in the book and used as a scare quote at the start of the work, summarized Duncan's position:

> Christians need to recognize the solemn fact that humanism is not an ally in making the world a better place in which to live. It is a deadly enemy for it is a religion without God and without hope in this world or the next.[65]

In true conspiracy-theory style, Duncan mused over President Carter's letter of support to the American Humanist Association in April of 1978, and his choice of Walter Mondale, a religious humanist, as vice president. "It is inconceivable that a good, born-again Southern Baptist would send such a message commending those who seek to destroy the very God whom he serves, but then I wonder."[66] Incredibly enough, the beliefs of Mondale were still being cited as an example of the perfidious influence of secular humanism more than two decades later, when the issue was brought up once more by Tim LaHaye and David Noebel in 2000![67] Books like this, and there were many, were, despite their breathtaking hollowness, very influential. No less a figure than Senator Jesse Helms wrote a preface for Duncan's work, describing it, apparently without irony, as a "thought-provoking analysis."[68] Only a few years after producing material as sweeping and inaccurate as this, Duncan acknowledged to *Free Inquiry* readers that humanists can't in fact be simply lumped together into a one-size-fits-all category and even that some fundamentalist Christians pose a threat to the open society.[69] Needless to say, these admissions did not find their way into any of his polemical writings.

But our downward spiral is not complete. Compared to some other works, Homer Duncan was moderate and fair-minded. A year after Duncan's work, Tim LaHaye wrote *The Battle for the Mind*, which was even more Manichean and extremist and even less concerned with the demands of accuracy than Duncan's work. LaHaye was even more determined to polarize Christianity and humanism and even more willing to demonize his opponents. LaHaye gave a summary of humanism in these terms:

> Humanism is pro-one world—America second, with an obsession to merge Western democracies, Eastern Communism, and third-world dictatorships into a one world, socialist state, where Plato's dream of "three classes of people" would be fulfilled: the elite *ruling* class; the omnipresent *military*; the *masses*, where there is no difference between the sexes: Men and women do the same work, and children are wards of the state. Naturally, the humanists will be the elite *ruling class*.[70]

The fact that such a vision bore no relationship with what humanists have actually advocated counted for nothing. At least Francis Schaeffer and even Homer Duncan had made some effort, however nominal, to understand the humanist position. But LaHaye's summary runs completely contrary to what prominent humanist thinkers have actually advanced; think of Bertrand Russell, Karl Popper, John Dewey, Sidney Hook, Ernest Gellner, or Paul Kurtz. LaHaye's caricature of humanism is worse than merely inaccurate. It actually summarizes what humanists from all political persuasions are most agreed that they oppose. Whether in so-called shilling shockers like Russell's *The Practice and Theory of Bolshevism* or in extended critiques like Popper's *The Open Society and Its Enemies* or Todorov's *Hope and Memory*, humanists have exercised their talents to decry just the sort of society LaHaye characterized as the essence of humanism. Even Corliss Lamont (who LaHaye does actually quote) held a much more nuanced view than he is portrayed as advancing.

But LaHaye's diatribes were not about accuracy. They were about stimulating a sense of disgust, one of the six basic human emotions, among his readers. Like the Nazi polemics against the Jews, this sort of fundamentalist attack has a moral purpose: to portray those being attacked as less than human and not deserving of the rules of conventional controversial engagement. LaHaye knew that people motivated by disgust will work harder and donate more to the cause, than those who merely find themselves in intellectual disagreement with some other section of society.[71] This is why we need to take the threat from fundamentalists like LaHaye seriously. It is important not simply to dismiss their writings as irrelevant yelping from the margins; often the preferred response of many religious humanists and progressive Christians. But it won't do to simply look away. Attacks such as these must be responded to, not swept under the carpet in the hope they will go away. And, as we know, LaHaye went on to dominate the fundamentalist attack on secular humanism right up to and including his *Left Behind* series. Despite their quite extraordinarily low quality, both intellectual and literary, they have enjoyed bestseller status and have been very influential in polarizing American opinion in the culture wars.

In Britain there has been a similar, though less severe, decline in the quality of apologetic literature, and secular humanism has not become the ritualized target that it has in the United States. In 1963, Lutterworth Press produced a series of short monographs in its "Christian Approach" series in which William Strawson, a Methodist minister, wrote the critique of humanism. Strawson was widely read in humanist literature and presented a fair and measured critique. Twenty-five years later, the evangelical polemic *Reason and Faith* by Roger Forster and Paul Marston combined a lesser familiarity with humanist opinion with a greater willingness to take cheap shots and rely on simple assertion. And two decades later again, Alister McGrath felt able to announce the twilight of atheism despite an almost total ignorance of humanist and atheist material produced since World War II.[72] Within months of McGrath's declaration of atheism's twilight, the New Atheists burst on the scene, bringing atheist opinion to a larger audience than had ever previously been the case.

LLOYD GEERING AND THE SPIRITUAL SCHIZOPHRENIA

Since the eclipse of the radical New Humanist theologies in the late 1960s and the subsequent resurgence of fundamentalism, the old faultline between Athens and Jerusalem has hardened and widened. Christian churches have been fracturing more along conservative and liberal wings—divisions that have more relevance than any of the old denominational distinctions. Caught in the no-man's-land between these two noncommunicating sections of Christianity is the general run of the believer, who is getting less and less information as to the actual state of scholarship on the foundations of their faith.

As Bishop John Shelby Spong, one of the highest-profile contemporary religious radicals put it: "Between the academy in which our clergy are trained and the pews in which our church members sit is a gap in knowledge of enormous proportions. Indeed, that gap might better be described as a void."[73] An ally of Spong, the New Zealand radical theologian Lloyd Geering has made the same observation:

> Much of what had been taught in seminaries for decades had never reached the people in the pews, let alone the public at large. This was partly because many ministers, afraid of causing dissension in their congregations, were reluctant to share with them the new understanding of the Bible, which even ministers themselves may have found disturbing at first. As a result, it was still widely assumed that everything in the Bible was to be taken literally.[74]

In the face of this threat a new group of Christian humanist thinkers has arisen to try to bridge the chasm. Each spent most of his life in the church, but most have been estranged from it to some extent or other. In Norway, for example, Lutheran Bishop Kristian Schjelderup (1894–1980) articulated what he called a "struggling humanism," the struggle being the attempt to reconcile what he believed to be almost irreconcilable.[75] In the English-speaking world, the best-known of them is the former Episcopalian bishop John Shelby Spong in the United States; Richard Holloway, Anthony Freeman, and Don Cupitt in Britain; and Lloyd Geering in New Zealand. We outlined Cupitt's thought in chapter 5, though it could just as easily be discussed here. This serves once again as a reminder that the chapter divisions in this book are porous and don't necessarily indicate important differences of approach. Spong and Freeman are generally thought of as the most conservative of this group, although that word should be used advisedly. Contrasted with most prominent churchmen of the early twenty-first century, they are very radical indeed. But compared with Geering, Holloway, or Cupitt, it is generally true that they are more willing to try to retain a Christian patina to their religious humanism. Holloway left the church in 2000, and Geering and Cupitt are Christian in very restricted senses. So much so that the distinction between *Christian humanist* and *religious humanist* at this point becomes pretty well impossible to maintain.

For no particular reason beyond that he is my countryman, I would like to focus on the work of Lloyd Geering as being representative of the latest attempts to give expression to a Christian humanism. Lloyd Geering (1918–) was born in Rangiora, a small town in the South Island of New Zealand, and rose to become the country's best-known theologian; he became, alongside Cupitt and Spong, one of the world's most influential exponents of a radical religious humanism. Geering became a household name in New Zealand in 1967 after hardliners in the Presbyterian Church brought him to trial for doctrinal irregularities—heresy to everyone else. This trial brought religion into the newspapers and living rooms of New Zealanders in way not seen before. His string of books, lectures, and public controversies over the next half century assured his place as New Zealand's best-known theologian and public intellectual on the big questions.

Though spending his adult life in the church, Geering was at heart a freethinker; he never embraced its teachings unthinkingly, as many of his fellow churchgoers did. So by the time the New Humanism, which we spoke of earlier in this chapter, came to prominence in the early 1960s, it was probably inevitable that Geering should be there amongst it. The people who mattered to Geering were Tillich, Martin Buber (1878–1965), the Scottish theologian Ronald Gregor Smith (1913–1968), and the Canadian theologian Wilfred Cantwell Smith (1916–2001).[76] The result was the clash between him and the traditionalists, culminating in the heresy trial that made his name heard around the country and determined his life. Geering made a career out of bridging the abyss between what the general Christian believer believes to be true about the Bible and what educated seminarians and theologians know to be true.

One of the most insightful diagnoses of the abyss separating Athens and Jerusalem came from Geering when he diagnosed the condition of spiritual schizophrenia. By *spiritual schizophrenia* he meant the attempt to inhabit the geocentric pre-Copernican world of the Bible and the heliocentric, post-Copernican world as unveiled by science at the same time.[77] Over the past five centuries, science has rendered untenable the human-centred universe the Bible was framed in. And only now are we beginning to appreciate that the error of anthropocentric thinking is reinforced each time we as a species behave with speciesist arrogance toward other living creatures on this world and toward our environment. And when anthropocentrism is allied with supernaturalism, a potentially disastrous mix is brought forth.

Geering has set himself the task of overcoming this schizophrenia by jettisoning all manifestations of Jerusalem that cannot pass the Athenian test of authenticity. But for Geering, as for many of the current cohort of prominent religious humanists, the test of authenticity is not limited to verifiable fact but to a world of lived experience. He is saying much the same thing as the Death of God theologians, although his prose is a great deal more accessible to the nonspecialist reader. And neither is he simply sweeping the Jerusalem strand away, as the Death of God theologians were widely accused of doing. Geering is enthusiastic about the spiritual value of myth, metaphor, and notions of green spirituality. This conscious replacement of the doctrinaire strand of faith with the more poetic appreciation of nonrational modes is the most significant contribution of religious humanism in the last half century.

Geering was eclectic in the labels he ascribed to himself. Rather in the style of Karl Jaspers, he called himself a Christian, despite having renounced every single item of Christian doctrine. But he was also happy to speak of himself as a humanist and has, when appropriate, defended what is good in humanism. Writing late in 1987, he commented on a work published by the New Zealand Rationalist Association that canvassed a general account of humanism. Geering agreed that humanism is civilized, broad-minded, and so on, but he felt, as religious humanists have long felt, that somehow it isn't enough. "Too often missing in humanism is the sense of mystery and wonder which in turn nurture the human spirit, foster the caring attitude and promote creativity."[78] The problem with this sort of rhetoric is that it assumes there is something else beyond the natural that can provide this extra dimension. It's tantamount to wanting to live in Athens while having periodic visiting rights to Jerusalem, even if only in one's dreams. It's another example of the criticisms Kaufmann and Howlett made against liberal religion. Having said this, Geering took pains to reprimand local fundamentalists who were intent on following the lead of their American coreligionists in drawing a Manichean picture of the struggle between Christianity and secular humanism, with humanism being bent on moral degradation and the ruin of all we hold dear. He has become increasingly impatient with fundamentalists as he has gotten older.[79]

Another evolution in Geering's thought has been the progressive jettisoning of larger and larger chunks of traditional Christianity. He was quick to see, for example, some serious difficulties with the doctrine of the Incarnation. It alienates other monotheistic faiths, which object to the gulf between humanity and God being bridged in a way that appears to them hubristic. But more important from our perspective is Geering's recognition that a view of Jesus in line with contemporary scholarship simply cannot be reconciled with a traditional view of God.[80] If the person we call Jesus was in fact Yeshua the Rabbi, who is understandable only in his Jewish context and who had no intention of undermining Judaism, let alone found a new religion hostile to the Jewish faith, then theological talk of an Incarnated Christ can only preserve the old, discredited account. Of all the Christian doctrines to interpret literally, the Incarnation is probably the most problematic. "The figure of Christ, the focal point of the doctrine of Incarnation, belongs not to the realm of historical data but to that of religious symbolism."[81] Geering went on to interpret the Incarnation in terms better understood as eco-spirituality than in anything recognizably Christian.

What has probably not been fully appreciated by Christian progressives is that making these long overdue concessions about the doctrine of Incarnation fatally undermines its ability to sustain a viable Christian humanism. Geering has, in a way, understood this, because of his continuing trajectory away from any recognizably Christian position. This is illustrated in his relatively late work, *Christianity without God* (2002). Reminiscent of Bonhoeffer's talk of "religionless Christianity," he writes: "In humankind's coming of age we have begun to move beyond the limited boundaries of Christian culture into a broader human culture."[82] He then sets himself two tasks, one negative and one positive. The negative task is to demonstrate that traditional, theistic Christianity has had its day and is part of the contemporary world's problems rather than part of the solution. The positive part of the book is devoted to arguing that contemporary secular society is not so much a rejection of traditional, theistic Christianity but is rather the logical continuation of it and that Geering's Christian humanism is the appropriate response to this new environment.

Little in the negative part of *Christianity without God* would be unfamiliar to the most secular-minded humanist. Geering observes that a morality based on expectation of heavenly reward or fear of hellish punishment is inferior to humanist ethics, which asks that good deeds be done simply because they are good deeds, and without thought to eternal punishment or reward.[83] He also draws our attention to some of the classic absurdities and iniquities of the Hebrew Bible. And he acknowledges that evolution posed a fundamental challenge to traditional Christian beliefs and assumptions. Rationalists were scorned for making these observations a century ago, but churchmen are now hailed as brave pioneers for saying the same things long after they have become common knowledge.

Geering argues for a naturalized spirituality of the earth, imbued with Christian impulses toward universal brotherhood. His brand of Christian humanism recognizes the dangers of anthropocentrism in fundamentalism and looks to reconcile believers to the facts of science and history. But the reconciliation comes at a cost few believers would be willing to pay. Most conventional Christians will be unable to relinquish as much traditional dogma as Geering has, and the more secular-minded humanist will be uncomfortable with the continued use of religious language. But these objections should not overlook the positive contribution Geering has made to square the circle of reconciling Athens and Jerusalem.

ALBERT SCHWEITZER AND THE REVERENCE FOR LIFE

More than anyone else, Albert Schweitzer deserves the title, "the twentieth century's most remarkable Christian."[84] And for that reason, we can end this chapter with an examination of this extraordinary man. *The Quest of the Historical Jesus* was and remains a landmark in the contemporary study of Jesus. But this was not his only significant book; he produced several highly respected theological works besides. He was also an accomplished organist and an authority on the works of Bach. But he became best known for his work as a medical doctor and missionary in what is now Gabon in Central Africa. Studying Christianity is one thing, he concluded, practicing it is altogether another. He was critical of the conformism, wealth, and comforts of the church, with all the hypocrisies, accommodations, and dissembling those privileges gave rise to. He was even more scathing of the accommodation, the Christian church came to with respect to offering itself up as a vehicle through which war could be justified to the people who would suffer most at its hands. Even more remarkable, Schweitzer was thoroughly well-read in the Asian traditions and went some way to appreciating their genius on their own terms, and not simply as examples of the barbarism and naiveté of pre-Christian beliefs, as so many of his fellow theologians were (and remain) wont to do.

Schweitzer was profoundly pessimistic about the prospects of civilization. He had not imbibed Schopenhauer and Nietzsche for nothing. Western civilization, he thought, had devoted too much time to developing life-affirming worldviews, but what came before worldviews was the more elemental life view, or our simple will to live. But this does not mean we are entitled to wallow in nihilism. Schweitzer was able to confine his pessimism to the realms of knowledge, while his willing and hoping remained—with effort—optimistic. The task, then, was to fuse the grim conclusion of one's intellect with the determination to remain positive and optimistic in one's conduct of life. This is the core dilemma of modernity as he saw it. How to survive and flourish as a human being in the knowledge of our staggering irrelevance to the cosmos as well as the observation that civilization carries within it the seeds of its own destruction? Does one lapse into blank nihilism or seek refuge in some consolation, be it intellectual or material? Schweitzer grew weary of theological system building and concluded a simple reverence for life was the foundation of any meaningful Christian living. He was seized by this insight in the unlikely context of watching a group of hippotami while making his way up the Ogowe river in Gabon. His watchword became *reverence for life*.

But reverence for life was not simply a feel-good slogan. Schweitzer thought it was the single most important breakthrough in the history of ethics. The problem of ethics until then, he argued, was that attempts had been made, all of them unsuccessful, to ground the meaning of life in some broader conception of the meaning of the universe. But hadn't all the failures shown that there was no necessary link?

> The hopelessness of the attempt to find the meaning of life within the meaning of the universe is shown first of all by the fact that in the course of nature there is no purposiveness to be seen in which the activities of men, and of mankind as a whole, could in any way intervene.[85]

Take stock for a moment of what is being said here, and how comprehensively the standard Christian metanarrative has been dumped. Schweitzer's account of reverence for life begins with remarkably similar cosmic assumptions Bertrand Russell had already made in "The Free Man's Worship," which we discussed in chapter 3. There are also strong parallels with Paul Kurtz's notion of eupraxsophy, which we discussed in chapter 6. What Schweitzer calls *active self-perfecting* comes very close to Kurtz's desire to fuse wisdom, goodness, and action. A more recent secular parallel for *reverence for life* could well be *biophilia*, as recommended by the American naturalist E. O. Wilson. *Biophilia* means "love of life," and comes from an attitude of seeing intrinsic value in all living forms and the environment that sustains them. We will return to this discussion in the final chapter.

The difference between Schweitzer and these others lies in their attitude to developing an ethical understanding of the world. Where the more secular-oriented humanists would see it as essential that an ethical understanding of the world be developed, Schweitzer listed it as that which should at all costs be avoided. Instead, he argued, we need to think cosmically and mystically, but without abstractions. "We are no longer obliged," he wrote, "to derive our life view from knowledge of the world."[86] He preferred we rely on our experience of the world and held that reverence for life is "rationalism thought to a conclusion."[87] Here is Schweitzer's attempt, the most brilliant yet, to reconcile Athens and Jerusalem. The problem is that managing a synthesis of this sort is possible only for someone of Schweitzer's intelligence and breadth of experience. But for most of us, disentangling any significant conclusion from rational processes threatens to quickly descend into any sort of fanciful theorizing. This is what Luther discovered to his horror, leading to his later authoritarianism.

Though Schweitzer spoke of mysticism as rationalism brought to a conclusion, he was by no means endorsing an ethic of disdain for reason (as Luther did) or a retreat from the world.[88] Here lay the heart of his Christian humanism, by which he meant the love of God manifested as working in the world, in the manner of the Sermon on the Mount. When he was asked his views by the American Humanist Association in 1951, Schweitzer replied:

> The world thinks it must raise itself above humanism; that it must look for a more profound spirituality. It has taken a false road. Humanism in all its simplicity is the only genuine spirituality. Only ethics and religion which include in themselves the humanitarian ideal have true value. And humanism is the most precious result of rational meditation upon our existence and that of the world.[89]

Schweitzer's path to this sort of affirmation of a Christian humanism began with his theological studies in the 1890s. Having worked his way through the enormous literature of German biblical criticism, he came to some unsettling conclusions. The core of Jesus' message was his preaching of the imminent coming of the Kingdom of God, and his career and words cannot be understood without recognition of this central fact. In particular, no sense can be gotten from Jesus' claim to be the Messiah, given the Jewish parameters he was working within, unless he believed literally that the world was coming rapidly to its supernatural denouement. The consequences of this approach on contemporary religious faith are profound, and Schweitzer was one of the few first-rate theologians to take seriously its consequences. The first point, of course, is that Jesus was wrong. His prophecy of an imminent Kingdom of God turned out not to be true. In this sense, all Christianity is built on this failure.[90] There was no need for "Christianity" while the end of the world was thought to be just around the corner. There was no need to worry unduly about moral or ethical issues, as all such considerations were about to rendered supernaturally irrelevant. But, as we now know, the Parousia did not happen, and "Christianity" was slowly developed to fill in the gap left by this primal failure.

Schweitzer understood the importance of his claims, and the scale of the adjustments Christians would need to make to accommodate the new understanding. And though not using the language of Athens and Jerusalem, he was articulating a similar problem when he said that if the Christ of Christian theology was a fiction, the living example of Jesus could still be a reality in people's lives. But unlike many previous attempts to outline a Christian humanism, Schweitzer was also careful to shed his talk of loaded Incarnational theology. He was unrepentant about being the bearer of these tidings. Are we acting in the spirit of Jesus, he asked, if "we attempt with hazardous and sophisticated explanations to force the sayings [of Jesus] into agreement with the dogmatic teaching of His absolute and universal incapability of error?"[91] By asking this question rhetorically, Schweitzer left little doubt as to the answer. At no point, he added, did Jesus ever demand that we sacrifice thinking to believing, a point lost on modern fundamentalists.

What makes Schweitzer's Christian humanism so attractive is his readiness to practice what he preached: a refreshing change. His years of work in Africa, notwithstanding the various criticisms it has attracted, remain an example of dedication to a cause. Yes, Schweitzer was something of a tyrant. Yes, his attitudes toward what he called "primitive and semiprimitive peoples" would not now pass muster. And yes, some doubt can reasonably be cast about his medical practices in Africa. But, in sharp contrast to the shameless posturing of so many contemporary Christian relief missions, Schweitzer did actually do good work. His statement from his autobiography remains the finest exposition of Christian humanism ever written and acted upon. "We of today do not, like those who were able to hear the preaching of Jesus, expect to see a Kingdom of God realizing itself in supernatural events. Our conviction is that it can only come into existence by the power of the spirit of Jesus working in our hearts and in the world."[92] We will see in the next chapter an interesting parallel with Schweitzer in the life and work of Rabindranath Tagore.

CHAPTER 9

INDIAN HUMANISM: ONE LONG, RICH ARGUMENT

It is best not to think of Hinduism as a religion. Rather, *Hinduism* is best seen as an acceptable shorthand term for the bewildering array of traditions that compose Indian civilization. Labeling all beliefs one finds in India as *Hinduism* is the same as an alien touching down in Missouri and, after a brief tour of the United States, lumping everything it saw—every sect, tradition, societal pattern, and social custom—in the blanket term *Americanism*, and expecting others to see that as a coherent body of thought with a static essence. Jawaharlal Nehru understood this when he called Hinduism "vague, amorphous, all things to all men." Anticipating the refrain of most religious studies scholars today, Nehru said it is hardly possible to define *Hinduism*, or indeed "to say definitely whether it is a religion or not, in the usual sense of the word."[1] In a striking parallel with humanism, we now appreciate that the cultural traditions of India are at least three thousand years old, and yet *Hinduism* became the word to describe them all in only the eighteenth century. The word came from the English, who were struck—and confused—by the variety of what they saw.

As befitting an ancient civilization, all manner of beliefs and practices can be found within what is now called *Hinduism*. Monotheism, polytheism, deism, pantheism, atheism, they are all there. Royalism, communism, neofascism, sectarianism, secularism and pluralism, they are all there too. The triumph of Indian civilization, in this respect, has been the value it has placed on this centuries-long argument. Amid all this variety, it comes as no surprise that Hinduism is not so much about believing this or that but about how one behaves. This is a core feature that unites the Asian traditions, all their other major differences in emphasis notwithstanding. The monotheistic religions—

Judaism, Christianity, and Islam—have, by contrast, been obsessed by what one believes. Or, less helpfully, by what one's neighbor believes.

And a procedural note is in order before we continue with this chapter and, by implication, the chapters that follow. Why corral Indian, Chinese, Muslim, and African thinkers into culturally confined chapters of their own? Why not have them take their place in the broad stream of humanist thinking? The answer made itself clear as I worked on this book. While there has been a fair amount of transcultural exchange between humanist traditions in Europe and Asia, in the end, humanist thought in India, China, the Middle East, and Africa have moved along different paths and at different paces than in the West. While integrating the thinkers in these chapters would seem warmly inclusive, it would be bad history. While the various humanisms discussed in this book are transnational in outlook, that does not mean that they are not firmly grounded in the soil of their native culture. Nor should they be. They are, as any good humanist system should be, both grounded and cosmopolitan. We will return to this idea in the last chapter.

TWO ANCIENT HUMANIST TRADITIONS OF INDIA

It is beyond the range of this book to give an account of the Indian humanist traditions beyond noting their existence and their long history.[2] Two brief surveys cannot be evaded, however. We should note the significant role Indian materialism has played over the past two and a half millennia, and we should also consider briefly the outlook of the Jains. Among the bewildering richness of Indian philosophical thought can be found some of the oldest naturalist traditions in the world. As early, perhaps, as the ninth century BCE, Uddalaka gave a naturalistic account of things and criticized the tendency to look to the Veda as a source of infallible scripture. Debates of this sort were carried around India by the sramanas, a movement of wandering teachers and ascetics. Centuries before the sophists performed a roughly similar role, the sramanas expressed skepticism about the more outlandish supernaturalist claims and were not afraid to question the authority of the brahmins. From these sramanas developed a range of philosophical schools, some of which went on to have major influence in India and around the world. Buddhism was one of them. The Carvakas and the Jains were among the others.

Carvaka is thought to be the name of the founder of the school, but nothing is known of him beyond his name, and even his historicity is uncertain. Tradition has Carvaka as the moral accuser of Yudisthira, a leading figure in the Hindu epic the *Mahabharata*. Alternatively, Carvaka also means "sweet-tongued," or "pleasant words," which may refer to the general perception of Carvaka philosophy as hedonist. As is common with naturalist movements from the ancient world, the main work representing Carvaka philosophy, the *Carvaka Sutra* (approximately 600 BCE), is lost and is known only through the works of its detractors. The traditional author of these sutras is given as Brihaspati, son of Loka. As with Buddhism, Carvaka doctrines rose in response to the growing dogmatism and formalism of Vedic philosophy. The Carvakas regarded the universe as interdependent and subject to perpetual evolution. Following from this, they believed that sacred literature should be regarded as false; that there is no deity or supernatural dimension, nor is there an immortal soul or afterlife; that karma is inoperative and illusory; that matter is the fundamental element; and that only direct perception, and neither religious injunctions nor sacerdotal classes, can give us true knowledge. The aim in life is to get the maximum amount of pleasure from it. This had various interpretations, from unalloyed hedonism on the one hand to altruistic service of one's fellows on the other. Contrary to most of the sramana schools, the Carvakas believed that happiness could indeed be achieved in this life.

Carvaka materialists are generally considered to be *nastika* (unorthodox), in that they reject or question the authority of the Veda. This does not mean, however, that materialists cannot be Hindus. It simply means that they are unorthodox Hindus. Most authorities acknowledge that the Carvaka tradition has saved Hinduism from lapsing into dogmatism or ritualism and has operated as an important irritant to majority patterns of thought. While the Carvaka tradition died out, the memory of it having once flourished has been retained. And the Carvakas made intellectual room in Hinduism for nastika thought. In the period this book is considering, the twentieth century, unorthodox thought has thrived.

Then there are the Jains, who pose more problems for scholars of religion than many other systems of belief because here we have perhaps the clearest example of an atheist religion. As with Hinduism, it's best to view Jain thought as a philosophy, rather than a religion.[3] It avoids having to unpack all the baggage people, especially Westerners, have about what a religion should entail. Jains specifically reject notions of God or gods, and most of their revered texts are explicitly atheist. They believe that the universe is uncreated and eternal, which sets them against arguments to design and generally to consider that the qualities attributed to God are contradictory and unreasonable. The Jain seer Archarya Mahaprajna (1920–) has written that to put all one's faith in religion or meditation is to betray the sense of equilibrium that should attend all one's thoughts.[4] And, of course, it follows from this that doing the same thing with respect to humanism and, presumably, even Jainism, shows the same level of balance. In the manner of many humanists around the world, Jains object that ideas of God end up underemphasizing personal ethical responsibility.

While broadly atheistic, Jainism is not entirely naturalistic. Jains argue that everything except souls and space are created from matter. Souls from the dead can, if having reached perfection, become a Parmatman, or supreme soul. But, contrary to other strands of Indian thought, Jains opposed the passive interpretations given to this process, preferring to emphasize the role the individual can play in perfecting him- or herself. A key to developing this sense of elevation is the development of the third eye, the Anekanta (which can also be translated as "nonextremism"), or the ability to see the world, and oneself, as the complex balance of opposites, each of which has a valid perspective.[5] On the foundation of this sort of cosmology, Jains have constructed a pluralistic and humanistic sociology. Whatever we call *truth* can only ever be the product of our own insight and experience, with all its gaps and flaws. Everyone must work out his or her own salvation, and liberated souls can only serve as guides, it being a mistake to consider them as infallible or supernatural. On the basis of these beliefs and practices, Jains have played a distinguished role in Indian culture, business, and intellectual life for more than two millennia.

The humanistic elements in Jainism and Carvaka materialism are not exceptional cases. The mainsprings of Indian humanism have their roots in Indian thought and Indian emphases. One interpreter of twentieth-century Indian thinkers, Basant Kumar Lal, has outlined the essentially humanistic drive of contemporary Indian philosophy. Classic Hinduism, Lal writes, understood the tragic sense of life and sought to escape its inexorable claims. But the great thinkers of twentieth-century Indian thought took the next step by incorporating the centrality of that suffering into our life in the here and now. Ancient Hindu thinkers spoke of *moksha* as the ultimate liberation from the suffering and illusion of life. But for many of the contemporary Indian thinkers, moksha became more a form of existential realization; and even after attaining moksha, the work of the individual is not done, for there is always more suffering to help alleviate.

So if the Indian thinkers Lal writes about are humanists, he insists they are not scientific humanists in the narrower sense of the term. He doesn't elaborate but clearly has a negative picture of scientific humanism as altogether too positivistic and this-worldly. He then goes on to add that "a modern humanist will be disgusted with the suggestion that contemporary Indian philosophy is also humanistic in its outlook."[6] Not true. It is one of the singular strengths of humanism that it can legitimately be employed in these areas. Lal is right to assert that humanism is a far broader style of thinking than is found among scientific humanism. This book exists to demonstrate that truth.

Another commentator on contemporary Indian thought, and a significant spokesman for humanism, is Vishwanath Prasad Varma (1924–), a political scientist educated in India and in the United States, with a wide familiarity with British thought. While Varma shares some of Lal's concerns with the more radical expressions of scientific humanism, he appreciates more than Lal the range of influences on modern Indian humanism. In *Philosophical Humanism and Contemporary India*, Varma suggests that modern Indian humanism derives from three sources. There is, first of all, the "positivistic and world-affirming gospel of the Upanishadic Vedantism, the *Bhagavad Gita* and Buddhism." Then there is the cross-fertilization of ancient Indian thought with Western scientific spirit and methods. And then there is the third strand, "the revival of the poetic spirit of the romantics"; he mentions Tagore in this context.[7]

Varma's threefold explanation helps explain the tremendous richness and variety of Indian humanism and will provide the structure we will use in this chapter. Varma himself advocated an idealist humanism that acknowledges a divine absolute, though he is careful to distinguish this from a personal God who would respond to human needs. "It is a pathetic desire of the human self," he writes, "to impose a total immanent hominocentric teleology on the whole universe as if the millions and millions of astronomical bodies were operative to act merely according to the dictates of the human mind."[8] Against this background of cosmic idealism, not at all out of place in Hindu thought, Varma speaks much more like a scientific humanist when addressing more down-to-earth subjects like the alleviation of poverty, transparent government, the value of education, and so on.

SWAMI VIVEKANANDA AND THE REALIZATION OF RELIGION

Few people articulated more fully the "world-affirming gospel of the Upanishadic Vedantism, the *Bhagavad Gita* and Buddhism" that Varma spoke of than Swami Vivekananda (1863–1902). Born into a privileged family in Calcutta, Narendranath Datta had a full education, including the Indian classics, Western philosophy, riding, and swimming. In 1881, Narendra came under the influence of Swami Ramakrishna (1836–1886), who became his mentor and guide for the rest of his life. After Ramakrishna's death, Vivekananda (as he had now become) wandered India as an ascetic monk. During his travels, he concluded that although India had a brilliant intellectual tradition, it needed more for its people to be lifted from the grinding poverty that blighted so many lives.

Talk of Vivekananda's intelligence and passion spread widely and quickly enough that, in 1893, he resolved to travel to Chicago to attend the World Parliament of Religions where he, in effect, became the spokesperson for Hinduism. His wide reading and fluent oratory, along with the exoticism of his person, won him celebrity status in the United States and Europe and was a significant factor in the new interest in Hinduism in the West at the time. He traveled through the West once again in 1899. Upon his first return to India, Vivekananda founded the Ramakrishna Ashram at Belur near Calcutta and undertook a program of social reform. The Ramakrishna Mission has gone on to become the largest charity in India. While in America, Vivekananda was offered the chair of Oriental Philosophy at Harvard University, but he turned it down to return to the poor of India. He died in 1902, aged only thirty-nine and after a public career of only ten years. A beautiful shrine to his memory was built at Kanniyakumari, a tiny islet at the southernmost tip of the Indian subcontinent. It is said that Vivekananda swam to the islet so he could contemplate whether to make his first trip to Europe.

Vivekananda's thought was grounded in a sophisticated understanding of Vedanta philosophy, although he was convinced that all ideas need to be reinterpreted for the conditions of the day. He was also influenced by Buddhism, Christianity, and Western philosophy and was happy to take wisdom from whatever source. He had little patience with superstition and mindless orthodoxy, and he favored the strict separation of church and state. For him, service to one's fellow human being constituted the essence of the godhead. As Ramakrishna had advised, if you seek God, seek him in other human beings.[9] This was an adaptation of the Vedantist teaching that one is not free until everyone is free. Vivekananda had a great impact on Mohandas Gandhi (1869–1948), who described his words as "great music."

Some people might raise their eyebrows at including Vivekananda in a book on humanism. Does he really deserve a place here? On the whole, yes. The context of his humanism was different from that of most Westerners, and the language he expressed himself with may not be to the taste of all humanists, but there is little doubt of his generally humanistic inclination. Vivekananda was as God-intoxicated as Spinoza, and on behalf of a similar notion of God. He was also as suspicious of book learning and abstract theorizing as the Buddha, a point reiterated throughout the eight volumes of his collected works. And Vivekananda, like Thomas Paine, was a passionate radical for the poor. The inspiration in Vivekananda's life, as we have seen, was Sri Ramakrishna, whose key insight was that all religions taught essentially the same message: not I but thou. And his key message was "be spiritual and realize truth for yourself." The core of religion was not books, doctrines, or ecclesiastical authority but the process of realization. And *realization* can have different meanings. It can be given a mystical rendering, but it can also refer to philosophical realization. In India, philosophy is called *darshana*, or "vision of the real," so in this sense, unburdening oneself of philosophical delusions is also a process of achieving a vision of the real. And for many people achieving a vision of the real involves shedding anthropocentric conceits such as a personal God. True to Indian thinking, Vivekananda said that God is not something one worships, for that only strengthens the error of seeing God and oneself as separate. Even using the word *God* is only because one has no better word. There is little in this that cannot be thought of as humanism. While in New York in 1894, Vivekananda wrote this to a friend back in India:

> I do not believe in a God, who cannot give me bread here, giving me eternal bliss in heaven! Pooh! India is to be raised, the poor are to be fed, education is to be spread, and the evil of priestcraft is to be removed.[10]

Spinoza, the Buddha, and Thomas Paine: each would have been proud to write that. Even if, at various times, Vivekananda skirted more closely to the wind with respect to supernaturalism than many humanists, myself included, are comfortable with. All the more reason to include this vibrant personality in this book. Vivekananda can be seen as complementary to aspects of religious humanism, but without some of its weaknesses. For instance, his philosophy of renunciation had a sense of a cosmic perspective to it. The West, he wrote "has solved the problem of how much a man can have: India has solved the problem of how little a man can have."[11] This is a more valuable insight to begin the twenty-first century with than a sunny forecast of unending progress.

Vivekananda died too early to be able to develop his wide-ranging insights. But he is remembered as one of India's most passionate reformers. His scathing criticisms of Hinduism served as a reforming jolt. And his success on foreign stages was an important contribution to the Indian people's growing sense of confidence in themselves and in their own future.

RABINDRANATH TAGORE AND THE RELIGION OF MAN

The person Vishwanath Varma immediately mentioned when speaking of the "poetic spirit of the romantics" that inspired Indian humanism was Rabindranath Tagore (1861–1941). A contemporary of Vivekananda, and someone who has been similarly typecast as nothing more than a mystic, Tagore was called by Albert Schweitzer the Goethe of India. He was born into the higher reaches of Bengal society, being the son of the Maharishi Debendranath Tagore, an important Hindu reformer. His mother, Shrimati Sharada Devi, died in his infancy. Tagore's prodigious output was inspired by the Bengali culture into which he was born. He was an accomplished playwright, artist, composer, singer, storyteller, and poet. But his experiences in England also instilled in him a lifelong appreciation for elements of English culture and literature. Even in his last years, as he became increasingly disillusioned with the unwillingness of the British government to acknowledge the inevitability of Indian independence, Tagore could never quite bring himself to wholly repudiate what was good in the British. But neither did he ever forget his roots in Bengal. His first major political work, from 1905, urged his fellow Bengalis toward self-sufficiency—culturally, economically, and otherwise. To this day, he is venerated by Bengalis and is seen as the most brilliant exponent of Bengali culture. Some of his more elitist contemporaries found it disquieting that Tagore wrote in the vernacular so that ordinary Bengalis could read his work.

In 1901, Tagore founded a school, Shantiniketan, with the intent of recapturing the rural simplicity of India while also incorporating what was valuable from the West. One of its most famous graduates has been Amartya Sen, the Nobel Prize–winning economist. Sen's grandfather, Kshiti Mohan Sen, a distinguished Sanskritist, taught there. Other important graduates include Indira Gandhi and the filmmaker Satyajit Ray. In 1921, Shantiniketan became a university. This imperative to found schools is a quintessentially humanist one, and in the chapters to follow we will see other pioneers have done the same thing.

People who found schools value education and the written word, but few have been as masterly in the art of writing as Tagore. Among his important works are the books *Nashtanir (The Broken Nest*, 1901) and *Chocher Bali (Eyesore*, 1903) and the short story *Punishment*, which spoke of the oppression of women in low-caste society. So important was Tagore that one of his songs was selected as India's national anthem and, a quarter century later, his poem "Our Golden Bengal" became the national anthem of Bangladesh. Tagore is probably the only person who has produced the national anthem for two countries. It's an ironic achievement for someone who was strongly critical of unthinking nationalism. As Amartya Sen noted, that the predominantly Muslim Bangladesh should adopt a work by a Hindu-born poet as its national anthem messes around with the fashionable "clash of civilizations" thesis.[12] Tagore won the Nobel Prize for Literature in 1913 for his collection of poems known as *Gitanjali*, or *Song Offerings* (1912). *Gitanjali* is rightly admired for its vividness and range of imagery. One of its most-quoted passages is from the thirty-fifth poem:

> Where the mind is without fear and the head is held high;
> Where knowledge is free;
> Where the world has not been broken up into fragments by narrow domestic walls;
> Where words come from the depth of truth;

> Where tireless striving stretches its arms towards perfection;
> Where the clear stream of reason has not lost its way into the dreary desert sand of
> dead habit;
> Where the mind is led forward by thee into ever-widening thought and action—
> Into that heaven of freedom, my Father, let my country awake.[13]

It is not taking Tagore's thoughts out of context to wish a planetary application for this ideal. Having said this, much of his other poetry resists easy interpretation, and Tagore, like so many other artists, insisted that there is no deep, underlying message lurking in his work and waiting to be unearthed in support of some cause or other.

> This utterance of feeling is not the statement of a fundamental truth or a scientific fact or a useful moral precept. Like a tear or a smile, a poem is but a picture of what is taking place within. If Science or Philosophy may gain anything from it, they are welcome, but that is not the reason of its being.[14]

Tagore was no less aware of the uselessness of musing after some lost perfection. In this and in other matters he remained rooted in the earth. Elsewhere in *Gitanjali* he wrote, "Only in the deepest silence of night the stars smile and whisper among themselves—'Vain is this seeking! Unbroken perfection is over all!'" There is something very Taoist in this insight. Sometimes the restless searching for perfection, wholeness, happiness masks the fact that it is all around us—if only we open our eyes and see it. So, it is not in the spirit of interpreting his work in support of one's own view of the world that makes Tagore a humanist. It is that, as a human being from another century and another culture, his utterances of feeling resonate with me as well. Simple human empathy is the core of humanism.

The Nobel Prize alerted European readers to Tagore's work, and he retained a wide European readership from then on. He was knighted in 1915, but in 1919 he renounced his knighthood in protest at the British policy in the Punjab, which had resulted in the massacre at Amritsar. While Tagore was an opponent of colonialism, he was reluctant to embrace the strong nationalism of the freedom struggle, which inevitably meant his relations with Mohandas Gandhi were at times strained, though the two men recognized the genius in each other. While Gandhi has become a name known around the world, India reflects Tagore's outlook a lot more closely than it does Gandhi's.[15]

People have argued for decades about where Tagore stood on questions of God. His father had been a prominent supporter of a monotheizing tendency of Hinduism, in part as a defense against the inroads of Christianity. Tagore remembered having nothing to do with the religious devotions of his family because, he said, "I had not accepted them for my own."[16] He has variously been described as monistic, theistic, pantheist, agnostic, and mystical, with all of them being correct at some point or other. Some commentators have detected his conscious application of anthropomorphic attributes to God, being of the view that the abstract Brahman was too distant for most people to comprehend. In defending these moves, Tagore said that in being anthropomorphic, humans are just being human. Humans can take an interest in the Absolute, he wrote, only when it is humanized.[17] Tagore saw *God* and *reality* as two words for the same thing, but without an anthropomorphic element added, how we could love such a thing? God and reality came together in the unity consciousness. And many people have noted that Tagore's descriptions of God have the sensual tone one would address to one's lover.

These sorts of sentiments were best expressed in his Hibbert lectures, which he gave in 1930 and which were subsequently published as *The Religion of Man*. The important point to note about these lectures is his frequent reminder that they were works of poetry rather than of philosophy, let alone of science. So if he sometimes appears to deify humanity, his real purpose was to bridge the divide between humans and the cosmos.

> The most perfect inward expression has been attained by man in his own body. But what has also been important of all is the fact that man has also attained in realization in a more subtle body outside his physical system. He misses himself when isolated; he finds his own larger and truer self in his wide human relationship. His multicellular body is born and it dies; his multipersonal humanity is immortal.[18]

The Religion of Man is vulnerable to the same sort of criticisms that H. G. Wells's *God the Invisible King* was because they are very similar. Tagore perhaps gets away with it a little more, if only because of his sublime writing and his candid admission that the work should be understood as poetry and imagination. *The Religion of Man* is best seen as an early plea for planetary humanism, albeit in a mystical vein. It could also be seen as an outstanding example of grounded cosmopolitanism, an idea we will explore in the final chapter. Tagore's humanism was deeply rooted in Indian philosophy and history, but he looked forward to the day when nationalism would be replaced by transnational values, what he called "unity consciousness." People are called to practice the religion they were brought up in, but genuine religion transcends these parochial limitations. This was what he called "the Religion of Man," the aim of which was realization of true kinship with all things. Institutional religions and escapist practices like asceticism were criticized as misleading and parochial. Tagore wrote:

> In dogmatic religion all questions are definitely answered, all doubts are finally laid to rest. . . . But the poet's religion is fluid, like the atmosphere around the earth where light and shadow play hide and seek . . . it never undertakes to lead anybody anywhere to any solid conclusion; yet it reveals endless spheres of light, because it has no walls around itself.[19]

Instead, there was Tagore's heartfelt humanism. Toward the end of his autobiography, he chose these words from his poem "Sharps and Flats" as his "prayer of the individual to the universal life." Tagore wrote, "This world is sweet—I do not want to die. I wish to dwell in the ever-living life of Man."[20]

The best way to approach Tagore's work, in my view, is to see it as a poetic contribution to the humanistic remythologization of the world. Postmodernists and other critics of humanism have accused it of a one-dimensional interest in *de*mythologizing and of leaving the world disenchanted. This has never been true. Whatever validity this claim has comes from factoring out of consideration those humanists inclined toward remythologizing the world. People like Rabindranath Tagore.

And a parallel can be drawn with Albert Schweitzer, who was an admirer of Tagore and a person whose spiritual trajectory was on a similar path. With his ethic of *reverence for life*, Schweitzer was trying to bridge the gap between recognition of the immensity of the cosmos and our near-total irrelevance to it, and a program of active work in the world. Tagore's wish to dwell in the ever-living life of Man resonates well with Schweitzer's *reverence for life*.

DR. AMBEDKAR AND THE PLIGHT OF THE DALITS

Few injustices in India disturb the conscience of humanists more than the inbuilt subjugation of the *dalits*, otherwise known as the *untouchables*. And it comes as no surprise that many of the most effective and dedicated campaigners against untouchability have been people also willing to criticize religion in more general terms. For example, Bairagi, Charan Misra (1885–1966) was a rationalist and humanist thinker and activist who fought against orthodoxy, caste, and superstition. And Nilakantha Das (1884–1969), who studied philosophy at Calcutta University only to turn down a job working for the British, preferring instead to return to his native Orissa, where he worked as a headmaster. Das was also politically active, serving on the state's legislative assembly. A powerful orator, his speeches denouncing untouchability and other social injustices became famous throughout Orissa.

The best-known campaigner against the plight of the dalits, however, was Bhimrao Ambedkar (1891–1956), the fourteenth child of a dalit family in what is now Madhya Pradesh. As a dalit child, he suffered continuous petty humiliation from all sides. He was refused permission by his teachers, for instance, to learn Sanskrit. But while the facts of inequality in India are clear enough, it is also true that real talent can receive the opportunities it deserves. This was Ambedkar's experience. Despite such inauspicious origins, his intelligence was quickly recognized and he was given access to education. One of his teachers, a brahmin, saw the child's promise and bestowed his surname on him. Thus Bhim Rao was now Bhimrao Ambedkar. In 1912 he graduated from Bombay University, studying politics and economics; and in the early 1920s he was awarded a doctorate from Columbia University for his dissertation on British provincial finance in India and a doctor of science from London on "The Problem of the Rupee." His education in America had been sponsored by the Maharaja of Baroda.

At this point Ambedkar could have easily embarked on a successful career in the top echelons of finance anywhere in the world. But he chose to return to India, and from then on he made it his business to advocate for the rights of dalits. Soon after his return in 1923, he established the Bahishkrit Hitkarini Sabha, or Outcastes Welfare Organization. His first two public struggles attracted national attention. In 1927, he led a campaign to secure for dalits the right to draw water from the same source as the others. And in 1930, he publicly burned a copy of the *Laws of Manu*, a strong source of justification for caste distinctions, at a famous temple that denied entrance to dalits. These successes secured for Ambedkar the right to speak for dalits at a national level. His next move was to claim that dalits, no less than Muslims, were an identifiable minority, and as such they deserved separate constituencies. For a short while, it looked as if it was going to happen. In August 1932, Britain announced the communal award, which would allocate constituencies to Hindus, Muslims, dalits, Europeans, and some other groups. Gandhi was strongly opposed to this and began a fast to the death to prevent it. On the fifth day, with Gandhi sinking fast, Ambedkar was persuaded to surrender his claim for separate constituencies. This became known as the Poona Pact, and for the rest of his life Ambedkar regretted his actions and resented Gandhi forcing his hand.

After the Poona Pact, Ambedkar also became increasingly critical of Gandhi's attitudes, which he saw as disingenuous. Gandhi patronized dalits with beautiful labels while leaving the caste system untouched. It is not simply that Gandhi supported the caste structure, Ambedkar maintained, he intertwined these differences "as a living faith." Such a view cannot function if India is to have a democratic future. "The man who condemns machinery and modern civilization simply does not understand their purpose and the ultimate aim [that] human society must strive to achieve."[21] The setback at Poona only encouraged Ambedkar to develop his critique of the religious underpinnings of the caste system. What loyalty do dalits owe the Hindu system when it is responsible for keeping them in subjection? He said in a speech in 1935, "I solemnly assure you that I will not die a Hindu." He kept that promise. But he was no less critical of Islam, Christianity, and Sikhism, all of which had accommodated themselves in various ways to the caste system. But inevitably the main focus of his anger was Hinduism. For Ambedkar, Hinduism was a brutalizing mockery of religion:

> Why do you remain in that religion which insults you at every step? A religion which prohibits righteous relations between man and man, is not a religion but a display of force. A religion which does not recognize a man as a human being is not a religion but a disease. A religion which allows the touch of animals but prohibits the touch of human beings is not a religion but a mockery. A religion which precludes one class from education, forbids

them to accumulate wealth, to bear arms, is not a religion but a mockery of the life of human beings. A religion that compels the illiterate to remain illiterate, and the poor to remain poor, is not a religion but a punishment.[22]

And behind this was the recognition that religion exists for human beings, not the other way around. This and his insistence that all human beings—without regard to the circumstances of birth—are, without qualification, centers of value are what make Ambedkar's career a humanist one. One scholar of Ambedkar, Dr. Bharathi Thummapudi, has spoken of Ambedkar's combination of theoretical acumen with practical action motivated by compassion as one of the twentieth century's premier examples of what she calls *total humanism*.[23]

Unlike many other champions of the underclass of India, Ambedkar was not bewitched by Marxism. He commented on several occasions that most of Marx's prophecies about how the revolution would develop had not transpired. It cannot be emphasized too much, he wrote, "that in producing equality society cannot afford to sacrifice fraternity or liberty. Equality will be of no value without fraternity or liberty."[24]

When India became independent in 1947, Jawaharlal Nehru asked Ambedkar to play an important role in devising the new state's constitution. Ambedkar was elected chairman of the drafting committee, and the emphasis in the constitution on equality before the law and a secular state were marks of his influence. But it is one thing to enshrine changes in a constitution and quite another to have those changes actually implemented. Many of the uniform principles Ambedkar wanted embedded in the constitution, with full coercive authority, were shifted sideways and given the more ambiguous status of being "Directive Principles of State Policy," which could not be enforceable in court. Ongoing frustration with the slow pace of change led Ambedkar out of the government in 1951. He was never elected to parliament again.

Ambedkar's last years were devoted to bringing to a head his twenty-year campaign to convince dalits of the need for a mass conversion. In 1956, shortly before his death and true to his promise twenty years previous Ambedkar publicly embraced Buddhism. All the religions, he told the BBC, bother themselves with talk of God and an afterlife. But Buddhism teaches a simple triad of understanding, love, and equality. "This is what man wants for a good and happy life on earth."[25] Ambedkar was also very well versed in Indian history and knew that much of the structure of discrimination against dalits arose from the brahmanical reaction to the challenge of Buddhism.[26] He chose to announce his conversion on October 14, the same day Ashoka was said to have become a Buddhist in the third century BCE. Inspired by his example, somewhere in the region of eight hundred thousand dalits followed him. This is thought to be the biggest single movement of people from one system of belief to another in history. Dr. Ambedkar issued twenty-two vows that underlined the extent of his departure from Hinduism. The fourth vow included renouncing any belief in an incarnate god. In 1990, Dr. Ambedkar was posthumously bestowed the honor of Bharat Ratna, and the 1990–1991 year was declared the year of social justice in his memory.

RATIONALISM IN INDIA

Vivekananda, Tagore, and Ambedkar were all larger-than-life individuals motivated toward fundamentally similar goals of emancipation and personal growth, however differently they understood and pursued these goals. But India has also spawned movements that have promoted rationalism, humanism, and atheism, each with varying emphases and degrees of success.

The earliest of the modern expressions of free thought to establish itself in India was rationalism. This was stimulated by the visit to India of Charles Bradlaugh, the British atheist parliamentarian. Having won, at enormous cost to his health, the right to sit in parliament as an atheist, Bradlaugh took an interest in freedom struggles outside the United Kingdom. India interested him in particular, and though exhausted by his campaign to take his seat in parliament, he traveled to India to attend the Fifth Indian National Congress over 1889 and 1890. His speech to the congressional conference was rhetorically rich, as all his speeches were, while also being honest. He made no declaration for Indian independence but repeated his support for the complete equality of Indians with all other citizens of the empire. He also praised the presence of women at the conference. His opponents in England had sneered that Bradlaugh was "the Member for India." He told his Indian listeners he was proud to own that title.[27]

Though Bradlaugh's visit gave rationalism a tremendous prestige among Indian intellectuals and leaders, it did not result in the formation of rationalist organizations. But it did color the complexion of the congress's movement, as we will see when we discuss the career of Jawarhalal Nehru. One of the earliest rationalist organizations was the Anti-Priestcraft Association, founded in Bombay in January 1930 and made up of influential men in that city, some of them with connections to the Rationalist Press Association in Britain. The following year, the Anti-Priestcraft Association changed its name to the Rationalist Association of India (RAI) and launched its quarterly journal, called *Reason*, under the editorship of Dr. Charles Lionel d'Avoine (1875–1945), a surgeon who hailed originally from Mauritius. *Reason* earned notoriety in September 1933 when d'Avoine wrote an article called "Religion and Morality," which gave offense to English ecclesiastical authorities in Bombay. The article congratulated a recent decision at the University of Bombay to reject a call for religious instruction of students, arguing that courses in comparative religion would be much more useful. It went on to say that followers of conventional religions often attach more importance to spectacle, ritual, and rites than to a moral code, and that one does not need to be religious in order to be moral.[28] The authorities slowly prepared a case against d'Avoine, including a police raid to seize copies of the offending article. D'Avoine was charged with "deliberate and malicious intention of outraging the religious feelings of any class of His Majesty's subjects."[29] In an admirable decision, the judge, Sir Hormuzdiar Dastur, acquitted d'Avoine, saying that no evidence of malice existed, nor had it been proved that religious feelings had been "outraged," and that a prosecution would involve an unacceptable diminution of freedom of speech.[30] The *Reason* case, as it became known, was a landmark decision for freedom of speech and separation of church and state in India. Press comment was overwhelmingly favorable to the decision. As the *Hindustan Times* put it, "The prosecution sought to make the King-Emperor not merely the 'Defender of the Faith' but also the 'Protector of Superstitions' and we are glad that the attempt has failed, as it deserved to fail."[31] The *Reason* case was the Rationalist Association of India's finest hour. The national attention the case stimulated also stimulated interest in rationalism. Soon after d'Avoine's acquittal, a Rationalist Youth League was formed, which nurtured some future leaders of Indian unbelief, such as Abraham Solomon. But this impetus did not last long. *Reason* suspended publication in 1936, starting up again in February 1937 under the editorship of Professor R. D. Karve (1881–1953), only to fold in 1942. The RAI became dormant after that.

Another prominent Indian rationalist at the time was Sir Raghunath Paranjpye (1876–1966), an educator, mathematician, and politician. Like d'Avoine, Paranjpye had links with the RPA going back to the 1910s, and in 1931, he became its first Indian honorary associate. That same year, Watts & Co., the RPA's publishing arm, published *The Crux of the Indian Problem*, which argued for a secular future for the Subcontinent if it was to achieve independence and then build on it constructively. Paranjpye was prominent in the reestablishment of the RAI in 1949, now called the Indian Rationalist Association. The new organization continued a fitful existence through the next three decades, troubled by financial and organizational difficulties. Under the editorship of S. Ramanathan, it published the *Indian Rationalist* intermittently through the 1950s and 1960s, finally ceasing publication in December 1966. The Indian Rationalist Association discontinued its activities at the end of 1970. Since then, it has been revived on several occasions in different parts of the country. Today there are at least two groups claiming the mantle of the Indian Rationalist Association.

Overall, it must be said that organizations calling themselves rationalist have not been a success. Their over-reliance on British rationalism limited the chance of securing genuine, broad-based appeal. But the rationalist organizations active today, particularly those in Kerala, Punjab, and Kolkata are much closer to the people and are more practically oriented than their predecessors and, as a result, are more successful. The Tarksheel Society of Punjab, for instance, was formed in 1984 and has been very active showing people of the state how the shabby tricks of the godmen are done, so as to insulate them from their threats and blandishments.

M. N. ROY AND RADICAL HUMANISM

Rationalism took root in the 1890s, but humanism did not arrive in India until after World War II. The person chiefly responsible for giving humanism an Indian face was M. N. Roy, whose early life seems almost impossibly romantic. Narendranath Bhattacharya was born in 1887 in Arbelia, near Calcutta, the son of a village priest and teacher of Sanskrit. Bhattacharya was deeply religious as a youth but became a revolutionary in his teens, participating in eight robberies with the purpose of collecting funds for the cause. He was sent to prison in 1910. During World War I, and under the name of

Charles A. Martin, he traveled Asia in search of arms for their planned insurrection. In 1916, he arrived in the United States, posing as a theology student. It was here he changed his name to Manavendra Nath Roy. He was arrested in 1917 and fled to Mexico while on parole. He stayed there for about two and a half years, and, under the influence of Michael Borodin, an official in the Communist International, he became a Marxist. In 1919, Roy traveled to the Soviet Union and lived there for the next ten years, during which time he rose to a senior position in the Comintern. But from 1927 onward, he fell out of favor with Stalin, and in 1929 he was expelled from the Comintern. The following year, he returned to India, where he remained for the rest of his life.

Soon after his return to India, he embarked on his Marxist-inspired history of Indian philosophy, which was published in 1940. *Materialism* outlined the naturalistic origins and beliefs of the Vaisesika, Samkhya, and Nyaya schools of Indian philosophy and gave an account of Indian intellectual history as a series of contests between essentially brahmanical and sacerdotal tendencies versus the naturalistic streams of thought. He was also an outspoken critic of what he saw as Gandhi's obscurantism, technophobia, and asceticism.

With views like this, Roy was never going to be comfortable in the Indian National Congress. He worked conscientiously for Congress for a few years but left early in the war to found the Radical Democratic Party in December 1940. His real problem was not with Congress or with his own party but with the entire political process. In December 1948, he wound his party up, turning his attention to educational and cultural activities. Alongside this process Roy slowly shed his Marxism in favor of what he came to call *radical humanism*. He founded a magazine in 1945 called *The Marxian Way*, which was later renamed *The Humanist Way*. At first, Roy distinguished between Marxism and Communism, the latter being simply a political expression of the former, but as he became increasingly disillusioned with Soviet Communism, so did his doubts mount about Communism as a totality. Like the earlier generations of Marxists, it was human freedom that motivated Roy, and he saw ever less evidence that Soviet Communism was a shining light in that respect. Eventually he came to see that Marxism itself was only slightly less ambivalent about human freedom than Soviet Communism had become.

By 1946, Roy had pretty much completed his transition to humanism, albeit one highly charged with Marxist presuppositions. In December of that year, his Radical Democratic Party adopted his *Twenty-Two Theses of Radical Humanism*. The theses assume a materialist conception of the universe with humanity being products of evolution. Most of them are devoted to charting a middle course between authoritarian and teleological communism on the one hand and laissez-faire capitalism on the other. They are an expression of a naturalist and materialist view of the world leading to a commitment to human freedom as the means by which the best can be made of the world for its citizens. The last thesis expresses the spirit best:

> Radicalism starts from the dictum that "man is the measure of everything" (Protagoras) or "man is the root of mankind" (Marx) and advocates reconstruction of the world as a commonwealth and fraternity of free men, by the collective endeavor of spiritually emancipated moral men.[32]

The Radical Humanist Movement, Roy's successor organization to the Radical Democratic Party, didn't survive his death in 1954 for long, and in 1969 the Radical Humanist Association (RHA) was established, whose principal figure, until 1980, was the jurist and thinker V. M. Tarkunde (1909–2004). His work *Radical Humanism* (1983) is the best single-volume summary of Indian radical humanism since Roy's own works. But, like Roy, Tarkunde took care not to simply theorize. His humanism was socially active and transnational. In particular, he continued Roy's close cooperation with humanist organizations abroad. Roy attended the Amsterdam congress in 1952 that created the International Humanist & Ethical Union (IHEU), even taking the office of vice chairman. Tarkunde carried on this close association, serving on the IHEU's board for forty years. This cooperation bore fruit in 1962 when the Radical Humanists persuaded the IHEU to support what became known as the Bihar Project, an ambitious program of rural development and education in one of India's poorest states. The underfunded and poorly coordinated project soon ran aground though. More impressive was the active opposition of prominent humanists during the Emergency, between 1975 and 1977, when Indira Gandhi shut down the democratic process and arrested prominent opposition leaders. In no uncertain terms, the Radical Humanists denounced the Emergency and all its correlates—the censorship, the postponement of elections, the arrests. Another significant opposition grouping was Citizens for Democracy, which Tarkunde co-led.

The Radical Humanists had another strong spell between 1986 and 2004 when the association was led by Dr. Indumati Parikh (1918–2004), a doctor based in Mumbai. Dr. Parikh had a long record of fighting for women's rights and health in that city. It is one of the ironies of contemporary life that Mother Teresa, whose actual charitable activities in India were minimal at best, is lionized around the world as the embodiment of virtue, while Indumati Parikh, whose record of achievement was incomparably greater, is unknown outside India. This comment could also apply to the work of A. B. Shah (1920–1981), who combined strong secularist advocacy with longstanding work directed toward the education of the children of prostitutes in Maharashtra. In 1964, alarmed by the burgeoning population in their city of Bombay (now Mumbai), Dr. Parikh and her husband sold their home in the affluent part of the city and moved to the slums, where she established Strihitakarini, a self-help organization dedicated to providing the women of the slums with contraceptives and advice on contraception. Strihitakarini, which means "women helper," soon expanded into a range of activities related to women's health and education. Acknowledging the influence of M. N. Roy, Dr. Parikh always sought to work *with* the women of Mumbai, rather than *for* them.

In 1992, Dr. Parikh took an active part in calming religious tensions in Mumbai after the destruction of the mosque in Ayodhya. In her later years, she was instrumental in beginning an ambitious project, to be called the M. N. Roy Development Centre, on the outskirts of Mumbai, to serve as the movement's headquarters as well as its educational center. Speaking about her beliefs, Dr. Parikh described humanism as "the only ideology that would cut across boundaries and help men and women to understand their basic humanness."

Why did Roy take up humanism, rather than rationalism, which still had some authority in India at the time? Rationalism, as expressed in India at the time, was not sufficiently engaged in real-world struggles to alleviate poverty. And most of its prominent leaders were men of the upper classes, something Roy was not able to ignore after many years in the communist movement. Neither could atheism supply Roy with the social activism he sought. He found what he was looking for in the language of scientific humanism, which, in the previous decade in the West, had moved along radical, left-wing lines without embracing dialectical materialism and other elements of Marxist theory.[33]

GORA AND THE ATHEIST CENTRE

Roy's radical humanism assumed atheism, feeling little need to stress that side of his program. But with the career of Gora, we find the opposite happened. Taking on this label is not without its social cost, even in India, but Gora's achievements deserve much wider recognition than they have so far achieved. Goparaju Ramachandra Rao (1902–1975) was born in Chatrapur, in what is now Orissa, to a high-caste family. *Gora* is an acronym of his full name, but one that drops the caste information embedded in it. Conventionally religious until his middle twenties, Gora carried around a sachet of sacred ash an aunt had given him. But as his hopes and dreams were slowly frustrated, he came to realize that sacred ash made no difference in his life. Neither did the devoted piety of his sister prevent her from losing three children in a row. In fact, soon after Gora threw his sacred ash away, his fortunes took a turn for the better, and he landed a good teaching job at the American Mission College in Madurai, Tamil Nadu.

Gora was a good teacher and soon attracted the attention of the principal, who offered him the chance for further study in the United States—if he embraced Christianity. Gora turned down the offer, justifiably feeling that such a conversion would not be honest. No longer welcome at the Mission College, he left soon afterward and took a position at the Agricultural Research Institute in Coimbatore. Here he was joined by his wife. The two had been married by arrangement of their parents in 1922, when Gora was twenty and Saraswathi, his bride, was ten. Now fourteen, Saraswathi was permitted to move in with the husband her family had chosen for her.

After a year at Coimbatore, Gora and his young bride moved to Ceylon, as Sri Lanka was then known, to teach at Ananda College, an institution run by the Buddhist Theosophical Society, where he taught botany. In 1928, he and his family returned to Kakinada in Andhra Pradesh to teach at PR College, his alma mater. By this time Gora and Saraswathi were both atheists. Gora taught well, and his informal teaching methods were greatly appreciated by the students, but his views were unacceptable to the school authorities, who engineered his dismissal, despite protests from the students. He had by this time ceased to wear Western clothing, preferring instead the *khadi*, or homespun woven cloth. More tellingly, he also stopped wearing the sacred thread, which helped identify the caste one belonged to. More than anything else, this caused heartache among his parents and colleagues. The growing discrimination against Gora came to the attention of Sarvepalli Radhakrishnan (1888–1975), later known as a prominent philosopher and president of India, but who at this time worked as vice chancellor of Andhra University. Though not agreeing with Gora, Radhakrishnan deplored the sacking and recommended he be appointed to teach botany at the Hindu College, Masulipatnam, also in Andhra Pradesh. Gora taught there for five years before resigning in 1940, after pressure from the college, which was trying to curtail his activities.

There seemed little point in finding yet another teaching position only, in all likelihood, to go through the same process all over again. An earlier attempt at establishing his own school, to be run on communal and democratic principles, foundered when he was offered most of the start-up money needed on condition he resumed wearing the sacred thread. It was time for a change of direction, so, with that in mind, Gora and his family went to the remote village of Mudunur in Andhra Pradesh to begin a new kind of life. It was a brave decision, as they had six children to support and no obvious means of earning a living. Living in two thatched huts built for them, Gora engaged in adult education in the village. He taught people of all castes, who sat together and drank from the same well. A big part of the new life at Mudunur was the more openly political nature of Gora's work. Responding to Gandhi's Quit India Movement, Gora led opposition activities in his region, for which he was imprisoned early in 1943. Saraswathi continued his work until her own arrest in April 1944. She was imprisoned for six months, despite being heavily pregnant with their seventh child. Imprisonment also impressed on Gora the woeful inadequacy of prisoner rehabilitation. He devoted considerable energy to this for the rest of his life.

Unlike Ambedkar or Roy, Gora was proud to call himself a Gandhian. Though not sharing all of Gandhi's opinions, Gora was much more inclined to see his essential greatness. And evidence exists that he was responsible for breaking down some of Gandhi's misconceptions about atheism. As a younger man, Gandhi had known and respected Charles Bradlaugh, without ever accepting his atheism. He said in his autobiography that he had crossed the "Sahara of atheism." Gandhi had less time for Annie Besant (1847–1933), Bradlaugh's former ally who had moved to India and had become a tireless campaigner for Indian independence and Theosophy.

After hearing about Gora's work and the persecution he had suffered, Gandhi invited him to the Sevagram Ashram in November 1944. Though not especially fruitful, it clearly stimulated Gandhi's interest enough for a second visit to be arranged. In January 1945, Gora returned to the Sevagram Ashram and stayed there for three months. At one point, Gora asked Gandhi why he would say *"Raghupathi Raghava"* (God Rama) when he should be saying *"Satyam, satyam"* (truth, truth). Gandhi replied "Do you think I am superstitious? I am Super-Atheist."[34] At another conversation, Gandhi said:

> I can neither say my theism is right or your atheism wrong. We are seekers after truth. We change whenever we find ourselves in the wrong.... Then I may go your way or you may come my way or both of us may go a third way. So go ahead with your work. I will help you though your method is against mine.[35]

This is not the condescending agreement to differ that a statement like this would be in the West. Gandhi was recognizing that Hinduism has no explicit bias for a theist or atheist outlook, seeing both as entirely valid means by which truth can be reached. Gora's question to Gandhi was in the context of the change Gandhi had made from speaking of "God is Truth" to "Truth is God." This trajectory away from specific god-talk escalated in the last year of his life, during the religious bloodletting in the months after independence. Shortly before his death, Gandhi wrote, "In the name of God we have indulged in lies, massacres of people, without caring whether they were innocent or guilty, men or women, children or infants ... [but] I am not aware if anybody has done these things in the name of Truth."[36] Days later, he was assassinated by a Hindu fanatic. And Gandhi meant what he said about helping Gora in his work. So much so that he agreed to officiate at the marriage of Gora's eldest daughter with an untouchable. Tragically, he was assassinated before the event took place. The marriage took place at the Sevagram Ashram on March 13, 1948.

After Gandhi's death, Gora withdrew from organized political activity because of his disgust with the widespread ignoring of Gandhi's call to simplicity and avoidance of pomp and short-term maneuvering for party advantage. He spent the rest of his life advocating democracy without political parties. In 1960, Gora led a march from Vijayawada to the state capital of Hyderabad to publicize his call for partyless democracy. And the following year, he led another march, this time all the way to New Delhi, which took ninety-nine days; there Gora spoke with Nehru about his concerns. Gora also campaigned for many years for elected representatives to use third-class carriages while traveling on trains, and for public buildings to grow vegetables rather than ornamental flowers. In all these campaigns, the influence of Gandhi was strong.

Gora went on to build the Atheist Centre and advocate what he called *positive atheism*. The Atheist Centre was founded by Gora in August 1940 in Mudunur, consisting of the rude, home-built huts he lived in. In 1941 he organized a three-day conference on atheism, which three hundred people attended. So successful were his various campaigns for improvement of sanitation, elimination of untouchability, and providing of adult education that Mudunur came to be known as "the godless village." In 1947, the Atheist Centre moved to Vijayawada in Andhra Pradesh. Two years after that, it began a Telugu weekly paper called *Sangham* (Society), which in 1954 was renamed *Arthik Samata* (Economic Equality). In 1969, an English-language monthly called *The Atheist* was included.

Central among the Atheist Centre's work over its career has been the promotion of inter-caste marriages, criminal rehabilitation, assistance to untouchables, and education. Gora broke new ground with respect to his views on gender equality. Among its subsidiary organizations is the Arthik Samata Mandal, or Association for Economic Equality, which was founded in 1951. The Arthik Samata Mandal operates in one hundred fifty villages around Andhra Pradesh in the fields of health, education, sanitation, and poverty relief. The Vasaya Mahila Mandali, founded in 1969, focuses more on the needs of women and children. This runs a small hospital and operates in fifty villages. The most recent is Samskar, which was founded by Lavanam (Gora's eldest son) and his wife, Hemalata, and which is devoted to the rehabilitation of ex-convicts. And we note, once again, the irony that while Mother Teresa was praised around the world for what in fact were negligible acts of charity, the Atheist Centre, which has an impeccable record of achievement, is unknown outside India.

Gora's version of positive atheism—not to be confused with the positive atheism as articulated by Antony Flew or Michael Martin—combines an active profession of atheism with a life of moral seriousness. It has a lot in common with Paul Kurtz's notion of eupraxsophy. Gora was not an original or systematic thinker. He was a passionate social activist, and the key point of positive atheism was its role as the agent of revolutionary liberation. In a culture as rooted in tradition as India, Gora saw no alternative to full atheism. During their first conversation, Gandhi asked Gora what the difference was between being an atheist and being godless. Gora said, "Godlessness is a negative. It merely denies the existence of God. Atheism is positive. It asserts the condition that results from the denial of God."[37]

His principal manifesto was *Positive Atheism* (1972), which grew out of an earlier treatise simply called *Atheism* (1938), which Gora's employers refused him permission to have published. Empowered by freedom and motivated by responsibility, Gora pictured the atheist as a socially active person working politically to eradicate suffering in all its forms. The many social programs of the Atheist Centre are a faithful reflection of Gora's vision of positive atheism. About humanism Gora was more circumspect and less consistent. He suspected, for instance, that humanism needed atheism before it could be fully activated into a social force for change. "Without avowed atheism, humanists compromise with nonhumanist habits and remain academic with little practical use."[38] But he also saw humanism as the vehicle for a common humanity. "Humanism is not a coalescence of different sects; it is the assertion of the homogeneity of all humanity. There are neither Hindus, Muslims, Christians, nor Jews; all are humans. There are neither Russians nor Chinese; all are humans. There are neither the rich nor the poor; all are humans. There are neither the white nor the black; all are humans. There should be wholesale proselytism into humans."[39] And in Gora's mind, this could only really be done via a forthright acceptance of atheism.

PERIYAR AND THE DRAVIDAR KAZAGHAM

At the southernmost tip of India is Tamil Nadu, home to one of the most extraordinary expressions of atheism in the world today. The organization is the Dravidar Kazagham (DK), and its founder was E. V. Ramasami Naicker (1879–1973), who is known as Periyar, which in Tamil means "great, great one." He was born in Erode, Tamil Nadu, on September 17, 1879, to a family of fair means and conventional Hindu belief. After a brief elementary education, he started work in his father's business, at which he did well. At nineteen he married Nagammai, who was at the time thirteen. They had one child, a girl who died after five months. Nagammai died in 1933, aged fifty-eight.

Periyar's leadership skills were seen early, and he held a variety of offices in his hometown. It is not known for certain when he became an atheist, but his visit to Varanasi in 1904 came as a shock to him when he saw this supposedly holy city was no more holy than anywhere else. (Shades of Martin Luther's reaction to Rome.) The distinctive feature of Periyar's atheism was its indissoluble link with his fervent nationalism. In 1919, he joined the Indian National Congress and worked actively in the party for several years. His leadership skills developed in these years, as when in 1924 he led a Congress agitation in Vaikam, in neighboring Kerala, against a custom whereby low-caste people were prohibited from walking down a street near a Hindu temple. Like Dr. Ambedkar, Periyar had a deep horror of the caste system, though his rejection of it was predicated along different lines to the northerner. Like many southern Indians, Periyar resented the born-to-rule assumptions of brahmins, which involved not only caste and class discrimination but also unwarranted northern domination. These differences notwithstanding, Periyar and the organization he founded remains one of the most constant champions of the work of Ambedkar. He led a *satyagraha* (a nonviolent protest involving fasts and civil disobedience, made popular by Gandhi) against the practice, was imprisoned for a month, and was told to leave Vaikam. He refused to do so and was imprisoned for an additional six months. But his activities attracted widespread support, and before long all the temples of Kerala rescinded this practice. Soon after this victory, Periyar left the Congress. Like Ambedkar, Periyar was dissatisfied with its attitude toward freeing low-caste people from restrictions. While giving some support to the Justice Party, Periyar devoted most of his efforts to the Self-Respect Movement, founded in 1926 by S. Ramanathan. But in 1944, Periyar founded his own organization, the Dravidar Kazagham. Dravidians are the indigenous people of South India, and *Dravidar Kazhagam* simply means "Dravidian Association."

By this time, Periyar had become convinced that no meaningful distinction could be made between the religious elements in Hinduism from the various social injustices practiced in its name. His focus, and that of the DK, has been to engender self-respect among Tamil people, who are so often at the bottom of the social and cultural ladder in India. Periyar campaigned fiercely against Hindi becoming the national language of independent India; Hindi being the language of the north alone. And, more provocatively, he was outspoken in his condemnation and ridicule of the *Ramayana*, which he saw as a protracted northern slight against Tamils.[40] In 1956, he led a series of public burnings of pictures of Rama, as a symbolic declaration of cultural independence against northern norms. Three years previous, he led a similar campaign against images of Ganesha.

As noted, Periyar's strongest opposition was reserved for brahminism, which often crossed the line into opposition to brahmins. The value of atheism and rationalism lay in the support they gave to nonbrahmins, Tamils in particular, having self-respect in the face of the immovable caste barriers. As he put it in 1936, "Hindu religion, scriptures, and gods are conceived in such a way as to be useful only to the Brahmins and to keep them at the top of all humans as a privileged lot. When Brahmins go, hate, religion, and god will also have gone. If there is no caste, there will be no Brahmins."[41] Nowhere is Periyar's no-holds-barred approach to religion illustrated better than on the plaque of the memorial statue to him in Chennai. The plaque reads, "There is no God. There is no God. There is no God at all. He who invented God is a fool. He who propagates God is a scoundrel. He who worships God is a barbarian."

Periyar was never far away from some controversy or other. He remarried in 1949, when he was seventy, to his twenty-eight-year-old secretary, Annaiyar Maniyammai. This led to widespread discontent among his followers. One of Periyar's main campaigns over the years had been for equality in marriage. His opponents felt that the age difference between them undermined the chance of any equality in the marriage. And in the same year, a breakaway grouping, the Dravida Munnetra Kazhagam (DMK) set itself up. Its leader, C. N. Annadurai complained that Periyar ran the organization too dictatorially and that his antibrahminism was too negatively charged. The DMK embarked on the long task of making itself electable, during which time it slowly abandoned its explicit support for atheism. The DMK has gone on to have an interesting career in the politics of Tamil Nadu, and Annadurai served successfully as chief minister for Tamil Nadu.

Periyar survived the splits and schisms and led the Dravidar Kazhagam until his death in 1973. He was succeeded by his second wife, Maniyammai. On her death in 1978, she was succeeded by Thiru K. Veeramani (1933–), a lawyer from the town of Cuddalore. Like Periyar, Veeramani has thrown himself into his position and has been imprisoned on several occasions as a result of various campaigns the organization has run. Under Veeramani's leadership, the DK has turned its attention in a more humanist direction by offering practical assistance to people through its range of educational and social institutions. Unlike religious organizations, the DK's institutions are almost entirely self-funded. It also runs its own daily newspaper called *Viduthalai* (Freedom), a fortnightly magazine called *Ummai* (Truth), and even an English-language journal called *The Modern Rationalist*.

Going back to Periyar's time, the Dravidar Kazhagam has condemned the exploitation of women. It was at a women's conference in 1938 that he was bestowed the honorific of Periyar. A significant feature of the organization's social program is the promotion of self-respect marriages. The marriages are performed without the presence of a priest, can be intercaste, and assume the equality of male and female. These marriages have been recognized as legal since 1967, and about fifty thousand such marriages are carried out each year.

An area of DK politics that has rarely failed to create controversy is its ambivalent attitude toward political independence for Tamil Nadu. There have even been accusations that the DK has links with the Tamil Tigers, the extremist separatists fighting a dogged civil war with the Singhalese authority in Sri Lanka. The Tamil Tigers claimed responsibility for the assassination of Rajiv Gandhi during a visit to Tamil Nadu in 1991. These accusations are stoutly rejected, although DK literature does acknowledge that Periyar dreamed of an independent Tamil Nadu and said as much at a meeting with Ambedkar and Muhammad Ali Jinnah early in 1940.[42] The issue is avoided in most current DK literature. The custom of wearing back shirts during mass DK rallies has also concerned some, particularly those with a sense of history.

The appeal of atheism for Periyar is clear: it helped cement the sense of difference the Tamil people would feel from their conventionally religious rivals from the north. He made no use of humanism as an idea because his movement was interested in notions of universal brotherhood only once the social and cultural independence of the Tamil people was clearly recognized. His successor, Veeramani, has occasionally spoken of humanism, as when he spoke to a conference of Rotarians in Tamil Nadu in 1998. Veeramani's version of humanism is unremarkable. He speaks of the value of empathy *with* others rather than sympathy *for* others, because empathy places us beside our neighbors, not above them.[43] More direct, as part of the DK's campaigns in the countryside, one of its slogans is "Raze down communalism, rear up humanism."[44] But Veeramani also places his humanism firmly in a Tamil framework, quoting only Tamil authors, notably the great first-century BCE humanist poet Tiruvalluvar. Incidentally, no less a person than Albert Schweitzer thought Tiruvalluvar a person of unique levels of wisdom.

JAWAHARLAL NEHRU AND INDIAN SECULARISM

At the beginning of this chapter, I mentioned two of Indian humanism's most important gifts to the world. One was the imperative to eliminate the gulf between this-worldly concerns and the construction of a sense of purpose not confined to the everyday world. Each person and organization discussed in this chapter has contributed to this in some way or another. The other significant contribution by Indian humanism is the articulation of the virtues of secularism. It is also India's genius to be able to do both these things together without supposing a contradiction exists. This chapter has also alternated between relating the stories of larger-than-life people and or various expressions of free thought, be it rationalism, humanism, or atheism. Here, both come together. Nehru was definitely a larger-than-life personality, and secularism is the most significant of the expressions of free thought in the Indian context. Rationalism, humanism, and atheism all presuppose a secular society where diversity is celebrated or at least tolerated. So it seems appropriate to end this chapter outlining the thoughts of Nehru and the importance of secularism to India and, by extension, to the world. And this is squarely Nehru's achievement because, we have seen, until the last year of his life Gandhi was insistent on fusing religion with politics. While he was able to do that at a lofty level, many of his countrymen in the months after independence expressed that fusion in more traditional, bloodthirsty ways.

Jawaharlal Nehru (1889–1964) deserves recognition as one of the twentieth century's most outstanding leaders. He was born into a very privileged family of brahmins originally from Kashmir. His father, Motilal Nehru (1861–1931), was a close friend and ally of Mohandas Gandhi. Jawaharlal was educated privately until 1905, when he was sent to Harrow, one of England's most prestigious private schools; then he went on to Trinity College, Cambridge, where he practiced law in London before returning to India in 1912. In 1916, he married Kamala Kaul (1899–1936). The couple had one daughter, Indira (1917–1984), who, using her married name Gandhi, went on to have a long and significant career in Indian politics.

At the same time, a growing interest in Indian independence led Nehru to become politically active. He met Gandhi at a meeting of the Indian National Congress in 1916 and one of the firmest, most important political partnerships of the twentieth century was underway. Gandhi and Nehru were very different personalities, and yet their contrasting strengths complemented each other. Nehru went to prison for the first time in 1921, the first of nine periods of incarceration under the British. Overall, Nehru spent nine years in prison in the cause of freedom. It was during his terms of imprisonment that Nehru did most of his writing.

After the death of Motilal Nehru in 1931, Jawaharlal became even more closely allied with Gandhi, and it was soon apparent that Nehru was Gandhi's preferred successor, although Gandhi did not make that specific until 1942. As another war became more likely, Nehru, despite struggling against the British for independence, made it quite clear that he, and India, was on the side of the Allies against fascism. Ironically, Nehru spent much of the war in prison. After the war, it was clear that British rule could not last, and Nehru took a central role in guiding the process to independence. He made a mistake, we can now see with the advantage of hindsight, in not involving the rival Muslim League more closely in the lead-up to independence. Although there is more than enough blame for the horrors of the partition and the bitter religious bloodletting that followed it. However, on August 15, 1947, India became independent, and Nehru was its first prime minister.

Until his death in 1964, Nehru was prime minister of India and was loved by the people—one of the few twentieth-century leaders about whom that can be said genuinely. Nehru's four guiding principles were democracy, socialism, national unity, and secularism. Each of these contributed substantially to making India the vibrant nation it has become. He was a leader of what became known as the *nonaligned countries*. And he helped steer India through the crisis of the assassination of Gandhi by a Hindu fanatic. Nehru's two biggest failures during his long term as leader of India were his inability to resolve the ongoing dispute over Kashmir and the disastrous war with China in 1962, in which Indian troops performed poorly and Indian territory was lost.

But for our purposes, it is Nehru's thoughts on religion and secularism that are important. Nehru helped set the intellectual tone in newly independent India by virtue of his writing. Books like *The Discovery of India* (1946) and his autobiography (1936) influenced millions of people for more than two generations. He didn't mince words when it came to his view of religion. When allied with theology, Nehru wrote, religion is more concerned with vested interests than with things of the spirit. "It produces narrowness and intolerance, credulity and superstition, emotionalism, and irrationalism. It tends to close and limit the mind of man, and to produce a temper of a dependent, unfree person."[45] Not much room for ambiguity there. For Nehru the two highest ideals of the modern age are humanism and the scientific spirit. Where these had formerly been in conflict, there "is a growing synthesis between humanism and the scientific spirit, resulting in a kind of scientific humanism."[46] And as he wrote that while languishing in Ahmadnagar Fort Prison, Nehru can perhaps escape the usual charge of being unduly optimistic or sanguine. Neither can he be accused of scientism, as in the pages leading up to that passage, he surveyed all the usual caveats about the scientific method and the fragility of reason. But, he went on, it is precisely because of their limitations that we must hold on to reason all the more thoroughly. "It is better to understand a part of truth and apply it to our lives, than to understand nothing at all and flounder helplessly in a vain attempt to pierce the mystery of existence."[47]

Nehru criticized the Indian propensity (although suggesting it is probably a universal vice) of succumbing to alternate bouts of self-glorification and self-pity. "We cannot lose ourselves," Nehru wrote, "in aimless and romantic quests unconnected with life's problems, for destiny marches on and does not wait for our leisure."[48] Nehru set for himself the practical aim of helping transform people's lives in the here and now. We have become so jaded about politicians whose breathless biographies (and not infrequently autobiographies) resound with declarations of this sort, that we are now inclined to doubt them in the few cases of those for whom, like Nehru, they remain true.

An underappreciated fact is the relative success during Nehru's lifetime to maintain Indian secularism. A proposed amendment to include mention of God in the preamble of the constitution was unsuccessful. More than any other country, India has continued exploring the meanings of secularism. India's philosophers and political scientists lead the world in their treatment of the question of secularism. Nehru was only one in a long line of Indian statesmen who have understood the need for toleration and secular neutrality of the state. When defending secularism at Oxford University on one occasion, Nehru told a student that Britain had an established religion and widespread indifference to religion whereas the India state had no religion and the people are deeply religious.[49] Others have since noted the same thing with respect to the United States. Well versed in Indian history, Nehru was always able to offer an Indian precedent. Ashoka in the third century BCE and Akbar (1542–1605) both set fine examples of toleration when they could as easily have simply dictated their will. In bringing together the third council of Buddhist thinkers in around 247 BCE, Ashoka was concerned to engage in disputation where each disputant would honor and respect his adversary and listen in a spirit of humility. And likewise, Akbar, while remaining a true (if heterodox) Muslim, nevertheless brought together representatives of all the major religions of India in a spirit of collective inquiry. He even listened to atheists.

Akbar's example has been followed by several prominent twentieth-century Indian politicians. And the best single example is Humayun Kabir (1906–1969), who devoted his life to Indian politics. Kabir was born into the upper reaches of Muslim society in West Bengal, where he was educated before going to Oxford. Back in India, he immersed himself in nationalist politics, looking for the independence of India. But unlike the majority of fellow Muslim leaders, Kabir opposed the partition of India along religious lines. He went on to become a leading politician of postindependence India, serving in a number of government positions and on some United Nations programs. As to be expected, Kabir was interested in issues of toleration and pluralism. And the experience of the huge Muslim minority in India has been a valuable training ground for these qualities. What made the experience a success, all things considered, was that they were part of a secular state. The only Muslim countries with populations larger than the Muslim minority in India are Indonesia and Pakistan. So this represents a significant social laboratory for Muslims.

Kushwant Singh, one of India's most respected journalists, wrote in 2002, "More than any other country in the world, India, which is a multireligious country, cannot afford to encourage religious exclusiveness in the name of God."[50] It has become fashionable in the West to sneer at secularism, to equate it with consumerism or another dominating religion or ideology. But in India, experience has shown that the secular state, and the values it promotes, has been absolutely vital to the ongoing health of the various faith traditions which are alive in it. The sophisticated articulation of a workable secularism constitutes one of India's gifts to the world.

CHAPTER 10

THE SPIRIT OF CHINESE HUMANISM

Speaking at the twenty-second World Congress of Philosophy in Seoul, Professor Kah Hyung Cho made the important observation that the West has taught the world how to make a living, but the East could teach the world how to live. The growing popularity of Eastern religions, meditative practices, and medicines in the West illustrates the point at one level. But if one looked beyond this often highly suspect form of faddish merchandizing, there is a far richer tradition of Chinese humanism there for millions of post-Christian Westerners to explore and learn from. Chinese humanism rested on two main foundations: it never separated humanity from nature, and it never separated the abstraction Man from the social phenomenon of humanity.[1] This important insight constitutes a significant element of China's gift to humanist thinking.

Chinese civilization cannot be understood without appreciating the central role humanistic assumptions and thinking have played in its development. In marked contrast to India, the basic lines of philosophical inquiry in China have tracked along this-worldly lines. The three basic questions of Chinese philosophy are *xing* ("human nature"), *li* ("principle"), and *ming* ("fate").[2] It is not just that naturalistic thinking can be traced back to the beginnings of the culture's distinctive philosophical quest, as is the case in India. In China, naturalistic thinking *is* the distinctive and normative feature of Chinese thinking. But this truth imposes real difficulties on a chapter devoted to "Chinese humanism," not the least of which is that little about Chinese humanism can be understood without going back two and a half thousand years.

CONFUCIUS AND THE WAY OF SHU

If we broke into Chinese history in 1808, the year Niethammer first spoke of humanism at the other end of the Eurasian landmass, we would see very little in the way of what would later be called *humanist*. The Qing dynasty (Ch'ing in the old spelling) had been in power for more than one hundred and fifty years, and the country felt entirely self-sufficient. A high-level British trade delegation had been sent packing in no uncertain terms a few years previous. The emperor told the British representative that China had no need for such trivial manufactures as those they were offering. By the standards of the twenty-first century, China was deeply conservative, complacent, hidebound, and immobile. Much of the history of twentieth-century China involved Confucianism getting the blame for the country's chronic inability to effectively meet the challenges of Western—and later Japanese—competition and encroachment.

So what is Confucianism, and is it reasonable to lay the blame at the feet of Confucius in this way? Kongfuzi (551–479 BCE), who is known in the West by his Latinized name Confucius, really does deserve to be thought one of the most outstanding humanists of all time. He was born into an aristocratic family in the state of Lu, now the western part of Shantung Province. Although aristocratic, his family had fallen on hard times and was impoverished, especially after his father's early death, when Confucius was only three. He overcame these difficulties, secured a government position in the state of Lu, and became successful, too successful for his own good. In 497 BCE, he left Lu after falling foul of government intrigue and became a wandering scholar, going from court to court in search of a sympathetic patron. It was during these dark years that he attracted a group of followers, and in about 485 BCE he returned to Lu, where he taught them. After his death, his students compiled a series of sayings and aphorisms of the Master which became known as the *Analects*.[3] Most of the other works attributed to him, while Confucian in flavor, were compiled by his followers.

Confucius did not so much create new concepts as skilfully develop those that were already in circulation. A brief look at the political culture of his day will illustrate this point. If we looked up a reference book, we would see that Confucius was born six hundred years into the Zhou dynasty (Chou in the old spelling), which had a further two hundred fifty years still to run, but the settled and peaceful conditions implied by this description is belied by the facts of the time. North China was run by a miscellany of principalities, all of which offered nominal allegiance to the Zhou emperors in Luoyang. Before long, the fragile peace between the principalities broke down, leading to what become known as the Warring States period, usually dated from 403–221 BCE. Zhou thinkers had, over the centuries, developed some sophisticated justifications for their earlier usurpation of control from the long-lived Shang dynasty. The Shang social system was tribal, with anthropomorphic gods who could bestow privileges as individual gods to individual mortals. Political legitimacy was thought to be bestowed on rulers by the Lord.

The problem the Zhou thinkers faced was to legitimize their rule in the face of Shang claims to have ruled at the behest of the Lord. What resulted has been described as the most radical development away from Shang thought. This was the concept of the *mandate of heaven*. It had a humanistic bias in that humanity's destiny depended upon its own words and deeds rather than the whim of Providence. In contrast to Shang anthropomorphism, the emphasis during the Zhou dynasty was more toward heaven as a non-specific repository of principle. Consequently, while Shang ancestors were identified with the Lord and therefore had powers to bestow, during the Zhou era, ancestors came to be seen more as part of heaven, and their power was more through their example and inspiration. And, most important of all, the mandate could be taken from rulers and transferred to a new source of power which, by virtue of having taken power, must now be seen as having heaven's favor.

It was into this political culture that Confucius was born. More than anyone else, Confucius molded Chinese culture and philosophy. And while humanism had been around before Confucius, it was he who "turned it into the strongest driving force in Chinese philosophy."[4] The main concern of Confucius was harmonious social relations inspired principally by the example of good government. Rulers would command the respect of the people by virtue and moral example rather than by punishment or force.

The greatness of Confucius's humanism lies in his subtle awareness of the interdependence between personal identity and obligation to society. He radically changed the concept of *junzi* (*chun-tzu* in the old spelling), which had traditionally meant "son of the ruler" but which he transformed into "superior man." He uses the term one hundred seven times in the *Analects*. The importance of this transition is critical. Confucius had transformed personal nobility, a Chinese version of bildung, from being something one is born *with* into something one *develops*. Being a superior man was a matter not of high birth, as hitherto thought, but of character. Confucius never spoke of *Ti* (the Lord), but to *T'ien-ming*, or the will, order, or mandate of heaven. This became known as *T'ien-li*, or the *way of heaven and nature*. And care should be taken not to import Western, supernaturalist conceptions of heaven into the Chinese version of the word. Each individual can achieve the greatness that lies within oneself, but this requires effort on one's part and the assistance of the wider society.

Confucius is often associated with conservative notions such as hierarchy and filial piety despite them predating him by centuries. Just as important to his thought is the notion of *jen*, which Confucius radically transformed from meaning "kindliness" to the more general "man of the golden rule," or perfect junzi. Jen was expressed in terms of *zhong* (*chung* in the old spelling) or "conscientiousness," and *shu* or "altruism." It was in this context that Confucius articulated his version of what we now call the Golden Rule. When asked whether his philosophy could be put into just one word, Confucius answered that it could, and the one word was *shu*, which can be translated as "Do not impose on others what you yourself do not desire."[5] In this way obligation becomes a two-way street, as it must be in any civilized society. Scholars disagree over whether or not zhong and shu can be considered separately, a debate we don't need to do anything with beyond simply noting it.

While Confucius only implied that human nature is good, it was left to Mengzi (371–289 BCE), or Mencius in Latinized spelling, to declare definitively that it is originally good. Evil is not inborn but due to our inability to resist external evil influences, hence our quest must be to "seek the lost mind," or rediscover our essential goodness. Mencius advocated *humane government*, which meant promoting the "kingly way" over "the way of the despot." And he valued a well-run polity to the point where he was happy to justify revolt against one that was badly run. The West had to wait two thousand years until Spinoza and Locke said similar things.

The social ideal of Confucius and Mencius is best illustrated in the short classic *The Great Learning*, which outlined the Confucian educational, moral, and political program in brief. The Three Ways of clear character, loving the people, and abiding in the highest good are to be achieved by the Eight Steps, which progress from extending one's own knowledge and sincerity, to properly managing one's family and country—and culminating in a world of peace. The core observation here is the central importance not of inalienable rights but of respect earned by the cultivation of virtue and the practical application of that virtue through selfless behavior in the world. Neither should the cultivation of virtue be mistaken for self-absorption or smug complacency. Confucius was critical of both these perversions. True humanity, one early classicist put it, lies in "making contact."[6]

It is difficult from all this to imagine the thought of Confucius and Mencius developing into the influential ideology that appealed to rulers. The humanist emphasis upon the goodness of humanity and the promise that anyone could achieve the status of junzi would probably have made these beliefs appear too impractical, not to say subversive, to be of any use in government. So while Mencius must be acknowledged as a valiant defender of Confucian thought against the attacks of Legalists, Taoists, and the followers of Mozi (Mo Tzu in the old spelling, 479–438 BCE), it was not in the field of intellectual debate that Confucianism first won its stripes.

CONFUCIANISM FROM QIN TO QING

Readers familiar with the history of Christianity know that there was a sea change in the four centuries from the death of Rabbi Yeshua to the establishment of a coercive religion justified in the name of something called *Jesus Christ*. The folksy truisms of a provincial Jewish prophet were gradually transformed into the ponderous tergiversations that became known as Christendom. And trying to unpick these developments has been hampered by the status of scripture accorded to the revered writings of this new religion. Some interesting parallels can be seen in China with the progressive divinization of Confucius, although, in the end, it is the differences that are more instructive. While Confucian scholars have been generally successful in opposing that trend, the record with respect to Confucianism and the state is a great deal more problematic.

It was during the short-lived Qin (Ch'in in the old spelling) dynasty, which ran from 221 to 207 BCE, that the moral and ethical observations of Confucius and his followers were transformed into a potent ideology of state. The Qin dynasty, despite its brevity, was one of the defining periods in Chinese political and intellectual history. Qin Shihuangdi (ca. 259–210 BCE), the first Qin emperor, sought to unite all China under a tightly disciplined centralist autocracy. His advisors came mainly from a school of political and social thought known as *Legalism*, and among the most prominent of such advisors were some disciples of Xun-zi (Hsun Tzu in the old spelling, 298–238 BCE). Xun-zi was harder and more authoritarian than was common among followers of Confucius and Mencius. Being less sanguine about the natural goodness of human nature, Xun-zi saw a greater place for control from the top. Few other Legalists claimed descent from Confucius, being more openly Hobbesian in their enthusiasm for raw power.

In 213 BCE, Qin Shihuangdi, on the advice of his Legalist advisors, inaugurated what became known as the "burning of the books." Altogether four hundred sixty scholars were buried alive during this short attempt to secure total intellectual and social homogeneity throughout China. Shihuangdi's reign was short, and his brutality ensured the early demise of his dynasty. It also spelled the end of any direct influence by Legalist thinkers. The calamities of the Qin dynasty had two far-reaching consequences. For Confucian scholars, the influence of Xun-zi's realpolitik was not lost, while among the people, the prestige of Confucian thinking, having been persecuted so thoroughly, resulted in an unprecedented growth of interest. It is reasonable now to speak of Confucian*ism*. There was a period of intense activity among the scholars in rewriting the texts that Shihuangdi had obliterated, but they were written in a different context to that of many of the originals. This allowed for changes in the texts to creep in, changes that suited the climate of the time. The common people were rapidly bringing Master Kung into their worldview, with the effect that stories about him became increasingly embellished. These additions, in turn, found themselves into the rewritten texts.

So, thanks to the historical accident of the Qin dynasty, the various works and thoughts of Confucius and his followers had become a powerful philosophy of social order and harmony, with the two main features it needed: an element of realpolitik in its political philosophy and the support of a very wide cross-section of society to enable the bonds of respect to be properly ordered. The Han dynasty, which succeeded the Qin, soon understood the value of this unique synthesis. In 195 BCE, only eighteen years after the burning of the books and only seven years after the dynasty was securely founded, the new emperor Gao Zu (Chao T'o in the old spelling, reigned 202–195 BCE) stopped at the grave of Confucius and sacrificed an ox, a sheep, and a pig, and in so doing began what became a common practice for Chinese rulers.

Later that century, Confucianism was further entrenched in the Chinese political psyche by yet another wayward reading of the Master's thought. Early in his reign, Wu Di (156–87 BCE), known as the Martial Emperor, sought greater national unity. Hearing of the emperor's wish, the scholar Dong Zhongshu (Tung Chung-shu in the old spelling, 179–104 BCE) sent him a memorandum lamenting the diversity among the people and advocated returning to the principles and disciplines of Master Kong. The Martial Emperor took the scholar's advice and announced that the Five Classics he were to become state doctrine; and in 124 BCE he created an imperial academy to train students in these works, thus inaugurating what became the examination system that was to last, off and on, for the better part of two thousand years.

It is not surprising that Dong's variation on Confucianism appealed to the Martial Emperor. Dong spoke of the Three Bonds: the ruler to the ruled, the father to the children, and the husband to the wife. People are naturally unenlightened and look to a king to instruct them. While Dong acknowledged, in true Confucian fashion, that human *nature* is good, he went on to add that human *feelings* are evil. To resolve this dichotomy, Dong emphasized the ruler's role as benign educator and mentor of the people. Confucius's emphasis on the ruler *deserving* the support of the people by virtue of meritorious rule was forgotten.

The appeal of such a doctrine to an intelligent and ambitious ruler who is able to exercise absolute power is obvious. While Wu Di's measures had the same goal of unification as Shihuangdi, the differences are instructive. Whereas the Qin emperor sought to achieve unity by destroying *all* schools of thought indiscriminately, Wu Di chose one of the contending "hundred schools" and gave it prominence, without proscribing the other schools. These extraordinary developments would not have happened unless the rulers could see the value in this body of thought, as opposed to any other body of thought, for their own rule.

The value of Confucian thought for harmonious social order continued to be apparent to most Former Han emperors. In 1 CE, for instance, emperor Pingdi (P'ing-ti in the old spelling, reigned 1 BCE–6 CE) ordered a general repair to the temples of Confucius and elevated him to the rank of duke. This was the first in a long line of honorifics that became increasingly extravagant. It was not until 1530 that this process was finally halted. On the advice of Confucian scholars, the Ming emperor Jia Jing (Chia Ching in the old spelling, reigned 1521–1567) revoked what by then had become a prodigious list of honorifics. From then on Confucius was to be known simply as "Master Kong, the Perfectly Holy Teacher of Antiquity." This de-escalation of flattery and honorifics is, it seems to me, a unique element of Confucius's legacy. It compares favorably with the more tortured and contested attempts over the past two centuries to rescue the historical character Rabbi Yeshua from the dross of the theological Christ.

By the beginning of the common era, the formative period of what we now know as Confucianism was at an end, and a period of textual criticism and systematization began. This is always a critical time for the development of any system of belief because it is at this stage that the initial goals and ideals of the belief can get lost in a welter of political and tactical exigencies. Confucianism was no exception to this rule, and indeed it faced the formidable challenge from a vibrant new foreign faith based on the teachings of the Buddha.

Before surveying that challenge, respects should be paid to the naturalist philosopher Wang Chong (Wang Ch'ung in the old spelling, 27–97 CE), not only for his role in opposing the growing tendency toward the deification of Confucius but also for his general contribution as China's preeminent rationalist and skeptic. Like Confucius, Wang never achieved the high office his ability would normally have made him eligible for. But he kept busy with vigorous cultural criticism. At a time when the intellectual quality of Confucian thought was in decline and Confucius himself was slowly being deified, Wang stood out as a stern critic of mysticism and irrationalism. Heaven, he argued, takes no action in the lives of human beings; natural events are simply that—natural events without any supernatural implications. Neither does moral virtue bring with it some essential connection with personal destiny. Anticipating W. K. Clifford by two millennia, he insisted that any theory must be tested by concrete evidence and tried at all times to argue in a rational manner, supporting his claims with appropriate levels of evidence.

Wang's thoughts appeared in *Lunheng* (*Discursive Equilibrium*), which was written over 82 and 83 CE. Sadly for Wang's posthumous reputation, he founded no school and attracted no lengthy commentary on his works, which are the usual paths to a lasting influence in China. It was Wang's bad luck to be overshadowed by the rise of Buddhism, which arrived in China roughly during his lifetime. The next seven hundred years were dominated by the growth of Buddhism, particularly among the common people. This growth of what was perceived as a vulgar, foreign religion was met occasionally by persecutions, sometimes at the behest of Confucian advisors. Both the Northern Wei and Northern Chou unleashed minor persecutions in 446 and 574, and Emperor Gaozu (formerly Li Yuan, 566–635 CE), the founder of the Tang dynasty, contemplated a major campaign against Buddhism but did not put the idea into action. Gaozu's son and successor Taizong (reigned 626–649) ordered in 630 that every prefecture in the empire erect a temple to Confucius with regular sacrifices. Tang emperors usually came twice a year to Confucius's grave and sacrificed with great pomp and ceremony. These ceremonies did much to show the provincial leaderships and even the common people that the mandate of heaven did indeed reside with the Tang.

More often, though, it was Buddhism that won the hearts of Tang emperors, and of many of the people. Emperor Xian Zong (Hsien Tsung, reigned 805–820) engaged in public rituals worshipping a bone of the Buddha and incurred the wrath of the Confucian scholar Han Yu (768–824). Han criticized Taoist passivity and Buddhist annihilation and was sent into exile for his troubles. Han would have found a much more appreciative audience in Wu-Zung (Wu-tsung, reigned 840–846), who, encouraged mainly by Taoist priests, undertook in the 840s a fierce persecution of Buddhism. Unlike several smaller religions, which were extinguished, Buddhism was too strongly rooted in the people's affections to be eradicated entirely, but it was never to be as strong again.

These persecutions, minor and infrequent by European standards, should not obscure the degree to which Confucianism, Buddhism, and Taoism interacted as peaceful rivals. It was in fact during the centuries of the Tang dynasty that Confucianism, Buddhism, and Taoism intertwined and enmeshed so completely as to become almost impossible to prise apart. And, within this trend of cooperation and interaction, a new variation of Confucianism emerged, that which scholars today call Neo-Confucianism. Neo-Confucianism would never have developed into as cohesive an ideology as it did without the remarkable synthesis of Zhu Xi (Chu Hsi, 1130–1200). For two hundred years, scholars had been studying the works of Master Kung and Master Meng with renewed vigor. Some, such as Zhou Dunyi (Chou Tun-i in the old spelling, 1017–1073) had done so under the influence of various Taoist texts and precepts. Others, like Zhang Zai (Chang Tsai in the old spelling, 1020–1077) and Cheng Yi (Ch'eng I in the old spelling, 1033–1107), returned to the more naturalistic and rationalistic heart of Confucian teachings.

It was Zhu Xi's contribution to effect an extraordinary synthesis of all these thinkers with the original classics. Zhu Xi brought together what had been little more than related concepts within an ever-broader Confucian framework; concepts such as jen, Mencius's doctrines of humanity and righteousness, the idea of the investigation of things in the *Great Learning*, the teaching of sincerity in the *Doctrine of the Mean*. Zhu Xi's greatest single amalgamation was that of Zhou Dunyi's Great Ultimate with the Cheng brothers' concept of principle that the Great Ultimate has no physical form but consists entirely of principle actual, and potential. That the Great Ultimate is nothing other than principle, is the central idea of Zhu Xi's philosophy. But Zhu Xi's most radical innovation was to select and group the Four Books: *Doctrine of the Mean, Great Learning, Analects,* and the *Book of Mencius*—the Confucian classic texts.

The relatively brief time Zhu's synthesis was permitted to take hold among the intellectuals proved enough to inoculate it from the incursions of the Mongols. While Zhu Xi was effecting a dramatic intellectual conquest, the Mongol chieftain Temujin was proving rather successful at a more conventional form of conquest. On several occasions Zhu Xi bitterly criticized the Song authorities for appeasement of the barbarians. Unsurprisingly, the Mongols took a dim view of the Confucian literati in the early days of their power, which took form in the establishment of the Yuan dynasty in 1260. The martial, spartan Mongols feared the subtle appeal of the civilized scholars and found the simpler magic and promises of help in war from Taoists and Tibetan Buddhists more to their liking. Within a short space of time, however, the Yuan leadership was well and truly sinicized, and by 1313 the examination system was reinstated and Zhu Xi's Four Books were prescribed as the main texts. That remained unchanged until 1905. This historical lesson was not lost on the Manchus, who established their dynasty in 1644. Despite also being foreigners and being anxious not to lose their identity, they were careful not to touch the examination system, and the Confucian literati were left largely untouched.

Several scholars have challenged the conventional view that Neo-Confucianism took on its ultimate flowering under Zhu Xi, pointing out that a great deal of the attention of Neo-Confucianist thought remained eminently this-worldly and humanistic. While in no way wanting to detract from Zhu Xi's remarkable synthesis, this point is worth bearing in mind. After all, it was the Song emperors who rearranged the priority of the pantheon of deities that were the focus of popular devotion. This was to have an important role in the further cross-fertilization of the three dominant systems of belief in China. The Song dynasty also listened patiently to Hu Yuan (993–1059), who criticized the already-revitalized examination system as nothing more than a repository for rote learning of the ancient texts, ignoring the pressing problems of the day.

CONFUCIANISM'S CENTURY FROM HELL

Despite many further interesting developments in the history of Confucianism, the essential point being made here has perhaps been given sufficient attention. Chinese history involves this continual rising and falling away of Confucianism as an agency of the state and as a humanist program. By the time of the Qing dynasty, Confucianism had become a formidable buttress to the state. It had successfully taken ideas from rival systems without being assimilated by them. Its precepts were intimately bound up in the national character. It provided feudal and semifeudal autocracies with a raison d'être and an explanation for their own magnificence and manifest destiny. Confucian*ism*, in other words, had mastered brilliantly a world of competing dynasties, or successive dynasties, and had learned to explain and administer the mandate of heaven to them, and from them to a grateful nation. What this whole system could not be expected to see coming was the maelstrom of change that turned this entire weltanschauung upside down. The century since the fall of the Qin dynasty has been the most challenging one for Confucian thought, but also, at least potentially, the most liberating. And this has enormous consequences for global humanism.

The facts of the change, we can go through quickly. In 1905, a desperate Qing dynasty finally abolished the by now widely unpopular examination that had survived untouched for almost six hundred years. The following year, in an attempt to placate an outraged literati, and mindful of the fate of the Yuan dynasty, the Manchus elevated the status of sacrifices to Confucius to equal that of those to heaven and earth. But all this was far too late to save the dynasty, which fell in 1911. A republic was formed that declared universal religious liberty, spurning attempts from the newly formed Confucian Society to have Confucianism declared the state religion. These events forced the Confucian scholar and erstwhile reformer Kang Youwei (Kang Yu-wei in the old spelling, 1858–1927) into the role of arch reactionary who supported two abortive attempts to restore the emperor, once in 1917 and again in 1924. He died in disgrace, although his reputation as a Confucian scholar lived on. He is still admired by scholars for his radical reworking of Confucian thought, even though for him it all came to naught.

In the chaotic decades following the collapse of the Qing dynasty, Confucianism was subjected to something totally new to it: the disapproval of educated public opinion. Among many exponents of the May Fourth Movement, which was influential in the decade from 1919, Confucianism was portrayed as outmoded and not suitable to a modern democracy such as China was striving to become. The younger generation of university-educated radicals competed among themselves in their denunciation of Confucian values, which were now seen as being responsible for China's parlous state. Autocracy, social immobility, lack of interest in technology, gender inequality—all these ills were laid at the feet of Confucianism. In 1928, the semiannual ceremonies (no longer an opportunity for emperors to demonstrate their continued right to claim the mandate of heaven) and compulsory study of Zhu Xi's four Confucian classics, were abolished.

From the perspective of this book, the irony of the May Fourth Movement's hostility to Confucianism is that we now have one form of humanism strongly attacking another form. Chinese civilization, as already said, is essentially humanist, and Confucianism has articulated that humanism more effectively and with more impact than any other system, and for longer. But the May Fourth Movement's zeal for an evolutionary progressionism and criticism of entrenched privilege and societal atrophy buttressed by outdated values also has clearly humanist roots. Much of modern Chinese history can be seen in terms of this dialogue—sometimes open conflict—between these alternative humanisms. And while the May Fourth range of solutions have had little long-term influence, their typecasting of Confucianism as antiquarian and reactionary has.

If the withdrawal of state sponsorship was, at one level, a disaster for Confucianism, a renewed interest from the Guomindang (Kuomintang in the old spelling) government in the 1930s was scarcely any better. The New Life Movement, launched by Chiang Kai-shek in 1934, was just as hostile to reactionary tradition as the May Fourth Movement had been but was less willing to paint Confucianism in those colors. The New Life Movement was sold as China's version of what the New Deal or the Soviet Five-Year Plans or fascism were attempting to do in their respective countries. It was a campaign by the state to create an atmosphere of order and control, expressed in language it hoped would resonate with the people. As such, it was no less strongly opposed to the Western-influenced individualism of the May Fourth Movement. The so-called Four Binding Principles of the New Life Movement were more conservative and communitarian: *li* ("courtesy"), *yi* ("duty"), *lian* ("honesty"), and *chi* ("high-mindedness"). Three years into the movement, a huge temple was erected in Nanjing with the portrait of Confucius placed above Sun Yatsen and a miscellany of Western thinkers. Most scholars are agreed that the New Life Movement was a travesty of Confucius's actual views. Even at his most conservative, the Sage never advocated blind obedience to the state, nor did he reduce his thought to easily digested maxims.[7] It was an attempt to corral the people in the service of the state, one which had not, and would not, ever come near to deserving that level of deference.

The prestige of Confucian thought was not helped by its misuse at the hands of the increasingly corrupt and authoritarian Guomindang government. And once the Communists won power in 1949, its association with the discredited regime further tarnished its reputation. But this did not happen overnight. For the first decade after the revolution, Confucius was discussed relatively openly and without undue criticism. Liu Shaoqi's (1898–1969) short work *How to Be a Good Communist* (1939) spoke of cultivating a sound Marxist-Leninist viewpoint in terms reminiscent of Confucianism. He even quoted Confucius and Mencius approvingly, highlighting their recognition that no one is born a sage. From this he drew a lesson for the good Communist. "As Communist Party members have to shoulder the unprecedentedly 'great office' of changing the world, it is all the more necessary for them to go through such steeling and self-cultivation."[8]

There were several stages to the hardening of attitudes among the Communists toward Confucianism, which paralleled their attitudes toward humanism. Each of these stages can now be seen as a marker in Mao Zedong's (1893–1976) rise to unchallenged power. The party's treatment of Li Yaotang (1904–2005), who wrote under the pseudonym Ba Jin (sometimes translated as Pa Chin or Ba Ren), can be given as an example. Li's assumed name was an acronym of Bakunin and Kropotkin, two of his heroes from his earlier days as an anarchist. Ba Jin is generally recognized as one of China's most famous writers of the twentieth century. During the brief experiment in semiopen criticism known as the Hundred Flowers Campaign, Ba was in his element. But his essay "On Humanity" (1957) and his book *On Literature*, expressed humanist sentiments that went beyond what the party would tolerate. Ba argued that one could only embody proletarian principles by expressing fine sentiments: to look for love, to enjoy life, to shun death, and to seek the company of those who have a strong sense of justice. The goal of class struggle is the full emancipation of humanity, not the victory of one group of humans over another. Ba's attempt to redefine proletarian principles in humanist terms was never going to work in Mao's China, even while during one of its intermittent phases of toleration. Like Stalin, Mao had nothing but contempt for humanism, which he saw as a bourgeois indulgence. The slapping down of Ba Jin served as a warning to others that speaking of humanism or even expressing humanist principles was not going to be tolerated. His thoughts came under attack from all quarters, and discussion of humanism vanished from the public forum. The Socialist Education Movement, embarked on in 1962, continued the trend when it emphasized the class struggle and stepped up criticism of Confucius as an agent of reaction. The criticism of scholars who had been less than emphatic in their denunciation in the previous years became more pronounced.

None of this criticism came anywhere close to the Anti-Confucius Campaign of 1973 and 1974, during which time Confucianism entered into a period of vilification unparalleled in Chinese history. This campaign was one facet of the Great Proletarian Cultural Revolution, which ran from 1966 until Mao's death in 1976. During this time, all but 300 of the 2,680 Confucian temples around the country were closed or destroyed, including Confucius's hometown temple at Qufu. While attacking Confucian virtues of filial piety, righteousness (transcending classes), and particularistic loyalty and ritualism, the Anti-Confucius Campaign doubled as a thinly veiled attack on Zhou Enlai (Chou En-lai in the old spelling, 1898–1976) and, later on, Lin Biao (1907–1971). Liu Shaoqi was already dead by this time, having already been tainted as a capitalist roader and toady of Confucius. This hostility intensified to such an extent during the Cultural Revolution that, following Mao's lead, *humanist* became one of the more bloodcurdling insults for Red Guards to throw around.

Much of the debate in the Anti-Confucius Campaign centered around the Qin dynasty, which was now seen as the historical means by which the necessary changes demanded by the current requirements of dialectical materialism were brought about. This shift had dire consequences for the approach taken to the Confucian advisors who opposed the Qin dynasty. Once seen as lonely heroes against tyranny, they now became selfish bourgeois conspirators seeking to return to pre-Qin conditions. And in a bizarre reversal of roles, Qin Shihuangdi's suppression of Confucian scholars two millennia previously was hailed as a noble precedent for the Anti-Confucius Campaign. Even the burning of the books was hailed as "a decisive revolutionary act."[9] The rest of the Anti-Confucius Campaign degenerated into an obscure debate about how to interpret history, most of which went over the heads of the masses. But as we have seen in previous chapters, while dialectical materialism is the paramount mechanism of Marxism, it can have little truck with humanism.

After Mao's death, and particularly during the 1980s, the Communist Party faced structural stresses and pressure to change that could no longer be buried in a tide of blood and xenophobia. Like their rivals in Moscow, Beijing undertook some half-hearted examinations as to whether embracing some suitably sanitized notion of humanism would help resolve its problems of legitimacy. While Mao was alive, the Chinese Communist Party had seen little need for what it dismissed as a bourgeois affectation. But after the death of Mao and the effective abandonment of orthodox Marxism, the Party explored some plausible alternatives to dialectical materialism. The tremendous advantage the Chinese enjoyed over their Russian neighbors was the existence in Confucianism of a homegrown variation of humanism that could be pressed into service.

The process of repositioning Marxism as an ideology and the Communist Party as its political organ took a major step forward with a symposium of Chinese philosophers held in October 1979 in Taiyuan, Shanxi Province. Under the unpromising heading "Symposium on the Problem of Methodology in Assessing Chinese Philosophy," the delegates set about dismantling the Zhdanovite doctrine of a Manichean struggle between materialism and idealism, a struggle that idealism must, in the end, lose. This doctrine had held sway in China throughout Mao's reign. It now became possible to actually study traditions rather than simply to criticize them from a preset position. One area explored with enthusiasm was Western humanism as well as a renewed interest in the so-called early Marx, in particular the *Economic and Philosophical Manuscripts*. Alongside these areas was a new level of interest in the humanist core of Confucianism. While stock criticisms of Confucianism persisted, older scholars such as Liang Shuming, belied his age (he was in his nineties) and stumped the country giving lectures on the fundamentally Confucian nature of Chinese society. The ten years after the Taiyuan conference are often thought of as among the most productive in modern Chinese intellectual history. As one participant remembered, "The liveliness of the debates, the many differences of opinion, and the healthy climate of contention were unprecedented since the founding of the People's Republic."[10]

The burning political relevance of these questions ensured that the Communist Party was just as interested in their outcome as the philosophers. After Mao's death, there was a revival of interest in humanism and some tentative reassessment of the relationship between Marxism and humanism. As with the Soviet Union, this dialogue was fitful and uncertain, and in the end it led nowhere. At the "Nationwide Academic Symposium for the 100th Anniversary of the Death of Karl Marx" held in March 1983, Zhou Yang, a prominent theorist, advocated a reevaluation of humanism. Among his criticisms was the observation that contemporary socialist society had not solved the problem of alienation. Recall that this was one of the principal insights of the socialist humanists. Now Zhou was no dissident, but his speech got him into the same sort of trouble a dissident might expect. The Communist Party's Propaganda Department and Party School, and the Academy of Social Science, and the Department of Education, all sponsors of the symposium, criticized Zhou. Later in 1983, at the Second Plenary Session of the Twelfth Central Committee, the tendency toward humanism was criticized. Socialism could not, by definition, be alienating, and humanism was strongly dissociated with Marxism. Within the Party, a demand was circulated that anyone who had expressed support for humanism should retract that support. Then, in January 1984, Hu Qiaomu, a senior Communist Party ideologue, published the official line in an article titled "On the Question of Humanism and Alienation." Humanism was dismissed as a capitalist ideology antithetical to the spirit of Marxism, but humanist morals, when properly understood as socialist humanism, were acceptable. Hu's article was the signal for a thorough and widespread criticism of humanism in the Chinese press.

Even in the face of this official disapproval, a few brave souls continued to discuss publicly the meaning of *humanism*. In 1986 Wang Ruo Shui published his collected works under the title *Defending Humanism*, and the following year Lei Yong-Sheng published a discussion of Marxism and humanism in more positive terms than was officially acceptable. And in 1989, Lei formed a "Study Group of the History of Western Humanism." A partial thaw on official disapproval of humanism lifted after 1990, although Lei noticed most scholars avoided using the word. After Tiananmen Square, clearly the Chinese authorities had realized that it was in fact possible to experience alienation under socialism.

While the debate on humanism was tying itself in knots, Confucianism was enjoying its modest return to favor. China's new leader Deng Xiaoping (1904–1997), once a supporter of Liu Shaoqi and who had suffered as a result, was looking to provide the country with a more stable political infrastructure from which it could pursue industrialization. With this in mind, he started speaking of Confucius in terms disturbingly reminiscent of the New Life Movement half a century earlier. Confucian values could once again be inveigled in the service of the state. In 1983, Confucius's home, which had been destroyed during the Cultural Revolution, was rebuilt; and the following year saw the return of annual celebrations on the occasion of the Sage's birthday. And in 1994, China hosted a huge conference convened on the occasion of Confucius's 2,545th birthday. But, as with previous cycles, whether from the Guomindang or the Communists, the Sage's return to favor came with a price tag. In 1995, Zheng Jiadong, a research fellow at the Academy of Social Science in Beijing, kept to safe ground when he acknowledged benevolence as the most important part of Confucian thought. But, in the post–Tiananmen Square climate, Zheng was probably echoing current government thinking when he said that Confucianism could play a role in the management of large numbers of people.

But the party was not finished with humanism. As the Marxist veneer has become ever less convincing over the years of booming capitalist expansion, the Communist Party has continued its search for some replacement ideology, much in the way the CPSU (Communist Party of the Soviet Union) had been doing in the last twenty years of its life. Humanism can still be spoken of, but in fairly ritualized ways. For example, the online version of the *Peking Daily* reported approvingly a visit to China late in 2004 of French president Jacques Chirac, who told a university audience that his country was the home of "freedom, equality, and humanism," which he also called the fundamental requirement of the Universal Declaration of Human Rights. He went on to suggest that Franco-Chinese relations could also be predicated on humanist principles. Somewhat more significant was the Communist Party's decision at the Fifth Plenary Session of the Sixteenth Central Committee in October 2005, which outlined the basics of the next Five-Year Plan. The three foci of the plan were the implementation of a "scientific view of development, humanism, and sustainable development." This would involve developing social services and other measures to create a "harmonious society."

The next step was in March 2006, when CCP (Chinese Communist Party) Secretary General Hu Jintao launched one of China's periodic morality campaigns when he spoke of the eight virtues and the eight disgraces. Speaking to the Chinese People's Political Consultative Conference, Hu declared it was time to recall the "socialist concept of honor and disgrace." The eight virtues and eight disgraces, however, also owed a substantial, and unacknowledged, debt to Confucius. And even more paradoxically, the campaign resembles the Guomindang's New Life Movement of 1934–1935.

> Love the Motherland, with the corresponding disgrace of harming the Motherland.
> Serve the people. Don't disserve the people.
> Be united. Don't gain benefits at the expense of others.
> Struggle hard and live plainly. Don't wallow in idle luxuries.
> Work hard. Don't be lazy.
> Advocate science. Don't be ignorant and unenlightened.
> Be honest. Don't be greedy for profit at the expense of others.
> Obey the law. Don't be chaotic or lawless.[11]

In 2005, government attitudes toward Confucius were radically different from those thirty years previous, when the Sage was attacked as upholding the virtues of feudalism. But in 2005, those same virtues were seen in a new light. Confucius's birthday was publicized very widely—and very expensively—and study of him in schools and universities was expanded from an already generous level. There has also been an ambitious program of seeding Confucius Institutes in universities around the Western world.

Humanism is so integral to Chinese civilization that it will never pass away entirely. But it is true that its being touted by the ruling Communist

Party at a time of rampant corruption and staggering lack of concern for the poor and disadvantaged will do it little good. The future of Confucianism is always going to be problematic so long as a dictatorship sees value in repackaging its current priorities in Confucian language, in the knowledge that one's own vocabulary is no longer meaningful. Most systems of belief, when taken on by rulers, tend to undergo changes more to the benefit of the rulers than to the system of belief, and the thoughts of Master Kong have been no exception to that rule. Difficult though the concept of separation of "church" and state may be in this context, it nonetheless seems essential for the future of Confucian thought.

THE RISE OF THE NEW CONFUCIANS

The discredit Confucianism fell into in the decades after the collapse of the Qing dynasty in 1911 is part and parcel of the fate of any intellectual system that allows itself to become the handmaiden of an autocracy. It is hard for humanism, of whichever variety, to prosper outside of democracies. It can't breathe in an atmosphere where questioning is frowned upon or carries with it social and even physical dangers. For this reason, some of the most fertile new thinking on Confucianism has taken place among the Chinese diaspora around the noncommunist world. As China looked desperately to find ways to rejuvenate its ancient beliefs and codes of conduct, it was inevitable that scholars should look to the West for assistance in that process. That was most noticeable among the May Fourth generation of scholars, who borrowed heavily from evolutionist thinkers like Herbert Spencer and Ernst Haeckel, as well as from American liberals, John Dewey in particular. The next generation looked increasingly to Marxism for guidance. Since 1949, a new series of quests for the liveable Confucius has taken place. They have been dubbed the "New Confucians," and their goal was best summed up by one of their number, the scholar Zhang Shuting, who wrote: "Use Chinese philosophy as *ti* [substance] and Western philosophy as *yong* [function]."[12]

Among this first wave of New Confucians since 1949 was Xu Fuguan (1903–1982). He is of particular interest here because of the clearly humanistic flavor of his Confucianism. Xu Fuguan was born in Hubei Province to a farming family. His family name was Binching, but he changed it to Fuguan, which served as a summary of a passage from the *Daodejing*, which says "All things come into being, and I see [*guan*] thereby their return [*fu*]." This passage epitomized Xu's outlook. He began his working life in the army, where he rose to the rank of major general, before retiring in mid-career, disillusioned with soldiers and politicians. The second half of his career was spent as a writer, journal editor, and university professor. By means of these various roles he worked to address the failings he had observed as a soldier and to revitalize the Chinese cultural tradition.

Xu is best known for the prominent role he played in the *Manifesto on China's Culture to the World*, which appeared in January 1958 and acknowledged China's debt to Western technology but added that the West has much to learn from Chinese, and especially Confucian, ethics. And as the discourse has developed, discussion has moved toward articulating what is meant by the *ti* and the *yong* and where, if any, boundaries between them can be drawn. Xu postulated a variation of anxiety as the basic characteristic of Chinese tradition. This was not anxiety in the existentialist sense of dread, fallenness, or despair, nor was it a variation of Christian sin or Buddhist suffering. It was rather a positive understanding of anxiety as the motivating agent for a life of virtue. In this way, Xu rearticulated Confucianism in the sense of virtue ethics: the opening up of a coherent inner world of moral character in dynamic relationship with the needs and demands of the world. He also defended Confucianism from the charge brought by the May Fourth generation of bearing responsibility for China's slide into autocracy and subsequent discord. He emphasized the essentially democratic elements in Confucian thinking, in particular the idea that a society is composed first and foremost of its people. He was quite clear that he was not reinventing the wheel. Nor was he interested in constructing a formal system of philosophy. He described his method as raking the sand so that the gold may be uncovered. Rather, he wanted to bring to light once again the values of Chinese civilization that were under threat or had in some way or other been forgotten. Xu went on to restate classical Chinese humanism as a life of practical virtue. Parallels can be drawn with Paul Kurtz's notion of eupraxsophy here.

Someone else who reworked Confucian thought, though who is not generally seen as one of the New Confucians, was Hu Shih (1891–1962). As a leading representative of the May Fourth generation, Hu was strongly critical of Confucianism as he perceived it. In Hu's mind, Confucianism meant passive acceptance of hierarchy and unthinking subservience to what is old, with the corresponding hostility to what is new. Unlike Xu Fuguan, Hu Shih was specific in singling out Confucianism for criticism. But Hu's solutions had elements no less essential to Confucianism than those he so consistently lamented. Hu was suspicious of the radicals who called for sweeping changes, or even for revolution. Change that actually helps people comes slowly, Hu argued. We need to know where we came from and to understand the implications of changes, and be prepared to learn from our mistakes.

Hu had been educated in the United States, taking his doctorate under John Dewey. That influence remained with him for the rest of his life. His experiences in America helped him connect with American audiences in a way few twentieth-century Chinese intellectuals have. Another Chinese intellectual relevant to our story is Lin Yutang (1895–1976), who, no less than Hu Shih, was very influential among Western readers. Lin Yutang was born in Zhangzhou (Changchow in the old spelling), Fujian Province, the son of a Presbyterian minister. He was fortunate to receive an education, starting at St John University in Shanghai. He abandoned his Christian beliefs while at St. John, both because he was only now appreciating the depths of Chinese culture, hitherto kept from him or slighted, and because he felt a sense of guilt that his older sister had been denied the same education by virtue of her sex. From there he moved to Harvard, where he studied under, and was heavily influenced by, Irving Babbitt.[13] But he did not complete his doctorate there; he moved on to France, and then to Germany, where he finished his doctorate at Leipzig. He returned to China to teach English literature at Beijing University and, for a while, become another prominent publicist for May Fourth ideals. His acerbic and witty essays earned him the attention of the prominent warlord "Dog Meat" Zhang Zongchang, who in 1926 forced him to flee Beijing. After 1936, he lived mostly in the United States. It was there he worked for many years on a Chinese typewriter. It had long been thought impossible that Chinese characters could conform to a typewriter—now a keyboard—format. Lin's invention became available in the 1940s.

The books that made Lin's reputation in the West were *My Country and My People* (1935), the first book by a Chinese author to reach the *New York Times* bestseller list; *The Importance of Living* (1938); and *The Wisdom of China and India* (1942). Lin spoke specifically of humanism which, in its Chinese sense, has three clear applications: "a just conception of the ends of human life"; "a complete devotion to these ends"; and "the attainment of these ends by the spirit of human reasonableness or the Doctrine of the

Golden Mean."[14] It is not that Chinese humanism has solved the riddle of the meaning of life. Indeed, he argued, the very act of asking such a question is a characteristically Western form of anthropocentric conceit. "If we must have a view of the universe," he wrote, "let us forget ourselves and not confine it to human life. Let us stretch it a little and include in our view the purpose of the entire creation—the rocks, the trees, and the animals."[15] The true end, as understood by Chinese humanism, said Lin, was "the enjoyment of a simple life, especially the family life, and in harmonious social relationships."[16]

Lin saw Chinese humanism as the unique blend of Confucian and Taoist influences. The rather priggish seriousness of the Confucian has to be lightened a little, while the irresponsibility of the Taoist recluse need also be mitigated. Chinese humanism sits in that middle ground between the two. Niethammer, whose humanism was also an exploration of a middle ground, would have approved. And in a way Bertrand Russell would surely have been proud of, Lin articulated a strong form of cosmic modesty and was suspicious of grand claims of the universe having a purpose for humans. But he was able to say all this with such a delightful lightness of touch that the prospect of our cosmic irrelevance is not merely inspiring, it is positively amusing. The single most attractive feature of Lin Yutang, however, is his generous praise of loafing. This is an underdeveloped though much-needed aspect of humanism.[17] Loafing is not the same as laziness; nor is it the same as having nothing to do. Loafing is doing nothing in full knowledge of it being a far finer way to spend time than rushing around busily doing things. Lin wrote, "The wisest man is therefore he who loafs most gracefully."[18] This is, of course, but a restatement of the old Taoist principle of *wuwei*, or nonaction. *Wuwei* can be understood in the sense of "Leave well enough alone," or "It'll get done when it needs to be done."

At this time, Lin had reacted against his Christian upbringing and was describing himself as a pagan. Lin's paganism was essentially humanistic. The Chinese pagan

> is one who starts out with this earthly life as all we can or need to bother about, wishes to live intently and happily as long as life lasts, often has a sense of the poignant sadness of this life and faces it cheerily, has a keen appreciation of the beautiful and the good in human life wherever he finds them, and regards doing good as its own satisfactory reward.[19]

Once we arrive at the so-called third generation of New Confucians, the situation becomes messier. One strand of thought from the 1980s ended up in territory oddly reminiscent of the New Life Movement, as when they spoke of "Asian Values." This is a blend of cultural triumphalism and support for the non- or semidemocratic systems of the highly performing Asian Tigers. Asian Values was usually said to involve emphasis not on rights, as in the West, but on duty—not on individualism but on harmony. Other values often described in this way include reliance on family and other close networks, delaying immediate gratification by taking a long-term view, and saving for the future. The key, and usually unspoken, corollary to this is passivity in the face of authoritarian rule. Once again, Confucius is usually held up as the quintessential exponent of Asian values, but this does him a disservice. To begin with, Confucius would have had little idea what *Asia* signified, let alone other civilizations whose values were different. And more important, while Confucius did stress the qualities the proponents of Asian Values admire, he did not do so to the exclusion of opposing tyranny. Talk of Asian Values as the qualities that underpin the economic success of the Asian Tigers petered out somewhat after the financial crisis in those economies at the end of the 1990s.

Among the scholars in the United States, the discourse has been more disengaged. In particular, the relationship between Confucianism and humanism has come in for critical comment from some quarters, the most important of them being Tu Weiming. Born in Kunming in the state of Yunnan, Tu Weiming (1940–) was educated in Taiwan and then in the United States. He ended up at Harvard, specializing in Chinese intellectual history. But he has a wider audience than most academics, being a member of the World Economic Forum at Davos, and is one of the Group of Eminent Persons on the Dialogue among Civilizations, which was convened by Kofi Annan during his term as secretary general of the United Nations.

Tu Weiming speaks enthusiastically about Confucian humanism and is looking not only to promote its values among the East Asian nations, he is exploring its potential as a foundational resource for a planetary humanism. When translated into Western political categories, Tu's version of Confucian humanism sounds a lot like social democracy in its blend of an interventionist style of government looking to enrich public needs and welfare. But his assertion of the family as the basic unit of society sounds closer to conservatism. The uniquely Confucian emphasis becomes apparent when he speaks of civil society as achieved by "dynamic interplay between family and state." And with an emphasis Confucius would have been proud of, Tu values education as "the civil religion of society." Confucian humanism's ideal has a lot of the qualities of bildung about it. Education's primary purpose is character building with respect to the individual and the accumulation of social capital through communication. The result is a seamless web of societal interdependence that Confucian humanism can articulate with authority: "Since self-cultivation is the root for the regulation of family, governance of state, and peace under heaven, the quality of life of a particular society depends on the level of self-cultivation of its members."[20] I doubt Friedrich Immanuel Niethammer would have found fault with that.

The major blight on Tu's otherwise admirable exposition is his anxiety—almost obsession—to stress the spiritual element of Confucian humanism, which for him involves making a sharp distinction between secular humanism, about which he takes a dim view. The stress he places on this distinction carries him away from majority opinion. Most scholars of Confucianism are not as concerned to accentuate this distinction, seeing it as rather missing the point of Confucianism's potential as a nondoctrinal seedbed for planetary humanism. And even while stressing this distinction, Tu is not saying Confucianism is a religion. He acknowledges one cannot convert to Confucianism, one cannot attend Confucian places of worship, and one should not confuse the sacred with the supernatural. At times he also insists that Confucius should not be held up as a moral paradigm to emulate, but at most other times, this is very much how it sounds. Confucianism, in Tu Weiming's view, is "a language of moral community flowing from a universal moral value."[21]

There is a trendline of pessimism in some contemporary scholarship on the subject. Confucianism has been through so many distortions, dislocations, and criticisms over the past century, so the argument goes, that it is seen as irrevocably tarnished. Confucianism is now widely understood as standing for group harmony with its implication of conformism (as opposed to the human rights of individuals), conservative hierarchies (as opposed to liberal democracy), and character (understood in a specifically Chinese way, rather than a generalized cosmopolitanism).[22] There is even less reason to see much future for a generalized, state-sanctioned humanism coming out of China. The Soviet experiment with humanism in the years leading up to its collapse and China's own flirtations with it in the years prior to Tiananmen

Square make it all too problematic. But this is no more than to be expected. A constant theme of this book is that humanism can never work when sponsored by an authoritarian state because it involves a fatal betrayal of humanism's core principles.

If the twentieth century was, by and large, a dreadful one for Confucianism, there is no reason why the twenty-first century need also be. The Confucian classics are readily available to any interested reader, and a whole new humanist journey can begin. What is more, in a century of planetary thinking, it is no longer the case that the future of Confucian humanism is the exclusive preserve of East Asian peoples. As the only genuinely transcultural trajectory of thought, humanism can, indeed *should*, look broadly for inspiration. And Confucian humanism is powerfully relevant in the twenty-first century as a corrective to the atomized, postmodern individualism that has become the norm. We can look once again in this direction, knowing full well that "Confucian humanism" is an abstraction that we are free to rework as we see fit. Not being a religion in the strict sense of the word, Confucianism has no scripture, so passages of works whose message no longer fits can be forgotten in good conscience. But most of what normally passes as Confucian humanism still has the capacity to guide and inspire. As Michael Nylan observed, since the time of Confucius himself, "the Way has been sought as remedy against cultural drift and foreign conquest, evils now inflicted less often by arms than by technology, consumer culture, and the global economy."[23] The Sage's awareness of the need for personal effort, the interdependence of personal effort with one's surroundings, and the moral duty of the rulers to earn the respect of the ruled—all in a natural context—can speak to us now more than ever.

THE VENERABLE MASTER XINGYUN AND HUMANISTIC BUDDHISM

We have spent this entire chapter looking at the varying fortunes of Confucianism as a vehicle for humanism. But in China, the division between Confucianism, Taoism, and Buddhism is in large part an artificial exercise that ignores their essential interdependence. They were traditionally known collectively as the *San Jiao* ("the three teachings"), including *Ju Jiao*, "teachings of the learned" [i.e., Confucianism]; *Tao Jiao*, "teachings of the Way" [i.e., Taoism]; and *Fo Jiao*, "teachings of the Buddha." There is a popular saying, "three ways to one goal." This fact alone constitutes an important point monotheistic religions should learn from.

This interdependence of the Asian traditions also makes it unsurprising, then, that we can also trace some interesting trends in humanistic thinking in South and East Asian Buddhism. This should come as no surprise. As sketched in the last chapter, Buddhism began as a naturalistic and humanistic protest to brahmanical formalism and supernaturalism. Theravada Buddhism, in particular, has remained largely humanistic in orientation. More recently we hear of *Engaged Buddhism*, which has developed strongly in Southeast Asia and latterly in the United States. The Vietnamese Thich Nhat Hanh is usually credited with developing the term, in the context of nonviolent antiwar protests in the 1960s. And Sulak Sivaraksa has championed Engaged Buddhism in his native Thailand. Thich Nhat Hanh's work forced him into exile in 1966, and Sulak Sivaraksa has had to spend periods away from his country at various times. And while Aung San Suu Kyi hasn't specifically spoken in these terms, her emphasis on nonviolent political activism for freedom and democracy in her homeland of Myanmar has all the same hallmarks of Engaged Buddhism.

Of particular interest to us, however, is the Foguangshan organization, an arm of Buddhism that has grown significantly, including in the West. The Foguangshan movement grew out of the corrupt and complacent state of Chinese Buddhism in the first half of the twentieth century and owed its development in part to the recognition that aspects of China's miserable condition could be alleviated by looking to the West. It also owes a considerable intellectual debt to Confucianism.

Li Kuoshen was born in Jiangsu Province on July 22, 1927, the third of four children. His father, a businessman, made a trip to Nanjing in 1937, only to get caught up in the Japanese occupation and subsequent massacre, never to be seen again. The following year, Li entered the Buddhist temple at Qixia, an important center of Chan Buddhism, and became known by his Dharma names of "Thorough Enlightenment" and "Instantaneous Awakening." With the approval of his superiors, he later took his own Dharma name Xingyun (Hsing Yun in the old spelling, which means "Star and Cloud"). After his move to the Jaioshan ("Flaming Mountain") Buddhist College in Zhenjian in 1945, Xingyun was exposed to Western thought for the first time.

There is a long pedigree of thinking in the Chan and Pure Land schools of Chinese Buddhism that predated Xingyun's thought. Among the more direct influences, Xingyun credits the Buddhist scholar-monk Taixu (T'ai Hsü in the old spelling, 1889–1947) with being the first to speak of *Humanistic Buddhism*. Taixu was concerned with the overemphasis on rites for the dying and the dead. Somewhere along the way, Buddhist concern for the living had fallen away. And among the living, the premier effort had gone into a bloated and corrupt monastic system that had long since ceased to work as an intellectual powerhouse for Buddhist philosophy and practice. In the face of this lassitude in Chinese Buddhism, he sought refreshment in Western philosophy, and it was from here that he came across the word *humanism*. Taixu was the first Chinese Buddhist cleric to travel through Europe and China, a trip he made in 1928 and 1929. I have not been able to discover who Taixu was reading when he came across the word *humanism*, but I suspect it would have been Ferdinand Schiller or, perhaps, Frank Doan.

It is not surprising that humanism would have attracted Taixu. A great deal of Chinese Buddhism is humanistic in orientation, and what would have seemed foreign in Western humanism could easily have been sidelined. This, after all, was what Chinese Buddhists had been doing for many centuries with the Buddhism that had come originally from India. Taixu spoke of Buddhism as *Rensheng Fojiao*, "Buddhism among the living." One attains as complete a humanness as one is capable by relying on the Buddha's example, as opposed to slavishly following each precept. In this way humanness perfected is the same as buddhahood attained. The combination of entrenched opposition from the Buddhist hierarchy and the ongoing war and disruption conspired to defeat Taixu's campaign. His influence became apparent only after his death, and then only in Taiwan.

Xingyun was influenced profoundly by Taixu's example, but circumstances were beginning to work against him. His career as a Buddhist cleric and teacher was imperiled by the civil war and was cut short by the victory of the Communists in 1949. That year he fled to Taiwan, where he promptly came under suspicion there as well, spending twenty-three days in detention on charges of subversion. Neither was Xingyun impressed with the state of Taiwanese Buddhism at the time, which was lackadaisical, mired in superstition, and busier tending to the dead rather than to the living. His brief brush with the law in Taiwan and the state of Buddhism on the island at the time meant that his career was going to have to be built from the ground up. With that in mind, he began his career in the unfancied and neglected backwater of Ilan, where over the next decade he built a strong following. From his base in Ilan, Xingyun established *Foguangshan*, "Buddha's Light Mountain." Clearly a very able organizer, Xingyun improved the number and quality of educational and promotional publications, broadened the range of social outlets for the people of Ilan, and generally overhauled the infrastructure of Buddhism in the province. The main components of Foguangshan were the Shoushan Temple and the Shoushan Buddhist College, completed in 1964 near the city of Kaohsiung. Three years later the college expanded, taking over a defunct Christian missionary center, and renamed itself the Tungfang Buddhist College. Foguangshan formed out of these various enterprises in 1967. Relations with the local community have not always been rosy, however. When the monastery complex closed its doors to tourists in 1997, the local economy suffered a severe blow.

Xingyun gradually emerged as one of the four pillars of postwar Taiwanese Buddhism. The other three were Shengyan (1930–), Zhengyan (1937–) and Weijue (1928–). Collectively the four are known as the *si dashan*, or the Four Major Mountains—in other words, the four most influential builders of Taiwanese Buddhism. Shengyan and Zhengyan's organizations also follow Humanistic Buddhism, differing only in details. Despite the relatively close ideological affinity between the si dashan, they operate as rivals, as each seeks the same political influence, donation money, and authority among the people. It took Xingyun many years to overcome the suspicion of him among the Taiwanese political establishment, but he knew he had "arrived" in 1973 when Jiang Jingguo (Chian Ching-Kuo in the old spelling), head of Taiwan's executive council, visited Foguangshan. Using his newfound status as an "insider," Xingyun expanded his operations abroad, often serving in an unofficial capacity as a cultural ambassador. Foguangshan temples were being developed around Asia and North America, and Xingyun became something of an international celebrity. In 1990, he founded the Buddha's Light International Association to help coordinate these efforts. In the decade that followed, Foguangshan founded almost a hundred centers around the world, some of them quite substantial buildings. At around this time Xingyun began to speak of himself as a "global person."

Through all this, he kept up a stream of publications and journalistic work to propagate his brand of Humanistic Buddhism. His first work,

Singing in Silence, was published in 1950, and in 1955 he wrote the first major life of the Buddha ever published in Taiwan. A steady flow of publications have continued ever since. After his retirement, Xingyun oversaw the production of the multivolume *Fo Guang Buddhist Dictionary*.

So what does Xingyun mean when he speaks of *Humanistic Buddhism*? To begin with, there is a great deal less emphasis on inward-focused meditation and retreat from the world that has been the staple of monasticism. The Buddha, one promotional publication tells us, "was born into this world, he sought the true nature of life during his time in this world, he attained enlightenment while in this world, he taught people in this world, and he entered nirvana while in this world. Sakyamuni Buddha is a Buddha for all of us in this world. His teachings truly embody Humanistic Buddhism."[24] And rather than dream irrelevantly of a Pure Land somewhere in the beyond, Humanistic Buddhism places great emphasis on establishing the pure land in the human realm. It was with this in mind that Xingyun took one step further than Taixu's understanding of Humanistic Buddhism. Where Taixu had spoken of *Rensheng Fojiao*, "Buddhism among the living," Xingyun spoke of *Renjian Fojiao* where *Renjian* translates as "in the midst of the people."[25]

Xingyun also carries on the great Buddhist insight that all sentient beings share a Buddha nature. This has an impact on his conception of human rights. While extolling the advance of human rights, he looks forward to the future when the principle is extended to recognition of what he calls life power in living things. This could be seen as taking a Buddhist perspective of E. O. Wilson's principle of Biophilia, or the love of the principle of life without regard to what manner of living each species has evolved. Both these insights, despite being expressed in the language of quite different intellectual and cultural traditions, represent an important advance from humanism as a form of anthropocentric conceit.

Xingyun isolated four principles of Humanistic Buddhism: educate the young, improve culture, benefit society, and purify the mind. These principles illustrate the role given to helping alleviate suffering and build the pure land in this mundane world. Too much emphasis has traditionally been given, he argues, to the supramundane world. And in doing that, Buddhism has become too inward-focused, too passive and tolerant of the suffering of others. Xingyun even questions the standard Buddhist stress on the centrality of suffering, insisting that he is a very happy person.[26] The Foguanshan's slogan (or mission statement, if you prefer) articulates the humanistic core of this brand of Buddhism: "Give others confidence, give others joy, give others convenience, and give others hope."[27] It is with this in mind that Foguangshan values choir groups and sports clubs as much as study groups and chanting sessions.

All this said, there are elements in Humanistic Buddhism many naturalistic humanists would be unhappy with. Master Xingyun's view of history has many features of teleology and easy progressionism that have been criticized elsewhere in this book. Sanguine confidence in unlimited progress in the sense of constant accumulation and enrichment is no longer something that can simply be assumed. It may even be that such an attitude is part of the problem rather than part of the solution. Also, Xingyun believes religion is a human condition and extols faith in a way familiar to readers of Paul Tillich. And he sticks with the *samsara* wheel of rebirth and sees suffering or happiness in this life as the just punishments or rewards for one's behavior in previous lives:

> Why do some dress well and eat like kings while others go hungry without three meals a day? This is because of the differences in the causes they have sown and the effects they reap, and it is not due to fate or the unfairness of the world.[28]

And while criticizing superstition in the form of *feng shui*, fortune telling, and the belief in days being auspicious or inauspicious, Xingyun is quite happy to attribute illness to things like "ghosts getting the upper hand, harassment by evil spirits, and bad karma."[29] And by Western standards he is unduly sanguine when dismissing the value of the separation of church and state. Government, he writes, "needs to be supplemented with the educating influence of Buddhism, while Buddhism can be spread with the protection and support of government."[30] This is a bit too win-win for Buddhism for comfort. Now, Buddhism's record of cooperation with governments has, by and large, been admirable, but one can't help feeling that an important principle is being set aside here altogether too lightly.

But if this book has any one major point to make, it is that humanism is a movable feast, not tied down solely by conformity to doctrine. After all these objections have been raised, it remains that Humanistic Buddhism seeks to enrich people's lives here and now. The emphasis on cultivation of the Way that Humanistic Buddhism shares with Confucianism and Taoism is an essentially humanistic priority. It also can be likened to an East Asian variation of bildung. Either way, the simple humanism taught by Confucius and the Buddha promise to become prominent features of twenty-first-century humanism. So long as they are not tied unduly to the state, Confucian and Buddhist humanism can indeed guide as how to live, rather than simply as how to make a living.

CHAPTER 11

HUMANISM IN THE MUSLIM WORLD: RETHINKING *IJTIHAD*

It has been said often enough but can bear repeating: there is more to Islam than Islamic fundamentalists. There has been no shortage of scholars lining up to offer convincing taxonomies of Islam, but the most useful for our purposes is Charles Kurzman's division into *customary*, *revivalist*, and *liberal* Islam. Customary Islam is the Islam as practiced by the people and may well include practices not condoned, or even specifically condemned, by the Qur'an. Kurzman mentions the drumming in West Africa, the veneration of saints in Morocco, the various ritual displays of belief in Indonesia, and the belief in jinn in Kurdistan. Then there is revivalist Islam, which calls on the past as a means to turn its back on modernity. This gives rise to the fundamentalism of the madrassas and what gets called *political Islam*. But then there is liberal Islam. Kurzman is careful to point out that *liberal* is nothing more than a term of convenience and hastens to add that many "liberal" Muslims would certainly not see themselves in those terms or use that word.[1] In some ways, *modernist* is a better word and conveys more clearly the modus operandi of these Muslim reformers. I will use *modernist* and *liberal* interchangeably in this context. All this said, the important point about modernist Islam is that, in contrast to the revivalists, it calls on the past *in the name of modernity*. No better example of this can be found than from Benazir Bhutto (1953–2007), who wrote shortly before her death, "Islam sanctifies the traditions of the past while embracing the hope for progress in the future."[2] Modernist Muslims (like Bhutto) are equally critical of customary and revivalist Islam for their perceived backwardness. It also needs to be said that no attempt will be made in this chapter to identify anything that could be called "true Islam." Religions, being human creations, develop or deteriorate alongside the human societies that nurtured them.

NURTURING A STRATEGY OF REFUSAL

Another insight relevant to this chapter is Mohammed Arkoun's notion of the unthought in Muslim thought. Arkoun is critical of the large areas of Muslim thought and practice that have been sealed off from free inquiry. He calls it the *dogmatic enclosure* whereby protected Muslim orthodoxy is allowed a free run, without competition or challenge. "A strategy of refusal, consisting of an arsenal of discursive constraints and procedures, permits the protection and, if necessary, the mobilization of what is uncritically called 'faith.'"[3] If we apply Kurzman's categories here, we can see that customary Islam and revivalist Islam are going to be more prone to this strategy of refusal, albeit for different reasons. Customary Islam simply has no need or wish for unnecessary complications in religious life; it may be more a case of strategy of incomprehension. But among revivalist Islam, a more direct and conscious refusal is taking place, and this has a lot to do with where the thrust of modernization is thought to hail from.

The critical point of divergence among these three strands of Islam is in their respective attitudes toward the West. For a religion accustomed to seeing itself as the final revelation of God to man, the slow realization of the growing power of the West from the sixteenth century onward provided more than a political problem. It was a major existential challenge to how Muslims saw the world. In his illuminating discussion of this long process, Bernard Lewis distinguishes between the modernizing element and the Westernizing element. The most blinkered Islamist can be a modernizer in the sense of employing Western technology to further his ends. But, clearly, the Islamist is not, at least not knowingly, a Westernizer. The whole focus of the Islamists' hatred is the West. But the modernist Muslim is in a more ambiguous position in recognizing some benefit both in modernizing and in Westernizing. A clear example Lewis gives of this is the treatment of women. To advocate gender equality is going to involve a degree of acceptance of norms and assumptions developed primarily in the West. He also cites the notion of the separation of church and state, which he sees as a uniquely Christian concept. While, in the narrowest sense, separation of church and state has long Western roots, it would be wrong to say the same thing of a broader secularism. As we saw in chapter 9, India has a long tradition of sophisticated thinking about secularism.

Another interesting parallel can be drawn here. We saw in the previous chapter that China's history, at least since the end of the nineteenth century, is also dominated by the ongoing dynamic of its reaction to the encroachments of the West. And China, too, produced its modernizers and its Westernizers. But without a monotheist worldview, the challenge of the West has not produced in China the same sorts of extreme reactions as the Muslim world has generated. Indeed, in adopting Marxism, China showed itself far more open to Western points of view than the Muslim world was. Whether that receptivity has been to China's benefit in that case is another question.

One of the many consequences of this growing recognition of having something to learn from the infidels was a reexamination of the Muslim ways of learning. A particularly important development in this area of Muslim thought and practice took place in the nineteenth century. This was when the two long-established concepts of *taqlid* and *ijtihad* started to be spoken of separately. The range of meanings for *taqlid* includes "to imitate" or "total submission" and refers to the requirement to follow Muslim clerics on all matters without asking for any sort of justification of their decisions. The taqlid doctrine states that there are no truths revealed beyond those revealed in the Qur'an. This sort of literalism had the effect of shutting down free inquiry and banishing scholars. It is the justification for the strategy of refusal. The Qur'an is inconsistent on this issue—as it is on many others— with passages that extol and condemn blind, uncritical faith. Revivalist Muslims are going to feel most at home in the tradition of taqlid, although, as we have already noted, they need not necessarily be opposed to taking from the West that which seems useful.

Ijtihad, by contrast, translates as "strenuous endeavor" or, more simply, "independent thinking" and refers to a conscientious examination of the sacred texts in order to discover for oneself the truths of Allah. It can also refer to the more problematic scenario of finding one's way in circumstances where believers find themselves uncertain of the proper Muslim response to a situation, where the sacred sources are unclear. In Sunni Islam it is permitted to make a decision oneself as to the correct course of action (albeit within strict bounds), whereas in Shiite Islam this is forbidden. Shiites believe there is no situation not foreseen in some capacity in either the Qur'an or the Hadith, or in sharia law. The practice of ijtihad in Sunni Islam became more problematic after the triumph of Qur'anic literalism and the doctrine of taqlid. And yet it is important to remember that the Wahhabis, whose brand of puritanical Sunni Islam now governs Saudi Arabia, began life extolling the virtues of ijtihad. So did several other prominent revivalists, like Shah Wali Allah (1702–1762) in India and Refa a Rafi al-Tahtawi (1801–1873) in Egypt.

Ijtihad, then, is not the exclusive preserve of reformist, humanistic Islam, although its potential for development probably lies with the reformers. Since the Cold War, and with rising fears of a clash of civilizations between Islam and the West, there have been conscious attempts to reinterpret *ijtihad* as a tradition of independent reasoning that encourages believers to reexamine their faith in the light of new knowledge or circumstances. This is too generous a reading of ijtihad for four reasons: (1) there is no room for inquiry that leads to a rejection of Islam; (2) the practice of ijtihad is usually restricted to scholars; (3) for the general public taqlid is the preferred option; and (4) individual study is generally frowned upon in favor of group study. And finally, it can legitimately be objected that ijtihad and taqlid cannot be separated in this way without doing serious conceptual violence to each of them. These legitimate objections notwithstanding, ijtihad stands as a dormant possibility for a reformation of Islam. As we saw in chapter 8, Christianity can be described as a not always happy compromise between the rational, philosophical tendency exemplified by Athens, and the tradition of faith and obedience exemplified by Jerusalem. The dialectic between ijtihad and taqlid works along the same trajectory.

In what context, then, should we think of humanism in the context of these debates within Islam? Humanism can be understood in several ways in the Middle East. It can refer to the relatively small number of apostates who have specifically repudiated the religion they were brought up in and now count themselves atheists, naturalists, and secularists in the Western sense. For them there is little quarter given, as the penalties for apostasy are grim and brutal. Apostates, if they are to live in accordance with their convictions, need to live in a Western secular democracy. But humanism can also be used with respect to the modernists and progressives within Islam who are looking to promoting the ijtihad tradition as means to combat fundamentalism and the deadening effect of taqlid. And one could also count as humanist the convinced Muslim who is looking to recapture the traditions of Muslim philosophy and rational thought as a means to rescue the religion from the harsher effects of the more primitive forms of supernaturalism. The minimum understanding of Muslim humanism in the context of this chapter is the refusal to leave any subject unthought. The abiding problem for Muslim humanists with these inclinations has been the ease with which their enemies can associate them and their objectives with the apostates. This chapter will survey each of these viewpoints.

MU'TAZILISM, IBN RUSHD, AND THE HEYDAY OF MUSLIM FREE THOUGHT

This is not the place to provide anything more than the briefest outline of the history of Islamic free thought. But it matters that Islam has a long history of rationalist, humanist, and freethinking philosophers. In what can serve as a warning to us all today, they were all overwhelmed in the end by the xenophobia and anti-intellectualism of the fundamentalists. But their having existed at all may serve as a rallying point for a revival in the fortunes of Islamic humanism.

One significant movement was Mu'tazilism, a school of Islamic rationalism that flourished from the eighth to eleventh centuries CE. Mu'tazilism was profoundly influenced by Greek philosophy, especially by Aristotle and the Neoplatonists. The first principle of Mu'tazili thinkers was that it is incumbent on all human beings to exercise speculative reason in order to know God. Speculative reason is to be based on rational argument, the scriptures, the paradigmatic practice of the Prophet, and the consensus of the community. On the basis of this first principle, Mu'tazili thinkers grouped around the Five Usul, or Fundamentals. These were divine unity, divine justice or theodicy, the promise of reward or threat of punishment in the hereafter, the intermediate position on who is and who is not a good Muslim, and the commanding of the good and prohibiting of the evil. For a while Mu'tazilism held sway among the leaders of political Islam, and some of them permitted authoritarian measures to ensure Mu'tazili doctrines be adhered to. Ironically, given they advocated open debate, the Mu'tazili theologians, acquiesced in this contradictory enforcement of their views.

By the eleventh century, Mu'tazilism was in decline and for many centuries the word *mu'tazili* became a term of abuse to mean little more than "unbeliever." In the twentieth century, Mu'tazilism underwent a limited revival as Muslim scholars have sought ways that contemporary Islam can resist the encroachments of the West while adopting Western practices felt to be necessary in order to preserve Muslim independence. Mu'tazilism has also been seen by some Muslim intellectuals as a necessary bulwark against Islamism, with its threats against democracy and free speech. In particular, the Mu'tazilite willingness to see ambiguous Qur'anic passages as best interpreted metaphorically has been popular.

The Mu'tazilite thinkers were, in the main, monotheists, but Islam has also produced a few more thoroughgoing skeptics, perhaps none more so than Ibn al-Rawandi (d. 910 CE). The Mu'tazilite theologians were usually able to balance their debt to Greek rationalism with their Islamic faith, but Ibn al-Rawandi took this line of questioning a great deal further. Al-Rawandi was prepared to question what to virtually all of his contemporaries was beyond question. And as is so often the case with early freethinkers, all of his works have been lost and destroyed, and we can only rebuild his thoughts through the passages attributed to him by his enemies. His enemies said that he repudiated the entire supernaturalist system of revelation and miracles and was frankly agnostic on the question of the existence of God. Other sources interpreted his views more in terms of denouncing revelation as unnecessary and irrelevant, in that unaided human reason was sufficient to determine knowledge of God and good and evil. Al-Rawandi was said to have rejected monotheism in favor of dualism, and to have disparaged the vanity of divine wisdom. He even parodied the Qur'an and Muhammad. He was accused of being an atheist (which, in all probability, he was) and executed.

A contemporary of Ibn al-Rawandi, and as radical a freethinker, was Abu Bakr Muhammad al-Razi (854–925/935 CE). Al-Razi was one of the first freethinkers to find the concept of God incompatible with a scientific outlook. Known to the West for many centuries as Rhazes, Abu Bakr Muhammad al-Razi was born in Rayy, where his youth was spent as a lute player or money-changer, according to different traditions. He soon gained recognition for his breadth of knowledge and was put in charge of the local hospital. His fame spread and he was later appointed in charge of the hospital in Baghdad. Al-Razi wrote widely, reputedly being responsible for more than two hundred works. His medical treatises remained influential until well into the sixteenth century. As with al-Rawandi, few of al-Razi's works survive, and he is mostly known through his detractors, who bitterly attacked his tendency to think independently. Symptomatic of this was al-Razi's criticisms of the pervasive Aristotelianism then dominating Muslim philosophy. His own views, those on the transmigration of the soul for instance, reflected more closely those of Plato and Pythagoras. Like al-Rawandi, al-Razi declared revelation to be superfluous (since reason was sufficient for knowledge of the truth) and morally questionable (because of the rivers of blood that have been spilled in the name of revelation). Along with this, al-Razi rejected the validity of prophecy. These views earned him long-lasting hatred from the orthodox as an infidel. The story of the end of his life has him refusing to have a cataract removed because he had seen enough of the world and didn't want to see any more.

And neither were al-Rawandi or al-Razi lone exceptions. From the days of the Prophet himself, Arabia knew of its *zindiqs*, "heretics." The first person known to have been put to death for heresy was in 742 or 743 CE when Dja'd Ibn Dirham was executed on the orders of the Umayyad caliph Hisham. By the eighth century, Muslim governance was established strongly enough to sustain the office of Sahih al-Zanadiqa (equivalent to Grand Inquisitor). This office went about its business with scrupulous efficiency over the next several centuries.

The most influential Muslim philosopher of all time was Ibn Rushd (1126–1198). Known in the West by his Latinized name Averroës, Rushd was also very influential in Christian circles. He was born into a privileged family of civil and religious professionals in Cordoba, the intellectual heart of Muslim Spain, and spent his life traveling between Cordoba and Seville in Spain, and Marrakesh in Morocco. In 1195 or so, he retired from public duties or was forced into exile, having come under a political cloud or in the face of rising opposition to him from conservative clerics. He was accused of atheism, and his books were burned. The charge of atheism was much less likely to be accurate than it was for al-Rawandi or al-Razi, but it did its job. Rushd's death, which has long been suspected of not being natural, spelled the beginning of the end for the golden age of Muslim philosophy.

A prime concern of Rushd was the reconciliation of philosophy and religion, which he approached through commentaries on the works of Aristotle. Many of Rushd's predecessors had been influenced by Aristotle—indeed the preservation of his philosophy is one of the great debts the world owes to Muslim philosophers—but where they were content to add layers of impenetrable Neoplatonist exegesis, Rushd developed the philosopher's work in new ways. His main work was called *The Incoherence of the Incoherence* (approximately 1180) and was a criticism of earlier philosophers who questioned the power and relevance of reason in all areas of human investigation. Rushd's harmonizing of religion and philosophy was sophisticated. On the one hand, he tried to avoid simply allegorizing the anthropomorphisms in the Qur'an as he felt the Mu'tazilites had done. But he was no less careful to avoid the crude literalism of Hanbal (d. 855 CE) and others. He did this by acknowledging that the Qur'an has passages that are ambiguous and passages that are unambiguous.[4] Following from this, he argued that the Qur'an addresses itself to different orders of people in different ways. What is appropriate to one group is not appropriate to others. While he accorded religion higher status than philosophy, he also said that reason has a vital part to play in religious life. Rushd's thoughts were later translated, not entirely correctly, as advocating a double truth idea that purportedly allowed religious truth to sit alongside conflicting philosophical truth.

The death of Rushd signaled the end of the golden centuries of Muslim philosophy. From then on, the voices of the isolationists became overwhelming. The damage done by the Crusades permanently soured relations with the Christians and made discussing works by Europeans (particularly the pagan Greeks who were not even People of the Book) ever more dangerous. Islam went into its shell and was from the thirteenth century largely content with commentary on scripture and unthinking literalism.

ISLAMIC MODERNISM AND THE REINVENTION OF *IJTIHAD*

The long, dogmatic slumber of Islam was rudely woken by the incursion of the West in the nineteenth century into its domain. Indeed, the dominant strand of debate in Islam in the last two centuries has been how best to respond to the West. Does one confront or accommodate? Or is it something in between? Historians have identified the century from around 1830 as the Liberal Age, when the first systematic attempts were made to look again at

Islam, this time in the light of what European thought had done with and to Christianity.

The common goal of the Muslim liberals was to find the balance between taking what was beneficial from the West while preserving the core of Arab or Muslim culture. They ranged from Muslim modernists to Arab secularists. These modernizers and Westernizers faced consistent opposition from the reactionary Islamists who dismissed as heretical any notion that the Umma needed to learn anything from the West and that the problem lay in not being sufficiently exclusivist and rigid. In Arkoun's language, they were determined to retain the expansive borders of the domain of the unthought. The first genuine Muslim modernist was Jamal-al-din al-Afghani (1838/1839–1897), who was probably born in Persia but spent most of his active life in Egypt and Turkey. He studied in France and Russia as well as in Teheran, then at Najaf in Iraq. While in France, he had befriended Ernest Renan, author of the humanistic *Life of Jesus* (1863). But where Renan postulated a complete dissonance between Islam and modernity, al-Afghani thought the gap more a product of Muslims' limited comprehension of their religion.[5] It was in this spirit that al-Afghani revived the ijtihad tradition within Islamic scholarship as the best means to effect a revival of the Muslim world, championing the Muʻtazilite doctrine of freedom over the current orthodoxy of fatalism. Science was the way to the future for the Muslim world, and the Islam that blithely ignores or downplays science is the Islam that needs to be abandoned. He likened religious dogma to the yoke that enslaves the ox. Though a sincerely religious man, al-Afghani was concerned to unite Islam once more and to modernize it in the face of the Western challenge.

Al-Afghani's modernism was met with a lot of criticism from traditionalists, some of whom resorted to ad hominem attacks and questioned his ethnic origin and religious affiliation. Nevertheless, al-Afghani was very influential among the intelligentsia of his day. His most important follower was the Egyptian Muhammad 'Abduh (1849–1905). After falling afoul of political swings and roundabouts, 'Abduh spent time in exile, returning to Egypt in 1889, where he took up lecturing at the influential al-Azhar University in Cairo. From 1899 he served as Grand Mufti of Egypt. 'Abduh also helped found the philosophy department at Fouad I (now Cairo) University. Like his mentor, 'Abduh was concerned to encourage the reform and revitalization of Islam by applying a freer approach to reading and interpreting

Muslim sources. Rather than strict rote learning of secondary texts, 'Abduh favored the more open-minded strands of Muslim thinking; the *qiyas* (or "argument by analogy"), the *istihsan* ("the principle of desirability") and the *al-masalih al-mursala* ("the general interests of the community"). 'Abduh has been called the first of the Muslim demythologizers.[6] His books and the journals run by his former students and supporters were influential around the Muslim world. Like al-Afghani, 'Abduh was a committed Muslim who opposed naturalist thinking and secularism. But even his strictly limited reformism was too much for the traditionalists, who accused him of straying from the path of orthodoxy. However, his legacy will be important in the future for the development of an Islamic reformation. The thought of these two men still has currency among moderate Islamists who reject both secularism and Islamic theocracy.[7]

In India the problem of Muslim reform was stimulated by the extra difficulty of being a minority. Indian Islam had long pondered this problem, going back to the centuries when the Moghuls ruled the Hindu majority in India. The examples of toleration set by Akbar and his grandson Dara Shikoh (1614–1659) at least had equal weight in the Indian Muslim memory as did the periods of intolerance. After the arrival of the British, the possibility of effecting change via the agency of the state disappeared. And after the failure of the Mutiny, the Muslim community turned its attention to the power of education. This was the approach taken by Syed Ahmad Khan (1817–1898), who taught that the work of God, as embodied in nature, and the word of God, as found in the Qur'an, cannot be contradictory. The Qur'an needs to be understood in the light of science and reason and, mediated in this way, could continue to exercise its authority in moral and spiritual matters. This approach was reminiscent of the Mu'tazilites and of Spinoza. Khan was also concerned to distinguish the authority of the Qur'an from the more problematic legacy of the Sunna, which he saw as a historical corpus without the theological authority normally ascribed to it.

In an attempt to bridge this divide, Khan founded in 1875 the Muhammadan Anglo-Oriental School in Aligarh, modeled largely on the British public school. He had already established two schools in other cities and a scientific society in 1864. These initiatives became known collectively as the Aligarh Movement. Khan hoped his movement would help bridge the divide between the British and the Muslims, a divide that was wide enough before the Indian Mutiny of 1857, which only further broadened the gulf between them. Khan made it his duty to try to walk a middle path between these two poles. He became known as the "Prophet of Education," even though the value of education was a guiding motif for most Muslim progressives at this time. All around the Muslim world, schools and universities were engaged to some degree or other in trying to accommodate Islam with modernity. It would be wrong to write him off as a collaborator, in the negative sense of that word. He opposed efforts to involve Muslims in the Indian National Congress, fearing it was dominated by Hindus. He advocated separate representation for Muslims and is credited as the progenitor of the "Two Nations" solution to the Indian problem.

The Aligarh Movement did not survive Khan's death in 1898, but his influence did. The school in Aligarh became the focal point of the movement, and in 1877 it became a college, and in 1913, a university that has since developed a reputation as the premier center for Islamic philosophy in India. Khan's work and the college he founded stimulated several progressive Muslim thinkers to continue his path. Syed Amir Ali (1849–1928) wrote *The Spirit of Islam* in this vein. And Abul Kalam Azad (1888–1958) devoted his life to commentaries on the Qur'an that were infused with this liberal spirit. And in what is now Bangladesh, the poet Kazi Nazrul Islam (1899–1976) propagated a tolerant, modernist variety of Islam. However, the most influential Muslim philosopher from the Subcontinent at this time was Mohammad Iqbal (1877–1938). Though he can't be called a humanist, Iqbal at least stressed the ijtihad element of Islam. Inevitably, though, Khan's modernist reformism provoked a xenophobic reaction from traditionalists. Tragically, it is their work that is today in the ascendant, but it is important that it be known it was not always that way.

As the nineteenth century turned into the twentieth, a greater variety of reformist voices began to be heard. At one end of the spectrum came a move away from Muslim reformism to a bolder secularism. Several scholars have noted the irony here. The traditionalists and revivalists, who had not accustomed themselves to the spirit of reform, accused modernists of being secularists. So when a new generation emerged who *were* actually secularists, the traditionalists thought their fears had been vindicated. The traditionalists were able to pose as the champions of "real" Islam against the lackeys of the West, with their foreign ideas of secularism and the freedoms that go with it. Modernizers never found a way to convincingly overcome this disadvantage.

It would be worth at this point to look briefly at some of these modernizers and see their various takes on Western thinking. One of the earliest of these genuine secularists was Shibli Shumayyil (1860–1917), a Lebanese-Egyptian popularizer of evolution. Shumayyil was the first Arab thinker to defend evolution to Muslim readers. Like the early Turkish secularists, Shumayyil was impressed by Ludwig Büchner, whose work *Force and Matter* he translated into Arabic. He also introduced his readers to the thoughts of Charles Darwin, Ernst Haeckel, Herbert Spencer, and other prominent evolutionists. A thoroughgoing naturalist, Shumayyil argued that only a naturalism informed by the sciences, evolution in particular, could serve as an antidote to superstition and reaction. From a later generation, Hamid Dalwai (1930–1977) combined a trenchant Muslim secularism inspired by similar authorities as Shumayyil with long-term work aiding the dispossessed of Mumbai. Shumayyil was too clearly a popularizer of Western trends to have much influence on Muslim thought at the time, quite apart from just how subversive his message was.

Another significant modernist was Ali Dashti (1896–1982), an Iranian politician and freelance scholar. In between a range of books on religious themes, usually with a Sufi flavor, Dashti wrote *Twenty Three Years: A Study of the Prophetic Life of Muhammad*. Muhammad's ministry lasted twenty-three years (610–632 CE), and this book was a biographical account of the Prophet's life shorn of the fanciful embellishments and pious frauds that have become associated with his story over the centuries. It was doing for Muhammad what Renan's *Life of Jesus* did for the Christian founder in the nineteenth century. *Twenty Three Years* took Muslims to task for taking an uncritical account of Muhammad's life and what he called "myth-making and miracle-mongering." The book was written in 1937 but was not published until 1974. Censorship in Iran was acute at the time, and the book was published in Beirut. His long record as a passionate Iranian patriot notwithstanding, Dashti came under serious scrutiny after the Muslim revolution in 1979. He was questioned by the police and violently manhandled, and he died in suspicious circumstances soon after. *Twenty Three Years* remains a favorite citation on dissident websites to this day.

Two Egyptian scholars, both from the Damietta region on the Nile Delta, can be cited as examples of more original thinkers who grafted elements of Western thinking into the Muslim context of their lives. One of them was Zaki Naguib Mahmoud (1905–1995), who, after many years teaching philosophy in secondary schools, emerged as an influential tertiary-level thinker. Mahmoud argued that we live in a scientific age and that abstract speculation in the manner of medieval philosophy or divine inspiration are no longer credible forms of thinking upon which to depend. In the manner of his mentors, Bertrand Russell and A. J. Ayer, Mahmoud argued that universal statements that range beyond the realm of verifiable particular facts are likely to be meaningless. In *The Renewal of Arabic Thought* (1971), he picked out authoritarianism, traditionalism, and verbalism as the three principal impediments to Arabic thought and advocated their replacement with modes of thinking that are not, as he put it, "fake" but that rest on reliable knowledge. Arab tradition is not written in fire across the cosmos, but, like any tradition, is an amalgam of techniques by which people lived. It was in that context that Mahmoud thought them fake. He was particularly concerned about the tendency to verbalism, by which he meant the veneration of the Arabic language in its own right, as an obstacle to progress. And it was a small step from this to oppose the power of religion to act as a brake to progressive thought and open debate in Arabic societies. Mahmoud's logical positivism would be open to criticism now, but his work will be an important resource for any future Muslim Renaissance.

Arriving at fundamentally similar conclusions but via a radically different route was Abdel-Rahman Badawi (1917–2002), a scholar of prodigious industry and breadth. In 1938, he joined the Philosophy Department at the Egyptian University, where he taught Greek philosophy and contemporary French thought. His doctorate, gained in 1944, was on the topic of "existentialist time." Over his career he held a variety of posts around the Muslim world and in Europe. His writings were extensive, including histories of atheism, humanism, and existentialism in Arabic thought. He singlehandedly wrote two encyclopedias and upward of one hundred twenty books. He was also an accomplished poet and translator. He never married.

Whereas Mahmoud looked to logical positivism as a way out of the sterile traditionalism, Badawi looked to a combination of German idealism and Sufi existentialist mysticism. A passionate Germanophile, Badawi was deeply read in German idealism, and his constructions of an Islam centered around self-knowledge founded upon intuition was, he thought, uniquely suitable to the Muslim mind. He was also politically active, which landed him in trouble more than once. He helped draft the Egyptian constitution after its formal independence in 1952, although this constitution was never implemented. He spent much of his life in self-imposed exile from Egypt after that. While teaching at Benghazi University in Libya in 1973, he was arrested and his books were publicly burned on the orders of Colonel Muammar Gadafi, who was incensed at being asked questions by Badawi's philosophy students during a visit there.

Other thinkers, like the Moroccan scholar Mohammed Aziz Lahbabi (1922–1993), made a career of stressing the ijtihad tradition of Islam. A novelist and poet as well as a philosopher, Lahbabi stressed the commonalities between the ijtihad traditions of Islam and Western humanism. He was nominated, though did not receive, the Nobel Prize for Literature in 1987.

Somebody entirely unknown outside his native land is the Bangladeshi rationalist Aroj Ali Matubbar (1900–1985). Born into a poor family in rural Bengal, Aroj Ali Matubbar had to take on the role of chief provider for his family at the age of eleven when his father died. His formal schooling lasted only one year, but he borrowed books from wealthier families in his locality, and later from public libraries. Matubbar became a rationalist after the death of his mother. When he went to a nearby town to develop a photograph of his dead mother, the local mullahs issued a fatwa, declaring that photographs could not be taken of dead people, especially of dead women. They insisted that prayers be sent to Allah for her soul instead. This led Matubbar to question Qur'anic teaching and then the existence of Allah himself.

Matubbar dedicated his life to alleviating poverty and ignorance and righting abuse of civil rights. Over his long life he worked quietly in his region to educate and empower some of the world's poorest people. His rationalism was not so much a doctrine but a system of learning the truth by the use of reason. Skepticism was the driving force of his rationalism. He put these thoughts together in *The Quest for Truth* in 1952, although it was not published until 1973. He had been under legal and social pressure from Muslim leaders not to publish, and it was only in the first years of newly independent Bangladesh, which declared itself a secular republic, that Matubbar was able to have his work published. Matubbar also published *Smaranika (Remembrance)* in 1982 and *Anumn (Conjectures)* in 1983 and left two unpublished works.

One Muslim thinker who spoke specifically of humanism was Mamadiou Dia (1911–2009), in turn a schoolteacher, journalist, and politician in Senegal. What makes Dia interesting is his articulation of what he called *Islamic humanism*. His earlier career was as a socialist, and after Senegal achieved independence in 1960 he collaborated with Leopold Senghor (1906–2001), the Catholic-humanist longtime president of the country. The two parted company in 1962, and Dia spent the next twelve years in prison— during which time he reconfigured his secularism and socialism into his conception of Islamic humanism. In a classic statement of Muslim modernism, Dia declared:

> Islamic authenticity requires a return to the sources, that is, to the Qur'an and to the [Sunna], not to take shelter there, to drown current cares there, but to draw from them elements for the renovation and revitalization of Islamic philosophy.[8]

Dia's blend of Islamic humanism reflected his close reading of twentieth-century French Christian theology with a criticism of previous reformism. He saw little to be gained, for instance, in stressing the virtues of ijtihad as some panacea for the future of Islam. But by the same token, he insisted that Islam has much to learn from Christianity, from Marxism, and even from atheism, which "has become a place for the formation of universalizing human values [that] no modern religion can allow itself to ignore."[9] His Islamic humanism looked to a radical theology that defines Allah not as a given, but as a giver, and that in return demands a constant relationship with the individual. But he also endorsed strongly the need to embrace science and technology as vehicles by which a new future could be built. The value of doing this was as much the opening up of lines of communication as the actual end products. What Dia feared was Islam closing in on itself and succumbing to "the temptation of a new metaphysics."[10]

We can bring this survey of contemporary humanist thought emanating from the Middle East to an end by examining in more detail the work of probably the most influential of all these thinkers, and the person whose thought we have used to frame this chapter: Mahommed Arkoun (1928–). Born in Algeria, Arkoun is a product of Francophone Africa. He studied at the Sorbonne and then joined the staff there as professor of Islamic thought in 1963. He has made it his duty to engage Muslim radicals in debate about the nature of their religion, in particular carrying the flag for a pluralist vision of Islam. The culmination of this project is the constructing of what he calls a *Critique of Islamic Reason*. He is deeply imbued with the language and presuppositions of Jacques Derrida and deconstruction, which has the unfortunate effect of bulking up his prose. But unlike most people so afflicted, Arkoun is worth the effort.

Arkoun has spoken of an Islamic humanism that is the combination of the two types of reason: the dogmatic and the secular. This, he argues, is a false dichotomy, and their creative fusion can produce a genuine Islamic humanism. Muslim thinkers worked to effect precisely this sort of fusion in the centuries between Muhammad and Ibn Rushd, only to be thwarted by an alliance of political power under the caliphs beginning with al-Qadir (reigned 991–1031 CE) and the Hanbal school of literalists. More recently Arkoun has been less inclined to speak of *humanism*, claiming the word is too hotly disputed to be useful.[11] He is also careful to say that he is not setting himself the task of developing a secularized theology of Revelation in the manner of modernizers. This is not because he disputes the need for such a shift, but that the conditions for it do not exist yet. "I would have done so," he apologizes, "had Islamic thought prepared the scientific conditions for such a difficult task, beginning in the nineteenth century."[12] This notwithstanding, Arkoun is clear in his exposure and criticism of what he calls "the unthought in Muslim thought." Among the significant areas of the unthought in Muslim thought he cites treating Qur'anic revelation as normative, and seeing no disconnect between the truth-claims made on behalf of the Qur'an and the historical record.

This area of scholarly exegesis of the Qur'an is going to grow in the twenty-first century and is likely to have the same effect on Islam that the same process had on Christianity in past centuries. The completion of the *Encyclopedia of the Qur'an*, a five-volume work published by Brill between 2001 and 2006, is an important stepping-stone in this direction. It takes the approach of "two parallel conversations," with articles from orthodox Muslims and from Western scholars of religion. One scholar who served on the editorial board of the encyclopedia was Nasr Abu Zayd, who caused an uproar in Egypt when he applied hermeneutical methods to the Qur'an. A fatwa was issued against him, and he was forced to flee the country. He now works in the Netherlands. The irony of this is that Zayd was as much reviving the Mu'tazilite forms of scholarship as he was importing Western forms of linguistic analysis. And, he insists, he is a pious Muslim.

THE DIFFICULT INTERSECTION BETWEEN ISLAM AND SECULARISM

With such a wealth of talented thinkers articulating a range of options, from Islamic modernism to outright atheism, we now need to look briefly at the troubled career of Arab secularism. On the face of it, it would be difficult to think of a cause as hopeless as that of Arab secularism, which, apart from in Turkey, has not been conspicuously successful. Saddam Hussein was only the latest in a series of disasters to have bedevilled secular politics in the Muslim world. Arab secularism suffered considerably from its perceived association with the West; either in the form of Christianity, liberalism or communism. As each of those worldviews became unacceptably foreign, secularism lost its footing. Coupled with the dismal record such supposedly secularist Arab states had—think of Algeria, Iraq, Syria, and (since 1991) Uzbekistan—secularism appears totally moribund as a liberating philosophy. And yet, the most successful face of secularism in the Muslim world is Turkey, which has consistently supported the West against communism, and stands as one of the least authoritarian, better-educated countries in the region. But as against this, Turkish secularism has needed the assiduous support of the army to remain a politically entrenched concept.

It is true that the secular principle is difficult to translate into Muslim terms. It is difficult to make a worthwhile distinction between the principles of relating humanity's relationship to God ('*ibadat*) and the principles of relating humanity's relationship to one another (*mu'amalat*). And it is hard for the separation of mosque and state to take hold on Muslim thinking without Islam itself being seen as under threat. Many contemporary Muslim writers are at pains to dissociate themselves from anything that smacks of the secular. To give but one example, Muhammad Al Naguib al-Attas, generally a well-informed commentator, makes his position quite clear. He says there is no meaningful distinction between secularism and secularization. Not only are both expressions "of an 'utterly unislamic worldview,' [they] are also 'set against Islam' in a manner that requires all Muslims to 'vigorously repulse' because they are 'deadly poison to true faith.'"[13] In Bernard Lewis's memorable phrase, Muhammad was his own Constantine.[14]

Other Muslim scholars beg to differ. Some have argued that the ideal of a secular society is not impossible in a country that is predominantly Muslim. Indeed, Mohammed Arkoun has insisted that secularism can be traced in Qur'anic discourse and in the "Medina historical experience."[15] He goes on to criticize scholars who assert the irrelevance of secularist thought and practice to Islam. To do so is to ignore the "confiscation of spiritual autonomy" by the state at the higher reaches, and by brotherhoods at the lower reaches of Muslim society. Far from being irrelevant, he argues, few debates are more important for Islam. Arkoun does not elaborate on this, but it is clear that a renewed appreciation of secularism will involve it undergoing some sort of reconceptualization. He is—rightly—critical of the unduly rigid interpretation of secularism as practiced in France, seeing it as unsuitable for any Muslim context. For the foreseeable future, at least, Muslim secularism may need to take the form of "one nation under God." This was the approach favored by modernizing politicians like Benazir Bhutto, who argued against speaking directly of secularism and for concentrating instead on providing the core "building blocks of democracy"—free elections, an independent judiciary, the rule of law, and gender equality. She was in no doubt, however, that secularism was fundamental to the successful implementation of those building blocks.[16] Like other progressive politicians, Bhutto looked to the past for examples of Muslim leaders being models of toleration. Pakistan's founder, Muhammad Ali Jinnah, was explicit in his belief that a person's religion was no concern to the state.[17] And the Moghul emperor Akbar set an outstanding example of toleration within a Muslim context, ruling his empire, in Bhutto's words "not by forced conversion but by the power of pluralism and multiculturalism."[18]

The problem of decline and subjugation was felt most strongly in the Ottoman Empire, which had been picked at, slapped around, amputated, and generally humiliated over the course of the nineteenth and early twentieth century, becoming known as the "Sick Man of Europe." In the face of this decline, many Ottoman thinkers and activists saw the need for a radical reform of society, politics, and religion. One of the more influential of these reforming trends was the movement that became known as the GarbcIlars, or "Westerners." Abdullah Cevdet (1869–1932) was raised a devout Muslim, but his medical training exposed him to Western science and the materialist philosophies then prominent, in particular Ludwig Büchner. He came to the conclusion that religion in general and Islam in particular were holding the Turkish people back.

To begin with, Cevdet spoke not of abolishing Islam so much as effecting a creative amalgamation of Muslim skepticism and Western materialism. He was critical of Turkish positivists who wished simply to replace Islam with positivism. Far better, he argued, to recast the reforming ideas as *hadiths*. He dreamt of stimulating a Muslim Reformation, and with that in mind his journal was called *Ijtihad*. But in the face of the combined effects of government censorship, popular indifference, and the Turkish losses in the Balkan Wars of 1912–1913, Cevdet became more radical and openly critical of Islam. He had translated and distributed widely a criticism of Islam by the Dutch writer Reinhardt Dozy (1820–1883). And he looked to more open and general criticisms of Islam. The façade of preserving a Muslim face on a process of Westernization was dropped.

The GarbcIlar movement was straightforwardly rationalist in direction. It was not Marxist, neither was it staunchly nationalist, as some other modernization movements were. It had no particular ideology beyond seeing Islam as a barrier to development. GarbcIlik literature was very widely read, especially as Ottoman fortunes went from bad to worse. *Ijtihad* was suppressed every now and then, only to reappear under a new name. Much of its program was taken up after World War I as modern Turkey tried to rebuild itself from the Ottoman ruins. In 1922, Cevdet publicly praised the Baha'i faith as the next step from Islam, and a faith more compatible with progressive attitudes. The long years of disseminating secular and rationalist thinking bore fruit in the 1920s as the new generation of leaders, brought up on GarbcIlar publications, began to create the secular Turkey that still exists today.

The most important of these new leaders was Mustapha Kemal (1881–1938), who, more than anyone else, galvanized the country to assert itself in the chaos after the empire's defeat in 1918, when it looked as if Turkey would be reduced to a rump state in northern Anatolia or even disappear altogether. In the five years after its defeat, Kemal led the fight against each of these invaders and saved Turkey from dismemberment. It was an incredible achievement, against all odds, and Kemal became known as Attatürk, or "father of the Turks." Attatürk did not just rescue Turkey from the consequences of military defeat. He can properly be called the father of modern Turkey. And the role the secularist and rationalist ideas of the GarbcIliks was considerable. In 1924 he abolished the Khalifat and established Turkey as a secular republic, an act that had far-reaching consequences in the Muslim world, not least for the future of secularism. Islamists have been able to associate secularism with irreligion ever since.[19] Inside Turkey it was Attatürk's changes in education that were probably the decisive factors in the success of the social revolution he achieved. He enacted the Law for the Unification of Education in Turkey in 1924. This law brought all the small, parochial schools in the country under the control of the Ministry of Education. Boys and girls received the same education; all convents run by religious sects were banned, and primary education was made secular and compulsory. And in 1928, the Arabic script was replaced by the Latin script. Most incredibe of all, Turkish women got the vote in 1934, the first country in the Middle East to take this step.

Attatürk's secularist legacy has been under attack for the past thirty years. After a military government took power in 1980, religious education was made compulsory and the number of Muslim clerics being trained increased by 300 percent. More recently, terrorist organizations have sought to destroy Attatürk's memorial in Ankara as a protest against secularism. However, the second article of the Turkish constitution states that Turkey is a "democratic, secular, and social state governed by the Rule of Law." The government of Tayyip Erdoğan, widely feared to be closet Islamist, has so far not lived down to those expectations. With respect to his views on religion and government, he insists he should be seen more as a Christian Democrat politician in the European sense. Today, Turkey stands on the brink of joining the European Union. It is inconceivable that this could be possible were it not for the reforms overseen by Attatürk. And the secular reforms in Turkey stand as an example of what can be achieved in the Middle East.

If Turkey was the principal laboratory for secularism, Egypt remained the most important source of theoretical thinking. The first proponents of secularism in Egypt were Christians, often migrants from the Ottoman lands, in most cases Syria. The first Muslim advocate of secularism was Ali Abd al-Raziq (1888–1966). In *Islam and the Bases of Rule* (1925), Abd al-Raziq argued that the khalifat had no basis in the Qur'an or Hadith and as such could be dispensed with at no serious cost to the Muslim world. He also outlined the history of the khalifat, showing it had brought little to the Muslim world in the way of peace, security, or prosperity. He went further by arguing that Islam was not a state but a religion, and that the differences should be kept in mind. For this he suffered persecution and was excommunicated. News today is dominated by Muslim fanatics and terrorists who seek the restoration of the khalifat as central to their political program. And yet a rival body of theory predates them and is in desperate need of wider dissemination.

It would be naïve to argue that Islam and secularism have had or can have an easy relationship. The very words used are sources of difficulty. The Arabic equivalent word for secularism is *almaniyya*, and a secularist is an *almani*. *Almaniyya* can claim derivation from *alam* ("world") or from *ilm* ("science" or "knowledge"), both of which pose problems because of the associations of a natural and inevitable split between religion and the world or between religion and science. The Islamists have succeeded in demonizing the term for the Muslim public. Once upon a time, being an *almani* meant one was a respected member of society, probably well educated, progressive, and part of the country's future. But now an *almani* is little better than an atheist (*mulhid*), a perverse traitor both to Allah and to all Muslim peoples. In such circumstances it is difficult not to be pessimistic about the future of Arab secularism. An interesting illustration of this came in 2005 from Jihad Fakhreddine, an Iraqi-born businessman and researcher then living in Dubai and who wrote to an English journal about the changing meaning of his given name. When he was named Jihad in the mid-1950s, his parents had in mind the secular values of national liberation and progressive development toward a fuller democracy in a world of democracies. But now, Fakhreddine wrote it is "dangerous to claim even to be secular, let alone to be a humanist."[20]

There is no shortage of evidence for this danger. We've already noted the persecution of Nasr Abu Zayd in Egypt, though his case was far from unique. In January 1985, Mahmud Muhammad Taha, an outspoken opponent of the slide into a fundamentalist version of sharia law in his native Sudan, was publicly hanged as an apostate. A year after Taha's execution, Subhi al-Salih, an enthusiastic exponent of ijtihad was assassinated by Shia hitmen. Taha argued that greater emphasis should be placed on Muhammad's more pluralistic and accommodating teachings while he was still in Mecca over the more strident and unforgiving teachings later in his career when he was based in Medina. Another supporter of his, Abdullahi Ahmed An-Na'im, developed his argument in the context of outlining ways in which Islam might contribute meaningfully to the improvement of human rights and international law. And in 1992 the Egyptian scholar Dr. Faraj Foda was murdered by the Islamic Jihad for his outspoken support of secularism and democracy. In the footsteps of Abd al-Raziq, Foda argued that the khalifat was a human institution and that a religious state would lead inevitably to dictatorship and disunity. An opponent of Foda's, Shaykh Muhammad al-Ghazali, publicly supported the killers, saying that a secularist had forfeited the right to life and that killing such a person was no great a crime than doing the proper thing that the authorities should already have done.

We could easily throw up our hands in despair at the magnitude of the problem. Secularism is at a low ebb in many parts of the Muslim world, not least because of its association with the hated West. The harassment and murder of outspoken secularists has done little to stimulate further debate in this area. And yet it surely stands as a priority of humanist scholars and commentators to articulate a new vision of secularism that does not equate with authoritarianism or with kowtowing to the West. This is easily said, from the safety of a Western democracy, but it is a tougher proposition in Egypt. Two Egyptian scholars active in this area were Ahmad Abd al-Mu'ti Hijazi and Mahmud Amin al-Alim. Both men have been brave enough to champion a moderate brand of secularism, stressing that it need not clash inevitably with Islam or resonate with foreign values. In the late 1980s, Hijazi stressed the compatibility of secularism with the "essence of Islam, which glorifies human life, rejects priesthood, encourages ijtihad, and makes the public interest the guiding principle of investigation and choice."[21] And Mahmud Amin al-Alim, a leftist Egyptian secularist, was slightly more assertive, being willing to admit there is a contradiction between secularism and fanatical Islamism, with its "rigidity, literalism, unhistoricalness, narrow-minded absolutism, and . . . condescending sense of superiority." Secularism, he argued in 1993, "does not mean losing one's identity, humanity, spiritual and cultural depth, or national peculiarity. . . . It is an outlook, a process, and a method, embodying the essential features of man's humanity and expressing his physical and spiritual ambition to overcome all obstacles [that] stand in the way of his advancement, happiness, and prosperity."[22]

Even more radical is Sadiq Jalal al-Azm, a prominent secularist thinker who rejects the modernist project of reforming Islam "from inside." The Syrian-based philosopher and author of *Critique of Religious Thought* (1969) calls himself the "official atheist of the Arab world." He has argued that claiming to reform Islam from the inside is disingenuous, not least because it presupposes a "real Islam" that can be reformed, once the apparently un-Islamic corruptions have been purged. Unsurprisingly al-Azm is finding it more dangerous to articulate this position openly in the Arab world. But while he spends some of his time in the United States or in the Netherlands, he still bases himself in Syria. Al-Azm was courageous enough to sign the *Humanist Manifesto 2000*, one of few Middle East scholars to make public their views. Al-Azm is disarmingly frank. Muslims need to realize that they are no more the masters of destiny than the Europeans were a century ago. Rather they are a politically underdeveloped minority of the global community. "Only when Muslims face this reality, they will be able to proceed."[23]

One of the more systematic efforts to reorient Muslim thinking in this way has been the brainchild of two Egyptian scholars, Mourad Wahba, a philosopher (and the only other Middle East–based scholar to sign the *Humanist Manifesto 2000*), and Mona Abousenna, a scholar of literature. In 1994, in the face of the growing fundamentalism, Wahba and Abousenna did what scholars are good at doing: they hosted a conference. On the face of it, the theme was unremarkable. In any university in the Western world, a conference on Ibn Rushd and the Enlightenment would attract no attention at all. The few specialists would fly in, present their papers, and leave, conscious of having improved their research rating. But this conference was held in Cairo and was opened by no less a figure than Boutros Boutros-Ghali, who was at the time the secretary general of the United Nations. Boutros-Ghali understood the importance of what was being discussed. There are parts of Rushd's writings, he said in his introduction, that "speak to us all today, on the importance of the masses in politics, on the need to address their problems and their happiness. Ibn Rushd also makes a strong case for the advancement of women, and their full participation in political and economic life."[24]

It has become a commonplace among commentators on the Middle East to lament it not having undergone a reformation. But this theme had been the governing idea of Mourad Wahba throughout his career. His principal question was, given that Ibn Rushd played a significant role in stimulating the Reformation and the Enlightenment in the West, why has his influence not been as great in his own culture? It was with a view to promoting these ideas that Wahba was instrumental in founding the Afro-Asian Philosophy Association. The idea was generated from a paper he read in Pakistan in 1975 on authenticity and modernization in the third world. Once again, Western scholars can make all of Wahba's points from the safety of a Western university seminar room (made safe thanks in no small part to the Reformation and the Enlightenment) but it is another thing altogether for these points to be made in the Middle East. The conference was held under the auspices of the Afro-Asian Philosophy Association and brought together scholars from the Middle East, Africa, Europe, and North America. Wahba and Abousenna went on to form the Averroës and Enlightenment International Association, which in 2004 became a branch of the Center for Inquiry movement. They put out a journal called *Averroës Today*.

Wahba and Abousenna have been criticized for making Rushd out to be more of a freethinker than was the case.[25] They're valid criticisms if one wants to be pedantic, but it seems to miss the main point of what Wahba and Abousenna are trying to do. In the context of the puritanical and anti-intellectual climate of the Almohads in which Rushd worked, he came across as a champion of reason. Wahba contends that at least part of the reason Rushd was persecuted was that his doctrine of interpretation legitimized diversity of interpretations of scripture. And once the principle of legitimate diversity in interpretation of scripture has been established, it is a short distance to see the value of some kind of secularism and for the process of reason and free inquiry.[26] Had the thought of Ibn Rushd exercised the same degree of influence over Muslim thought that it did over European thought, it could well have helped generate the Reformation in Islam so many people yearn for. It is Wahba and Abousenna's aim to show that secularism is not the preserve of the West; a legitimate secularism with a Muslim face can be achieved. A daunting enough goal on its own, before adding to the mix the anti-Western, victim mentality stimulated by Edward Said's shilling shocker *Orientalism* (1978) and apparently underlined a decade later by the Rushdie affair, which was presented to the Muslim world as evidence of the West's implacable hostility to Islam. But beyond the media glare, good work is being done. As if in support of Wahba and Abousenna, the University for Humanistics in the Netherlands has established the Ibn Rushd Chair for the Study of Humanism and Islam.

THE RISE OF THE REFUSENIKS

The maintenance of a secular society is an indispensable first step in developing an open society where scholarship may thrive. Another condition needed for any reformation of Islam to get underway is the availability of scholarly work of Qur'anic criticism. Some of the most radical work in this area comes from former Muslims who have devoted themselves to the criticism of the religion that once dominated their lives. Three examples, all from the Indian subcontinent, illustrate the process. Anwar Shaikh (1928–2006) was one of these people. Brought up a deeply religious Muslim, he was a young man during the partition of the Indian subcontinent in 1947. Filled with religious indignation at the suffering of his coreligionists, the young man prayed to Allah for guidance, then went around his town looking for non-Muslims to kill. After killing the first three non-Muslims he came across, Shaikh went through a major crisis of faith that lasted many years. He came to read the Qur'an more critically and devoted the rest of his life to writing critical accounts of what the Muslim holy book actually says.[27]

Shaikh's works are intelligent and passionate, but, being self-published, they are destined for a restricted readership. Another rebel from the Subcontinent is Taslima Nasrin (1962–), the Bangladeshi author and activist. Unlike Shaikh, Nasrin's father was a progressive secularist, though her mother was an unsophisticated Muslim believer. Nasrin recalled the frightening descriptions of hell and the penalties for uppity women that were spoken about by the local Muslim cleric her mother took her to. On her father's urging, Nasrin had a thorough education and was able to build a reputation as a poet and author. She won national awards in 1992 and 1993, but it was only when her first novel, *Lajja* (*Shame*) was banned by the Bangladesh government that Nasrin developed an international reputation. *Shame* records the smoldering Muslim reaction to the destruction of the Babri Masjid mosque in Ayodhya, which ignited religious violence in the Subcontinent that has still not abated. *Shame* was translated into English in 1994.

Since being forced into exile, Nasrin has lived a restless existence, pining for her native Bengal, yet unable to live there safely. In 2005, she ignored the dangers and relocated to Kolkata, but it wasn't long before her presence once again became an issue for those Muslims unable to live at peace with their neighbors. A new series of fatwas were issued against her, and the Indian government had to intervene to ensure her safety. In March 2008, she—very reluctantly—returned to Europe.

Incredibly, some people manage to find fault in Nasrin in all this, accusing her of being too radical, of outraging religious sensibilities. To this Nasrin replies:

> I criticize all religions, not particularly Islam. I also criticize Hinduism because of the discrimination against women that it justifies. But only the

> Muslims take offense at my criticism and threaten me with their fatwas. The others do not attack me. Does that mean there is no room for criticism in Islam? But how can a society evolve, lift itself out of stagnation, if it rejects all form of criticism?[28]

How indeed. And against the backdrop of these accusations of provoking religious sensibilities, in 2004, Nasrin was awarded the UNESCO-Madanjeet Singh Prize for the Promotion of Tolerance and Non-Violence.

Another critic, one whose contributions in this area could be reasonably called seminal, is Ibn Warraq, who has been called the Bertrand Russell of Islam. The name is a pseudonym and refers to the freethinking scholar Abu Isa Muhammad bin Harun Warraq (d. 909 CE), who was the teacher to Ibn al-Rawandi. Ibn Warraq came to public attention with his first book, *Why I Am Not a Muslim* (1995), which has become a bestseller. In the tradition of Russell's *Why I Am Not a Christian*, Warraq subjects Islam to a thorough criticism, looking at Islamic theology, Muslim history, and social practices in Muslim societies. Since then he has edited several important collections of scholarly essays on various aspects of Islamic Studies and Qur'anic criticism: *The Origins of the Koran* (1998), *The Quest for the Historical Muhammad* (2000), and *What the Koran Really Says* (2002). He then turned to a more popular work called *Leaving Islam* (2003), which featured a series of accounts, some of them very moving, of people's paths away from Muslim belief, and the prices they paid for doing so. Warraq sees little good in religion in general or Islam in particular and is scornful of the gambit, used by many, of distinguishing the "Islamic" from the "fundamentalist." He is also critical of many humanists whom he sees as too wishy-washy in their desire to overlook the dark and dangerous in Islam. Conversely, he has been criticized for being too rigid in his criticisms, but his edited collections of essays contain a broader range of criticism than his critics allow for. Ibn Warraq's books are thought by many to lay the foundations for a long-overdue era of Qur'anic criticism.

Working at a more popular level is Irshad Manji, a Ugandan-born Canadian woman who, in *The Trouble with Islam*, produced a racy polemic against the misogyny and paranoia of much of what passes for contemporary Islam. Manji, a lesbian, describes herself as a "Muslim refusenik." She has launched Project Ijtihad, which is seeking some way forward for a tolerant, intellectually engaged Islam.[29] In Europe the refusenik cause has been taken up by Aayan Hirsi Ali. Her autobiography, *Infidel* (2007), movingly outlines the slow emergence of a refusenik. Manji and Hirsi Ali are both fully alive to the fact that the freedoms and opportunities open to them are specifically Western ones. Not only would a traditional Islamic society not make opportunities available to them, but also it would scorn the idea that women should have choices to make in the first place. Hirsi Ali has gone a step further than Manji in publicly renouncing Islam. The events of September 11, 2001, brought to a head a long process of withdrawal from being a practicing Muslim. And unlike so much of the tortured analysis in the Western media after the attacks, Hirsi Ali had few doubts that Islam as a religion had a part to play. Where many Western pundits were anxious to create distance between the "real Islam" of peace and tolerance, Hirsi Ali knew from personal experience how prevalent these attitudes were. "This was belief," she wrote. "Not frustration, poverty, colonialism, or Israel; it was about religious belief, a one-way ticket to heaven."[30] She also gave expression to the strategy of refusal that Arkoun had identified and that we began this chapter with:

> For centuries we [Muslims] had been behaving as though all knowledge was in the Qur'an, refusing to question anything, refusing to progress. We had been hiding from reason for so long because we were incapable of facing up to the need to integrate it into our beliefs. All this was not working; it was leading to hideous pain and monstrous behavior.[31]

Hirsi Ali's indignation at the depths to which her coreligionists had plunged was by no means felt by her alone. At a time when dark fears are surfacing about the Islamization of Europe—people speak of *Eurabia*—it is well to take note of some other types of response. In June 2007, the British Council of Ex-Muslims was created, replicating similar organizations already established in Germany and Scandinavia. These councils meet a need for people who are publicly identified as Muslims despite having renounced their religion and who no longer wish to seen in this way. They are also a reaction to, in Britain's case, the Muslim Council of Britain, which is anxious to be seen as the voice of "Muslim" opinion. And it is convenient for policymakers to accede to this simple form of communitarianism. But growing numbers of Britons—for this is how they want to be seen—do not want to represented by an organization that identifies itself by religion. The spokesperson for the

Council of Ex-Muslims had this to say:

> Those of us who have come forward with our names and photographs represent countless others who are unable or unwilling to do so because of the threats faced by those considered "apostates"—punishable by death in countries under Islamic law. By doing so, we are breaking the taboo that comes with renouncing Islam but also taking a stand for reason, universal rights and values, and secularism. We are quite certain we represent a majority in Europe and a vast secular and humanist protest movement in countries like Iran.[32]

Only in a secular state would it be feasible to conceive, let alone actually establish, an organization devoted to the needs of former Muslims. Muslim hostility to apostasy is so deep that the very idea of an honest, upright former Muslim is unthinkable. The Council of Ex-Muslims has struck at one of the central citadels of the unthought in Islam: the idea of an honest apostate. It is not surprising, then, that the council advances a clearly humanist program when it talks of universal human rights and equal citizenship for all. It also supports the right to freedom from religion and the right to subject religion to the same sorts of criticism any other social organization is exposed to. And, of course, it is specifically secular, objecting to the privileging of religious institutions by the state. Not only is religion a private affair, so is being nonreligious, with all the implications this has on the need for the neutrality of the state. The Council of Ex-Muslims is highlighting a very twenty-first-century issue: the politics of identity. The time has passed when we can be branded at birth with a single mark. In a globalized world, our identity is a multilayered thing, and one's self-perception plays a larger role in determining identity than has ever been the case. And those perceptions may change.[33]

Needless to say, the dangers these people face are real. Prominent council members in Germany and the Netherlands had to go into hiding in 2007 after threats of violence and death were made against them by Muslim fanatics. And in the case of the Netherlands, the murder of the filmmaker Theo van Gogh and the forcing into exile of Ayaan Hirsi Ali is evidence enough that the threats are to be taken seriously. The reality of physical threats from Muslim fundamentalists was sufficiently real to force the disbanding of the Dutch chapter of the council in April 2008.

Several smaller groups operate in the United States. The best organized is ISIS, the Institute for the Secularization of Islamic Society. ISIS operates mainly as a website and by organizing conferences. Then there is Advocates of Article 18, a California-based group seeking to popularize Article 18 of the Universal Declaration of Human Rights, which says:

> Everyone has the right to freedom of thought, conscience, and religion; this right includes freedom to change his religion or belief, and freedom, either alone or in community with others and in public or private, to manifest his religion or belief in teaching, practice, worship, and observance.

All groups catering to the needs of former Muslims are only too aware that this article is sadly neglected in most Muslim countries. The United Nations Declaration of Human Rights enshrines the right to leave the religion of one's birth, but many Muslim religious scholars are reluctant to acknowledge such a right exists. Most Muslim countries are signatories to the declaration, but few take Article 18 seriously, and some retain legislation that identifies apostasy as a capital crime.

The existence of significant numbers of ex-Muslims, especially in Europe, has largely gone unreported, as people have been fixated on the so-called Islamization of Europe. But it is a fear that underrates the attractiveness of living in a secular society. The conscious articulation of the virtues of a secular society must surely be one of the principal goals for twenty-first-century humanism. Aayan Hirsi Ali's story needs to be understood by all twenty-first-century humanists.

Of the most successful initiatives of a group of these refuseniks was the Secular Islam Summit, which met in March 2007 in St. Petersburg, Florida. Comprising ex-Muslim secularists and reformist Muslims, the summit was an attempt to articulate a coherent vision of Muslim secularism. The summit produced the St. Petersburg Declaration.

> We are secular Muslims, and secular persons of Muslim societies. We are believers, doubters, and unbelievers, brought together by a great struggle, not between the West and Islam, but between the free and the unfree. We affirm the inviolable freedom of the individual conscience. We believe in the equality of all human persons. We insist upon the separation of religion from state and the observance of universal human rights.

We find traditions of liberty, rationality, and tolerance in the rich histories of pre-Islamic and Islamic societies. These values do not belong to the West or the East; they are the common moral heritage of humankind. We see no colonialism, racism, or so-called Islamophobia in submitting Islamic practices to criticism or condemnation when they violate human reason or rights.[34]

The declaration issued a call to reject sharia law, to recognize the separation of mosque and state, to withdraw penalties for blasphemy and apostasy, and to foster a climate of gender equality and freedom of expression. It insisted that Islam has a glorious future as a personal faith but not as a political doctrine.

Reaction to the declaration was mixed. Most media commentators saw it as a positive contribution. Of particular interest was the relatively positive comment it attracted in several Middle East news sources. Several news agencies and papers acknowledged that the summit was at least a contribution in the "dialogue of civilizations." Other groups were predictable in their opposition. The Council of American-Islamic Relations (CAIR) reacted to the event with hostility, denouncing it as the tool of nonpracticing Muslims and believers willing to act as pawns of Islamophobes. Some of the signatories hoped the declaration would help stimulate the new Islamic Reformation, with its focus on a reform from within the fundamental tenets of the faith. Others were more keen on an Islamic Enlightenment, with its emphasis on a systematic criticism of the pretensions of religion. But if the declaration served any purpose, it showed that some measure of dialogue is possible. There need not be a clash of civilizations. With a little more effort, we could just manage a dialogue of, and within, civilizations.

ARE THERE GROUNDS FOR HOPE?

In the end, the refuseniks will only ever be a minority among Muslims, although their role as irritant and stimulus to change will be only to the good. And whether the conservative mullahs like it or not, the Muslim world is changing; one of the more significant changes is the increasing difficulty in preserving the fiction of a uniform "Muslim world." The reality is that the Muslim world is divided along lines of theology, language, region, and culture; and a new difference between generations is also beginning to make itself felt. In an age where undemocratic governments can no longer control all the means of communication, young Muslims across the Middle East are hearing things their elders would barely comprehend, let alone approve of. The successful career of the Egyptian-based televangelist Moez Masoud serves as a good an illustration of the changes taking place. Masoud, barely thirty at the time of writing, is a successful televangelist whose brand of Islam is geared toward the Generation X of the Middle East. Yes, sex outside marriage is wrong and one should pray five times a day, but sex, music, and art are there to be enjoyed. Masoud even extends his goodwill toward homosexuals and unbelievers who are, after all, "our brothers." Masoud's brand of Islam resonates with large numbers of young Muslims his age. It is not unthinkingly anti-Western, nor is it reactively fundamentalist. Masoud, who was educated at the American University in Cairo, is but the latest in the long line of humanistically oriented Muslim reformists that go back a century and a half. Like many of the thinkers mentioned in this chapter, Masoud has looked at the West and seen what can be brought back to his homeland and used for the good of his religion. At a forum on the question of Muslim extremism held in Qatar in 2008, Masoud declared suicide bombers to be *haram*, scripturally forbidden. And the four-hundred-strong audience agreed overwhelmingly to the moot for the event: "This house believes Muslims are failing to combat terrorism."[35] Looking to the next generation again, the so-called Generation Y, some indication of the burgeoning pluralism can be gleaned from the popular website Facebook, where "Muslim atheist" and "Palestinian atheist" converse with one another with little sense of incongruity.

A large part of Masoud's influence comes from his also having learned from Shaikh Ali Gomaa, the grand mufti of Cairo, the second most important religious office in Egypt. Ali Gomaa (1953–) was responsible for a fatwa in November 2006 that denounced female genital mutilation. The practice had long been illegal in Egypt, but was still practiced widely. He is sympathetic to Sufi mysticism and describes himself as a liberal and a Muslim. He opposes theocracy while carefully denying he is a secularist. He has specifically criticized Muslim political parties on the grounds that they create more divisions between Muslims than opportunities for unity. He has made some guarded criticisms of domestic violence in Muslim society and has even declared certain contexts in which a person may leave Islam without deserving death.

When looking at the prospects of Islamic humanism, it is difficult to avoid the clichés about being at the crossroads, the moment of decision, and so on. There is no shortage of reasons to be despondent. The murder of Benazir Bhutto, the death in suspicious circumstances of the Bangladeshi scholar Humayun Azad (1947–2004), the flight of many intellectuals from Middle Eastern nations to the West, and the continuing resistance of the "shabby dictatorships" (in Bernard Lewis's words) of the Middle East to open their countries up to democracy, the lamentable state of tertiary education in most Muslim countries—the list is long. But against this, the influence of young Muslim preachers like Masoud and older figures of authority like Ali Gomaa, the unrest among Iran's younger generation at the conservative theocracy of the mullahs, and the slow effect of criticism from Muslims and refuseniks living in the West all give some suggestion that the battle is not lost.

Islamic humanism has several competing strands that range from mildly unorthodox theism preferring the ijtihad tradition, to radical unbelief. Islam is capacious enough to sustain these quite different attitudes toward the West, toward democracy, toward extending rights to women, and toward other key issues. But all strands of Islamic humanism are needed in the debate that is to come. For these strands, their differences notwithstanding, agree that revivalist Islam (to return to the categories we began the chapter with), insofar as it supports an uncritical acceptance of the clash of civilizations thesis—and its allied xenophobia—and nurtures a culture of refusal, can do no good for the billion Muslims of the world. Benazir Bhutto was right to see the principal faultline of conflict running not between civilizations but within the Muslim world, "between the forces of moderation and modernity and the competing forces of extremism and fanaticism."[36] Islamic humanism has a future, but it is going to have to struggle for all it's worth to win through and persuade coreligionists that one can be Muslim and be open-minded, tolerant of differences, and open to the challenges of democratic ways of governance.

CHAPTER 12

HUMANISM IN AFRICA: FROM *UHURU* TO *UBUNTU*

If this book has one overriding point to make, it is that humanism, alone among the great worldviews of today, is genuinely transnational in character. By *transnational* I mean *above and beyond* nations, not merely *between* nations, as is implied by a word like *international*. But if humanism is genuinely transnational, we know all too well that this does not mean it is strong everywhere. Speaking at a conference in Kampala in 2004, Deo Ssekitooleko, secretary of the Uganda Humanist Association, stated bluntly that "Africa needs humanism more than any other continent." The reasons he gave for this make grim reading: massive poverty, poor education, poor politics, the fatalism implicit in much African mysticism, and the parasitism of imported religions (particularly the American evangelical sects, each competing for funds no less than for souls). These factors have combined to make the expression of humanism rare and quite frequently dangerous in Africa. Gebregeorgis Yohannes, the founder of the Ethiopian Humanist Organization, said from personal experience that it takes "a great deal of courage to go against established beliefs and superstitions in Africa."[1]

And no continent can lament the baneful influence of religion more than Africa. Even once full acknowledgement of noble figures such as Archbishop Tutu is made, for every person of his standing there are several hucksters, charlatans, and even psychopaths. Several countries have suffered from or are threatened by religious war, as in southern Sudan and northern Nigeria. In Rwanda, religious leaders led the way in whipping people up into a frenzy of bloodletting, in some cases even leading the murderers to the victims. Witchcraft and sorcery keep millions of people needlessly poor, ignorant, and fearful of change and outsiders. In country after country we see evidence of pervasive religion from the highest ranks of society living alongside, and often covering up, endemic corruption. Many church leaders have been outspoken opponents of making condoms available to their flock, even when they are being decimated by AIDS. Others lead the way in reactionary and literalist interpretation of the Bible so as to marginalize or force homosexuals and women priests out of their church. Several African nations have been led by men whose claims to religious prophethood have been made as vehemently as their claims to political power. To name only one, Charles Taylor (1948–), whose murderous rule of Liberia was brought short in 2003, took himself very seriously as a Baptist visionary. And then there are those still thirsting for power and who fight brutal guerilla wars in the name of God. Uganda has fought a long and bloody war against a guerilla group that calls itself the Lord's Resistance Army, led by Joseph Kony. In the Democratic Republic of the Congo, the guerilla leader Laurent Nkunda issued badges to his fighters that said "Rebels for Christ." More ominous, this has been taken seriously by a number of wealthy American Christian evangelicals who have supported Nkunda's warmaking.[2] Is it any wonder, then, that a new generation of Africans is asking whether the continent might not be better off looking elsewhere for guidance.

WHAT IS MEANT BY *AFRICAN HUMANISM*?

The need for humanism is one thing, but can one truly expect it to grow and flourish in Africa? As with preceding chapters, it depends what you mean by *humanism*. There is a general scholarly consensus that traditional African thought was essentially humanist, being grounded in mutual respect and a sense of place in the social, natural, and cosmic order. African humanism, writes Richard Bell is "rooted in *lived dependencies*."[3] It is not that supernatural agencies did not exist. What made traditional African thought humanistic was that human goods were valued for that reason alone, with no attempts to then claim the goods as being so because the gods wished it.[4] A much-cited Yoruba proverb illustrates this well: "If humanity were not, the gods would not be."

As Africa slowly constructs a postcolonial view of itself and of the world, one of the concepts receiving a great deal of attention is *ubuntu*. The word I remember as a child in Kenya in the last days before independence was *uhuru*, or "freedom." *Uhuru*, at least in its more obvious forms, has been achieved, but *ubuntu* has still to be fully realized. A Zulu word, *ubuntu* can be understood as understanding one's humanity is intrinsically bound up with recognizing the humanity in others and, on that basis, living harmoniously with others.[5] Parallels with bildung can be drawn, in particular its emphasis on the completion of the individual. But where bildung can be seen as focusing on the individual through the individual, ubuntu places the individual squarely in a social context and completes individuality by and through participation in one's family and social setting. In a globalized world of atomized individualism, the appeal of ubuntu should be apparent.

Attempts have been made to corral ubuntu into having an exclusively religious underpinning, but there is no convincing reason why this should be accepted, and it runs the risk of preserving the now largely discredited stereotype of the "naturally religious African." Ubuntu is equally an idea with strong humanist implications. Whether one is religious or nonreligious, one can see the positive in ubuntu. In the process of establishing the boundary between a cloying communalism and an affirmative community where all members are valued, *ubuntu* has the potential to become the watchword for African humanism. One African philosopher, Joe Teffo, has claimed that ubuntu has the potential to be African philosophy's gift to the world.[6]

Before getting too carried away, however, we need to deal with the question of just how commensurable ubuntu actually is with humanism. Mogobe Ramose, one of Africa's leading theorists of ubuntu, has dealt with this question, arguing that the two words are not "readily translatable." He prefers *humaneness*, claiming it is more multilayered and open-ended and less suggestive of a closed system than *humanism*, or indeed any ism word. If *humanism* did in fact necessarily imply a closed and dogmatic system, I would agree with Ramose on this point.[7] Hopefully readers who have persevered with this book so far will agree that this is not, in fact, the case. Ever since the nineteenth century, humanism has been concerned with questions about what we might become or about precisely the questions Ramose associates with *humaneness*. *Humanism* is simply *humaneness* with a different suffix. How *humaneness* is understood differs across cultures and times, although the disposition toward humaneness is a universal condition, as is the propensity to esteem it highly as a virtue.

The interest in ubuntu is relatively recent in African circles, and care needs to be taken not to universalize ubuntu across all Africa, regardless of the very significant regional, linguistic, and other differences. Various attempts at this type of essentialism have dogged African philosophy over the past half century and more. It remains the case, though, that most of the significant African languages have a word similar to *ubuntu*, and which carries most of the same meanings. Time alone will tell whether ubuntu can carry itself across the continent and become the force for good it clearly has the potential to be.

Another problem specific to African humanism is that some of the earlier forms of essentialist thought had humanist connections. This is not surprising and, on its own, does humanism no discredit. Faced with the inescapable fact of colonialism in the first half of the twentieth century, the need was felt for a stronger form of race consciousness. There were two styles of response to this challenge from people who spoke in terms of humanism, neither being without problems. The first was the violent *new humanism* preached by Frantz Fanon (1925–1961). Often cited as a founder of the whole genre of postcolonial studies, Fanon was born in Martinique, then a colony of France (now a department), and experienced racist ill-treatment by stranded Vichy soldiers there. After heroic war service in France, Fanon spent the last years of his life in North Africa. His two best-known works are *Black Skin, White Masks* (1952), where he announced his new humanism; and his signature work, *The Wretched of the Earth*, which he dictated on his deathbed in 1961. Fanon was critical of nonviolent anticolonial movements, seeing them as not engaging with the core outrageousness of colonialism. The racism of Europe and America must be met, violently if necessary, by the new type of person that only total liberation from colonialism could create. Fanon's writing made for good inflaming rhetoric, but his fundamentalist binaries were at the extreme end of being Manichean. The objections to Fanon's conception of humanism are similar to those of Marx and Engels of *The Communist Manifesto*.

Not motivated by violence, though problematic in other ways, was the movement known as *Négritude*. Coming out of Francophone Africa, Négritude was deeply concerned, as was Fanon, with creating a new type of person. The Nigerian critic Wole Soyinka has described Négritude as a theory of race retrieval. Negritude sought to make a virtue of all the things Europeans were saying were weaknesses in the African. If the European said the African was incapable of rationality, the Négritudinists spoke of the virtue of the African sense of harmony. But, as Soyinka has persuasively observed, this gave Négritude a reactive and defeatist flavor. Indeed, the very idea of "separating the manifestations of the human genius is foreign to the African worldview."[8] One could add that it's foreign to the humanist worldview. Soyinka does not write off Négritude entirely, but it is a valid criticism that notions of race retrieval sit uncomfortably with humanist preferences to look beyond culture as a means by which we can be divided.

That said, the possibility of some degree of compatibility between Négritude and humanism exists is demonstrated by Leopold Senghor (1906–2001), a very significant spokesman for Négritude and longtime leader of Senegal, Senghor served from 1991 until his death as a laureate of the International Academy of Humanism. Senghor argued for a humanism with a local focus but a transnational outlook. "The one 'Pan-ism' that meets twentieth-century requirements is, I dare say, pan-humanism—a humanism that includes all men on the basis of their contributions and their comprehension."[9] We shall return to this theme in the final chapter when we speak of *grounded cosmopolitanism*. Senghor's humanism reflected an eclectic bundle of influences: Marxism, Catholicism, and pan-Africanism. He admired Karl Marx and was deeply influenced by socialism, but he rejected its materialism. Another important influence was Claude McKay, the Jamaican-American poet and mentor of the Harlem Renaissance in the United States, whom we mentioned briefly in chapter 6. For a time, he stressed the humanistic element in Marx's writing before moving on to Pierre Teilhard de Chardin's cosmic evolutionism.[10] Either way, Senghor's variation of humanism was too eclectic a mix of ideas to be stable.

Although there exist several strands of African humanist thought beside the debate on ubuntu, none exist as yet in any great depth. At this stage there exist only various snippets that could be developed into a fuller humanist account of being African. Many of these have emerged in the form of critique of the earlier essentializing outlooks of Négritudinists and religiously inclined scholars. The Ghanaian philosopher Kwasi Wiredu (1931–) has spent much of his philosophical career criticizing essentialist notions of what Africans can or cannot do. What many Négritudinists saw as inviolable essences of being African, Wiredu relabeled *folk philosophy*. The set of social norms, proverbs, and folk wisdom is not being disparaged by this term. He places a high value on many of its values (consensus and reconciliation, for instance). But it is this folk philosophy that is culturally specific to Africans and that should be distinguished from the language of formal, analytical philosophy that Africans can involve themselves in, just like any other people on the planet. And, Wiredu adds, all cultures possess folk philosophies, their specific grab-bag of cultural particularisms. Wiredu's purpose here is fundamentally humanistic in that it rejects notions of African culture being by definition inferior to any other culture by virtue of lacking this or that feature.[11] He also argues that, of all the areas of African thought in need of decolonization, nowhere is this more apparent than in the field of religion.[12] Against this, he speaks of humanism, which for him is "the point of view according to which morality is founded exclusively on considerations of human well-being."[13] This concise, even brilliant, understanding of humanism captures the spirit both of traditional African humanism and of the tradition of Western liberal humanism.

Many consider the boldest and most original African thinker to be Henry Odera Oruka (1944–1995), who worked on a project in Kenya that became known as *Sage Philosophy*. Oruka sought out a range of older Kenyans renown for wisdom and recorded their views on a number of issues. These people Oruka called *sages*. Oruka's Sage Philosophy project helped dispel two hitherto powerful misperceptions, even among some African thinkers. Not only did Sage Philosophy dent seriously the idea that Africans were naturally religious, but also it upset the presumption that there could be such a uniform thing as "African philosophy." Several of Oruka's sages were quite clearly atheist, and there was also a willingness to criticize the communalism of traditional African society.

Oruka struggled even in his own university. At the time he was active, the Department of Religion and Philosophy at Nairobi University was headed by former Anglican bishop Stephen Neill (1900–1984), who preserved the notion of a particular unsuitability among Africans for abstract thought. And African philosophy courses were at this time dominated by the work of another Anglican priest, John S. Mbiti (1931–), whose *African Religions and Philosophy* (1969) was then the most influential book by an African thinker. While Mbiti challenged the standard Christian claim that traditional African religious thought was uninteresting heathenism, he was just as anxious to portray African thinking as inevitably and comprehensively religious. "It is religion," he wrote, "more than anything else, which colors [Africans'] understanding of the universe and their empirical participation in that universe, making life a profoundly religious phenomenon."[14]

This, and Mbiti's other notion that Africans have a sense of the short present and of the long past but not of the future—which they have had to acquire from the Europeans—has been seen by many later critics as limiting African possibilities along stereotyped lines.

Much of African philosophy since the 1980s has been directed toward breaking down this form of essentialism. Oruka's first move to break this stranglehold came in his 1972 article "Mythologies as African Philosophy." Here he conceded that myths are valuable cultural items but objected to their being seen as, for Africans at any rate, a satisfactory alternative to critical thinking. What Oruka found among the people he identified as sages was an ability to think as a critically minded individual. To simply expound traditional lore is not the work of a sage. But neither is knee-jerk contrarianism. More recently, some prominent West African scholars have taken up this line of inquiry. The Ghanaian scholar Kwame Gyekye has contributed significantly here. Speaking of the Akan people in Ghana, Gyekye has argued that their moral culture is best seen as humanist, in the sense that the good is not determined by supernatural constructs but by human beings. This is not to say, of course, that the Akan have no place for the supernatural in their lives. But in the end it is the welfare of the community that comes first. Segun Gbadegesin has argued along similar lines from his studies of Yoruba culture in Nigeria.

The humanism implied by Wiredu, Oruka, Gyekye, and Gbadegesin is social, methodological, local, practical, and nondogmatic. In none of these cases is it necessarily atheistic, but neither does it qualify comfortably as religious humanism in the Western sense. We could almost call it *ubuntu humanism*. A term like this would acknowledge the specifically African contribution to a universal approach, but without sidelining it into an irrelevant cul-de-sac. African humanism is not a pale import of Western models any more than Indian, Chinese, or Middle Eastern humanism is. The title of this book is not intended as a mere slogan.

A SHORT HISTORY OF ORGANIZED HUMANISM IN AFRICA

For many years, organized humanism in Africa attracted little interest in the West, even from the humanist movement. Occasionally, the British humanist press would run a story about a new free thought organization being formed, which, like the one in Ghana in 1957, was the work of British and local activists.[15] But in most cases, nothing more was heard of African humanists. One of the first expressions of interest among humanists in the situation in Africa came from the Rationalist Press Association (RPA), which hosted in 1961 its annual conference on the theme of "The African Revolution: A Challenge to Humanists" at Girton College, Cambridge. Much of Africa had become independent from its colonial rulers the year before, and humanists were aware of the wind of change. A significant feature of this conference was the participation of African speakers: this was not just another instance of Europeans talking about Africa. The RPA followed this up with some good articles on the situation in Africa in its journal *The Humanist*, over the next couple of years, but interest waned after that as the early hopes of independent Africa dissolved in blood and chaos.

Then, as will be outlined later in this chapter, there was the rise and fall of Zambian humanism, a movement that bore some interesting similarities with Négritude. Zambian humanism began life as a private commitment of Kenneth Kaunda (1924–) and ended up as a state-supported ideology working in tandem with an extravagant cult of personality around an increasingly autocratic leader. The saving grace of Zambian humanism was that Kaunda was willing—eventually—to dismantle the one-party state he had created and to abide by the people's rejection of his leadership.

Western unconcern in African humanism did not change until Paul Kurtz visited Gabon, Zambia, Zimbabwe, and South Africa in 1984. In each country he gave lectures and spoke to broadcasters and reporters. He noted that apartheid South Africa was prepared to hear criticism of the paranormal, but even opposition journals were afraid to print criticism of religion. Several prominent journals decided not to run interviews of him, for fear of reprisal from outraged Christians. The visit of Kurtz to South Africa also gave a boost to a recently formed Humanist Association in that country.[16] That same year, Kurtz established the Growth and Development Committee of the International Humanist and Ethical Union (IHEU), with a view to broadening its area of interest away from Europe and the English-speaking world and toward Africa, Asia, and Latin America. He was also instrumental in having the IHEU pass a resolution condemning apartheid and calling for a multiracial, democratic South Africa.

Humanism in Africa was not going to develop if left to its own resources.

A good case could be made that the outside organization that has achieved the most with respect to African humanism was one whose original focus was not directed to Africa at all. After sporadic spells of interest in Africa from European humanist organizations, the next major initiative in this direction came from the United States when Paul Kurtz employed Norm Allen to establish African Americans for Humanism (AAH) in August 1989. As outlined in chapter 6, AAH was originally established with a view to addressing the needs of African Americans, but it soon became apparent that a vast constituency existed in Africa itself, so AAH has slowly extended its area of interest across the Atlantic. With this in mind, prominent humanists from Ghana and Nigeria were invited to serve on the advisory board of the AAH and appear as contributors to *African American Humanism: An Anthology*, a work that Allen edited and that was published by Prometheus Books in 1991. Among the thousands of titles by Prometheus Books that have been distributed for free or at nominal cost on the African continent, this is one of the most commonly seen. In fact, when the story of African humanism comes to be written a century from now, *African American Humanism: An Anthology* should be seen as a foundational text. In 2003, Allen oversaw another collection of readings called *The Black Humanist Experience*, which features humanists from Nigeria, Ghana, and Ethiopia as well as the United States.

A good example of the sort of work AAH did in Africa comes from Ghana, one of the first countries where an indigenous humanism was struggling to emerge. Early in the 1990s, a young Ghanaian, Hope Tawiah, established what he called the Rational Centre. At this stage the center was little more than a post-office box, but for a while it was hoped to establish a center in Poukasi, a village (now a suburb) on the outskirts of Accra. The chief of Poukasi, Nii Otto Kwame III, who had worked as an accountant before taking up his chiefly responsibilities, considered himself a rationalist and was willing to donate land for the center. AAH sent a large consignment of humanist works for the fledgling library there. As well as the general range of books and magazines, AAH had its own publication. Edited by Allen and funded by the Center for Inquiry, the *AAH Examiner* remains the only transnational periodical devoted to the development of humanism in Africa and by Africans. It is one of the least appreciated journals of world humanism. The Rational Centre did not develop as hoped, but the AAH presence in Ghana had its effect. In 1991, Micah Lamptey was a student in

Ghana. Having come home one weekend, Lamptey was watching television, and there was Norm Allen talking about humanism.

> What he said sounded very interesting and appealing to me, and immediately after the show, I told my sister that I had found where I belonged. She said I was crazy, but the next day I went to the office where the show originated and made inquiries as to how I could contact Allen.[17]

Having established contact, Lamptey read a number of books and *Free Inquiry* magazine, sent to him by Allen. As Lamptey said, "I have enjoyed being a secular humanist ever since."

It is the constant flow of material to humanist organizations and individuals in Africa that represents the AAH's single most significant contribution to the development of humanism there. *Free Inquiry, Skeptical Inquirer*, the *AAH Examiner*, as well as literally thousands of Prometheus Books titles have been given away in Africa since the early 1990s. These titles became the core of the library at the Rational Centre in Ghana, when that library was put together. AAH has also sent *Free Inquiry* and several hundred Prometheus Books titles to the Ethiopian Humanist Organization for distribution there. The AAH also helped the Ethiopians establish a presence on the World Wide Web. There are now fledgling humanist organizations around the continent, two of which we will examine in greater depth later in this chapter.

HUMANISM IN SOUTH AFRICA

We have, then, the seeming paradox that humanist thinking, approaches, and practices are widespread in African culture, while humanist organizations are rare and fragile. But, given the broad nature of humanism, this is less paradoxical than it might at first sight appear. Neither is it peculiar to Africa. This paradox can be illustrated by looking at the story of humanism in South Africa. In all probability, the first modern humanist organization on the African continent was formed in the late 1940s or early 1950s by Edward Roux (1903–1966), a botanist at the University of the Witwatersrand in South Africa. Eddie Roux, as he was known, was a capable and popular man, the son of a freethinking Afrikaner father and English mother. He grew up on the Far Left, helping found the Young Communists League in 1921 and joining the Communist Party of South Africa (CPSA) two years later. After graduating at the University of the Witwatersrand, Roux completed a doctorate at Cambridge in 1929, doing research on plant physiology. Between 1929 and 1936, Roux was deeply committed to Communism, attending in 1928 the Sixth Congress of the Communist International in the Soviet Union. Back in South Africa, Roux was active in Communist Party politics until falling afoul of a purge in 1935 and leaving the party altogether the following year. In 1945, he joined the faculty at the University of the Witwatersrand, where he became professor of botany in 1962.

In 1957, Roux returned to active politics by joining the Liberal Party of South Africa, which was committed to a multiracial future for South Africa. One of his more important books was called *Longer Than Rope* (1948), the first history of African nationalism in South Africa. At about this time he also founded a rationalist association. His activities did not go unnoticed by the apartheid regime, and early in the 1960s Roux was listed officially as dangerous to the regime, and as such came under a raft of restrictions. The South African authorities had been alerted to the threat posed by humanists after Julian Huxley's ringing condemnation of apartheid at a lecture at Cape Town University in 1960 to a capacity crowd. Under these new restrictions, in 1963 Roux was forcibly retired from his position at the university and was barred from any teaching and political activity, and even from being quoted. His health suffered under this persecution, and he died, it was said, of a broken heart, in 1966, aged only sixty-three. The rationalist association he founded did not long survive him, although a small amount of money from that organization was bequeathed to a humanist society, which formed in 1979. There remains a small humanist presence in South Africa to this day.

So if we measure the contribution of humanism in South Africa by the scale of humanist organizations, we shall have little more to say. But if we look through a wider lens, interesting vistas open. The struggle against apartheid has, like the civil rights movement in the United States, often been portrayed as the exclusive creation of progressive Christianity. This disguises two important facts: the no-less-prominent role played by organized Christianity in buttressing apartheid, and the significant role played by non-Christians against it. Here we can speak positively about the contribution played by communists, whose role in the antiapartheid struggle was critical. Indeed, the role played by communists in the antiapartheid struggle stands out as the single most noble action undertaken by communists in the twentieth century.

The antiapartheid struggle, in African National Congress (ANC) at least, brought together two ideological tendencies. On the one hand were the progressive Christians and on the other were the communists. But the communists who worked so selflessly for the ANC were less ideologically immobile than their colleagues who remained in the Communist Party. Both the Christian wing and the communist wing were, in effect, operating more as humanists than as ideologues whose main concern was for the purity of the program.

One of the key events in South African humanism was the Freedom Charter, an exercise in mobilization led by the ANC. Nelson Mandela credits the idea of the Charter to Zachariah Keodirelang Matthews (1901–1968), who had just returned from a year in the United States as a visiting professor. Matthews, or "ZK," as he was known, operated within the Christian framework but was viscerally hostile to the official face of South African Christianity, which underwrote and justified apartheid, and the whole organization of missionary schools, which supported a colonial mind-set among its charges. It was ZK's idea to go out among ANC members around the country and ask them what sort of country they wanted to live in. The idea was taken seriously, and members' views were sought from one end of the country to the other. The idea took hold, and people responded wholeheartedly.

Lionel "Rusty" Bernstein (1920–2002), a longtime leftist activist, had a role in drafting the Freedom Charter, based on the submissions that thousands of Africans sent in over a period of months. The humanist aspects of the charter did not please the more extreme wings of the antiapartheid opposition. The more doctrinaire Marxists, reacting to the absence of any reference to class war and the dictatorship of the proletariat, sneered at the "petty bourgeois" charter; and the more racially exclusive Pan-Africanist Congress split off from the ANC after the charter was adopted, in protest against its multiracial policies. The ideologues and exclusivists were right to object to the humanist tone of the document. The main points of the Freedom Charter are:

> The people shall govern.
> All national groups shall have equal rights.
> The people shall share in the country's wealth.
> The land shall be shared among the people who work it.
> All shall be equal before the law.

All shall enjoy equal human rights.
There shall be work and security.
The doors of culture and learning shall be opened.
There shall be houses, security, and comfort.
There shall be peace and friendship.

Each item of the Freedom Charter was passed by acclamation by the three thousand or so delegates who gathered at Kliptown, near Soweto, on June 25 and 26, 1955, at the so-called Congress of the People. Nelson Mandela had to attend the congress in disguise. On its second day, the Congress was broken up by the police.

When the ANC came to power in May 1994, the newly written constitution of South Africa was amended to include the general tenor of the Freedom Charter. That postapartheid South Africa has not realized these ideals is another story. The third and fourth goals, in particular, stand in need of attention.[18] But the Freedom Charter served as the galvanizing ideal for the ANC goals throughout its long struggle with apartheid and remains so to this day.

A good case could be made that the ANC Freedom Charter could stand out as the most impressive humanist manifesto of the twentieth century. John Stuart Mill would have been proud of its concern for liberty, and the social democratic tradition would have applauded its commitment to equality of opportunity in all fields of human flourishing. Nelson Mandela likened it to other "enduring political documents," including the American Declaration of Independence, the French *Declaration of the Rights of Man and of the Citizen* and *The Communist Manifesto*.[19] And, as Mandela also noted, the charter pandered to no exclusivist ideology or creed and involved dialogue and a certain compromise to come together as a unifying document. And it makes no reference whatsoever to any sort of supernatural construct.[20]

KENNETH KAUNDA AND CHRISTIAN HUMANISM

The highest-profile example of indigenous humanism in Africa is also the one few people would want to recall. It is also represents the only experiment in humanism becoming a state ideology. Kenneth Kaunda (1924–) was the first president of Zambia and was one of Africa's leading political figures for at least twenty years. The son of a Presbyterian minister, Kaunda was a staunchly religious man, given to singing hymns with his family and beginning public meetings with a sermon liberally infused with biblical references. And yet Kaunda described himself as a humanist, while acknowledging he had read none of the "standard works on the subject."[21] What books he did read were sent to him by a friend and longtime correspondent, Reverend Colin Morris. Kaunda enjoyed and responded favorably to Teilhard de Chardin's work *The Future of Man* (1964), but he responded negatively to *Objections to Humanism* (1963), a more secular-oriented work edited by H. J. Blackham. It was the clear sense of purpose and direction in Teilhard that Kaunda warmed to, and the specific rejection of such a notion in Blackham that he rejected. Kaunda described himself specifically as a *Christian humanist*, by which he meant "that we discover all that is worth knowing about God through our fellow men and unconditional service to our fellow men [as] the purest form of the service to God."[22] Kaunda's Christian humanism was, like Kaunda himself, sentimental. "I have a passionate belief in the worth and possibilities of man, and I expect him some day to achieve perfection."[23] He was impatient with many elements of Christian dogma, original sin in particular, and he was quite content with acknowledging the truth of evolution while also speaking of the dignity of man. He also criticized the uncritical indoctrination of children into religion and the unthinking piety of people who attend church on Sundays, only to resume uncharitable and exploitative activities on Monday.

In a manner more reminiscent of the early postindependence trend toward essentialism, Kaunda distinguished between the Western problem-solving mentality with what he called the African "situation-experiencing" mentality. Such an outlook makes no distinction between natural and supernatural, rational and nonrational. It is possible, Kaunda said, to be right in the problem-solving sense but also to betray one's integrity.[24] There is something reminiscent of Négritude in some of Kaunda's views. For instance, "Let the West have its technology and Asia its mysticism! Africa's gift to world culture must be in the realm of human relationships."[25] This, he thought, lay at the heart of African humanism. Also, his praise for what he saw as core African values: tribal solidarity, communitarianism, and a relaxed attitude toward time was reminiscent of the Négritudinists. But Kaunda's humanism also shared the weakness more similar to the American religious humanists. Being close to nature and under no illusions as to its beneficence, African people take more trouble to talk with one another, to live among one another. And tribal society had the great strengths of communality, acceptance, and sharing. He hoped that Africa would be able to take on the benefits of Western technology without losing that core insight of spirituality. Most of his more optimistic effusions were written in the years immediately after independence, when the promise of a prosperous future as a free nation lay ahead. But, as with the American religious humanists, it did not take long for his sentimental optimism to appear hopelessly sanguine.

Like many of his fellow African leaders, Kaunda was enamored of socialism, but a socialism with an African face. His friend and ally Julius Nyerere of Tanzania had brokered a form of African socialism he called *Ujamaa*. Some commentators have suggested that Kaunda's use of humanism was just a way of distinguishing his program from Nyerere's socialism. This is probably not the case, however. John Hatch, an Africa-watcher better informed than most, was of the opinion that Kaunda genuinely preferred the term. For Kaunda, *humanism* was the name of the ideal society that came *after* socialism. Like Senghor, Kaunda disliked communism as the goal of socialism because of the materialist assumptions that underlay it. Humanism, by contrast, was the materially satisfied society as created by socialism but with a spiritual dimension, in particular the recognition that humanity can not live by bread alone.[26] One could be a socialist without being a humanist, Kaunda argued, but one couldn't be a humanist without being a socialist.

In the early stages of Kaunda's presidency, this easy confidence was understandable, but as the real-world pressures of politics began to make themselves felt, Kaunda's humanism started to show some cracks. All opposition parties were banned in 1968; Zambia was declared a one-party state in 1972; and parliament was dissolved in 1973. And through all this, Kaunda encouraged a cult of personality around himself and built his brand of humanism into something akin to a national ideology. Zambian humanism was developed into a national rallying cry, similar to the African socialism, or Ujamaa, of his friend and ally, Julius Nyerere of Tanzania. Parallels can also be drawn with what Sekou Toure (1922–1984), Guinea's first postindependence leader, called "national democracy," and with the thought of Kwame Nkrumah (1909–1972), Ghana's first postindependence leader. Nkrumah called his thought *philosophical consciencism*, which he said was a natural development of the humanism implicit in traditional African thought.

The various attempts to ground socialism in African soil failed to take root, as did Kaunda's attempt to do the same with humanism. The fragility of Kaunda's humanism was apparent once he needed to present a justification for banning multiparty democracy in favor of a one-party state. Like so many other African rulers doing the same thing at the time, he returned to arguments based on African exceptionalism: the concept of a loyal opposition was contrary to the African way of doing things, and the communalism of African society is better manifested in one-party rule. This, and the general state of Zambia, was not likely to impress Paul Kurtz during his visit to the country in 1984. Kurtz criticized the inefficient nationalized industries, the corruption, and the absence of democracy. His understanding of humanism had little in common with Kaunda's. Kaunda may call himself a humanist, Kurtz wrote, but that "does not mean that the country expresses humanist values or that there is a strong humanist movement."[27] Kurtz's criticism here is instructive because it shows two strands of humanism in conflict. Kurtz was expressing the values of liberal humanism in opposition to Kaunda's state-backed Christian humanism. Most Africans, certainly most Africans who call themselves humanist, would agree with Kurtz against Kaunda.

Kaunda hung on to power until 1991 when, to his credit, he saw the game was up and stepped down. In response to growing unrest at home and pressure from people he trusted, like Nyerere, Kaunda dismantled the one-party state he had created, called elections, and abided by the result that saw him ejected from office. In old age, Kaunda maintained a website that described him, rather improbably, as the Gandhi of Africa. If anyone deserves that title it is, surely, Nelson Mandela, whose spirit of reconciliation and willingness to reach out to former enemies following his release from imprisonment in 1994 contributed mightily to a peaceful transition to a postapartheid South Africa.

HUMANISM IN NIGERIA FROM TAI SOLARIN TO WOLE SOYINKA

The Zambian experience was unique. The story in Nigeria is more representative of the humanist experience in Africa. The country has maintained a fig leaf of secularity to cover an increasingly bitter and ideological struggle between the Muslim and Christian populations. Section 10 of the country's 1999 constitution declares that neither the federal nor any state government shall adopt any formal religious affiliation. But since then, many of the northern states have adopted variations of sharia law, and many southern states as well as the federal government are run by what is called the *theocratic class* of evangelical Christians. So strong are the divisions that many have feared for the future integrity of the country.

Forgotten amid all the sectarian blare is a long and interesting strand of humanism. One of the first African humanists to achieve a national reputation was the Nigerian educator Tai Solarin (1922–1994). While the first humanist organization was in South Africa, the first major humanist project was the Mayflower School in Nigeria, which was the creation of Solarin, a man Wole Soyinka described as a "passionate warrior in the cause of democracy." Solarin was a very prominent educator and social critic in Nigeria, reaching wide audiences there through the Nigerian newspaper the *Guardian*. After an education in missionary schools, Solarin received higher education in the United Kingdom, where he discovered the writings of H. G. Wells, Robert Ingersoll, and others. From his readings, Solarin became convinced that religion served only to instill submissive attitudes to white domination, and later, to a general underdevelopment and passivity that worked in the interest of ruling elites.

Solarin returned to Nigeria in 1952 and became the headmaster of a local school, only to be sacked when he tried to remove religious instruction from the school. In 1956, he established his own school, calling it the Mayflower, which went on to become one of the leading educational institutions in his country. Mayflower graduates developed a reputation for working harder, and for having greater technological competence and independence of mind. The first woman engineer in Nigeria was a graduate of the Mayflower. Solarin was a fearless and public advocate of atheism, humanism, and democracy in a country used to uncritical acceptance of religious dogmas and superstitions.[28] He suffered detention on several occasions, the longest in 1984–1985, when he was imprisoned for seventeen months for criticizing the military regime then in power. He died in 1994, the day after participating in the Walk for Justice in Lagos in opposition to the dictatorship of Sani Abacha. Tai Solarin was survived by his wife Sheila, who has carried on his work.

Outside of what was happening at Mayflower School, there was little in the way of an organized humanist movement in Nigeria before the 1990s. A small humanist organization made itself known to the IHEU in the 1950s, but little was heard of it. Most expressions of humanism came from individuals, among them was Sanya Onabamiro, a biologist at University College, Ibadan. Onabamiro went on to write widely on history and philosophy and had a very prominent role in Nigerian intellectual and political life. Small groups (like Action for Humanism, led by Emmanuel Kofi Mensah in Ogun State, and the Humanist Friendship Center, led by Charles Ufomadu in Imo State) did what they could with their limited resources to advance humanist thinking. What transformed these sporadic initiatives into something larger and more organized was the emergence of bitter sectarian feeling in the 1990s between the growing Muslim population in the north of the country and evangelical Christianity, funded in large part from the United States, in the south. The increasingly sectarian nature of Nigerian politics and society has made it crucial that a secular voice for toleration and pluralism be heard.

As well as providing literature, African Americans for Humanism did what it could to help develop an indigenous humanist literature. In 1991, the AAH funded the first Nigerian humanist newsletter, called the *Sunray*. Alongside the indigenous literature, the Center for Inquiry has also been active in developing a cadre of leaders. Over the decade, the center provided airfares for Ghanaian and Nigerian delegates to attend international humanist meetings in Belgium, in the Netherland,s and in Mexico.

It was not long before a leader emerged in the form of a young activist named Leo Igwe. Born into a Catholic family, Igwe tells of a violent and vulgar father amid an upbringing punctuated with prayers and rosaries. He lost whatever faith he had as a teenager studying at a seminary. "My Lord," he recalled telling his bishop, "I want to go and think."[29] When Igwe attended the International Humanist & Ethical Union congress in Mumbai in January 1999, Nigerian humanism made its first major foray into the world since Tai Solarin went to study in England half a century previous. His speech outlined the urgent need for humanism in Nigeria and across Africa and condemned the intrusion of foreign religions with their sectarian ways that shattered the cohesion that once marked the traditional life of African people. Under Igwe's energetic leadership, the Nigerian Humanist Movement (NHM) led a series of campaigns, including one against the imposition of sharia law in the northern provinces of the country. It has also campaigned against child killing, a practice common among practitioners of traditional beliefs. The movement produces a journal called the *Humanist Inquirer.*

Ten years of work in Africa came to a head late in 2001 with the inaugural conference of the Nigerian Humanist Movement, held at the University of Ibadan. Funded by the Center for Inquiry (the parent body of African Americans for Humanism) and organized by Igwe, the theme of the conference was "Science, Humanism, and the African Renaissance." Conferences are two a penny in the West, but events like this are still momentous developments in Africa, and this conference was attended by a broad range of Nigerian academics, teachers, and activists, as well as several nongovernmental organizations (NGOs). A Ugandan delegate was also there, and reports of the situation in Ethiopia and Tanzania were heard. Most delegates were strongly secular in outlook and deplored the breakdown in commitment to a secular state in Nigeria. Dr. G. A. Akinola, a historian from the University of Ibadan, spoke for many delegates when he stressed the need to revive the Nigerian rationalist tradition. This was reiterated by speakers from the health sector who lamented the influence of primitive health practices frequently peddled by charlatans out for a quick profit. Not all delegates were of the same mind though. Jerry Obi-Ikogbuo, a senior lecturer at the Federal University of Technology at Owerri in Nigeria, worried that *secular humanism*, which he distinguished from *sacred humanism*, alienated people from God. There was also disagreement over the role genetically modified foods should play in alleviating hunger on the continent.

Another aspect of humanism in Nigeria is the example of Wole Soyinka (1934–) whose thoughts on Négritude we explored earlier in this chapter. Soyinka was born in Abeokuta, in southwestern Nigeria. This is Yoruba country, and he recalls being brought up in a Christian family, with Muslim neighbors. He studied at Ibadan and at Leeds University in England. He abandoned his budding career in theater and returned to Nigeria after his homeland became independent in 1960. There he became politically active in opposition to the military regime led by General Gowon, serving a term of imprisonment between 1967 and 1969, most of it in solitary confinement. This became the subject of his book *The Man Died* (1972), which bristles with a fierce determination to live. Its withering indictment of Gowon and his regime meant he could not return to Nigeria until the general's dismissal in a coup d'état in 1975. Upon his release, Soyinka was involved in academia in Nigeria and abroad and was particularly active as a writer. His literary criticism and cultural-studies work won him the Nobel Prize for Literature in 1986, the first black African to win this distinction.

Growing respectability did not prevent Soyinka from continuing to oppose military regimes in Nigeria. Things got so bad during the dictatorship of Sani Abacha (1993–1998) that he fled the country once more, this time to escape a death sentence. While in exile, Soyinka wrote *The Open Sore of a Continent* (1996), a strong criticism of misrule in Africa, particularly in Nigeria. Soyinka dedicated that book to Tai Solarin. In this and other writings, Soyinka made no secret of his opinion that religious extremism played an important role in the problems besetting Africa. As if to vindicate this view, a Muslim cleric issued a fatwa calling for Soyinka's death.

Soyinka pays great heed to the Yoruba worldview he was born into. In line with the work of philosophers like Kwame Gyekye and Segun Gbadegesin, whom we discussed earlier in this chapter, Soyinka claims Yoruba religion is among the most humanistic in the world, as their deities have next to supernatural authority and derive their status from their relationship with human needs and priorities. It is in this context that the Yoruba proverb recited early in this chapter ("If humanity were not, the gods would not be") is relevant. On the basis of an understanding of humanism in these terms, Soyinka is guardedly optimistic for the future of humanism in Africa. Of his own humanism, he has written, "Humanism for me represents taking the human entity as the center of world perception, of social organization, and indeed of ethics, deciding in other words what is primarily of the greatest value for humans as opposed to some remote extraterrestrial or ideological authority."[30]

Soyinka's courage has set an outstanding example of practical, active humanism. But he would be the first to agree that in Nigeria, as in the rest of Africa, the real cause of humanism is at a much more basic level. The two principal battles are to ensure the full separation of church and state and to combat superstition. Separation of church and state in Nigeria came with the British, and so, after independence it was natural that this, as with all other aspects of colonization, should be reexamined. In the constitution that was enacted in 1979, a formal separation of church and state remained while permitting the actual imposition of sharia law in the Muslim states in the north and the quasi-official propagation of Christianity in the south. The result is unsatisfactory on so many levels. Religious tensions have escalated into violence on many occasions, and the treatment of women has become little better than barbaric, as the case of Amina Lawal illustrated. In March 2002, Lawal was found guilty of adultery by a local sharia court. As is consistent with sharia law, she was not provided any defense counsel. The punishment for women found guilty of adultery is death by stoning. The man escaped any charge when he declared on the Qur'an that he was not responsible.

News of the case spread around the world when, on August 19, 2002, a sharia court of appeal upheld the decision, and by implication, the method of punishment. Over the next year, the case became a *cause célèbre*. Lawal was offered asylum and intense pressure was put on the sharia system and on Nigeria's president Obasanjo, a born-again Christian. Eventually the sharia court acquitted Lawal on a technicality rather than risk threats from the Obasanjo government to overrule any decision that would entail death by stoning.

The Lawal saga demonstrated that separation of church and state is not some abstract academic argument. People's livelihoods, even their lives, depend on full separation. And in Nigeria, the separation issue is tied in with the question of the pervasive reach of superstition. To give an example, Leo Igwe writes of the incidence of untouchability in his country. In south of the country lies Igboland, where people are either *Nwadiala* (freeborn), or *Osu* (in which case they are strangers, aliens, and marginalized). The Osu are thought to be the offspring of slaves to early tribal gods, and proscriptions against them are every bit as severe as faced by dalits in India. Laws, going back to the British, have been passed against the practice, but to little effect. The Christian churches in Igboland have accommodated themselves to the practice. The only consistent condemnation of the practice comes from the Nigerian humanists, but it will be a long process to break down the old taboos in Igboland.

The challenges faced by Nigerian humanists are daunting in the extreme. Poverty, overpopulation, violence, corruption, superstition, and the theocratizing of politics—all work together to make for a lethal mix. In the words of one Nigerian humanist, "If you fight for the cause of your religion or culture alone, you are part of the problem. A healthy environment makes room for the proper practice of religion. Hence a cause for the Nigerian nation is a cause for our individual freedom, which includes freedom of worship. It is not our religion that makes us Nigerians but the soil of Nigeria on which we are all born."[31]

UGANDAN HUMANISM AND THE PROMISE OF EDUCATION

Like Nigeria, Uganda has more than enough reasons to be skeptical about the value of religion. Once called by Winston Churchill the "pearl of Africa," Uganda has had more than its fair share of obsessive dictators, misgovernance, and murderous sectarianism. And Uganda's experience serves to act as a reminder that superstition, with all the negative associations customarily attached to that word, is still a reality in people's lives. It has become problematic throughout the Western world to speak of *reason* or *superstition* without resorting to scare quotes. To talk of them is naïve, logocentric, culturally imperialist, or some other fashionable pejorative. But wrap these sorts of words in scare quotes, and we can affect a pleasing irony.

Why has this happened? Probably because people in the West who think and speak in this way have lost a firsthand sense of what reason or superstition mean in people's lives. One needs to go to Uganda to see superstition for the danger it really is. In Uganda, superstition is not simply a brand name, it is a real danger that blights real people's lives. And reason is not a token of Western imperialism but a real means by which people can take back responsibility for their own lives from those who seek to enslave them.

To recount the story of Ugandan humanism, we could begin with the story of the Buganda king Mutesa I (1856–1884) being courted by Catholic, Protestant, and Muslim missionaries. Mutesa was so bemused by the mutual excoriating of each other's beliefs and scriptures that he remained a pagan till his dying day. He was, at any rate, more interested in the Western weaponry he could acquire from them, in order to pursue his local wars more effectively. But after Mutesa's death and the slow decline and dismemberment of Buganda and the other kingdoms of the region into the British colony, the missionaries had a free hand, which they used to great advantage. Since then, Uganda has counted itself a strongly religious country, but one that has suffered more than its share of bloodshed in religion's name, from intertribal wars to fundamentalist banditry and cult slayings.

The earliest evidence of any indigenous humanist activity in Africa can be found in the British humanist press. The value of the British humanist journals for isolated freethinkers in various parts of the world is difficult to exaggerate. So when in 1953 Aloni Lubwama was starting out on what would certainly have been a lonely road of secular humanism in Uganda, it was understandable he would write to the *Literary Guide*, then the most prestigious humanist journal in the world. Lubwama's path from religion began at the Church of England school he attended. After reading Bishop Gore's *New Commentary of Holy Scripture*, he questioned the teachers about the veracity of the Gospel accounts of creation. The unsatisfactory answers he received led him on to H. G. Wells's *The Outline of History*, with its entirely naturalistic account of origins. The parallel here with Tai Solarin is interesting. Wells's writings were hugely influential outside Europe, something that deserves proper exploration. Now no longer a believer, Lubwama was at odds with his headmaster, who involved the archbishop of Uganda. After indicating a desire to become a teacher, he was told in a letter from the archbishop of Uganda that no school in Uganda would employ him. At the time of writing, he was setting up a rationalist study group in Kampala. "Wish us well," he ended his letter.[32]

As in Nigeria, organized humanism started very modestly and began to acquire a national reputation only after Western humanist organizations began to take notice. Once again, it was African Americans for Humanism that had the longest track record of cooperation. In collaboration with the Center for Inquiry, the Ugandan humanists run a small office in Kampala, just down the road from Makerere University. With two hundred or so books donated by Prometheus Books, and a couple of computers, humanism had a presence in Uganda. Ugandan humanism's moment in the sun came in 2004 when the International Humanist & Ethical Union held its annual congress, as well as that of its youth wing, in Kampala. The Ugandan Humanist Association (UHASSO) was formally established at this time. It was also an opportunity to promote the African Humanist Alliance (AHAL), under whose auspices the conference was run. AHAL is an attempt to coordinate humanism across the continent. Some anecdotes from this conference will help give a picture of the Ugandan humanism and of the problems faced.

The first impression a European attendee of the conference in Uganda would have had is of the youth and passion of the African humanists. Many of the African attendees had struggled to Kampala on buses, even hitchhiking. A young teacher from Tanzania spoke of the discrimination he faced by the religious authorities of his school for not subscribing to the orthodox line. A group of students from Nairobi University spoke of their sense of isolation in an environment expecting conformity to religious norms. And from Western Uganda, a man who had been a practicing witch doctor spoke about his journey from superstition to reason. No scare quotes needed here, this man's journey really was from superstition to reason. He was now actively engaged in his region, showing people how the witch doctors' tricks are done and encouraging them to resist their blandishments. But the most memorable talk came from a young Rwandan woman about the genocide in her country. In a deeply moving account, she gave a full sense of the horror the country had undergone, not omitting the shameful role of many church leaders in encouraging the genocide, leading the murderers to victims, or at the very least taking no action to prevent the killings.

Another feature of the conference was the expression given to other forms of discrimination. In Uganda homosexuality carries with it a maximum of life imprisonment, with severe punishments even for those who fail to report homosexual activity to the police. Unsurprisingly, then, the few Ugandan homosexuals brave enough to show their faces began speaking up at the conference. The conference agreed that this form of discrimination was unacceptable in an open society.

Nobody was ready for the press reaction. One city paper, the *New Vision*, carried an article the next day under the headline "Homos meet in Kampala." All of a sudden a series of humanist conferences had become "the first ever conference to discuss the rights of homosexuals."[33] And the cartoon in the following day's paper plumbed the depths of bad taste when it portrayed some very caricatured gays mincing off to a conference, taunting police in full confidence of not being arrested while the other large conferences of donor nations were still in town. The policeman replies to the homosexual with the veiled threat to dare continue the conference after the donor conferences have finished.[34]

Coverage as hostile as this did the conference a grave disservice but, more to the point, starkly showed the problems African humanism face. All the other issues the humanist conferences discussed over five days dissolved into irrelevance as it had now been branded a "homos conference." The hotel where the conferences were held was visited by the police, though no arrests were made. The *New Vision* ran a major op-ed piece a few days later in which one correspondent confessed to being "gravely amazed" to hear that Ugandan law had been flouted in so cavalier a fashion by "two associations I have never heard of, namely the Uganda Humanist Association and the International Humanist and Ethical Union."[35] Roy Brown, at the time president of the IHEU, went out of his way to correct the misinformation, but to little effect. Had the *New Vision* reporters stayed longer, they could have had more material with which to berate the humanists. Dr. Sylvia Tamale of Makerere University gave a fiery indictment of the patriarchal conservatism in Ugandan society that conspires to hold women down. There were also some good presentations on third world debt, globalization, and the rise of Islam. And it's worthwhile to note that a colleague of Dr. Tamale, Ernest Beyeraza, had spoken at the Cairo conference on Averroës and the Enlightenment that we discussed in the previous chapter. Professor Beyeraza had made an impassioned plea for the enlightenment to develop scientifically and technologically.

All this said, once the conferences were over, the key to humanism in Africa is the value placed on education. And what better way to ensure people are educated than to found a school? UHASSO has founded the Humanist Academy at the village of Kampiringisa in the Mpigi district. And eighty miles southwest of Kampala, near the township of Makasa, is the Isaac Newton School, which in 2006 served eighty-three pupils in two classrooms. Children, many of whom are orphans, help grow crops on the school's site for their meals. And at Busota, seventy-five miles northeast of the capital, is the Mustard Seed School, which educates children along humanist lines. The story of Mustard Seed's founder, Moses Kamya, is reminiscent of Gora and Tagore in India and Tai Solarin in Nigeria. Kamya decided to found his own school after having been dismissed twice from Christian schools because of his beliefs. He began with just four students, but within months this had risen to more than one hundred fifty. His pupils are either too poor to be educated anywhere else or too female. Both schools receive ongoing support from humanist organizations in Britain and Norway.

Organized humanism is only beginning in Africa, but it has a rich seedbed of cultural thought upon which to grow. Signs of humanist activity are apparent in Kenya, in Cameroon, in Ethiopia, and in Senegal. And hopefully the African Humanist Alliance can slowly build itself up as an effective coordinating agent for these disparate activities. The case studies of Nigeria and Uganda show, among other things, the tremendous resilience of liberal humanism. From their various standpoints, Marxists, evangelical Christians, and postmodernists have all declared, at some point or another, the death of this strand of thought. They have also claimed to have superseded it, and yet this has not happened. The liberal humanist vision of the world—free; secular; respectful of tradition, yet open to the future; human-oriented while not human-confined—continues to inspire people from all cultures. And some of them, as in Nigeria and Uganda, have more reasons than most to understand the full import of these values and the full horror of their absence.

This is not to say, of course, that African humanism can only prosper insofar as it meekly assimilates Western liberal humanism. The truly exciting prospect is of an African humanism developing from within its own cultural resources. The Cameroonian scholar and technocrat Daniel Etounga-Manguelle describes African culture as "one of the most—if not *the* most—humanistic culture in existence." These humanistic values he described as "the solidarity beyond age classification and social status; social interaction; the love of neighbor, whatever the color of his skin; the defense of the environment, and so many others."[36] From this broad, humanistic foundation, Etounga-Manguelle sees education as the key to Africa's future—a secular, technical, and practical education. The sort of education Tai Solarin offered and Moses Kamya would like to offer, if only he had the resources. Meanwhile, the rest of the world would profit greatly from a conscientious study of ubuntu humanism.

CHAPTER 13

A WORLD WITHOUT WALLS: PLANETARY HUMANISM

In this final chapter we need to consider the state of humanism in the twenty-first century and ask what planetary humanism means. Is it nothing more than a pious dream? Plenty have argued that it is. Some, like John Gray, go further and accuse liberal humanists of all manner of follies, crudities, and delusions. Liberal humanists, he argues, are inheritors of Christian apocalyptic myths of history having a purpose. But for an accusation of this sort to work, the long line of humanist thinkers over the past two centuries who have opposed teleological strands of thinking needs to be ignored. Neither are Gray's sneers at liberal humanism made in the name of some rival coherent system of thought he thinks superior. Toward the end of one of his books, after having slapped around all varieties of defender of liberal societies, he quietly acknowledges that liberal societies are indeed worth defending.[1] This wish to have one's cake and eat it too is, as we saw in chapter 7, also a feature of some postmodern antihumanism. In Gray's case, it is hard to see his preferred solution as any less utopian than those of his opponents. His solution? Throw one's hands in the air and "seek the company of mystics, poets, and pleasure lovers rather than utopian dreamers."[2] Other critics of humanism, like David Cooper, have agreed that such company is preferable to that of humanists because of the latter's supposed hubris. I cannot help agreeing at this point with Sidney Hook, who saw this form of dogmatic preference for mystery not so much as evidence of humility, as of a failure of nerve.[3]

If one is of a mind to take a more active role than Gray or Cooper in doing what one can to help realign humanity's destructive priorities and methods, then we will need some sort of program by which to operate. The humanist version of this has been called *planetary humanism*. This chapter will first look at some of the thoughts and motivations behind planetary humanism, then range back over the past century or so and see how it developed. And finally, we'll examine what people are saying now about planetary humanism.

ECOHUMANISM AND THE AWARENESS OF INTERDEPENDENCE

The core insight of planetary humanism is the recognition that our principal form of identification is as inhabitants of a coherent though fragile and interdependent ecosystem known as planet Earth. It is the planet that sustains us, rather than some supernaturalist abstraction. This means that *Homo sapiens* need to be understood in the context of being members of this system of nature.[4] Ecology, in this sense, is a consequence of Charles Darwin, and it is not accidental that the word *ecology* was coined by Darwin's chief advocate in Germany, Ernest Haeckel (1834–1919). It is also important that an ecological humanism, or *ecohumanism* as it has been called, should establish a coherent theoretical framework by which to operate. David Cooper sees this as unlikely by virtue of the hubris he believes "scientific realists" display when they believe themselves to have access to an account of the world that is both true and clean (in the sense of being uncontaminated by the interests, purposes, and values of a competing human world).[5] This accusation remains credible until one actually examines the fallibilism and ecological awareness of "scientific realists." Humanists have repeatedly warned of the tentative nature of scientific hypotheses, of how little is really known, of how every conundrum solved raises more questions, and so on. In fact, science is so much better equipped to stimulate attitudes of awe and wonder at the universe than most primitive theological takes of mystery.[6]

Any valid articulation of an ecologically aware humanism, however, is going to have to do more than act as apologist for scientific method. As this book is primarily a historical account, let us once again survey what humanists have actually said on the issue, rather than what people think they have said. One of the first people to speak of humans as part of an interdependent whole was John Stuart Mill. In his brilliant essay "Nature," written in the

1850s, Mill placed human beings squarely in the natural realm, which, in its broadest sense, he spoke of as "a collective name for all facts, actual and possible."[7] He drew the important distinction that human beings have little option but to obey the laws of nature, but he noted that we are not necessarily guided by them.[8] And neither should we be, given nature's indifference to any living thing. Rather, our job as a species is to improve on the sorry condition nature fits us to be. The significance of Mill's essay for our purposes is the absence of anthropocentric conceit, of any cult of progress, or of a sense that nature owes humanity a living. Frederick Woodbridge continues this theme in *An Essay on Nature*, which we will examine shortly.

Someone else who was ahead of his time with respect to humanity's relation to nature was H. G. Wells, who stressed the importance of the conservation of resources as central to human survival. He was even conscious, in the 1940s, of the need to save the whale. From the 1960s, attention in the humanist magazines, as elsewhere, turned to overpopulation, but more pressing political and social issues resumed pride of place in the 1970s and 1980s. The question of humanism and the environment returned as a major issue in the 1990s.

There have been at least two attempts to devise a big-picture ecological humanism. As we saw in chapter 5, the last version of Julian Huxley's evolutionary humanism arrived at a workable confluence of evolutionary and ecological thought. But most attempts at an ecological humanism did little more than contrive some sort of transcendental uplift. For instance, Henryk Skolimowski, a Polish-born philosopher who taught in the United States, was critical of most previous varieties of humanism, in particular what he saw as the raw scientism of naturalistic humanism. To replace them, he wrote *Ecological Humanism* (1974), a reworking of vitalist evolutionism and the thoughts of Albert Schweitzer with a nod toward Teilhard de Chardin. Skolimowski was working for a morality that was neither God-centered nor human-centered but evolution-centered. But this did not stop him articulating the most anthropocentric cosmology. "We should feel comfortable," he wrote, "in this universe. For we are not an anomaly, but its crowning glory. We are not lost in it, or alienated from it, for it is us."[9]

Skolimowski's thought, which has become known as *eco-philosophy*, has not been especially influential outside some religious humanist and Gaia circles. Certainly, among most secularly inclined humanists, his teleological anthropocentrism found little favor. In fact, central to the cosmology of naturalistically inclined humanists over the past century has been a tremendous awareness of our utter irrelevance to the cosmos. This was made plain by Bertrand Russell and George Santayana at the beginning of the twentieth century and by Carl Sagan and Steven Weinberg at its end. But few people expressed it more clearly than the English classicist Gilbert Murray. Speaking in 1939, Murray made it clear that

> our earth is not the center of the cosmos; it is not even the center of the solar system; and the solar system itself is only one out of very many systems, incalculably vast, incalculably numerous, to which the welfare or misery of us human beings is, as far as we can make out, of no consequence whatever. The sun was not created to give us light by day, nor the moon by night. The animals were not, after all, made for men's sake, so as to provide with food by eating them, with clothes by skinning them or with healthy amusement by trapping, hunting, shooting, and tormenting them. All such anthropocentric thinking proves to have been just a part of our inordinate human conceit.[10]

Far from placing man at the center of the cosmos, as popular apologists have liked to insist, humanists, especially the more naturalistically inclined among them, have been concerned to articulate a meaningful way to live in the face of being peripheral to the nth degree. It follows from this that humanism is not anthropocentric in the sense of placing a grandly articulated construct called "Man" on a pedestal and then falling to one's knees in wonder. The key insight of humanism since Darwin is that human beings, like all other animals, are part of nature. The shift in emphasis at the start of the twenty-first century is that all living beings, and all inanimate things, are bound indissolubly in a fragile interdependence. Being a humanist in the twenty-first century involves recognizing the central fact of this interdependence. And one aspect of this recognition is to eschew any supernaturalist constructs that can serve as sops to our anthropocentric conceit.

We know about humanists rejecting supernaturalism, but less emphasis has been given to their thoughts on broader ecological issues. This has gone on long enough to establish a general tendency to place *humanist* and *ecologist* in different boxes. This is a mistake, explained in part by the restricted view of who has been labeled *humanist*. The great ecologist Aldo Leopold (1887–1948), who developed what he called the *land ethic*, expressed a core humanist insight when wrote, "We now know that men are only fellow voyagers with other creatures in the odyssey of evolution. This new knowledge should have given us, by this time, a sense of kinship with fellow creatures; a wish to live and let live."[11] From a different perspective Gerhard Szczesny, whose work we outlined in chapter 7, thought this realization was the essential point of difference with preceding generations. Where "modern man differs in essence from earlier generations is in his feeling of being expressly dependent on external circumstance. He knows himself to be environmentally bound."[12]

But the most systematic treatment of these themes came from Frederick Woodbridge, Corliss Lamont's mentor and one of the most significant expositors of American philosophical naturalism in the twentieth century. His beautifully written and closely reasoned work, *An Essay on Nature*, sets humanity in a natural setting, with none of the hubris or geocentrism that is said to attend humanist cosmology. It is in the face of nature's indifference, Woodbridge writes, that humans contrive some means by which nature can be outflanked. "Now the desire arises for the personal possession of a knowledge [that] would give us security, only the knowledge must not be like physics, biology, or history. They and their like do not deliver the kind of security desired."[13] The notion of the supernatural arose to fit this need. The answer to nature's indifference is to reduce nature to something standing alongside humans, and then to pay respects to the ultimate expression of supernaturalism: God. Human beings seek justification "by prayer and praise and sacrifice and by confessing that he and Nature belong, not to himself, but to God." Woodbridge cited Psalm 8:3–9 as an example of this hubris.[14] In this way, the dualism between natural and supernatural arises not from the pursuit of knowledge but from the pursuit of happiness and is therefore a product of human egotism. The lesson to take from Woodbridge is that our pursuit of happiness can only take place in the natural realm, with all the consequences that brings as to what form our pursuit of happiness should take and the resources we can justifiably allocate it.

The issue that arises from Woodbridge's inquiry is the attitude human beings should then adopt, and the actions that should then follow, with respect to nature. The next major step toward a consistent ecological humanism came from John Passmore. Born in Australia and raised a Catholic, Passmore (1914–2004) rebelled against the moral consequences of the Christian story. He came to describe himself as a "pessimistic humanist" in light of humanity's ongoing capacity for wickedness and stupidity. He studied philosophy at the University of Sydney under John Anderson (1893–1962), one of that country's most important philosophers and an outspoken rationalist. Most of Passmore's career was spent at the Australian National University in Canberra.

Passmore was more than just another clever philosopher. He also helped shape his discipline. Much of what is now called *applied philosophy* developed under his influence. Reflecting Anderson's interests, Passmore was interested in the larger context in which philosophical ideas play themselves out. His work in applied philosophy surveyed political theory, art, science, and, most important, the environment. But the work of interest to us is *Man's Responsibility for Nature* (1974), in which he argued that *Homo sapiens* needs to change its attitudes toward the environment. Nature, he wrote "helps to preserve men from hubris, to make them more conscious that things go in their own way, indifferent to man's concerns."[15] This observation was not original to Passmore, of course, although his ability to make it without then succumbing to some brand of antiscience was. Science and reason are essential tools by which we may survive.

Passmore rejected the earlier claims that ecological disaster could be laid squarely at the doorstep of Christianity. While that religion's triumphalist emphasis on dominion and hierarchy has been massively destructive and unhelpful, he noted the heritage was as much Graeco-Christian as Judeo-Christian.[16] He also criticized the Romantic urge to call nature sacred, but even here his objections were not merely to the extravagance of such a move; he objected to the way it would undermine serious ecological thinking. To call something sacred is to assume it has extraordinary powers, including that of recuperation. It also has the, often unintended, effect of re-admitting an element of anthropocentric conceit, as humanity can take on the mantle of sacredness as well, by virtue of its place in nature. In contrast to this, Passmore concentrated on humanity's utter dependence on nature and the fragility of the whole system. "And this means that neither man nor nature is sacred or quasi-divine."[17] Far from embracing talk of sacredness, it is important, he argued, that we reject it if we are to fully appreciate that humans—and humans alone—can make the adjustments necessary to save the world.[18] Despite these criticisms, I doubt that Passmore would endorse a blanket rejection of this sort of language, particularly if anthropocentric conceit is not being smuggled in through the back door. When David Suzuki, for instance, writes of the sacred balance between humanity and nature, it would be churlish to object to the use of language when his argument is thoroughly humanistic in orientation.[19] Passmore's response was constructive. He went on to articulate more fully than had been done before the ethos of stewardship of nature. *Man's Responsibility for Nature* should be seen as one of the humanist classics of the twentieth century.

Woodbridge, Passmore, and many who have followed them have argued that humanism not only *accommodates* recognition of our interdependence with nature, it *requires* it. Anything less would involve ignoring the lessons of science over the past several centuries. Humans are a product of evolution, as are all other living species. Where monotheistic religions have gifted humans a special destiny by virtue of having an immortal soul fashioned in the image of God, most humanists are naturalists, seeing only a difference in degree between the consciousness of *Homo sapiens* and that of other animals. When we come, then, to measure humanist ecology against what can be taken as core ecological values, we do not find an abyss, rather we find a necessary symmetry. The core ecological values, according to Tim Hayward, are to live in harmony with nature, to overcome anthropocentric prejudice, and to recognize intrinsic value in nonhuman beings.[20] These are humanist values.

The reorienting of humanity and nature that Woodbridge and Passmore articulated has been continued by a range of humanist thinkers since then, with perhaps Richard Dawkins and Peter Singer as the most prominent among them. Until *The God Delusion*, Dawkins had become one of the principal spokesmen for an awareness of nature's intricacy that could almost be described as reverential. He has rarely spoken directly of humanism, beyond noting it is an ethical system that often accompanies atheism.[21] I suspect Dawkins shares Bertrand Russell's ambivalence about humanism, and for similar reasons.

Among Chinese and African humanists, there has been less need for a reorientation of values in an ecological direction because significant elements of their worldviews are already geared toward an understanding of our place in nature and the need for harmonious relations within it. Speaking of the ecophilosophical dimension of ubuntu, Mogobe Ramose notes its core principle is that of motion, or permanent, directionless change, which allows no place for an individual ego arrogating to itself a position at the center of the universe.[22] How can one do this coherently, when the universe has no center? Having said this, it would be one-eyed not to notice the appalling environmental damage being done in Africa, China, and India at the moment. The solution lies not in the wholesale adoption of exotic standards of behavior, but in the intelligent appropriation of the best from each culture.

A prevailing charge against humanism is that it is the most rampant form of speciesism, the prejudice that accords an unacceptable level of privilege to *Homo sapiens*, simply by virtue of being *Homo sapiens*. In contrast to the grand anthropocentric conceits of the doctrine of Incarnation or of theistic humanism as practiced in the Renaissance, human beings necessarily accord importance to being human. This is not to say that this sense of importance is in any way written in fire across the cosmos. It is to make the simple point that Bernard Williams made: human beings are important to human beings.[23] The good ecologists understand this as well. Stephen Kellert, codeveloper with E. O. Wilson of the Biophilia thesis, has noted that human beings are an integral part of nature, and that little good can come from seeing ourselves as "some kind of exogonous, alien, or added layer to the natural world."[24] So it won't do to simply equate speciesism with any other form of prejudice, such as racism or sexism. Identifying ethically as a species is not a crime. In this sense, it is a very rare person who is *not* a humanist, as we all have, presumably, some interest in being human.[25] It seems Protagoras was right after all. From recognizing the anthropomorphic quality of human thought, it does not follow that humanists must then rush off to an anthropocentric triumphalism. Williams is simply warning against taking speciesism up as a form of self-hatred. Other humanist writers have noted this strain of self-hatred operating at a cultural level, as when Robert C. Solomon criticized Thomas Berry's sentimental work *Dream of the Earth* (1988), which resurrected a noble savage theme when he pleaded we all live like Native Americans.[26]

One humanist who *has* explored the consequences of speciesism (indeed, he's credited with inventing the term) is Peter Singer. It's important, he argues, that humans do not simply rest content with the general recognition of the existence of a global ecosystem. This must be followed up with an active unwillingness to inflict needless suffering on nonhuman animals. The issue of the treatment of nonhuman animals is not going to go away. As well as the animal rights perspective, there is a growing awareness of the environmental element to this argument. Several people have argued that vegetarianism would be just as worthwhile a contribution to eliminating global warming than our token efforts at recycling or avoiding too many plane or car trips. The ten billion animals killed each year in the United

States alone pose more than an ethical challenge. Greenhouse gases produced by these animals contribute significantly to global warming, and the resources needed to feed them contribute to resource depletion. "There is no nonreligious reason," Singer argues, "why the pains and pleasures of nonhuman animals should not be given equal weight with the similar pains and pleasures of human beings."[27]

The speciesism issue has serious implications for the far older philosophical debate on what gets called "human nature." The old free-will-versus-determinism debate now seems unnecessary, as it seems apparent that human nature is an intricate balance between nature and nurture. Human nature has no clear beginning or end, either in evolutionary time or horizontally, across species barriers. To assert a distinctive coherence for human nature is, in fact, just another form of anthropocentric conceit. One extreme reading of this insight comes in the form of transhumanism, which looks forward to the day when self-enhancement through genetic remodeling is a reality for us all.[28] Like many others, I must confess to finding the implications of this deeply troubling, but I want to avoid rushing into a knee-jerk reaction on behalf of some misplaced "uniqueness of man" delusion. The transhumanism debate is at least offering some insights on what constitutes "normal" or "standard" human limitations. It is also exploring where the boundary is between supposedly legitimate *external* assistance for various conditions or imperfections that are now available, to the newer ones that will be attachable *internally*.[29]

Returning to the historical survey, the first specific recognition from the mainstream humanist community of the new ecological awareness was the *Humanist Manifesto II*, published a year before Passmore's book. Paul Kurtz was the key figure behind this new articulation of a humanist ecology. The fourteenth article called for cooperative planning at a world level.

> The planet Earth must be considered a single *ecosystem*. Ecological damage, resource depletion, and excessive growth must be checked by international concord. The cultivation and conservation of nature is a moral value; we should perceive ourselves as integral to the sources of our being in nature.[30]

The next major milestone in humanist advocacy about the environment came in the form of the Declaration of Interdependence. Written by Paul Kurtz, the declaration was unveiled at the Tenth World Congress of the International Humanist & Ethical Union, held in Buffalo, New York, in August 1988, and it was signed by some very prominent humanist scholars, like E. O. Wilson, Isaac Asimov, Jean-Claude Pecker, Gerald Larue, Mario Bunge, and Adolf Grünbaum, all laureates of the International Academy of Humanism. The declaration called for the creation of a world community built upon shared transnational values. It began with the recognition that we need a new global consensus, the core of which was the understanding of our common humanity and of the moral truisms shared by us all. "It is time that we clearly enunciate these ethical principles so that they may be extended toward all members of the human family living on this planet." It went on to itemize a range of rights and responsibilities that are common to us all. And it ended with a set of observations on the ethics of a global community:

> The basic imperative faced by humankind is the need to develop a worldwide ethical awareness of our mutual interdependence and a willingness to modify time-hardened attitudes that prevent such a consensus.
>
> We face a common challenge to develop scientific education on a global scale and an appreciation for critical intelligence and reason as a way to solve human problems and enhance human welfare.
>
> It is necessary to create on a global scale new democratic and pluralistic institutions that protect the rights and freedoms of all people.
>
> A new global economic system based on economic cooperation and international solidarity needs to emerge.
>
> We need to firmly defend the ideals of political democracy on a worldwide basis and to encourage the further extensions of democracy.
>
> We urgently need to enlarge our common ground. We should encourage the intermingling of peoples in every way we can.
>
> We urge the establishment of an international environmental monitoring agency and recommend the development of appropriate standards for the disposal of industrial waste and the control of toxic emissions.
>
> We have a clear duty to future generations to curtail excessive population growth, to maintain a healthy environment, and to preserve the earth's precious resources.[31]

The same year the Declaration of Interdependence was framed, our global interdependence became a subject of international political action. It was in 1988 when the UN Environment Program and the World Meteoro-

A World without Walls 423

logical Office jointly established the Intergovernmental Panel on Climate Change, which has monitored the changes taking place and has provided the scientific evidence for not only climate change itself but also the significance of human activity in generating these changes. And in 1994, Donald Worster proposed the principle of interdependency with respect to ecology. That principle says, "No organism or species of organism has any chance of surviving without the aid of others."[32] What the Declaration of Interdependence had already done was make clear that this applied to human beings, as it did to all other species.

It is not unreasonable to claim that the humanist movement has played a significant, if unacknowledged, role in providing leadership in understanding the grim new realities humanity faces. It is not that these developments arose directly from a humanist initiative; that is not what is being claimed. What is being claimed is that humanist thinking has been in harmony with the need of the times and has not displayed anthropocentric thinking, let alone the human-at-the-center-of-the-universe hubris it is often accused of displaying. Five years after the Declaration of Interdependence, a remarkably similar document was issued by the dissident Catholic theologian Hans Küng and endorsed by the Parliament of World Religions in Chicago in 1993. Küng had been inspired by the First Colloquium on Religion, held by UNESCO in Paris in 1989. He went on to write *Global Responsibility: In Search of a New World Ethic*, for which he was much praised. Nowhere was the priority of the Declaration of Interdependence acknowledged.

In the end, a passionate concern for, and record of work on behalf of, the environment that sustains us is a quintessentially humanist venture. The 1987 World Commission on Environment and Development Report, chaired by the former Norwegian prime minister Gro Harlem Brundtland, outlined three main categories. As well as the protection of resources and the combating of pollution, the Brundtland report added the ideas of equity with respect to the equal access to resources, and futurity (ensuring the sustainable use of those resources). Twenty-first-century humanists can undertake work in whichever of these areas they find their skills most useful.

H. G. WELLS AND THE FEDERATION OF HUMANITY

If humanists have argued for the interdependence *between* species, so have they also argued for our interdependence *as* a species. Yet again, we can go back to H. G. Wells as a good starting point. It took World War I to bring the internationalist out in Wells. Between the Treaty of Versailles and Hiroshima he became ever more concerned about our tendency to think in parochial ways. His first major foray into this area was his classic single-volume work, *The Outline of History* (1920), which ended with his vision of the federation of humanity. The problems he thought beset the world of 1920 have an extraordinarily contemporary feel to them. Wells listed five main trends and problems: the growing destructiveness of the technology of war; the "fusion of the world's economic affairs into one system"; planetary health needs in the wake of growing mobility of peoples; the growing disparity in the labor conditions of the educated and the uneducated; and the growing need for regulation of air travel.[33]

In the face of these planetary problems, Wells looked to a world where things were handled on a planetary scale. He listed what he thought would be the broad fundamentals of the future world state. The first feature he predicted was a common world belief. "This will not be Christianity nor Islam nor Buddhism nor any such specialized form of religion, but religion itself pure and undefiled; the Eightfold Way, the Kingdom of Heaven, brotherhood, creative service, and self-forgetfulness."[34] Wells's common world belief anticipates what John Dewey had in mind with his idea of a common faith. Upon this foundation would be an attitude toward education that would be a lifetime quest for everybody on earth. He hoped for fully 10 percent of the entire population of the world being employed in education. Following from this it was a relatively small step to look forward to world disarmament; incomparably superior resources given to scientific research; a planetary-wide circulation of free literature, criticism, and discussion (an idea he later expanded in *World Brain*, his groping toward the idea of the Internet); a democratic, responsive world political organization; rational exploitation of the world's resources with state and private enterprise working together. And finally, Wells called for reform of electoral methods and currency reform.

Humanists have often been accused of speaking arrogantly about harnessing the forces of nature in order that they should be exploited all the more effectively. This has never been true of humanists as a whole, and it certainly wasn't true of Wells, who had a greater appreciation for ecological thought than was customary at the time. "There will still be mountains and the sea, there will be jungles and great forests, *cared for indeed and treasured and protected*."[35] Wells was also aware of the fear that a federation of humanity would end up producing a dull, homogeneous humanity, with all the local color washed out. He deprecated the idea that his future state will mean the imprisonment of humanity in sterile, institutional orderliness. Communities, he wrote, "all to one pattern, like boxes of toy soldiers, are things of the past rather than the future."[36] Returning to the theme at a speech at the Sorbonne in 1927, Wells anticipated the problem of what we now call *globalization*.

> The master problem before us all, before our race, is how to achieve this world economic unity, how to produce a system of world controls with as little blind experiment as possible, without the sacrifice of countless millions of whole generations, in the throes of this inevitable reconstruction.[37]

Thirteen years later, in conditions altogether less favorable, Wells returned to the theme of world peace as part of the discussion about the war aims that Britain should announce as part of its struggle against Nazi Germany. Coming out during the Phoney War, Wells's plans generated a lot of interest. Remembering how badly the whole war-aims debate had been handled between 1914 and 1918, he urged that rather than specifying in advance what national boundaries would change and what penalties would be enforced, there should be a free and general discussion of the principles the Allies were defending. In that spirit, Wells then proposed the ten-point Declaration of Rights. Beginning with the subsistence rights of nourishment, shelter, and medical care, he went on to outline rights to a measure of education, the possession of property, and a series of negative rights (for example, freedom from unreasonable state coercion).[38] Just as interesting as the content of the declaration, was the *process* it went through, something Wells made a point of making transparent. To his enormous credit, he began the book with an early version and then proceeded to survey the various corrections, amendments, objections, and alternatives that the ensuing discussion threw up. In this way, the reader could see not just a statement of aims that could stand as a reason why Nazism was being fought but an illustration of a process of public engagement with an issue of importance. He also included, in full, other attempts at a similar document and discussed their merits openly. He then set off, a man in his midseventies, for a speaking tour of the United States to promote the declaration. Along the way he sought the opinion of world leaders, many of whom he had already met and befriended. Franklin Delano Roosevelt and Gandhi, among others, responded to Wells and commented on the document. David Smith, Wells's most thorough biographer, records the impact the declaration had on the Atlantic Charter and on Roosevelt's Four Freedoms.[39] Wells continued to revise it in later publications, up to 1944.[40]

In twenty-first-century language, Wells was outlining what is now called *planetary humanism*. It has become customary to dismiss humanists who are bold enough to offer visions such as this as dreamers and utopians. But among mystical traditions, much less plausible or attractive offerings are regularly hailed as visionary and inspiring forecasts of the future. H. G. Wells was a utopian in the best sense of the word. Secular societies are no less in need than religious ones of hopeful projections of a future vastly better organized and more fulfilled than our own. But supernaturalist religions confuse utopia with pie in the sky when they offer the transcendental temptation—what Marx so perceptively called the *opium of the people*. A secular utopia doesn't have this luxury. A secular utopia is always tempered by the recognition that humans will have to build it themselves. Wells recognized this in his famous statement, written in the very last paragraphs of *The Outline of History* that human history "becomes more and more a race between education and catastrophe."[41] This remains as true now as it was then.

JULIAN HUXLEY, BOYD ORR, AND THE UNITED NATIONS PROGRAMS

Wells provided the inspiration for a whole generation of thinkers, politicians, and activists. Their opportunity to create the sort of world he had written about came after the defeat of Hitler. The attempts to create a framework for international cooperation after World War I had died stillborn, but now, at the end of World War II, people had another chance. Lessons had been learned about the League of Nations: why it had failed and what needed to be done to rectify it. And there was no shortage of people who were committed to making a better job of this second chance.

One of them was Julian Huxley. There have been plenty of opportunities in this book to be critical of Huxley's whimsical blend of mysticism and humanism, and most of them have been taken up. But here, at last, we can warmly admire something he did. Julian Huxley's work after the war for the United Nations Educational, Scientific and Cultural Organization (UNESCO) was foundational for that body. Indeed, he was instrumental in adding the *scientific* to what was originally an organization devoted solely to cultural cooperation.[42] After a long and varied career in a range of educational, scientific, and cultural positions, and with an illustrious surname, Huxley was ideally suited to leading this arm of the United Nations. Before the war, he had served as president of the International Institute for Intellectual Cooperation (IIIC), the League of Nations' predecessor to UNESCO. He served as secretary to UNESCO during its formative phase and, after November 1946, as its inaugural director-general. In his two-year stint, Huxley worked frenetically to build up the organization, to persuade UN nations to take an interest in UNESCO activities, and to provide the fledgling body with a mission.

One of his first duties was to write a pamphlet outlining its philosophy. In *UNESCO: Its Purpose and Its Philosophy*, Huxley spoke of promoting cultural exchanges, fostering educational development in underdeveloped countries, and making serious efforts toward the preservation of natural resources and habitats. And, of course, UNESCO could not associate itself with any of the competing religious creeds or philosophies. So far so good, but then Huxley added that the underlying philosophy of UNESCO should be Scientific Humanism, based as it is on undisputed facts of science with respect to evolution and the need for progress. Unsurprisingly, this attracted some opposition, mainly from religiously oriented UNESCO supporters. The pamphlet still went out, but it was tagged as Huxley's personal view rather than that of UNESCO as a body. To his credit, Huxley admitted in his autobiography that his critics were right.[43] Scientific Humanism, especially when graced in capitals, cannot legitimately claim to be the default philosophy. It is true that UNESCO's aims are essentially humanistic, but there is a big difference between something being humanistic and it officially espousing Scientific Humanism. Danger lurks in the uppercase.

All this said, UNESCO's program was, and remains, inescapably humanistic. It was set down at the inaugural General Conference in Paris at the end of 1946. Its aims included: fostering education, especially in underdeveloped nations; cultural exchanges around the world in order to foster understanding of our common humanity; and scientific cooperation, especially with respect to the preservation of resources and the maintenance of a stable population. And a project Huxley took particular interest in was a world history that stressed common threads of human development rather than endless succession of kings and courtiers. The influence of Wells's *The Outline of History* is apparent here. Admirable though the project may have been, it is doubtful this mammoth thirteen-volume set has ever been read in its entirety.

Huxley continued to make a positive contribution after formally stepping down as UNESCO director-general. He traveled continuously, advising governments on establishing national parks and other conservation programs, or else helping assess educational facilities with a view to having the best of them upgraded to university status. Many of the universities in developing countries, and many of the now world-famous national parks, owe their existence at least in part to Julian Huxley.

A contemporary of Julian Huxley was John Boyd Orr (1880–1971), who, after a long career as director of the Rowett Institute in Aberdeen, Scotland, became the first director of the Food and Agriculture Organization (FAO). The Rowett Institute was a pioneering body in the study of nutrition, animal husbandry, and other matters relating to improving agricultural productivity. Boyd Orr had overseen the foundation and growth of the institute to a world-class establishment and was a natural choice for the FAO. He was a passionate man, totally committed to eliminating hunger and malnutrition and not afraid to tell people getting in his way what he thought of them. His autobiography is punctuated with his response—always the same—to dissembling politicians or bureaucrats: "At this stage I'm afraid I lost my temper...." Boyd Orr got things done, even if it meant offering some brisk encouragement along the way. His indefatigable energy in the first years of the FAO was widely credited with helping cope with the chronic food shortages the whole world was facing in the two years after the war's end. It was for this work he was awarded the Nobel Peace Prize in 1949. He donated most of his Nobel Prize money to organizations devoted to world government.

THE INTERNATIONAL HUMANIST AND ETHICAL UNION

As well as their work with United Nations agencies, Huxley and Boyd Orr devoted time to a more specifically humanist international network organization. Soon after the war in Europe finished, freethinkers of various persuasions started looking at an ambitious plan to cooperate internationally and export the humanist message further afield. There had at one stage been two international organizations representing different strands of humanist opinion: the World Union of Freethinkers (WUF), founded in 1880, and the International Ethical Union (IEU), founded in 1896 but now dormant.

In 1946, a small delegation of British humanists traveled to the Netherlands at the invitation of the recently reformed Dutch Freethinkers. Their intention was to revive the World Union of Freethinkers (WUF), which had not met since 1938. As a result of their work, the WUF convened in Rome in 1949. Three main topics for discussion were education, the Vatican, and humanism. To a lot of delegates' surprise, it was the third issue that generated the most heat. The core of the disagreement revolved around the merits of the word *humanism* and the benefits it was thought to have which older words like *rationalist* and *freethinker* lacked. As already commented on, this is one of those arguments that matters a great deal to people whose lives have been spent within a movement but that seems quite pointless to those outside it. The argument raised once again the old line of division within free thought between the *abolitionists*, who see the prime task of free thought to liberate people through the criticism of the religious dogmas that shackle them, and *substitutionists*, who place less emphasis on criticism, preferring to compete with religions by providing similar ranges of services and activities.[44] It's not that abolitionists are uninterested in being positive, or that substitutionists are uninterested in the criticism of religion. The differences are ones of perception, priority, and personality, rather than differences of substance. Sadly, however, that doesn't make them any less real.

One of the delegates to the Rome Congress was Charles Bradlaugh Bonner (1890–1966, Charles Bradlaugh's grandson). As is evident from his account of the final resolution, Bradlaugh Bonner was suspicious of what he saw as the pussyfooting of the humanists:

The congress finally voted a resolution expressing their approval of the social aims of the humanists, which had (though the humanists seemed unaware of it) been advocated in congress after congress and put into practice by many supporters of militant free thought: at the same time the congress asked the humanists not to overlook the need for a more active and sustained effort against the great religious organizations than ever before if the highest aims of humanism were to be subserved.[45]

Bradlaugh Bonner was gently skeptical about humanism when compared to the anti-clericals from Spain, France and Italy. Fresh from the struggle against the pro-fascist church in their respective countries, the anti-clericals were in no mood to talk of the religion of humanism. What made things even more difficult was the staunch pro-communism of many of the WUF anti-clericals. Coming away from the 1949 WUF congress, it was clear to most humanists that it would be easier, in the long run, to found a new humanist international. This came to fruition in 1952 when representatives of organizations from the Netherlands, Britain, the United States, Belgium, India and Austria came together to found the International Humanist & Ethical Union. The driving force behind the creation of IHEU was Jaap van Praag, the Netherlands' most prominent twentieth-century humanist. Even without the WUF it was not all plain sailing. It took fourteen hours of debate to agree on the organization's title. The European delegates generally preferred to speak of humanism, which the Americans distrusted on account of its links with rationalism and pragmatism.[46] Being clear in his own mind what was needed, Van Praag was able to navigate difficult waters. "Our duty is to develop our national movements and to gather the scattered sparks of humanism all over the world." He added, perhaps with the WUF in mind: "We must first have a hand before making a fist."[47]

The congress ended with a statement of principles that became known as the Amsterdam Declaration. It consisted in five points:

- Humanism is democratic, aiming at the fullest possible development of every human being;
- Humanism seeks to use science creatively;
- Humanism is ethical, affirming the right of everyone to the greatest possible freedom compatible with the rights of others;
- Humanism insists that personal liberty needs to be balanced with social responsibility;

- Humanism is "a way of life, aiming at the maximum possible fulfillment, through the cultivation of ethical and creative living."[48]

The Amsterdam declaration was superseded at one stage by a longer, ten-point program outlined in Paris in 1966. But at the time of its half-century congress, held once again in Amsterdam, the IHEU returned to a revised version of the original declaration, now grown to seven points. The current Amsterdam Declaration now begins with the point, suitably expanded, about humanism being ethical, which originally sat third in the list. The second point about the creative use of science has also changed a bit, focusing now on the process of reason and its relations with science. Since the collapse of Communism, the need to make a specific commitment to democracy has been less crucial, so the point about humanism being democratic has been relegated to third place.[49] The fourth point on liberty balancing with social responsibility remaining largely unchanged. The two new points, coming in fifth and sixth, are as follows:

(5) Humanism is a response to the widespread demand for an alternative to dogmatic religion; and
(6) Humanism values artistic creativity and imagination and recognizes the transforming power of art.

The seventh point remains fundamentally the same as the original fifth point, only now having adopted the term *lifestance*.[50] The addition of point six is a standard piece of cultural humanism of the bildung tradition. More controversial is the fifth point, which reflects the growing recognition that sanguine confidence that the nastier elements of religion will eventually fade away is no longer tenable. This was one of the less helpful legacies of European humanism, which has (or thinks it has) long since defanged the uglier sides of religion and can safely move on. In the post-9/11 world, one can no longer simply assume the dangerous excesses of religion will simply wither away. As has been commented upon already, this sanguine attitude has been one of twentieth-century humanism's less inspired features.

The IHEU's main problem has always been money. Impecunious humanists around the world may or may not pay their dues, so the reliable flow of funding cannot be relied upon. Very few countries subsidize humanist organizations, absolve them of taxes or rates, or provide them the other privileges that churches around the world take for granted. It's not the intention here to offer any sort of history of the IHEU beyond noting its existence and commenting on the nature of its humanism.[51] But within the limitations of its modest budget, the IHEU has worked admirably in two areas: providing an umbrella for humanists around the world to meet and draw strength from one another's experiences; and promoting among world leaders and NGOs a civilized, multifaceted planetary humanism.

BERTRAND RUSSELL AND THE PERIL OF MAN

Julian Huxley, Boyd Orr, and others worked as technocrats to help put together the first strands of global governance. The IHEU has sought to influence decision-making bodies with an informed humanist perspective. Bertrand Russell's role was more of the international gadfly, critic, and prophet of world government. His views on world government, and indeed on world politics and foreign policy in general, have not received a great deal of support, even from his admirers.[52] With some justification, Russell has been criticized for the varying means he recommended world government could be brought about. In years between the end of World War II and the Soviet Union acquiring nuclear weapons in 1949, he expressed support for a single hyperpower managing the world by virtue of unassailable military power. Events since his death will have disabused most people of the wisdom of that idea. And, most scandalously of all, at the height of the Cold War Russell even supported a preemptive nuclear strike against the Soviet Union, in the interests of preserving hyperpower status for the United States. From the end of the 1950s, however, he had settled on the United Nations or some similar body as the best vehicle to exercise planetary authority. But, having lived through the League of Nations, Russell knew full well that that the world authority would need sole use of military options for its power to be meaningful.

In the end, Russell's thoughts on world government are less important than his work as visionary for world peace. And of that work, the single most outstanding episode was his collaboration with Albert Einstein to wake people from their complacent slumbers as to the imminent danger the planet faced from nuclear war. At the end of 1954, Russell returned to public life with a radio broadcast titled "Man's Peril," which spelled out graphically what was at stake in the event of a nuclear war. "Man's Peril" deserves to be thought of as one of the classics of twentieth-century humanism. He began his broadcast with the stark opening:

> I am speaking on this occasion not as a Briton, not as a European, not as a member of a Western democracy, but as a human being, a member of the species Man, whose continued existence is in doubt.[53]

Russell then outlined the nature of the problem, emphasizing that the ill-effects of a nuclear exchange would befall everyone equally, even the animals, "whom no one can accuse of Communism or anti-Communism."[54] He ended the broadcast with perhaps the most concentrated humanist declaration ever made: "Remember your humanity, and forget the rest."[55] In the first half of 1955, he expanded "Man's Peril" and sent it to Albert Einstein in America, asking him to endorse it as part of a manifesto for world peace. Einstein signed it enthusiastically, doing so only two days before he died, making his signature his last public act. It soon became known as the *Russell-Einstein Manifesto* and was endorsed by a large number of very prominent scientists.

Later in that decade, Russell moved on to more radical forms of protest against the nuclear danger. He was instrumental in founding the Campaign for Nuclear Disarmament, the Committee of 100, and the Bertrand Russell Peace Foundation, each more radical than those before. It was during his association with the Committee of 100 that Russell took part in the huge sit-down protest in Trafalgar Square in August 1961. For the second time in his life, he was arrested and went to prison, if only for a week this time (the first time was during World War I as a pacifist).

The *Russell-Einstein Manifesto* helped create a momentum for other citizens to make some contribution toward world peace. A generation of protestors counted their memory of Russell's actions between 1955 and 1961 as their original inspiration. One person inspired by these events was Cyrus Eaton (1883–1979), a wealthy Canadian-born industrialist, who in 1957 offered to fund a series of high-profile peace conferences. These were called the "Pugwash Conferences," after Eaton's hometown in Nova Scotia, where the first conference was held. At a time when these conferences were denounced in hysterical tones as Communist fronts, the IHEU made a point of endorsing Eaton's work at their second congress, also held in 1957.

The Pugwash Conferences broke new ground in that, for the first time, scientists from both sides of the Iron Curtain were able to speak about peace in the same room. Eaton was also instrumental in persuading Khrushchev to visit the United States and to extend an invitation to Eisenhower to visit the Soviet Union. Eisenhower's visit never happened, but that was not for lack of effort on Eaton's part. Eaton was an active humanist and, like Corliss Lamont, a left-leaning capitalist. Pugwash has been widely credited with helping to create the atmosphere in which the partial Test-Ban Treaty of 1964 was signed. In 1995, the Pugwash Conferences, along with nuclear physicist Joseph Rotblat (1908–2005), were awarded the Nobel Peace Prize for their efforts toward world peace.

Russell's reputation has taken more than the usual posthumous dive. Even his friends recognize his naiveté as a political thinker. Among his growing cohort of detractors, his work is seen variously as useless, self-defeating, unfocused, or simply foolish. But none of his critics could match Russell's practical achievement of alerting millions of people to the extent of the threat nuclear war posed and inspiring many thousands to campaign for peace. Russell may never have been that keen on the idea of humanism, but he was still one of the twentieth century's greatest humanists.

JOHN RAWLS AND THE LAW OF PEOPLES

Moving from ecohumanism to varying thoughts on planetary government and international cooperation, we need now consider the more recent philosophical underpinning of planetary humanism. Philosophers have long mused on the basis for world peace. In an essay from 1795, Immanuel Kant expressed his thought that for world peace to be a possibility monarchy would need to be replaced by republicanism, that no nationality should govern any other nationality, and that the world should disarm. World peace would be administered by a general federation of nations, and eventually a planetary republic would govern on behalf of all people. And the foundation for all this would be a solid body of international law.[56] As Europe was on the threshold of Romanticism and nationalism, this counsel was consigned to the draw marked "utopia."

More than two centuries have passed since Kant first articulated the conditions needed for all peoples to live together harmoniously. Since then, many able and dedicated men and women have committed themselves to some aspect of that vision: thinkers like Wells and Russell, men of affairs like Boyd Orr, Julian Huxley, and Cyrus Eaton. The most recent significant contributor to the ideal of planetary humanism was the American philosopher John Rawls (1921–2002). Widely regarded as the most prominent political philosopher of the second half of the twentieth century, Rawls was born in Maryland to a prosperous, socially active, and liberal family. He originally planned to enter the ministry, but his experiences during World War II led him to change his mind. Rawls enrolled at Princeton in 1946 and was awarded a doctorate in 1950. He taught there and at Oxford, Cornell, and MIT before moving to Harvard in 1962, where he stayed until his retirement.

Rawls's career was devoted to the very Kantian project of establishing how to arrange fair terms of cooperation between rational citizens who hold different political, philosophical, and religious worldviews. In doing this, he restated and revitalized liberal philosophy in a way not achieved since John Stuart Mill. Rawls's classic was *A Theory of Justice* (1971), which has been translated into twenty-seven languages and has become a bestseller, despite being neither an easy nor an elegant read. Not since *Das Kapital* has a work of political theory been so influential among politicians and activists; *A Theory of Justice* was a significant influence among prodemocracy protesters at Tiananmen Square in China in 1989. Rawls went on to develop his ideas in *Political Liberalism* (1993) and *The Laws of Peoples* (1999), and a revised edition of *A Theory of Justice* appeared in 1999.

The work that matters most for our purposes is *The Law of Peoples*, which extended the arguments in the earlier books to a transnational setting, though without using exactly the same justifications. Rawls never spoke of *planetary humanism*, preferring his term, *political liberalism*. Indeed, he would almost certainly object to this pairing, being anxious to distinguish political liberalism from any sort of comprehensive doctrine, even liberalism itself. Whether this distinction is valid, or even possible, has dominated much of the debate about Rawls's work. I do not want to enter this fractious debate beyond claiming that planetary humanism is not an unreasonable match for political liberalism.

Rawls spoke of a realistic utopia, or the condition where imagining a world run according to the Law of Peoples is possible. There is no element of the coercion that John Gray has claimed lies at the heart of utopian thinking. It is merely something that is possible. And if it is possible, and good, it is not unreasonable to work for it. Like Wells and Russell, Rawls placed great value in developing planetary institutions, though unlike Russell, he was less sanguine about world government, agreeing with Kant that world government would most likely involve misrule and corruption. Again, without using the phrase, Rawls was happier with notions of global governance than with world government. Global governance is the messier reality of nation-states, the United Nations, international treaties like the Kyoto Treaty, major multinational corporations, international governmental organizations (IGOs), and nongovernmental organizations (NGOs) all having some input in preserving the planet for the future. Global governance doesn't presuppose the end of the nation-state, nor does it seek to usurp all power into the hands of a tiny elite that decides what is good for the rest of us. World government would be more likely to give rise to some form of hegemonic globalism than the looser process of global governance. Global governance is the product not of globalism, in the negative sense of being a coercive ideology, but of the barely controlled process of transformation given the collective name of *globalization*.[57]

Rawls constructed the means by which liberal and democratic societies can work with their nondemocratic neighbors in a state of mutual respect on the world stage. Contrary to the criticisms of John Gray and others, Rawls does not require all societies to become liberal and democratic and is not simply calling for *Pax Americana*. He posited an alliance of, as he called them, *well-ordered peoples* who can agree to disagree on their internal arrangements but can cooperate on the world stage. The dangers come from outlaw states and from unstable dictatorships. He even revisited the "just war" doctrine and established the legitimate criteria for intervention. Another criticism from within the humanist tradition has drawn attention to Rawls's preference to speak of peoples, rather than scaling down the focus so that individual people come into view. Peter Singer, for instance, has charged Rawls with indifference to the fate of actually poor individuals, because of his preference for longer-term improvements in the standards of the society in which those individuals live.[58] This criticism seems unfair because Rawls is not indifferent to the existence of inequality at an individual level. It is just that he sees it as not something a law of peoples, properly understood, can address. Straight after acknowledging the indifference to transnational inequality that Singer referred to, Rawls said: "The cosmopolitan view, on the other hand, is not indifferent. It is concerned with the well-being of individuals and hence with whether the well-being of the globally worst-off person can be improved."[59]

Rawls devoted relatively little time to outlining what the principles of the Law of Peoples actually are, being content to itemize once more the "familiar and traditional principles of justice among free and democratic peoples." He listed eight items:

(1) Peoples are free and independent, and their freedom and independence are to be respected by other peoples.
(2) Peoples are to observe treaties and undertakings.
(3) Peoples are equal and are parties to the agreements that bind them.
(4) Peoples are to observe a duty of nonintervention.
(5) Peoples have the right of self-defense but no right to instigate war for reasons other than self-defense.
(6) Peoples are to honor human rights.
(7) Peoples are to observe certain specified restrictions in the conduct of war.
(8) Peoples have a duty to assist other peoples living under unfavorable conditions that prevent their having a just or decent political and social regime.[60]

The last of these points, Rawls acknowledged, is the most controversial, but one could look to Amartya Sen here for an extended treatment of this point, in works like *Development as Freedom*. It does not, of course, mean a blanket authorization for military exercises in "regime change." And the previous four chapters should be enough to repel the charge that Rawls's Law of Peoples is some sort of homogenizing Western narrative.

PLANETARY HUMANISM AND THE TWENTY-FIRST CENTURY

We have followed the careers of all sorts of hyphenated humanisms: *scientific*, *evolutionary*, *religious*, and *secular*, to name only the most significant of them. And as we have seen through the course of this book, none of them has been free from problems, and none has been universally accepted. It may well be, in the wake of this discussion, that, of all the prefixes given to humanism over the past century, *planetary* will be the most useful. Planetary humanism places us not at some evolutionary apex nor in a Eurocentric bubble but fairly and squarely on our planet, our pale blue dot, which astronauts say is indescribably beautiful when seen from space. Its core insight is that no major problems can be solved on anything less than a planetary scale. Climate change, preservation of resources like water, the maintenance of clean air, population pressure, technological change, globalization—these are all planetwide problems that cannot be solved by this or that legislature working in isolation. Any proper understanding of planetwide interdependence means that *Homo sapiens* isn't the only species to be taken into account. All species on the planet are inextricably interwoven in complex webs of interdependence. We are only beginning to grasp the significance of this.

These core insights have been expressed in a variety of intellectual milieu. Christian progressives have spoken of the greening of Christianity. The Universist movement deriving from several sources has developed recently. And of course the green movement has given voice to elements of these concerns, although sometimes with a Romantic and antiscience tinge that has confused the issue. Moving further along that spectrum, the New Age movement and Gaia enthusiasts have also been active. Planetary humanism is the humanist response to this commonly felt need of a planetary response to planetwide problems. It need not be set up *against* these other expressions of planetary concern or consciousness, it can run harmoniously alongside them. Planetary humanism is another way of speaking, as Tzvetan Todorov did, of the universality of the you.

One of the first things a comprehensive account of planetary humanism needs is some set of principles as to what constitutes human well-being. We saw John Rawls list what he saw as the "traditional principles of justice among free and democratic peoples," but the British humanist philosopher Ted Honderich has gone one step further. He has articulated what he calls the *principle of humanity*, which is understood in terms of the extension of six fundamental human goods. These human goods are:

- *subsistence*, a reasonable life expectancy and health;
- *material goods*, a home, food, shelter, medical care sufficient to sustain and extend life's possibilities;
- *freedom*, particularly political and social freedom;

- *respect and self-respect*, from one's neighbors and peers;
- *human relationships*, both personal and on a wider level that sustain a sense of belonging;
- *culture*, the awarenesses of an education and cultural understanding.[61]

Actions that preserve and extend these goods are consistent with the principle of humanity, and those that don't, aren't. He sees the principle as the property of the political left, but it may well be that this unduly narrows the universal scope of this principle. In fact, Honderich's principle of humanity stands in the tradition of John Stuart Mill's religion of humanity, which he articulated in the 1850s. In the wake of a discredited supernaturalism, Mill argued, the "sense of a unity with mankind, and a deep feeling for the general good, may be cultivated into a sentiment and a principle capable of fulfilling every important function of religion and itself justly entitled to the name."[62] Whether or not we accord the principle of a deep sense of commitment to humanity a religion is a question we can leave specialists to ponder. My inclination would be not to. But what we know in the twenty-first century, and which we knew imperfectly at best in the nineteenth century, is that any commitment to a principle of humanity involves a sense of commitment no less deep to the environment that sustains the species, and to all the others species we share it with.

In few times in history has the need for some sort of principle of humanity been as apparent as it is in our globalized world. There is no need to essay, once again, the contracting of the planet by instant communication and mass travel that is a feature of the early twenty-first century. But it is worthwhile to note the unprecedented development in the clarity, range, and depth of international law since the end of World War II. What governments do within their own borders was once thought outside the legitimate scope of citizens of another country, unless it threatened regional stability in some way, or unless some other political advantage could be had by intervention. We now know that this luxury of unfettered sovereignty is no longer practicable.

Contemporary international law began with the Atlantic Charter, which was signed by the Allied powers on August 14, 1941, during the darkest months of the war against Hitler. As noted earlier, the thoughts of H. G. Wells were influential in the wording of the charter, which committed the signatories to a few key principles: an end to territorial aggrandizement or changes; respect for self-government; social security; peace and freedom from fear or want; freedom of the high seas; and restraints on the use of force.[63] Once the war was won, it was a natural transition that these principles play a significant role in the foundation of the United Nations. Called "the Magna Carta for all humanity," the Universal Declaration of Human Rights is the most significant humanist vision ever created. After two years deliberation, the Declaration was adopted by the United Nations on December 10, 1948, since designated as Human Rights Day.

The declaration has thirty articles. Articles 1–19 deal with individual liberties, articles 20–26 deal with issues of social and economic equality, and the last four articles are about rights associated with community. One of the people responsible for drawing up the declaration was the Nobel Peace Prize winner and human rights campaigner René Cassin (1887–1976), who took inspiration from the battle cry of the French Revolution and identified the declaration's four main pillars as "dignity, liberty, equality, and brotherhood." Its successful passage through the United Nations owed a great deal to the skill and dedication of Eleanor Roosevelt (1884–1962). It is not a binding document but was intended to serve as a common vision of what all peoples of the earth should come to enjoy. And this common vision has come to take an ever more central place in the lives of all human beings. Globalization and the growth of technology have meant that human rights abuses, though just as widespread, are at least much more difficult to hide than they used to be.

The unprecedented growth in international law and its associated global governance does not imply that planetary humanism is irrevocably tied to a triumphalist globalism. Seeing value in increased opportunities for dialogue between peoples, brought about in no small part by the breaking down of political barriers, does not require one to accept the globalist mantras of free trade, corporate gigantism, or exploitative employment practices. Many would go further and say that a degree of skepticism toward globalism is an important component of planetary humanism, in the interests of the growing abyss between the rich and poor.[64]

The most significant recent expression of a strictly nonglobalist planetary humanism has been the *Humanist Manifesto 2000*. Building on earlier statements of humanism, including the Declaration of Interdependence, *Humanist Manifesto 2000* outlined the central importance of understanding that planetary problems can only be solved at a planetary level and then went on to offer a practical charter for the realization of that vision. As part of outlining a new global agenda, the manifesto called for:

- backing the United Nations as the principal coercive agency of the world;
- recognizing overpopulation as one of the most fundamental causes of world distress;
- support for the existing international conventions regarding human rights;
- fighting tax avoidance among the largest multinational corporations;
- developing a suitably transnational system of international law; and
- greater effort to raise awareness of, and to combat, environmental deterioration.

In order to put this agenda into effect, the *Humanist Manifesto 2000* advocated:

- an effective global governance based on popular elections;
- a workable international security system;
- increasing the powers of the World Court;
- creating an effective planetary environment–monitoring body;
- planning an international system of taxation for the sole purpose of assisting the underdeveloped nations;
- developing global institutions to monitor and regulate the behavior of multinational corporations; and
- keeping alive the free market of ideas.[65]

Manifestoes such as this are unpopular among some sections of the humanist movement, as they are seen as rhetorical declarations signifying nothing. On the surface, it's a valid criticism, but it seems to ignore the value of presenting an outline of what humanism stands *for*, as opposed to what it stands *against*. It's easy to find fault from the margins, less so to offer a vision for people. And the *Humanist Manifesto 2000* was careful to add all the usual caveats about offering itself simply as a contribution to constructive dialogue.[66] Even more important is that there is now a tradition of manifestoes being periodically replaced and revised. And here lies the true significance of the manifestoes: humanist conclusions at any one time are less important than the intellectual restlessness that provokes them in the first place. When we talk of humanism as first and foremost an attitude of inquiry, this is what we mean.

The recent work of the American former diplomat Carlton Coon has reworked some of the priorities of the *Humanist Manifesto 2000*. Coon makes the point that the nation-state represents a transitional stage in our development. "It is but a stepping-stone from an ethic based on culture to an ethic [that] embraces a global community."[67] This is the goal to work for, but it rests on a simple statement of fact: nation-states have considerably less autonomy than they had sixty years ago. And more than anywhere else, it is here where we can see the most dramatic shift in thought over the last two centuries that emerging from the shadow of Hegel has required. No planetary humanist, Hegel was uncompromising in his avowal of the nation-state as "the absolute power on earth."[68] But where earlier generations of humanist internationalists spoke of world government, Coon speaks of global governance, the differences between which we outlined above. World government has never been able to offer convincing evidence that it would not end up as the most powerful hegemonic system yet devised by virtue of its planetary reach. Global governance, by contrast, is not some utopian dream of the future: it is the reality we have now. Global governance is shorthand for the myriad of multinational treaties and protocols, the many important transnational agencies, the United Nations, the NGOs. All these are important elements in the transnational reality of managing our planet. The clear need is for more decisions to be made at a global level and for better coordination between the various agencies. This is the reality of global governance.

None of the solutions to our current problems are attainable at the level of the nation-state. The changes being brought about by globalization are beyond the power of any one country to turn back. And neither do international boundaries act as a barrier to filthy air or polluted water. Human beings can be cloned wherever the technology exists. So, planetary problems require planetary solutions. And planetary solutions are realistic only once what Coon calls "the big tent of global humanism" can give shelter to everyone.[69] Coon is not, of course, insisting that everyone should become humanists in order that the world be saved. The subtitle of his book on this subject is "Beyond 'Us' versus 'Them.'" But his vision is of a future world order that is democratic, humane, secular, and progressive. These ideals are brought about by focusing on the core principles of diversity and human rights.

The most significant practical example of planetary humanism came in the form of the Millennium Development Goals (MDGs), announced by the then United Nations secretary general, Kofi Annan, on September 8, 2000. The Millennium Development Goals are an ambitious program for the eradication of poverty, which all 191 member-nations of the United Nations have agreed to ratify by 2015. The goals are:

(1) Eradicate extreme poverty and hunger.
(2) Achieve universal primary education.
(3) Promote gender equality and empower women.
(4) Reduce child mortality.
(5) Improve maternal health.
(6) Combat HIV/AIDS, malaria, and other diseases.
(7) Ensure environmental sustainability.
(8) Develop a global partnership for development.

These goals are not simply a set of fine words, although they could easily end up as little more than that if the will to implement them falters. The United Nations has been devoting as many resources as it has available to bringing about these goals. It is coordinating the work on inter- and non-governmental organizations around the world to bring these goals to fruition. Needless to say, many of the governments that have signed their assent to these goals are less than conspicuous in realizing them. Mike Moore, former head of the World Trade Organization, has noted how modest the cost of implementation the MDGs would be, if the will to implement existed.[70] Each of these goals could be achieved at about the same cost of the subsidies the European Community provides each year to insulate their farmers from cheap imports.

Five years after setting the MDGs out, the United Nations decided, very wisely, to come together and evaluate what progress was being made. The news at World Summit, held in New York in September 2005, was not good. With only ten years left to go to implement the goals, it was apparent that a massive amount of work remained to be done. As if to remind people of the continuing urgency of the goals, the United Nations issued a report card of progress. It noted that as of 2005, someone died of starvation every 3.6 seconds (recall goal 1); 115 million children received no education of any sort (goal 2); two thirds of the world's illiterate were women (goal 3); four million babies died each year before they were a month old (goal 4); a woman died in pregnancy or childbirth every minute (goal 5); over three million people—500,000 of which were children—died of AIDS in 2004 alone (goal 6); 940,000 square kilometers of forest were destroyed in the 1990s alone (goal

7); and 61 percent of aid from the G8 nations never reach the target recipients, being chewed up in goods and services from domestic suppliers or administrative costs (goal 8). Sustainable development and world peace are clearly not possible in such conditions.

The Millennium Development Goals are clearly compatible with the principles of planetary humanism, so working toward their successful implementation is one of the best ways to give practical expression to twenty-first-century humanism. Given this, generating public knowledge of and support for the MDGs should be seen as a priority for humanists while they remain operative. There is no shortage of worthwhile organizations one can devote time and donate money to. It is a question of seeking some out that resonate most closely with one's own beliefs and priorities and then putting one's thoughts into deeds.

GROUNDED COSMOPOLITANISM AND THE IDENTITY OF THE FUTURE

This book has returned time and again to the dangers anthropocentric thinking contribute to the crisis the planet faces. Anthropocentrism, it has argued, is built into monotheistic systems, with the assurance of an all-powerful God taking an interest in our every move. But we have also seen that anthropocentric thinking can reappear in secular guise as dialectical or metaphysical abstractions. In place of anthropocentrism, whether religiously or humanistically motivated, attention has been drawn to a wealth of insights generated by humanist thinkers of the last two centuries. But we should also take care not to wander into the bland terraces of multiculturalism, where any identification of cultural identity is seen as obscurantist and any criticism seen as intolerance.

With all these things to avoid, how do we combine a cosmic perspective with a sense of identification with a place or a people? Perhaps Kwame Anthony Appiah's notion of *rooted cosmopolitanism* suggests the right balance for a twenty-first-century sense of identity. Personally, I would prefer to speak of *grounded cosmopolitanism*, as the antipodean slang I am familiar with has an altogether more earthy take on things that are "rooted." There is a large literature critical of the rootlessness and superficiality of cosmopolitanism. Cosmopolitans, so this critique goes, are urban and selfish and will move on to the next job in the next city rather than commit to where they are. Anti-Semites have applied this critique to Jews as people having no real grounding in the soil and so living parasitically on the soil of others, and inevitably fouling it in the process. Some of the more xenophobic Christian fundamentalists have used similar tactics in their linking secular humanists and the United Nations in a sinister coven of evil. Less fanatically, many of the concerns over atomized societies could have been made in earlier conditions in the context of cosmopolitanism. Much postmodern theory has reflected the less helpful aspects of this sort of cosmopolitanism.

But cosmopolitanism, properly understood, has also had its defenders. Cosmopolitan people are free from many of the prejudices of their more narrowly rooted neighbors. Their wider perspective and broader education have been the engines for change and development. Cosmopolitans are people who can genuinely call themselves citizens of the world. Appiah sets himself the task of showing that we are not restricted to an either/or choice here. It is quite possible to be fully grounded in our local culture and milieu while also maintaining a transnational and transcultural perspective. Although he recognizes that *Homo sapiens* share a common biological human nature, he criticizes what he calls the *older humanism* that posits humanity coming together by virtue of commonly held principles that can be applied universally. Without endorsing the more excitable polemics against "Eurocentrism," Appiah makes the simpler observation that in fact "we often respond to the situations of others with shared judgments about particular cases."[71] Maybe those great declarations of common humanity get in the way of the more localized way we can respond to another human being. If it is our local commitments that can allow us to empathize with a stranger, through shared judgments on particular cases, then it follows that our being grounded in our own particular society is a good thing. Hilary Putnam said much the same thing when he argued for producing more rational conceptions of rationality and better conceptions of morality when we operate within our own culture. Knowing others are doing the same, the groundwork for "truly human dialogue" is enhanced, not least because the risk of a brutalizing globalist rationality and morality has been avoided.[72] This is an important point, but I would be reluctant to jettison entirely Ted Honderich's principle of humanity, for example.

An extension of grounded cosmopolitanism can be found in Rawls's notion of proper patriotism, which he characterized as "an attachment to one's people and country, and a willingness to defend its legitimate claims while fully respecting the legitimate claims of other peoples."[73] No matter the title given it, the core insight of grounded cosmopolitanism is not new to the humanist tradition. In fact, one could go further and add that grounded cosmopolitanism is one of the few ideas all humanists share. There is a long tradition in humanism of extolling this ideal, some of it predating the centuries covered in this book. Thomas Paine, who died in 1809, just when the word *humanism* was born, declared the world to be his country, yet he never saw fit to decry or renounce his roots in English soil. Friedrich Immanuel Niethammer was able to be deeply concerned for the future of his native Germany (then still a geographical expression) while also being able to see the value in the ideas coming out of France, something his more xenophobic acquaintances were unable to do. H. G. Wells and Bertrand Russell both loved England very much, while being sternly critical of imperialism. Muslim modernists loved their culture enough to see that things could be learned from the West. Albert Einstein and Isaiah Berlin could reconcile their strongly felt Zionism with an equally strongly felt internationalism. Rabindranath Tagore expressed a similar trend of thought when he spoke of his wish to dwell in the ever-living life of Man. And Karl Jaspers's notion of limitless communication moved in the direction of grounded cosmopolitanism when he spoke of the unity of mankind determined not by doctrine nor common language nor governance but by "boundless communication of the historically different in never-ending dialogue, rising to heights of noble emulation."[74] Less poetically but in the same spirit, Xingyun has spoken of himself as a global person. And, more to the point, he has directed a significant proportion of Foguangshan's resources toward developing an outreach beyond Taiwan. And from the United States, Paul Kurtz has emphasized the transnational nature of planetary humanism. And one could point to Amartya Sen as a clear example of grounded cosmopolitanism, despite not having used this language. Few readers of his less technical writings would be unaware of his Bengali roots. He can combine a public appreciation of being Bengali with his role as a global citizen. What's more, Sen's appreciation of his Bengali origins lends texture and color to his work as an ambassador of planetary humanism. Neither Sen nor Tagore nor Xingyun nor Kurtz would be understandable without reference to the cultures that nurtured them, but each draws strength from his roots in articulating his cosmopolitan outlook to the world. And on a more popular level, grounded cosmopolitanism is a variation on the truism of "think globally, act locally."

In a world of planetary humanism and grounded cosmopolitanism, what will be the fate of the notion of bildung we have followed through this book? What challenges will the twenty-first century pose to our notions of self? The British neuroscientist Susan Greenfield has written intelligently on this. Greenfield poses two personality types dominant in the twentieth century: *Someone*, who has achieved a degree of individuality but at the cost of a sense of community or fulfillment; and *Anyone*, who has buried his or her individuality by being absorbed in some mass creed or faith. But as the twenty-first century began, a new option became available: *Nobody*, who has lost a sense of individuality and of fulfillment by being absorbed in the hedonism of the moment. But rather than simply say we must resist and overcome the lesser options, Greenfield says the twenty-first-century identity is going to need aspects of all three, plus a fourth ingredient. The sense of autonomy that *Someone* has achieved is obviously an important achievement, but at a high cost in terms of unsustainable consumption and social isolation. But there is also value in being *Anyone* at various times. When on mass public transport, we are *Anyone*, and this is preferable to being the *Someone* commuting to work alone in a car, with all the environmental and infrastructural cost we know that entails. And there is even value in being *Nobody* at various times in our lives, as when we forget notions of self while engrossed in some recreational activity. The trick, of course, is in the balance between the three. Here Greenfield adds the fourth ingredient: *creativity*. It is creativity that will enable us to navigate the unprecedented challenges technology will pose to our sense of identity in the twenty-first century. Limited to the resources of *Someone* or *Anyone* or *Nobody*, we will surely falter. But with all three, garnished with a generous topping of creativity, we might just make it. "The wonderful thing about creativity is that it cannot be contrived because it is not a specific trait, a set of beliefs, an operationally defined skill or corpus of knowledge."[75] What we need now is an ethicist who can look at Todorov's three pillars of humanist morality, at Schweitzer's notion of reverence for life, at Paul Kurtz's eupraxsophy, at Confucian ethics, and at ubuntu, and devise a formula for humanist living in the twenty-first century. And preferably it would be shot through with the humor and lightness of touch we associate with the British. I believe that humanist thinkers have generated such a wealth of insights here that is of tremendous importance for our survival in the century to come.

EPILOGUE:

THE MAIN FEATURES OF TWENTY-FIRST-CENTURY HUMANISM

Out of the wealth of insights generated by such different people from different cultures over the past two centuries, we are not going to reach some tidy consensus. What follows is not a manifesto of any sort. It is rather a summary of attitudes that seem common to most of the people we have studied, and which appear to still be valuable for the difficult years ahead. And, if we are of a mind, we could call this range of attitudes and preferences humanism.

LIFE IS INTRINSICALLY WORTH LIVING

Humanists of all stripes have agreed that life is worth living, for the simple pleasures that life can bring. Tzvetan Todorov expressed this beautifully from a secular perspective, while Lin Yutang drew on his knowledge of the extensive Chinese literature in this area to restate the classic Chinese virtues of cultivation and simple enjoyment in this life. When Herbert Read spoke of the "sensuous apprehension of being," he was talking, in the end, of the same thing E. O. Wilson was when he spoke of Biophilia. Biophilia is Wilson's way of encapsulating in one word the maxim of treating the world as if there is none other. This can also be expressed in a religious way, as Albert Schweitzer did when he exhorted us to have reverence for life. It is only the language used that is different.

Virtually all humanists over the past two centuries have rejected notions of life as some sort of trial or cosmic test of character in preparation for a more important assignment after our death. It is something to be lived to the full and cherished at every moment. What distinguishes the twenty-first-century humanist understanding of this is that "life" is understood more broadly than to simply mean "Man." In fact, it goes one step further. Expressing a love and reverence for life is to expressly deny that any one genus has a privileged position on the planet. The other development of twenty-first-century humanism is that the fragility of the interdependent systems that sustain life is better appreciated, as is the need to nurture and sustain the system as a whole, even when such an exercise becomes inconvenient and costly.

A SUFFICIENT GROUNDING IN HUMILITY

The principal difference between the humanism of the Renaissance and that of the twenty-first century is in their attitudes to the universe. Renaissance humanists, enthused as they were by variations of mystical Platonism, were full of the dignity of man and man's central place in the cosmos. This has not been a helpful legacy. And when anti-humanist critics speak of humanism replacing God at the center of the universe with man, the point is at least partially valid with respect to Renaissance humanists. But it is no longer true. It is not overstating the case to say that the principal lesson of science with respect to humans is that they are not the center of the universe, but are in fact carbon-based animals in a state of fragile interdependence with all other things, animate and inanimate, whose home is planet earth, one planet among a number we cannot even begin to count. Humanist thinkers in the last two centuries have been open to this message and prepared in their various ways to act upon it in their lives.

We saw Gilbert Murray express this as clearly as can be done. Albert Camus and Bertrand Russell also took this message to heart. Russell put it this way: "Even within the life of our own planet man is only a brief interlude."[1] Lin Yutang expressed similar sentiments, but was more directly critical of Christian presumption, particularly with respect to personal immortality. And, as discussed in chapter 7, it was in the context of his distrust of humanism as an idea that he expressed his cosmic perspective.

Irving Babbitt thought that humanism could not live without religion, though religion could live without humanism. This was because while humanism exemplified decorum and the proper employment of the inner check, it was religion that provided the other essential ingredient; humility. What Babbitt did not grasp (unlike Russell) was that it is science, not monotheistic religion, which is the principal means by which human beings learn their place in the cosmos, and that their place in the cosmos is a very modest one indeed. But, if we find fault with Babbitt for his misplacement of the source of humility, he should be applauded for his motives, which make more sense for the twenty-first century than those of many of his contemporaries. Babbitt wrote in 1919 that a humanism "sufficiently grounded in humility is not only desirable at all times but there are reasons for thinking that it would be especially desirable today."[2] Almost a century on, that is still true.

NOT AGAINST OR BEYOND NATURE, BUT WITHIN IT

It is not a case of man replacing God at the center of the cosmos, as anti-humanists of various stripes have claimed, or even of the natural replacing the supernatural as the principal means by which we understand the cosmos. Thinking in terms of the supernatural is not something *against* or *beyond* nature, because, like everything else, such thinking happens *within* nature and is determined by its possibilities and limitations. In this way, humanists of all shades can dispute and, hopefully, co-operate in finding solutions to the global crisis we face in the twenty-first century.

It is tempting to see this as a rather obvious point, but it's more problematic than it might seem. The main bone of contention here is the degree to which humanism rejects the supernatural, and the language used in the course of the rejection. As we have seen, people calling themselves humanists have ranged across the spectrum on this question. There are the atheists, who predicate their moral code on a rejection of supernaturalism. Then there are agnostics, who work without reference to the question. Slightly different are the European humanists who have got so used to their irreligion they see the whole question as irrelevant to the more pressing question of building an ethos of toleration. Then there are religious humanists who reject the "hairy thunderer" notion of God but retain some role for the divine—variously conceived—in their lives. And then there are a few religious believers who nonetheless see themselves as humanist by virtue (for Christians at least) of a theology of Incarnation, whereby God's love is best nurtured and experienced through active living in the world of people.

Humanists have probably been overly concerned with the minutiae of definition and distinction around this point. What seems important inside the base-camp can seem crashingly uninteresting outside it. The one feature common to almost all aspects of humanism we have examined in this book is some level of awareness that the traditionally-empowered God of the omnis; omniscience, omnipotence and so on, is no longer a credible idea. Beyond this, it would be a mistake to go. So, if I find it difficult to see how a conception of God before which human beings feel the need to placate and mollify can be reconciled with a humanist outlook, maybe this is evidence of a limitation on my part. This may prove unsatisfactory to the hardliners, but there you are. In humanism there has to be room for Mamadiou Dia as there is for Christopher Hitchens.

LEARNING FROM AND VALUING THE PAST

From Friedrich Immanuel Niethammer through Edward Howard Griggs and on to Clive James, humanists have valued what can be learned from the past. Among Europeans it has been the example of Classical Greece which has provided the outstanding example. If at times it has looked like an unhelpful cry of "back to the Greeks," the call has just as frequently been "forward with the Greeks." We can see a similar dynamic in China, where the slogan "Antiquity is now," captures the central relevance of many classical Confucian ideas in the twenty-first century. And in Africa, the Sage philosophy of Henry Oruka helps us see that the past isn't some distant abstraction. We might find it in our elderly neighbors. Or our parents.

What is exciting about humanism at the start of the twenty-first century is the opportunity to learn from the past among all the great cultures of the world. India, China, the Muslim world and Africa have as many exemplars of humanist living as the North Atlantic cultures, people from whom anyone around the world can learn from and be enriched by.

GROUNDED IN OUR CULTURE, YET BEYOND NATIONS

Twenty-first-century humanism is not just international. It is transnational. *International* simply means something operates *between* nations. But when something is transnational it has taken the next step and operates *above and beyond* nations. In a way no other lifestance has done, humanist ideas have long, independent histories in China, in India and in Europe. It is the only genuinely transcultural intellectual program the world has ever seen. This has been a refrain of humanists since Thomas Paine who have taken pride in the idea of being citizens of the world. More recently, people like Julian Huxley, Boyd Orr and Paul Kurtz devoted large parts of their lives to this ideal. Rabindranath Tagore and Vivekananda expressed this ideal better than most.

As Kwame Appiah has demonstrated, we can be deeply grounded in, and derive immense pleasure and sense of identity from, the land of our birth while at the same time have a truly global perspective on the need to cooperate across cultures and beyond borders. We can call it planetary humanism or we could call it grounded cosmopolitanism. In the end it doesn't matter what we call it.

PLACING A HIGH VALUE ON LEARNING

To place a high value on learning presupposes we have a real need to learn, because of the breadth of our ignorance. This is as good a place to end as any. It is an attitude grounded in humility and skepticism toward pretentious displays of what H. G. Wells called "Big Thinks." Confucius emphasized education as the key to happy and successful living, "to go on learning so that you do not notice yourself growing old."[3] And Hu Shih, even while criticizing Confucius, retained the Master's reverence for a life spent in study. And when Karl Jaspers praised the notion of limitless communication, he had in mind our constant need to subject our own thoughts to criticism and to learn from others. There would be little point in limitless communication if we thought we had already had all the answers. And for half a century Paul Kurtz has spoken of humanism as first and foremost a method of inquiry. This, at least, will not change.

NOTES

INTRODUCTION

1. Clive James, *Cultural Amnesia: Necessary Memories from History and the Arts* (New York: W. W. Norton, 2007), p. xviii.
2. Ibid., p. 308.
3. David E. Cooper, *The Measure of Things: Humanism, Humility, and Mystery* (Oxford: Clarendon Press, 2002), pp. 7–8.

CHAPTER 1: OUT OF THE SHADOW OF HEGEL

1. Eric Hobsbawm, *The Age of Revolution* (London: Weidenfeld & Nicolson, 1995 [1961]), p. 1.
2. Raymond Williams, *Culture and Society* (London: Penguin, 1985 [1958]), pp. 14–18.
3. Immanuel Kant, "Answer to the Question: What Is 'Enlightening'?" in *The Age of Enlightenment: An Anthology of Eighteenth-century Texts*, ed. Simon Eliot and Beverley Stern (London: Ward Lock/Open University, 1984 [1979]), 2:250.
4. Scholars have debated for a long time whether Kant can legitimately be seen as a humanist, with most people deciding that he can't. David E. Cooper thought not because for Kant, human beings are activated by something more abstract than machinelike agency of earlier Enlightenment thinkers like Holbach or La Mettrie. See David E. Cooper, *The Measure of Things: Humanism, Humility, and Mystery* (Oxford: Clarendon Press, 2002), especially chapter 3. And, working from a quite different (and more sound) understanding of humanism, John Luik also denies that Kant qualifies, by virtue of arguing for a foundation of evil in human beings in *Religion within the Limits of Reason Alone*. See John Luik, "An Old Question Raised Yet Again: Is Kant an Enlightenment Humanist?" in *The Question of Humanism: Challenges and Possibilities*, ed. David Goicoechea, John Luik, and Tim Madigan (Amherst, NY: Prometheus Books, 1991), pp. 117–37. By contrast, the Norwegian philosopher Finngeir Hiorth says that, though not a humanist himself, Kant is clearly one of contemporary humanism's most influential forbearers. See Finngeir Hiorth, *Introduction to Humanism* (Oslo: Human-Etisk Forbund, 2007), p. 171.

5. Jaap van Praag, *Foundations of Humanism* (Amherst, NY: Prometheus Books, 1982), p. 15.

6. Vito Giustiniani, "Homo, 'Humanus,' and the Meanings of 'Humanism,'" *Journal of the History of Ideas* 46, no. 2 (April/June 1985): 175.

7. Albert Schweitzer, *Civilization and Ethics* (London: Adam & Charles Black, 1946 [1923]), p. 133.

8. Georg Henrik von Wright, *What Is Humanism?* (Topeka: University of Kansas, 1977), p. 16.

9. This is not to say that Hegel could be counted as a humanist, at least not in the contemporary sense. David E. Cooper is correct to observe that there is nothing especially human about Hegel's *Geist*, which is the cause of the world. See Cooper, *Measure of Things*, p. 78.

10. John Edward Toews, *Hegelianism: The Path toward Dialectical Humanism, 1805–1841* (Cambridge: Cambridge University Press, 1980), p. 32.

11. Von Wright, *What Is Humanism?* p. 23.

12. Toews, *Hegelianism*, p. 58.

13. Friedrich Immanuel Niethammer, *Philanthropinismus—Humanismus* (Weinheim, Berlin, Basle: Verlag Julius Beltz, 1968 [1808]), p. 95. I am grateful to Sascha Nolden for translating excerpts of this book and for providing me with insights about the history of Philanthropinism.

14. Ibid., p. 162.

15. Nicolas Walter, *Humanism: What's in the Word* (London: Rationalist Press Association, 1997), pp. 25–27.

16. Poignant though this phrase is, it was anticipated in Feuerbach, who spoke of God as a "tear of love, shed in the deepest concealment over human misery." See Ludwig Feuerbach, *The Essence of Christianity* (Amherst, NY: Prometheus Books, 1989 [1841]), p. 122. And Feuerbach was taking this thought from the German mystic Sebastian Franck (1499–1542).

17. Sidney Hook, *From Hegel to Marx: Studies in the Intellectual Development of Karl Marx* (New York: Humanities Press, 1958 [1950]), p. 129.

18. Walter, *Humanism*, p. 27.

19. Hook, *From Hegel to Marx*, p. 227.

20. Feuerbach, *Essence of Christianity*, p. 23.

21. Ibid., p. 107. This insight also anticipates William James's important observation that religion is a monument to human egoism. See William James, *The Varieties of Religious Experience* (London: Longmans, Green, 1908 [1902]), p. 491.

22. J. M. Robertson, *A History of Freethought in the Nineteenth Century* (London: Watts, 1929), p. 196.

23. Hiorth, *Introduction to Humanism*, pp. 7–10.

24. Quoted in David Boulton, *The Trouble with God* (Alresford, Hants: John Hunt Publishing, 2002), p. 161.

25. George Jacob Holyoake, *The Origin and Nature of Secularism* (London: Watts, 1896), p. 73.

26. Ibid.

27. Ibid., pp. 74–75.

28. Ibid., p. 75.

29. Although it is important to acknowledge the differences between the philosophical radicals and liberals, as Bertrand Russell noted in *Freedom and Organization* (London: George Allen & Unwin, 1952 [1934]), pp. 389–90.

30. Jeremy Bentham, *A Fragment on Government and an Introduction to the Principles of Morals and Legislation*, ed. Wilfred Harrison (Oxford: Basil Blackwell, 1967 [1948]), p. 412. Bentham's insight was endorsed enthusiastically as recently as 2002 by a prominent group of British humanist philosophers. See Humanist Philosophers' Group, *What Is Humanism?* (London: British Humanist Association, 2002), p. 16.

31. E. Royston Pike, *Pioneers of Social Change* (London: Barrie & Rockliff, 1963), p. 95.

32. I have in mind works like Bertrand Russell, *Authority and the Individual* (London: George Allen & Unwin, 1949) and A. C. Grayling, *Towards the Light* (London: Bloomsbury, 2007).

33. Kwame Appiah, *The Ethics of Identity* (Princeton, NJ: Princeton University Press, 2005), p. 142. It's worth noting Mill's favorable comparison of the Indian record of female leadership with that in European history. See John Stuart Mill, *On Liberty and the Subjection of Women* (London: Wordsworth, 1996), p. 169.

34. Owen did this in a famous speech on August 21, 1817. Mill also anticipated Richard Dawkins by a century and a half when he said it was high time that nonreligious people made their views public. "On religion in particular the time appears to me to have come when it is the duty of all who, being qualified in point of knowledge, have on mature consideration satisfied themselves that the current opinions are not only false but hurtful, to make their dissent known; at least, if they are among those whose station or reputation gives their opinion a chance of being attended to." John Stuart Mill, *Autobiography* (New York: New American Library, 1964 [1873]), p. 52.

35. I have in mind the following works: Ninian Smart, *The Religious Experience of Mankind* (Glasgow: Collins, 1980 [1969]), p. 647; and Basil Mitchell, *Morality: Religious and Secular* (Oxford: Clarendon Press, 1985 [1980]), chapter 4.

36. The popularity of rationalism was helped in no small way by the publication in 1865 of *The History of the Rise and Influence of the Spirit of Rationalism in Europe* by the liberal historian William Lecky (1838–1903).

37. Herman J. Saatkamp, ed., *Rorty and Pragmatism* (Nashville: Vanderbilt University Press, 1995), p. 197.

38. Karl Löwith, *From Hegel to Nietzsche: The Revolution in Nineteenth-century Thought* (London: Constable, 1965 [1941]), p. 63. More recently the same point was made in Jürgen Habermas, *The Philosophical Discourse of Modernity* (Cambridge: Polity Press, 1987), p. 51.

39. G. W. F. Hegel, *The Philosophy of History* (New York: Dover, 1956), p. 424.

40. Richard Rorty, *Philosophy and Social Hope* (London: Penguin, 1999), p. 16.

41. Löwith, *From Hegel to Nietzsche*, p. 75.

42. See Walter Kaufmann, *From Shakespeare to Existentialism* (Boston: Beacon Press, 1959). Kaufmann also deserves the title of the century's greatest exponent of existentialism, one of the few who has not become dated.

43. Walter, *Humanism*, p. 20.

44. Robert Southey and Samuel Taylor Coleridge, eds., *Omniana* (Fontwell, Sussex: Centaur, 1969 [1812]), p. 350.

45. John Addington Symonds, *Renaissance in Italy* (London: Smith, Elder, 1902 [1875–86]), 2:52.

46. William Kingdon Clifford, "The Influence upon Morality of a Decline in Religious Belief," *The Ethics of Belief and Other Essays* (Amherst, NY: Prometheus Books, 1999 [1947]), p. 126.

47. William James, "The Will to Believe," in *The Will to Believe and Other Essays in Popular Philosophy* (New York: Dover, 1956 [1897]), p. 17.

48. J. M. Robertson, *Modern Humanists Reconsidered* (London: Watts, 1927), p. 105.

49. A. W. Benn, *A History of Modern Philosophy* (London: Watts, 1912), p. 124.

50. Edward Howard Griggs, *The New Humanism* (Croton-on-Hudson, NY: Orchard Hill Press, 1922 [1899]), p. 230.

51. Ibid., p. 194.

52. Fred Donnelly, "The Tale of Two World Histories," *Open Society* 80, no. 4 (Summer 2007): 6–9.

53. Winwood Reade, *The Martyrdom of Man* (London, Trubner, 1877 [1872]), p. 492.

54. Ibid., pp. 543–44.

55. I owe this insight to John Bowle, *Politics and Opinion in the Nineteenth Century* (London: Jonathan Cape, 1966 [1954]), p. 278.

CHAPTER 2: PROTAGORAS'S CHEERLEADER

1. F. C. S. Schiller, *Humanism: Philosophical Essays* (London: Macmillan, 1912 [1903]), p. xxi. Schiller's works are hard to get now, so I am grateful to John Shook and Hugh McDonald for overseeing the publication of *F. C. S. Schiller on Humanism and Pragmatism: Selected Writings, 1891–1939* (Amherst, NY: Prometheus Books, 2007). I strongly recommend this work.

2. F. C. S. Schiller, *Our Human Truths* (New York: Columbia University Press, 1939), p. 18.

3. F. C. S. Schiller, *Studies in Humanism* (London: Macmillan, 1907), p. 305.

4. Ibid., pp. 4–5, emphasis in the original.

5. Ibid., p. 7, emphasis in the original.

6. William James, *Pragmatism and Other Essays* (New York: Washington Square, 1963 [1907]), p. 32. James dedicated *Pragmatism* to the memory of John Stuart Mill.

7. Schiller, *Studies in Humanism*, p. 11, emphasis in the original.

8. Ibid., p. 12, emphasis in the original.

9. Ibid.

10. Louis Menand, *The Metaphysical Club* (London: Flamingo, 2002 [2001]), p. 350.

11. William James, *Selected Papers on Philosophy* (London: J. M. Dent, 1956 [1917]), p. 219.

12. James, *Pragmatism*, p. 106.

13. Schiller, *Our Human Truths*, p. 76.

14. Schiller, *Humanism*, p. 12, emphasis in the original.

15. Ibid., p. 13.

16. Bernard Williams, *Ethics and the Limits of Philosophy* (London: Fontana/Collins, 1985), p. 119. This insight was expanded on in his essay "The Human Prejudice," in Bernard Williams, *Philosophy as a Humanistic Discipline* (Princeton, NJ: Princeton University Press, 2006), pp. 135–52.

17. Schiller, *Humanism*, p. 347.

18. Ibid., p. 348.

19. Ibid., pp. 278–79.

20. Ibid., p. 282.

21. Benedict Spinoza, *Tractatus Theologico-Politicus* (London: George Routledge & Sons, n.d. [1885]), p. 182.

22. Colin Campbell, *Towards a Sociology of Irreligion* (London: Macmillan, 1971), p. 43.

23. Schiller, *Studies in Humanism*, p. 276.

24. Schiller, *Our Human Truths*, p. 19.

25. Ibid., p. 20.
26. Ibid., p. 79.
27. Schiller, *Humanism*, p. 302.
28. Ibid., p. 152.
29. Ibid., p. 155.
30. Ibid., p. 153.
31. Ibid., p. 134.
32. Ibid., p. 152, emphasis in the original.
33. Ibid., p. 155.
34. Ibid., p. 288.
35. Reuben Abel, ed., *Humanistic Pragmatism: The Philosophy of F. C. S. Schiller* (New York: Free Press, 1966), p. 7.
36. Alan Wood, *Bertrand Russell: The Passionate Skeptic* (London: George Allen & Unwin, 1957), p. 83. Wood's comment is also interesting for what he conceives humanism to be, and for how little it owes Schiller.
37. Schiller, *Our Human Truths*, p. viii.
38. Schiller, *Humanism*, p. 231.
39. Richard Rorty, *Consequences of Pragmatism (Essays: 1972–1980)* (Minneapolis: University of Minnesota Press, 1982), p. xl.
40. William F. Schulz, *Making the Manifesto: The Birth of Religious Humanism* (Boston: Skinner House Books, 2002), p. 107.
41. Schiller, *Humanism*, p. xii.
42. Schiller, *Studies in Humanism*, p. 206.
43. Abel, *Humanistic Pragmatism*, p. 10.

CHAPTER 3: MAKING THE MANIFESTO

1. *Humanist* (November 1, 1918): 168.
2. F. J. Gould, *The Life Story of a Humanist* (London: Watts, 1923), p. 164.
3. F. J. Gould, "1906 and 1907," *Literary Guide* (January 1, 1907): 5.
4. William F. Schulz, *Making the Manifesto: The Birth of Religious Humanism* (Boston: Skinner House Books, 2002), p. 20.
5. Gould, *Life Story of a Humanist*, pp. 53–54.
6. F. J. Gould, "The New Humanism," *Literary Guide* (September 1931): 164.
7. Ibid.
8. Joseph McCabe, *The Religion of Woman* (London: Watts, 1905), p. 172.
9. Ibid., p. 188.

10. Joseph McCabe, "Fore-gleams of Humanism in Dante," *Agnostic Annual* (London: Watts, 1907), pp. 53–57.

11. Adam Gowans Whyte, *The Religion of the Open Mind* (London: Watts, 1913), p. 13.

12. Ibid., p. 39.

13. Ibid., p. 183.

14. Richard Holloway, *Looking in the Distance* (Edinburgh: Canongate, 2005 [2004]).

15. Jim Dakin, "Humanism as It Was in New Zealand," *New Zealand Humanist* 115 (September 1992): 7. Seddon's comments were reported in the *Evening Post*, Wellington's evening newspaper, on May 1, 1906.

16. Bertrand Russell, "A Free Man's Worship," in *Mysticism and Logic* (London: George Allen & Unwin, 1959 [1917]), pp. 47–48. The essay's title was changed to "A Free Man's Worship" during publication.

17. Ibid., p. 48.

18. Russell thought that Greek philosophy went astray after Democritus for placing an undue emphasis on man rather than the universe, see *History of Western Philosophy* (London: George Allen & Unwin, 1946), p. 93. Feuerbach's attitude is also relevant here: "Whence stem the lacunae and limitations of our knowledge of nature? From the fact that knowledge is neither the basis nor the goal of nature." Quoted from Eugene Kamenka, *The Philosophy of Ludwig Feuerbach* (London: Routledge & Kegan Paul, 1970), p. 86.

19. Ronald W. Clark, *The Life of Bertrand Russell* (London: Jonathan Cape & Weidenfeld & Nicolson, 1975), pp. 95–96.

20. John McCormick, *George Santayana: A Biography* (New York: Alfred A. Knopf, 1987), p. 183.

21. For a fuller discussion of this, see Bill Cooke, "The Fatal Flaw in Religious Liberalism and How to Avoid It" (keynote speech, Sea of Faith Network [New Zealand], 14th annual conference, September 29–October 1, 2006), www.sof.wellington.net.nz/2006cookekeynote.pdf.

22. McCormick, *George Santayana*, pp. 183–84.

23. George Santayana, *Persons and Places: The Background of My Life* (New York: Scribner, 1944), p. 240.

24. Russell, *History of Western Philosophy*, p. 19.

25. George Santayana, "Platonism and the Spiritual Life," in *Winds of Doctrine and Platonism and the Spiritual Life* (New York: Harper & Brothers, 1957), p. 249.

26. George Santayana, *The Genteel Tradition at Bay* (New York: Scribner, 1931), p. 42.

27. Daniel Cory, ed., *The Letters of George Santayana* (New York: Scribner, 1955), p. 389.

28. Irving Babbitt, "What I Believe: Rousseau and Religion," in *Character and Culture* (New Brunswick, NJ: Transaction, 1995 [1940]), pp. 229–30.
29. R. B. Haldane, *The Philosophy of Humanism* (London: John Murray, 1922), p. 87.
30. Ibid., pp. 92–93.
31. Frank Carleton Doan, *Religion and the Modern Mind* (Boston: Sherman, French, 1909), p. 35.
32. Ibid., p. 198.
33. Frank Carleton Doan, "Just Being Human," in *Humanist Sermons*, ed. Curtis Reese (Chicago: Open Court, 1927), p. 232.
34. Roy Wood Sellars, *Reflections on American Philosophy from Within* (Notre Dame, IN: University of Notre Dame Press, 1969), p. 94.
35. Roy Wood Sellars, *Religion Coming of Age* (New York: Macmillan, 1928), p. 10.
36. Sellars, *Reflections on American Philosophy*, p. 153.
37. Ibid., p. 156.
38. Ibid., p. 157.
39. Ibid., p. 164.
40. Charles Francis Potter, *Humanism: The New Religion* (New York: Simon & Schuster, 1930), p. 14, emphasis in the original.
41. Curtis Reese, ed., preface to *Humanist Sermons* (Chicago: Open Court, 1927), p. xv.
42. Potter, *Humanism*, p. 42.
43. Reese, preface to *Humanist Sermons*, pp. ix–x.
44. A. Wakefield Slaten, "Modernism and Humanism," in *Humanist Sermons*, ed. Curtis Reese (Chicago: Open Court, 1927), p. 92.
45. Finngeir Hiorth, *Introduction to Humanism* (Oslo: Human-Etisk Forbund, 2007 [1996]), p. 20.
46. Schulz, *Making the Manifesto*, pp. 59–60.
47. Paul Kurtz, *Humanist Manifestos I and II* (Amherst, NY: Prometheus Books, 1973), p. 8.
48. Ibid., p. 9.
49. Ibid., p. 7.
50. Ibid., p. 10.
51. Schulz, *Making the Manifesto*, p. 87.
52. F. C. S. Schiller, *Our Human Truths* (New York: Columbia University Press, 1939), p. 76.
53. Ibid.
54. Theodore Schroeder, "Religious Humanism," *Truth Seeker* (August 6, 1927): 503.

55. "Humanism and the Modern Revolt," *Inquirer* (October 22, 1932): 532. Thanks to Wayne Facer for both directing my attention to this material and making it available to me.

CHAPTER 4: THE RISE AND FALL OF SCIENTIFIC HUMANISM

1. One of the few examples of blatant racism in a published work of an unbeliever was from *Essays of an Atheist* (New York: Truth Seeker, 1945), by Woolsey Teller (1890–1954), who was also an outspoken critic of humanism, preferring what he saw as the more straightforward term *atheist*.

2. Julian Huxley, *Religion without Revelation* (London: Ernest Benn, 1927), p. 9.

3. Ibid., p. 250.

4. Ibid., p. 315.

5. The main tenets of Christian belief that Darwinism undermined include: belief in essentialism; belief in the simpler notions of causality in nature in the tradition of Newton and, more particularly, Descartes; and belief in final causes or teleology. See Ernst Mayr, *One Long Argument: Charles Darwin and the Genesis of Modern Evolutionary Thought* (London: Penguin, 1993 [1991]), p. 39.

6. Huxley, *Religion without Revelation*, p. 9.

7. Julian Huxley, *What Dare I Think?* (London: Chatto & Windus, 1931), p. 150.

8. Ibid., p. 165.

9. Julian Huxley, *The Uniqueness of Man* (London: Chatto & Windus, 1941), p. 34.

10. This is why I shall speak of *Homo sapiens*, despite Raimond Gaita's concern that such a classification is to trivialize humanity. See *A Common Humanity* (Melbourne: Text Publishing, 2000), p. 268. It's possible that this risk exists, but it seems less ominous than the risk of anthropocentric conceit being enflamed by speaking of *souls*, even though Gaita is careful to deny any supernaturalist association with the word.

11. Huxley, *Uniqueness of Man*, p. 32.

12. There is a good account of Hogben's struggle against eugenics in Gary Werskey, *The Visible College* (London: Allen Lane, 1978), pp. 105–10. For McCabe's views, see Bill Cooke, *A Rebel to His Last Breath: Joseph McCabe and Rationalism* (Amherst, NY: Prometheus Books, 2001), pp. 128–30. Bertrand Russell's views are scattered throughout his writings, so an anthology like Al Seckel's *Bertrand Russell on Ethics, Sex and Marriage* (Amherst, NY: Prometheus Books, 1987) is the quickest way to follow his views.

13. Julian Huxley, *Memories I* (London: Penguin, 1978 [1970]), p. 147.

14. John Bowle, *Politics and Opinion in the Nineteenth Century* (London: Jonathan Cape, 1966 [1954]), p. 318.

15. Michael Ignatieff, *Isaiah Berlin: A Life* (London: Vintage, 2000 [1998]), p. 251. Also it is worth looking at Finngeir Hiorth, *Marxism* (Oslo: Human-Etisk Forbund, 2004), p. 32; and Bertrand Russell, *Freedom and Organization, 1814–1914* (London: George Allen & Unwin, 1952 [1934]), p. 210. Coming from a quite different perspective, Louis Althusser was of much the same opinion. For him the difference between the *1844 Manuscripts* and his mature works was simply one of language. See Louis Althusser, *For Marx* (New York: Vintage, 1970 [1965]), p. 61.

16. By the time he was writing *The German Ideology*, Marx was dismissing humanism as an assortment of "airy" theories on human essence.

17. Dimitri Volkogonov, *Stalin: Triumph and Tragedy* (New York: Grove Weidenfeld, 1991 [1988]), p. 70. It would be so good if American evangelicals could take note of this, but it's probably unlikely.

18. David McLellan, *The Thought of Karl Marx* (London: Papermac, 1980 [1971]), p. 124.

19. Ibid., p. 244.

20. Althusser opposed the idea that Marx "superseded" Hegel, that being too Hegelian a concept. It was, for Althusser, not so much a supersession as a movement from illusion to reality. See Althusser, *For Marx*, pp. 79–81.

21. See Russell, *Freedom and Organization*, p. 220. The most comprehensive humanist refutations of dialectical materialism came from Karl Popper in *The Poverty of Historicism* (London: Routledge & Kegan Paul, 1957) and *The Open Society and Its Enemies* (London: Routledge & Kegan Paul, 1963 [1945]), notwithstanding the many legitimate objections that can be made against Popper's misreading of Plato and Hegel.

22. J. B. S. Haldane, *The Marxist Philosophy and the Sciences* (London: George Allen & Unwin, 1939), p. 16.

23. Susan Haack, *Defending Science—Within Reason* (Amherst, NY: Prometheus, 2003), p. 19.

24. C. H. Waddington, *The Scientific Attitude* (London: Penguin, 1948 [1941]), p. viii.

25. Ibid., p. 103.

26. Alan Ryan, *Bertrand Russell: A Political Life* (London: Allen Lane, 1988), p. 92. Mention has already been made of Bertrand Russell and Karl Popper's works in this area. No less active was H. G. Wells's work through the 1930s, many works by Sidney Hook, and on to Ernest Gellner's *Conditions of Liberty* (London: Hamish Hamilton, 1994). Among the more recent works in this long tradition of humanist

criticism of dialectical materialism and Marxism would be Tzvetan Todorov's *Hope and Memory* (London: Atlantic, 2005 [2003]).

27. J. B. Coates, "Scientific Humanism and the RPA," *Literary Guide* (August 1931): 155.

28. F. J. Gould, "The New Humanism," *Literary Guide* (September 1931): 164.

29. J. B. S. Haldane, "The Rationalist Outlook from Varying Standpoints," *Literary Guide* (September 1931): 166.

30. J. M. Robertson, "Notes and Queries about 'Scientific Humanism,'" *Literary Guide* (October 1931): 179–81.

31. Bill Cooke, *The Gathering of Infidels: A Hundred Years of the Rationalist Press Association* (Amherst, NY: Prometheus Books, 2004), pp. 99–103.

32. C. E. M. Joad, *The Book of Joad* (London: Faber & Faber, 1945 [1932]), p. 168.

33. C. E. M. Joad, ed., *Manifesto* (London: George Allen & Unwin, 1934), pp. 23–25.

34. John Dewey, *Philosophy and Civilization* (New York: G. P. Putnam's Sons, 1931), p. 19.

35. Reuben Abel, ed., *Humanistic Pragmatism: The Philosophy of F. C. S. Schiller* (New York: Free Press, 1966), p. 9.

36. John Dewey, *The Quest for Certainty* (London: George Allen & Unwin, 1930), p. 12.

37. Ibid., pp. 217–18.

38. John Dewey, *Human Nature and Conduct* (New York: Modern Library, 1930 [1922]), p. 285.

39. John Dewey, *A Common Faith* (New Haven, CT: Yale University Press, 1947 [1934]), p. 51.

40. Corliss Lamont, *Yes to Life: Memoirs of Corliss Lamont* (New York: Horizon Press, 1981), p. 81.

41. Alan Ryan, *John Dewey and the High Tide of American Liberalism* (New York: W. W. Norton, 1995), p. 274.

42. Dewey, *Common Faith*, p. 53.

43. Ibid., p. 86.

44. Ibid., p. 54.

45. Ryan, *John Dewey and the High Tide of American Liberalism*, pp. 236–37.

46. Dewey, *Common Faith*, p. 87.

47. Oliver Reiser, *Scientific Humanism* (Girard, KS: Haldeman-Julius, 1946), pp. 5–6. It should also be mentioned that Reiser incorrectly attributed the origins of scientific humanism to Henry C. Tracy in 1927. We have seen that Lothrop Stoddard used the phrase a year earlier.

48. William F. Schulz, *Making the Manifesto: The Birth of Religious Humanism* (Boston: Skinner House Books, 2002), p. 71.

49. Bertrand Russell, "Why I Am Not a Christian," in *Why I Am Not a Christian* (London: George Allen & Unwin, 1957), p. 16. It's worth noting here Russell's anticipation of Dennett's talk half a century later of cranes and skyhooks. See Daniel C. Dennett, *Darwin's Dangerous Idea* (London: Allen Lane, 1995), especially pp. 75–77.

50. Bertrand Russell, "Dreams and Facts," in *Sceptical Essays* (London: George Allen & Unwin, 1928), p. 34.

51. Russell, Bertrand, "My Mental Development," in *The Philosophy of Bertrand Russell*, ed. Paul Arthur Schilpp (Evanston, IL: Northwestern University, 1944), pp. 19–20.

52. H. G. Wells, *God the Invisible King* (London: Cassell, 1917), p. 52.

53. Ibid., p. xiii.

54. Ibid., p. 205.

55. H. G. Wells, *The Soul of a Bishop* (London: Cassell, 1918), p. 283.

56. H. G. Wells, *The Undying Fire* (London: Cassell, 1919), pp. 94–95.

57. Ibid., p. 159.

58. H. G. Wells, *The Fate of Homo Sapiens* (London: Secker & Warburg, 1939), p. 178.

59. Gordon N. Ray, *H. G. Wells and Rebecca West* (London: Macmillan, 1974), p. 106.

60. H. G. Wells, *Experiment in Autobiography* (London: Victor Gollancz, 1934), p. 677.

61. Krishnan Kumar, "Wells and 'the So-called Science of Sociology,'" in *H. G. Wells under Revision*, ed. Patrick Parrinder and Christopher Rolfe (Selinsgrove, PA: Susquehanna University Press, 1990), p. 194.

62. H. G. Wells, *The Outline of History* (London: Waverley, 1921 [1920]), p. vii.

63. A worthwhile tribute to *The Outline of History* is Peter Watson's ambitious work *Ideas: A History of Thought and Invention from Fire to Freud* (New York: HarperCollins, 2005). Watson's fine study owes a huge debt to *The Outline of History*, both in conception and execution. It can stand as a twenty-first-century continuation of and tribute to Wells's work.

64. Wells, *Fate of* Homo Sapiens, p. 29.

65. H. G. Wells, *The War of the Worlds* (London: Penguin, 1946 [1898]), p. 11.

66. Wells, *Fate of* Homo Sapiens, p. 24.

67. Ibid., p. 25.

68. H. G. Wells, *You Can't Be Too Careful* (London: Secker & Warburg, 1941), p. 286.

69. Antony Flew, "Scientific Humanism," in *The Humanist Alternative*, ed. Paul Kurtz (London: Pemberton Books, 1973), p. 109.

70. Jacob Bronowski, "The Value of Science," in *Rationalist Annual*, ed. Hector Hawton (London: Watts, 1960), pp. 26–34.

71. Jacob Bronowski, *The Ascent of Man* (London: BBC, 1979 [1973]), p. 374. Less poetically, though in a similar vein, Alfred Hobson and Neil Jenkins provide a fair summary of the relations of science and humanism in *Modern Humanism* (Newcastle-upon-Tyne: Dene Books, 1989).

72. Letter to the editor, *Humanist* 78, no. 2 (February 1963): 57.

73. Karl Jaspers, *Way to Wisdom* (London: Victor Gollancz, 1951), p. 91.

74. Haack, *Defending Science*, pp. 20–26.

CHAPTER 5: BRITISH HUMANISM SINCE WORLD WAR II

1. Ian MacKillop, *The British Ethical Societies* (Cambridge: Cambridge University Press, 1986), p. 117.

2. Stanton Coit, *The Soul of America* (New York: Macmillan, 1914), p. 335.

3. Harold Blackham, "Organized Rationalism," in *Reason in Action*, ed. Hector Hawton (London: Watts, 1956), p. 115. Unfortunately, this rather tortured emphasis isn't entirely coherent. Presumably it's the other way around—to replace you need to destroy—which supports the abolitionist argument.

4. John A. Hobson, *Rationalism and Humanism* (London: Watts, 1933).

5. H. J. Blackham, *Humanism* (London: Penguin, 1968), p. 21.

6. H. J. Blackham, "A Definition of Humanism," in *The Humanist Alternative*, ed. Paul Kurtz (London: Pemberton Books, 1973), p. 35.

7. Blackham, *Humanism*, p. 15.

8. Ibid., p. 81.

9. Bertrand Russell, *Human Knowledge: Its Scope and Limits* (London: George Allen & Unwin, 1948), p. 13.

10. Bertrand Russell, *Philosophy and Politics* (London: National Book League, 1947), p. 21.

11. Morris Cohen, *The Faith of a Liberal* (New York: Henry Holt, 1946). Of special interest is the prologue, "What I Believe," and the penultimate essay, "The Open Mind."

12. Bertrand Russell, *The Faith of a Rationalist* (Auckland: New Zealand Rationalist Association, n.d. [1960]), p. 5.

13. Karl Popper, *The Open Society and Its Enemies* (London: Routledge, 1963 [1945]), 2:225. Popper could just as easily be mentioned in the chapter on European humanism or even in the chapter on scientific humanism, showing once again how porous these chapter divisions are.

14. Karl Popper, *Conjectures and Refutations: The Growth of Scientific Knowledge* (London: Routledge, 1989 [1963]), p. 384.

15. Russell had been an honorary associate since 1927.

16. *Humanist* 11, no. 5 (October/November 1951): 199. Schulz, in his history of American religious humanism, mentions this as well, although in a different context. See William F. Schulz, *Making the Manifesto: The Birth of Religious Humanism* (Boston: Skinner House Books, 2002), p. 71.

17. Bertrand Russell, *New Hopes for a Changing World* (London: George Allen & Unwin, 1951), p. 14. Russell shared this concern with Blackham through these years.

18. Herbert Read, *The Forms of Things Unknown* (London: Faber & Faber, 1960), p. 175. Like so many people of his generation, Read owed a huge philosophical debt to Bertrand Russell, which helped act as a corrective to other influences. See Herbert Read, "A Philosophical Debt" in *Bertrand Russell: Philosopher of the Century*, ed. Ralph Schoenman (New York: Little, Brown, 1967), pp. 95–99.

19. Read, *Forms of Things Unknown*, p. 177.

20. H. G. Wells, *H. G. Wells in Love*, ed. G. P. Wells (London: Faber & Faber, 1984), p. 89.

21. Ruth Fry, *Maud and Amber* (Christchurch: Canterbury University Press, 1992), p. 109.

22. Amber Blanco White, *Ethics for Unbelievers* (London: Routledge & Kegan Paul, 1949), p. 211.

23. Ibid., p. 195.

24. *Literary Guide* 64, no. 12 (December 1949): 247–48.

25. Bill Cooke, *The Blasphemy Depot: A Hundred Years of the Rationalist Press Association* (London: Rationalist Press Association, 2003). This was published the following year in the United States as *The Gathering of Infidels: A Hundred Years of the Rationalist Press Association* (Amherst, NY: Prometheus Books, 2004); see pp. 246–49.

26. Margaret Knight, *Morals without Religion* (London: Dennis Dobson, 1955), p. 14.

27. Ibid., p. 27.

28. Hector Hawton, "Freedom of the Air," *Literary Guide* 70, no. 2 (February 1955): 4.

29. Knight, *Morals without Religion*, pp. 58–59.

30. Ibid., p. 54.

31. Margaret Knight, ed., *The Humanist Anthology* (London: Barrie & Rockliff, 1961), p. xiii.

32. See Cooke, *Gathering of Infidels*, chapter 5, for a fuller discussion of this.

33. Hector Hawton, "Humanist Aims," *Humanist* 74, no. 9 (September 1959): 3.

34. Hector Hawton, *The Humanist Revolution* (London: Barrie & Rockliff, 1963), p. 66.

35. Ibid., p. 75.

36. The changes made weren't considerable, but care needs to be taken with respect to them, and several people have run aground being insufficiently watchful. For instance, an appreciation of Huxley by the American humanist Timothy Madigan is undermined by his confusing the first edition of *Religion without Revelation* with the revised edition. The most important change in the revised edition was a new final chapter. And where the first edition spoke of *scientific humanism*, the revised edition spoke of *evolutionary humanism*. Unaware of this change, Madigan attributes Huxley's discussion of evolutionary humanism to the 1920s and not to the 1950s, where it belongs. This gives the impression Huxley's thinking was considerably more stable than it actually was. See Timothy J. Madigan, "Evolutionary Humanism Revisited: The Continuing Relevance of Julian Huxley," *Religious Humanism* 32, nos. 3 and 4 (Summer/Fall 1998): 73–82.

37. Julian Huxley, ed., *The Humanist Frame* (London: George Allen & Unwin, 1961), p. 13.

38. Ibid., p. 38.

39. Ibid., p. 48.

40. Ibid., p. 41.

41. Ibid., p. 14.

42. Aldous Huxley, "Human Potentialities," in *The Humanist Frame*, ed. Julian Huxley (London: George Allen & Unwin, 1961), pp. 423–25.

43. Ibid., p. 426.

44. Julian Huxley, "The Late Aldous Huxley," *Humanist* 79, no. 3 (March 1964): 91–92.

45. Julian Huxley, *Essays of a Humanist* (London: Chatto & Windus, 1964), p. 121.

46. Ibid., p. 125.

47. Cyril Bibby, "Towards a Scientific Humanist Culture," in *The Humanist Outlook*, ed. A. J. Ayer (London: Pemberton Books, 1968), p. 22.

48. A. J. Ayer, "Humanism and Reform," *Encounter* (June 6, 1966), quoted from Ben Rogers, *A. J. Ayer: A Life* (New York: Grove Press, 1999), p. 281.

49. Hector Hawton, "Introducing Question 1," in *Question 1*, Hawton (London: Pemberton Publishing, 1968), pp. 3–4.

50. Ronald Fletcher, *Ten Non-Commandments: A Humanist's Decalogue* (London: Pioneer, 1964).

51. Ronald Fletcher, "A Definition of Humanism," in Hawton, *Question 1*, p. 7 (see note 49).

52. Ibid., pp. 9–10.

53. Ibid., p. 15.

54. "Alan Bullock and Humanism in the West," *New Humanist* 101, no. 1 (Winter 1986): 8.

55. Alan Bullock, *The Humanist Tradition in the West* (London: Thames & Hudson, 1985), p. 98.

56. Ibid., p. 9.

57. Ibid., pp. 155–57.

58. Ibid., p. 160.

59. Ibid., p. 180.

60. Ibid., p. 16.

61. Ibid., p. 195.

62. Ramin Jahanbegloo, *Conversations with Isaiah Berlin* (London: Phoenix, 1993 [1991]), pp. 47–48. As if to underscore the value of Berlin's pluralism, Jahanbegloo was imprisoned in 2006 by the Iranian authorities for his work as an exponent of cultural dialogue.

63. Ibid., p. 70.

64. Isaiah Berlin, *The Crooked Timber of Humanity* (New York: Vintage, 1992 [1990]), pp. 17–18.

65. Ibid., p. 19.

66. Michael Ignatieff, *Isaiah Berlin: A Life* (London: Vintage, 2000 [1998]), p. 294.

67. Richard Harries, "A Fellow Humanist," in *Richard Dawkins*, ed. Alan Grafen and Mark Ridley (Oxford: Oxford University Press, 2006), p. 241. For a fuller look at the strength of atheist and humanist outlooks in the academy on both sides of the Atlantic, see Louise M. Antony, ed., *Philosophers without Gods: Meditations on Atheism and the Secular Life* (Oxford: Oxford University Press, 2007). A simpler illustration can be found in a dialogue on the merits of humanism between two English philosophers, Tim Crane and Peter Cave. The two shared so many humanistic assumptions and beliefs that the debate was limited largely to discussing terms and picking over details. See Tim Crane and Peter Cave, "What on Earth Is Humanism?" *Philosophers' Magazine* 41 (2nd quarter 2008): 55–62.

68. David Boulton, *The Trouble with God* (Alresford, Hants: John Hunt Publishing, 2002), p. 187. In an otherwise competent exposition of religious humanism, Boulton manages a string of factual errors in his historical account of secular humanism: George Jacob Holyoake is credited with founding the RPA; the founding of the American Humanist Association is given as 1973, not 1941; Harold Blackham is repeatedly referred to as Harold Blackman, and so on.

69. Simon Blackburn is also relevant here, when he said that "if religious practitioners are not even in the business of representing the world truly, it is a pity that they chose a story told so like a recital of plain truth, in an apparently descriptive, factual language, in order to do whatever it is that they are doing instead." See Simon Blackburn, *Truth: A Guide for the Perplexed* (London: Allen Lane, 2005), p. 16.

70. Don Cupitt, *After God: The Future of Religion* (London: Phoenix, 1998 [1997]), p. 82.

71. Ibid., p. xiii.

72. A. C. Grayling, *What Is Good? The Search for the Best Way to Live* (London: Weidenfeld & Nicolson, 2003), p. 203. In the chapters to come, you will notice the similarities between Grayling's list of humanist values and those as articulated by Corliss Lamont, Tzvetan Todorov, and Confucius. In particular, note the order in which these values are listed.

73. Ibid., p. 219.

74. A. C. Grayling, *Towards the Light: The Story of the Struggles for Liberty and Rights that Made the Modern West* (London: Bloomsbury, 2007), p. 239.

75. Jim Herrick, *Humanism: An Introduction* (London: Rationalist Press Association, 2003), p. 1.

76. See Cooke, *Gathering of Infidels*, pp. 175–88, for a fuller discussion of this.

77. Nicholas Walter, "Are Humanists Human?" *New Humanist* 104, no. 3 (November 1989): 16.

78. Ibid., p. 14.

79. Ibid., p. 16.

80. Fowler, Jeaneane, *Humanism: Beliefs and Practices* (Brighton: Sussex Academic Press, 1999), p. 3.

81. Ibid., p. 7.

82. Ibid., p. 33.

83. Richard Norman, *On Humanism* (London: Routledge, 2004), p. 14. This point is amply illustrated by reference to people like Edward Howard Griggs, Herbert Read, and Clive James.

84. British Humanist Association, http://www.humanism.org.uk/.

85. Humanist Philosophers' Group, *What Is Humanism?* (London: British Humanist Association, 2002), p. 23.

86. E. M. Forster, "How I Lost My Faith," *Humanist* 78, no. 9 (September 1963): 265.

CHAPTER 6: AMERICAN HUMANISM SINCE WORLD WAR II

1. Sidney Hook, *Out of Step: An Unquiet Life in the 20th Century* (New York: Harper & Row, 1987), p. 237.

2. Corliss Lamont, *The Illusion of Immortality* (New York: Philosophical Library, 1959 [1935]), pp. 22–24.

3. Wells dedicated his novel *Men Like Gods* (London: Cassell, 1923) to Florence Lamont.

4. Frederick J. E. Woodbridge, *An Essay on Nature* (New York: Columbia University Press, 1940), p. 125.

5. Corliss Lamont, *Humanism as a Philosophy* (New York: Philosophical Library, 1949), p. xvii.

6. Ibid., p. 183.

7. Ibid., pp. 19–21.

8. Corliss Lamont, *The Philosophy of Humanism* (New York: Frederick Ungar Publishing, 1965), p. 13.

9. Ibid., p. 14.

10. Lamont, *Humanism as a Philosophy*, p. 144.

11. Ibid., p. 40.

12. Ibid.

13. Ibid., p. 213.

14. Ibid., pp. 313–29.

15. Ibid., p. 330.

16. Sidney Hook, *Convictions* (Amherst, NY: Prometheus Books, 1990), p. 18.

17. See "Modern Knowledge and the Concept of God," in Sidney Hook, *The Quest for Being* (New York: St. Martin's Press, 1961), pp. 115–35.

18. This was a very similar insight to that which Isaiah Berlin made central to his thinking. See the previous chapter.

19. Sidney Hook, "Pragmatism and the Tragic Sense of Life," in *American Philosophy in the Twentieth Century*, ed. Paul Kurtz (New York: Macmillan, 1967 [1966]), p. 535.

20. Paul Kurtz, "The Moral Crisis in Humanism," *Humanist* 27, no. 5 (September/December 1967): 151.

21. *Humanist* 23, no. 1 (January/February 1973): 15.

22. Ibid., p. 19.

23. Paul Kurtz, *Humanist Manifestos I and II* (Amherst, NY: Prometheus Books, 1973), p. 16.

24. The most egregious example, if only because of its pretensions to academic integrity, is David Noebel, J. F. Baldwin, and Kevin Bywater, eds., *Clergy in the Classroom: The Religion of Secular Humanism* (Manitou Springs, CO: Summit, 2001 [1995]).

25. Kurtz, *Humanist Manifestos I and II*, p. 13.

26. Ibid., p. 23.

27. Harold Blackham, "Call to Thought," *New Humanist* 90, no. 2 (June 1974): 66. Elsewhere he dismissed the manifesto as "rather rhetorical and necessarily

cliché-ridden." See Harold Blackham, "Humanist Statement," *New Humanist* 91, no. 2 (June 1975): 44.

28. Paul Kurtz, ed., *The Humanist Alternative* (London: Pemberton Books, 1973), pp. 185–86.

29. Kurtz, *Humanist Manifestos I and II*, p. 24.

30. Eric Hobsbawm, *Age of Extremes: The Short Twentieth Century, 1914–1991* (London: Michael Joseph, 1995 [1994]), p. 403.

31. James Davison Hunter, "The Liberal Reaction," in *The New Christian Right*, ed. Robert Liebman and Robert Wuthrow (New York: Aldine, 1983), p. 160.

32. Paul Kurtz, *Exuberance: An Affirmative Philosophy of Life* (Amherst, NY: Prometheus Books, 1985 [1978]), p. 174.

33. Paul Kurtz, "Announcing a New Magazine," *Free Inquiry* 1, no. 1 (Winter 1980–81): 1.

34. Paul Kurtz, "A Secular Humanist Declaration," in ibid., pp. 3–4.

35. Ibid., p. 6.

36. "The Secular Humanist Declaration: Pro and Con," *Free Inquiry* 1, no. 2 (Spring 1981): 6–11.

37. Letter to the editor, *New Humanist* 96, no. 4 (Spring 1981): 28.

38. Leo Pfeffer, *Creeds in Competition: A Creative Force in American Culture* (New York: Harper & Brothers, 1958), p. 29.

39. Paul Kurtz, "On Criticizing Religion," *Free Inquiry* 1, no. 2 (Spring 1981): 1.

40. Paul Beattie, "The Religion of Secular Humanism," *Free Inquiry* 6, no. 1 (Winter 1985–86): 16.

41. Joseph Fletcher, "Residual Religion," *Free Inquiry* 6, no. 1 (Winter 1985–86): 19, emphasis in the original.

42. Beattie, "Religion of Secular Humanism," p. 13, emphasis in the original.

43. Howard Radest, *The Devil and Secular Humanism* (New York: Praeger, 1990), p. 123.

44. Tom Flynn, *Secular Humanism Defined* (Amherst, NY: Council for Secular Humanism, 2002), p. 19.

45. An example of this attempt to define boundaries can be found in *Free Inquiry* 22, no. 4 (Fall 2002). The front page heading announced the issue was devoted to "Drawing Clear Boundaries: Secular and Religious Humanism."

46. An honorable exception can be found in Jeaneane Fowler, *Humanism: Beliefs and Practices* (Brighton: Sussex Academic Press, 1999), p. 21.

47. "Free Inquiry's Second Decade," *Free Inquiry* 10, no. 1 (Winter 1989–90): back page. The article is unsigned but there is no doubt that Paul Kurtz wrote it.

48. Tim Madigan, "The Need for Eupraxophy," *Free Inquiry* 9, no. 3 (Summer 1989): 8–10.

49. Molleen Matsumura, letter to the editor, *Free Inquiry* 8, no. 2 (Spring 1988): 3.

50. Daniel O'Hara, "Humanism and Creationism," *New Humanist* 104, no. 2 (August 1989): 24.

51. Christopher Lyon, letter to the editor, *Free Inquiry* 19, no. 2 (Spring 1990): 3.

52. Anthony B. Pinn, *African American Humanist Principles* (New York: Palgrave Macmillan, 2004), p. 6.

53. Ibid., p. 7.

54. Ibid., p. 104.

55. Ibid., p. 21.

56. Through his marriage to Marcella Walker, McGee was stepfather to Joan Harris (1928–2006), the prominent sociologist who later attributed her strong religious humanist commitment to McGee.

57. Norm Allen Jr., ed., *The Black Humanist Experience* (Amherst, NY: Prometheus Books, 2003), p. 147.

58. "An African-American Humanist Declaration," *Free Inquiry* 10, no. 2 (Spring 1990): 13–15.

59. Richard Rorty, *Consequences of Pragmatism—Essays: 1972–1980* (Minneapolis: University of Minnesota Press, 1982), p. 218.

60. Edward Said, *Humanism and Democratic Criticism* (New York: Columbia University Press, 2004), p. 136.

61. Danny Postel, "Obituary," *New Humanist* 122, no. 4 (2007): 38–39. For Rorty himself expressing this idea, see "Solidarity or Objectivity?" in *Objectivity, Relativism, and Truth* (Cambridge: Cambridge University Press, 1995 [1991]), p. 34; and "Religion as a Conversation Stopper" in *Philosophy and Social Hope* (London: Penguin, 1999), p. 168.

62. Said, *Humanism and Democratic Criticism*, pp. 53–54. It has to be said that Said's contribution to humanist discourse in the Middle East has been ambivalent at best in the wake of the victim culture his work *Orientalism* (1978) encouraged.

63. Daniel C. Dennett, *Darwin's Dangerous Idea* (London: Allen Lane, 1995), pp. 476–77.

64. Daniel C. Dennett, *Breaking the Spell: Religion as a Natural Phenomenon* (London: Allen Lane, 2006), p. 263.

65. Ibid., p. 25.

66. For instance, see Woodbridge, *Essay on Nature*, pp. 6–7.

67. John R. Shook, ed., *Pragmatic Naturalism and Realism* (Amherst, NY: Prometheus Books, 2003), p. 8.

68. Kurt Baier, *Problems of Life and Death: A Humanist Perspective* (Amherst, NY: Prometheus Books, 1997), p. 5.

69. Charles Taylor, *A Secular Age* (Cambridge, MA: Belknap, 2007), p. 525.

70. Susan Jacoby, *Freethinkers: A History of American Secularism* (New York: Metropolitan Books, 2004).

CHAPTER 7: *BILDUNG* TO *LAÏCITÉ*

1. Preface to vol. 1, *Sammtliche Werke* (1846), pp. xiv–xv. Quoted from Eugene Kamenka, *The Philosophy of Ludwig Feuerbach* (London: Routledge & Kegan Paul, 1970), p. 17.

2. Sidney Hook, *From Hegel to Marx: Studies in the Intellectual Development of Karl Marx* (New York: Humanities Press, 1958 [1950]), p. 225. This contrasts with *volo ergo sum*, or "I will, therefore I am," which Isaiah Berlin described as the slogan of the Romantics. See Isaiah Berlin, *Roots of Romanticism* (London: Chatto & Windus, 1999), p. 97. Walter Kaufmann made the same point as Hook when he said that God-talk can be meaningful and even verifiable without implying that such an entity exists. This gets to the core of European humanism. See Walter Kaufmann, *Critique of Religion and Philosophy* (New York: Harper Torchbooks, 1972 [1958]), p. 176.

3. Karl Löwith, *From Hegel to Nietzsche: The Revolution in Nineteenth-century Thought* (London: Constable, 1965 [1941]), p. 20.

4. For a fuller discussion of this, see Peter Gay, *The Pleasure Wars* (London: HarperCollins, 1998).

5. Thomas Mann, *The Magic Mountain* (London: Penguin, 1960 [1924]), p. 249.

6. Letter to Arthur Schnitzler, in *The Letters of Thomas Mann*, ed. Richard Winston and Clara Winston (London: Penguin, 1975 [1970]), p. 108.

7. Ronald Hayman, *Thomas Mann: A Biography* (New York: Scribner, 1995), p. 426.

8. *Humanist* 11, no. 5 (October/November 1951), p. 199.

9. Anonymous, *I Believe* (London: George Allen & Unwin, 1941 [1940]), pp. 219–20.

10. Herbert R. Lottman, *Albert Camus: A Biography* (London: Weidenfeld & Nicolson, 1979), p. 339.

11. Albert Camus, *The Myth of Sisyphus* (London: Hamish Hamilton, 1965 [1942]), p. 44.

12. Ibid., p. 45.

13. Albert Camus, *The Plague* (London: Penguin, 1968 [1947]), p. 34.

14. Ibid., p. 178.

15. Albert Camus, *Resistance, Rebellion and Death* (London: Hamish Hamilton, 1963 [1960]), pp. 51–52.

16. Lottman, *Albert Camus*, p. 1.

17. Bertrand Russell, *Power: A New Social Analysis* (London: George Allen & Unwin, 1938), p. 263.

18. Erik Wielenberg, *Value and Virtue in a Godless Universe* (Amherst, NY: Prometheus Books, 2005), p. 126. It's also worth noting that Wielenberg has a high opinion of Bertrand Russell's "The Free Man's Worship," the value of which was canvassed in chapter 3.

19. Clive James, *Cultural Amnesia: Necessary Memories from History and the Arts* (New York: W. W. Norton, 2007), pp. 671–72.

20. Sartre is credited with coining the word *existentialism*, and, as with humanism, the *ism* version of the word came after people spoke of a "philosophy of existence," of even "existential philosophy."

21. Jean-Paul Sartre, *Existentialism and Humanism* (London: Methuen, 1970 [1946]), pp. 55–56.

22. Martin Heidegger, "Letter on Humanism," in *Martin Heidegger: Basic Writings*, ed. David Farrell Krell (New York: Harper & Row, 1977), p. 203.

23. Ibid., p. 204.
24. Ibid., p. 205.
25. Ibid., p. 210.
26. Ibid., p. 213.
27. Ibid., p. 231.
28. Ibid., p. 222.
29. Ibid., p. 228.
30. Ibid., p. 237.
31. Ibid., p. 213.
32. Ibid., p. 214.
33. Ibid., p. 224.
34. Ibid., p. 210.

35. Paul Edwards, *Heidegger's Confusions* (Amherst, NY: Prometheus Books, 2004), pp. 28–30.

36. Richard Rorty, *Objectivity, Relativism and Truth* (Cambridge: Cambridge University Press, 1995 [1991]), p. 71.

37. Edwards, *Heidegger's Confusions*, pp. 28–30.

38. Heidegger, "Letter on Humanism," p. 203.

39. Paul Tillich, "Heidegger and Jaspers," in *Heidegger and Jaspers*, ed. Alan M. Olson (Philadelphia: Temple University Press, 1994), p. 17. Even Hector Hawton, in his severe, though intelligent, critique of existentialism, conceded Jaspers was the "least exasperating and the most persuasive of all the existentialists." See Hector Hawton, *The Feast of Unreason* (London: Watts, 1952), p. 197.

40. Karl Jaspers, *Way to Wisdom* (London: Victor Gollancz, 1951), p. 179.

41. Ibid., p. 90.

42. Ibid., p. 70.

43. Stephen Eriksen, "The Space of Transcendence in Jaspers and Heidegger," in Olson, *Heidegger and Jaspers* (see note 39); Jaspers, *Way to Wisdom*, p. 131. This, despite Jaspers's deep ambivalence about Aristotle through his career.

44. Jürgen Habermas, *Philosophical-Political Profiles* (Cambridge, MA: MIT Press, 1983), pp. 45–52.

45. This idea will be explored in more detail in chapter 8.

46. www.humanistiche-union.de.

47. Jaap van Praag, *Foundations of Humanism* (Amherst, NY: Prometheus Books, 1982), pp. 15–52. The examples used here are more transcultural than those Van Praag employed. And no claim is being made that there is a direct line of intellectual descent from, say, Confucius to Jeremy Bentham.

48. Jaap van Praag, "The Humanist Outlook," in *A Catholic/Humanist Dialogue*, ed. Paul Kurtz and Albert Dondeyne (London: Pemberton Books, 1972), p. 5. Van Praag probably had Bertrand Russell's postulates at the end of *Human Knowledge* in mind.

49. This has been comprehensively demolished by Kaufmann in *Critique of Religion and Philosophy*, pp. 331–47.

50. Veljko Korac, quoted in Oskar Gruenwald, "The Silencing of the Marxist Avant-Garde in Yugoslavia," *Humanist* 35, no. 3 (May/June 1975): 34.

51. Ibid.

52. Hans van Deukeren, "From Theory to Practice—A History of the IHEU 1952–2002," in *International Humanist & Ethical Union, 1952–2002*, ed. Bert Gasenbeek and Babu Gogineni (Utrecht: De Tijdstroom, 2002), p. 62.

53. George Novack, *Humanism and Socialism* (New York: Pathfinder, 1980 [1973]), p. 113.

54. Louis Althusser, *For Marx* (New York: Vintage, 1970 [1965]), p. 26, emphasis in the original.

55. Ibid., p. 227.

56. Ibid., pp. 229–31.

57. E. P. Thompson, *The Poverty of Theory* (London: Merlin, 1978), p. 236.

58. Ibid., p. 360. Thompson was not, of course, the first person to say this. He was anticipated, for instance, by Bertrand Russell in *Freedom and Organization, 1814–1914* (London: George Allen & Unwin), p. 253.

59. Quoted in Paul Kurtz, "Is Everyone a Humanist?" *The Humanist Alternative*, ed. Paul Kurtz (London: Pemberton Books, 1973), p. 175.

60. Maria Petrosyan, *Humanism: Its Philosophical, Ethical and Sociological Aspects* (Moscow: Progress Publishers, 1972).

61. Paul Kurtz, "Militant Atheism versus Freedom of Conscience," *Free Inquiry* 9, no. 4 (Fall 1989): 32.

62. Michel Foucault, *The Order of Things* (London: Vintage, 1973), pp. 386–87.

63. Tzvetan Todorov, *Imperfect Garden: The Legacy of Humanism* (Princeton, NJ: Princeton University Press, 2002), p. 34.

64. Friedrich Nietzsche, *Thus Spake Zarathustra* (Amherst, NY: Prometheus Books, 1993 [1885]), p. 222.

65. Friedrich Nietzsche, *Beyond Good and Evil* (London: Penguin, 1988 [1886]), pt. 2, p. 32. See also David Goicoechea, "Zarathustra and Enlightenment Humanism," in *The Question of Humanism: Challenges and Possibilities*, ed. David Goicoechea, John Luik, and Tim Madigan (Amherst, NY: Prometheus Books, 1991).

66. Gregory Bruce Smith, *Nietzsche, Heidegger and the Transition to Postmodernity* (Chicago: University of Chicago Press, 1996), p. 329.

67. Norman Levitt, *Prometheus Bedeviled: Science and the Contradictions of Contemporary Culture* (New Brunswick, NJ: Rutgers University Press, 1999), p. 183. One doesn't even need to be irrevocably set against postmodernism to acknowledge this point. Christopher Butler, in his admirably evenhanded assessment, says the same thing. See Christopher Butler, *Postmodernism: A Very Short Introduction* (Oxford: Oxford University Press, 2002), p. 114.

68. This observation comes from Alain Finkelkraut, who was quoted in Martin Halliwell and Andy Mousley, *Critical Humanisms: Humanist/Anti-Humanist Dialogues* (Edinburgh: Edinburgh University Press, 2003), p. 14.

69. Tony Davies, *Humanism* (London: Routledge, 1997), pp. 131–32.

70. Stephen Yarbrough, *Deliberate Criticism: Toward a Postmodern Humanism* (Athens: University of Georgia Press, 1992), p. 35.

71. Ibid., p. 23.

72. Ibid., p. 13.

73. Halliwell and Mousley, *Critical Humanisms*, p. 16.

74. Edward Said, *Humanism and Democratic Criticism* (New York: Columbia University Press, 2004), pp. 42–43.

75. Gaby Jacobs, "Humanistics: Reflection and Action in the Transitional Space of the Political and the Existential," in *Empowering Humanity: State of the Art in Humanistics*, ed. Annemie Halsema and Douwe van Houten (Utrecht: De Tijdstroom Uitgeverij, 2004), p. 243.

76. Todorov, *Imperfect Garden*, p. 233. See also Todorov's *Hope and Memory* (London: Atlantic Books, 2005 [2003]), p. 313, where he says this is *the* task of twenty-first-century humanism.

77. Todorov, *Imperfect Garden*, p. 30. And just to see that this observation can also be made from within the English-speaking humanist tradition, if in more prosaic language, see Jeaneane Fowler, *Humanism: Beliefs and Practices* (Brighton: Sussex Academic Press, 1999), pp. 55–57.

78. Todorov, *Hope and Memory*, p. 34. Jaspers understood this as well, when he

said that we "are independent only when we are at the same time enmeshed in the world." See Jaspers, *Way to Wisdom*, p. 115.

79. Ibid., p. 313. And this is also very much the message in James's recent work *Cultural Amnesia*, which made an examination of many of the same people Todorov looked at the main vehicle by which contemporary humanism can be understood.

80. Todorov, *Imperfect Garden*, p. 235.

81. Ibid., p. 236.

CHAPTER 8: CHRISTIAN HUMANISM

1. Leszek Kolakowski, *Religion* (London: Fontana, 1993), pp. 55–56.

2. Thomas J. J. Altizer, "Theology and the Death of God," in *Radical Theology and the Death of God*, ed. Thomas J. J. Altizer and William Hamilton (Indianapolis: Bobbs-Merrill, 1966), p. 96.

3. Roger L. Shinn, *Man: The New Humanism* (London: Lutterworth, 1968), p. 95.

4. Altizer, "Theology and the Death of God," p. 111.

5. Charles Taylor, *A Secular Age* (Cambridge, MA: Belknap, 2007), pp. 544, 549.

6. Jacques Maritain, *True Humanism* (London: Geoffrey Bles, 1954 [1938]), p. 19.

7. Ibid., p. 27.

8. Ibid., p. 81.

9. The perceptive rationalist and former Catholic, Hector Hawton, whom we discussed in chapter 5, was characteristically succinct in his response to this line. "To suppose that a word can have a 'true meaning' is one of the fallacies [that] we are only just beginning to outgrow." See Hector Hawton, "Humanism and God," *Literary Guide* 67, no. 3 (March 1952): 41.

10. Werner Jaeger, *Humanism and Theology* (Milwaukee: Marquette University Press, 1943), p. 20.

11. Ibid., p. 45.

12. Ibid., p. 55.

13. Letter dated January 12, 1941, quoted in Shinn, *Man* (see note 3), p. 47.

14. Pierre Teilhard de Chardin, *The Phenomenon of Man* (London: Collins, 1960), p. 35.

15. Ibid., p. 211.

16. Ibid., p. 209.

17. Ibid., p. 210.

18. Ibid., p. 298.

19. Martin D'Arcy, *Humanism and Christianity* (New York: World Publishing, 1969), p. 162.

20. Edward Stourton, *Absolute Truth: The Catholic Church Today* (London: Penguin, 1999 [1998]), p. 40.

21. Vatican, The Holy See, http://www.vatican.va/. This encyclical also spoke of "exclusive humanism," which Charles Taylor later took up as his motif in *A Secular Age*.

22. Albert Dondeyne, "Modern Humanism and Christian Faith in God," in *A Catholic/Humanist Dialogue*, ed. Paul Kurtz and Albert Dondeyne (London: Pemberton Books, 1972), p. 15.

23. D'Arcy, *Humanism and Christianity*, p. 54.

24. D'Arcy was warmly remembered by the *New Humanist* after his death as "one of the first English Catholics prepared to take modern humanism seriously." See Nicholas Walter, "Rationally Speaking," *New Humanist* 92, no. 5 (January/February 1977): 160.

25. John Carroll, *Humanism: The Wreck of Western Culture* (London: Fontana, 1993), p. 138.

26. Ibid., p. 6.

27. In particular, see John F. Haught, *God after Darwin: A Theology of Evolution* (Boulder, CO: Westview, 2000).

28. Maureen Fiedler and Linda Rabben, eds., *Rome Has Spoken* (New York: Crossroad, 1998). This is the sort of book the Rationalist Press Association would have published a century ago—and would have been lambasted as being anti-Christian for so doing.

29. The only noteworthy point among an otherwise uninteresting argument is his anticipation of a point made by Antony Flew many years later that what was really being discussed was an argument *to* design, rather than an argument *from* design. See Arthur Balfour, *Theism and Humanism* (London: Hodder & Stoughton, 1915), p. 44.

30. Ibid., p. 248.

31. Charles Hartshorne, *Beyond Humanism: Essays in the Philosophy of Nature* (Lincoln: University of Nebraska Press, 1968 [1937]), p. 9.

32. Ibid., p. 7.

33. Ibid., p. 19.

34. Ibid., p. 98.

35. Ibid., p. 101.

36. Ibid., p. 106.

37. Letter dated July 16, 1944, quoted in William Hamilton, "Dietrich Bonhoeffer," in Altizer and Hamilton, *Radical Theology and the Death of God*, p. 115. It is significant that this passage was also the starting point for Paul van Buren. See Paul van Buren, *The Secular Meaning of the Gospel* (London: SCM, 1963), p. 1.

38. Rudolf Bultmann, "Christianity and Humanism," *Journal of Religion* 32, no. 2 (April 1952): 80.

39. Ibid., p. 81.
40. Ibid., p. 83.
41. See, for example, Shinn's positive discussion of this tension in *Man*, pp. 174–75.
42. Paul Tillich, *The Shaking of the Foundations* (London: Penguin, 1969 [1949]), p. 53.
43. Ibid., pp. 63–64.
44. Ibid., p. 108.
45. Ibid., p. 95.
46. See Walter Kaufmann, *Critique of Religion and Philosophy* (New York: Harper Torchbooks, 1972 [1958]), pp. 195–96. The quoted passage is on page 223.
47. J. A. T. Robinson, *Honest to God* (London: SCM, 1963), p. 8. A BBC talk on the meaning of God-language by Robinson and Bernard Williams was published by the first issue of *Question*, the Rationalist Press Association's academic journal, in 1968. See Bernard Williams and the bishop of Woolwich, "Has 'God' a Meaning? (A Discussion)," in *Question 1*, ed. Hector Hawton (London: Pemberton Publishing, 1968), pp. 49–61.
48. The reference by Hegel to the death of God came in an early essay, usually translated as "Faith and Knowledge," published in 1802. Hegel argued that the age of dogmatic philosophies had come to an end and that "the supreme totality in all its seriousness can and must arise again from its deepest ground, all-embracing into the serenest freedom of form." Quoted from Ronald Gregor Smith, *Secular Christianity* (London: Collins, 1966), p. 160.
49. Thomas J. J. Altizer, "America and the Future of Theology," in Altizer, *Radical Theology and the Death of God*, p. 12.
50. See the preface of Altizer, *Radical Theology and the Death of God*, p. xii.
51. Thomas J. J. Altizer, "America and the Future of Theology," in Altizer, *Radical Theology and the Death of God*, p. 11.
52. Ibid., p. 16.
53. Smith, *Secular Christianity*, p. 103.
54. Shinn, *Man*, p. 138.
55. William Franklin and Joseph M. Shaw, *The Case for Christian Humanism* (Grand Rapids, MI: William B. Eerdmans, 1991), p. xvii.
56. Ibid., p. xi.
57. Ibid., p. 4.
58. Anthony Freeman, *God in Us: A Case for Christian Humanism* (London: SCM, 1993), pp. 9–10.
59. See in particular, John Hick, ed., *The Myth of God Incarnate* (London: SCM, 1977). Hick later followed up with *The Metaphor of God Incarnate* (London: SCM, 1993).
60. Walter Kaufmann, *Critique of Religion and Society*, p. 295.

61. Duncan Howlett, *The Fatal Flaw at the Heart of Religious Liberalism* (Amherst, NY: Prometheus Books, 1995), especially p. 55.

62. I owe this observation to Gerhard Szczesny. See Gerhard Szczesny, *The Future of Unbelief* (New York: George Braziller, 1961 [1958]), p. 198.

63. David Ehrenfeld, *The Arrogance of Humanism* (Oxford: Oxford University Press, 1981 [1978]), p. 5.

64. Francis Schaeffer, *How Should We Then Live?* (Old Tappan, NJ: Fleming H. Revell, 1976), p. 190.

65. Homer Duncan, *Humanism: The Most Dangerous Religion in America* (Lubbock, TX: Missionary Crusader, 1979), p. 12.

66. Ibid., p. 13.

67. Tim LaHaye and David Noebel, *Mind Siege: The Battle for Truth in the New Millennium* (Nashville: World Publishing, 2000), pp. 171–72. One sociologist from 1983 correctly observed that LaHaye's *The Battle for the Mind* became "the key tract in the attack on secular humanism." Robert Liebman, "Mobilizing the Moral Majority," in *The New Christian Right*, ed. Robert Liebman and Robert Wuthrow (New York: Aldine, 1983), p. 59.

68. Duncan, *Humanism: The Most Dangerous Religion in America*, p. 4.

69. Letter to the editor, *Free Inquiry* 3, no. 3 (Summer 1983): 63.

70. Tim LaHaye, *The Battle for the Mind* (Old Tappan, NJ: Fleming H. Revell, 1980), p. 83.

71. For a fuller discussion of this important insight, see Susan Greenfield, *ID: The Quest for Identity in the 21st Century* (London: Sceptre, 2008), especially chapter 12.

72. See William Strawson, *The Christian Approach to the Humanist* (London: Lutterworth, 1970 [1963]); Roger Forster and Paul Marston, *Reason and Faith* (Eastbourne: Monarch Publications, 1989); and Alister McGrath, *The Twilight of Atheism* (London: Rider, 2004).

73. John Shelby Spong, *Liberating the Gospels: Reading the Bible through Jewish Eyes* (New York: HarperCollins, 1996), p. 235.

74. Lloyd Geering, *Wrestling with God: The Story of My Life* (Wellington: Bridget Williams Books, 2006), p. 150.

75. I owe this point to Finngeir Hiorth, *Introduction to Humanism* (Oslo: Human-Etisk Forbund, 2007), p. 93.

76. Buber spoke of a "believing humanism" that integrated existentially humanism and faith. See Martin Buber, *A Believing Humanism*, ed. Ruth Nanda Anshen (New York: Simon & Schuster, 1969 [1967]), p. 118. Geering appreciated this point in his own study of Buber, where he wrote approvingly of Buber's humanism as that which sought a true sense of community where the secular and the spiritual were wholly integrated. See Lloyd Geering, *The World of Relation: An*

Introduction to Martin Buber's I and Thou (Wellington: Victoria University Press, 1983), p. 4.

77. Lloyd Geering, *God in the New World* (London: Hodder & Stoughton, 1968), p. 39. It's interesting to note that Gerhard Szczesny made the same point, even speaking of schizophrenia. See Gerhard Szczesny, *The Future of Unbelief* (New York: George Braziller, 1961 [1958]), pp. 20–21, 202.

78. Lloyd Geering, "Humanism: Is It Enough?" *Listener* (October 10, 1987): 105. Geering was responding to the short work *Humanism: Its History and Nature* (Auckland: NZARH, 1987), by Edwin Tapp, a New Zealand historian. As well as providing a standard account of secular humanism, Tapp was also keen to reconcile the free thought movement in the country, which had broken into humanist and rationalist factions.

79. Lloyd Geering, *Fundamentalism: The Challenge to the Secular World* (Wellington: St. Andrew's Trust, 2003).

80. Lloyd Geering, *Faith's New Age* (London: Collins, 1980), p. 295.

81. Ibid., p. 296.

82. Lloyd Geering, *Christianity without God* (Wellington: Bridget Williams Books, 2002), p. 14.

83. This insight is commonly made by humanist thinkers. See, for instance, Paul Kurtz, *Forbidden Fruit: The Ethics of Humanism* (Amherst, NY: Prometheus Books, 1988), p. 53.

84. Rachael Kohn, *The New Believers: Reimagining God* (Pymble, NSW: HarperCollins, 2003), p. 180.

85. Albert Schweitzer, *Civilization and Ethics* (London: Adam & Charles Black, 1946 [1923]), p. 204.

86. Albert Schweitzer, *Out of My Life and Thought* (New York: Mentor, 1960 [1933]), p. 157.

87. Ibid., p. 158. Also see Schweitzer, *Civilization and Ethics*, p. xviii.

88. Schweitzer, *Civilization and Ethics*, p. 265.

89. *Humanist* 11, no. 5 (October/November 1951): 197. Neither was this a one-off flourish. He said much the same in *Civilization and Ethics*, p. 270.

90. Albert Schweitzer, *The Quest of the Historical Jesus* (London: Adam & Charles Black, 1950), p. 358.

91. Schweitzer, *Out of My Life and Thought*, p. 49.

92. Ibid., pp. 46–47.

CHAPTER 9: INDIAN HUMANISM

1. Jawaharlal Nehru, *The Discovery of India* (London: Asia Publishing, 1960 [1946]), p. 63.

2. The definitive account of Indian naturalist thought remains Dale Riepe, *The Naturalistic Tradition of Indian Thought* (Seattle: University of Washington Press, 1961).

3. This is the approach, for instance, of Samani Chaitanya Prajna, ed., *The Role of Jainism in Evolving a New Paradigm of Philosophy* (Ladnun: Jain Vishva Bharati, 2008). This was the handbook prepared for the 22nd World Congress of Philosophy, held in Seoul, South Korea.

4. Acharya Mahaprajnak, *Anekanta: The Third Eye* (Ladnun: Jain Vishva Bharati Institute, 2002), p. 195.

5. Ibid., pp. 1–12.

6. Basant Kumar Lal, *Contemporary Indian Philosophy* (New Delhi: Motilal Banarsidass, 1992 [1973]), p. xx.

7. Vishwanath Prasad Varma, *Philosophical Humanism and Contemporary India* (New Delhi: Motilal Banarsidass, 1979), pp. 189–91.

8. Ibid., p. 13.

9. Sri Ramakrishna, *Teachings of Sri Ramakrishna* (Kolkata: Advaita Ashrama, 2004 [1916]), p. 44.

10. Swami Vivekananda, *The Complete Works of Swami Vivekananda* (Calcutta: Advaita Ashrama, 1972), 4:368.

11. Ibid., p. 75.

12. Amartya Sen, *The Argumentative Indian* (London: Penguin, 2006 [2005]), p. 90.

13. Rabindranath Tagore, *Collected Poems and Plays of Rabindranath Tagore* (London: Macmillan, 1973 [1936]), p. 16.

14. Rabindranath Tagore, *My Reminiscences* (London: Macmillan, 1921 [1917]), p. 222.

15. I owe this point to Krishna Dutta and Andrew Robinson's excellent biography; *Rabindranath Tagore: The Myriad-Minded Man* (London: Bloomsbury, 1997 [1995]), p. 237.

16. Tagore, *My Reminiscences*, p. 186.

17. Lal, *Contemporary Indian Philosophy*, p. 15.

18. Rabindranath Tagore, *The Religion of Man* (Boston: Beacon, 1961 [1931]), p. 15.

19. Quoted in Lal, *Contemporary Indian Philosophy*, p. 73.

20. Tagore, *My Reminiscences*, p. 266.

21. B. R. Ambedkar, "What Congress and Gandhi Have Done to the Untouchables," in *Dr. Babasaheb Ambedkar, Writings and Speeches*, ed. Vascant Moon

(Bombay: Education Department, Government of Maharashtra, 1989 [1979]), 9:284.

22. B. R. Ambedkar, *Conversion as Emancipation* (New Delhi: Critical Quest, 2004), p. 30.

23. Bharathi Thummapudi, "Dr. Ambedkar's Philosophy: A Step towards Total Humanism" (conference presentation delivered August 3, 2008, at the 22nd World Congress of Philosophy, Seoul, South Korea, July 30–August 6, 2008).

24. B. R. Ambedkar, "Buddha or Karl Marx," in *Dr. Babasaheb Ambedkar, Writings and Speeches* (see note 21), 3:462.

25. Subbarao Maradani, "Dr. Bhim Rao Ramji Ambedkar: Some Little-known and Unknown Facts," *Rationalist Voice* 3, no. 6 (March/April 2004): 7.

26. This is outlined well in R. Srinivasam, "Dr. Ambedkar's Search for Roots," *New Quest*, no. 116 (March/April 1996): 81–90. Srinivasam argues that Ambedkar's challenge was to build among dalits any sense of community with a common history.

27. Charles Bradlaugh, *Speeches* (London: Freethought Publishing, 1890), p. 155.

28. For a full reprint of the article, see V. K. Sinha, ed., *The Reason Case* (Pune: Indian Secular Society, 1995), pp. 24–26.

29. Ibid., p. 33.

30. Ibid., pp. 39–44.

31. Ibid., p. 54.

32. Innaiah Narisetti, ed., *M. N. Roy: Selected Writings* (Amherst, NY: Prometheus Books, 2004), p. 194.

33. Roy's radical humanism is a variation of scientific humanism, a link that V. M. Tarkunde made specific. See V. M. Tarkunde, *Radical Humanism* (New Delhi: Ajanta Publications, 1991 [1983]), pp. 1–4.

34. Lavanam, *Of Gandhi, Atheism and Social Experimentalism*, ed. K. H. S. S. Sundar (Vijayawada: Atheist Centre, 2003), p. 29.

35. Sunanda Shet, *Gora: His Life and Work* (Podanur, Tamilnadu: CSICOP India, n.d. [ca. 2000]), p. 129.

36. Lavanam, *Of Gandhi, Atheism and Social Experimentalism*, p. 29.

37. Gora, *An Atheist with Gandhi* (Ahmedabad: Navajivan Publishing, 2003 [1951]), pp. 32–33.

38. Gora, *The Need of Atheism* (Vijayawada: Atheist Centre, 1991 [1980]), p. 57.

39. Ibid., p. 38.

40. See his work *The* Ramayana *(A True Meaning)* (Chennai: DK Publications, 1998 [1959]).

41. Periyar, "We Cannot Eradicate Caste without Becoming Atheists," *Modern Rationalist* 30, no. 9 (September 2005): 5.

42. K. Veeramani, *Periyar's Movement: A Short Summary* (Chennai: DK Publications, 2002), p. 8.

43. K. Veeramani, *Humanism* (Chennai: Periyar Self-Respect Institution, 1998), p. 13.
44. Veeramani, *Periyar's Movement*, p. 8.
45. Nehru, *Discovery of India*, p. 526.
46. Ibid., p. 573.
47. Ibid., p. 525.
48. Ibid., p. 576.
49. Asghar Ali Engineer, "The Future of Secularism in India," *Modern Rationalist* 28, no. 10 (October 2003): 16.
50. Kushwant Singh, "Belief in God and Loyalty to the Country," *Modern Rationalist* 30, no. 4 (April 2005): 19.

CHAPTER 10: THE SPIRIT OF CHINESE HUMANISM

1. I owe this insight to Joseph Needham's *Within the Four Seas: The Dialogue of East and West* (London: George Allen & Unwin, 1969), p. 94.
2. Keping Wang, "Wang Guowei: Philosophy of Aesthetic Criticism," in *Contemporary Chinese Philosophy*, ed. Chung-ying Cheng and Nicholas Bunnin (Oxford: Blackwell, 2002), p. 41.
3. I recommend Jonathan Clements, *Confucius: A Biography* (Stroud: Sutton Publishing, 2008 [2004]), for a well-written and straightforward account of Confucius's life.
4. Wing-tsit Chan, *A Source Book in Chinese Philosophy* (Princeton, NJ: Princeton University Press, 1973 [1963]), p. 15.
5. Confucius, *The Analects* (London: Penguin, 1987 [1979]), 15:24.
6. Michael Nylan, *The Five "Confucian" Classics* (New Haven, CT: Yale University Press, 2001), p. 357. This core humanist insight was reproduced in Edwardian England by E. M. Forster, who coined the epigram "Only connect," as a concentration of human priorities. See *Howards End* (London: Penguin, 1983 [1910]), p. 188.
7. Nylan, *Five "Confucian" Classics*, p. 326.
8. Liu Shaoqi, *How to Be a Good Communist* (Beijing: Foreign Languages Press, 1952 [1939]), p. 8. During the anti-Confucius campaign of 1973–1974, Liu was lumped in with Lin Biao and "Soviet revisionist social-imperialists" of "raising the sinister flag of pro-Confucianism and anti-Legalism in their vain attempts to subvert the proletarian dictatorship and restore capitalism in China." See Lo Szu-ting "Evolution of the Debate between the Confucians and Legalists as Seen from Wang

An-shih's Reform," in *Selected Articles Criticizing Lin Piao and Confucius* (Peking: Foreign Languages Press, 1974), pp. 210–11.

9. Lo, "Evolution of the Debate" (see note 8), p. 200.

10. Shi Yanping, "Developments in Chinese Philosophy over the Last Ten Years," *Philosophy East and West* 43, no. 1 (January 1993): 117.

11. *Guardian Weekly* 174, no. 15, March 31–April 6, 2006, 8.

12. Chung-ying Cheng, "An Onto-Hermeneutic Interpretation of Twentieth-century Chinese Philosophy: Identity and Vision," in *Contemporary Chinese Philosophy* (see note 2), p. 376.

13. Babbitt's influence is clear when Lin says that humanism occupies "a mean position between the other-worldliness of religion and the materialism of the modern world." See Lin Yutang, *Chinese Ideals of Life* (London: Watts, 1944), p. 6. Another strong influence on Lin was George Santayana.

14. Ibid., p. 5.

15. Lin, *The Importance of Living* (London: William Heinemann, 1941 [1938]), pp. 135–36.

16. Lin, *Chinese Ideals of Life*, pp. 5–6.

17. Bertrand Russell wrote in a similar vein in *In Praise of Idleness* (London: George Allen & Unwin, 1935), although with the more serious intention of highlighting the madness of overwork for some while others languish with no work at all.

18. Lin, *Importance of Living*, p. 163.

19. Ibid., p. 436. In all fairness it should be noted that in his last years, Lin renounced his paganism and returned to the Presbyterian Christianity of his youth.

20. Tu Weiming, "Multiple Modernities: A Preliminary Inquiry into the Implications of East Asian Modernity," in *Culture Matters: How Values Shape Human Progress*, ed. Lawrence E. Harrison and Samuel P. Huntington (New York: Basic Books, 2000), p. 263.

21. Tu Weiming and Alan Wachman, "Workshop on Confucian Humanism," *Bulletin of the American Academy of Arts and Sciences* 43, no. 6 (March 1990): 24.

22. Lynn Struve, review of *Confucianism and Human Rights*, edited by Wm. Theodore de Bary and Tu Weiming (New York: Columbia University Press, 1998), *The China Journal*, no. 43 (January 2000): 166–68.

23. Nylan, *Five "Confucian" Classics*, p. 351.

24. Hsing Yun [Xingyun], *Star and Cloud: The Biography of Venerable Master Hsing Yun*, trans. Madelon Wheeler-Gibb (Hacienda Heights, CA: Buddha's Light Publishing, 2003), p. 138.

25. Stuart Chandler, *Establishing a Pure Land on Earth* (Honolulu: University of Hawaii Press, 2004), p. 43.

26. Ibid., p. 60.

27. Hsing, *Star and Cloud*, p. 138.
28. Hsing Yun [Xingyun], *Humanistic Buddhism: A Blueprint for Life* (Hacienda Heights, CA: Buddha's Light Publishing, 2005 [2003]), p. 68.
29. Ibid., pp. 52–53.
30. Ibid., p. 106.

CHAPTER 11: HUMANISM IN THE MUSLIM WORLD

1. Charles Kurzman, ed., *Liberal Islam: A Sourcebook* (New York: Oxford University Press, 1998), pp. 5–6.
2. Benazir Bhutto, *Reconciliation: Islam, Democracy and the West* (London: Simon & Schuster, 2008), p. 20.
3. Mohammed Arkoun, *The Unthought in Contemporary Islamic Thought* (London: Saqi Books/Institute of Ismaili Studies, 2002), p. 61.
4. It's worth noting that the Qur'an itself acknowledges this in 3:7, which distinguishes between "decisive" and "allegorical" passages and states that none know truly the proper interpretation except Allah.
5. I owe this point to Nasr Abû Zayd, *Rethinking the Qur'ân: Toward a Humanistic Hermeneutics* (Utrecht: Humanistics University Press, 2004), p. 40.
6. Ibid., p. 58.
7. Fauzi M. Najjar, "The Debate on Secularism in Egypt," *Arab Studies Quarterly* 18, no. 2 (Spring 1996): 8.
8. Kurzman, *Liberal Islam*, p. 295.
9. Ibid., p. 300.
10. Ibid., p. 301.
11. Arkoun, *Unthought in Contemporary Islamic Thought*, p. 265.
12. Ibid., p. 69.
13. Muhammad al Naquib al-Attas, *Islam and Secularism* (New Delhi: New Crescent Publishing, 2002 [1984]), p. 49.
14. Bernard Lewis, *What Went Wrong?* (London: Phoenix, 2002), p. 110.
15. Arkoun, *Unthought in Contemporary Islamic Thought*, p. 248.
16. Bhutto, *Reconciliation*, pp. 76–77.
17. Mohammad Ali Jinnah, speech of August 11, 1947, *Speeches as Governor General 1947–1948* (Karachi: Pakistan Publications, 1960), quoted in Mohiuddin Ahmad, "Politics and Religion: South Asian Perspectives," in *One Civilisation: Many Cultures*, ed. Mourad Wahba and Abousenna Mona (Cairo: Anglo-Egyptian Bookshop, 2002), p. 65.

18. Ibid., p. 160.

19. Najjar, "Debate on Secularism in Egypt," p. 2. For a full account of the GarbcIlar movement, see Şükrü Hanioglu, "GarbcIlar: Their Attitudes toward Religion and Their Impact on the Official Ideology of the Turkish Republic," *Studia Islamica*, no. 86 (1997): 133–58.

20. Jihad Fakhreddine, "What's in a Name?" *New Humanist* (March/April 2006): 9. It is noteworthy that *jihad* and *ijtihad* share the same root in Arabic. *Jihad*, which has come to be associated with holy war and righteous violence against the unbeliever, can also mean "strenuous endeavor against one's own various weaknesses and inadequacies."

21. Najjar, "Debate on Secularism in Egypt," pp. 13–14.

22. Ibid., p. 14.

23. Radio interview with Michael Hoebink, Radio Netherlands Worldwide, March 27, 2007, www.radionetherlands.nl/current affairs/is1070327.

24. Boutros Boutros Ghali, foreword to *Averroës and the Enlightenment*, ed. Mourad Wahba and Mona Abousenna (Amherst, NY: Prometheus Books, 1996), p. 9.

25. Craig Martin, "Rethinking Renaissance Averroism," *Intellectual History Review* 17, no. 1 (2007): 3–19.

26. Mourad Wahba, "Philosophy in North Africa," in *A Companion to African Philosophy*, ed. Kwasi Wiredu (Oxford: Blackwell, 2004), p. 162.

27. Anwar Shaikh's odyssey, along with many others no less moving, can be found in *Leaving Islam: Apostates Speak Out*, ed. Ibn Warraq (Amherst, NY: Prometheus Books, 2003), pp. 285–93.

28. Frédéric Robin, "Trapped, Waiting for Meaning," *Guardian Weekly*, June 13, 2008, 29.

29. See "Project Ijtihad," IrshadManji.com: For Muslim Reform and Moral Courage, http://www.irshadmanji.com/project-ijtihad.

30. Ayaan Hirsi Ali, *Infidel* (New York: Free Press, 2007), p. 270.

31. Ibid., p. 271.

32. See Council of Ex-Muslims of Britain, http://www.ex-muslim.org.uk/.

33. For a fuller discussion of this, see Amartya Sen, *Identity and Violence: The Illusion of Destiny* (London: Allen Lane, 2006).

34. Institution for the Secularization of the Islamic Society, "The St. Petersburg Delcaration," Center for Inquiry, http://www.secularislam.org/blog/post/SI_Blog/21/The-St-Petersburg-Declaration.

35. Ed Husain, "Arabs Can Help Us Reframe the Debate," *Guardian Weekly*, March 14, 2008, 19.

36. Bhutto, *Reconciliation*, p. 256.

CHAPTER 12: HUMANISM IN AFRICA

1. Norm Allen, "Report from Nigeria," *Free Inquiry* 22, no. 1 (Winter 2001–2002), p. 52.
2. Chris McGreal and Sephanie McCrummen, "The DRC Was the Host of Africa's First World War. Can It Now Hope for Peace?" *Guardian Weekly*, May 30–June 5, 2008, 23.
3. Richard Bell, *Understanding African Philosophy* (New York: Routledge, 2002), p. 40.
4. Kwasi Wiredu, *Philosophy and an African Culture* (Cambridge: Cambridge University Press, 1980), p. 6.
5. Mogobe Ramose, *African Philosophy through Ubuntu* (Harare: Mond Books, 2002 [1999]), p. 42. Also worth consulting is Dirk J. Louw, "Ubuntu: An African Assessment of the Religious Other" (paper given at the Twentieth World Congress of Philosophy in Boston, MA, August 10–15, 1998), http://www.bu.edu/wcp/Papers/Afri/AfriLouw.htm.
6. Joe Teffo, "Toward Understanding African Humanism," *AAH Examiner* 5, no. 2 (Summer 1995): 6.
7. Ramose, *African Philosophy through Ubuntu*, pp. 123–24.
8. Wole Soyinka, *Myth, Literature and the African World* (Cambridge: Cambridge University Press, 1980 [1976]), p. 130.
9. Olefumo Taiwo, "Post-Independence African Political Philosophy" in *A Companion to African Philosophy*, ed. Kwasi Wiredu (Oxford: Blackwell, 2004), p. 246.
10. Léopold Senghor, "Socialism Is a Humanism," in *Socialist Humanism*, ed. Erich Fromm (London: Penguin, 1967 [1965]), pp. 50–62.
11. Barry Hallen, "Contemporary Anglophone African Philosophy: A Survey," in *Companion to African Philosophy* (see note 9), p. 109.
12. Kwasi Wiredu, "Introduction: African Philosophy in Our Time," in *Companion to African Philosophy* (see note 9), p. 16.
13. Wiredu, *Philosophy and an African Culture*, p. 5.
14. John S. Mbiti, *African Religions and Philosophy* (London: Heinemann, 1971 [1969]), p. 262.
15. A. N. Ezeabasili, "Christianity in West Africa," *Humanist* 72, no. 11 (November 1957): 12–13.
16. For a fuller account, see Paul Kurtz, "Humanism in Africa: Paradox and Illusion," *Free Inquiry* 4, no. 4 (Fall 1984): 44–49.
17. Micah Lamptey, "Rebel with a Cause," in *The Black Humanist Experience*, ed. Norm Allen (Amherst, NY: Prometheus Books, 2003), p. 114.

18. This story is well told in Naomi Klein, *The Shock Doctrine: The Rise of Disaster Capitalism* (London: Allen Lane, 2007), especially chapter 10.

19. Nelson Mandela, *Long Walk to Freedom* (London: Little, Brown, 1994), pp. 161–62.

20. Many groups have claimed Mandela as their own, something I will not attempt here beyond noting Mabogo More's description of him as a "humanist pacifist," as against the Christian pacifism of Albert Luthuli (1898–1967), an earlier ANC leader and recipient of the Nobel Peace Prize in 1961.

21. Kenneth Kaunda, *A Humanist in Africa: Letters to Colin Morris* (London: Longmans, 1966), p. 19.

22. Ibid., p. 39.

23. Ibid., p. 19.

24. Ibid., p. 31.

25. Ibid., p. 22.

26. John Hatch, *Two African Statesmen: Kaunda of Zambia and Nyerere of Tanzania* (London: Secker & Warburg, 1976), p. 246.

27. Kurtz, "Humanism in Africa," p. 45.

28. Solarin described the product of Nigerian missionary schools in this memorable passage: "[education] bestowed on them the rudiments of English grammar, the definitions of all conceivable jargons in topographical geography, the chronology of all the kings and queens of England, live, inconsequential or moribund from AD 1066; an unmatched knowledge of the insane wars of the Old Testament flanked by parrotlike acquaintance with the church catechism." See Tai Solarin, "Christian Education: Nigeria's Unwanted Legacy," *Humanist* 26, no. 1 (January/February 1966): 15.

29. See the interesting account of Igwe's path to humanism, "My Lord, I Want to Go and Think: Choosing Reason over Faith," in *Black Humanist Experience* (see note 17), pp. 53–57.

30. "Why I Am a Secular Humanist: An Interview with Nobel Laureate Wole Soyinka," *Free Inquiry* 17, no. 4 (Fall 1997): 48–49.

31. Collins Uche Okeke, "Religion and the Decay of the Nigerian Nation," *AAH Examiner* 6, no. 3 (Fall 1996): 7.

32. *Literary Guide* 68, no. 5 (May 1953): 73.

33. *New Vision*, May 27, 2004, 4.

34. *New Vision*, May 28, 2004, 15.

35. *New Vision*, May 31, 2004, 12.

36. Daniel Etounga-Manguelle, "Does Africa Need a Cultural Adjustment Program?" in *Culture Matters: How Values Shape Human Progress*, ed. Lawrence E. Harrison and Samuel P. Huntington (New York: Basic Books, 2000), p. 75.

CHAPTER 13: A WORLD WITHOUT WALLS

1. John Gray, *Black Mass: Apocalyptic Religion and the Death of Utopia* (London: Allen Lane, 2000), p. 191.
2. Ibid., p. 206.
3. See Sidney Hook, "Naturalism and Democracy," in *Naturalism and the Human Spirit*, ed. Yervent Krikorian (New York: Columbia University Press, 1944), pp. 40–44.
4. See note 10 in chapter 4 for a brief justification of speaking of *Homo sapiens*.
5. David E. Cooper, *The Measure of Things: Humanism, Humility, and Mystery* (Oxford: Clarendon Press, 2002), p. 174.
6. For fuller discussions of this, see Richard Dawkins, *Unweaving the Rainbow* (London: Penguin, 1998); as well as Frederick Woodbridge, *An Essay on Nature* (New York: Columbia University Press, 1940); and E. O. Wilson, *Consilience, the Unity of Knowledge* (London: Little, Brown, 1998).
7. John Stuart Mill, "Nature," in *Three Essays on Religion* (London: Longmans Green, Reader, and Dyer, 1874), p. 6.
8. Ibid., pp. 16–17.
9. Quoted in "A New Humanism?" *New Humanist* 92, no. 5 (January/February 1977): 161.
10. Gilbert Murray, *Stoic, Christian and Humanist* (London: George Allen & Unwin, 1940), pp. 175–76.
11. Reed Noss, "Aldo Leopold Was a Conservation Biologist," in *Aldo Leopold and the Ecological Conscience*, ed. Richard L. Knight and Suzanne Riedel (Oxford: Oxford University Press, 2002), p. 110.
12. Gerhard Szczesny, *The Future of Unbelief* (New York: George Braziller, 1961 [1958]) p. 181.
13. Frederick J. E. Woodbridge, *An Essay on Nature* (New York: Columbia University Press, 1940), p. 278.
14. Ibid., p. 288. Feuerbach had pointed this out a century earlier in *The Essence of Christianity* (Amherst, NY: Prometheus Books, 1989 [1841]), p. 107. See also the comments on this in chapter 1.
15. John Passmore, *Man's Responsibility for Nature* (London: Duckworth, 1974), p. 106. Also, for a similar view, see Georg Henrik von Wright, *What Is Humanism?* (Topeka: University of Kansas, 1977), p. 15.
16. Passmore, *Man's Responsibility for Nature*, p. 17.
17. Ibid., p. 176.
18. Ibid., p. 184.

19. See David Suzuki with Amanda McConnell, *The Sacred Balance* (Crows Nest, NSW: Allen & Unwin, 1999 [1997]).

20. Tim Hayward, *Ecological Thought: An Introduction* (Cambridge: Polity Press, 1995), pp. 31–32.

21. Richard Dawkins, *The God Delusion* (London: Bantam, 2006), p. 229.

22. Mogobe Ramose, *African Philosophy through Ubuntu* (Harare: Mond Books, 2002 [1999]), p. 124. There is an interesting parallel here with the Jain principle of Anekanta, which posits the ongoing coexistence of opposites in a dynamic sea of change.

23. Bernard Williams, *Philosophy as a Humanistic Discipline* (Princeton, NJ: Princeton University Press, 2006), p. 139.

24. Stephen Kellert, "Aldo Leopold and the Value of Nature," in *Aldo Leopold and the Ecological Conscience* (see note 11), p. 135.

25. Jeaneane Fowler, *Humanism: Beliefs and Practices* (Brighton: Sussex Academic Press, 1999), p. 5.

26. Robert C. Solomon, *Entertaining Ideas: Popular Philosophical Essays, 1970–1990* (Amherst, NY: Prometheus Books, 1992), p. 241.

27. Peter Singer, "Taking Humanism beyond Speciesism," *Free Inquiry* 24, no. 6 (October/November 2004): 19–21. I note this not from the moral high ground of already being a vegetarian but as a meat eater.

28. James Hughes, "From Human-Racism to Personhood," in *Science and Ethics: Can Science Help Us Make Wise Moral Judgments?* ed. Paul Kurtz, with the assistance of David Koepsell (Amherst, NY: Prometheus Books, 2007), pp. 166–76.

29. For a refreshingly levelheaded discussion on transhumanism, see Susan Greenfield, *ID: The Quest for Identity in the 21st Century* (London: Sceptre, 2008), especially pp. 102–108.

30. Paul Kurtz, *Humanist Manifestos I and II* (Amherst, NY: Prometheus Books, 1973), pp. 21–22.

31. Paul Kurtz, "A Declaration of Interdependence: A New Global Ethics," *Free Inquiry* 8, no. 4 (Fall 1988): 4–7.

32. J. Baird Callicott, "The Land Ethic in a Time of Change," in *Aldo Leopold and the Ecological Conscience* (see note 11), p. 96.

33. H. G. Wells, *The Outline of History* (London: Waverley, 1921 [1920]), p. 604.

34. Ibid.

35. Ibid., p. 607, emphasis added.

36. Ibid.

37. H. G. Wells, *The Way the World Is Going* (London: Ernest Benn, 1928), pp. 64–65.

38. H. G. Wells, *The Rights of Man* (London: Penguin, 1940), especially pp. 31–69.

39. David C. Smith, *H. G. Wells: Desperately Mortal* (New Haven, CT: Yale University Press, 1986), p. 604n16. Another Wells biography suggests that his work was also influential on Wendell Willkie's bestseller *One World*. See Norman MacKenzie and Jeanne MacKenzie, *H. G. Wells* (New York: Touchstone, 1973), p. 424.

40. See H. G. Wells, *The Outlook of* Homo Sapiens (London: Secker & Warburg, 1946 [1942]), especially pp. 240–48; and H. G. Wells, *42 to 44: A Contemporary Memoir upon Human Behavior during the Crisis of the World Revolution* (London: Secker & Warburg, 1944), pp. 36–48.

41. Wells, *Outline of History*, p. 608.

42. Julian Huxley, *Memories II* (London: Penguin, 1978 [1973]), p. 9.

43. Ibid., pp. 11–12.

44. See note 21 in chapter 2.

45. Charles Bradlaugh Bonner, "How It Was at Rome," *Literary Guide* 64, no. 11 (November 1949): 217, bracketing in the original.

46. Hans van Deukeren, "From Theory to Practice—A History of the IHEU 1952–2002," in *International Humanist & Ethical Union, 1952–2002*, ed. Bert Gasenbeek and Babu Gogineni (Utrecht: De Tijdstroom, 2002), p. 21.

47. Ibid., p. 23.

48. Ibid., p. 26.

49. This mirrors a change made in 1996 when the Council for Democratic and Secular Humanism renamed itself the Council for Secular Humanism. In the wake of the collapse of Communism, the need to differentiate democratic humanism from socialist humanism was no longer apparent.

50. "The IHEU Amsterdam Declaration 2002," *International Humanist News*, November 2002, 15.

51. This has been done well by Van Deukeren, "From Theory to Practice," pp. 15–103.

52. Alan Ryan, *Bertrand Russell: A Political Life* (London: Allen Lane, 1988), p. 163.

53. Bertrand Russell, *Portraits from Memory and Other Essays* (London: George Allen & Unwin, 1956), p. 215.

54. Ibid., p. 219.

55. Ibid., p. 220. This saying served as a source of lifelong inspiration for the American billionaire, entrepreneur, and philanthropist Warren Buffett.

56. Manfred Kuehn, *Kant: A Biography* (Cambridge: Cambridge University Press, 2001), pp. 383–84.

57. Two people worth reading on global governance are Mike Moore, *A World without Walls: Freedom, Development, Free Trade, and Global Governance* (Cambridge: Cambridge University Press, 2003); and Carl Coon, *One Planet, One People: Beyond "Us" vs. "Them"* (Amherst, NY: Prometheus Books, 2004).

58. Peter Singer, *One World: The Ethics of Globalisation* (Melbourne: Text Publishing, 2006 [2002]), pp. 193–97.

59. John Rawls, *The Law of Peoples* (Cambridge, MA: Harvard University Press, 2002 [1999]), p. 120.

60. Ibid., p. 37.

61. Ted Honderich, *On Political Means and Social Ends* (Edinburgh: Edinburgh University Press, 2003), pp. 87–89.

62. John Stuart Mill, *Three Essays on Religion* (London: Henry Holt, 1874), p. 110.

63. Philippe Sands, *Lawless World* (Camberwell, Victoria: Penguin, 2005), pp. 8–9.

64. John Ralston Saul's discussion of this is useful. See John Ralston Saul, *The Collapse of Globalism and the Reinvention of the World* (Sydney: Viking, 2005).

65. Paul Kurtz, *Humanist Manifesto 2000: A Call for a New Planetary Humanism* (Amherst, NY: Prometheus Books, 2000), especially pp. 35–61.

66. Ibid., p. 64.

67. Coon, *One Planet, One People*, p. 99.

68. G. W. F. Hegel, *Hegel's Philosophy of Right*, trans. T. M. Knox (London: Oxford University Press, 1967 [1952]), p. 212. This is not to endorse Karl Popper's view (among others) that Hegel can be seen as an apologist for totalitarianism. This view was comprehensively squashed by Walter Kaufmann. See Walter Kaufmann, *From Shakespeare to Existentialism* (Boston: Beacon Press, 1959), especially chapter 7.

69. Coon, *One Planet, One People*, p. 134.

70. Moore, *World without Walls*, pp. 167–68. And Peter Singer has noted the World Bank calculation that implementing the MDGs would require the relatively modest increase of no more than $60 billion more in aid money per year. See Singer, *One World*, p. 202.

71. Kwame Appiah, *The Ethics of Identity* (Princeton, NJ: Princeton University Press, 2005), p. 256.

72. Hilary Putnam, *Reason, Truth and History* (Cambridge: Cambridge University Press, 1981), p. 216.

73. Rawls, *Law of Peoples*, pp. 111–12.

74. Karl Jaspers, *Way to Wisdom* (London: Victor Gollancz, 1951), p. 106. Later in the same book he said that only as "determinate men, each in his specificity, can we experience humanity as such" (p. 130).

75. Greenfield, *ID*, p. 289.

EPILOGUE: THE MAIN FEATURES OF TWENTY-FIRST-CENTURY HUMANISM

1. Bertrand Russell, *The Faith of a Rationalist* (Auckland: NZRA, 1960 [1947]), p. 5.

2. Irving Babbitt, *Rousseau and Romanticism* (Cleveland, OH: Meridian, 1947 [1919]), p. 289.

3. Confucius, *The Analects* (London: Penguin, 1987 [1979]), 7:19.

BIBLIOGRAPHY

Note: in order to keep this bibliography within the bounds of reason, only book titles, articles in refereed journals, and reputable website sources are cited. All other sources are cited in full in the notes.

Abel, Reuben, ed. *Humanistic Pragmatism: The Philosophy of F. C. S. Schiller*. New York: Free Press, 1966.
Abû Zayd, Nasr. *Rethinking the Qur'ân: Toward a Humanistic Hermeneutics*. Utrecht: Humanistics University Press, 2004.
Allen, Norm Jr. ed. *African American Humanism: An Anthology*. Amherst, NY: Prometheus Books, 1991.
———, ed. *The Black Humanist Experience*. Amherst, NY: Prometheus Books, 2003.
Althusser, Louis. *For Marx*. New York: Vintage, 1970 [1965].
Altizer, Thomas J. J., and William Hamilton. *Radical Theology and the Death of God*. Indianapolis, IN: Bobbs-Merrill, 1966.
Ambedkar, B. R. *Conversion as Emancipation*. New Delhi: Critical Quest, 2004.
———. *Dr. Babasaheb Ambedkar, Writings and Speeches*. 11 vols. Bombay: Education Department, Government of Maharashtra, 1989 [1979].
An-Na'im, Abdullahi Ahmed. *Toward an Islamic Reformation: Civil Liberties, Human Rights, and International Law*. Syracuse: Syracuse University Press, 1990.
Antony, Louise M., ed. *Philosophers without Gods: Meditations on Atheism and the Secular Life*. Oxford: Oxford University Press, 2007.
Appiah, Kwame. *The Ethics of Identity*. Princeton, NJ: Princeton University Press, 2005.
Arkoun, Mohammed. *The Unthought in Contemporary Islamic Thought*. London: Saqi Books, 2002.
Auden, W. H., et al. *I Believe*. London: George Allen & Unwin, 1941 [1940].
Ayer, A. J., ed. *The Humanist Outlook*. London: Pemberton Books, 1968.
———. *Part of My Life*. London: Collins, 1977.
———. *Philosophy in the Twentieth Century*. London: Unwin Paperbacks, 1984.
Babbitt, Irving. *Character and Culture: Essays on East and West*. With an introduction by Claes G. Ryn. New Brunswick, NJ: Transaction Publishers, 1994 [1940].
———. *Rousseau and Romanticism*. Cleveland, OH: Meridian, 1947 [1919].

Baier, Kurt. *Problems of Life and Death: A Humanist Perspective.* Amherst, NY: Prometheus Books, 1997.
Balfour, Arthur. *Theism and Humanism.* London: Hodder & Stoughton, 1915.
Bandiste, D. D. *Humanist Values: A Source Book.* Delhi: BR Publishing, 1999.
Bell, Richard H. *Understanding African Philosophy.* New York: Routledge, 2002.
Benn, A. W. *A History of Modern Philosophy.* London: Watts, 1912.
———. "Pragmatism as a Method of Religious Belief." In *RPA Annual and Ethical Review for 1910,* by the Rationalist Press Association, 3–8. London: Watts, 1910.
Bentham, Jeremy. *A Fragment on Government and an Introduction to the Principles of Morals and Legislation.* Edited by Wilfred Harrison. Oxford: Basil Blackwell, 1967 [1948].
Berlin, Isaiah. *The Crooked Timber of Humanity.* New York: Vintage, 1992 [1990].
———. *Karl Marx.* Oxford: Oxford University Press, 1980 [1939].
———. *The Roots of Romanticism.* London: Chatto & Windus, 1999.
———. *The Sense of Reality.* London: Chatto & Windus, 1996.
Berman, David. *A History of Atheism in Britain: From Hobbes to Russell.* London: Routledge, 1990 [1988].
Berman, Paul. *Terror and Liberalism.* New York: W. W. Norton, 2003.
Beuttler, Fred W. "Failed Nerves and the Problem of Religion on the American Left—The Partisan Review, 1935–1962." *Intellectual News,* no. 15 (Winter 2005): 43–55.
Bhutto, Benazir. *Reconciliation: Islam, Democracy and the West.* London: Simon & Schuster, 2008.
Birus, Hendrik. "The Archaeology of Humanism." *Surfaces* 4 (1997).
Blackburn, Simon. *Truth: A Guide for the Perplexed.* London: Allen Lane, 2005.
Blackham, H. J. *Blackham's Best.* Selected by Barbara Smoker. London: Barbara Smoker, 2003 [1988].
———. *Humanism.* London: Penguin, 1968.
———. *Six Existentialist Thinkers.* New York: Harper Torchbooks, 1959 [1952].
———. *Stanton Coit: 1857–1944.* London: Favil Press, n.d. [ca. 1957].
Blanco White, Amber. *Ethics for Unbelievers.* London: Routledge & Kegan Paul, 1949.
Boulton, David. *The Trouble with God.* Alresford, Hants: John Hunt Publishing, 2002.
Bowden, John, ed. *Thirty Years of Honesty: Honest to God Then and Now.* London: SCM, 1993.
Bowle, John. *Politics and Opinion in the Nineteenth Century.* London: Jonathan Cape, 1966 [1954].
Boyd Orr, John. *As I Recall.* London: Macgibbon & Kee, 1967 [1966].

Bradlaugh, Charles. *Speeches*. London: Freethought Publishing, 1890.
Brendon, Piers. *Eminent Edwardians*. London: Penguin, 1981 [1979].
British Humanist Association. *Humanism and the British Humanist Association*. London: British Humanist Association, n.d. [ca. 1970].
———. *Towards an Open Society: Ends and Means in British Politics*. London: British Humanist Association, 1971.
Bronowski, Jacob. *The Ascent of Man*. London: BBC, 1979 [1973].
———. *A Sense of the Future*. Cambridge, MA: MIT Press, 1978 [1977].
Buber, Martin. *A Believing Humanism*. Edited by Ruth Nanda Anshen. New York: Simon & Schuster, 1969 [1967].
Budd, Susan. *Varieties of Unbelief*. London: Heinemann, 1977.
Bullock, Alan. *The Humanist Tradition in the West*. London: Thames & Hudson, 1985.
Bullough, Vern, and Tim Madigan, eds. *Toward a New Enlightenment: The Philosophy of Paul Kurtz*. New Brunswick, NJ: Transaction, 1994.
Bultmann, Rudolf. "Christianity and Humanism." *Journal of Religion* 32, no. 2 (April 1952): 77–86.
Burckhardt, Jacob. *The Civilization of the Renaissance in Italy*. London: Penguin, 1990 [1860].
Campbell, Colin. *Towards a Sociology of Irreligion*. London: Macmillan, 1971.
Camus, Albert. *The Myth of Sisyphus*. London: Hamish Hamilton, 1965 [1942].
———. *The Plague*. London: Penguin, 1968 [1947].
———. *The Rebel: An Essay on Man in Revolt*. New York: Alfred A. Knopf, 1957 [1951].
———. *Resistance, Rebellion and Death*. London: Hamish Hamilton, 1963 [1960].
Carroll, John. *Humanism: The Wreck of Western Culture*. London: Fontana, 1993.
Catholic University of America. *New Catholic Encyclopaedia*. New York: McGraw-Hill, 1967.
Chakrabarti, Mohit. *Swami Vivekananda: Vibrant Humanist*. New Delhi: Kanishka Publishers, 2001.
Chan, Wing-tsit. *A Source Book in Chinese Philosophy*. Princeton, NJ: Princeton University Press, 1973 [1963].
Chandler, Stuart. *Establishing a Pure Land on Earth*. Honolulu: University of Hawaii Press, 2004.
Chattopadhyaya, Debiprasad. *Carvaka/Lokayata: An Anthology of Source Materials and Some Recent Studies*. New Delhi: Indian Council of Philosophical Research, 1994 [1990].
———. *Indian Atheism*. New Delhi: People's Publishing, 1991 [1969].
Cheng, Chung-ying, and Nicholas Bunnin, eds. *Contemporary Chinese Philosophy*. Oxford: Blackwell, 2002.

Clark, Ronald W. *The Life of Bertrand Russell*. London: Jonathan Cape, 1975.
Clements, Jonathan. *Confucius: A Biography*. Stroud: Sutton Publishing, 2008 [2004].
Clifford, William Kingdon. *The Ethics of Belief and Other Essays*. With introduction by Timothy J. Madigan. Amherst, NY: Prometheus Books, 1999 [1947].
Coates, J. B. *A Challenge to Christianity*. London: Watts, 1958.
———. *Ten Modern Prophets*. London: Frederick Muller, 1944.
Cohen, Morris. *The Faith of a Liberal*. New York: Henry Holt, 1946.
Cohen-Solal, Annie. *Sartre: A Life*. London: Heinemann, 1987.
Coit, Stanton. *The Soul of America*. New York: Macmillan, 1914.
Confucius. *The Analects*. London: Penguin, 1987 [1979].
Cooke, Bill. "Atheism and Social Progress." In *Atheism and Social Progress, Fifth World Atheist Conference*, edited by Vijayam and Vikas Gora, 3–4. Vijayawada: Atheist Centre, 2005.
———. *Dictionary of Atheism, Skepticism, and Humanism*. Amherst, NY: Prometheus Books, 2006.
———. *The Gathering of Infidels: A Hundred Years of the Rationalist Press Association*. Amherst, NY: Prometheus Books, 2004.
———. *Heathen in Godzone: Seventy Years of Rationalism in New Zealand*. Auckland: NZARH, 1998.
———. "The Necessity of Atheism." In *Sixth World Atheist Conference*, edited by Vijayam and Vikas Gora, 33–36. Vijayawada: Atheist Centre, 2007.
———. *A Rebel to His Last Breath: Joseph McCabe and Rationalism*. Amherst, NY: Prometheus Books, 2001.
Coon, Carl. *One Planet, One People: Beyond "Us" vs. "Them."* Amherst, NY: Prometheus Books, 2004.
Cooper, David E. *The Measure of Things: Humanism, Humility, and Mystery*. Oxford: Clarendon Press, 2002.
Cory, Daniel, ed. *The Letters of George Santayana*. New York: Scribner, 1955.
Cupitt, Don. *After God: The Future of Religion*. London: Phoenix, 1998 [1997].
Dahlitz, Ray. *Secular Who's Who*. Melbourne: Ray Dahlitz, 1994.
D'Arcy, Martin. *Humanism and Christianity*. New York: World Publishing, 1969.
Darrow, Clarence, and Wallace Rice, eds. *Infidels and Heretics: An Agnostic's Anthology*. Boston: Stratford, 1929.
Davies, Tony. *Humanism*. London: Routledge, 1997.
Dawkins, Richard. *The God Delusion*. London: Bantam, 2006.
———. *Unweaving the Rainbow*. London: Penguin, 1998.
Dennett, Daniel C. *Breaking the Spell: Religion as a Natural Phenomenon*. London: Allen Lane, 2006.
———. *Darwin's Dangerous Idea*. London: Allen Lane, 1995.
Desmond, Adrian. *Huxley*. London: Penguin, 1998.

Dewey, John. *A Common Faith*. New Haven, CT: Yale University Press, 1947 [1934].
———. *Human Nature and Conduct*. New York: Modern Library, 1930 [1922].
———. *Philosophy and Civilization*. New York: G. P. Putnam's Sons, 1931.
———. *The Quest for Certainty*. London: George Allen & Unwin, 1930.
———. *Reconstruction in Philosophy*. New York: Mentor, 1953 [1920].
Doan, Frank Carleton. *Religion and the Modern Mind*. Boston: Sherman, French, 1909.
Dooley, Patrick Kiaran. *Pragmatism as Humanism: The Philosophy of William James*. Totowa, NJ: Littlefield, Adams, 1975.
Duncan, Homer. *Humanism: The Most Dangerous Religion in America*. Lubbock, TX: Missionary Crusader, 1979.
Dutta, Krishna, and Andrew Robinson. *Rabindranath Tagore: The Myriad-Minded Man*. London: Bloomsbury, 1997 [1995].
Easterman, Daniel. *New Jerusalems: Reflections on Islam, Fundamentalism and the Rushdie Affair*. London: Grafton, 1992.
Edwards, Paul, ed. *The Encyclopedia of Philosophy*. New York: Macmillan, 1972 [1967].
———. *Heidegger's Confusions*. Amherst, NY: Prometheus Books, 2004.
Ehrenfeld, David. *The Arrogance of Humanism*. Oxford: Oxford University Press, 1981 [1978].
Eliade, Mircea, ed. *The Encyclopaedia of Religion*. New York: Macmillan, 1987.
Eliot, Simon, and Beverley Stern, eds. *The Age of Enlightenment: An Anthology of Eighteenth-Century Texts*. London: Ward Lock, 1984 [1979].
Eliot, T. S. *Selected Essays*. London: Faber & Faber, 1949 [1932].
Fakhry, Majid. *A History of Islamic Philosophy*. New York: Columbia University Press, 1983 [1970].
Feuerbach, Ludwig. *The Essence of Christianity*. Amherst, NY: Prometheus Books, 1989 [1841].
Fiedler, Maureen, and Linda Rabben, eds. *Rome Has Spoken*. New York: Crossroad, 1998.
Fletcher, Joseph. *Situation Ethics*. London: SCM Press, 1966.
Fletcher, Ronald. "A Definition of Humanism." In *Question 1*, 5–16. London: Pemberton Books, 1968.
———. *Ten Non-Commandments: A Humanist's Decalogue*. London: Pioneer, 1964.
Flynn, Tom. *The New Encyclopaedia of Unbelief*. Amherst, NY: Prometheus Books, 2007.
———, ed. *Secular Humanism Defined*. Amherst, NY: Council for Secular Humanism, 2002.
Foote, G. W. *Secularism: The True Philosophy of Life*. London: G. W. Foote, 1998 [1879].

Forster, Roger, and Paul Marston. *Reason and Faith*. Eastbourne: Monarch Publications, 1989.
Foucault, Michel. *The Order of Things*. London: Vintage, 1973.
Fowler, Jeaneane. *Humanism: Beliefs and Practices*. Brighton: Sussex Academic Press, 1999.
Franklin, William, and Joseph M. Shaw. *The Case for Christian Humanism*. Grand Rapids, MI: William B. Eerdmans, 1991.
Freeman, Anthony. *God in Us: A Case for Christian Humanism*. London: SCM, 1993.
Fry, Ruth. *Maud and Amber*. Christchurch: Canterbury University Press, 1992.
Fung, Yu-lan. *A Short History of Chinese Philosophy*. New York: Macmillan, 1960 [1948].
Gaita, Raimond. *A Common Humanity: Thinking about Love, and Truth and Justice*. Melbourne: Text Publishing, 2000 [1999].
Gasenbeek, Bert, and Babu Gogineni, eds. *International Humanist & Ethical Union, 1952–2002*. Utrecht: De Tijdstroom, 2002.
Gaskin, J. C. A., ed. *Varieties of Unbelief from Epicurus to Sartre*. New York: Macmillan, 1989.
Gay, Peter. *The Enlightenment: An Interpretation*. London: Wildwood House, 1973 [1966].
———. *The Pleasure Wars*. London: HarperCollins, 1998.
Geering, Lloyd. *Christianity without God*. Wellington: Bridget Williams Books, 2002.
———. *Faith's New Age*. London: Collins, 1980.
———. *Fundamentalism: The Challenge to the Secular World*. Wellington: St. Andrew's Trust, 2003.
———. *God in the New World*. London: Hodder & Stoughton, 1968.
———. *The Greening of Christianity*. Wellington: St. Andrew's Trust, 2005.
———. *In Praise of the Secular*. Wellington: St. Andrew's Trust, 2007.
———. *The World of Relation: An Introduction to Martin Buber's "I and Thou."* Wellington: Victoria University Press, 1983.
———. *Wrestling with God: The Story of My Life*. Wellington: Bridget Williams Books, 2006.
Gellner, Ernest. *Conditions of Liberty: Civil Society and Its Rivals*. London: Hamish Hamilton, 1994.
———. *Legitimation of Belief*. Cambridge: Cambridge University Press, 1974.
———. *Reason and Culture*. Oxford: Blackwell, 1992.
Giustiniani, Vito. "Homo, 'Humanus,' and the Meanings of 'Humanism.'" *Journal of the History of Ideas* 46, no. 2 (April/June 1985): 167–95.

Goicoechea, David, John Luik, and Tim Madigan, eds. *The Question of Humanism: Challenges and Possibilities*. Amherst, NY: Prometheus Books, 1991.

Gora. *Atheism: Questions and Answers*. Vijayawada: Atheist Centre, 1992.

———. *An Atheist around the World*. Vijayawada: Atheist Centre, 1987.

———. *An Atheist with Gandhi*. Ahmedabad: Navajivan Publishing, 2003 [1951].

———. *The Need of Atheism*. Vijayawada: Atheist Centre, 1991 [1980].

———. *Positive Atheism*. Vijayawada: Atheist Centre, 1999 [1972].

Gorham, Charles. *The Gospel of Rationalism*. London: Watts, 1942.

Gould, F. J. *The Life-Story of a Humanist*. London: Watts, 1923.

Grafen, Alan, and Mark Ridley, eds. *Richard Dawkins*. Oxford: Oxford University Press, 2006.

Gray, John. *Black Mass: Apocalyptic Religion and the Death of Utopia*. London: Allen Lane, 2005.

Grayling, A. C. *The Choice of Hercules*. London: Weidenfeld & Nicolson, 2008.

———. *Towards the Light: The Story of the Struggles for Liberty and Rights That Made the Modern West*. London: Bloomsbury, 2007.

———. *What Is Good? The Search for the Best Way to Live*. London: Weidenfeld & Nicolson, 2003.

Green, Maia. "Confronting Categorical Assumptions about the Power of Religion in Africa." *Review of African Political Economy*, no. 110: 635–50.

Greenfield, Susan. *ID: The Quest for Identity in the 21st Century*. London: Sceptre, 2008.

Grieder, Jerome. *Hu Shih and the Chinese Renaissance*. Cambridge, MA: Harvard University Press, 1970.

Griffin, Nicholas, ed. *The Selected Letters of Bertrand Russell: The Public Years, 1914–1970*. London: Routledge & Kegan Paul, 2001.

Griggs, Edward Howard. *The New Humanism*. Croton-on-Hudson, NY: Orchard Hill Press, 1922 [1899].

Haack, Susan. *Defending Science—Within Reason*. Amherst, NY: Prometheus Books, 2003.

Habermas, Jürgen. *The Philosophical Discourse of Modernity*. Cambridge: Polity Press, 1987.

———. *Philosophical-Political Profiles*. Cambridge, MA: MIT Press, 1983.

Haldane, J. B. S. *The Marxist Philosophy and the Sciences*. London: George Allen & Unwin, 1939.

Haldane, R. B. *The Philosophy of Humanism*. London: John Murray, 1922.

———. *Richard Burdon Haldane: An Autobiography*. London: Hodder & Stoughton, 1929.

Halliwell, Martin, and Andy Mousley. *Critical Humanisms: Humanist/Anti-Humanist Dialogues*. Edinburgh: Edinburgh University Press, 2003.

Halsema, Annemie, and Douwe van Houten, eds. *Empowering Humanity: State of the Art in Humanistics*. Utrecht: De Tijdstroom Uitgeverij, 2004.

Hanioglu, Şükrü. "Garbcīlar: Their Attitudes toward Religion and Their Impact on the Official Ideology of the Turkish Republic." *Studia Islamica*, no. 86 (1997): 133–58.

Hardwick, Elizabeth, ed. *The Selected Letters of William James*. New York: Farrar, Straus & Cudahy, 1961.

Harrison, Lawrence E., and Samuel P. Huntington, eds. *Culture Matters: How Values Shape Human Progress*. New York: Basic Books, 2000.

Hartshorne, Charles. *Beyond Humanism: Essays in the Philosophy of Nature*. Lincoln: University of Nebraska Press, 1968 [1937].

Hatch, John. *Two African Statesmen: Kaunda of Zambia and Nyerere of Tanzania*. London: Secker & Warburg, 1976.

Haught, John F. *God after Darwin: A Theology of Evolution*. Boulder, CO: Westview Press, 2000.

Hawton, Hector. *Controversy: The Humanist/Christian Encounter*. London: Pemberton Books, 1971.

———. *The Feast of Unreason*. London: Watts, 1952.

———. *Humanism Explained*. London Ethical Union, n.d. [ca. 1953].

———. *The Humanist Revolution*. London: Barrie & Rockliff, 1963.

———. *Philosophy for Pleasure*. London: Watts, 1952 [1949].

———, ed. *Reason in Action*. London: Watts, 1956.

———. *The Thinker's Handbook*. London: Watts, 1950.

Hayman, Ronald. *Thomas Mann: A Biography*. New York: Scribner, 1995.

Hayward, Tim. *Ecological Thought: An Introduction*. Cambridge: Polity Press, 1995.

Hecht, Jennifer Michael. *Doubt: A History*. New York: HarperSanFrancisco, 2003.

Hegel, G. W. F. *Hegel's Philosophy of Right*. Translated by T. M. Knox. London: Oxford University Press, 1967 [1952].

———. *The Philosophy of Hegel*. Edited by Carl Friedrich. New York: Modern Library, 1954 [1953].

———. *The Philosophy of History*. New York: Dover, 1956.

Herman, Arthur. *The Idea of Decline in Western History*. New York: Free Press, 1997.

Herrick, Jim. *Humanism: An Introduction*. London: Rationalist Press Association, 2003.

Hick, John, ed. *The Myth of God Incarnate*. London: SCM, 1977.

Hiorth, Finngeir. *Atheism in India*. Pune: Indian Secular Society, 1998.

———. *Introduction to Atheism*. Pune: Indian Secular Society, 1995.

———. *Introduction to Humanism*. Oslo: Human-Etisk Forbund, 2007.

———. *Marxism*. Oslo: Human-Etisk Forbund, 2004.
Hirsi Ali, Ayaan. *Infidel*. New York: Free Press, 2007.
Hobhouse, L. T. *The Rational Good*. London: George Allen & Unwin, 1921.
Hobsbawm, Eric. *Age of Extremes: The Short Twentieth Century, 1914–1991*. London: Michael Joseph, 1995 [1994].
———. *The Age of Revolution*. London: Weidenfeld & Nicolson, 1995 [1961].
Hobson, Alfred, and Neil Jenkins. *Modern Humanism*. Newcastle-upon-Tyne: Dene Books, 1989.
Hobson, John A. *Rationalism and Humanism*. London: Watts, 1933.
Holloway, Richard. *Godless Morality: Keeping Religion out of Ethics*. Edinburgh: Canongate, 2000 [1999].
———. *Looking in the Distance*. Edinburgh: Canongate, 2005 [2004].
Holyoake, George Jacob. *Sixty Years of an Agitator's Life*. London: T. Fisher Unwin, 1906 [1892].
———. *The Origin and Nature of Secularism*. London: Watts, 1896.
Honderich, Ted. *On Political Means and Social Ends*. Edinburgh: Edinburgh University Press, 2003.
Hook, Sidney. *Convictions*. Amherst, NY: Prometheus Books, 1990.
———. *From Hegel to Marx: Studies in the Intellectual Development of Karl Marx*. New York: Humanities Press, 1958 [1950].
———. *Out of Step: An Unquiet Life in the 20th Century*. New York: Harper & Row, 1987.
———. "Pragmatism and the Tragic Sense of Life." In *American Philosophy in the Twentieth Century*, edited by Paul Kurtz, 523–38. New York: Macmillan, 1967 [1966].
———. *The Quest for Being*. New York: St Martin's Press, 1961.
Houf, Horace T. "Is Humanism Religion?" *Journal of Bible and Religion* 14, no. 2 (May 1946): 101–106.
Hourani, George. *Reason and Tradition in Islamic Ethics*. Cambridge: Cambridge University Press, 1985.
Howlett, Duncan. *The Fatal Flaw at the Heart of Religious Liberalism*. Amherst, NY: Prometheus Books, 1995.
Hsing, Yun [Xingyun]. *Humanistic Buddhism: A Blueprint for Life*. Hacienda Heights, CA: Buddha's Light Publishing, 2005 [2003].
———. *Star and Cloud: The Biography of Venerable Master Hsing Yun*. Translated by Madelon Wheeler-Gibb. Hacienda Heights, CA: Buddha's Light Publishing, 2003.
Hughes, H. Stuart. *Consciousness and Society: The Reorientation of European Thought 1890–1930*. London: Macgibbon & Kee, 1959.

Humanist Association. *What Humanism Is*. London: Humanist Association, n.d. [ca. 1958].

Humanist Philosophers' Group. *What Is Humanism?* London: British Humanist Association, 2002.

Hunter, Michael, and David Wootton, eds. *Atheism from the Reformation to the Enlightenment*. Oxford: Oxford University Press, 1992.

Huxley, Aldous. *The Doors of Perception*. London: Chatto & Windus, 1957 [1954].

Huxley, Julian. *Essays of a Humanist*. London: Chatto & Windus, 1964.

———, ed. *The Humanist Frame*. London: George Allen & Unwin, 1961.

———. *Life Can Be Worth Living*. London: Watts, 1939.

———. *Memories I*. London: Penguin, 1978 [1970].

———. *Memories II*. London: Penguin, 1978 [1973].

———. *New Bottles for New Wine*. London: Readers Union/Chatto & Windus, 1959 [1957].

———. *Religion without Revelation*. London: Ernest Benn, 1928 [1927].

———. *The Uniqueness of Man*. London: Chatto & Windus, 1941.

———. *What Dare I Think?* London: Chatto & Windus, 1931.

Hynes, Samuel. *The Edwardian Turn of Mind*. Princeton, NJ: Princeton University Press, 1975 [1968].

Ignatieff, Michael. *Isaiah Berlin: A Life*. London: Vintage, 2000 [1998].

International Commission for a History of the Scientific and Cultural Development of Mankind. *History of Mankind: Cultural and Scientific Development*. 6 vols. London: George Allen & Unwin, 1963–1966.

Jack, Homer A., ed. *The Gandhi Reader*. London: Dennis Dobson, 1958 [1956].

Jacoby, Susan. *Freethinkers: A History of American Secularism*. New York: Metropolitan Books, 2004.

Jaeger, Werner. *Humanism and Theology*. Milwaukee: Marquette University Press, 1943.

Jager, Ronald. *The Development of Bertrand Russell's Philosophy*. London: George Allen & Unwin, 1972.

Jahanbegloo, Ramin. *Conversations with Isaiah Berlin*. London: Phoenix, 1993 [1991].

James, Clive. *Cultural Amnesia: Necessary Memories from History and the Arts*. New York: W. W. Norton, 2007.

James, William. *Pragmatism and Other Essays*. New York: Washington Square, 1963 [1907].

———. *Selected Papers on Philosophy*. London: J. M. Dent, 1956 [1917].

———. *The Varieties of Religious Experience*. London: Longmans, Green, 1908 [1902].

———. *The Will to Believe and Other Essays in Popular Philosophy*. New York: Dover, 1956 [1897].

Jaspers, Karl. *Way to Wisdom*. London: Victor Gollancz, 1951.
Jeyifo, Biodun, ed. *Perspectives on Wole Soyinka: Freedom and Complexity*. Jackson, MS: University Press of Mississippi, 2001.
Joad, C. E. M. *The Book of Joad*. London: Faber & Faber, 1945 [1932].
———, ed. *Manifesto*. London: George Allen & Unwin, 1934.
Judelson, Catherine, trans. *Dictionary for Believers and Nonbelievers*. Moscow: Progress Publishers, 1985.
Jung-Kuo, Yang, et al. *Selected Articles Criticizing Lin Piao and Confucius*. Peking: Foreign Languages Press, 1974.
Kamenka, Eugene. *The Philosophy of Ludwig Feuerbach*. London: Routledge & Kegan Paul, 1970.
Kaufmann, Walter. *Critique of Religion and Philosophy*. New York: Harper Torchbooks, 1972 [1958].
———. *From Shakespeare to Existentialism*. Boston: Beacon Press, 1959.
Kaunda, Kenneth. *A Humanist in Africa: Letters to Colin Morris*. London: Longmans, 1966.
Kaye, Harvey. *The British Marxist Historians*. London: Polity Press, 1990 [1984].
Kaye, Harvey, and Keith McClelland, eds. *E. P. Thompson: Critical Perspectives*. London: Polity Press, 1990.
Keyser, Cassius J. "Humanism and Pseudo-Humanism." *Hibbert Journal* 29, no. 2 (January 1931): 227–39.
Knight, Margaret. *Honest to Man*. Amherst, NY: Prometheus Books, 1974.
———, ed. *The Humanist Anthology*. Revised by Jim Herrick. Amherst, NY: Prometheus Books, 1995. First published 1961 by Barrie & Rockliff in London.
———. *Morals without Religion*. London: Dennis Dobson, 1955.
Knight, Margaret, C. A. Mace, Cyril Bibby, et al. *Religion and Your Child*. London: Rationalist Press Association, 1959.
Knight, Richard L., and Suzanne Riedel, eds. *Aldo Leopold and the Ecological Conscience*. Oxford: Oxford University Press, 2002.
Kohn, Rachael. *The New Believers: Re-imagining God*. Pymble, NSW: HarperCollins, 2003.
Kolakowski, Leszek. *Religion*. London: Fontana, 1993.
Krell, David Farrell, ed. *Martin Heidegger: Basic Writings*. New York: Harper & Row, 1977.
Krikorian, Yervent, ed. *Naturalism and the Human Spirit*. New York: Columbia University Press, 1944.
Kuehn, Manfred. *Kant: A Biography*. Cambridge: Cambridge University Press, 2001.
Kurtz, Paul, ed. *American Philosophy in the Twentieth Century*. New York: Macmillan, 1967 [1966].

———. *The Courage to Become*. Westport, CT: Praeger, 1997.
———. *In Defense of Secular Humanism*. Amherst, NY: Prometheus Books, 1983.
———. *Eupraxophy: Living without Religion*. Amherst, NY: Prometheus Books, 1989.
———. *Exuberance: An Affirmative Philosophy of Life*. Amherst, NY: Prometheus Books, 1985 [1978].
———. *Forbidden Fruit: The Ethics of Humanism*. Amherst, NY: Prometheus Books, 1988.
———. *The Fullness of Life*. New York: Horizon Books, 1974.
———, ed. *The Humanist Alternative*. London: Pemberton Books, 1973.
———. *Humanist Manifestos I and II*. Amherst, NY: Prometheus Books, 1973.
———. *Humanist Manifesto 2000: A Call for a New Planetary Humanism*. Amherst, NY: Prometheus Books, 2000.
———, ed. *Moral Problems in Contemporary Society*. Amherst, NY: Prometheus Books, 1973 [1969].
———. *The New Skepticism: Inquiry and Reliable Knowledge*. Amherst, NY: Prometheus Books, 1992.
———, ed. *Science and Ethics: Can Science Help Us Make Wise Moral Judgments?* With the assistance of David Koepsell. Amherst, NY: Prometheus Books, 2007.
———. *A Secular Humanist Declaration*. Amherst, NY: Free Inquiry, 1980.
———. *The Transcendental Temptation: A Critique of Religion and the Paranormal*. Amherst, NY: Prometheus Books, 1986.
———. *What Is Secular Humanism?* Amherst, NY: Prometheus Books, 2007.
Kurtz, Paul, and Albert Dondeyne, eds. *A Catholic/Humanist Dialogue*. London: Pemberton Books, 1972.
Kurzman, Charles, ed. *Liberal Islam: A Sourcebook*. New York: Oxford University Press, 1998.
LaHaye, Tim. *The Battle for the Mind*. Old Tappan, NJ: Fleming H. Revell, 1980.
LaHaye, Tim, and David Noebel. *Mind Siege: The Battle for Truth in the New Millennium*. Nashville: World Publishing, 2000.
Lal, Basant Kumar. *Contemporary Indian Philosophy*. New Delhi: Motilal Banarsidass, 1992 [1973].
Lamont, Corliss. *Freedom of Choice Affirmed*. London: Pemberton Books, 1971 [1967].
———. *Humanism as a Philosophy*. New York: Philosophical Library, 1949.
———. *The Illusion of Immortality*. New York: Philosophical Library, 1959 [1935].
———. *The Independent Mind*. New York: Horizon Press, 1951.
———. *A Lifetime of Dissent*. Amherst, NY: Prometheus Books, 1988.
———. *The Philosophy of Humanism*. New York: Frederick Ungar Publishing, 1965.

———. *Yes to Life: Memoirs of Corliss Lamont*. New York: Horizon Press, 1981.
Lavanam. *Of Gandhi, Atheism and Social Experimentalism*. Edited by K. H. S. S. Sundar. Vijayawada: Atheist Centre, 2003.
Lecky, W. E. H. *History of the Rise and Influence of the Spirit of Rationalism in Europe*. 2 vols. London: Longmans, Green, 1904 [1865].
Lenz, John R. "Pugwash and Russell's Legacy." *Bertrand Russell Quarterly*, no. 89 (February 1996): 18–24.
Levine, Peter. *Nietzsche and the Modern Crisis of the Humanities*. Albany: State University of New York Press, 1995.
Levitt, Norman. *Prometheus Bedevilled: Science and the Contradictions of Contemporary Culture*. New Brunswick, NJ: Rutgers University Press, 1999.
Lewis, Bernard. *What Went Wrong?* London: Phoenix, 2002.
Lewis, John. *Bertrand Russell: Philosopher and Humanist*. London: Lawrence & Wishart, 1968.
Liebman, Robert, and Robert Wuthrow, eds. *The New Christian Right*. New York: Aldine, 1983.
Lin, Yutang. *Chinese Ideals of Life*. London: Watts, 1944.
———. *The Importance of Living*. London: William Heinemann, 1941 [1938].
Lipson, Leslie. *The Ethical Crises of Civilization*. Newbury Park, CA: Sage Publications, 1993.
Liu, Shaoqi. *How to Be a Good Communist*. Beijing: Foreign Languages Press, 1952 [1939].
Lottman, Herbert R. *Albert Camus: A Biography*. London: Weidenfeld & Nicolson, 1979.
Louw, Dirk. "Ubuntu: An African Assessment of the Religious Other." Paper given at the Twentieth World Congress of Philosophy in Boston, MA, August 10–15, 1998.
Löwith, Karl. *From Hegel to Nietzsche: The Revolution in Nineteenth-century Thought*. London: Constable, 1965 [1941].
Mackenzie, John Stuart. *Manual of Ethics*. London: University Tutorial Press, 1946 [1883].
MacKenzie, Norman, and Jeanne MacKenzie. *H. G. Wells*. New York: Touchstone, 1973.
MacKillop, Ian. *The British Ethical Societies*. Cambridge: Cambridge University Press, 1986.
Macquarrie, John. *God and Secularity*. London: Lutterworth, 1968.
Macy, Christopher, ed. *Rationalism and Humanism in the New Europe*. London: Pemberton Books, 1973.
Madigan, Timothy J. "Evolutionary Humanism Revisited: The Continuing Relevance of Julian Huxley." *Religious Humanism* 32, nos. 3 and 4 (Summer/Fall 1998): 73–82.

Mahaprajna, Acharya. *Anekanta: The Third Eye*. Ladnun: Jain Vishva Bharati Institute, 2002.
Mahto, Sneha Prabha. "Imagery in Rabindranath Tagore's *Gitanjali.*" *New Quest* 119 (September/October 1996): 293–97.
Mandela, Nelson. *Long Walk to Freedom*. London: Little, Brown, 1994.
Manji, Irshad. *The Trouble with Islam*. New York: St. Martin's Press, 2003.
Mann, Thomas. *Dr. Faustus*. New York: Alfred A. Knopf, 1948 [1947].
———. *The Magic Mountain*. London: Penguin, 1960 [1924].
———. *Stories of Three Decades*. London: Secker & Warburg, 1946 [1936].
Maritain, Jacques. *True Humanism*. London: Geoffrey Bles, 1954 [1938].
Marsh, P. T. *The Victorian Church in Decline*. London: Routledge & Kegan Paul, 1969.
Martin, Craig. "Rethinking Renaissance Averroism." *Intellectual History Review* 17, no. 1 (2007): 3–19.
Martin, Richard C., Mark R. Woodward, and Dwi S. Atmaja. *Defenders of Reason in Islam*. Oxford: Oneworld, 1997.
Marx, Karl. *Early Writings*. London: Penguin, 1992 [1975].
Marx, Karl, and Friedrich Engels. *On Religion*. Moscow: Progress Publishers, 1976 [1957].
Mayr, Ernst. *One Long Argument: Charles Darwin and the Genesis of Modern Evolutionary Thought*. London: Penguin, 1993 [1991].
McCabe, Joseph. *A Biographical Dictionary of Modern Rationalists*. London: Watts, 1920.
———. "Fore-gleams of Humanism in Dante." In *Agnostic Annual and Ethical Review, 1907*, edited by Charles A. Watts, 53–57. London: Watts, 1907.
———. *Key to Culture*. Girard, KS: Haldeman-Julius, 1929.
———. *The Life and Letters of George Jacob Holyoake*. 2 vols. London: Watts, 1908.
———. *A Rationalist Encyclopaedia*. London: Watts, 1948.
———. *The Religion of Woman*. London: Watts, 1905.
McCormick, John. *George Santayana: A Biography*. New York: Alfred A. Knopf, 1987.
McGee, John Edwin. *A History of the British Secular Movement*. Girard, KS: Haldeman-Julius, 1948.
McGrath, Alister. *The Twilight of Atheism*. London: Rider, 2004.
McIlroy, William. *Foundations of Modern Humanism*. Sheffield: Sheffield Humanist Society, 1995.
McLellan, David. *The Thought of Karl Marx*. London: Papermac, 1980 [1971].
Menand, Louis. *The Metaphysical Club*. London: Flamingo, 2002 [2001].
Mencius. *Mencius*. Translated by D. C. Lau. London: Penguin, 1970.

Middleton, Christopher, ed. *Selected Letters of Friedrich Nietzsche*. Chicago: University of Chicago Press, 1969.

Mill, John Stuart. *Autobiography*. New York: New American Library, 1964 [1873].

———. *On Liberty and the Subjection of Women*. London: Wordsworth, 1996.

———. *Three Essays on Religion*. London: Longmans, Green, Reader, and Dyer, 1874.

Mitchell, Basil. *Morality: Religious and Secular*. Oxford: Clarendon Press, 1985 [1980].

Mitter, Rana. *A Bitter Revolution: China's Struggle with the Modern World*. Oxford: Oxford University Press, 2004.

Moore, Mike. *A World without Walls: Freedom, Development, Free Trade, and Global Governance*. Cambridge: Cambridge University Press, 2003.

Mouat, Kit. *What Humanism Is About*. London: Barrie & Rockliff, 1963.

Muirhead, J. H., ed. *Contemporary British Philosophy: Personal Statements*. London: George Allen & Unwin, 1924.

Murdoch, Iris. *Existentialists and Mystics: Writings on Philosophy and Literature*. London: Chatto & Windus, 1997.

———. *Sartre: Romantic Rationalist*. London: Chatto & Windus, 1987 [1953].

Murray, Gilbert. *Stoic, Christian and Humanist*. London: George Allen & Unwin, 1940.

Murty, K. Satchidananda. *Philosophy in India: Traditions, Teaching and Research*. New Delhi: Motilal Banarsidass, 1991 [1985].

Najjar, Fauzi M. "The Debate on Secularism in Egypt." *Arab Studies Quarterly* 18, no. 2 (Spring 1996).

Naquib al-Attar, Muhammad al-. *Islam and Secularism*. New Delhi: New Crescent Publishing, 2002 [1984].

Narisetti, Innaiah, ed. *M. N. Roy: Radical Humanist: Selected Writings*. Amherst, NY: Prometheus Books, 2004.

Needham, Joseph. *Within the Four Seas: The Dialogue of East and West*. London: George Allen & Unwin, 1969.

Nehru, Jawaharlal. *The Discovery of India*. London: Asia Publishing, 1960 [1946].

Newman, Francis William. *Phases of Faith, or, Passages from the History of My Creed*. London: Watts, 1907 [1850].

Niethammer, Friedrich Immanuel. *Philanthropinismus—Humanismus*. Weinheim: Verlag Julius Beltz, 1968 [1808].

Nietzsche, Friedrich. *Beyond Good and Evil*. London: Penguin, 1988 [1886].

———. *The Will to Power*. New York: Vintage, 1968 [1901].

———. *Thus Spake Zarathustra*. Amherst, NY: Prometheus Books, 1993 [1885].

Noebel, David, J. F. Baldwin, and Kevin Bywater, eds. *Clergy in the Classroom: The Religion of Secular Humanism*. Manitou Springs, CO: Summit Press, 2001 [1995].

Norman, Richard. *On Humanism*. London: Routledge, 2004.
Norris, Pippa, and Ronald Inglehart. *Sacred and Secular: Religion and Politics Worldwide*. Cambridge: Cambridge University Press, 2004.
Novack, George. *Humanism and Socialism*. New York: Pathfinder Press, 1980 [1973].
Nylan, Michael. *The Five "Confucian" Classics*. New Haven, CT: Yale University Press, 2001.
Obadare, Ebenezer. "Pentecostal Presidency? The Lagos-Ibadan 'Theocratic Class' and the Muslim 'Other.'" *Review of African Political Economy*, no. 110: 665–78.
Olds, Mason. *American Religious Humanism*. Minneapolis, MN: Fellowship of Religious Humanists, 1996.
Olson, Alan M., ed. *Heidegger and Jaspers*. Philadelphia: Temple University Press, 1994.
Parrinder, Patrick, and Christopher Rolfe, eds. *H.G. Wells under Revision*. Selinsgrove, PA: Susquehanna University Press, 1990.
Passmore, John. *A Hundred Years of Philosophy*. London: Penguin, 1962 [1957].
———. *Man's Responsibility for Nature*. London: Duckworth, 1974.
———. *The Perfectibility of Man*. New York: Scribner, 1970.
Paul, J. T. *Humanism in Politics: The New Zealand Labour Party in Retrospect*. Wellington: New Zealand Labour Party, 1946.
Peake, Arthur S., and R. G. Parsons, eds. *An Outline of Christianity: The Story of Our Civilisation*. London: Waverley, n.d. [ca. 1928].
Perkins, Ray, Jr. *Yours Faithfully, Bertrand Russell*. Chicago: Open Court, 2002.
Petrosyan, Maria. *Humanism: Its Philosophical, Ethical and Sociological Aspects*. Moscow: Progress Publishers, 1972.
Pfeffer, Leo. *Creeds in Competition: A Creative Force in American Culture*. New York: Harper & Brothers, 1958.
Pike, E. Royston. *Pioneers of Social Change*. London: Barrie & Rockliff, 1963.
———. "What Wells Meant to My Generation." In *The Rationalist Annual*, 70–78. London: Watts, 1947.
Pinkard, Terry. *German Philosophy 1760–1860: The Legacy of Idealism*. Cambridge: Cambridge University Press, 2002.
———. *Hegel: A Biography*. Cambridge: Cambridge University Press, 2000.
Pinn, Anthony B. *African American Humanist Principles*. New York: Palgrave Macmillan, 2004.
Popper, Karl. *Conjectures and Refutations: The Growth of Scientific Knowledge*. London: Routledge, 1989 [1963].
———. *The Open Society and Its Enemies*. London, Routledge, 1963 [1945].
———. *The Poverty of Historicism*. London: Routledge & Kegan Paul, 1957.

Potter, Charles Francis. *Humanism: The New Religion*. New York: Simon & Schuster, 1930.
Prajna, Samani Chaitanya, ed. *The Role of Jainism in Evolving a New Paradigm of Philosophy*. Ladnun: Jain Vishva Bharati, 2008.
Putnam, Hilary. *Reason, Truth and History*. Cambridge: Cambridge University Press, 1981.
Ramakrishna, Sri. *Teachings of Sri Ramakrishna*. Kolkata: Advaita Ashrama, 2004 [1916].
Ramose, Mogobe. *African Philosophy through Ubuntu*. Harare: Mond Books, 2002 [1999].
Ranganathananda, Swami. *Swami Vivekananda: His Humanism*. Kolkata: Advaita Ashrama, 1996 [1980–81].
Rawls, John. *The Law of Peoples*. Cambridge, MA: Harvard University Press, 2002 [1999].
Ray, Gordon N. *H. G. Wells and Rebecca West*. London: Macmillan, 1974.
Read, Herbert. *The Forms of Things Unknown*. London: Faber & Faber, 1960.
Reade, Winwood. *The Martyrdom of Man*. London, Trubner, 1877 [1872].
Reese, Curtis, ed. *Humanist Sermons*. Chicago: Open Court, 1927.
Reiser, Oliver. *Scientific Humanism*. Girard, KS: Haldeman-Julius, 1946.
Riepe, Dale. *The Naturalistic Tradition of Indian Thought*. Seattle: University of Washington Press, 1961.
Robertson, Archibald. *Man His Own Master: An Essay in Humanism*. London: Watts, 1948.
Robertson, J. M. *Explorations*. London: Watts, n.d. [ca. 1923].
———. *A History of Freethought: Ancient and Modern*. London: Watts, 1936.
———. *A History of Freethought in the Nineteenth Century*. London: Watts, 1929.
———. *Modern Humanists Reconsidered*. London: Watts, 1927.
———. *Pioneer Humanists*. London: Watts, 1907.
Robinson, J. A. T. *Honest to God*. London: SCM, 1963.
Rogers, Ben. *A. J. Ayer: A Life*. New York: Grove Press, 1999.
Rorty, Richard. *Consequences of Pragmatism. Essays: 1972–1980*. Minneapolis: University of Minnesota Press, 1982.
———. *Objectivity, Relativism, and Truth*. Cambridge: Cambridge University Press, 1995 [1991].
———. *Philosophy and Social Hope*. London: Penguin, 1999.
Roshwald, M. *Humanism in Practice*. London: Watts, 1955.
Royle, Edward. *Radicals, Secularists and Republicans*. Manchester: Manchester University Press, 1980.
———. *Victorian Infidels*. Manchester: Manchester University Press, 1974.

Russell, Bertrand. *The Autobiography of Bertrand Russell*. 3 vols. London: George Allen & Unwin, 1967–69.

———. *Common Sense and Nuclear Warfare*. London: George Allen & Unwin, 1959.

———. *The Faith of a Rationalist*. Auckland: New Zealand Rationalist Association, n.d. [ca. 1960].

———. *Freedom and Organization, 1814–1914*. London: George Allen & Unwin, 1952 [1934].

———. *Has Man a Future?* London: George Allen & Unwin, 1961.

———. *History of Western Philosophy*. London: George Allen & Unwin, 1946.

———. *Human Knowledge: Its Scope and Limits*. London: George Allen & Unwin, 1948.

———. *Human Society in Ethics and Politics*. London: George Allen & Unwin, 1954.

———. *In Praise of Idleness*. London: George Allen & Unwin, 1935.

———. *John Dewey and the High Tide of American Liberalism*. New York: W. W. Norton, 1995.

———. *My Philosophical Development*. London: George Allen & Unwin, 1959.

———. *Mysticism and Logic*. London: George Allen & Unwin, 1959 [1917].

———. *New Hopes for a Changing World*. London: George Allen & Unwin, 1951.

———. *Philosophy and Politics*. London: National Book League, 1947.

———. *Portraits from Memory and Other Essays*. London: George Allen & Unwin, 1956.

———. *Power: A New Social Analysis*. London: George Allen & Unwin, 1938.

———. *Religion and Science*. Oxford: Oxford University Press, 1960 [1935].

———. *Skeptical Essays*. London: George Allen & Unwin, 1928.

———. *Why I Am Not a Christian*. London: George Allen & Unwin, 1957.

Ryan, Alan. *Bertrand Russell: A Political Life*. London: Allen Lane, 1988.

Saatkamp, Herman J., ed. *Rorty and Pragmatism*. Nashville: Vanderbilt University Press, 1995.

Safranski, Rüdiger. *Martin Heidegger: Between Good and Evil*. Cambridge, MA: Harvard University Press, 1998.

Said, Edward. *Humanism and Democratic Criticism*. New York: Columbia University Press, 2004.

Sands, Philippe. *Lawless World*. Camberwell, Victoria: Penguin, 2005.

Santayana, George. *The Genteel Tradition at Bay*. New York: Scribner, 1931.

———. *The Life of Reason*. New York: Scribner, 1954.

———. *Middle Span: The Background of My Life*. London: Constable, 1947.

———. *Persons and Places: The Background of My Life*. New York: Scribner, 1944.

———. *Winds of Doctrine and Platonism and the Spiritual Life*. New York: Harper & Brothers, 1957.
Sartre, Jean-Paul. *Existentialism and Humanism*. London: Methuen, 1970 [1946].
Saul, John Ralston. *The Collapse of Globalism and the Reinvention of the World*. Sydney: Viking, 2005.
Schaeffer, Francis. *How Should We Then Live?* Old Tappan, NJ: Fleming H. Revell, 1976.
Schiller, F. C. S. *Humanism: Philosophical Essays*. London: Macmillan, 1912 [1903].
———. *Our Human Truths*. New York: Columbia University Press, 1939.
———. *Studies in Humanism*. London: Macmillan, 1907.
———. "Why Humanism?" In *Contemporary British Philosophy: Personal Statements*, edited by J. H. Muirhead. London: George Allen & Unwin, 1924.
Schilpp, Paul Arthur, ed. *The Philosophy of Bertrand Russell*. Evanston, IL: Northwestern University, 1944.
Schoenman, Ralph, ed. *Bertrand Russell: Philosopher of the Century*. New York: Little, Brown, 1967.
Schulz, William F. *Making the Manifesto: The Birth of Religious Humanism*. Boston: Skinner House Books, 2002.
Schweitzer, Albert. *Civilization and Ethics*. London: Adam & Charles Black, 1946 [1923].
———. *Out of My Life and Thought*. New York: Mentor, 1960 [1933].
Seaver, George. *Albert Schweitzer: The Man and His Mind*. London: Adam & Charles Black, 1955 [1947].
Seckel, Al, ed. *Bertrand Russell on God and Religion*. Amherst, NY: Prometheus Books, 1986.
Sellars, Roy Wood. *The Essentials of Philosophy*. New York: Macmillan, 1924 [1917].
———. *Reflections on American Philosophy from Within*. Notre Dame, IN: University of Notre Dame Press, 1969.
———. *Religion Coming of Age*. New York: Macmillan, 1928.
Sen, Amartya. *The Argumentative Indian*. London: Penguin, 2006 [2005].
———. *Development as Freedom*. New York: Anchor Books, 2000 [1999].
———. *Identity and Violence: The Illusion of Destiny*. London: Allen Lane, 2006.
Shet, Sunanda. *Gora: His Life and Work*. Podanur, Tamilnadu: CSICOP India, n.d. [ca. 2000].
Shi, Yanping. "Developments in Chinese Philosophy over the Last Ten Years." *Philosophy East and West* 43, no. 1 (January 1993): 113–25.
Shinn, Roger L. *Man: The New Humanism*. London: Lutterworth, 1968.
Shook, John R., ed. *Pragmatic Naturalism and Realism*. Amherst, NY: Prometheus Books, 2003.

Shook, John R., and Hugh McDonald, eds. *F. C. S. Schiller on Humanism and Pragmatism: Selected Writings, 1891–1939*. Amherst, NY: Prometheus Books, 2007.

Shotwell, J. T. *The Religious Revolution of Today*. London: Watts, 1915.

Singer, Peter. *How Are We to Live?* Milsons Point, NSW: Random House Australia, 1997 [1993].

———. *One World: The Ethics of Globalisation*. Melbourne: Text Publishing, 2006 [2002].

Sinha, V. K. *The Reason Case: In Defence of Freedom of Speech*. Pune: Indian Secular Society, 1995.

Sluga, Hans. *Heidegger's Crisis: Philosophy and Politics in Nazi Germany*. Cambridge, MA: Harvard University Press, 1993.

Smart, Ninian. *The Religious Experience of Mankind*. Glasgow: Collins, 1980 [1969].

Smith, David C. *H. G. Wells: Desperately Mortal*. New Haven, CT: Yale University Press, 1986.

Smith, Gregory Bruce. *Nietzsche, Heidegger and the Transition to Postmodernity*. Chicago: University of Chicago Press, 1996.

Smith, Ronald Gregor. *Secular Christianity*. London: Collins, 1966.

Smith, Warren Sylvester. *London Heretics 1870–1914*. London: Constable, 1967.

Solomon, Robert C. *Entertaining Ideas: Popular Philosophical Essays, 1970–1990*. Amherst, NY: Prometheus Books, 1992.

———. *Spirituality for the Skeptic*. Oxford: Oxford University Press, 2002.

Southey, Robert, and Samuel Taylor Coleridge, eds. *Omniana*. Fontwell, Sussex: Centaur Press, 1969 [1812].

Soyinka, Wole. *The Man Died*. London: Vintage, 1994 [1972].

———. *Myth, Literature and the African World*. Cambridge: Cambridge University Press, 1980 [1976].

Spiller, G., ed. *A Generation of Religious Progress*. London: Watts, 1916.

Spinoza, Benedict. *Tractatus Theologico-Politicus*. London: George Routledge & Sons, n.d. [ca. 1885].

Spong, John Shelby. *Liberating the Gospels: Reading the Bible through Jewish Eyes*. New York: HarperCollins, 1996.

Stein, Gordon, ed. *An Anthology of Atheism and Rationalism*. Amherst, NY: Prometheus Books, 1980.

———, ed. *The Encyclopaedia of Unbelief*. Amherst, NY: Prometheus Books, 1985.

———. *Freethought in the United Kingdom and the Commonwealth: A Descriptive Bibliography*. Westport, CT: Greenwood Publishing, 1981.

———, ed. *A Second Anthology of Atheism and Rationalism*. Amherst, NY: Prometheus Books, 1987.

Stoddard, Lothrop. *Scientific Humanism*. New York: Scribner, 1926.

Stopes-Roe, Harry. "The Presuppositions of Dialogue: A Fair Vocabulary." *Journal for the Critical Study of Religion, Ethics and Society* 1, no. 2 (Summer/Fall 1996).
Storer, Morris, ed. *Humanist Ethics: Dialogue on Basics*. Amherst, NY: Prometheus Books, 1980.
Stourton, Edward. *Absolute Truth: The Catholic Church Today*. London: Penguin, 1999 [1998].
Strawson, William. *The Christian Approach to the Humanist*. London: Lutterworth, 1972 [1963].
Suzuki, David, and Amanda McConnell. *The Sacred Balance*. Crows Nest, NSW: Allen & Unwin, 1999 [1997].
Symonds, John Addington. *Renaissance in Italy*. 7 vols. London: Smith, Elder, 1902 [1875–86].
Szczesny, Gerhard. *The Future of Unbelief*. New York: George Braziller, 1961 [1958].
Tagore, Rabindranath. *Collected Poems and Plays of Rabindranath Tagore*. London: Macmillan, 1973 [1936].
———. *My Reminiscences*. London: Macmillan, 1921 [1917].
———. *The Religion of Man*. Boston: Beacon, 1961 [1931].
Tallis, Raymond. *Enemies of Hope: A Critique of Contemporary Pessimism*. New York: St Martin's Press, 1997.
Tapp, E. J. *Humanism: Its History and Nature*. Auckland: NZARH, 1987.
Tarkunde, V. M. *Radical Humanism*. New Delhi: Ajanta Publications, 1991 [1983].
Taylor, Charles. *A Secular Age*. Cambridge, MA: Belknap, 2007.
Teilhard de Chardin, Pierre. *The Phenomenon of Man*. London: Collins, 1960.
Teller, Woolsey. *Essays of an Atheist*. New York: Truth Seeker, 1945.
Thompson, E. P. *The Poverty of Theory*. London: Merlin, 1978.
Thrower, James. *The Alternative Tradition: Unbelief in the Ancient World*. The Hague: Mouton, 1980.
———. *A Short History of Western Atheism*. London: Pemberton Books, 1971.
Tillich, Paul. *The Shaking of the Foundations*. London: Penguin, 1969 [1949].
Todorov, Tzvetan. *Hope and Memory*. London: Atlantic Books, 2005 [2003].
———. *Imperfect Garden: The Legacy of Humanism*. Princeton, NJ: Princeton University Press, 2002.
Toews, John Edward. *Hegelianism: The Path toward Dialectical Humanism, 1805–1841*. Cambridge: Cambridge University Press, 1980.
Trainor, Chad. "Solitary, Poor, Nasty, Brutish and Short: Russell's Views on Life without World Government." *Bertrand Russell Society Quarterly*, nos. 128 and 129 (December 2005/February 2006): 23–34.
Tribe, David. *Nucleoethics*. London: Paladin, 1973 [1972].

———. *100 Years of Freethought*. London: Elek, 1967.
———. *President Charles Bradlaugh MP*. London: Elek, 1971.
Van Buren, Paul. *The Secular Meaning of the Gospel*. London: SCM, 1963.
Van Praag, J. P. *Foundations of Humanism*. Amherst, NY: Prometheus Books, 1982.
Varma, Vishwanath Prasad. *Philosophical Humanism and Contemporary India*. New Delhi: Motilal Banarsidass, 1979.
Veeramani, K. *Humanism*. Chennai: Periyar Self-Respect Institution, 1998.
———. *Periyar's Movement: A Short Summary*. Chennai: DK Publications, 2002.
Vivekananda, Swami. *The Complete Works of Swami Vivekananda*. Calcutta: Advaita Ashrama, 1972.
Volkogonov, Dimitri. *Stalin: Triumph and Tragedy*. New York: Grove Weidenfeld, 1991 [1988].
Von Wright, Georg Henrik. *What Is Humanism?* Topeka: University of Kansas, 1977.
Waddington. C. H. *The Scientific Attitude*. London: Penguin, 1948 [1941].
Wagar, W. Warren, ed. *H. G. Wells: Journalism and Prophecy 1893–1946*. London: Bodley Head, 1965 [1964].
Wahba, Mourad, and Mona Abousenna, eds. *Averroës and the Enlightenment*. Amherst, NY: Prometheus Books, 1996.
Wallraff, Charles. *Karl Jaspers: An Introduction to His Philosophy*. Princeton, NJ: Princeton University Press, 1970.
Walter, Nicolas. *Blasphemy: Ancient and Modern*. London: Rationalist Press Association, 1990.
———. *Humanism: What's in the Word*. London: Rationalist Press Association, 1997.
Warder, A. K. *Indian Buddhism*. New Delhi: Motilal Banarsidass, 1980 [1970].
Warnock, Mary. *Existentialist Ethics*. London: Macmillan, 1970 [1967].
Warraq, Ibn, ed. *Leaving Islam: Apostates Speak Out*. Amherst, NY: Prometheus Books, 2003.
———. *Why I Am Not a Muslim*. Amherst, NY: Prometheus Books, 1995.
Watson, Peter. *Ideas: A History of Thought and Invention from Fire to Freud*. New York: HarperCollins, 2005.
Wells, G. A., ed. *J. M. Robertson, 1856–1933: Liberal, Rationalist, and Scholar*. London: Pemberton Books, 1987.
Wells, H. G. *After Democracy*. London: Watts, 1932.
———. *Ann Veronica*. London: Eveleigh Nash & Grayson, n.d. [1909].
———. *The Conquest of Time*. London: Watts, 1942.
———. *Experiment in Autobiography*. London: Victor Gollancz, 1934.
———. *The Fate of Homo Sapiens*. London: Secker & Warburg, 1939.
———. *First and Last Things*. London: Watts, 1929 [1909].

———. *42 to 44: A Contemporary Memoir upon Human Behavior during the Crisis of the World Revolution.* London: Secker & Warburg, 1944.
———. *God the Invisible King.* London: Cassell, 1917.
———. *H. G. Wells in Love.* Edited by G. P. Wells. London: Faber & Faber, 1984.
———. *Joan and Peter.* London: Cassell, 1918.
———. *Mind at the End of Its Tether.* London: William Heinemann, 1945.
———. *Mr. Blettsworthy on Rampole Island.* London: Ernest Benn, 1928.
———. *The Open Conspiracy: Blueprints for a World Revolution.* London: Victor Gollancz, 1928.
———. *The Outline of History.* London: Waverley, 1921 [1920].
———. *The Outlook of* Homo Sapiens. London: Secker & Warburg, 1946 [1942].
———. *The Rights of Man.* London: Penguin, 1940.
———. *The Soul of a Bishop.* London: Cassell, 1918.
———. *The Undying Fire.* London: Cassell, 1919.
———. *The War of the Worlds.* London: Penguin, 1946 [1898].
———. *The Way the World Is Going.* London: Ernest Benn, 1928.
———. *What Are We to Do with Our Lives?* London: William Heinemann, 1931.
———. *The Work, Wealth and Happiness of Mankind.* London: William Heinemann, 1932.
———. *The World of William Clissold.* London: Ernest Benn, 1926.
———. *You Can't Be Too Careful.* London: Secker & Warburg, 1941.
Wells, H. G., Julian Huxley, and G. P. Wells. *The Science of Life.* London: Cassell, 1931.
Werskey, Gary. *The Visible College.* London: Penguin, 1978.
Wheeler, J. M. *A Biographical Dictionary of Freethinkers of All Ages and Nations.* London: Progressive Publishing, 1889.
Whyte, Adam Gowans. *The Religion of the Open Mind.* London: Watts, 1913.
Wielenberg, Erik J. *Value and Virtue in a Godless Universe.* Cambridge: Cambridge University Press, 2005.
Wiener, Philip P., ed. *Dictionary of the History of Ideas.* New York: Scribner, 1978.
Williams, Bernard. *Ethics and the Limits of Philosophy.* London: Fontana, 1985.
———. *Philosophy as a Humanistic Discipline.* Princeton, NJ: Princeton University Press, 2006.
Williams, Raymond. *Culture and Society.* London: Penguin, 1985 [1958].
Wilson, A. N. *God's Funeral.* London: John Murray, 1999.
Wilson, Edward O. *Consilience, The Unity of Knowledge.* London: Little, Brown, 1998.
Winetrout, Kenneth. *F. C. S. Schiller and the Dimension of Pragmatism.* Columbus: Ohio State University Press, 1967.

Winston, Richard, and Clara Winston. *The Letters of Thomas Mann*. London: Penguin, 1975 [1970].
Wiredu, Kwasi, ed. *A Companion to African Philosophy*. Oxford: Blackwell, 2004.
———. *Philosophy and an African Culture*. Cambridge: Cambridge University Press,1980.
Wood, Alan. *Bertrand Russell: The Passionate Skeptic*. London: George Allen & Unwin, 1957.
Wood, H. G. *Belief and Unbelief since 1850*. Cambridge: Cambridge University Press, 1950.
Woodbridge, Frederick J. E. *An Essay on Nature*. New York: Columbia University Press, 1940.
Yarbrough, Stephen. *Deliberate Criticism: Toward a Postmodern Humanism*. Athens: University of Georgia Press, 1992.

INDEX

'Abduh, Muhammad, 363–64
Abousenna, Mona, 377–78
Acton, Lord, 256
African Americans for Humanism, 204–5, 395–96, 404
al-Afghani, Jamal-al-din, 14, 363
al-Azm, Sadiq Jalal, 376–77
Allen, Norm R., Jr., 17, 204, 395–96
al-Razi, Abu Bakr Muhammad, 360–61
al-Raziq, Ali Abd, 374
Althusser, Louis, 239–40, 464
Ambedkar, Bhimrao, 301–4, 315, 485
American Humanist Association, 138, 173, 183–84, 189–90, 194, 219, 286, 470
antihumanists, 227–30, 233, 239–40, 244–49, 262–63, 275–79, 336
Appiah, Kwame Anthony, 444–47, 453
Aristotle, 198–99, 258, 359, 361, 477
Arkoun, Mohammed, 356–59, 363, 369–70, 372
Arnold, Matthew, 48, 51, 163
Asian values, 345
Atheist Centre, 310–14
Averroës. *See* Rushd, Ibn
Averroës and Enlightenment International Association, 377–78
Ayer, A. J., 153, 154–56, 169, 186, 367

Babbitt, Irving, 14, 49, 80–82, 160–61, 250, 343, 450–51, 487
Badawi, Abdel-Rahman, 367–68
Baldwin, James, 202

Balfour, Arthur, 263–64
Barth, Karl, 266–67
Basedow, Johann Bernard, 28
Beattie, Paul, 195–96
Benn, Alfred William, 48
Bennett, Arnold, 111
Bentham, Jeremy, 21, 38–39, 43, 51, 234, 457
Bergson, Henri, 69, 260
Berlin, Isaiah, 105, 161–63, 165, 446, 472, 475
Bhutto, Benazir, 355–56, 372, 386
biophilia, 285, 350, 420, 449
Blackham, Harold J., 133–35, 150, 186, 400, 467, 470, 472–73
Blanco White, Amber, 108, 141–42, 149
Bonhoeffer, Dietrich, 266–67, 269, 283
Bradlaugh, Charles, 37, 40, 161, 304–5, 311
Bragg, Raymond, 94, 173
British Humanist Association, 155, 169–71
Bronowski, Jacob, 129–30
Brown, Egbert Ethelred, 204
Buber, Martin, 281, 482–83
Büchner, Ludwig, 64, 366
Bullock, Alan, 158–61, 165
Bultmann, Rudolf, 266–68
Burckhardt, Jacob, 45–46

Camus, Albert, 220–24, 251, 450
Carvaka materialism, 290–92

Center for Inquiry, 395, 409
Cevdet, Abdullah, 372–73
Christian thought and humanism, 253–87
   Athens versus Jerusalem dilemma, 214, 253–55, 275, 279, 281, 283, 358
   Catholic thinkers and humanism, 182, 221, 256–63, 391, 400, 415
   Death of God theology, 232, 267–75, 281
   evangelical reactions to humanism, 180, 188–89, 192, 275–79, 472, 482
   Incarnation, doctrine of, 254–55, 270–75, 282–83, 287, 420
   Protestant thinkers and humanism, 244, 263–66, 279–87
Clifford, William Kingdon, 47, 55, 330
Coates, J. B., 110–12
Cohen, Morris, 137
Coit, Stanton, 133–34
Coleridge, Samuel Taylor, 44
Committee for the Scientific Investigation of Claims of the Paranormal, 189–90
Confucius. *See* Kongfuzi
Cooper, David E., 13, 413–14
Council for Secular Humanism, 190
Council of Ex-Muslims, 381–82
Cupitt, Don, 163–64, 280

D'Arcy, Martin, 260–62, 480
Darwinism, 64, 101, 110, 127, 255, 262, 366, 416, 463
Dashti, Ali, 366
Davies, Tony, 246–47
d'Avoine, Charles Lionel, 305
Dawkins, Richard, 163, 165, 419
Declaration of Interdependence, 421–23, 440

Dennett, Daniel C., 195, 207–8, 246
Dewey, John, 13, 89, 95, 114–19, 174, 183, 190, 199, 202, 233, 246, 265, 278, 341, 343, 424
Dia, Mamadiou, 369–70, 452
dialectical materialism, 104–9, 235–44
Dietrich, John H., 70, 90, 121
DK. *See* Dravidar Kazagham
Doan, Frank C., 85–87, 122, 349
Dravidar Kazagham (DK), 314–18

Eaton, Cyrus, 433–34
Ehrenfeld, David, 275–76
Einstein, Albert, 146, 265, 432–33, 446
Eliot, George, 39, 178
Eliot, T. S., 82
Engels, Friedrich, 107
Enlightenment, 9, 21–23, 25, 161–63, 205–6, 260
Erasmus, 178, 255
Ethical Societies, Union of, 68–69, 75, 79, 96, 133–35, 169
eupraxsophy, 198–200, 215, 285, 313, 342, 447

Fanon, Frantz, 390
Farmer, James, 202–3
Farrington, Benjamin, 131–32
Feuerbach, Ludwig, 33–35, 43, 54, 81, 104, 174, 208, 213, 456, 461
Fichte, Johann Gottlieb, 24–26
Fletcher, Joseph, 196, 198
Fletcher, Ronald, 156–58, 168
Flew, Antony, 129–30, 313
Flynn, Tom, 197
Forster, E. M., 146, 171, 486
Foucault, Michel, 245
Fowler, Jeaneane, 167–68
Freedom Charter, 398–99
Freeman, Anthony, 273, 280

Freud, Sigmund, 110, 139, 142, 160
Frolov, Ivan, 242–43
Fromm, Erich, 236

Gandhi, Mohandas, 295, 298–99, 302, 307, 311–15, 318–19, 426
Gardner, James, 44
Geering, Lloyd, 279–83, 482–83
God, 21, 34, 75, 92, 101, 116–17, 121–25, 213, 232, 251, 266–75, 279–83, 295, 316, 444, 451–52, 481
Goethe, Johann Wolfgang, 214–16
Gora, 187, 310–14, 411
Gorham, Charles T., 68
Gould, F. J., 69–70, 111, 133
Gray, John, 413–14, 435
Grayling, A. C., 165–66, 471
Greenfield, Susan, 447
Griggs, Edward Howard, 49–50, 85–86, 159, 452
Gyekye, Kwame, 393, 406

Haack, Susan, 108, 132, 230
Habermas, Jürgen, 233
Haeckel, Ernst, 64, 341, 366, 414
Haldane, John Burdon Sanderson, 108, 111
Haldane, Richard Burdon, 67, 73, 83–84
Harries, Richard, 163, 470
Hartshorne, Charles, 263–66, 268
Haught, John, 263
Hawton, Hector, 134, 148–49, 156–57, 190, 225, 476, 479
Hedenius, Ingemar, 224
Hegel, G. W. F., 24–28, 30–35, 41–43, 214–15, 271, 276, 442, 456, 481, 495
Hegelians, 30–35, 42, 64
Heidegger, Martin, 63, 227–30, 245, 266, 268
Herrick, Jim, 160, 166

Hinduism, 289–91, 294–96, 301–4, 310–12, 316
Hirsi Ali, Aayan, 380–83
Hitchens, Christopher, 452
Hitler, Adolf, 98, 107
Hobhouse, L. T., 52, 77
Hobsbawm, Eric, 21, 188
Hobson, J. A., 135
Hogben, Lancelot, 103–4
Holloway, Richard, 73, 280
Holyoake, George Jacob, 35–41, 135, 215, 470
Homo religiosus, 101
Honderich, Ted, 438–39, 445
Hook, Sidney, 174, 180–83, 186, 190, 213, 244, 413, 475
Howlett, Duncan, 274–75, 282
Hsing Yun. *See* Xingyun
Hughes, Langston, 203
humanism
  African humanism, 387–412
  and atheism, 52, 55, 77, 117–18, 165, 209, 221–22, 232, 242–43, 310–18, 451–52, 463
  as *bildung*, 26, 28–29, 49, 135, 140, 213–20, 249, 447
  Buddhist humanism, 303–4, 347–53
  Christian humanism, 254–55, 266–75, 279–83, 286–87, 399–402
  and Christianity, 32–33, 44, 58–59, 63, 78, 80–82, 143–47, 163–64, 217–18, 221–23, 232, 251, 253–87, 387–88, 400
  Confucian humanism, 142, 146, 215, 323–47, 447, 452, 453
  core insights of, 11–13, 15, 27, 29–30, 36–37, 42–43, 72–73, 82, 94, 120, 135, 144, 158, 159, 168, 176–77, 215, 223–24, 234–35, 250–51, 285–87, 323, 416, 433, 449–53

cultural humanism, 11–15, 23–30, 43–46, 49–50, 78–82, 85, 139–40, 158–161, 168, 178, 215–24, 249, 344, 431, 452–53
and democracy, 21–23, 31–32, 40, 73, 179–80, 187, 216–20, 251, 342–43, 383–85, 403–7, 430–31, 435–37, 439–40
ecohumanism, 34, 126–28, 414–23, 425
and eugenics, 61–62, 98, 103–4, 112
evolutionary, 149–54, 415–16
"exclusive," 12–13, 480
and grounded cosmopolitanism, 391, 444–47, 453
history of, 11–15, 21–23, 30, 42–46, 52–53, 68–69, 96, 158–61, 165–66, 226, 452
and humor, 62–63, 169–71, 447
Indian, 11, 289–322
Jain, 290–92, 493
liberal, 40–41, 52, 137–39, 142, 161–63, 185–86, 191, 243–44, 411–12, 430–31, 435–37
as a lifestance, 80–82, 94, 167–68, 197, 430–31
Muslim. *See* Muslim thought and humanism
and naturalism, 33–34, 74–76, 87–89, 106, 175–80, 205–8, 290–94, 323, 366, 417, 451–52
and naturalistic humility, 13, 34, 58–59, 62–63, 74–76, 80, 89, 96, 103, 119–21, 127, 137–38, 154, 156, 168, 179, 208, 223–24, 293, 344, 351, 414–23, 463
New Humanism, 70, 98, 220, 266–75, 280–81
origins of, 12, 21–30, 45–46, 52
planetary, 11–12, 128, 154, 185, 350, 387, 413–23, 424–26, 432–34, 437–44, 453
and postmodernism, 12, 115, 164, 194, 225, 244–49, 262–63, 266–71, 277, 330, 413
and pragmatism, 47, 53–65, 182, 208–10
and progress, 27–28, 32, 36–37, 41–43, 46–51, 61–62, 94, 115–18, 185, 451–52
and rationalism, 39, 41, 47, 72–73, 100–101, 109–14, 119–20, 137–38, 151, 156–58, 161–63, 286, 304–6, 309, 429–30
and religion, 33–34, 44, 59–60, 77, 82, 92, 94, 99–104, 109–12, 116–17, 148–149, 151–54, 160–61, 183–87, 190, 193–98, 207–8, 253–88, 402, 451–52
religious, 50, 70, 78, 85–96, 99–104, 121–24, 163–64, 195–98, 208–10, 220, 279–87, 299–300, 470
Renaissance, 23, 27–28, 45–47, 50, 72, 98, 257–58, 420, 450
and Romanticism, 32, 39, 49, 76–77, 79–82, 418, 475
and science, 51, 83–84, 97–132, 136, 232, 430–31, 450, 453
scientific, 97–132, 152–54, 320, 427, 465, 485
secular, 182, 187–200, 207–10, 346
and secularism, 35–37, 41, 215, 318–22, 371–78, 426
socialist, 235–44, 307–8, 337–41
Soviet, 105–6, 235–44
and speciesism, 284–85, 420–21
and spirituality, 33–34, 74–75, 80, 153, 164, 220, 295–96, 299–300, 401
and teleology, 41–43, 46–47, 52, 60–61, 68, 83, 101, 106–7, 415–16

humanismus, 30, 32
humanist, 23
humanistics, 236, 248–49
Humanist Manifesto I, 63, 93–96, 113–14, 118, 173, 184
Humanist Manifesto II, 183–87, 203, 421
Humanist Manifesto 2000, 203, 377, 440–42
humanity, principle of, 438–39, 445
Humboldt, Karl Wilhelm, 214
Hume, David, 129, 155
Hu Shih, 342–43, 453
Huxley, Aldous, 153
Huxley, Julian, 89, 99–104, 122, 126–27, 149–54, 169, 186, 242, 269, 397, 415, 426–28, 453, 469
Huxley, Thomas Henry, 99–102, 120, 199

Igwe, Leo, 404–7
IHEU. *See* International Humanist and Ethical Union
ijtihad. *See* Muslim thought and humanism
Interdependence, Declaration of, 421–23, 440
International Humanist and Ethical Union (IHEU), 234, 238, 308, 394, 404, 409, 411, 422, 429–32, 433
Iqbal, Mohammad, 365
Islam. *See* Muslim thought and humanism

Jacobi, Friedrich Heinrich, 23
Jacoby, Susan, 210
Jaeger, Werner, 257–58, 265
Jain humanism, 290–92, 493
James, Clive, 11–12, 225, 452, 479
James, William, 47, 53–65, 77–78, 114, 121, 264, 456
Jaspers, Karl, 77, 132, 159, 230–35, 281, 446, 453, 476–77, 495
Joad, C. E. M., 68–69, 109–14
junzi, 215, 325–26

Kant, Immanuel, 22, 25, 53, 162, 434–35, 455
Kaufmann, Walter, 43, 269, 274, 282, 458, 475, 495
Kaunda, Kenneth, 14, 394, 399–402
Kemal, Mustapha, 373–74
Khan, Syed Ahmad, 14, 364–65
Kierkegaard, Søren, 222, 253, 271
Knight, Margaret, 143–47
Kolakowski, Leszek, 253
Kongfuzi, 142, 146, 177–78, 234, 324–47, 453, 471
Küng, Hans, 262, 423
Kurtz, Paul, 182, 183–200, 204–7, 215, 242, 285, 313, 342, 394, 402, 421–22, 446–47, 453

La Haye, Tim, 180, 277–78, 482
Lahbabi, Mohammed Aziz, 368
laïcité, 215, 234–35
Lamont, Corliss, 80, 114–15, 119, 143, 153, 173–80, 184, 209, 278, 434, 471
land ethic. *See* Leopold, Aldo
Leopold, Aldo, 416–17
Lin Yutang, 343–45, 449, 450, 487
Lippmann, Walter, 98, 110
Lotze, Rudolf Hermann, 62
Lovejoy, Arthur O., 88

MacIntyre, Alasdair, 129
Mackenzie, John Stuart, 67–69, 75
Madigan, Timothy, 199, 469
Mahmoud, Zaki Naguib, 366–67
Mandela, Nelson, 398–99, 491
Manji, Irshad, 380–81

Mann, Thomas, 160, 215–20, 249
Mao Zedong, 181, 335–41
Maritain, Jacques, 257, 260–61
Markovic, Mihailo, 237–38
Marx, Karl, 31, 34, 42, 115, 424
Marxism, 34, 42, 52, 104–9, 128, 131, 175–81, 191, 221, 226–27, 235–44, 303, 306–9, 335–47, 357, 391, 396–99
Masoud, Moez, 385
Matubbar, Aroj Ali, 368
Mbiti, John, 201, 392–93
McCabe, Joseph, 71–72, 104, 223
McCarthy, Joseph, 175, 180
McGee, Lewis A., 204, 474
McGrath, Alister, 279
McKay, Claude, 203–4, 391
McTaggart, J. M. E., 62, 143
MDGs, 442–44
meliorism, 36–37, 42, 51, 115–16, 125, 182, 221
Mencius. *See* Mengzi
Mengzi, 250, 326–27
Mill, John Stuart, 35, 38–41, 43, 51, 137, 165, 240, 245, 414–15, 439, 457
Millennium Development Goals (MDGs), 442–44
Monty Python's Flying Circus (television series), 171
Morley, John, 100
Murray, Gilbert, 126, 416, 450
Muslim thought and humanism, 355–87
  customary Islam, 355–56
  ijtihad, 357–59, 373, 380–81, 489
  liberal/modernist/humanist Islam, 355–59, 370, 383–86
  Mu'tazilism, 359–62, 370
  Mughals, 321, 364–65, 372
  refuseniks, 378–84
  revivalist Islam, 355–56
  and secularism, 321, 365, 371–78, 381–83
  taqlid, 357–59

Nasrin, Taslima, 379–80
National Secular Society, 73, 102, 121, 147, 166, 169
nature, 414–25, 451–52
Nazism, 191, 218–19, 227–31, 257, 267, 278, 425
Negritude, 390–92, 400
Nehru, Jawaharlal, 289, 303, 318–22
New Atheists, 209, 279
New Confucians, 341–47
Niethammer, Friedrich Immanuel, 23–30, 87, 140, 146, 183, 215, 220, 234–35, 258, 346, 446, 452
Nietzsche, Friedrich, 43, 78–79, 215, 245, 271, 284
Norman, Richard, 168, 190
Novack, George, 238

O'Hair, Madalyn Murray, 198
Orr, John Boyd, 426–28, 453
Oruka, Henry, 392–93, 452
Orwell, George, 50, 109
Owen, Robert, 23, 39, 42, 55, 457

paideia, 215, 257–58
Paine, Thomas, 37, 41, 147, 155, 295, 446, 453
Paranjpye, Raghunath, 306
Parikh, Indumati, 309
Parmenides, 229
Passmore, John, 417–18
Peirce, Charles Sanders, 61, 64, 114
Periyar, 314–18
Petrosyan, Maria, 241–42
Pfeffer, Leo, 193–94
philanthropinism, 28–30, 44, 49

Pike, E. Royston, 39
Pinn, Anthony B., 201, 224
Popper, Karl, 137–38, 181, 278, 467, 495
postmodernism, 12, 164, 207, 245–49, 250–51, 300, 478
Potter, Charles Francis, 90–91
Protagoras, 55, 222, 229, 258, 420

Radest, Howard, 196–97
Ramakrishna, Swami, 294–96
Ramose, Mogobe, 17, 389, 419–20
Rationalist Press Association (RPA), 39, 48, 68–69, 72–73, 79, 96, 110–14, 131, 134–35, 148–50, 155–56, 167, 169, 173, 306, 394, 470, 480
Rawandi, Ibn, 360
Rawls, John, 434–38, 445–46
Read, Herbert, 139–40, 168, 449, 468
Reade, Winwood, 50–51, 125
Reese, Curtis W., 68, 90–91
Reeves, Amber. *See* Blanco White, Amber
Reiser, Oliver, 118–19
relativism, 60–61
relativity, 60–61, 83–84
reverence for life, 284–87, 300, 447, 450
Robertson, J. M., 34, 47–48, 70, 111–12
Robinson, J. A. T., 164, 269–70, 273, 481
Roosevelt, Eleanor, 440
Rorty, Richard, 41–43, 47, 63, 205–7, 229, 233
Rousseau, Jean-Jacques, 28, 49, 81, 250, 257
Roux, Edward, 396–97
Roy, M. N., 234, 306–9
RPA. *See* Rationalist Press Association
Ruge, Arnold, 30–35, 37, 43, 51, 88, 105, 128
Rushd, Ibn, 361–62, 370, 377–78

Russell, Bertrand, 13, 62, 74–77, 79–82, 104, 107, 109, 119–20, 136–39, 223–42, 278, 285, 367, 380, 419, 432–34, 446, 450, 461, 466, 477
Ryan, Alan, 109, 117, 118

Said, Edward, 207, 248, 378, 474
St. Petersburg Declaration, 383–84
Sakharov, Andrei, 186
Samson, Leon, 104–5, 114
Santayana, George, 76–80, 88, 174, 245
Sartre, Jean-Paul, 221, 225–27, 236
Schiller, Ferdinand Canning Scott, 53–65, 67, 69, 88, 109, 114–15, 147, 222, 258, 349
Schiller, Johann Cristoph Friedrich, 24, 214
Schleiermacher, Friedrich, 255
Schulz, William F., 86, 90, 468
Schweitzer, Albert, 159, 284–87, 296, 300, 415, 447, 449
Sea of Faith, 163–64
Secular Humanist Declaration, 187–93
Seddon, Richard John, 73–74
Sellars, Roy Wood, 64, 87–89, 94, 110, 184
Sen, Amartya, 297, 437, 446
Senghor, Leopold, 369, 391, 401
Shinn, Roger, 254–55
Shumayyil, Shibli, 366
Sibbern, Gabriel, 34–35, 43–44, 55, 84
Singer, Peter, 420–21, 436
Skolimowski, Henrik, 415–16
Smith, Linda, 170–71
Smith, Ronald Gregor, 272, 281
Smoker, Barbara, 161, 166–67
Snow, C. P., 84
Solarin, Tai, 403–7, 409, 411–12, 491
South Place Ethical Society, 135, 148, 166

Soyinka, Wole, 390, 403–7
Spencer, Herbert, 42, 341, 366
Spinoza, Benedict, 40, 76, 123, 147, 174, 295
Spong, John Shelby, 279–80
Stalin, Joseph, 106, 107, 181, 307
Stoddard, Lothrop, 14, 97–99, 102–3, 145
Stojanovic, Svetozar, 186
Strauss, David Friedrich, 31, 83
Suzuki, David, 418–19
Symonds, John Addington, 45–46, 92
Szczesny, Gerhard, 233–34, 417, 483

Tagore, Rabindranath, 118–19, 122, 296–300, 411, 446, 453
Taixu, 349–51
taqlid. See Muslim thought and humanism
Tarkunde, V. M., 308–9
Taylor, Charles, 12–13, 209, 255, 272
Teilhard de Chardin, Pierre, 149, 152–53, 258–60, 263, 391, 400, 415
Thompson, E. P., 239–40
Tillich, Paul, 230, 266–69, 281, 352
Todorov, Tzvetan, 119, 245, 250–51, 278, 438, 447, 449, 464–65, 471
Toulmin, Stephen, 131
transhumanism, 421
Tu Weiming, 345–47

ubuntu, 388–93, 419–20
umanista, 44–45
Union of Ethical Societies, 68–69, 75, 79, 96, 133–35, 169
Unitarianism, 75, 85–87, 94–97, 158, 204
United Nations, 422–23, 426–28, 439–40, 445

Universal Declaration of Human Rights, 383, 440

Van Gogh, Theo, 382
Van Praag, Jaap, 24, 234–35, 430–31, 477
Varma, Vishwanath Prasad, 293–94, 296
Veeramani, Thiru K., 317–18
Vivekananda, Swami, 294–96, 453
Voigt, Georg, 44–45

Waddington, C. H., 108–9
Wahba, Mourad, 377–78
Wallas, Graham, 52
Walter, Nicholas, 30, 167
Wang Chong, 330–31
Ward, Mrs. Humphry, 104, 141, 152
Warraq, Ibn, 380
Wells, H. G., 51, 110–14, 120–28, 141, 151, 175, 299, 403, 409, 415, 424–26, 439, 446, 453
Whyte, Adam Gowans, 72–73
Wielenberg, Erik J., 224
Williams, Bernard, 58–59, 420, 459, 481
Williams, Raymond, 21
Wilson, Edwin H., 70, 100, 121, 173
Wiredu, Kwasi, 391–92
Woodbridge, Frederick, 33, 64, 174–76, 208, 415, 417, 419
Wright, Georg Henrik von, 27

Xingyun, 347–53, 446
Xu Fuguan, 341–42

Yarbrough, Stephen, 247